"A valuable collection that interpret
the perspective of the classical Refc
sources for the wider church, the vc   ……, lucid, patient,
and temperate exposition of key themes. It reflects the dual capacity of Reformed theology to accommodate a measure of diversity while never losing
sight of its catholicity."

—**David Fergusson**, New College, University of Edinburgh

"Behaving for all the world as if we were living in some kind of golden age of
vibrant Reformed orthodoxy, the editors have brought together a multiauthor
confessional theology, with significant contributions from a range of respected
scholars. This is a gift to the entire church: the solidity, maturity, resourcefulness, and sagacity of these chapters provide theologians from all confessions
with a statement of Christian doctrine from an identifiably Protestant perspective. I would not have thought such a thing possible in our time, but here
it is: further evidence of Reformed catholicity's helpfulness."

—**Fred Sanders**, Torrey Honors Institute, Biola University

"An outstanding collection on Reformed dogmatics from some of the sharp-
est minds in the contemporary business. Insisting upon the centrality of the
scriptural gospel of the Triune God for every area of Christian confession, the
contributors also demonstrate how the hearing of that gospel in the company
of the church catholic and Reformed presents true hope for theological renewal
in today's world. This book instructs, challenges, and inspires, abundantly
illustrating the privilege and delight as well as demands that attend our ongoing reckoning with the church's historic faith. Why does dogmatic reasoning
continue to matter so much, and what must dogmatics seek—in the strength
of God—to say if it is to speak the gospel afresh in the church and to the
world? Read here, and find out."

—**Ivor J. Davidson**, University of St. Andrews

"With this volume, Michael Allen and Scott Swain continue their promising
project of Reformed catholicity. Those of us who identify as confessional
Reformed Christians should embrace their call to center our faith and life
around the Scriptures, yet to do so as participants in an ancient and enduring
community of believers who have mined the Scriptures and confessed the faith
before us. *Christian Dogmatics* brings together a diverse group of thoughtful
and accomplished theologians who take up the editors' call for retrieval and
reflect upon most of the main themes of Christian theology. Their constructive
proposals embrace a variety of classical and revisionist ideas, and although
no reader will embrace everything proposed herein, no one will fail to be
challenged, edified, and spurred on to further study of Scripture with the
help of our theological forebears."

—**David VanDrunen**, Westminster Seminary California

CHRISTIAN DOGMATICS

REFORMED THEOLOGY FOR THE CHURCH CATHOLIC

Edited by

Michael Allen and
Scott R. Swain

B
Baker Academic
a division of Baker Publishing Group
Grand Rapids, Michigan

© 2016 by Michael Allen and Scott R. Swain

Published by Baker Academic
a division of Baker Publishing Group
P.O. Box 6287, Grand Rapids, MI 49516-6287
www.bakeracademic.com

Printed in the United States of America

Library of Congress Cataloging-in-Publication Data
Names: Allen, Michael, 1981– editor.
Title: Christian dogmatics : reformed theology for the church catholic / edited by Michael Allen and Scott R. Swain.
Description: Grand Rapids, MI : Baker Academic, 2016. | Includes bibliographical references and index.
Identifiers: LCCN 2015043722 | ISBN 9780801048944 (pbk.)
Subjects: LCSH: Theology, Doctrinal.
Classification: LCC BT75.3 .C46 2016 | DDC 230—dc23
LC record available at http://lccn.loc.gov/2015043722

Chapter 7 is published by kind permission of Bloomsbury Publishing Plc / T&T Clark.

16 17 18 19 20 21 22   7 6 5 4 3 2 1

For our children:
Jackson and Will Allen
and
Caroline, Sophia, Josiah, and Micah Swain

CONTENTS

INTRODUCTION

MICHAEL ALLEN AND SCOTT R. SWAIN

Christian Dogmatics and the Theological Task

Dogmatic reasoning is the concerted attempt of the church to discipline its hearing of and testimony to the gospel according to that same gospel, specifically, to the promise that God makes himself known to and by his people. As Lutheran theologian Robert Jenson has articulated so well, "The church has a mission: to see to the speaking of the gospel, whether to the world as message of salvation or to God as appeal and praise."[1] This is no easy mission, for the world is not eager to hear this message, and we are not naturally prone to profess it. Even regenerate Christians continue to resist the shape of the gospel at times and to return to their sinful ways. The practice of dogmatics nevertheless goes forward in its mission vis-à-vis the gospel because it is moved along by the promise and provision of the Lord. The possibility of faithful service in the task of dogmatics does not arise from within the resources of dogmatics itself but from within the infinite depths of the Triune God who speaks to his church and who wills through his church to shed abroad the knowledge and love of himself.

This volume includes essays on most of the major topics (*loci*) of dogmatics. They are written by accomplished theologians from across the world. The contributors bring differing areas of specialization and theological affiliation to the table and therefore do not constitute a unified school of thought

---

1. Robert Jenson, *Systematic Theology*, vol. 1, *The Triune God* (New York: Oxford University Press, 1997), 11.

on various methodological and theological matters (including some matters discussed herein). What binds the different essays together is their attempt to draw on the fecund resources of Holy Scripture within the context of the catholic church of the Reformed confessions.[2] The contributors to this volume are all committed to the proposition that theological renewal comes through dependence upon the generative resources of the Triune God in and through the gospel and that such dependence is best expressed in our particular historical moment by way of retrieval. In other words, theological fruitfulness in the future will be possible only if we first tend faithfully to the past: specifically, to the confession of our ancestors in the faith and to the root of that confession in the scriptural witness that God has generated through his Word and Spirit. Thus this volume seeks to bridge the classical and the contemporary by enlisting the contribution of some of today's leading theologians and by aligning itself with the catholic and Reformational heritage of the church. In this manner, these essays are meant to contribute to the flourishing of theology within the church today.

Because this commitment to renewal through retrieval functions on the margins of contemporary strategies for market success in our contemporary society (where it is invoked only when the retro might sell), and, still further, because it often exists even on the periphery of contemporary church life (where it is mostly perpetuated only for sentimental rather than principled reasons), we will reflect briefly on the theological impetus for such a commitment as more than a mere stratagem for success but, profoundly, as a promise of the gospel itself.

Renewal

Theology does not come easily. Better put, faithful theology comes by grace or not at all, while idolatry comes quite naturally to those of us who make our bed east of Eden. John Calvin famously referred to our hearts as idol-making factories.[3] In a world of spin and with a heart full of idols, true wisdom and

2. In parallel to the intent expressed thirty years ago to address the catholic church from the Lutheran confession specifically, as stated by Carl E. Braaten and Robert W. Jenson, eds., preface to *Christian Dogmatics* (Philadelphia: Fortress, 1984), 1:xviii. That multiauthor confessional dogmatics exemplified for the editors what was needed now in addressing the catholic church from the Reformed confessional theology.

3. John Calvin, *Institutes of the Christian Religion*, ed. John T. McNeill, trans. Ford Lewis Battles (Louisville: Westminster John Knox, 2006), 1.11.8. Calvin made similar comments in his exegetical material, e.g., *Commentary on Ezekiel* 1:13, 80; *Commentary on 2 Corinthians* 11:3, 141.

genuinely faithful speech seem impossible. Idolatry without and within appears to throw all theological efforts into question. So, "The central theological principle of the Bible [is] the rejection of idolatry."[4]

But grace does come, and it brings theology along with it. God sends a Word, and his Word does not return void. God speaks into the chaos, and his speech does bring order, beauty, and goodness. God does these things, so theology is by grace or not at all. Grace does not undercut or circumvent intellectual reflection. Rather, grace comes as this promise: "Think over what I say, for the Lord will give you understanding in everything" (2 Tim. 2:7). The nature of God's gift is illumining. It does not augment our intellectual activity; it provides the context, conditions, and character for its proper functioning. B. B. Warfield, the noted twentieth-century Presbyterian theologian from Princeton Seminary, was asked which was more vital to theological work: ten hours of study or ten minutes on one's knees in prayer. Warfield retorted that ten hours of prayerful study on one's knees was surely the order of the day.[5] His pastoral reminder points to a profound theological truth: the life of faith does not manifest itself in habits of inactivity but in free service and loving self-sacrifice. And Karl Barth, another famed Reformed theologian of the twentieth century, concurred with his assessment that "prayer without study would be empty; study without prayer would be blind."[6]

Theology is not easy, and it is not natural, not for those of us who are sons of Adam and daughters of Eve, plagued by sin's onset. But theology is a genuinely human practice and really does take shape in the context of the body of Christ. Minds are renewed. Eyes are opened. Congregations do hear. Grace takes the common, even the corrupt, and sets it apart for a sacred use. "The light shines in the darkness, and the darkness has not overcome it" (John 1:5). Indeed, "The true light, which gives light to everyone, was coming into the world . . . the only God, who is at the Father's side, he has made him known" (John 1:9, 18). So the saints do know their Lord and, in knowing him, love him. Our theological ventures are premised upon this promise: behold, the Lord makes all things new, including our sinful reason and our darkened suppression of the knowledge of the one true God.

4. Moshe Halbertal and Avishai Margalit, *Idolatry*, trans. Naomi Goldblum (Cambridge, MA: Harvard University Press, 1992), 10.
5. "The Religious Life of Theological Students," in *Selected Shorter Writings of Benjamin B. Warfield*, ed. John E. Meeter (Phillipsburg, NJ: P&R, 2001), 1:412.
6. Karl Barth, *Evangelical Theology: An Introduction*, trans. Grover Foley (New York: Anchor, 1964), 151.

Retrieval

Renewal is promised by the "giver of life," but we do well to ask how his lordly grace is bestowed and what effect his *modus operandi* should exercise on our intellectual efforts. A healthy dose of Christian anthropology puts the lie to any premonition that the path forward lies in cutting ties with the past. While we must put to death our sin, the way to glory surely does not involve a detachment from nature or from our history, at least not our history within the economy of salvation. Indeed, what we find is that the "great cloud of witnesses" draws us out of our delusions and overwhelms us with an illuminating testimony. With Nicholas Lash we confess, "Christian doctrine . . . functions, or should function, as a set of protocols against idolatry."[7]

Many evangelicals have felt duty bound to shirk tradition and, specifically, the role of creeds and confessions in the church for the sake of maintaining an emphasis on God's action in revealing himself to us. For these saints, tradition has become a surrogate or substitute for God's own revelation. Contrary to the words of Lash, they view tradition as itself an idol, not a protocol against idolatry. Yet this sort of maneuver fails to honor the biblical emphasis on the way in which Jesus Christ reveals himself to us through the ongoing practices of his people. To keep the heritage of the church at bay, then, is not merely to make a judgment call about its history or to adopt a particular path for intellectual progress; no, to do so is to adopt a posture of disbelief in the promise of Jesus. Hilary of Poitiers writes that "only in receiving can we know," and the Lord has determined that our reception of this knowledge come through the witness of one generation to another.[8] To do so is to honor the fifth commandment, believing that in doing so we might live long and blessed in the divine kingdom.

Dogmatics is the disciplined effort to have our eyes and mouths retrained by the gospel. In so doing we inhabit the classroom of the communion of saints, and we seek to learn from its instruction. We read the creeds of the ecumenical church, and we study the confessions of the Protestant Reformation. We go to school in the texts of the ancient church fathers and the medieval doctors of the faith. We consider the modern articulations of the gospel and the contemporary testimonies to God's Word. Dogmatics is receptive, believing that the Word of Christ dwells richly not merely when savored by individuals but also when sung and spoken by the people of God (Col. 3:16–17).

7. Nicholas Lash, *The Beginning and End of "Religion"* (Cambridge: Cambridge University Press, 1996), 194.

8. Hilary of Poitiers, *The Trinity*, in vol. 6 of *Nicene and Post-Nicene Fathers*, series 2, ed. W. Sanday, trans. E. W. Watson and L. Pullan (Peabody, MA: Hendrickson, 2004), 2.35.

Whereas some approaches to dogmatics suggest a pacified relation between the gospel and tradition, our approach cannot be so sanguine. The gospel does generate a tradition (1 Cor. 15:3; 2 Tim. 2:2): this Christ does give birth to Christians. Yet the history of the church is one of conflict marked by that famed Reformational claim that we are simultaneously the just and the sinful people of God. Thus our appropriation of ecclesial tradition must always be a critical traditioning wherein we seek to be shaped by the truth, goodness, and beauty of our heritage and not to be drawn into a pathology of untruth, evil, and ugliness by our native resources. Such critique goes back not only to the way our incarnate Lord addressed the religious traditions of his day but to the prophetic witness of old as well. Catholicity and tradition are not about calm conservatism, then, but about honoring the context within which God names and makes Christians and speaks and sustains Christian reasoning. We entrust ourselves to the guidance of the church because we believe the Triune God and because we honor the path he has set before us, not because we find any of our ancestors to offer infallible readings of the Holy Scriptures.[9] Holy Scripture calls us to embrace "tradition"—the faithful transmission of biblical truth through time, rather than mere "custom"—which may simply be the historical perpetuation of error. We find a precious touchstone to this faithful tradition in the creeds and confessions of the church.

Renewal through Retrieval: Reformed Catholicity and the Theological Task

The essays that follow chart a catholic and Reformed path forward, then, by pointing backward. In varying places and to different ends, they look to a number of figures and texts as resources for the journey.

These essays are not merely ecclesial but also dogmatic in that they seek to reflect intellectually and synthetically on the task of the Christian confession. They are not systematic if that means unpacking doctrines by way of logical deduction from a principle. But they are systematic in a synthetic sense in that they attend to the full breadth of the biblical witness as well as the order, emphases, and coherence of that full swathe of canonical teaching. The attentive reader will notice that the Triune God is the center of reflection in the essays that follow, since Christian theology is about God and all things as they relate to him. More often than not, chapters move explicitly from reflection

9. For further reflection on a distinctly Reformed approach to catholicity and tradition, see Michael Allen and Scott R. Swain, *Reformed Catholicity: The Promise of Retrieval for Theology and Biblical Interpretation* (Grand Rapids: Baker Academic, 2015).

on God's character (in and of himself) and only then (in light of the fullness and life that are his alone) to consider his works and wonders done for the sake of others: whether creation writ large or his covenant people.

This collection—and the wider practice of dogmatic theology of which it is but a piece—is not meant to replace the reading of Holy Scripture but to illuminate it. Just as pastors and evangelists serve to equip the saints for the work of ministry (Eph. 4:12), so these essays seek to equip saints for a more faithful hearing of and testimony to the words of the prophets and apostles. Zacharius Ursinus reflected that the "highest" purpose for studying church doctrine is to prepare us "for the reading, understanding, and exposition of the holy Scriptures. For as the doctrine of the catechism and common places (*loci communes*) are taken out of the Scriptures, and are directed by them as their rule, so they again lead us, as it were, by the hand to the Scriptures."[10] Dogmatic reasoning is meant to flow from and send one back to the task of exegesis. Like good art criticism, it is drawn from careful viewing of a specimen, but it is beneficial only if it aids further interaction with the specimen itself.

Such is our hope for this volume: that readers will find its chapters a reliable guide to the mysteries of the faith attested by the prophets and apostles and a prompt in the ongoing journey of theological reason between the darkness of Egypt and the light of Canaan. By listening to the witness of pilgrims before us and by attending to the broader terrain in which we roam, we hope that the task of journeying well—that is, faithfully—will be aided and encouraged.

Recognizing that faithfulness on this path depends wholly on the resources of the one who has accompanied the church even before the onset of our own pilgrimage, we conclude with a plea for divine assistance.

> May our most great and wonderful God, who begat his own eternal Son Jesus Christ, our Redeemer, by eternal generation and sanctifies him to us by eternal predestination, that he may be our wisdom, righteousness, sanctification and redemption—may that same God also bestow upon us the spirit of wisdom, that growing stronger by his power we may increase in the saving treasures of this knowledge and wisdom unto the unity of faith and recognition of him, until we become a complete man according to the proper measure of the stature which is fitting for that most distinguished and glorious body in Christ Jesus our head and Savior, for his glory. Amen.[11]

---

10. Zacharias Ursinus, *Commentary on the Heidelberg Catechism*, trans. G. W. Williard (Phillipsburg, NJ: P&R, 1985), 10.

11. Franciscus Junius, *A Treatise on True Theology: With the Life of Franciscus Junius*, trans. David C. Noe (Grand Rapids: Reformation Heritage Books, 2014), 234.

1

Knowledge of God

MICHAEL ALLEN

A Theology of Knowing God

Christian theology is human reason disciplined by the gospel. Reason is not aloof or alone. It is implicated in the story of God's generosity. Reason is not shaped in only a parochial way, by things like sociocultural influences and partisan biases. It is baptized in the common life of the saints. Disorder arises when reason is considered apart from the rule of the gospel. When the context for intellectual self-awareness shifts from the country of the gospel to another land, fissures and imbalances set in.

The ills of recent thinking about thinking can be traced to a relocation of such reflection, no longer in the economy of sin and grace but instead transplanted to the orbit of (scientific) technique or (cultural) training. In his essay "What Is Enlightenment?," Immanuel Kant belittled reliance on religious formation, arguing for a moral necessity to question such indoctrination and proceed to reason independently of ecclesiastical and familial order. By now a veritable industry has arisen, offering intellectual histories of the Enlightenment and its roots in earlier shifts in thinking about reality as such, our minds, and the connection between the two.[1] We need not buy in hook, line,

---

1. For the most influential in recent years, see Charles Taylor, *A Secular Age* (Cambridge, MA: Belknap, 2007); David Bentley Hart, *The Beauty of the Infinite: The Aesthetics of Christian*

and sinker to any given genealogy, though we can surely see that the broad emphases of Enlightenment thinking about thinking located the knowing subject as one with direct and immediate access to the known (irrespective of its nature: whether creaturely or, as we are considering, the Creator himself).

And supposed rejections of Enlightenment rationality tend to be predictable responses made by those who throw their arms up in protest without changing the fundamental terms of the game. Scientific technique may be trusted no longer as a reliable broker of truth, but now knowledge is political power. In place of objectivity comes spin. The mind no longer needs to learn a certain set of methods; the mind needs to be liberated from groupthink by having the biases of one's parents, priests, or president exposed and alternative approaches of "the other" articulated. Knowledge is reduced to angle, perspective, and approach. It may not be perceived as technique, but it is no less restricted to the realm of human action: now it is social rather than scientific, perhaps, but describable by means of materialistic processes just the same.

Roger Lundin has traced such a maneuver ably in his volume *From Nature to Experience*, focusing on the nineteenth century as a time of shifting beliefs about knowledge and truth. For a variety of reasons—ranging from Darwinian naturalism to the violence of the American Civil War—Lundin argues that faith in the idea of a nature that was given order from above and might communicate truth to those below sunk in this long nineteenth century. Biological evolution seemed to raise questions about nature and order in the world, while the moral ambiguities and failures of the American strife seemed to raise questions about anything like a natural law or common conscience granted from above.[2] Whereas Kant had turned us from revelation to natural order, the experiences of struggle (biologically and politically) in the modern era seemed to raise questions about nature itself. Some other source of reason and wisdom must be sought. The failure to perceive an illuminating order

Truth (Grand Rapids: Eerdmans, 2003), part 1; J. B. Schneewind, *The Invention of Autonomy: A History of Modern Moral Philosophy* (Cambridge: Cambridge University Press, 1997); John Milbank, *Theology and Social Theory: Beyond Secular Reason* (Oxford: Blackwell, 1993); Charles Taylor, *Sources of the Self: The Making of the Modern Identity* (Cambridge, MA: Harvard University Press, 1992); Amos Funkenstein, *Theology and the Scientific Imagination: From the Middle Ages to the Seventeenth Century* (Princeton, NJ: Princeton University Press, 1986); Alasdair MacIntyre, *After Virtue: A Study in Moral Theory* (Notre Dame, IN: University of Notre Dame Press, 1981). The most recent intellectual history of this scale is Brad S. Gregory, *The Unintended Reformation: How a Religious Revolution Secularized Society* (Cambridge, MA: Belknap, 2012); the most accessible entry to this genre may be Stanley Hauerwas, *With the Grain of the Universe: The Church's Witness and Natural Theology* (Grand Rapids: Brazos, 2001).

2. Roger Lundin, *From Nature to Experience: The American Search for Cultural Authority* (Lanham, MD: Rowman & Littlefield, 2005), 3, 19; see also Louis Menand, *The Metaphysical Club: A Story of Ideas in America* (New York: Farrar, Straus and Giroux, 2001), 69.

led, first, to the search for a cohesive aesthetic (experience) and, second, to a focus on pragmatic means (of varying sorts). Thus pragmatism became the philosophy of the twentieth century over against more metaphysical approaches to truth and knowledge.

We will not attempt to locate a theological fall from grace, whether in the rise of nominalism, the person of Scotus, or the philosophy of a René Descartes or (later) a Christian Wolff. Yet we must note that for various reasons, reason has been plausibly thought within very different contexts: no longer the space of sin and its overcoming, now the territory of technical mastery or political pull. Of such approaches, completely fixed on creaturely activity as they are, the verdict of William Butler Yeats is proven true: "Things fall apart; the centre cannot hold."[3] When centered fully in the creaturely realm, reason does fall apart, and wisdom cannot hold.

If we are to avoid such maladies, then our task is reflective, namely, to address the various ways that the gospel chastens our thinking about human reason. Elsewhere I have argued that the gospel can be summarized thus: "The gospel is the glorious news that the God who has life in himself freely shares that life with us and, when we refuse that life in sin, graciously gives us life yet again in Christ."[4] Life involves truth. Indeed, a theology of knowing God will focus on this aspect of the life we have with God in Christ. God gives truth as an essential facet of that ever-bountiful blessing of life. So we can modify our thesis statement and fix our eyes on this aspect of the gospel: *The gospel is the glorious news that the God who is truth himself freely shares that truth with us and, when we refuse that truth in sin, graciously gives us truth yet again in Christ.* Our reflections on the place of intellectual reason within the gospel are prompted by the confession of the first of the Ten Theses of Berne (1528): "The holy, Christian Church, whose only Head is Christ, is born of the Word of God, abides in the same, and does not listen to the voice of a stranger."[5] Knowledge is provided for by divine communication—the very Word of God—and we do well to consider the metaphysics and ethics of its communication. In the following reflections, we will address matters metaphysical by considering the context of theology within the economy of God's external works, and we will then reflect on the ethics of theology by defining the character of theology within this same economy, according to its own rules.

3. William Butler Yeats, "The Second Coming" (1919), www.poetryfoundation.org/poem/172062.
4. Michael Allen, *Justification and the Gospel: A Dogmatic Sketch* (Grand Rapids: Baker Academic, 2013), 3.
5. Ten Theses of Berne (1528), in *Reformed Confessions of the Sixteenth Century*, ed. Arthur C. Cochrane (Louisville: Westminster John Knox, 2003), 49.

The Context of Theology

The discipline of the gospel can be best expressed by considering the story of the gospel. Human reason has a history, and its everyday exercise can be appreciated only when its biography is understood. To that end, we will consider the impact on human reason of the key moments of the redemptive-historical movement from eternity to economy: God's eternity, creation, sin, and reconciliation. At each point I will highlight a key distinction that has been employed by theologians to emphasize the operative nature of this doctrine. Such distinctions are not employed to tone down or cordon off the effects of doctrines; rather, they are flags reminding one of the doctrines and insisting that no side of the divide be ignored or obfuscated. Distinctions in doctrine serve to keep us alive to the breadth of God's address to us in Scripture. Thus these classical doctrines, if retrieved as exegetical signals, may well help to renew our efforts to think well in light of the gospel.

First, *the gospel is the glorious news that God is truth himself.* The God who has truth in himself *elects* to share that truth with others. "God is know-able to Himself; the Son to the Father, but also the Father to the Son. This is the first and last thing which is to be said about the knowability of God even from the point of view of the readiness of man."[6]

Scholastic theologians noted this truth of God's own self-knowledge by distinguishing between theology *ad nostra* (our theology) and theology *in se* (theology in himself). Duns Scotus employed the distinction to emphasize that only God's mind is proportionate to knowing God.[7] John Calvin would point out that "there is a measure of impropriety (*improprium quodammodo*) in what is taken from earthly things and applied to the hidden majesty of God," showing that he employed the distinction between what is and is not propor-tional to its mental object.[8] Many Protestant scholastics concurred, but other Protestants suggested that "theology" really applies—strictly speaking—only to our knowledge and talk of God.[9] Richard Muller argues that William Perkins, William Ames, and John Owen each focus on human knowledge of God; they do not deny that God knows himself, but they refuse to speak of

6. Karl Barth, *Church Dogmatics* II/1, ed. G. W. Bromiley and T. F. Torrance, trans. T. H. L. Parker et al. (Edinburgh: T&T Clark, 1957), 151.
7. Duns Scotus, *Ordinatio* prologue 3.1–3.
8. John Calvin, *The Epistle of Paul to the Hebrews and the First and Second Epistles of Peter,* ed. David W. Torrance and Thomas F. Torrance, trans. William B. Johnston (Grand Rapids: Eerdmans, 1963), 7–8 (on Heb. 1:3).
9. Many Reformed scholastics employed the language of Scotus while radically disagreeing with his repudiation of the analogy of being (*analogia entis*), wherein he argued that there is no proportion between theology *in se* and theology *ad nostra.*

this divine wisdom as "theology."[10] There may be other ways for these theologians to remember that knowledge of God begins in and with God, but refusal to speak of God's self-knowledge as "theology" seems to set one up for one of two errors. Either one will lose the distinction between creaturely and divine knowledge of God (without a distinction to ward off the confusion) or one will believe the two wisdoms drift apart into completely different, that is, equivocal knowledge (without the distinction to remind us of their fundamentally analogous and participatory nature).

It is good news that God has knowledge in himself before any interaction with or even determination to bring about creatures. God knows all. God knows himself. Thus God is quite aware that any economy, that is, any interaction between God and creatures, will be for his glory and their good rather than mutual hostility or harm. God needs no experimental groups to learn of his fullness, and God has no need of history to demonstrate to himself the character of the Trinity or of creatures. From the foundations of all time, God knows. We should join Job and the prophets in returning to this fundamental truth (see Job 38–41).

Second, *the God who is truth himself freely shares that truth with us.* This inclusion tells us something fundamental about both God and ourselves. Regarding God, it shows us that his knowledge is relational in nature. His inner communication freely spills over into creative and covenantal speech. Regarding ourselves, it points to the type of existence and knowledge we can possess. Jesus Christ is the author and perfecter of faith (Heb. 12:2). This tells us something fundamental about knowledge of the divine. It occurs first in God (its author) even as it reaches out to include genuine human subjects (its perfection in faith).

Such knowledge is inclusive, that is, it participates within the knowledge that God has of himself.[11] Augustine addressed this idea in the conclusion to his *Confessions*: "When people see [your works] with the help of your Spirit, it is you who are seeing in them. . . . So also no one knows the things of God except the Spirit of God."[12] In Christ we do live and move and have our knowledge, as an epistemological extension of Colossians 1 would have it. Knowledge is by means of revelation: either God makes himself known,

10. Richard A. Muller, *Post-Reformation Reformed Dogmatics: The Rise and Development of Reformed Orthodoxy, ca. 1520 to ca. 1725*, vol. 1, *Prolegomena to Theology*, 2nd ed. (Grand Rapids: Baker Academic, 2003), 232–33. Muller also lists Turretin, but the quotation cited below (see note 14) proves this to be an inaccurate interpretation of his theology.

11. For an account of participation that is disciplined by the gospel, specifically by the Creator/creature distinction, see Allen, *Justification and the Gospel*, 33–70.

12. Augustine, *Confessions*, trans. Maria Boulding (Hyde Park, NY: New City, 1997), 13.31.46.

or he will not be known (1 Cor. 2:11–12). Thus knowledge must be participatory or nonexistent.

The shape of created knowledge is thus good yet limited. Here another distinction was cast to highlight its particular nature: whereas God possessed archetypal knowledge, humans were able to reason in ectypal ways.[13] Francis Turretin provides an instructive description:

> True theology is divided into: (1) infinite and uncreated, which is God's essential knowledge of himself (Matt. 11:27) in which he alone is at the same time the object known (*epistēton*), the knowledge (*epistēmōn*), and the knower (*epistēmē*), and that which he decreed to reveal to us concerning himself which is commonly called archetypal; and (2) finite and created, which is the image and ectype (*ektypon*) of the infinite and archetypal (*prōtotypou*) (viz., the ideas which creatures possess concerning God and divine things, taking form from that supreme knowledge and communicated to intelligent creatures, either by hypostatical union with the soul of Christ . . . ; or by beatific vision . . . ; or by revelation . . .).[14]

Both forms are "true theology," though they are markedly different in shape. In one case, the knower is the known. But in the other case, the knower is a dependent—whether self-aware or not, faithful or not—of the known. And this plumbs down to a deep spiritual insight: grace precedes and creates the freedom for us to name and invoke God in worship, prayer, and witness. We follow the Word of God, given freely by the gracious Trinity of love. The key principle is that the gospel includes its telling; the way we come to know about God is itself gracious. "By grace alone" (*sola gratia*) applies across the theological board, affecting the very way that sinners come to reason about a holy God.

Knowledge of this God by these creatures is mysterious. And contrary to our immediate impulse, this is not necessarily a sign of a failure. As Katherine Sonderegger reminds us, "Divine mystery is not a sign of our failure in knowledge; but rather our success. It is because we know truly and properly—because we obey in faith the First Commandment—that God is mystery."[15]

13. For the pedigree of this distinction, see Willem J. van Asselt, "The Fundamental Meaning of Theology: Archetypal and Ectypal Theology in Seventeenth-Century Reformed Thought," *Westminster Theological Journal* 64, no. 2 (2002): 319–35.

14. Francis Turretin, *Institutes of Elenctic Theology*, ed. James T. Dennison Jr., trans. George Musgrave Giger (Phillipsburg, NJ: P&R, 1992), 1.2.6. This distinction (archetypal/ectypal) is doing similar work to a patristic distinction (theology/economy) found in texts such as Basil of Caesarea, *Against Eunomius*, trans. Mark DelCogliano and Andrew Radde-Gallwitz (Washington, DC: Catholic University of America Press, 2011), 1.14.

15. Katherine Sonderegger, *Systematic Theology*, vol. 1, *The Doctrine of God* (Minneapolis: Fortress, 2015), 24. For similar sentiments, see Barth, *Church Dogmatics* II/1, 3: "[God] remains a

Mystery can be the result of sheer ungivenness. "The secret things belong to the LORD," says Moses (Deut. 29:29). The vice of curiosity leads one to pursue or pontificate on things outside one's knowledge. This vice is the noetic manifestation of pride: overconfidence in one's own capacities and unbelief in one's need to depend on the gift of another (which, in this case, has not been rendered).[16] Humans are constantly inclined to describe the inner workings of reality rather than to depend on the Word in whom reality is upheld.

But mystery also comes from revealedness. Barth is instructive:

> A fully restrained and fully alive doctrine of God's attributes will take as its fundamental point of departure the truth that God is for us fully revealed and fully concealed in his self-disclosure. We cannot say partly revealed and partly concealed, but we must actually say wholly revealed and wholly concealed at one and the same time. We must say wholly revealed because by the grace of revelation our human views and concepts are invited and exalted to share in the truth of God and therefore in a marvelous way made instruments of a real knowledge of God (in his being for us and as he is in himself). We must say wholly concealed because our human views and concepts . . . have not in themselves the smallest capacity to apprehend God.[17]

The holy God really does show himself, yet that revelation is no simple possession. Our knowledge is in no way univocal (strictly identical) with God's knowledge or reality, even though it is also not equivocal (strictly different) from them either. Hence medieval and post-Reformation scholastic theologians alike speak of the analogy between divine and human wisdom. We have true theology, but we have it mysteriously and imperfectly; this is no flaw, for in itself finitude is a good. Thus "the true goal of theological inquiry is not the resolution of theological problems, but the discernment of what the mystery of faith is."[18]

---

mystery to us *because* He Himself has made Himself so clear and certain to us" (emphasis mine). Note that the mystery comes precisely because of the clarity and certainty, not in spite of it.

16. On the vice of curiosity, see John Webster, *The Domain of the Word: Scripture and Theological Reason* (London: T&T Clark, 2012), 193–202; John Calvin, *The Second Epistle of Paul the Apostle to the Corinthians and the Epistles to Timothy, Titus, and Philemon*, ed. David W. Torrance and Thomas F. Torrance, trans. T. A. Smail (Grand Rapids: Eerdmans, 1964), 157 (on 2 Cor. 12:4).

17. Barth, *Church Dogmatics* II/1, 341–42. Robert Price has observed that this distinction between veiling and unveiling functions similarly to a doctrine of analogy, though Barth seems allergic to such a doctrine at this point due to his worries about natural theology (*Letters of the Divine Word: The Perfections of God in Karl Barth's Church Dogmatics* [London: T&T Clark, 2011], 41–42).

18. Thomas Weinandy, *Does God Suffer?* (Notre Dame, IN: University of Notre Dame Press, 2000), 32.

As Protestants, we need not fear language of an analogy of being (*analogia entis*).[19] By God's grace, we do participate in his knowledge: we do not possess it as he does (univocally), but we are also not left bereft of divine truth to find our own way to knowledge (equivocally). Rather, God is our light who illumines the world (John 1:4–5). God himself needs no illumination, for he is light. Thus our knowledge certainly is not possessed as God's. But God is our light, and we do see through his effulgence and radiance. If covenant includes communication, and if that communication is self-communication, and if that self-communication includes the other in one's own knowledge of oneself, then we must speak of a participation by grace in the knowledge of God that is God's by nature and, furthermore, this participatory knowledge must take the form of analogous knowledge (neither univocal nor equivocal).[20] All this talk of an analogy of being and of participation in God's knowledge by grace is a reminder to tend to the words of the psalmist: "For with you is the fountain of life; in your light do we see light" (Ps. 36:9).

Third, though *the God who is truth himself freely shares that truth with us, we refuse that truth in sin.* That is, the truthful God *was disbelieved* by those creatures who instead cast their lot in with the lie. While we have confessed that finitude is no flaw, we fail to believe this and buy into the lie that finitude is to be fled. We seek as sons of Adam and daughters of Eve to possess the divine knowledge in our timing and on our own terms: we think east of Eden.

Martin Luther reminds us that the exercise of human reason remains constitutively linked to the history of sin and its aftereffects. He employed the terms "theologian of glory" and "theologian of the cross" to signal the difference

19. Protests to the analogy of being stem largely from Karl Barth (who referred to it as the "invention of the Antichrist"). He protested ways in which late nineteenth- and early twentieth-century Roman Catholic theologians employed this terminology without truly upholding the distinction between Creator and creature; over the next few decades, to some degree because of Barth's protest, Roman Catholic theologians recovered a robust approach to the doctrine that maintained that crucial distinction in a traditional and biblical manner (see Keith Johnson, *Karl Barth and the* Analogia Entis [London: T&T Clark, 2010]). Unlike Johnson and Barth, however, I would argue that the time has come for a Protestant return to our own classical resources, wherein the analogy of being was upheld. Barth's concern that this analogous knowledge can be enjoyed (that is, participated in) now only by those who experience grace as mortification and vivification before perfection can be upheld within the orbit of the traditional doctrine (even as held by Thomas Aquinas), according to Thomas Joseph White, "'Through Him All Things Were Made' (John 1:3): The Analogy of the Word Incarnate according to St. Thomas Aquinas and Its Ontological Presuppositions," in *The Analogy of Being: Invention of the Antichrist or the Wisdom of God?*, ed. Thomas Joseph White (Grand Rapids: Eerdmans, 2011), 277.

20. On the link between participation and analogy, see Reinhard Hütter, "Attending to the Wisdom of God—from Effect to Cause, from Creation to God: A *relecture* of the Analogy of Being according to Thomas Aquinas," in White, ed., *Analogy of Being*, 209–45; contra Bruce D. Marshall, "Christ the End of Analogy," in White, ed., *Analogy of Being*, 280–313.

between one who thinks him- or herself to be on a paradisal journey upward and onward and one who thinks him- or herself to be within a confrontational challenge marked by thrusts and parries, by being put to death and being made alive.[21] "A theologian of glory calls evil good and good evil," says Luther, suggesting that one who seeks to find glory in their own power will go the way of the lie. By contrast, "a theologian of the cross calls the thing what it actually is," for this one "comprehends the visible and manifest things of God seen through suffering and the cross."[22] Luther's distinction, like others before it, is meant to remind us of all the Scriptures teach: In this case we should not forget the words of 1 Corinthians 1–2, where Christ is not only our redemption but also our wisdom from God (1:30). And this wisdom will seem foolish to the natural intuition (1 Cor. 2:12, 14–15). Sin does affect all things—corporate and individual, cosmic and personal, physical and mental—and the intellectual faculties and their exercise surely reside within this terrain of destruction and despair. This side of Eden, there is a "wisdom of this age," and we do well to remember that it is "doomed to pass away" (1 Cor. 2:6).

It is important to note that the tides of intellectual disarray do not simply occur out there in the world or the present age over against the settled and sanctified borders of the church. The plague of sin battles on within all creatures of our God and King. The mire of transgression stains our sight and deprives us of discerning wisdom. Even those in Christ must continue to pray—with the apostle—for "a spirit of wisdom and of revelation in the knowledge of him [the Father of glory]" and that the eyes of their heart might be opened (Eph. 1:18 NASB). While the church is unlike the world in battling the falsehood by grace, the church is like the world in being beset by the lie's temptation. The church does fall into lapses in wisdom and discernment from time to time, looking to resources other than God's self-revelation for guidance and spurning the very notion of dependence in favor of self-constitution and self-preservation. But the Lord does not leave the church to its own devices: he pledges his Spirit to lead and keep the church in his truth (John 14–17). But we have moved ahead of ourselves: as we do remember that sin's effects continue to plague even Christian knowledge of God, so we must see the sting of sin brushed aside by God's life-giving work.

Fourth, *the gospel is the glorious news that the God who is truth himself freely shares that truth with us and, when we refuse that truth in sin, graciously gives us truth yet again in Christ.* The God who has truth in himself *gave*

---

21. Martin Luther, "Heidelberg Disputation, 1518," in *Career of the Reformer 1*, ed. Harold J. Grimm, vol. 31 of *Luther's Works* (Philadelphia: Fortress, 1957), 39–79.
22. Ibid., 53, 52.

truth yet again in Christ Jesus. Up to this point, the story sounds like little good news, of opportunity lost and none else. Indeed, the truth known by God of himself seems to hover over the darkened recesses of this rebellious country, where the sons of Adam and the daughters of Eve recede back into the abyss of ignorance. Becoming wise, they turn foolish.

> Of course, at this point man still seems to stand outside. Everything still seems to be invalid for him. For we are not God. Indeed we are not. But God is man. For Jesus Christ, the Lord attested in the Old and New Testaments, is as little God in Himself and as such as He is man in himself and as such. He is God who is man. This is Jesus Christ. In Him we do not stand outside but inside; we participate in the first and last.[23]

The language of theological principles signals the dependence human reason maintains on the gifts of the Triune God for any knowledge of God. The seventeenth-century divine Johannes Wollebius prods us toward a distinction: "The principle of the being of theology is God; the principle by which it is known is the Word of God."[24] That is, the ontological principle of all such knowledge is God himself, the only one who possesses this knowledge. God's overflowing wisdom comes to humans in two forms. "The Church is *creatura verbi divini*: the creature of the divine Word. The Church is constituted by God's action and not by any human action. . . . And the way in which the Church is constituted by divine action determines the character and scope of human action in the Church."[25] The church's life and knowledge are enjoyed in a creaturely manner determined—in both character and scope—by their dependence on the divine Word. The Word's activity takes two forms: external and internal.

The external principle is a person, the incarnate Son of God. His hypostatic union provides the surety that humans can know the only true God in a faithful and fitting way. This humanity of Christ in its stark actuality is essential to God's self-revelation. In Jesus Christ, God's truth has become actual for us in space and time. Jesus Christ is the truth, the mystery in whom are

23. Barth, *Church Dogmatics* II/1, 151.
24. Johannes Wollebius, *Compendium theologiae christianae* prol. 1.3, in *Reformed Dogmatics*, ed. J. W. Beardslee (Grand Rapids: Baker, 1977), 30.
25. Christoph Schwöbel, "The Creature of the Word: Recovering the Ecclesiology of the Reformers," in *On Being the Church: Essays on the Christian Community*, ed. Colin E. Gunton and Daniel W. Hardy (Edinburgh: T&T Clark, 1989), 122; see also Oswald Bayer, *Authorität und Kritik: Leibliches Wort. Reformation und Neuzeit im Konflikt* (Tübingen: Mohr Siebeck, 1992), 149: "Because Christians owe their freedom to this word, they never really gain control of that freedom."

hidden all the treasures of wisdom and knowledge, and from whose fullness we may all benefit. The astounding thing is that the eternal Word by whom all things were created became a creature without ceasing to be that eternal Word, and therefore his very creatureliness constitutes the act of revelation and is the guarantee that revelation is here within creation and accessible to humans. It is the guarantee that God's revelation is revelation to creaturely humanity within the limitations of time and space. Because the eternal has become temporal, men and women can know the eternal truth in creaturely temporal form, the eternal truth in time.[26]

The incarnate Son is the true image of God and the faithful last Adam. No one knows the Father but the Son and those to whom the Son reveals him. It is the Son's knowledge—genuine human knowledge—upon which the whole doctrine of revelation pivots.

The internal principle is the pledged Spirit, who illumines the Word and not only enables but also actualizes reception of that Word in the minds of God's people. The prophet recounts: "Thus says the LORD God: Behold, I will open your graves and raise you from your graves, O my people. . . . And I will put my Spirit within you, and you shall live, and I will place you in your own land. Then you shall know that I am the LORD; I have spoken, and I will do it, declares the LORD" (Ezek. 37:12–14). The giving of life takes the form of a Spirit coming to indwell and thus to enable knowledge ("then you shall know"). The objective word of the King requires loyal and dependent acceptance in a pliable mind and attentive heart. The Spirit is this agent of interpersonal translation, enabling the hearer to grasp the communicative work of the speaker.[27]

Inside and outside, then, the principle of our living and our knowing remains the one true God. Across the board revelation comes in Christ alone. Calvin reminds us that the Triune God works in his elect: though this comes in two ways or principles, the Word and Spirit work the mission of the one God.[28] Fresh knowledge of God is birthed like creation from the deep: "For God, who said, 'Let light shine out of darkness,' has shone in our hearts to give the light of the knowledge of the glory of God in the face of Jesus Christ" (2 Cor. 4:6). This glorious light is not native to sinners, though it was natural in Eden. Indeed, "the god of this world has blinded the minds of the

---

26. Thomas F. Torrance, *The Incarnation: The Person and Life of Christ*, ed. Robert T. Walker (Downers Grove, IL: IVP Academic, 2008), 185–86. See also Dietrich Bonhoeffer, *Ethics*, ed. Clifford J. Green, trans. Reinhard Krauss, Charles C. West, and Douglas W. Stott, vol. 6 of *Dietrich Bonhoeffer Works*, ed. Wayne Whitson Floyd Jr. (Minneapolis: Fortress, 2005), 54.

27. See also 1 Cor. 2:9–16; John 14:26; 15:26–27; 16:8–11, 13–15.

28. John Calvin, *Institutes of the Christian Religion*, ed. John T. McNeill, trans. Ford Lewis Battles (Philadelphia: Westminster, 1960), 2.5.5.

unbelievers, to keep them from seeing the light of the gospel of the glory of Christ, who is the image of God" (2 Cor. 4:4). In the "face of Jesus Christ," however, we see God shine all the way "in our hearts." Knowledge reborn in the Son's grace is not merely knowledge *of such* but wisdom *with such*: it is the presence of the Son by his Spirit that makes his blessings known.[29]

Clarity needs to be sought regarding the nature of this christological context for theological knowledge because it has led to some fairly lush proposals in the name of avoiding speculation and disciplining the human tendency toward idolatry. We confess: God is seen in the face of Jesus Christ.

> Once God was incomprehensible and inaccessible, invisible and entirely unthinkable. But now he wanted to be seen, he wanted to be understood, he wanted to be known. How was this done, you ask? God lay in a manger and lay on the Virgin's breast. He preached on a mountain, prayed through the night, and hung on a cross. He lay pale in death, was free among the dead, and was master of hell. He rose on the third day, showed the apostles the signs of victory where nails once were, and ascended before their eyes to the inner recesses of heaven. . . . When I think on any of these things, I am thinking of God, and in all these things he is now my God.[30]

Bernard is extrapolating the statement of John 1:18: "No one has ever seen God; the only God, who is at the Father's side, he has made him known." The Word comes to give life, and John 1 describes this beneficent work as involving (among other things) the giving of light (1:4–5). Indeed, the Son was "the true light, which gives light to everyone" (1:9). The prologue of this Gospel according to John then reveals that light is given only with glory that "we have seen" (1:14) and glory is the personal revelation of God's own character: "glory as of the only Son from the Father, full of grace and truth" (1:14).

Karl Barth found this teaching to be both profoundly informative as well as frequently forgotten.[31] During his days in Germany, he grew appalled at the ways in which the leaders of the National Socialist Movement were able to identify their cause as the ongoing revelation of God's character and will. Barth led the composition of the Theological Declaration of Barmen (1934),

29. On the importance of presence for wisdom, see Thomas Aquinas, *Summa theologiae* Ia.43.5, *ad* 2; IIaIIae.45.2, resp.; IIaIIae.97.2, *ad* 2; see also the reflections on this theme in patristic writings in A. N. Williams, *The Divine Sense: The Intellect in Patristic Theology* (Cambridge: Cambridge University Press, 2007), 179–80, 235–36.

30. Bernard of Clairvaux, *Sermo in nativitate B. Mariae* 11, in *The Analogy of Being*, ed. Thomas Joseph White, trans. Bruce D. Marshall (Grand Rapids: Eerdmans, 2011), 313.

31. See, e.g., Karl Barth, *Erklärung des Johannesevangeliums (Kapital 1–8). Vorlesung Münster Wintersemester 1925/1926, wiederbolt in Bonn, Sommersemester 1933* (Zurich: TVZ, 1999), 113–14.

the clarion call of the Confessing Church movement in Germany to oppose the idolatrous claims of the Nazis. The document's first confession regarding the "evangelical truth" was that "Jesus Christ, as he is attested for us in Holy Scripture, is the one Word of God which we have to hear and which we have to trust and obey in life and in death."[32] The text purports to offer explicit exposition of two biblical passages (John 10:1, 9; 14:6). It does not hesitate to offer a negative statement as well: "We reject the false doctrine, as though the Church could and would have to acknowledge as a source of its proclamation, apart from and besides this one Word of God, still other events and powers, figures and truths, as God's revelation."[33]

The polemical concern of Barth is to rule out natural theology and any speculation that is supported by purported revelations other than that of Jesus Christ. As in the Theological Declaration of Barmen, so in his own theology, Barth reminded us that theology that is not always and everywhere Christology is not Christian at all. In the work of a number of theologians after Barth, this christological lens has become an eschatological and historicist criterion. George Hunsinger has traced the way in which "eternity was historicized and subjected to an eschatological scheme" in the work of Jürgen Moltmann, Wolfhart Pannenberg, and Eberhard Jüngel.[34] Hunsinger argues that each of these theologians—a Reformed thinker and two Lutherans—illustrates a hard version of Rahner's Rule, the trinitarian principle proposed by the twentieth-century Roman Catholic Karl Rahner: "The economic Trinity *is* the immanent Trinity, and the immanent Trinity *is* the economic Trinity."[35] Rahner's Rule can be taken simply to mean that the eternal Trinity (the "immanent Trinity") is revealed or manifested to us in the external works of God (the "economic Trinity"). This epistemological reading is a soft version of Rahner's Rule. But Hunsinger argues that these three theologians—and we could add more, for they represent a groundswell of recent theologians—take a harder reading that interprets Rahner's Rule in an ontological fashion: the eternal Trinity is constituted by and coterminous with the Trinity in its external works.[36]

---

32. "The Theological Declaration of Barmen," in *Book of Confessions: Study Edition: Part I of the Constitution of the Presbyterian Church (U.S.A.)* (Louisville: Geneva, 1996), 311.

33. Ibid.

34. George Hunsinger, "Karl Barth's Doctrine of the Trinity and Some Protestant Doctrines after Barth," in *The Oxford Handbook of the Trinity*, ed. Gilles Emery and Matthew Levering (New York: Oxford University Press, 2011), 312.

35. Karl Rahner, *The Trinity* (New York: Herder and Herder, 1972), 22.

36. For astute analysis of two more recent examples, Robert Jenson and Bruce McCormack, each of whom has achieved remarkable prestige in the English-speaking world, see Scott R. Swain, *The God of the Gospel: Robert Jenson's Trinitarian Theology* (Downers Grove, IL: IVP Academic, 2013).

This development fails to honor the biblical principle that God's presence follows from God's perfection. Intrinsic to the gospel are its eternal roots in the life of God, who has all life in himself and only then freely determines to share that life with others. The fundamental provenience of God's life solidifies the freedom and grace that characterize the existence of creatures (in a wider sense) and Christians (in a narrower sense). Eternity does reveal itself in history; hence, the soft reading of Rahner's Rule can prove helpful against speculation about God. Yet eternity does energize God's engagement of history; therefore, the hard reading cannot be accepted without emptying the gospel of its potency.

A still further development involves exegetical narrowing. At times in the work of Barth and still further in the developments of some of his followers, the suggestion is put forward that theology must begin with the canonical Gospels or the apostolic witness in order to be Christocentric. And yet the Word has ruled a domain of divine discourse that predates his incarnate sojourn through the realm of Galilee, Gethsemane, and Golgotha. The external principle is the Son in all his revelatory speech, not merely in its fleshly form from the lips of Jesus of Nazareth. G. C. Berkouwer sees Barth's worry as an aberration that does not disprove the validity of general revelation or of genuine revelation amid Israel before the incarnation: "The basic mistake of this method [of Karl Barth] is that it calls abstract what *may* not be called abstract."[37]

"God spoke to our fathers in many times and various ways" (Heb. 1:1), so the whole ministry of the Son must be attended to.[38] While Hebrews, for example, mentions the "once for all" character of God's revelation and reconciliation in Christ—no doubt more so than any other text—it also portrays this pointed work of grace in terms and categories revealed in the Word's earlier prophetic activity in the divine economy, that is, through the writings of the prophets.[39] Not only Hebrews but that other great Christocentric book of the New Testament, the Gospel according to John, also locates the revelation of God in Christ (1:14, 17) amid a wider and prevenient self-revelation of God through this Word's light (1:4–5).[40] As Hebrews 1 and John 1 make clear, a particular God (the one revealed most fully in Jesus) can be revealed universally. That the fullness of God's identity is not revealed everywhere does not mean that real revelation has not occurred; that it may be skewed and

37. G. C. Berkouwer, *General Revelation* (Grand Rapids: Eerdmans, 1955), 249.
38. Herman Bavinck, *Reformed Dogmatics*, vol. 1, *Prolegomena*, ed. John Bolt, trans. John Vriend (Grand Rapids: Baker Academic, 2003), 110.
39. Berkouwer, *General Revelation*, 104.
40. Ibid., 236–50.

misused (whether in the shape of Rom. 1:20 or in the guise of Nazism) does not disprove the giving of the revelation. It proves only that sinful humans thwart God's gifts. (This occurs with special revelation as well; see the history of Israelite religion and the debates with false teachers present in virtually every text of the New Testament itself.)

We are called to be Christocentric, and doing so attentively means being canonical in our thinking. The story of the Son is definitive, and it begins with a genealogy that lays its very groundwork "in the beginning with God" and then through the history of this God's interaction with Israel.[41]

All things hold together in the Son. The truth of any reality finds its roots in his very gift. So we can rightly speak of all truth participating in his light; yet there is a more specific sense in which certain truths are his and are given by him. Elsewhere, Kevin Vanhoozer has distinguished between "a general cosmological participation in the Son through whom all things were made (Col. 1:16) and a more particular christological abiding in the Son in whom there is reconciliation (2 Cor. 5:17)."[42] That we may entrust ourselves to the God of the gospel depends on real knowledge not simply of a divine being, but of and with this one. So Calvin says, "Put briefly, the entire authority of the Gospel collapses unless we know that the living Christ speaks to us from the heavens."[43] The God who is truth himself will eventually bring us to perfect knowledge.[44] Completion is not simply a calling given to the individual. The gospel rules our thinking about progress and possibility by fixing our sights first on the actuality pledged by the Triune God. Barth notes, "Because we do not in any sense begin with ourselves, with our own capacity for faith and knowledge, we are secured against having to end with ourselves, i.e., with our own incapacity."[45] To think with Calvin and Barth, our capacity leaves

41. For further reflections on the biblical order of teaching (*ordo docendi*), see part 2 of Michael Allen and Scott Swain, "The Obedience of the Eternal Son," *International Journal of Systematic Theology* 15, no. 2 (2013): 117–21.

42. Kevin J. Vanhoozer, *Remythologizing Theology: Divine Action, Passion, and Authorship* (Cambridge: Cambridge University Press, 2010), 281–82. Later Vanhoozer clarifies various aspects of this second union with Christ (what he calls "christodramatic participation"): it is both dialogical and sapiential, which we might translate as communicative and intellectual (291–92).

43. John Calvin, *The Acts of the Apostles 1–13*, ed. David W. Torrance and Thomas F. Torrance, trans. John W. Fraser and W. J. G. McDonald (Grand Rapids: Eerdmans, 1965), 24 (on Acts 1:3).

44. It is worth noting that perfection does not mean a return to Edenic knowledge but an escalation to eschatological wisdom. First Cor. 15:44–45 shows that the "last Adam" brings not merely a gracious return to nature but grace that perfects nature. First Cor. 13:8–12 anticipates the escalating nature of perfect knowledge in Christ: now as pilgrims, later as those beholding his glory (13:12); "when the perfect comes, the partial will pass away" (13:10).

45. Barth, *Church Dogmatics* II/1, 43.

us in danger of collapse; thank God that we are not left with our capacity alone but with a commitment from the God of the gospel. We are promised his prophetic Word and his indwelling Spirit's illumination. From glory to glory, then, the human mind is being illumined to see and be satisfied in the glory of the Triune God.

Thus far we have traced the order of the gospel and sketched its rule over the reason exercised by humans. Truth has been given, truth is being declared, and truth will be cherished. As we survey the story of the gospel, we see the march through falsehood toward the truth's eventual triumph: not a story of upward human progress in ascent to heaven but of divine presence pledged to descend to and accommodate itself to needy creatures. And we appreciate how theologians have formulated various distinctions in each case for the purpose of keeping each moment in the story in play. Even here, in thinking about the knowledge of God, we see that doctrine serves an ostensive role: reminding us to tend to hearing and testifying to the gospel in its fullness.

The Character of Theology

Ethics follows ontology.[46] That is, thinking about how theology is practiced follows careful reflection on the way in which its nature is disciplined by the gospel of Jesus Christ. It remains to reflect briefly on the way in which theology is practiced in this space described in the previous section. Five points will suffice for our introductory purposes.

First, the knowledge of God remains, strictly speaking, reason's apprehension of truth regarding this particular being, the Father, Son, and Spirit, the one God of the gospel. Yet this one being, the Triune God of glory, is the maker and sustainer of all things and, further, the God of the covenant. Whereas we often speak of someone being a "man of his times," incapable of being understood apart from his own cultural milieu, God is surely a being of his economy: his character in all its perfection and presence is displayed in these outer works. Of course, this is meant in a noetic and not ontic sense: God is not dependent on the economy, but our knowledge of God is dependent on the economy. But this does generate a concrete connection owing to God's gloriously humble commitment to reveal himself among us: while theology is about God, it is also about everything else insofar as it relates to God.

All the doctrines treated in dogmatics—whether they concern the universe, humanity, Christ, and so forth—are but the explication of the one central dogma

46. Bavinck, *Reformed Dogmatics*, 1:58.

of the knowledge of God. All things are considered in light of God, subsumed under him, traced back to him as the starting point. Dogmatics is always called upon to ponder and describe God and God alone, whose glory is in creation and re-creation, in nature and grace, in the world and in the church. It is the knowledge of him alone that dogmatics must put on display.[47]

Herman Bavinck is well aware that other topics must be addressed, but here he locates any such endeavor as reason's exercise *sub species divinitatis*. Theology must remain theological, or it loses its purpose and energy.[48]

Second, the journey of theology must be one of faith: "Only in receiving can we know."[49] And this faith is trust expressed in the form of hopeful prayer. Prayer may take the form "Maranatha" or that of a great divine: "I pray, O God, that I may know thee, that I may love thee, so that I may rejoice in thee. And if I cannot do this to the full in this life, at least let me go forward from day to day until that joy comes to fullness."[50] And prayer is not wistful aspiration; it is rooted in the promise of a God who is light and who sheds his knowledge abroad. Though God is seated in the heavens, still his name and its praise resound across the globe and through the centuries. With Gregory the Great, we are astonished at this mystery of grace: "Though our lips can only stammer, yet we chant the high things of God."[51]

The prayerful posture of theology should not, however, be construed in any way that renders its intellectual caliber moot. Theology will be done by divine illumination or not at all. But illumination renders intellectual reason operative, not optional. As Irenaeus put it, "The glory of God is man fully alive, and the life of man is the vision of God."[52] Theology is work done by humans. It is done as the vision of the self-presenting God whose glory makes us fully alive: spiritually, relationally, and, yes, intellectually.

Lydia Schumacher has offered a wonderful account of the doctrine of divine illumination as it was classically construed by Augustine as well as its fate throughout the middle ages and into the post-Reformation era. Schumacher

47. Herman Bavinck, *Reformed Dogmatics*, vol. 2, *God and Creation*, ed. John Bolt, trans. John Vriend (Grand Rapids: Baker Academic, 2004), 29. See also Turretin, *Institutes of Elenctic Theology* 1.5.4; Thomas Aquinas, *Summa theologiae* Ia.3.7.

48. John Webster, "Theological Theology," in *Confessing God: Essays in Christian Dogmatics II* (London: T&T Clark, 2005), 11–32.

49. Hilary of Poitiers, *The Trinity*, in vol. 6 of *Nicene and Post-Nicene Fathers*, series 2, ed. W. Sanday, trans. E. W. Watson and L. Pullan (Peabody, MA: Hendrickson, 2004), 2.35.

50. Anselm, "Proslogion," in *A Scholastic Miscellany: Anselm to Ockham*, ed. Eugene Fairweather (Philadelphia: Westminster, 1956), 92.

51. Gregory the Great, *Moralia* (Louisville: Ex Fontibus, 2012), 5.26.29.

52. Irenaeus, *Adversus Haereses*, in vol. 1 of *The Ante-Nicene Fathers*, ed. A. Cleveland Coxe (Peabody, MA: Hendrickson, 2004), 4.20.6.

argues that divine illumination shapes our "intrinsic intellectual capacity" and thus cannot be construed as a divine action that "undermines the integrity of the intellect."[53] She argues this point convincingly by considering a wider range of Augustine's writings before turning to his specifically epistemological discussions where he considers divine illumination explicitly.[54] "With all this in mind, one can conclude that the illumination of Christ does not bear on cognition in any way that undermines the autonomy or integrity of the intellect but in a way that reinstates it, at least for the intellect that stokes rather than extinguishes his light through a decision to work with faith in him."[55]

In Schumacher's account Thomas Aquinas becomes the faithful disciple of Augustine, contrary to many standard readings that pit Thomas's use of Aristotle against Augustine's reliance on Plato. Thomas does not continue to use the same philosophical apparatus to describe how humans think, but he continues to hold to the fundamental theological framework (regarding God, creation, anthropology, sin, and redemption) present in Augustine's work. Thomas does introduce Aristotelian psychology into his reflections on illumination, but he allows his reflection on theology and the nature of the divine economy to chasten their function. At the end of the day, because he shares Augustine's commitment to a participatory epistemology wherein humans really can come to share in God's own knowledge by the missions of his Son and Spirit, Thomas is compelled to articulate a robust account of how human reason can be operative in theology.[56] Hence he introduces Aristotle (with all his concern for detail regarding creaturely processing) precisely because he is so committed to Augustine's vision of participation (drawn from both the canon of Scripture and his retooling of Platonic *methexis*).[57] One

---

53. Lydia Schumacher, *Divine Illumination: The History and Future of Augustine's Theory of Knowledge* (Oxford: Blackwell, 2011), 62–65.

54. Not all of Schumacher's historical proposals are convincing. Her assessment of Bonaventure is questionable. She suggests that far from following Augustine's path, Bonaventure identified illumination as the direct implanting of knowledge that does not follow natural pathways of cognition (see Schumacher, *Divine Illumination*, 98, 114, 146; for another account of Bonaventure's classic text "Reduction of the Arts to Theology," as well as his "Collations on the Seven Gifts of the Holy Spirit," see John Webster, "*Regina atrium*: Theology and the Humanities," in *The Domain of the Word: Scripture and Theological Reason* [London: T&T Clark, 2012], 171–92 [esp. 173–87]: "For Bonaventure the arts of intelligence are intrinsically illuminated by the Father of lights" [184]).

55. Schumacher, *Divine Illumination*, 65.

56. Ibid., 160, 178.

57. This link between participation and individuation in Thomas is made to great effect also in Adrian Pabst, *Metaphysics: The Creation of Hierarchy* (Grand Rapids: Eerdmans, 2012). For ways in which the doctrine of creation *ex nihilo* is crucial to understanding his approach to participation as well as his critical appropriation of Aristotle, see Janet Martin Soskice, "Naming God: A Study in Faith and Reason," in *Reason and the Reasons of Faith* (London: T&T Clark,

must be committed to the proper functioning of the mind (and, as best we can, to understanding it in terms of faculties and functions) if one believes that it really participates in God's own wisdom by grace.

A counterexample could be offered to Thomas: Jonathan Edwards. Edwards also shows concern to describe divine illumination as essential to human knowledge. Edwards will speak of illumination (in the pagan's case, what he calls "common illumination") not only in the believer's knowledge from nature and from Scripture but even in the pagan's grasp of certain truths of God. But Edwards presents an account of reason that is markedly shaped by his occasionalist metaphysics.[58] As he puts it, "Our perceptions, or ideas that we passively receive by our bodies, are communicated to us immediately by God."[59] For Edwards, there seems to be a competitive relationship between divine illumination and the mediated use of reason.[60] As with his teaching on free will and divine sovereignty, so here his account modifies the deep Augustinian tradition and instead posits a relationship whereby divine provision involves some loss of human agency.[61]

Reformational thinking about divine illumination would do well to return to its catholic posture wherein the operation of Word and Spirit renders human mental work operative rather than optional.[62] We dare not oppose naturalism (in an Enlightenment form or a postmodern historicist form) with

2005), 241–54; Reinhard Hütter, "Is There a Cure for Reason's Presumption and Despair?—Why Thomas Matters Today," in *Dust Bound for Heaven: Explorations in the Theology of Thomas Aquinas* (Grand Rapids: Eerdmans, 2012), 29–74.

58. For an attempt to argue that Edwards does not hold to an occasionalist metaphysic, see Stephen H. Daniel, "Edwards as Philosopher," in *The Cambridge Companion to Jonathan Edwards*, ed. Stephen J. Stein (Cambridge: Cambridge University Press, 2007), 168. Given the quotations that Daniel provides, however, one wonders what it would take for him to refer to someone as an occasionalist. Daniel's argument does prove that Edwards has a fundamentally relational notion of substance metaphysics (ibid., 169), but he does not disprove its occasionalist basis in the will of God.

59. Jonathan Edwards, "The Mind," in *Scientific and Philosophical Writings*, Works of Jonathan Edwards 6, ed. Wallace E. Anderson (New Haven: Yale University Press, 1980), 339. Edwards does not deny a mind-body connection (see entry 4 on the same page), but he speaks of immediacy in the mind's grasp of illumined truth.

60. On his approach to divine communicativeness and the immediacy of divine illumination, see William M. Schweitzer, *God Is a Communicative Being: Divine Communicativeness and Harmony in the Theology of Jonathan Edwards* (London: T&T Clark, 2012), 22–23.

61. For reflection on the ways in which Edwards modifies the Augustinian and Reformed approach to predestination, see Richard A. Muller, "Jonathan Edwards and the Absence of Free Choice: A Parting of Ways in the Reformed Tradition," *Jonathan Edwards Studies* 1, no. 1 (2011): 3–22.

62. For a robust account along these lines, see John Webster, "Illumination," in *The Domain of the Word: Scripture and Theological Reason* (London: T&T Clark, 2012), 50–64; see also Bavinck, *Reformed Dogmatics*, 1:226, 333, and esp. 361–62, 566.

supernaturalism: the doctrine of revelation neither leaves us with bare nature nor locates our knowledge elsewhere than in human intellectual reasoning done under the metaphysical (though not overtly psychological) compulsion of grace. We do well to remember the words of Bavinck: "Nature precedes grace; grace perfects nature. Reason is perfected by faith; faith presupposes nature."[63]

Third, the knowledge of God and all things in him takes the form of following the economy of God's works. There is a sequence to Christian theology, and it is not an order drawn from the realm of logic or philosophy outside of the biblical revelation. Theology follows the biblical order itself: God, then all other things as they play out in redemptive history (election, creation, fall, promise of redemption in Israel, incarnation, sending of the Spirit, church, application of salvation, last things). Other topics, when deemed important, can be considered within this canonical structure at various points (whether dropped in somewhere or distributed across the range of topics).

Here our approach to the order of Christian theology cuts across some common claims regarding the supposed distinction between biblical theology and systematic theology. When done according to the discipline of the gospel, systematic theology follows the canon's own order. It does so with greater resolve than most biblical theology, inasmuch as it realizes that the Bible begins with theology proper ("In the beginning *God* . . ."). Redemptive history must be rooted in God's own character; its salvific missions flow from the inner divine processions of Son and Spirit. Biblical theology can easily sound like nothing more than ancient history precisely because it lacks a doctrine of God to provide a metaphysical framework for its narrative.[64]

This biblical order fits the discipline of the gospel and follows the guidance of the ecumenical creeds. These rules of faith sketch out the basic contours of the canon's own teaching. They confess faith in God and chart the broad strokes of a narrative of God's economy. Regarding the sequence of theology, then, the creeds point us to the deep grammar or logic of the canon. They prompt us to shape the very form of theology according to the self-presentation of God in the Holy Scriptures. While certain doctrines are distributed in various places across the canon and thus may appear in a number of given spots, the broad shape of the gospel guides the course of our reflection.

Fourth, the context of the knowledge of God takes various cultural forms, though it remains within a catholic space. Any theological reflection on

63. Ibid., 1:322.
64. Ibid., 1:104: "the order that is theological and at the same time historical-genetic in character deserves preference. It, too, takes its point of departure in God and views all creatures only in relation to him. But proceeding from God, it descends to his works, in order through them to ascend to and end in him" (112).

theology's context must focus primarily on canon, creed, and clergy prior to any helpful attention given to matters sociological, ethnographic, or political.

So-called postmodern approaches to knowledge focus on the importance of context in shaping our vision and understanding. He thinks as he does because his parents taught him that. She approaches life as she does because she went to that school. They follow that practice because they are emulating some influential figure in the religious sphere or world of entertainment.

The response to such accounts must be a call to be more contextual than the contextualizers. Foucault, Lyotard, and Derrida are correct to highlight the shaping powers of society in its various facets. They are myopic in that they focus only on the economies of this world and miss the most fundamentally defining economy for all humans: the divine economy rooted not in class, race, gender, or education but in God's eternal fullness and his covenantal election.

The Triune God has determined to grace his children with wisdom from on high through various horizontal means of grace. What one finds in reading the Bible—whether the witness of Israel's Scriptures or the writings of the apostles—is that the Holy Scriptures themselves point to an ongoing traditioning process whereby readers and hearers are to be shaped (see Deut. 7:6; 9:4–6; 2 Tim. 1:8–14; 2:2). There is need not only for the Word but also for interpretive helps. The Word dwells richly among a community—specifically, his church—not among individuals (Col. 3:16–17).[65]

In recent years Kevin Vanhoozer has provided an analogy by which the role of the church in the economy of God's wisdom may be better grasped.[66] Vanhoozer suggests that the economy of God's grace is an epic drama, and doctrine is meant to help us more wisely inhabit our roles, whereby we offer worship to God and witness to the world. The traditions of the church—most especially its creeds and confessions—are Spirit-enabled guides to help the understudies go about their dramatic callings.[67] They are binding guides:

---

65. Because there is a churchly and even a catholic context for hearing the Word, the supposed individualistic flaw of the Scripture Principle of Protestantism is shown false. Christian Smith and Brad Gregory have each sought to demonstrate that the Reformation has unintentionally spawned what Smith calls "pervasive interpretive pluralism"; further, each suggests that the only way out of this morass is to ditch Reformational ecclesiology and return to Rome (see Smith, *The Bible Made Impossible: Why Biblicism Is Not a Truly Evangelical Doctrine of Scripture* [Grand Rapids: Brazos, 2011]; Brad Gregory, *The Unintended Reformation*). But see the arguments in response in Michael Allen and Scott Swain, *Reformed Catholicity: The Promise of Retrieval for Theology and Biblical Interpretation* (Grand Rapids: Baker Academic, 2015).

66. Kevin J. Vanhoozer, *The Drama of Doctrine: A Canonical-Linguistic Approach to Christian Theology* (Louisville: Westminster John Knox, 2005).

67. See ibid., chaps. 5–7, for his account of Scripture and tradition.

ecclesial expectations for worship and witness shaped by canonical speech of the Triune God.[68] Indeed, the role of creeds and confessions helps to shape the very title of this volume: *Christian Dogmatics* rather than merely *Christian Theology* or *Systematic Theology*. Dogmatics involves a churchly engagement of doctrine within the lived reality of the communion of the saints and attention to her ecclesiastical guidance in the form of her creeds and confessions. Paul tells Timothy to "follow the pattern of the sound words that you have heard from me" (2 Tim. 1:13), and the church has seen itself ever since as an apostolic community that passes on that gospel pattern from generation to generation. Like Israel of old, the prophecies of God must be passed along as "one generation shall commend your works to another, and shall declare your mighty acts" (Ps. 145:4). Biblical reasoning, by its own demands, calls for creedal and confessional reasoning.[69]

Fifth, the calling of theology should be examined. The knowledge of God is summoned for the sake of missional purposes: worship and witness. Psalm 145 locates the work of theology within the context of testimony and praise. The psalm begins and ends with adoring speech about God: "I will extol you . . . and bless your name forever and ever. Every day I will bless you and praise your name forever and ever" (145:1–2); "My mouth will speak the praise of the LORD, and let all flesh bless his holy name forever and ever" (v. 21). Throughout this psalm, speech about the works of God is a constant refrain (vv. 3–4, 6–7, 10–11). An intergenerational conduit of communication is affirmed: "One generation shall commend your works to another, and shall declare your mighty acts" (v. 4; see also vv. 6–7). The psalm makes plain that this testimony is not merely among a clique or an ethnic group, for God is creator of all and satisfies "the desire of every living thing" (v. 16).

---

68. James Bannerman, *The Church of Christ: A Treatise on the Nature, Powers, Ordinances, Discipline and Government of the Christian Church* (Edinburgh: Banner of Truth Trust, 1960), 1:306–7. It is crucial to reiterate the subordinate authority of the creeds and confessions—as well as the clergy—vis-à-vis the fundamental authority of God speaking through his prophets and apostles, i.e., in Holy Scripture. The doctrine of the canon has served well to highlight the breadth of authorities affirmed by Reformed catholics as well as the hierarchy of authorities (with Scripture alone as the *norma normans*, that is, the norming norm of all faith and practice) contra the reductive account of Reformational Christianity in William J. Abraham, *Canon and Criterion in Christian Theology* (Oxford: Clarendon, 1998). Abraham undersells the breadth of authorities genuinely affirmed by Protestants as well as the need for a hierarchy of authority: in so doing *sola Scriptura* becomes *nuda Scriptura* (ibid., 147).

69. On the role of creeds and confessions, see Scott R. Swain, "A Ruled Reading Reformed: The Role of the Church's Confession in Biblical Interpretation," *International Journal of Systematic Theology* 14, no. 2 (2012): 177–93; Henri Blocher, "The 'Analogy of Faith' in the Study of Scripture," in *The Challenge of Evangelical Theology: Essays in Approach and Method*, ed. Nigel M. de S. Cameron (Edinburgh: Scottish Bulletin of Evangelical Theology, 1987), 17–38.

So theology is second-order reflection on first-order speech. Christians are called, first, to hear God's Word and respond in kind: to God with praise, to neighbors with proclamation. Christians do this by God's grace. Theology functions like a good critic, simply to help draw together the shape of God's Word and Christian practice and to seek to analyze the ways in which the latter befits the former. It sends Christians back to the Word and on to the task of employing their own words before God and the world. Thus theology is for the sake of exegesis, which is for the sake of life with God and others.

Theology goes terribly awry when it becomes a surrogate for either listening to the Word or speaking the gospel. In so doing, failures of faith and love are evident. We either run into a position whereby we entrust ourselves to the tradition of the church's reflection or the intellectual vitality of the present day rather than fundamentally throwing ourselves on the life-giving Word of God. The dogmatic task is meant to enable the exegetical task to run more faithfully, attentive in fresh and new ways to the life-giving Word of God. Indeed, the work of doctrine is nothing more than a reflective prompt to be mindful of the ways in which God's presence is promised and practiced. But the living is in the presence itself, not the prompting.

To sum up, we have considered an ontology and ethics of the knowledge of God, that is, the nature and practice of theology. In creation and new creation alike, knowledge of God comes by faithful entrusting of oneself, including one's mind and wisdom, to another: the Triune God of light and love. This is good news for humans, finite and fallen as they are, for this God is light himself and love shone forth. Thus we can pray, "Let the words of my mouth and the meditation of my heart be acceptable in your sight, O LORD, my rock and my redeemer" (Ps. 19:14).

2

Holy Scripture

KEVIN J. VANHOOZER

Introduction: The Word of God in the Words of Men

"This is the Word of the Lord"; "*Thanks be to God*." This exchange between pastor and congregation that typically follows the public reading of Scripture in the order of worship also sums up the task of a doctrine of Holy Scripture: to say what Scripture *is* and to give thanks for what it *does*—or rather, for what God does in and through the Scripture.[1] Holy Scripture is the Word of God in the words of men, a message from one who is beyond space and time (because he is their Creator) to earthbound humans (creatures). How ought we to describe this marvel?

In 1974 scientists working with the SETI (Search for Extra-Terrestrial Intelligence) Institute transmitted a message from earth into space via a signal from the Arecibo Radar Telescope in Puerto Rico. The message used not words but symbols (binary digits) depicting our solar system, the structure of the DNA molecule, and the human body. Alexander Zaitsev, a Russian

---

1. Cf. Olof Herrlin: "The liturgy of the Church, like its preaching, is the assertion of Scripture as God's Word" (*Divine Service: Liturgy in Perspective* [Philadelphia: Fortress, 1966], 3). For a Roman Catholic reflection, see *The Word of the Lord: Verbum Domini. Post-Synodal Apostolic Exhortation of the Holy Father Benedict XVI* (Boston: Pauline Books & Media, 2010).

astronomer, argues that transmission of messages into the cosmos is one of the most pressing needs of an advanced civilization.[2] It also requires considerable patience: if the nearest civilization is one hundred light-years away, as some scientists think, it would take two hundred years to receive a reply. Nevertheless, SETI has had for several years now a radio telescope listening for any interstellar gossip. There is also a branch that focuses on writing and interpreting messages that could theoretically be used for communication with extraterrestrial intelligence, or CETI.

Contrast these space signals with time capsules: deliberately sealed deposits of messages or other objects intended to communicate something of the past to future generations. Whereas ancient Mesopotamian and Egyptian deposits were intended simply to preserve something of the past for an indefinite time period, in the nineteenth century people began to deposit information for retrieval on specific later dates. The purpose of such time capsules is "to transfer cultural information across the millennia."[3] Yet ancient writings too "can be time capsule-like phenomena and their interpretations can evoke time capsule experiences."[4]

The Bible is neither a message from beyond the world (i.e., outer space) nor a time capsule from the ancient world. The Bible transcends such analogies, for it is both like and unlike every other book. It is *like* every other book because it has human authors. It is *unlike* every other book because (1) it has God for its ultimate author; (2) it has God (Jesus Christ) as its ultimate content; (3) it has God (the Holy Spirit) for its ultimate interpreter; and (4) it has the church for its ultimate interpretive community. The first challenge of a doctrine of Scripture, however, is to say how these human words are also "of God": how can we confess the words of Moses, Mark, and Paul to be also "the Word of the Lord"?

Holy Scripture and the God-World Relationship

God's relationship to Scripture is a microcosm of theology in general inasmuch as the latter deals with God's relationship to the world. Accounts of Scripture quickly go wrong when they start with pictures of the God-world relationship taken from elsewhere than the Bible. Attempts to reason to knowledge of God from the notion of perfect being, when not disciplined by the gospel, dwindle into mere human projections that tell us more about the people who made

2. Alexander L. Zaitsev, "Rationale for METI," n.d., arxiv.org/pdf/1105.0910v1.pdf.
3. William E. Jarvis, *Time Capsules: A Cultural History* (Jefferson, NC: McFarland, 2003), 2.
4. Ibid., 175.

them than they do about God. Attempts to say what a perfect book *must* be like typically go wrong for the same reason. The only way to know the God who is beyond creation is to attend to his self-presentation.

The Bible presents itself as one of the chief means of God's self-presentation to humankind. We thus do well to attend to Scripture, both as a record of God's self-presentation in history and as itself a prime instance of this self-presentation. Scripture depicts God's Word in trinitarian covenantal terms, namely, as an ingredient in the missions of the Son and the Spirit to communicate the Father's light, life, and love to his chosen people. Before expounding on this thesis further, however, it will be instructive to contrast this with other approaches.

Naturalistic approaches to Scripture view the Bible as a merely human product to be studied, like other ancient texts, with a variety of critical methods that seek to understand it in terms of its original context (i.e., without recourse to any kind of supernaturalistic causal explanation). This perspective systematically excludes any appeal to God in accounting for Scripture's composition, canonization, or interpretation. James Barr's position is typical of the methodological naturalist: "We do not have any idea of ways in which God might straightforwardly communicate articulate thoughts or sentences to men; it just doesn't happen."[5] The Bible may involve "God" inasmuch as it contains descriptions of religious experience. However, while the Bible may teach *of* God, Barr cannot say it is "taught *by* God."[6] In sum: naturalistic approaches to Scripture ascribe no causal agency to God in relation to Scripture or anything else.[7]

At the other extreme are descriptions of the God-world relationship that exaggerate divine agency, making God the sovereign determiner and sole efficient cause of every worldly event. The assumption here is that in order for God truly to author Scripture, his would be the only operative intelligence, and that the men responsible for writing Scripture functioned only as scribes, not as genuine authors. We can call this hypothetical position *extreme* (divine) authorship.[8] According to its critics, extreme divine authorship presupposes divine sovereignty, for God can ensure a cognitive identity

5. James Barr, *The Bible in the Modern World* (London: SCM, 1973), 17.
6. The implied contrast is with the medieval definition of theology as *Deum docet, a Deo docetur, ad Deum ducit* ("teaches of God, is taught by God, and leads to God").
7. For arguments in favor of viewing revelation as a form of divine self-testimony, see Rolfe King, *Obstacles to Divine Revelation: God and the Reorientation of Human Reason* (London: Continuum, 2008), chap. 11; Mats Wahlberg, *Revelation as Testimony: A Philosophical-Theological Study* (Grand Rapids: Eerdmans, 2014).
8. "This 'dictation theory' is a man of straw. It is safe to say that no Protestant theologian, from the Reformation until now, has ever held it; and certainly modern Evangelicals do not

only between what he wills to communicate and what human authors actually say if he controls them.[9] The problem is that this proves too much: if God can control human history, including the human words of Scripture, then he is either responsible for all of it, including its horrors and injustices, or neglectful of some of it (i.e., everything not concerned with salvation history). Either way, say its critics, extreme authorship leads to the problem of evil.[10] Extreme authorship entails a dictation theory, according to which Scripture's human authors are passive mouthpieces, mere puppets in the hands of God. In turn, the dictation theory assumes a dictatorial (and I would say *nonbiblical*) picture of divine determination, as if God's will and human freedom were locked into a zero-sum game in which there can be only one survivor.

Other theologians, largely in reaction to the preceding view, espouse a different model of the God-world relationship, according to which God does not determine but only influences events: call it (very) *weak* authorship. According to Clark Pinnock, "God is present, not normally in the mode of control, but in the way of stimulation and guidance."[11] The problem with the notion of divine influence is that there is no guarantee that the human authors will go along with it, in which case what they say leads to *unreliable* knowledge of God.[12] According to Kenton Sparks, God does not control the human authors but "accommodates" his communication to human finitude and fallenness, adapting his word to the prevailing historical and cultural conditions of the day (if you can't beat them, join them), with the result that there are not only factual but ideological (and theological) errors in the biblical texts.[13] Sparks goes so far as to contradict Jesus's statement that "Scripture cannot be broken" (John 10:35) by speaking of the *brokenness* of Scripture, which follows from his belief that the biblical authors "sometimes thought and wrote *ungodly*

---

hold it" (J. I. Packer, *"Fundamentalism" and the Word of God* [Grand Rapids: Eerdmans, 1968], 79).

9. Cf. Edward Farley: "The principle of identity . . . is the basis for attributing infallibility and inerrancy to what appears to be human and creaturely" (*Ecclesial Reflection: An Anatomy of Theological Method* [Philadelphia: Fortress, 1982], 39).

10. "God's activity as heteronomous causality violates creaturely freedom and autonomy and therefore divine goodness and love are sacrificed" (ibid., 157).

11. Clark Pinnock with Barry L. Callen, *The Scripture Principle*, 2nd ed. (Grand Rapids: Baker Academic, 2006), 131.

12. Pinnock assumes that Scripture's unfailing truth requires strong divine authorship: "Inerrancy thinking is deductive, rooted in the assumption of total divine control" (ibid., 128).

13. Kenton Sparks's underlying assumption is that "in many cases God does not correct our mistaken human viewpoints but merely assumes them in order to communicate with us" (*God's Word in Human Words: An Evangelical Appropriation of Critical Biblical Scholarship* [Grand Rapids: Baker Academic, 2008], 231).

things."[14] The moral is clear: if sinful humans are left to their own devices, their words will not convey the Word of God.

What the above discussion shows is the extent to which one's doctrine of Scripture depends on one's doctrine of God and the God-world relationship. The problem with the approaches we have just examined is that they each begin with a view of the God-world relationship that fails to accord with the biblical testimony. Naturalistic approaches omit God altogether. Approaches that rely on extreme authorship view God as the most powerful causal force in the created realm but fail to do justice to the Creator/creature distinction (i.e., God is not simply the greatest causal force *in* the created realm because God reigns *over* it).[15] Conversely, approaches that presuppose weak authorship fail to do justice to Scripture's clear teaching about God's lordship over all creation, including the human creature.

This chapter sets out to discuss God and God's Word together, and to do so according to the Scriptures. Scripture regularly depicts God as a personal speaker: a communicative agent who uses words to do things, mostly in relation to administering covenants and addressing his covenant people. Indeed, "the Word of the Lord" plays the central role in the Old Testament's description of God's relationship to Israel, just as "the Word made flesh" plays the central role in the New Testament: "What we find in Scripture is an astoundingly close relationship between God himself and the words through which he speaks."[16] God makes communicative initiatives in order to share what is his with others, and he does so with words, the most supple and sophisticated medium of interpersonal relationship. God, according to the Scriptures, is not an impersonal causal force manipulating puppets but rather a personal communicative agent in lordly covenantal relation with responsible human covenant servants: call it *strong* authorship (see below). The purpose of Scripture as God's Word is to invite and orient us to be in right relationship to God. From this vantage point, Mary's response should be the template for the disciple's response: when addressed by God through an angelic messenger, Mary answered, "Behold, I am the servant of the Lord; let it be to me according to your word" (Luke 1:38).

14. Kenton Sparks, *Sacred Word, Broken Word: Biblical Authority and the Dark Side of Scripture* (Grand Rapids: Eerdmans, 2012), 47 (emphasis mine).

15. A more technical way of making this distinction would be to differentiate creaturely power (secondary causality) from the distinct and unique power of the Creator (primary causality), which is of a different order and on a different level. See Michael J. Dodds, *Unlocking Divine Action: Contemporary Science and Thomas Aquinas* (Washington, DC: Catholic University of America Press, 2012), chap. 1.

16. Timothy Ward, *Words of Life: Scripture as the Living and Active Word of God* (Downers Grove, IL: InterVarsity, 2009), 27.

Locating the Doctrine of Scripture: Historical and Contemporary Approaches

To study the history of the doctrine of Scripture from the early church to the present is to confront four issues: (1) how to view Scripture and patristic tradition in the pattern of authority; (2) where to locate the doctrine of Scripture vis-à-vis the doctrine of God; (3) where to locate the doctrine of Scripture vis-à-vis other doctrines; and (4) how Scripture (the written form of God's Word) relates to Jesus Christ (the living Word of God made flesh).

Scripture in the Creeds: The Pattern of Authority

Christian doctrine is "what the church of Jesus Christ believes, teaches, and confesses on the basis of the word of God."[17] Orthodox tradition (e.g., the creeds) was thought to preserve the right interpretation of Scripture in contrast to heretics who claimed to be biblical but failed to grasp Scripture's message. There is a kind of circularity at work: "The Scripture is to be understood as the tradition and this particular creed interpret it, but this particular creed . . . is subject to the Scripture."[18] The circularity is not vicious but virtuous: the Apostles' Creed is a summary of the basic plot that ties the various books together, and subsequent creeds (e.g., Nicaea, Chalcedon) work out further implications of what the story entails, especially as concerns its divine protagonists.[19]

What must the church of Jesus Christ believe, teach, and confess about Scripture on the basis of the Word of God? Origen, commenting on John 1:17 ("grace and truth came through Jesus Christ"), argued that the words of Christ included not only what he spoke while he was in the flesh but also what he spoke as Word of God through the prophets in the Old Testament.[20] Virtually everyone in the early church acknowledged the authority of Scripture; the real question was what it taught about Jesus Christ. The Niceno-Constantinopolitan Creed (381) identifies the Holy as the one *qui locutus*

---

17. Jaroslav Pelikan, *The Christian Tradition: A History of the Development of Doctrine*, vol. 1, *The Emergence of the Catholic Tradition (100–600)* (Chicago: University of Chicago Press, 1971), 1.

18. Jaroslav Pelikan, *Credo: Historical and Theological Guide to Creeds and Confessions of Faith in the Christian Tradition* (New Haven: Yale University Press, 2003), 127. Cf. Telford Work: "A systematic . . . doctrine of Scripture is necessarily circular: all the categories that describe it also emerge from it" (*Living and Active: Scripture in the Economy of Salvation* [Grand Rapids: Eerdmans, 2002], 9).

19. Cf. Augustine's comment that the catholic faith "is not a bundle of opinions and prejudices but a summary of biblical testimonies" (Augustine, "Sermons," 52.2).

20. Origen, *On First Principles* pref. 1.

est per prophetas ("who spoke through the prophets") and confesses that
Christ "was raised on the third day in accordance with the Scriptures" (1 Cor.
15:4). It was the consensus of the early church that what the Spirit spoke
concerns the mystery of salvation in Jesus Christ. After all, the risen Christ
himself interpreted the Old Testament as prefiguring his person and work
(Luke 24:27). Irenaeus appealed to 1 Corinthians 2:10–16 to argue that only
those enlightened by the Holy Spirit could discern the true christological
sense of the Old Testament.

In general, the church fathers considered Holy Scripture to be a divinely
authored (and thus authoritative) text that reveals the mystery of God's salvation: his plan for the fullness of time to unite all things on heaven and earth
in Christ (Eph. 1:10). As the apostles recognized that only Jesus taught the
words of life, so the early church fathers acknowledged that the church is born
from and lives by the Word of God written that presents Christ.

Scripture in the Reformed Confessions: First Theology

The Reformation was in large part a protest against the ways in which
the medieval Roman Catholic Church corrupted the gospel through the addition of nonbiblical teachings, such as the doctrine of indulgences, on the
authority of church tradition. Martin Luther and Ulrich Zwingli each based
his proposal to reform the church on the authority of Scripture. Zwingli's
preface to his "Sixty-Seven Articles" (1523) makes this explicit: "The articles
and opinions below, I, Ulrich Zwingli, confess to have preached . . . as based
upon the Scripture which are called inspired by God [*theopneustos*—2 Tim.
3:16] . . . and where I have not now correctly understood [the] said Scriptures
I shall allow myself to be taught better, but only from said Scriptures."[21]

In light of the absolute (magisterial) authority of God, the dispute over
the relative (ministerial) authority in church tradition, and the prominence
of Scripture as the foundation for the Reformers' prescriptions to reform
church tradition, it is not surprising to learn that Reformed confessions of
faith sometimes began with the doctrine of God and at other times with
the doctrine of Scripture.[22] For example, the French Confession (1559), the
Scots Confession (1560), the Belgic Confession (1561), and the Thirty-Nine

21. Cited in *Thy Word Is Still Truth: Essential Writings on the Doctrine of Scripture from
the Reformation to Today*, eds. Peter A. Lillback and Richard B. Gaffin Jr. (Phillipsburg, NJ:
P&R, 2013), 88.
22. "First theology" is the attempt to say which comes first: the doctrine of God or the doctrine of Scripture. On the one hand, we know only about the God of Jesus Christ by reading
Scripture; on the other hand, we appeal only to the Bible as authoritative because it is the Word
of God. The solution, I shall suggest, is to begin with both together, that is, with the Bible as

Articles of the Church of England (1571) all begin with an article on the doctrine of God.

A doctrine develops when the need arises. It was precisely because of the conflict over the locus of authority in the church that the doctrine of Scripture came into its own in Reformation confessions and post-Reformation Reformed dogmatics.[23] Instead of being the implicit authoritative basis, as it was in patristic theology, the Protestant Reformers made the doctrine of Scripture an explicit doctrinal locus of its own: "The logical priority of Scripture over all other means of religious knowing in the church—tradition, present day corporate or official doctrine, and individual insight or illumination—lies at the heart of the teaching of the Reformation and of its great confessional documents."[24] In elevating Scripture into the place of the first article, the Ten Conclusions of Bern (1528), the Geneva Confession (1536), the First (1536) and Second (1566) Helvetic Confessions, the Irish Articles of Religion (1615), and the Westminster Confession of Faith (1647) all demonstrate the belief that Scripture is the cognitive foundation (*principium cognoscendi*) of revealed theology.

In spite of Scripture's prominence in the Confessions, Reformed theology is not simply a "religion of the book." It is rather a "religion of the Word of God," and it is crucial not to miss this point. The First Helvetic Confession begins by identifying the canonical Scriptures with the Word of God, delivered by the Holy Spirit by the prophets and apostles. Article 1 of the Ten Theses of Bern says that the church "is born of the Word of God, and listens not to the voice of a stranger." Even when the doctrine of Scripture is not treated until later, as in the Scots Confession, it is clear that Scripture is "of God," that it is "sufficient to instruct and make the man of God perfect," and that the church is to hearken to and obey only "the voice of her own Spouse and Pastor."[25] The Westminster Confession states that the authority of Holy Scripture, which commands our trust and obedience, "dependeth not upon the testimony of any man or Church, but wholly upon God (who is truth itself), the author thereof."[26] As God's Word, Scripture ultimately serves his authorial purposes, chief among which is to serve as means for gathering, governing,

---

a communicative act of God. See further Kevin J. Vanhoozer, *First Theology: God, Scripture, and Hermeneutics* (Downers Grove, IL: InterVarsity, 2002), 15–41.

23. Richard A. Muller, *Post-Reformation Reformed Dogmatics*, vol. 2, *Holy Scripture: The Cognitive Foundation of Theology*, 2nd ed. (Grand Rapids: Baker, 2003), 152.

24. Ibid., 2:151.

25. Scots Confession (1560), article 19, in *Reformed Confessions of the Sixteenth Century*, ed. Arthur C. Cochrane (Louisville: Westminster John Knox, 2003), 178.

26. Westminster Confession of Faith (1647), in *The Constitution of the Presbyterian Church (U.S.A.)*, Part I: *Book of Confessions* (Louisville: Office of the General Assembly, 1996), 1.4.

and putting the finishing touches on those who will be his treasured possession (Exod. 19:5; Deut. 7:6; cf. 1 Pet. 2:9). In this respect, the church figures
in "first theology" too, namely, as the addressee of God's Word.

Scripture in the System of Theology: Room, Hallway, or Foundation?

Theology is systematic because it seeks to relate everything to God in an "orderly account" (cf. Luke 1:4). Where should we locate Scripture in the economy
of God's external works, the plan (*oikonomia*) to unite all things in Christ
(Eph. 1:10)? Stated differently: Where in the system or structure (the "house")
of theology does Scripture belong? Does Scripture have its own room (i.e., is it
a distinct doctrinal *locus*) or is it the hallway that connects the various rooms
(i.e., doctrines)? What is the place of Scripture in the Christian dogmatic inn?

Calvin begins his *Institutes* with the insight that there is no knowledge of God
without knowledge of self, and no knowledge of self without knowledge of God.
Post-Reformation Protestant theologians add that there is no knowledge of salvation apart from revelation in Scripture: "Just as the good architect provides a good
foundation for his proposed edifice, so must the theologian place his teaching
concerning Scripture first in the discussion of theology."[27] Only God can make
himself known, and Scripture is "the principle instrument" of his self-revelation.[28]
Because the primary function of Scripture was conveying knowledge of God,
Scripture quickly found its home in the doctrine of revelation.[29]

If theology were a house, revelation would probably be the room in which
the doctrine of Scripture has spent most of its time in the era of modernity,
though theologians have variously sought to say what makes Scripture "holy"
(i.e., how it is "of God") by appealing to other doctrines, including providence,
ecclesiology, sanctification, the sacraments, and pneumatology.[30] Telford Work
goes further, viewing Scripture as the hall that connects all the rooms in the
house of theology rather than merely the foundation on which the house is
built.[31] By and large, however, the doctrine of Scripture resided for much of
the modern period in the land of theological prolegomena.

27. Muller, *Post-Reformation Reformed Dogmatics*, 2:157.
28. From the Leiden *Synopsis*, cited in Muller, *Post-Reformation Reformed Dogmatics*, 2:158.
29. "Special revelation is God whispering his secrets to his servants, the prophets" (Bernard
Ramm, *Special Revelation and the Word of God: An Essay on the Contemporary Problem of
Revelation* [Grand Rapids: Eerdmans, 1961], 27).
30. See, e.g., A. T. B. McGowan, *The Divine Authenticity of Scripture: Retrieving an Evangelical Heritage* (Downers Grove, IL: InterVarsity, 2007).
31. Work describes his project as one that approaches the doctrine of Holy Scripture "as
more than simply foundational for the rest of Christian doctrine. Systematic bibliology draws
on the developed categories of the rest of systematic theology" (*Living and Active*, 9–10).

William Abraham speaks for those who worry that viewing Scripture as the cognitive foundation of theology reduces its role to that of an independent epistemic criterion: a standard for knowing to be used, like a slide rule, to determine whether a given doctrinal formulation measures up.[32] Abraham thinks it is a mistake to view Scripture as the solution to an epistemological problem (i.e., a criterion with which to discern truth from falsehood) rather than as the solution to a soteriological problem (i.e., sin).[33] John Webster raises the further concern that a preoccupation with Scripture as a deposit of propositional revelation could lead to "the isolation of the text both from its place in God's revelatory activity and from its reception in the community of faith."[34] Holy Scripture is not a textbook of divinely revealed data on which scientific theologians set to work developing doctrine. It is rather God's life- and light-giving loving overture to humans stumbling in the darkness of sin and death: it is God's presentation of Jesus Christ. Scripture is not merely the source and norm of other doctrines (a formal principle in the economy of revelation) but also an ingredient in the economy of redemption.

Scripture in Relation to Christ: Words and the Word

Karl Barth is well known for his insistence that revelation is a free act of God whereby he discloses not information about himself but himself, in the person of Jesus Christ: "God's Word is God Himself in His revelation."[35] Only God can make God known: God reveals himself through himself. Barth unpacks this in a distinctly trinitarian manner: the Father is the revealer, the Son is the revelation, and the Spirit is the "revealedness" (i.e., the reception of the revelation): "We arrive at the doctrine of the Trinity by no other way than that of an analysis of the concept of revelation."[36]

Where does Scripture fit in Barth's account of trinitarian revelation? Barth resists treating the Bible on its own, as if it were a holy object that could be studied on its own apart from its role in witnessing to Christ. Barth insists that the Bible *becomes* the Word of God (which is what God has determined

---

32. See, e.g., William Whitaker, who insists, "All doctrine is to be judged by the scriptures" (*A Disputation on Holy Scripture against the Papists*, trans. William Fitzgerald [Cambridge: Cambridge University Press, 1849], 457).

33. William J. Abraham, *The Bible: Beyond the Impasse* (Dallas: Highland Loch, 2012), 64. See also idem, *Canon and Criterion in Christian Theology: From the Fathers to Feminism* (Oxford: Oxford University Press, 1998).

34. John Webster, *Holy Scripture: A Dogmatic Sketch* (Cambridge: Cambridge University Press, 2003), 6.

35. Karl Barth, *Church Dogmatics* I/1, ed. G. W. Bromiley and T. F. Torrance, trans. T. H. L. Parker et al. (Edinburgh: T&T Clark, 1975), 295.

36. Ibid., 312.

that it be) when God in his gracious freedom co-opts the human words of
Scripture to present Christ. To treat the Bible as an independent deposit of
God-given truth is to "propositionalize" revelation, as if revelation were a
worldly entity (a thing of nature) rather than a divine event (a happening of
grace). Barth consistently refuses to view Scripture as if it were "grounded
upon itself apart from the mystery of Christ and the Holy Ghost."[37] The
Bible must not become "a part of the natural knowledge of God, i.e., of that
knowledge of God which man can have without the free grace of God."[38]

Barth's dogmatic theology is clearly Christocentric. Indeed, Christology—
God's eternal decision to be with and for humanity in human form—is argu-
ably Barth's "first theology," thus raising the question: if Jesus Christ is the
Word of God, is it a dogmatic mistake to identify the Bible too with God's
Word? Barth himself views Scripture (along with preaching) as a "form" of
the Word of God. When through the Spirit Scripture witnesses to or echoes
revelation in Jesus Christ, then the Bible has its being in its becoming the Word
of God, which is what God in his grace freely wills it to be again and again.[39]
John Webster makes a similar point when he observes that the Bible and its
interpretation "are elements in the domain of the Word . . . constituted by the
communicative presence of the risen and ascended Son of God who governs
all things."[40] The salient point, brought home anew in the twentieth century
by Barth, is that "forgetfulness of this wider economy is a large part of the
disarray of the church's apprehension of Scripture."[41] Scripture belongs not
in an abstract account of how humans acquire supernatural knowledge (i.e.,
revelation) but in the concrete account of how the testimony of the prophets
and apostles is caught up in the redemptive history of Israel and the church.
In Webster's words, "Holy Scripture is dogmatically explicated in terms of
its role in God's self-communication, that is, the acts of Father, Son, and
Spirit which establish and maintain that saving fellowship with humankind
in which God makes himself known to us and by us."[42]

37. Barth, *Church Dogmatics* I/2, 525.
38. Ibid., 522–23. Barth sees natural theology as "the doctrine of a union of man with God
existing outside God's revelation in Jesus Christ" (*Church Dogmatics* II/1, 168).
39. See Bruce L. McCormack, "The Being of Holy Scripture Is in Becoming: Karl Barth
in Conversation with American Evangelical Criticism," in *Evangelicals and Scripture: Tradition, Authority, and Hermeneutics*, ed. Vincent Bacote, Laura Miguélez, and Dennis Okholm
(Downers Grove, IL: InterVarsity, 2004), 555–75.
40. John Webster, *The Domain of the Word: Scripture and Theological Reason* (London:
T&T Clark, 2012), viii. See also Peter H. Nafziger, *"These Are Written": Toward a Cruciform
Theology of Scripture* (Eugene, OR: Pickwick, 2013), esp. chap. 2.
41. Webster, *Domain of the Word*, 7.
42. Webster, *Holy Scripture*, 8. Cf. Donald Wood's remark: "By locating the doctrine of
scripture within a trinitarian doctrine of revelation . . . Barth is guarding against the possibility

Some scholars, encouraged by Barth's emphasis on Christ as the revelation of God, have exaggerated the difference between Christ as perfect
Word and the human witnesses whose imperfect words make up Scripture.[43]
These scholars further contend that Protestant orthodox theologians tended
to make the Scriptures, not Christ, the *principium cognoscendi* of theology,
collapsing the Word into the words of Scripture, as it were.[44] Fortunately,
Richard Muller has set the historical record straight by showing how Calvin
and subsequent Reformed theologians always understood Scripture in relation
to God's Word and Spirit.[45] Calvin, for example, makes a trinitarian point
in distinguishing the "eternal and essential Word" who was with God from
the beginning (John 1:1) from the words spoken by the prophets, yet insisting that this same Son, the Second Person of the Trinity, is the source and
subject of all prophecy ("the wellspring of all oracles") and that the Spirit,
who spoke through the prophets, is "the Spirit of the Word."[46] Muller's
conclusion is worth citing: "For the Protestant orthodox, the Word incarnate stands not as the revelation itself but as the final revealer of God. The
doctrine of Scripture and Word, in short, reflects the Reformed doctrine of
the prophetic office of Christ."[47]

Triune Discourse: A Dogmatic Account of Holy Scripture

The moral of the previous section is that Scripture belongs not with the
doctrine of revelation, understood as an independent theological locus of its
own, but rather with the doctrine of the Trinity, especially as this concerns
the sending of the Word and Spirit in the history of redemption. With Calvin,
we must refuse to allow Scripture to become "a static, rationalizing norm
divorced from personal acceptance of the living Christ and from the active
presence of Christ's Spirit."[48] To the extent that Barth's trinitarian interpretation of revelation served to remind us of this truth, we owe him thanks. To
the extent that Barth's understanding of Scripture fails to do justice to that

---

that the scripture principle will be set up as a norm without content" (*Barth's Theology of
Interpretation* [Aldershot, UK: Ashgate, 2007], 107).

43. See, e.g., Heinrich Heppe, *Reformed Dogmatics* (Grand Rapids: Baker, 1978), 14–15.

44. See the discussion in Richard Muller, "A Note on 'Christocentrism' and the Imprudent
Use of Such Terminology," *Westminster Theological Journal* 66 (2006): 255–56.

45. See Muller, *Post-Reformation Reformed Dogmatics*, 2:182–206.

46. John Calvin, *Institutes of the Christian Religion*, ed. John T. McNeill, trans. Ford Lewis
Battles (Philadelphia: Westminster, 1960), 1.13.7.

47. Muller, *Post-Reformation Reformed Dogmatics*, 2:193.

48. Richard Muller, "The Foundation of Calvin's Theology: Scripture as Revealing God's
Word," *Duke Divinity School Review* 44, no. 1 (1979), 21.

economy, we need to correct him, not least by retrieving insights from his Reformed forebears.

From Revelation to Divine Discourse

That *God* speaks human words to humans is a conspicuous theme in Scripture from Genesis onward. God speaks *to* humans ("Be fruitful and multiply"; Gen. 1:28), and God *does* things by speaking even when no humans are present (e.g., "Let there be light"; Gen. 1:3): "Speaking is not incidental to God, as if it were simply one more thing he happens to do. It is central to who he is, what he does, and how he relates to his creation."[49] Of particular interest to the biblical authors are the episodes of God's *covenanting*: making promises and soliciting obedience. It is this covenantal "Word of the Lord," together with the people's response (or lack thereof), that drives the history of Israel forward, and it is this same covenantal phrase (now focused on the gospel) that impels the mission of the church (Acts 13:48–49; 19:10, 20; 1 Thess. 1:8; 2 Thess. 3:1). It is important to note, especially in the context of a dogmatic account of Holy Scripture as God's Word, that God makes covenants by speaking. Indeed, in promising, commanding, forgiving, and so on, speaking and acting are one and the same thing. No word, no promise (or forgiveness).[50]

Nicholas Wolterstorff wonders whether Barth does justice to the Bible's depictions of God speaking and to the statement in the Apostles' Creed that the Holy Spirit "spake by the prophets." For Barth, God is the author of Jesus Christ (so to speak) but not, strictly speaking, of Scripture. As to the Bible "becoming" revelation, Wolterstorff objects that whatever happens does not count as speech but something else: "God must so act on me that I am 'grabbed' by the content of what God has already said [in Jesus Christ]. I see no reason to call this action 'speech.' "[51]

Wolterstorff breaks from Barth by insisting that the Bible is indeed divine speech and that speaking is not the same thing as revealing. To *reveal* is to dispel ignorance, to make known what was previously unknown. But the thrust of promising, commanding, or warning is something other than making the

49. Nafziger, *"These Are Written,"* 67. For more on God as a communicative agent, see Kevin J. Vanhoozer, *Remythologizing Theology: Divine Action, Passion, and Authorship* (Cambridge: Cambridge University Press, 2010).

50. God uses other things to signify his covenant, yet as with the sacraments, these other elements must be accompanied by the divine Word. For example, God appoints the rainbow as the sign of his covenant with Noah, but it would not function as a covenant sign with the divine word that appoints it (Gen. 9:9–17).

51. Nicholas Wolterstorff, *Divine Discourse: Philosophical Reflections on the Claim That God Speaks* (Cambridge: Cambridge University Press, 1995), 72.

unknown known.[52] Revealing is only one form of discourse, only one way for
someone to say something about something for some purpose. Wolterstorff
also offers an account of the Bible as double-agency discourse that explains
how the words of the biblical authors may be deemed God's Word. To be
sure, the human authors produce the sentences that comprise Scripture: they
are its *locutionary* agents. Yet it is one thing to *utter* or *write* a sentence and
another to *do* something with it. An *illocutionary* act is what we *do* in saying
something (e.g., we promise, warn, command, assert, question, narrate, etc.).

Wolterstorff describes two ways that one person's locutionary act counts
as another person's illocutionary act: "If the ambassador was deputized to
say what he did in the name of his head of state, then the head of state speaks
(discourses) by way of the uttering of the ambassador; locutionary acts of the
ambassador count as illocutionary acts of the head of state."[53] God does indeed
appoint such deputies: Scripture calls them "prophets" (Deut. 18:15–22). The
second way to speak by means of another's discourse is to appropriate it, in
effect to declare "let this text serve as medium of my discoursing."[54] Wolterstorff thus provides two ways of thinking about the Bible as God's Word (i.e.,
divine discourse), neither of which requires a theory of divine origination
(i.e., inspiration).[55] However, conspicuous by its absence in Wolterstorff's account is the very thing Barth thought was central: attention to the trinitarian
framework of God's Word.

From Divine to Triune Discourse

A dogmatic account of Scripture must build both on Wolterstorff's insight
that God does things by means of human discourse (instead of restricting
God's Word to revelation in the person and history of Christ) and on Barth's
insight that the Word of God belongs to a triune economy of revelation and
redemption that revolves around Jesus Christ. Such an account must also
retrieve the Reformed doctrine of inspiration: God does not simply deputize
or appropriate discourse but *authors* it. The human words of the Bible are
the means in which the singular Word of God is heard. The result of this
three-stranded cord (Wolterstorff, Barth, Reformed orthodoxy) is an account
of Scripture as product of and medium for triune communicative action.

The Bible is discourse, and, like all God's works, it is triune: *opera trinitatis
ad extra indivisa sunt* ("the external operations of the Trinity are undivided").

---

52. See further ibid., chap. 2.
53. Ibid., 45.
54. Ibid., 41.
55. Wolterstorff distinguishes divine discourse from divine inspiration in ibid., 283–84.

In Calvin's words: "To the Father is attributed the beginning of activity . . . to the Son . . . the ordered disposition of all things; but to the Spirit is assigned the power and efficacy of that activity."[56] Christian dogmatics attends first and foremost to the divine economy in which the Father sends the Son and Spirit to make good on his covenant promise (and eternal purpose) to communicate himself to those creatures whom he has chosen for eternal fellowship: "And you shall be my people, and I will be your God" (Jer. 30:22; cf. Exod. 6:7; Lev. 26:12; Ezek. 36:28). A doctrine of Scripture must never lose sight of its covenantal content and context or its dependence at every point on trinitarian communicative agency.[57] Hence my thesis: *Scripture is holy because God, its ultimate author, commissions just these texts to play a vital and authoritative role in the triune economy of covenantal communication whereby the Lord dispenses his light (i.e., revelation, knowledge, truth) and life (i.e., redemption, fellowship, salvation). The Father initiates, the Son effectuates, and the Spirit consummates the discourse that Holy Scripture preserves in writing. Scripture is a means of God's self-presentation, a collection of diverse forms of discourse that, taken together, are ingredient in the extraordinary ministry of God's Word by which the risen Christ announces the gospel, administers his new creational kingdom, and imparts his light and life to readers made right-minded and right-hearted—fit for communion with God—through the illumination of the Holy Spirit.*

The remainder of this chapter unpacks this thesis in three parts, corresponding to the roles of Father, Son, and Spirit, respectively, in the economy of communication.[58] Here I need make only three brief points.

First, *discourse*—"something someone says to someone about something at some time in some way for some purpose"—better catches all the things God does in and through Scripture to communicate than *statement* or *proposition*.[59] To be sure, all discourse has a propositional component (i.e., cognitive

---

56. Calvin, *Institutes* 1.13.18.

57. On these connections see especially Ward, *Words of Life*, chap. 3, and Scott R. Swain, *Trinity, Revelation, and Reading: A Theological Introduction to the Bible and Its Interpretation* (London: T&T Clark, 2011), chaps. 1–2.

58. Though the external operations of the Trinity are undivided (i.e., each person is involved in everything God does), it is nevertheless fitting to ascribe certain aspects of actions to particular persons in light of what we learn about the work of Father, Son, and Spirit by attending to the history of redemption. For more on these so-called "divine appropriations," see Kevin J. Vanhoozer, "Triune Discourse, Part 2," in *Trinitarian Theology for the Church: Scripture, Community, Worship*, ed. Daniel J. Treier and David Lauber (Downers Grove, IL: InterVarsity, 2009), esp. 58–63.

59. My definition of discourse derives from Paul Ricoeur's seminal study, *Interpretation Theory: Discourse and the Surplus of Meaning* (Fort Worth: Texas Christian University Press, 1976).

content; the *something said*), and statements (affirmations of propositions) are an important part of biblical discourse.[60] *Discourse* nevertheless gives us a better purchase on all the aspects of God's verbal self-communication by distinguishing

the *who* of communication action (the subject of discourse: God and/or man);

the *to whom* (the recipient of discourse: original and/or contemporary reader);

the *what* (the predicate of discourse: what is being said/done);

the *about what* (the reference of discourse: history of Israel and/or mystery of Jesus Christ);

the *when* (the time of discourse: past and/or present); and

the *why* (the purpose of discourse: proximate and/or ultimate).[61]

Second, Jesus Christ is the ultimate subject and substance of triune discourse; communicating Christ—the self-communication of the Father and the turning point of the ages—for the sake of covenantal communion in Christ is the chief purpose of the Bible's *communicative action* taken as a whole (Luke 24:27). That Jesus is both subject and substance of God's self-communication comes into focus in the opening words of the last book of the Bible: "The revelation of Jesus Christ" (Rev. 1:1).[62] J. I. Packer describes Scripture as "God the Father preaching God the Son in the power of God the Holy Ghost."[63] Dogmatics, we might add, is the attempt to give an orderly account of the biblical logic of God's "gospel preaching." The Bible is not merely a bare "word" from God but an account of "his ways to Moses, his acts to the people of Israel" (Ps. 103:7). The biblical narrative is a "passing by" of the glorious ways of God that Moses asked to be shown to him (Exod. 33:13). And those "ways" of God—his steadfast love (*hesed*) and faithfulness (*emeth*)—that make up the content of God's name (Exod. 34:6–7) are

60. A proposition is *what* gets asserted in the act of asserting: "Assertions, commands, and questions are not propositions; they are speech-acts that do things with propositions" (Wahlberg, *Revelation as Testimony*, 26).

61. For a slightly different parsing of discourse, see Kevin J. Vanhoozer, "The Apostolic Discourse and Its Developments," in *Scripture's Doctrine and Theology's Bible: How the New Testament Shapes Christian Dogmatics*, ed. Markus Bockmuehl and Alan J. Torrance (Grand Rapids: Baker Academic, 2008), 191–207.

62. Joseph Mangina comments that the book of Revelation presents Jesus as "both the revealer and the revealed" (*Revelation* [Grand Rapids: Brazos, 2010], 40).

63. J. I. Packer, *God Has Spoken: Revelation and the Bible* (Grand Rapids: Baker, 1979), 97.

eventually summed up by another name ("Jesus Christ"), whose narrative
is also full of covenant love and faithfulness, grace and truth (John 1:14).
"The content of the New Testament is solely the name Jesus Christ."[64] Like
dogmatic theology, Scripture is more than a merely formal structure, a house
with a number of empty rooms (i.e., doctrines). On the contrary: the house
is not empty. Someone lives there. It is Christ's house. A dogmatic account of
Scripture attends to its place in this house and to its role in the Triune God's
household management.

Third, those who read Scripture stand on holy ground: "*To encounter the
words of Scripture is to encounter God in action.*"[65] Stated differently: readers too are caught up in the economy of God's triune self-communication.[66]
God ultimately communicates Christ in and through Scripture in order to
conform readers to Christ. It is the Spirit who sets right readers' cognitive,
volitional, and affective capacities so that they can understand Scripture and
bathe in its communicative effects, of which the most important is the reader's
transformation from faith to faith.

Triune Communicative Agent: Authorship and the Covenantal Ontology of Scripture

This is the first of three sections that unpack my thesis statement concerning the self-communicative activity of the Father, Son, and Spirit in terms of
Scripture's ontology, function, and teleology, respectively. Each section begins
with a biblical verse that orients the discussion and continues by restating classical Reformed categories in the idiom of triune covenantal communication.

Ontology: What Scripture Is

And we also thank God constantly for this, that when you received the word
of God, which you heard from us, you accepted it not as the word of men but
as what it really is, the word of God. (1 Thess. 2:13)

According to the Scriptures, the God who spoke creation into existence also
stoops to speak into creation. In particular, God makes covenants: binding
words—words sealed by an oath—by which God promises to be there and
do things for his people. Scripture often depicts God entering into covenantal

64. Barth, *Church Dogmatics* I/2, 15.
65. Ward, *Words of Life*, 48 (emphasis original).
66. Whereas Barth spoke of revealer, revelation, and revealedness, I think in terms of com-
municator, communication, and communicatedness.

relationships with people through specific acts of discourse (Gen. 17:6–7; 2 Sam. 7:13; Jer. 30:18). Only God can initiate a divine-human covenant, and the way God takes the initiative is by speaking words, sometimes directly (e.g., Exod. 20:1–17), sometimes indirectly, through authorized spokesmen (e.g., angels, prophets), and occasionally by writing texts (Exod. 31:18).

In the New Testament, the voice of God, heard again on a mountain, says of the transfigured Jesus, "Listen to him" (Matt. 17:5). The words of Jesus are the words of God incarnate, and this same Jesus commissions his apostles to continue communicating the good news that the long-awaited covenant with God has attained in Christ a new and unlooked for wonderful fulfillment. Throughout the biblical narrative, however, there are false prophets and false teachers. Not all words are gospel, nor are all words of God. The Bible is "holy" because its discourse is set apart as the medium of triune communicative activity and thus an extension of God's own personal communicative presence. Scripture does not have a divine nature but a divine Author (and origin).

Inspiration: Strong (Triune) Authorship

To speak of the Bible as Holy Scripture is to indicate "what it really is [*kathōs estin alēthōs*], the word of God" (1 Thess. 2:13). The human words of the prophets and apostles, the "extraordinary ministers"[67] of the word, are the means by which the eternal Word of God spoke to Israel and speaks to the church. First Samuel 15:1 speaks of the "voice of the words [*qôl dabar*] of Jehovah," an unusual construction that highlights the one who is heard speaking in these words. The apostle Paul's way of describing this phenomenon is to say, "All Scripture is breathed out by God [*theopneustos*]" (2 Tim. 3:16). The other biblical text that loomed large over Reformed confessions was 2 Peter 1:21: "Men spoke from God as they were carried along by the Holy Spirit." The biblical texts are therefore "given by inspiration of God."[68] B. B. Warfield's classic definition is instructive: "Inspiration is that extraordinary, supernatural influence . . . exerted by the Holy Ghost on the writers of our Sacred Books, by which their words were rendered also the words of God."[69]

The Father is the source of the economic activity of the Son and Spirit. It is the Father's voice that eternally utters the Word (John 1:1). Jesus is the

67. William Ames, *The Marrow of Theology*, trans. John Dystra Eusden (Grand Rapids: Baker, 1968), 185.
68. Westminster Confession of Faith (1647), 1.2.
69. B. B. Warfield, *The Inspiration and Authority of the Bible* (Phillipsburg, NJ: P&R, 1970), 420.

communication of the Father in human form: "For I have not spoken on my own authority, but the Father who sent me has himself given me a commandment—what to say and what to speak" (John 12:49). Similarly, the Spirit of truth "will not speak on his own authority, but whatever he hears he will speak" (John 16:13; cf. 5:19). In the pattern of triune communication, the Father is the originating Voice, the Son the Word, and the Spirit that carries the Word.

That the Bible is the Word of God implies verbal inspiration, as well as a strong (rather than weak or extreme) account of divine authorship: *triune* authorship. What God inspires (breathes out) is not authors or ideas but *discourse*. Consider the strong identity between Jeremiah's discourse and God's: "But neither [Zedekiah] nor his servants nor the people of the land listened to the word of the LORD that he spoke through Jeremiah the prophet" (Jer. 37:2). Clearly, the words themselves (i.e., the locutions) are Hebrew, not some heavenly tongue, yet this does not prevent them from conveying God's message. The difference between God's discourse and Jeremiah's lies not in ontology but origin: "Yet when we claim as an attribute of the text that it is in substance the words of God, while we have not thereby divinized the text, we have made an ontological claim in respect of it."[70] The words of the Bible are not divine, but the discourse is, and it is fixed in writing. What Scripture says, God says. The Triune God speaks in and through the various books of the Bible. God's Word is God's bond.[71]

Inspiration is the confession that God is the strong author of Holy Scripture. In confessing Scripture as inspired discourse, the accent is on the product, not the process. As to the process itself, Herman Bavinck says it is "organic": God in his infinite wisdom leads the human authors to say the right words not through a mechanical or coercive process but by working with and through their created personalities, histories, and intelligence.[72] There is therefore no competition between human and divine communicative agency. The human authors are divinely commissioned witnesses who offer creaturely testimony that is both their own and prompted by the Spirit. John Webster suggests that biblical inspiration is a matter of sanctification: "not a unilateral cognitive force but a compound act in which the creator and reconciler takes creatures and their powers, acts and products into his service."[73]

---

70. Andrew Shead, *A Mouth Full of Fire: The Word of God in the Words of Jeremiah* (Downers Grove, IL: InterVarsity, 2012), 277.

71. Barth was reluctant to identify God's Word (the act of revelation) with the Bible for fear of compromising God's freedom. My argument is that God is free to speak or not to speak but, having spoken/written, God freely chooses not to deny himself and thus to stand by his words.

72. Herman Bavinck, *Reformed Dogmatics*, vol. 1, *Prolegomena*, ed. John Bolt, trans. John Vriend (Grand Rapids: Baker Academic, 2003), 430–39.

73. Webster, *Domain of the Word*, ix. See also Webster, *Holy Scripture*, chap. 1.

Holy Scripture is human discourse commissioned and confirmed as the servant form of God's communicative initiative: *strong* (i.e., triune) authorship. The prophets and apostles were set apart by God as creaturely means to advance the communicative economy by which the Voice of God utters the Word of God by the Breath of God. "You will be my witnesses," the risen Christ tells the apostles, "when the Holy Spirit has come upon you" (Acts 1:8). And this is the key point about divine inspiration: the prophets and apostles speak and write what the Spirit of Christ leads them to say. The Father speaks a Word (the Son) who in turn commissions human agents to speak words on his behalf through the enabling power of the Holy Spirit.[74] Strong triune authorship does not suppress but rather sanctifies the human discourse, making it a fit verbal temple for the communicative presence and activity of God.[75]

Canonization: Locating the Triune Discourse

The Reformed confessions rightly listed the books of the Bible that Protestant churches acknowledge as "of God." But the canon is much more than a list. It is an indication that just these texts count as the communicative works of God, and hence the church's rule (Greek κανών) for faith and life. The canon is the answer to the question of where the church should go to hear the words of eternal life (John 6:68). Further, taken as a whole—the "collected works" of God, as it were—the canon provides the context for discerning the divine authorial intent.[76]

The canon has a "natural history," but we cannot fully explain the ontology of the canon in terms of this-worldly causality only. To be sure, on a merely historical level, it appears as if the church created the canon. Calvin is closer to the mark in affirming the *autopistia* (Greek αὐτοπιστια) or self-convincing character of Scripture, and ascribing this quality to the testimony of the Holy Spirit.[77] The canon too is part of the economy of triune communication. The church does not declare but acknowledges canonical Scripture. A dogmatic account of the canon is ultimately "an account of Christ's active, communicative presence in the Spirit's power through the commissioned apostolic testimony."[78] In Jesus's words, "My sheep hear my voice" (John 10:27).

74. Cf. Webster: "God speaks as in the Spirit Jesus Christ speaks" (*Domain of the Word*, 8).
75. See further Swain, *Trinity, Revelation, and Reading*, 62–70.
76. See further Kevin J. Vanhoozer, *Is There a Meaning in This Text? The Bible, the Reader, and the Morality of Literary Knowledge* (Grand Rapids: Zondervan, 1998), 264–65.
77. See Henk van den Belt, *The Authority of Scripture in Reformed Theology: Truth and Trust* (Leiden: Brill, 2010).
78. Webster, *Holy Scripture*, 59. See also idem, "The Dogmatic Location of the Canon," in *Word and Church: Essays in Christian Dogmatics* (Edinburgh: T&T Clark, 2001), 9–46.

Triune Communicative Action: The Covenantal Form, Content, and Function of Scripture

Function: What Scripture Does

For the word of God is living and active. (Heb. 4:12)

God's voice sounds through the human words of Scripture: "God spoke to our fathers by the prophets" (Heb. 1:1). To maintain that God's speech is only a thing of the past is to hold a quasi-deistic view of the canon: God created it and then left it to its own devices. We have been suggesting, however, that Scripture is a creaturely ingredient that continues to function as part of the economy of triune communicative action. The Holy Spirit uses Old Testament locutions to speak "today": "Today, if you hear his voice . . ." (Heb. 3:7).[79] The point is that God's personal word—what he has spoken through the prophets, in his Son, and in Scripture—is "living and active" (Heb. 4:12), and that it solicits a personal response on the part of its hearer or reader, on pain of not entering into God's Sabbath rest (Heb. 4:11).

Scripture is the creaturely instrument of God's living and active Word and will accomplish the purpose for which it was sent (Isa. 55:11). To be sent is to set out on a mission (Latin *missio* = "sending"). Scripture contains not merely mission statements but statements (and songs, stories, etc.) on a mission: to present Christ, the substance of the new covenant. Scripture displays single-mindedness, in both senses: the canon is ultimately the product of a single Author, and its parts cohere "as a company of emissaries appointed to do [Christ's] bidding as the history of his revelation to creatures unfolds."[80]

Authority: Rightful Say So

The risen Christ declares, "All authority in heaven and on earth has been given to me" (Matt. 28:18). We may draw two inferences: (1) because he *lives*, Christ continues to speak in and through Scripture; and (2) because he *rules*, everything he says is authoritative. Jesus's voice has an intrinsic right to be heard and *heeded*. Scripture is both the cradle where the incarnate Christ lies and the scepter by which the ascended Christ now rules the church (Luther). As John Webster has said, "Scripture is both the announcement of the reality of his exaltation to the right hand of the Father and itself an instrument

79. See Daniel J. Treier, "Speech Acts, Hearing Hearts, and Other Senses: The Doctrine of Scripture as Practiced in Hebrews," in *The Epistle to the Hebrews and Christian Theology*, ed. Richard Bauckham et al. (Grand Rapids: Eerdmans, 2009), 338–44.
80. Webster, *Domain of the Word*, 18.

through which his governance is exercised."[81] Scripture is the personal discourse of the Word, the Second Person of the Trinity, addressed to the church, the "creature of the word" and his particular domain. Scripture is the founding covenant document of the covenant community, the constitution of God's holy nation (1 Pet. 2:9).[82] The Bible recounts the mighty acts that identify God as Lord of the covenant (Deut. 1:6–3:29), records the making and renewing of covenants (Josh. 8:30–35; 1 Sam. 12; 2 Sam. 7; 2 Kings 22:2–3; Ezra 9–10; Neh. 9–10; Luke 22:20; 1 Cor. 11:25; 2 Cor. 3:6; cf. Heb. 9:15), and regulates the life of the covenant community.

Sola scriptura ("Scripture alone") means that Scripture is supremely authoritative in (and over) the church. It is the final court of appeal for understanding the gospel—identifying Jesus as the Christ and saying what God was doing in Christ—or anything else that pertains to Christian faith and life. What Scripture says, God says.[83] Tradition, the moon to Scripture's sun, has a derivative authority insofar as creeds and confessions rightly reflect the light the Spirit shines/speaks from the biblical text. Scripture's authority stems from its place in the economy of triune communication, where it functions not only to convey information about the covenant but also to *administer* it, not least by training people in the ways of covenant obedience (e.g., truthful speech and righteous action). Scripture is an authoritative guide to the privileges and responsibilities of those whose citizenship is in heaven, where Christ is: "Its *form* fits its *function* of communicating the unfolding drama of Christ and covenant."[84] Scripture is the curriculum of the new covenant, "profitable for teaching, for reproof, for correction, and for training in righteousness" (2 Tim. 3:16).

Infallibility: The Utter Reliability of Triune Discourse

As Jesus was impeccable, truly human yet not liable to fail (i.e., sin), so Scripture is infallible, truly human but not liable to fail (e.g., to err).[85] Jesus

81. John Webster, "Resurrection and Scripture," in *Christology and Scripture: Interdisciplinary Perspectives*, ed. Andrew T. Lincoln and Angus Paddison (London: T&T Clark, 2008), 152.

82. Steven L. McKenzie calls Deuteronomy "Israel's *constitution*" (*Covenant* [St. Louis: Chalice, 2000], 135).

83. Cf. B. B. Warfield, "'It Says:' 'Scripture Says:' 'God says:'" in *Inspiration and Authority of the Bible*, 299–348. I have been arguing in this chapter that what "God says" is triune discourse. The Trinity is our Scripture principle because the supreme authority in the church is the Triune God speaking in the Scriptures (see Vanhoozer, "Triune Discourse, Part 2," 76).

84. Swain, *Trinity, Revelation, and Reading*, 71 (emphasis original).

85. Scripture is reliable because whatever the form of discourse, God's Word is infallible (i.e., it will not fail to accomplish the purpose for which it was written). I understand inerrancy— the affirmation of Scripture's truth—to be a subset of infallibility: i.e., when the discourse in

Christ is the name of God—"steadfast love" (*hesed*) and "faithfulness" (*emeth*)—made flesh. That Scripture is made up of human language and literature no more disqualifies it from being a vehicle for God's Word than does Jesus's humanity: both are servant forms.[86] Jesus is God's corporeal discourse (the Word incarnate); Scripture is God's canonical discourse (the Word inscribed). We should not impose our concept of perfection on Scripture but rather acknowledge that God in his wisdom chose to employ just these forms of human discourse to present Christ and administer his covenant. What we can say is that each servant form of biblical discourse perfectly performs its communicative and covenantal function, whether to state facts, issue warnings, tell stories, proffer wisdom, or provide consolation.

Holy Scripture is infallible not because the text is a quasi-divine object with supernatural powers of its own but because God has appointed it to play a part in the economy of triune communication, namely, as that which preserves the divine discourse, and God's covenant, in writing. The words of Scripture are powerful and profitable because they are the words of the Word, the One who sits on the great white throne and says, "Write this down, for these words are trustworthy and true" (Rev. 21:5). These words are trustworthy and true because they present Jesus Christ—the proof of God's covenanting faithfulness and steadfast love. All the forms of the Bible's covenant discourse—laws, promises, prophecies, wisdom, history, gospel, apocalyptic, and the like—are utterly reliable because they correspond to what is ultimately real.

"Let God be proved true" (Rom. 3:4 NRSV); "Your word is truth" (John 17:17). Holy Scripture is true because it is the utterly reliable personal word of the Triune God. God proves himself true by time and time again keeping his word. Jesus says, "Heaven and earth will pass away, but my words will not pass away" (Matt. 24:35). The Word of the Lord endures forever (1 Pet. 1:25; cf. Ps. 119:160) because God is as good—as true, utterly reliable—as his word. "Your word is truth," yes, and so is God's name: steadfast love and covenant faithfulness (Exod. 34:6–7). There is a covenantal correspondence, a faithful fit, between God's words and God's deeds. God's discourse is trustworthy and true because God is trustworthy and true (i.e., utterly reliable). Scripture is infallible because God stands by his words.

---

question is indicative (e.g., statements, affirmations), it will not fail to correspond to what is the case—assuming, of course, that interpreters understand what they are reading.

86. On the "servant-form" of Scripture, see G. C. Berkouwer, *Holy Scripture* (Grand Rapids: Eerdmans, 1975), chap. 7; Richard B. Gaffin Jr., *God's Word in Servant-Form: Abraham Kuyper and Herman Bavinck and the Doctrine of Scripture* (Jackson, MS: Reformed Academic Press, 2007).

Jesus is the truth (John 14:6) because he is the fulfillment of the covenant promises and because he communicates who and what God is. True words communicate what is.[87] Words that purport to say *what is*, yet fail in doing so, are false: unreliable and untrustworthy. The triune discourse in Scripture treats "all things necessary for . . . man's salvation, faith, and life."[88] This is not to say that the Bible provides encyclopedic knowledge on every topic that it touches. The overarching function of Scripture is "to communicate Christ and covenant."[89]

Triune Communicative Achievement: Reading and the Covenantal Purpose of Scripture

Teleology: Why Scripture Is and Does

Let the word of Christ dwell in you richly. (Col. 3:16)

Why is there Scripture rather than nothing? God speaks in order to be heard. Communication is short-circuited unless and until it is received: discourse is something said *to someone, for some purpose*. God speaks in Scripture in order to make a difference—or rather, to make *all* the difference in the world, for what God says concerns his reconciliation with the world through Christ (2 Cor. 5:18–19). The purpose of Scripture is to communicate "the word of Christ": "So faith comes from hearing, and hearing through the word of Christ" (Rom. 10:17).

Faith comes by hearing but matures by attending to the gospel (Col. 1:5), the Word from and about Christ: "Let the word of Christ dwell in you richly" (Col. 3:16). The *telos*, or end, of the biblical discourse about Jesus Christ is not merely to *inform* but also to *transform* the reader—to *form* Christ in us. Scripture is the Word of Christ that rules the domain of Christ (i.e., everything!), particularly the community of believers who worship in Spirit and truth. It follows from the purpose of communication that the community

---

87. The Chicago Statement on Biblical Inerrancy (1978) affirms Scripture's truth "in all the matters it addresses" (article 11). Inerrancy is the position that the Bible's discourse is true in all that it affirms (when the authors make affirmations) and will eventually be seen as true (when right-minded readers read rightly). For more on the relationship of infallibility and inerrancy, see Kevin J. Vanhoozer, "Augustinian Inerrancy: Literary Meaning, Literal Truth, and Literate Interpretation in the Economy of Biblical Discourse," in *Five Views on Biblical Inerrancy*, ed. J. Merrick and Stephen Garrett (Grand Rapids: Zondervan, 2013), 199–235.

88. Westminster Confession of Faith (1647), 1, 6.

89. Swain, *Trinity, Revelation, and Reading*, 78. Cf. Ward's covenantally oriented definition of the sufficiency of Scripture: "Scripture is sufficient as the means by which God continues to present himself to us such that we can know him, repeating through Scripture the covenant promise he has brought to fulfillment in Jesus Christ" (*Words of Life*, 113).

of readers is part of the economy. Scripture accomplishes its purpose not merely when it is read but when it is used by the Holy Spirit to minister—to *form*—Christ in its readers ("let the peace of Christ rule in your hearts"; Col. 3:15). The Word dwells richly in believing readers because there is a wealth in what it conveys: in a word, it conveys every spiritual blessing with which we have been blessed in Christ (Eph. 1:3), especially the covenant blessing of life in God's life-giving presence.

Interpretation: Right Reception

The interpretation of the Bible—the way readers receive and act in response to it—is also part of the domain of God's Word. To be sure, it is possible to read the Bible "like any other book," yet Scripture, unlike every other book, is a set-apart (i.e., holy) vehicle of triune discourse and therefore requires special treatment: "The natural person does not accept the things of the Spirit of God, for they are folly to him, and he is not able to understand them because they are spiritually discerned" (1 Cor. 2:14). We cannot describe what it is to read Scripture rightly as if human agents were able to understand triune discourse simply through the employment of their natural abilities. Readers are sinners who "by their unrighteousness suppress the truth" (Rom. 1:18).

Readers too are, therefore, part of the economy of triune discourse (what God says *to someone*). The Creator of heaven and earth does not speak futilely into the air but effectively into human hearts and minds. The reader's role in the economy is not to author Scripture or to confer authority on it but rather to receive and revere it as the Word of Christ, giving thanks for it with others in the church and letting it dwell in the core of their being in order gradually to conform them to Christ, its subject matter.[90] The goal of interpretation is to create right-minded and right-hearted readers who will rejoice in the truth, not least by willingly participating in it. The reader's place in the economy of communication is to perform or live out the reality held out by the biblical text: fellowship with God or, in a word, *communion*.[91]

Illumination: The Spirit of Enlightenment

The Holy Spirit consummates triune discourse by creating right-hearted readers, first, through regenerating their natures and renewing their minds

90. "The Spirit who enables and sustains our reading of Holy Scripture also provides a community to aid us in our reading . . . the church" (Swain, *Trinity, Revelation, and Reading*, 100).

91. On the importance of viewing readers and the activity of reading in a theological framework, see Darren Sarisky, *Scriptural Interpretation: A Theological Exploration* (Oxford: Wiley-Blackwell, 2013), esp. chap. 9.

(Rom. 12:2) and, second, by leading the church—the community of its right-hearted and right-minded readers—into all truth (John 16:13). "Spiritual interpretation" is the response of the covenant servant to the act of the covenant Lord. The meaning of Scripture does not depend on readers' activity, however, for "Scripture interprets Scripture." The vocation of the reader is to think Scripture's interpretations after it—or rather, after the Spirit, its strong divine Author.

The Spirit is the perfecter of both the writing and reading of Scripture, the executor of inspiration and illumination alike. Of special concern now is the place of illumination in the economy of communication: "Illumination refers to the ways in which the operation of creaturely intelligence is caused, preserved and directed by divine light, whose radiance makes creatures to know."[92] What links communication and illumination to Scripture is the latter's role in communicating light. Scripture is "the sword of the Spirit" (Eph. 6:17) whose piercing light divides truth from falsehood and discerns the thoughts and intentions of the heart (Heb. 4:12).

"God is light" (1 John 1:5). Jesus Christ is "the radiance of God's glory" (Heb. 1:3), "the true light, which gives light to everyone" (John 1:9; cf. John 9:5). The Son communicates the light and life of God (John 8:12). Yet Scripture too is part of this economy of illumination, a means by which the Triune God advances the dominion of light: "Your word is a lamp to my feet and a light to my path" (Ps. 119:105). In particular, what shines in Scripture is "the light of the gospel of the glory of Christ" (2 Cor. 4:4). It is not the Bible that needs illumining but its readers.

The Spirit completes the process of enlightening—the communication of the "light of life" (John 8:12)—by removing the veil of ignorance that shrouds readers' hearts (2 Cor. 3:18). The Spirit's illumination allows readers not only to see but also to taste—to appreciate the excellence—of what God communicates in Scripture: the sweetness of salvation in Christ. "The Spirit's role—or goal—in interpretation is to allow the interpreter to understand the text in such a way that the text transforms the interpreter into the image of Christ."[93] Word and Spirit thus work together to communicate—to speak, show, and share—Christ.

92. Webster, *Domain of the Word*, 50.
93. Gary L. Nebeker, "The Holy Spirit, Hermeneutics, and Transformation: From Present to Future Glory," *Evangelical Review of Theology* 27 (2003): 47. Cf. Kevin J. Vanhoozer, "The Spirit of Light after the Age of Enlightenment: Reforming/Renewing Pneumatic Hermeneutics via the Economy of Illumination," in *Spirit of God: Christian Renewal in the Community of Faith*, ed. Jeffrey W. Barbeau and Beth Felker Jones (Downers Grove, IL: InterVarsity, 2015).

Conclusion: Cultivating the Love of God, the Mind of Christ, and the Fellowship of the Holy Spirit

The Bible is Holy Scripture not because it has dropped down from heaven or been dug up from the past but because it is a vital ingredient in the ongoing economy of triune communication: "God the Father is the giver of Holy Scripture; God the Son is the theme of Holy Scripture; and God the Spirit . . . is the author, authenticator, and interpreter of Holy Scripture."[94] In the final dogmatic analysis, Holy Scripture is the Word of God that presents the word of Christ with the illumining power concomitant with the sword of the Spirit. *The Holy Spirit, the Spirit of Christ, effectually communicates the mind of Christ to human authors of Scripture, the word of Christ, so that Jesus's disciples can hear, read, and respond to Scripture in ways that build up the church, the body of Christ.*

Holy Scripture is written in ordinary language but communicates an extraordinary culture: a set of beliefs, values, and practices that correspond to the new created order "in Christ." God gives us Scripture to help us understand what is in Christ and to render us right-minded and right-hearted readers, able to play our parts in the drama of redemption as witnesses to this eschatological reality with both scriptural fidelity and improvisational freedom. Scripture's role in the economy of revelation and redemption is that of finishing school: it is the Spirit's curriculum for uniting believers to Christ and then cultivating the mind of Christ in his disciples by imparting habits of right thinking and desiring that conform to the word of Christ.

We conclude with a collect from Thomas Cranmer, which expresses gratitude for the word of the Triune God, a gift that both educates and edifies the church:

> Blessed Lord, who hast caused all Holy Scriptures to be written for our learning, grant that we may in such wise hear them, read, mark, learn, and inwardly digest them, that by the patience and comfort of Thy holy Word we may embrace, and ever hold fast, the blessed hope of everlasting life, which Thou hast given us, in our Savior Jesus Christ, who liveth and reigneth with Thee and the Holy Ghost, ever one God, world without end.[95]

94. Packer, *God Has Spoken*, 97.
95. Collect for the Second Sunday in Advent, *Book of Common Prayer* (1662). Peter Toon's commentary on the collect is also worth citing: "Thus a basic theme of the Collect is the right use of Scripture as a means of preparing for the Second Advent as we live in the Light of the First Advent" ("Second Sunday in Advent," The Prayer Book Society, n.d., www.pbs.org.uk /the-bcp/second-sunday-in-advent).

3

Divine Attributes

MICHAEL ALLEN

The most fundamental matter in Christian theology is the character of God. "All the doctrines in dogmatics . . . are but the explication of the one central dogma of the knowledge of God. All things are considered in light of God, subsumed under him, traced back to him as the starting point."[1] All other matters being understood in light of God (*sub species divinitatis*), the nature of God is determinative for all theological reflection, indeed, for Christian worship and witness itself. "The more principal end of founded things is God's glory or goodness; not, indeed, to be acquired or enlarged, but man tested and communicated."[2] As humans are to give God glory, we do well to know him accurately so as to render him trust, love, and worship. Traditionally theologians have reflected on the nature of the Christian God by focusing on two aspects of his being: his attributes and his triunity. This book follows this course. In doing so, however, it does not suggest that the attributes of God might refer to a deeper, singular deity behind the three persons of the Godhead. In doing so, it also does not purport to treat the attributes and the

1. Herman Bavinck, *Reformed Dogmatics*, vol. 2, *God and Creation*, ed. John Bolt, trans. John Vriend (Grand Rapids: Baker Academic, 2004), 29.
2. Bonaventure, *Commentaria in quatuor libros sententiarum 2*, vol. 2, *Opera omnia S. Bonaventurae* (Quaracchi: Collegium S. Bonaventurae, 1885), 1.2.2.

triune persons as parallel realities, as if attributes are persons or vice versa. These categories are aspectival, not partitive. The triunity of God refers to the entirety of God's nature, while the attributes of God also refer to that same entirety albeit from a different angle or aspect.

In this chapter we will unpack a thesis: *The doctrine of the divine attributes summons the church to confess the incomparably beautiful name of God, manifest in the works of the divine economy and rooted in his eternal triunity, as the almighty God and the Father of the gospel.*

Avoiding Idolatry and Speculation

The doctrine of the divine attributes summons the church to confess the incomparably beautiful name of God. The incomparable nature of the divine being provokes reflection on the not simply difficult but also dangerous work of theology. Thinking about God is no blasé matter. It is playing with live ammo. Thinking about God is no free intellectual speculation. It is engaging with the living God. Were we creatures attuned to constant integrity, honesty, and charity, this would be no matter for concern. But given our finitude and fallenness, this is no small matter. God dwells in unapproachable light (1 Tim. 6:16), and his appearance is, in a very real sense, our undoing (Isa. 6:5).

The Bible rejects idolatry in a blistering and polemical manner. The Old Testament addresses this threat with force and repetition. The creation account of Genesis 1 locates God's activity amid that of other religious figures in the ancient Near Eastern world (for example, the lights and the seas). But it links these figures by noting that God made them by simple fiat. The great competitors of the God of Israel are but productions of his. No doubt Genesis tells the story of creation in this way to prepare Israel for entry into the promised land, wherein the people will be tried and tempted to worship the gods of the neighboring people. The exodus account also highlights the need to put the idols in their place. As Jon Levenson has argued, the major message of the book of Exodus is not liberation per se but the sovereignty of YHWH over Pharaoh (and, with him, all the gods of Egypt).[3] Thus the course to freedom takes time enough for the symbols of Egyptian religion to be mocked one by one in the plague cycle.[4] Again the story of Israel's freedom

3. Jon D. Levenson, "Exodus and Liberation," in *The Hebrew Bible, the Old Testament, and Historical Criticism: Jews and Christians in Biblical Studies* (Louisville: Westminster John Knox, 1993), 140–51 (where Levenson employs the Song of the Sea in Exod. 15 as a theological framework for understanding the entirety of the text).

4. John D. Currid, *Ancient Egypt and the Old Testament* (Grand Rapids: Baker, 1997), 104–20.

is told in a certain way, no doubt, to prepare its children for entry into another polytheistic environment in Canaan. There will be many kings and lords in this terrain, yet only YHWH is King of kings and Lord of lords.

Idolatry is not merely a problem to be warded off in the beginnings, whether Genesis, Exodus, or Deuteronomy. That is, idolatry is not something that can be dealt with once and for all, as if Israel could, before entering the land, assure that she would never fall prey to the lures and testimonies of her neighbors and their gods, or as if the Christian, having "turned to God from idols to serve the living and true God" (1 Thess. 1:9), is never to feel the temptation or tendency to commit idolatry again. No, the prophecies of Isaiah 40–66 serve as a reminder that idolatry is an ever-present threat and, more so, one into which God's people can and do fall.[5] With texts like this in mind, Calvin said that the human heart was an idol-making factory.[6] Nicholas Lash has spoken of theology as an exercise to flee idolatry by providing a set of "protocols against idolatry."[7] We might focus our attention on the divine attributes as particular tools in this battle. The attributes point against certain tendencies to think of God in various ways: by either contradicting or reducing the biblical witness to who God has revealed himself to be.

The Reformed confessions identified the Reformational emphasis on *sola fide* with the singularity of the Triune God. The Genevan Confession (1536) affirmed that "there is only one God" and "therefore we think it an abomination to put our confidence or hope in any created thing, to worship anything else than him, whether angels or any other creatures, and to recognize any other Saviour of our souls than him alone."[8] Just over two decades later, John Knox showed similar sentiments in the opening words to the Scots Confession: "We confess and acknowledge one God alone, to whom alone we must cleave, whom alone we must serve, whom only we must worship, and in whom alone we put our trust."[9] These citations manifest a fascinating theological point with powerful historiographic and methodological ramifications. First, the confessions both interpret biblical monotheism as necessarily calling for total trust in this one divine being. In other words, theology shapes ethics; *solus*

5. The link between origins and ongoing temptation can be seen in the way Israel's doctrine of creation was fashioned amid her theological-ethical reflections; see Gerhard von Rad, "The Theological Problem of the Old Testament Doctrine of Creation," in *The Problem of the Hexateuch and Other Essays*, trans. E. W. Trueman Dicken (New York: McGraw-Hill, 1966), 131–43.

6. John Calvin, *Institutes of the Christian Religion*, ed. John T. McNeill, trans. Fort Lewis Battles (Louisville: Westminster, 2006), 1.11.8.

7. Nicholas Lash, "Considering the Trinity," *Modern Theology* 2 (1986): 187.

8. The Geneva Confession of 1536, in *Reformed Confessions of the Sixteenth Century*, ed. Arthur Cochrane (Louisville: Westminster John Knox, 2003), 120.

9. The Scots Confession, 1560, in *Reformed Confessions of the Sixteenth Century*, 166.

Deus brings forth a corresponding claim *sola fide*; if God is Lord of all, then we depend on him for all things. Second, this link helps to reframe the way we view the Reformational movement. Its concerns regarding salvation and assurance were not an addition to the catholic heritage of the Western church; rather, its emphasis on life *sola fide* was simply the extension of the catholic doctrine of God to its soteriological implications. Because Christians have always believed in this (singular) God, the salvific and ethical ramifications are to recast human life as "by faith" across the board and all the way down. In so doing, the Reformed confessions offer doctrinal and ethical expansion upon the teaching of Moses to the Israelites: "Hear, O Israel: The LORD our God, the LORD is one. You shall love the LORD your God with all your heart and with all your soul and with all your might" (Deut. 6:4–5). A fully sufficient benefactor—Israel's covenant LORD—calls for total trust.

The doctrine of the divine attributes summons the church to confess the incomparably beautiful name of God, manifest in the works of the divine economy and rooted in his eternal triunity.

Where human ingenuity leads to idols, the manifestation of God in his gracious works brings truth. Idols, by definition, involve the taking of the common and classing it divine. Whether physical or intellectual, such maneuvers render a god in the stock of the everyday (even if the everyday ideal rather than the everyday experience). God becomes, in such an approach, the apogee of truth, beauty, goodness, satisfaction, and closure, as construed in some human register or according to some cultural standard. Such occurrences can be identified as instances of projection, wherein God is found interesting for the sake of other things or helpful for the sake of finding that which we already knew we needed. Paul Tillich noted that "when applied to God, superlatives become diminutives."[10] But Eberhard Jüngel reminds us that the Christian God is "interesting for his own sake."[11] Unlike idols, this particular God cannot be marked off as simply a provider of generic goods. He is the unique and final—the ultimate—Good (*summum bonum*).

This particularity and uniqueness is manifest in the divine economy. "A Christian dogmatics of the divine perfections is a positive science in the church of Jesus Christ whose task is the rational articulation of the singular identity of God the Holy Trinity, freely presented in the works of God's triune being."[12] The identity of God is presented to us inasmuch as God makes himself present

10. Paul Tillich, *Systematic Theology* (Chicago: University of Chicago Press, 1951), 1:235.
11. Eberhard Jüngel, *Justification: The Heart of the Christian Faith*, trans. Jeffrey Cayzer (Edinburgh: T&T Clark, 2001), 54.
12. John Webster, "The Holiness and Love of God," in *Confessing God: Essays in Christian Dogmatics 2* (London: T&T Clark, 2005), 110.

to us: among Israel, in Jesus of Nazareth, through the church, and in the testimony of the apostles and prophets. We are called to faith, intellectually as well as spiritually.[13] Psalm 145 is illustrative in its description of the economy: "the works" and "mighty acts" of God are the focus of theological reasoning (Ps. 145:4–6, 10, 12, [13], 17). Thus theology is a positive and not poetic science: we receive knowledge; we do not make it as such. Surely no one has reflected on this receptive nature of theology more than Karl Barth.

> Lead us not into the temptation of the false opinion that Thou art an object like other objects which we can undertake to know or not just as we wish, which we are free to know in this way, or even in that. Lead us not into the temptation of wanting to know Thee in Thy objectivity as if we were spectators, as if we could know, speak and hear about Thee in the slightest degree without at once taking part, without at once making that correspondence actual, without at once beginning with obedience.[14]

Here we are reminded that theology is done amid an economy, and that means in the wake of God's communicative presence. Barth spoke often of the importance of the first commandment as an axiom for theology, inasmuch as the particular presence of God renders theology responsible to listen well. But it also means that theology is possible, because we have been addressed from on high. "Seek the LORD while he may be found" (Isa. 55:6)—this is the imperative and the indicative of theology, the intellectual form of the first commandment.

"He was foreknown before the foundation of the world but was made manifest in the last times for the sake of you who through him are believers in God, who raised him from the dead and gave him glory" (1 Pet. 1:20–21). There is an order that is evangelically basic. "He was foreknown before." He "was made manifest in the last times." The patristic theologians employed the terms "theology" and "economy" to signal this distinction, which remains of crucial importance. He did possess eternal life and glory in God's fullness. He then underwent his divine mission that terminated in not only creaturely life but also an appropriate glory as a creature (as v. 21 has it). Thus all his attributes—like glory itself—bear this shape: true and full in the

13. "Only in receiving can we know" (Hilary of Poitiers, *The Trinity*, in vol. 6 of *Nicene and Post-Nicene Fathers*, series 2, ed. W. Sanday, trans. E. W. Watson and L. Pullan [Peabody, MA: Hendrickson, 2004], 2.35).

14. Karl Barth, *Church Dogmatics* II/1, ed. G. W. Bromiley and T. F. Torrance (Edinburgh: T&T Clark, 1957), 26. See also Karl Barth, "The First Commandment as a Theological Axiom," in *The Way of Theology in Karl Barth: Essays and Comments*, ed. H. M. Rumscheidt (Allison Park, PA: Pickwick, 1986), 63–78.

divine repose of eternity, manifest and of benefit or, perhaps better, inclusive of others in the divine missions of the gospel economy. His character revealed in the economy really goes all the way down. Calvin notes that this is crucial, for "we cannot confidently put trust in Christ unless we are convinced that eternal salvation is in Him, and always has been."[15] And this is the decisive matter: the attributes are, as Webster puts it, "freely presented," meaning that they are genuinely presented but they are shown forth by the one true God in his freedom (thus out of his fullness and at his determination). He was all these things. These characteristics are not coerced by others or contingent on certain states of affairs—they are basic to his identity. And yet he shows himself to be all these things. They are revealed in the ups and downs of history, in the nooks and crannies of covenantal life. So, with the apostle we may say, "He was," and then "he was made manifest in the last times." While not equivalent statements, the first does bring the second, and the second does manifest the first.

Barth addressed the link between theology and economy with great vigor: "God is who he is in his works. He is the same even in himself, even before and after and over his works, and without them. . . . He is, not, therefore, who he is *only* in his works. Yet in himself he is not another than he is in his works."[16] Interpreters debate whether Barth maintained this approach to the eternal being of God and his determined engagement of history; such matters are not our immediate concern. Barth's statement here points to the profound truth of the gospel: God is revealed in Jesus Christ (John 1:18). Yet the God revealed in Jesus Christ first "was" in the beginning (John 1:1–3). His life was to be the "light of men" (John 1:4). Only when the "Word became flesh and dwelt among us" could John confess that "we have seen his glory."[17] And yet when the Word did become flesh and tabernacle in our midst, his was "glory as of the only Son from the Father, full of grace and truth" (John 1:14). While God existed without his economy, God is shown to be none other than the one revealed in the economy. The gospel does reveal the truth of humanity—Jesus as the *imago*—but it just as surely puts the truth of God before us. "And we all, with unveiled face, beholding the glory of the Lord, are being transformed" (2 Cor. 3:18).

15. John Calvin, *The Epistle of Paul the Apostle to the Hebrews and the First and Second Epistles of St. Peter*, ed. D. W. Torrance and T. F. Torrance, trans. William B. Johnston (Grand Rapids: Eerdmans, 1963), 249 (on 1 Pet. 1:20).
16. Barth, *Church Dogmatics* II/1, 260 (see also 257).
17. Note that the verb "to become" (*ginomai*) is already used for a genuine event (a becoming) twice in John 1:2. While the Word is not "created" as a human, he is nonetheless genuinely "born" and truly "becomes" flesh. The economy is a move beyond the repose of the immanent Trinity.

In a slew of essays, Bruce McCormack has presented a particular form of theism that is opposed to classical theism and process theism, suggesting that both of these approaches are rooted ultimately in natural theology. He argues by making four observations that he suggests are common to both the classical approach and its process detractors. "What they have in common, in the first place, is the belief that the 'order of knowing' runs in the opposite direction to the 'order of being.'" He clarifies: "That is to say, though the being of God is above and prior to the being of all else that exists . . . , our knowledge of God proceeds from a prior knowledge of some aspect or aspects of creaturely reality." He suggests a result: "The consequence of this methodological decision is that the way taken to knowledge of God controls and determines the kind of God-concept one is able to generate; thus, epistemology controls and determines divine ontology."[18]

McCormack, second, links the approaches of classical theism and process theology as the positive and negative reactions to these prior commitments that shape possible knowledge of God: "Both conceptions are the result of an exercise in metaphysical thinking in the strict sense of the term. Whether one seeks to liken God to some aspect of creaturely existence . . . or to deny to God any similarity to created reality through a process of negating the limits thought to belong to the creaturely does not really matter at the end of the day." He points to the path of projection, whether ideal affirmed or denied of God: "Both are exercises in metaphysics because both take up a starting point 'from below' in some creaturely reality or magnitude and proceed through a process of inferential reasoning to establish the nature of divine reality."[19] In other words, classical theists and process theologians join together in beginning with creaturely ideals or experiences: classical theologians affirm some and deny others of God, while process theologians tend to reverse the judgments. In so doing, however, they share a modus operandi even if they come to different material judgments at the end of the day.

McCormack argues that we must begin with Christology.[20] The doctrine of God cannot be thought "from below" precisely because it must be thought from the person and work of Jesus Christ. This relates to McCormack's third observation regarding these purported versions of Christian theism (classical theism and process theology): "Both claim to know what God is before

---

18. Bruce L. McCormack, "The Actuality of God: Karl Barth in Conversation with Open Theism," in *Engaging the Doctrine of God: Contemporary Protestant Distinctives*, ed. Bruce L. McCormack (Grand Rapids: Eerdmans, 2008), 187.

19. Ibid., 187–88.

20. McCormack's own leanings—here in the form of an exercise in thinking with Barth and beyond Barth—appear in ibid., 210–42.

a consideration of Christology. At the point at which Christology is finally introduced, its central terms ('deity' or 'divinity,' the divine 'nature' or 'person') have already been filled with content." He refers to both, then, as exercises in "abstractive" reasoning.[21] Their fundamental concerns are projected from the universally human and thus abstracted from the christologically particular.

There is much to be appreciated in McCormack's approach. That there is a version of theism—sometimes going by the name "classical theism" or "perfect being theology"—that projects or maximalizes the ideals of creaturely existence and calls it divine cannot be denied. That the God of process theology looks very much like the inverse, in so many fundamental ways, of this God of philosophical theology, also cannot be rejected. McCormack, then, has provided help in showing that vastly different material judgments may flow from a shared formal approach to theology. In this his analysis is not unlike that which Barth had of Roman Catholicism and liberal Protestantism, suggesting that while they looked vastly different (right and left, as it were) on the surface in their material judgments, they shared a formally similar theological epistemology.

Yet McCormack's view seems flawed in two crucial ways. First, his polemics paint with too wide a brush. Consider his fourth observation about classical theism and process theology: "Fourth and finally, both conceptions rely heavily on an independent doctrine of creation." What does he mean? Specifically addressing classical theism, we read that it is "buttressed by the notion of a *creatio ex nihilo* . . . [which is] 'independent' in the specific sense that like the doctrines of God they support, their content has been filled out without reference to Christology." The consequence? "Such teleology as can be found . . . will (where consistency prevails) be elaborated without reference to God's reconciling and redeeming activity in Jesus Christ."[22] As stated above, it is impossible to avoid noting that McCormack's critique finds a valid target in many versions of theism that do note creaturely ideals or ills and then maximalize or deny those creaturely traits of God. Yet the catholic stream of classical theism is anything but committed to a Christ-less doctrine of creation or a secular teleology. It is hard to avoid judging that McCormack has conflated God's two words. As Calvin and the Reformed confessions affirm, God reveals himself in creation and in his Word by his Spirit.

A second flaw can be found as well: his positive argument fails to honor the lead and pace of the canon itself. If one is to be led by Christology, one will be compelled to begin with the Old Testament, for Jesus constantly does

21. Ibid., 188.
22. Ibid.

so in his own self-presentation. It is hard to avoid judging that McCormack has conflated God's two Testaments and two covenants. As the Reformers and the prevening catholic tradition have seen, the Old Testament and the covenant of nature are preparatory for the New Testament and the covenant of grace. The creeds do not begin with the second paragraph—the Bible does not begin with the apostles—and the economy does not begin with the incarnation. To suggest otherwise is to border on the terrain of Marcion.[23] Better to be Christ-centered in our thinking of God and to follow Christ's own pedagogy, wherein he continually identifies himself in light of and within the framework of the economy with Israel, the witness of the prophets, and what we know to be the first article of the creeds. This is not to go secular, abstract, or nonchristological; it is to listen well to where Jesus himself begins.

The attributes are not only rooted in God's eternal being, but they are also shaped by God's triune nature. One crucial tenet of God's almightiness is divine aseity. Strictly speaking, this is a confession that God has life in himself. The doctrine of aseity must be teased out in trinitarian fashion. It is not the case that God is Stoic needlessness, or that God is self-causal force.[24] Rather, God is life in and of himself—Father, Son, and Spirit—sharing that life one with the others.

Again, the trinitarian shape of aseity must define its character. Each person is *a se* in essence (*agenētos*); this is their common glory. Yet only the Father is *a se* with respect to person (*agennētos*); this is his proper personal quality. Thus John Calvin could argue that the divine Son is *autotheos* (God *a se*), and yet he could affirm simultaneously the eternal generation of the Son. In affirming these two things, Calvin believed he was honoring the principles set forth in texts like John 5:26: "For as the Father has life in himself, so he has granted the Son also to have life in himself."[25] The Father and Son share the property of having "life in himself," yet the Father has it of himself while the Son has this property receptively from the Father. Aseity is shared

23. Khaled Anatolios demonstrates that having a christologically determined approach to the doctrine of God does not hinder Gregory of Nyssa from beginning his reflections on the scandal of the incarnation with the doctrine of creation, referencing the argument of both *Against Eunomius* and the *Catechetical Orations* (*Retrieving Nicaea: The Development and Meaning of Trinitarian Doctrine* [Grand Rapids: Baker Academic, 2011], 199).

24. Contra the famous exegesis of Eph. 3:15 by Jerome in Roland E. Heine, ed., *The Commentaries of Origen and Jerome on St. Paul's Epistle to the Ephesians* (New York: Oxford University Press, 2002), 158.

25. For further elaboration on this text and its implications for catholic Trinitarianism and Reformed Christology, see Michael Allen and Scott Swain, "The Obedience of the Eternal Son," *International Journal of Systematic Theology* 15, no. 2 (2013): 114–34.

in common, yet it is possessed by each in his proper, personal way. Further, aseity is not only enjoyed in trinitarian ways, but it is also defined as such. That is, aseity is not a statement of a monolithic monad but of a tripersonal God in himself. The love and life of God is enjoyed among Father, Son, and Spirit, not apart from any personal engagement. So aseity as such is defined by triune personal being.

As with the example of aseity, so other attributes are employed to fill out the notion of God as the Almighty LORD. While these terms may be employed also in natural theology or certain strands of philosophical theology, they are disciplined by the economy of God as published in the canon of Scripture, that is, by the manifestation of God as eternally triune. Whether aseity, infinity, or otherwise, these terms are defined by the revealed nature of God, not by certain preconceived notions or category assumptions based on creaturely experience (good, bad, or otherwise). Thus theological definitions of any attribute must be derived from the trinitarian shape of the divine being.

The doctrine of the divine attributes summons the church to confess the incomparably beautiful name of God, manifest in the works of the divine economy and rooted in his eternal triunity, as the almighty God and the Father of the gospel.

The attributes of God encompass the full range of his perfections. As Moses sees, this one proclaims himself to be: "The LORD, the LORD, a God merciful and gracious, slow to anger and abounding in steadfast love and faithfulness, keeping steadfast love for thousands, forgiving iniquity and transgression and sin, but who will by no means clear the guilty, visiting the iniquity of the fathers on the children and the children's children, to the third and the fourth generation" (Exod. 34:6–7).

All this is one instance of revelation. Still other texts would address other perfections. Irenaeus spoke of certain attributes: "God, the Father, uncreated, incomprehensible, invisible, one God, creator of all."[26] The Augsburg Confession of the Lutheran Church also briefly spoke to God's character as such: "There is one divine essence which is called God and is God: eternal, incorporeal, indivisible, of immeasurable power, wisdom, and goodness."[27] In my thesis, I have shortened the list to God's almightiness as well as his being the God and Father of the gospel. It is worthwhile, however, to appreciate how abbreviated such a statement is before unpacking its usefulness.

---

26. Robert Louis Wilken, *The Spirit of Early Christian Thought: Seeking the Face of God* (New Haven: Yale University Press, 2003), 65.

27. "The Augsburg Confession—Latin Text," in *The Book of Concord: The Confessions of the Evangelical Lutheran Church*, ed. Robert Kolb and Timothy J. Wengert (Minneapolis: Fortress, 2000), 37.

The Westminster Confession of Faith also offers a select testimony to the biblical perfections of the Triune God.

> There is but one only living and true God, who is infinite in being and perfection, a most pure spirit, invisible, without body, parts, or passions, immutable, immense, eternal, incomprehensible, almighty; most wise, most holy, most free, most absolute, working all things according to the counsel of his own immutable and most righteous will, for his own glory; most loving, gracious, merciful, long-suffering, abundant in goodness and truth, forgiving iniquity, transgression and sin; the rewarder of them that diligently seek him; and withal most just and terrible in his judgments; hating all sin, and who will by no means clear the guilty.
>
> God hath all life, glory, goodness, blessedness, in and of himself; and is alone in and unto himself all-sufficient, not standing in need of any creatures which he hath made, nor deriving any glory from them, but only manifesting his own glory in, by, unto, and upon them: he is the alone foundation of all being, of whom, through whom, and to whom are all things; and hath most sovereign dominion over them, to do by them, for them, or upon them whatsoever himself pleaseth. In his sight all things are open and manifest; his knowledge is infinite, infallible, and independent upon the creature; so as nothing is to him contingent or uncertain. He is most holy in all his counsels, in all his works, and in all his commands. To him is due from angels and men, and every other creature, whatsoever worship, service, or obedience, he is pleased to require of them.[28]

Westminster clearly speaks with wider purview than Irenaeus, Augsburg, or my thesis statement, yet it still remains a cursory read of the canonical witness. It lists many Scripture proofs for each point, yet it leaves dozens, if not hundreds, unmentioned for the sake of time and space.

What Is God?

For a still tighter focus on the most emphatic attributes found in the Bible, the Westminster Shorter Catechism serves as a useful tool. "God is a Spirit, infinite, eternal, and unchanging in his being, wisdom, power, holiness, justice, goodness, and truth."

This description offers a number of instructive features. First, it manifestly links the attributes (e.g., God is infinite, eternal, and unchanging in his being as well as his wisdom). Attributes cannot be parceled out or treated piecemeal.

---

28. Westminster Confession of Faith, in *The Creeds of the Churches: A Reader in Christian Doctrine from the Bible to the Present*, ed. John H. Leith, 3rd ed. (Louisville: John Knox, 1982), 197.

In other words, the catechism here shows a lived embrace of the doctrine of divine simplicity, that is, the belief that God has no parts.[29] Second, it seems to order attributes in layers of priority and emphasis. This is not to say that one or another is more or less true, only that some have more or less extensive formative power and influence. Westminster here orders Spirit as of highest significance, followed by infinity, eternality, and unchangeableness, followed by existence, wisdom, power, holiness, justice, goodness, and truth.

We might approach the attributes in a simpler framework that both provides a general schematic for organizing them and yet, in so doing, allows them all to exist in their particularity and in their breadth. We can make some headway in thinking about the attributes by beginning at the canonical beginning for the revelation of God: Exodus 3.[30] As we read this passage we will see two primary characteristics noted: God is almighty, and God is Father.

Throughout the tradition, these two attributes have served signal roles in shaping Christian thinking about God. Of course, the Apostles' Creed identifies God in two primary ways at its inception: "I believe in God the Father Almighty." The Heidelberg Catechism identifies these as not merely personal descriptions of the first person of the Trinity but as primary attributes of the whole Trinity. In question 26, the confession of the first article of the creed is exposited, and the Heidelberg Catechism describes trust in this God as Lord of all things. It suggests that even evil and troubles are within his providential will and "whatever evil he sends upon me in this troubled life he will turn to my good, for he is able to do it, being almighty God, and is determined to do it, being a faithful Father."[31] Two qualifications underwrite God's loving dispensations in the economy: "being almighty God" and "being a faithful Father." I will suggest that these can serve as governing principles for thinking about the full range of divine attributes, and they are flagged as early as the formative teaching given in Exodus 3.

The people of God experienced terrible enmity at the hands of Pharaoh and his Egyptian slavemasters. The Israelites cried to the God of the patriarchs, and "God heard their groaning, and God remembered his covenant with Abraham, with Isaac, and with Jacob. God saw the people of Israel—and God knew" (Exod. 2:24–25). As God moves into redemptive action, he began by

29. Westminster Confession, 1.1, makes the point that God is "*without* body, *parts*, and passions" (emphasis mine).
30. I have addressed the history of interpretation of this text in "Exodus 3 after the Hellenization Thesis," *Journal of Theological Interpretation* 3, no. 2 (2009): 179–96, and offered theological exegesis of the passage in "Exodus 3," in *Theological Commentary: Evangelical Essays*, ed. Michael Allen (London: T&T Clark, 2011), 25–40.
31. Heidelberg Catechism, Q. 26, in *Reformed Confessions of the Sixteenth Century*, 309.

calling Moses as his voice. From the burning bush he called Moses into service as an ambassador and prophet. Moses replied with a host of objections, among which was a concern that his own people would not even recognize his divine mandate unless he could signal divine warrant with a fresh revelation of God (Exod. 3:13). The question is not an honest one. Moses is grasping at straws, but God can erect a theological vista without straw. God responds to Moses by offering not one but two divine names that prove formative for Israel's understanding of God.

First, God names himself: "I AM WHO I AM" (Exod. 3:14). The translation has been debated for centuries; it might be rendered "I have been who I have been," "I AM WHO I AM," or "I will be who I will be." More profound than debates about the tense is its self-referential nature. Whereas most identifications work by way of reference ("so-and-so is taller than this one, but younger and thinner than that one"), God refuses to be known in such a manner. Comparative analysis is denied. Strictly speaking, God is in a class by himself and cannot be classed with others as a peer (*Deus non est in genere*).

Kathryn Tanner has argued that the Christian doctrine of divine transcendence is qualitative and not merely quantitative.[32] This distinction proves helpful in grasping what is being revealed here in Exodus 3:14. Note, first, that something is being revealed. Contrary to some suggestions, God is not silent. God answers the inquiry. However, second, God answers by distinguishing himself from the categories of human thought, the ideals, forms, and grids of human reason. God does not say "I am more this or that" or even "I am the perfect instantiation of this ideal." Such approaches—what often, in its elegant forms, goes by the way of "perfect being theology"—would seem to present a quantitative view of divine transcendence, wherein God is like others, only more and, we might add, perfectly more. But, third, God demurs from such comparative analysis. "I AM WHO I AM" prevents comparative analysis. God is qualitatively different from all other beings. As Stanley Hauerwas puts it, "God, the creator of all that is, cannot be . . . part of the metaphysical furniture of the universe."[33]

This name of mystery shapes our understanding of theological knowledge. That God is qualitatively different from all other beings rules out some simple

32. For historical analysis, see Kathryn Tanner, *God and Creation in Christian Theology: Tyranny or Empowerment?* (Oxford: Blackwell, 1988); for this analysis put to constructive work, see idem, *Jesus, Humanity, and the Trinity: A Brief Systematic Theology* (Minneapolis: Fortress, 2001), 1–35. Tanner's work is supported by William C. Placher, *The Domestication of Transcendance: How Modern Thinking about God Went Wrong* (Louisville: Westminster John Knox, 1997).

33. Stanley Hauerwas, *With the Grain of the Universe: The Church's Witness and Natural Theology* (Grand Rapids: Brazos, 2001), 28.

movement from human aspirations or ideals to divine perfection. Any attribution of terms from human to divine or in reverse must traverse an analogical path. That is, our words and ideas cannot be univocally true of God and created beings, lest we forget the qualitative distinction. Yet, at the very same time we dare not say knowledge is equivocal and thus impossible, or else we deny the answer of God at the burning bush (and the whole economy with it). We do know God, the catholic and Reformational tradition argues, and we do so analogically.[34] So Augustine: "We should understand God, if we can and as far as we can, to be good without quality, great without quantity, creative without need or necessity, presiding without position, holding all things together without possession, wholly everywhere without place, everlasting without time, without any change in himself making changeable things, and undergoing nothing." What does Augustine believe has been revealed in these claims of God's almighty transcendence? "Whoever thinks of God like that may not yet be able to discover altogether what he is, but is at least piously on his guard against thinking about him anything that he is not."[35] Here Augustine reminds us that the Lord is the holy one in our midst (Isa. 12:6), not a component in some set. A whole set of attributes have been employed to help explain this almighty or transcendent character of God: aseity, simplicity, incomprehensibility, immensity, immutability, impassibility, eternality, infinity, holiness, and so on. They are not meant to refer to parts of his character but various aspects of his whole triune being.

The question of translation has become crucial. How do the biblical words shape contemporary life in its various forms? Throughout the centuries, the church has translated biblical teachings into certain philosophical tones. It did so in an effort to remind a philosophically attuned culture to attend to a host of biblical texts: to synthesize the full breadth of them rather than picking and choosing, much less providing an alien or opposing portrait of the Trinity. But it did employ primarily Hellenistic philosophical terms to connote the biblical judgments that must guide the church's faith and practice.

Some claim that creedal language and pastoral language ought never use extrabiblical words. This has been used by some radical reformers as an argument against creedal language and any employment of philosophical or synthetic terms to convey biblical teaching. And this argument was used as

34. The classic argument against univocal and equivocal language and in favor of analogical language remains Thomas Aquinas, *Summa theologiae* Ia.13.5.

35. Augustine, *The Trinity*, ed. John Rotelle, trans. Edmund Hill (Hyde Park, NY: New City, 1991), prologue 5. See also Gregory Nazianzus, "Theological Oration 28," in *On God and Christ: The Five Theological Orations and Two Letters to Cledonius* (Crestwood, NY: St. Vladimir's Seminary Press, 2002), 28.3.

a polemic against Protestantism by many Roman Catholic interlocutors. Yet the Reformers did not mean such restrictiveness to be the result of their affirmation of theology *sola Scriptura*. Calvin noted, "If they call a foreign word one that cannot be shown to stand written syllable by syllable in Scripture, they are indeed imposing upon us an unjust law . . . what prevents us from explaining in clearer words those matters in Scripture which perplex and hinder our understanding, yet which conscientiously and faithfully serve the truth of Scripture itself."[36]

Heinrich Bullinger agrees and goes still further: "The pastors of the church have been forced, in response to quarrels about vicious teachings, with careful precision to devise terms for certain things that explain what is meant by them and leave quarrelsome persons with nowhere to hide."[37] Here the Reformed theological tradition has distinguished between the *verbum* (word) and the *res* (subject matter) of Scripture, arguing that the *res* may and must be translated into extrabiblical words faithfully. *Sola Scriptura* was intended to govern the *res* of theology, not its verbal form.[38]

Many have questioned this heritage. The so-called Hellenization thesis suggests that the gospel was lost at some point when the alien thought forms of the Hellenistic world overwhelmed or modified the Hebraic shape of Jesus's work and message. Some suggest that this occurred during the time of the New Testament; others point to later dates in the first four centuries of the church's life. Adolf von Harnack and other historians of the early twentieth century shaped the way in which thinkers of this past century viewed their forebears, suggesting that the route to faithfulness involves shedding this Greek heritage and returning to a more pristine form of the gospel. Harnack viewed this Hellenization as an understandable translation of the gospel for a particular time, but he found it to be both inconsistent with its original impulse and unhelpful for our continuing efforts.

Recent patristic studies have found the Hellenization thesis wanting. In his magisterial study of early Christianity, Robert Louis Wilken addresses

---

36. Calvin, *Institutes* 1.13.3.

37. Heinrich Bullinger, *Ad Ioannis Cochlei de canonicae scripturae & Catholicae ecclesiae authoritate libellum, pro solida Scripturae canonicae authoritate, tum & absoluta eius perfectione, ueraque Catholicae ecclesiae dignitate, Heinrychi Bullingeri orthodoxa Responsio* (Zurich: Christoph Froschauer, 1544), f. 14.

38. For further reflection on the movement from scriptural language to scriptural reasoning, see Michael Allen and Scott Swain, "In Defense of Proof-Texting," *Journal of the Evangelical Theological Society* 54, no. 3 (2011): 589–606; and Richard A. Muller, "'Either Expressly Set Down . . . Or by Good and Necessary Consequence': Exegesis and Formulation in the *Annotations* and the Confession," in *Scripture and Worship: Biblical Interpretation and the Directory for Worship* (Phillipsburg, NJ: P&R, 2007), 59–82.

it head-on: "The notion that the development of early Christian thought represented a Hellenization of Christianity has outlived its usefulness . . . a more apt expression would be the Christianization of Hellenism, though that phrase does not capture the originality of Christian thought nor the debt owed to Jewish ways of thinking and to the Jewish Bible."[39] Similar judgments can be found in the works of the most significant patristic historians of our time. Yet the "Hellenization thesis," by now, has shaped the approach with which many contemporary theologians and biblical scholars view the history of doctrine and its relationship to ongoing faith and practice.

An example might prove instructive here. Paul Gavrilyuk terms this historical Hellenization thesis the Theory of Theology's Fall into Hellenistic Philosophy (TTFHP)." By focusing on the doctrine of God's immutability, Gavrilyuk suggests the TTFHP includes the following judgments:

1. Divine impassibility is an attribute of God in Greek and Hellenistic philosophy.
2. Divine impassibility was adopted by the early fathers uncritically from the philosophers.
3. Divine impassibility does not leave room for any sound account of divine emotions and divine involvement in history, as attested in the Bible.
4. Divine impassibility is incompatible with the revelation of the suffering God in Jesus Christ.
5. The latter fact was recognized by a minority group of theologians who affirmed that God is passible, going against the majority opinion.[40]

Against the TTFHP, however, Gavrilyuk shows that matters are not so simple in at least two ways. First, Hellenistic thought was anything but unified when it came to reflection on theology.[41] Pick up Plato alongside Greek mythology, and one quickly catches this notion of diversity within the Greco-Roman world. When it comes to the doctrine of impassibility in particular, Gavrilyuk points out that divine *apatheia* (impassibility) was anything but a common confession of the divine. For instance, Stoics might idealize *apatheia* among creatures, but they did not consistently view the divine as impassible.[42]

---

39. Wilken, *Spirit of Early Christian Thought*, xvi.
40. Paul Gavrilyuk, *The Suffering of the Impassible God: The Dialectics of Patristic Thought* (New York: Oxford University Press, 2004), 176.
41. See esp. the argument of W. V. Rowe, "Adolf von Harnack and the Concept of Hellenization," in *Hellenization Revisited: Shaping a Christian Response within the Greco-Roman World* (Lanham, MD: University Press of America, 1994), 69–98.
42. Gavrilyuk, *Suffering of the Impassible God*, 29–34.

Second, the way in which impassibility was affirmed among Christians was markedly different from its reference in the world of Greek philosophy. Cyril spoke of the "suffering of the impassible God."[43] Gavrilyuk argues that impassibility was affirmed of God when "the Fathers sought to distance God the creator from the gods of mythology."[44] Impassibility was an analogical qualifier, an element of what we call "apophatic theology," meant to keep us from interpreting divine emotions as mere counterparts to human emotional experience. Thus Augustine, Cyril, and other early Christian theologians affirmed divine emotions alongside divine impassibility.

Therefore, the TTFHP will not make sense of the data in either the world of Hellenism or the intellectual world of early Christianity and ought to be jettisoned. Gavrilyuk rightly shows that patristic thinkers viewed various divine attributes as a web of correlated confessions of divine transcendence rooted in the distinction between Creator and creature.[45] He keenly shows that Hellenistic categories are already being adopted critically within the world of the apostles (e.g., the Gospel of John and the Epistle to the Hebrews).

In giving a second divine name, God names himself "the Lord, the God of your fathers, the God of Abraham, of Isaac, and the God of Jacob" (Exod. 3:15). Augustine appreciates the dilemma Moses must have felt. "Perhaps it was hard even for Moses himself, as it is much also for us, and much more for us, to understand what was said, 'I am who I am' and 'He who is has sent me to you.' And if by chance Moses understood, when would they to whom he was being sent understand?" Augustine heard a second name given immediately thereafter: "Therefore the Lord put aside what man could not grasp and added what he could grasp. For he added and said, 'I am the God of Abraham, and the God of Isaac, and the God of Jacob.' This you can grasp. But what mind can grasp, 'I am who I am'?"[46] Augustine refers to this second name as a "name of mercy." Whereas the first name speaks of God's transcendence, this second name points to God's identification with the patriarchs of Israel: he is their God, and they are his people.

The Almighty nature of the Lord is what enables him to be our loving Father in such proximity. "You were more intimately present to me than my innermost

43. Cyril, "Scholia on the Incarnation," in John McGuckin, *St. Cyril of Alexandria and the Christological Controversy* (Crestwood, NY: St. Vladimir's Seminary Press, 2004), 327–35.

44. Gavrilyuk, *Suffering of the Impassible God*, 48.

45. Ibid., 60–61. For similar demonstration, see Andrew Radde-Gallwitz, *Basil of Caesarea, Gregory of Nyssa, and the Transformation of Divine Simplicity* (New York: Oxford University Press, 2009), 225.

46. Augustine, *Homilies on the Gospel of John 1–40*, ed. Allan Fitzgerald, trans. Edmund Hill (Hyde Park, NY: New City, 2009), 38.8.3.

being and higher than the highest peak of my spirit."[47] Augustine's confession points not only to spiritual perception of divine presence in the soul but also to the manifestation of God more widely in the divine economy. This second name is elaborated just three chapters later in Exodus 6, when God reiterates his identity and his commitment to Israel: "Say therefore to the people of Israel, 'I am the LORD, and I will bring you out . . . and I will deliver you . . . and I will redeem you . . . I will take you to be my people, and I will be your God, and you shall know that I am the LORD your God'" (Exod. 6:6–7). The liberating promise of this Lord culminates in the provision of land, a pledge given to the patriarchs (see Exod. 3:15–17; 6:8). The plague cycle and the wilderness journey show God to be intimately involved in the lives of Israel and its neighbors; further, these events show God to be Lord in this history.

Throughout the Bible, this rhythm is recapitulated.[48] It occurs perhaps most explicitly in the prophecies of Isaiah, whereby the Lord of hosts governs history and yet maintains his commitments to his people, even this side of their sin and spurning of him. Huldrych Zwingli took the whole of Isaiah 40 to be commentary on the divine name found in Exodus 3:14–15. Isaiah 40, and the whole of Isaiah 40–48, offers vivid description of God's transcendence and sovereign rule over the nations. Because he rules over and above all nations, God can employ various political powers for his purposes and then judge them for their sins. At every point, however, God's transcendent rule is linked to the course of human history and tangible experience. While God is not to be identified with history or anything therein (à la G. F. W. Hegel's *Geist*), God governs and guides history to his purposes. As has been shown by a number of biblical scholars, there are numerous lexical allusions to the exodus in Isaiah, where the deliverance of Israel is construed as an anticipated "new exodus."[49] Even more telling are thematic parallels that clearly exist: in both texts, the message is that God reigns over all threats, so God's people must trust him to provide.[50] The character of God instills the confidence of

47. Augustine, *Confessions*, ed. John Rotelle, trans. Maria Boulding (Hyde Park, NY: New City, 1997), 3.6.11.

48. This paragraph is taken from Allen, "Exodus 3," in *Theological Commentary*, 29.

49. Brevard S. Childs, *Isaiah: A Commentary* (Louisville: Westminster John Knox, 2000), 110–11, as well as a host of studies on the intertextual use of the exodus imagery in Isaiah and then in the New Testament: Joel Marcus, *The Way of the Lord: Christological Exegesis of the Old Testament in the Gospel of Mark* (Edinburgh: T&T Clark, 1992), chap. 2; Rikki E. Watts, *Isaiah's New Exodus in Mark* (Tübingen: Mohr-Siebeck, 1997); David W. Pao, *Acts and the Isaianic New Exodus* (Tübingen: Mohr-Siebeck, 2002).

50. Indeed, Levenson argues that the first message of the exodus is "a story of the enthronement of YHWH and the glad acceptance of his endless reign by his redeemed, the whole House of Israel" ("Exodus and Liberation," 142).

salvation to come and the credence of God's prophet (see repeated references to YHWH in Isa. 45:14, 21–24).

But God's presence is not merely found amid Israel. His electing love reaches still farther, as can be seen in the book of Job. Once Job has suffered repartee with his three friends as well as Elihu, God intervenes and addresses Job twice. Both times the divine address is introduced in this way: "Then the LORD answered Job out of the whirlwind and said . . ." (Job 38:1; 40:6). Two things should be observed. First, it is the Lord speaking; the transcendent character of this voice is flagged by saying that he speaks "out of the whirlwind," a biblical image for a lofty and holy Lord (Exod. 34). Second, the Lord does speak and answers Job, which is no small matter given that Job and his friends have been less than commendable in their theological and spiritual conversation (Job 40:2). God truly condescends to engage a human in conversation, to answer sinners in their debate.

Ultimately, of course, the presence of God climaxes in the incarnation of the Son. Neither the divine lordship of Israel's history nor triune sovereignty over Job's fate demonstrates the kind of personal union with the human that is present here in Jesus of Nazareth. This one alone is Immanuel. Here we see majesty in the manger and glory on Golgotha. Jesus is the carpenter's son and the child of Mary, yet he calls the Lord his heavenly Father and says, "Before Abraham was, I AM" (John 8:58). In Christ, we have the fulfillment of all the promises of God (2 Cor. 1:20), including that great pledge given to the patriarchs and to Moses: "I will be your God, and you will be my people." Even in his incarnate presence, the Triune God—yes, even the Son—retains his almighty glory: while he is our "wonderful counselor," "mighty God," and "prince of peace," he is still our "everlasting father" (Isa. 9:6).[51]

Before proceeding, we do well to note the order of revelation. Almightiness is declared before fatherhood is attested. Barth speaks of transcendence and immanence: "It is just the absoluteness of God properly understood which can signify not only his freedom to transcend all that is other than himself, but also his freedom to be immanent within it, and at such a depth of immanence as simply does not exist in the fellowship between other beings."[52] Here in

---

51. In this vein, the confession of the *extra Calvinisticum* characterizes the incarnate presence of the Second Person of the Trinity, showing that while he is wholly present in Jesus, he is not circumscribed by this local presence as Jesus. David Willis has shown that this famous tenet of Reformed Christology is simply the application of catholic teaching regarding the doctrine of God to the economy of redemption (*Calvin's Catholic Christology: The Function of the So-Called* Extra Calvinisticum *in Calvin's Theology* [Leiden: Brill, 1966], 26–60); see also Andrew McGinnis, *The Son of God beyond the Flesh: A Historical and Theological Study of the* Extra Calvinisticum (London: T&T Clark, 2014).

52. Barth, *Church Dogmatics* II/1, 313; see also Isaak A. Dorner, *System of Christian Doctrine*, trans. Alfred Cave (Eugene, OR: Wipf & Stock, 2005), 1:338.

Exodus and in what Walter Moberly has called "the Old Testament of the Old Testament,"[53] the book of Genesis, God's lordship is revealed en route to God's covenantal presence. There in Genesis, the primeval history reveals God to be lord of all: sovereign over all competitors, which he created, and sustainer of all things, which he governs. The rest of Genesis reveals God's particular commitment to the patriarchs and their descendants. These two emphases provide the theological foundation for God's involvement in the book of Exodus, specifically in the inception of his involvement as found here in Exodus 3. The Israelites must know that God is Lord of all—even Pharaoh and the Egyptian powers—and that God is their Lord and Father, the very God of their patriarchs.

We must return, however, to the divine presence. God's perfection does not remove him from our midst. Rather, his perfection characterizes the shape of his very near presence. For example, God's omnipresence—one aspect of his perfection, aseity, and almightiness—does not suggest that God is not present to this world or even that God is evenly present to this world. Rather it connotes God's lordship over space—God is free with respect to space and not bound by it. It reminds us that God exceeds any exact location (e.g., 1 Kings 8:27; Ps. 139:7). It also deflects from blasé assumptions of divine presence based on tradition or proximity to places of previous blessing (e.g., Jer. 7:4; 23:23). Thus God's very near presence is marked by genuine might and freedom. So Bavinck notes the mysterious force of God's triune presence: "It is completely incomprehensible to us how God can reveal himself and to some extent make himself known in created beings: eternity in time, immensity in space, infinity in the finite, immutability in change, being in becoming, the all, as it were, in that which is nothing."[54] God is almighty in his Fatherly presence, and this Triune God is fatherly in his almightiness.

We might conclude by asking, Is this metaphysical teaching?[55] Étienne Gilson claimed, "Of course we do not maintain that the text of Exodus is a revealed metaphysical definition of God; but if there is no metaphysic *in* Exodus there is nevertheless a metaphysic *of* Exodus."[56] We do well to follow Matthew Levering in observing that metaphysics is not thought about abstract things; rather, metaphysics is abstract thought about very concrete things.[57] In this

53. R. W. L. Moberly, *The Old Testament of the Old Testament: Patriarchal Narratives and Mosaic Yahwism*, Overtures to Biblical Theology (Minneapolis: Fortress, 1992).

54. Bavinck, *Reformed Dogmatics*, 2:49.

55. This paragraph is taken from Allen, "Exodus 3," in *Theological Commentary*, 35.

56. Étienne Gilson, *The Spirit of Medieval Philosophy* (New York: Charles Scribner's Sons, 1940), 433.

57. Matthew Levering, *Scripture and Metaphysics: Aquinas and the Renewal of Trinitarian Theology* (Oxford: Blackwell, 2003).

case, Exodus 3:14 identifies a particular character (YHWH) as a unique being in a class all by himself (*sui generis*). As Augustine says in *De Trinitate*, Exodus 3:14 makes God "difficult to contemplate."[58] But it provides a prompt for reading well the economic engagements of this God attested in Exodus 3:15–16, Exodus 6, Isaiah, Job, and ultimately in the Gospels. The divine attributes are metaphysical and moral characterizations of the Triune God that help us to render his fatherly care in its almighty shape and to remember that his almighty power has been willed toward our flourishing.

58. Augustine, *The Trinity* 1.3.

4

Divine Trinity

SCOTT R. SWAIN

Introduction

The doctrine of the Trinity is not simply one article among many within the Christian confession. It is the first and fundamental article of the faith, and the framework within which all other articles receive their meaning and import, because the Triune God is the efficient, restorative, and perfecting principle of all things in nature, grace, and glory.[1] For this reason too the doctrine of the Trinity is the heart of Christian piety and religion. In confessing faith in the Trinity, the Christian is not

> saying just how he thinks about God. He is not there giving out a notion of God, nor saying that God has such and such attributes, and that he exists in this and that wise. Instead, he confesses: I believe *in* God the Father, and *in* Jesus Christ his only-begotten Son, and *in* the Holy Spirit: I believe in the Triune God. . . . The Christian owes everything to him. It is his joy and comfort that he may believe *in* that God, trust him, and expect everything from him.[2]

1. Bonaventure, *Breviloquium*, Works of St. Bonaventure, vol. 9 (Saint Bonaventure, NY: Franciscan Institute Publications, 2005), 1.1–2.
2. Herman Bavinck, *Our Reasonable Faith: A Survey of Christian Doctrine*, trans. Henry Zylstra (Grand Rapids: Baker, 1977), 144.

Trust in God the Father, of majesty unbounded, in his beloved, true, and only Son, and in the Holy Spirit, the Comforter, is the ground of all saving consolation, the animating source of the blessed hope, and the wellspring of Christian love. To this Triune God, from whom and through whom and to whom are all things, the church has bound itself throughout the ages, in peace and in controversy, in life and in death.

No doctrine received more attention in modern theology than the doctrine of the Trinity. Convinced that the Reformation failed to apply its newly discovered anthropological and soteriological insights to the doctrine of the Trinity, Protestant theologians in the nineteenth century called for renewed reflection on the Triune God.[3] In their estimation, renewing trinitarian theology would require subjecting the older form of the doctrine to "thoroughgoing criticism"[4] and would result in "a new formulation of the concept of God more generally."[5] Twentieth century theology, both Protestant and Catholic, responded to this call, reconceiving the task and the subject matter of trinitarian theology, often with quite radical results. In formal terms, following widespread loss of confidence in the Bible's status as the product of God's revelatory goodness and, consequently, as a reliable witness to God's triune nature, theologians attempted to ground trinitarian doctrine either internally, within the subjective field of the experience of grace, or externally, in the field of historical events. In material terms, following widespread rejection of classical Christian metaphysics of God's simple perfection, theologians sought to conceptualize God's triune nature via categories of personal subjectivity and history.[6] To be sure, modern trinitarian theology was not a monolithic

3. Friedrich Schleiermacher, *The Christian Faith*, ed. H. R. Mackintosh and J. S. Stewart (Edinburgh: T&T Clark, 1989), 747.

4. Ibid., 749.

5. Isaak A. Dorner, *A System of Christian Doctrine*, trans. Alfred Cave and J. S. Banks (Edinburgh: T&T Clark, 1897), 1:413.

6. The literature here is vast. Representative studies include: Karl Barth, *Church Dogmatics* I/1, ed. G. W. Bromiley and T. F. Torrance (Edinburgh: T&T Clark, 1975); Karl Rahner, *The Trinity*, trans. Joseph Donceel (New York: Herder and Herder, 1970); Wolfhart Pannenberg, *Systematic Theology*, vol. 1, trans. Geoffrey Bromiley (Grand Rapids: Eerdmans, 1991); Hans Urs von Balthasar, *Theo-Drama*, vol. 3 (San Francisco: Ignatius, 1992); Jürgen Moltmann, *The Trinity and the Kingdom: The Doctrine of God*, trans. Margaret Kohl (Minneapolis: Fortress, 1993); Peter C. Hodgson, *God in History: Shapes of Freedom* (Nashville: Abingdon, 1989); Catherine Mowry LaCugna, *God for Us: The Trinity and Christian Life* (San Francisco: HarperCollins, 1991); Elizabeth Johnson, *She Who Is: The Mystery of God in Feminist Theological Discourse* (New York: Crossroad, 1992); Robert Jenson, *Systematic Theology*, vol. 1 (New York: Oxford University Press, 1997). The most helpful surveys include Ted Peters, *God as Trinity: Relationality and Temporality in Divine Life* (Louisville: Westminster John Knox, 1993); John Thompson, *Modern Trinitarian Perspectives* (New York: Oxford University Press, 1994); Stanley J. Grenz, *Rediscovering the Triune God: The Trinity in Contemporary Theology* (Minneapolis:

enterprise. Churchly theologians such as Herman Bavinck maintained a free relation to modern Protestantism's revisionist program in their constructive trinitarian dogmatics, while others deeply indebted to that program—one thinks here of Isaak Dorner or Karl Barth—deployed the resources of Scripture and tradition with a deftness that enabled them to preserve much of the substance of the traditional doctrine even as they pursued the modern quest for "a new formulation of the concept of God." These exceptions notwithstanding, the largely revisionist nature of modern trinitarian theology has led recent studies to question whether it has amounted to real progress in dogmatics.[7]

Given the significance of the Trinity for Christian dogmatics and piety, the desire to renew trinitarian theology cannot be gainsaid. One may doubt, however, the wisdom of treating the catholic tradition of trinitarian doctrine as a problem to be overcome rather than as a potential resource for theological enrichment, whether it be in the name of a more radical Enlightenment or a more purified Protestantism.[8] Indeed, there are specifically trinitarian reasons to believe the tradition of the church will prove a fruitful resource for constructive dogmatics. It is to the church that the Son has promised the ongoing revelation of his Father's name: "I made known your name to them, and I will continue to make it known" (John 17:26). And it is within the church that we may expect to apprehend the meaning of that name—the name that the Son shares with the Father (John 17:11)—through the Spirit's ministry of inspiration and illumination (John 16:13–15; 1 John 2:27).[9] These realities suggest that we should regard the church's traditional tasks, sources, and forms of trinitarian doctrine as resources rather than obstacles for renewing trinitarian theology.

Fundamental to the task of retrieving classical Christian doctrine is the requirement to retrieve the patterns of biblical reasoning within which that

---

Fortress, 2004); Samuel M. Powell, *The Trinity in German Thought* (Cambridge: Cambridge University Press, 2001); and Fred Sanders, "The Trinity," in *Mapping Modern Theology: A Thematic and Historical Introduction*, ed. Kelly M. Kapic and Bruce L. McCormack (Grand Rapids: Baker Academic, 2012).

7. Bruce Marshall sounded the alarm; Stephen Holmes assessed the extent of the damage. See Bruce D. Marshall, "Trinity," in *The Blackwell Companion to Modern Theology*, ed. Gareth Jones (Oxford: Blackwell, 2004), chap. 12; and Stephen R. Holmes, *The Quest for the Trinity: The Doctrine of God in Scripture, History and Modernity* (Downers Grove, IL: IVP Academic, 2012).

8. Holmes, *Quest for the Trinity*, 199.

9. For more extensive dogmatic argument in support of this point, see Michael Allen and Scott R. Swain, *Reformed Catholicity: The Promise of Retrieval for Theology and Biblical Interpretation* (Grand Rapids: Baker Academic, 2015), chap. 1. More broadly on the nature and importance of retrieval in trinitarian theology, see Lewis Ayres, *Nicaea and Its Legacy: An Approach to Fourth-Century Trinitarian Theology* (Oxford: Oxford University Press, 2004), chap. 16; and Khaled Anatolios, *Retrieving Nicaea: The Development and Meaning of Trinitarian Doctrine* (Grand Rapids: Baker Academic, 2011).

doctrine emerges. As David Yeago observes, "No theory of the development of doctrine which attempts to save the classical doctrines without accounting for the unanimous conviction of the Christian tradition that they are the teaching of Scripture can overcome the marginalization of the doctrines which is so evident in the contemporary western church and theology."[10] The purpose in what follows, therefore, is to trace the patterns of biblical reasoning from which the church's doctrine of the Trinity arises, and (if only briefly) to exhibit how that doctrine enriches our understanding of God's perfect being and action and promotes human bliss in communion with God. We will discover along the way that pursuing a path of retrieval in trinitarian theology does not require us to abandon many of the questions and tasks of modern trinitarian theology but instead puts us within the company of those fitted to address those questions and tasks with deeper, and more biblical, wisdom and insight.

The following dogmatic thesis will govern our discussion: *The doctrine of the Trinity is the church's interpretation of God's revealed name, "the name of the Father and of the Son and of the Holy Spirit" (Matt. 28:19). God makes his triune name known to us through an unfolding economy of revelation that disciplines us at once to distinguish the one true God from all who bear the name "god" but lack the characteristic marks of God's unique and indivisible nature and to identify the Father, the Son, and the Holy Spirit with the one true God without eliding the distinctions signified by their personal names. Interpretation of God's triune name in turn gives rise to trinitarian language and metaphysics, along with the illuminating concept of divine "person," which serve to elucidate further the significance of God's triune name and to expose errors that would mask that name's significance. Because it concerns the supreme mystery of revelation, the doctrine of the Trinity sheds light on our understanding of divine perfection and divine action and deepens our communion with God.*

"Because That Is How God Is Revealed in God's Own Word"

Question 25 of the Heidelberg Catechism asks, "Since there is only one divine being, why do you speak of three, Father, Son, and Holy Spirit?" It answers, "Because that is how God is revealed in God's own Word; these three distinct persons are one, true, eternal God." The doctrine of the Trinity, according to the church's confession, is a deliverance of God's revelation in his Word.

10. David S. Yeago, "The New Testament and the Nicene Dogma: A Contribution to the Recovery of Theological Exegesis," *Pro Ecclesia* 3 (1994): 153. Similarly, Ayres, *Nicaea and Its Legacy*, 416–20.

The Revelation of God's Triune Name

Creation bears witness to the existence of "one, true, eternal God." According to the apostle Paul, "His invisible attributes, namely, his eternal power and divine nature, have been clearly perceived, ever since the creation of the world, in the things that have been made" (Rom. 1:20). Similarly, according to the psalmist, "The heavens declare the glory of God, and the sky above proclaims his handiwork" (Ps. 19:1). The being and existence of God is the atmosphere within which "we live and move and have our being" (Acts 17:28). Even when sinful humanity suppresses the truth of God in unrighteousness (Rom. 1:18), creation maintains its eloquent witness to God's most excellent nature: "We are not your God, look beyond us. . . . He made us."[11] God's created effects lead us to their eternal, immutable, and simple source, and their existence cannot be explained apart from his existence. And yet, though we may search the heights of heaven and fathom the depths of the sea, creation does not tell us this God's name, nor does it tell us his Son's name (Prov. 30:4; with Job 28). In this case we have the supreme instance of the principle that the cause exceeds its effect.[12] God's created effects do not, indeed cannot, disclose to us that God's name is YHWH, nor can they disclose to us God's threefold subsistence as Father, Son, and Holy Spirit. The disclosure of this sublime truth belongs to God's self-revelation in his Word alone.

Why must this be the case? Because the truth of the Trinity does not concern relations *external* to God's most excellent being, for example, the relation of creator to creature or of divine king to creaturely subject. The truth of the Trinity concerns relations *internal* to God's being: the relation between the Father and the Son, in mutual fellowship of the Holy Spirit, who proceeds from them both. The truth of the Trinity is internal to the hidden depths of God's being and therefore is known to the tripersonal God alone: "No one knows the Son except the Father, and no one knows the Father except the Son" (Matt. 11:27); "no one comprehends the thoughts of God except the Spirit of God" (1 Cor. 2:11). The good news is that God does not will that his triune existence remain a mystery hidden from our eyes. Because the depths of God "are also depths of love,"[13] God's infinitely deep self-knowledge graciously accommodates itself to us in a creaturely form of knowledge: "No one knows the Father except the Son and anyone to whom the Son chooses to reveal

11. Augustine, *Confessions*, trans. Henry Chadwick (Oxford: Oxford University Press, 1991), 10.6.
12. Basil of Caesarea, *Against Eunomius*, trans. Mark DelCogliano and Andrew Radde-Gallwitz (Washington, DC: Catholic University of America Press, 2011), 2.32.
13. Dorner, *System of Christian Doctrine*, 413.

him" (Matt. 11:27); "now we have received not the spirit of the world, but the Spirit who is from God, that we might understand the things freely given us by God" (1 Cor. 2:12).[14] Because God has revealed himself to us through the embassy of his Son and Spirit, we may know, confess, and adore—in a manner suitable to creatures—the deep and mysterious reality of his triune being. The truth of the Trinity is vouchsafed to the friends of YHWH, to whom God makes known his covenant (Ps. 25:14).

God's *name* is the mode of revelation that most fully and faithfully indicates the inexhaustible reality of God's *being*. God's name signifies God's nature. Though one may know something of the divine artist through his art, apart from the disclosure of the divine artist's name (being much more than simply his signature!), he remains anonymous, an "unknown God" (Acts 17:23). God's name discloses his personal character and quiddity (Exod. 34:5–7; John 17:6, 26); it is therefore the distinguishing mark by which he blesses his people (Exod. 20:24; Deut. 21:5) and by which he is blessed (Ps. 113). The name whereby God discloses his identity to us is a triune name. Under Jesus's messianic mandate, the church baptizes in "the name of the Father and of the Son and of the Holy Spirit" (Matt. 28:19). Following apostolic example, the church blesses this triune name: professing faith in one God the Father of all, in one Lord, and in one Spirit (1 Cor. 8:6; 12:3; Eph. 4:4–6), and pronouncing benediction by the grace of our Lord Jesus Christ, by the love of God, and by the fellowship of the Holy Spirit (2 Cor. 13:14).

According to John Owen, the triune name into which we are baptized "compriseth the whole of the truth" of the doctrine of the Trinity.[15] Again, the reason for this is that God's triune name reveals God's triune being. The character of this revelation is worth pausing over, for God's triune name exhibits a peculiar grammar.

God's Singular Name and Nature

"The name" into which we are baptized (Matt. 28:19) is *one* name. The singular name in Matthew's baptismal formula is undoubtedly an "oblique reference" to the Tetragrammaton, the proper name of the God of Israel.[16] As in the case of other proper names such as "Stephen" or "Sarah," the fundamental

---

14. In more formal terms, "archetypal theology," God's infinitely deep knowledge of himself, is the basis and guarantee of "ectypal theology," our creaturely knowledge of God.

15. John Owen, *Vindication of the Doctrine of the Trinity in the Works of John Owen*, ed. William H. Goold (Edinburgh: Banner of Truth, 1965), 2:374.

16. R. Kendall Soulen, *The Divine Name(s) and the Holy Trinity*, vol. 1, *Distinguishing the Voices* (Louisville: Westminster John Knox, 2011), 176.

role of God's proper name YHWH "is not to describe but simply to point: this one and not another."[17] The Tetragrammaton is "the linguistic token of God's uniqueness par excellence,"[18] identifying the one true God of Israel and distinguishing him from all creatures and from all rival gods: "YHWH is his name" (Exod. 15:3; Jer. 33:2; Amos 5:8; etc.). Building on its fundamental role of identifying the one true God, God's proper name gathers around it a host of other "names" or identity descriptions that serve to "exegete" the meaning and significance of God's proper name, "bringing the sheer darkness of its infinite depths to light."[19] To borrow Kendall Soulen's striking image, "The Tetragrammaton is surrounded by a corona of connotation that reflects the one who bears it."[20] Preeminent among these other "names" is God's sovereign self-exposition of the Tetragrammaton in Exodus 3:14: "I AM WHO I AM." Drawing on Exodus 3:14 as well as other Old Testament texts (e.g., Isa. 44:24–26), Francis Turretin argues that this name "implies three things" about God: (1) "the eternity and independence of God, inasmuch as he is a necessary being, and existing of himself, independent of any other, self-existent"; (2) "causality and efficiency because what is the first and most perfect in each genus is the cause of the rest (for God is by himself so that he is the cause of being to all others, Isa. 44:24)"; (3) "immutability and constancy in promises because he really performs and does what he has promised by giving to his promises being."[21]

Along with God's sovereign self-exposition of the Tetragrammaton in Exodus 3:14, we may summarize the additional "names" by which YHWH is characterized under two categories: names that "identify God in his relation to all reality" and names that "identify God in his relationship to Israel."[22] The first category includes the naming of YHWH as sole creator and ruler of all things. YHWH is "God Almighty" (Gen. 17:1) who brought all creaturely being into existence through his Word and Spirit (Gen. 1; Ps. 33:6, 9), who blessed the patriarchs (Gen. 12:1–3; 49:25–26), who rules history in accordance with his sovereign purpose—often overruling the misdeeds of human agents (Gen.

17. Ibid., 3. Perhaps in distinction from Soulen, I would emphasize that identification is the fundamental but not exclusive role of proper names.
18. Ibid., 160.
19. Ibid., 161.
20. Ibid., 211.
21. Francis Turretin, *Institutes of Elenctic Theology*, vol. 1, *First through Tenth Topics*, ed. James T. Dennison Jr., trans. George Musgrave Giger (Phillipsburg, NJ: P&R, 1992), 3.4.5.
22. Richard Bauckham, *God Crucified: Monotheism and Christology in the New Testament* (Grand Rapids: Eerdmans, 1998), 9–10. Here I have reversed the order in which Bauckham presents these two categories in order to reflect the canonical *ordo docendi* wherein YHWH is first identified as the creator and ruler of all things (Gen. 1:1–2:3) and then as the God of the covenant (Gen. 2:4–25; see also Exod. 6:3).

45:5, 7; 50:20), in whom the patriarchs hoped for life out of death (Gen. 15:2; 50:24–25). As God Almighty, YHWH is the one "who gives life to the dead and calls into existence the things that do not exist" (Rom. 4:17). The second category includes the naming of YHWH by his great redemptive acts toward Israel, his covenant people: YHWH is the one "who brought you out of the land of Egypt" (Exod. 20:2). This category also includes the naming of YHWH through the proclamation of his character as "a God merciful and gracious, slow to anger, and abounding in steadfast love and faithfulness" (Exod. 34:6).[23]

The identification of God by his proper name and its "corona of connotation" reveals that YHWH is *one* and serves to indicate *what sort of one* he is.[24] YHWH's great redemptive acts toward his covenant people cause Israel to know that YHWH alone is the "God; there is no other besides him" (Deut. 4:35, 39; 6:4). YHWH's almighty acts in creation and history manifest the unrivaled nature of his divine power and expose the worthless nature of the nations' gods (Isa. 40:26, 28; 44:24; 45:18). And thus, while the Old Testament acknowledges the existence of many gods, it also insists that the term "god" applies only to YHWH in truth, for he alone bears the characteristic marks of the one true God: almighty, eternal, and imperishable being. YHWH "is the true God; he is the living God and the everlasting King. . . . It is he who made the earth by his power, who established the world by his wisdom, and by his understanding stretched out the heavens" (Jer. 10:10, 12; see also Ps. 102:25–27; Isa. 40:12–31). In contrast to YHWH, other so-called gods, "who did not make the heavens and the earth," are characterized by their nondivinity: they "shall perish from the earth and from under the heavens" (Jer. 10:11; see also Deut. 32:17, 21).

Characterization of YHWH as the one true God is not confined to the Old Testament. The New Testament confirms this characterization as well.[25] The

---

23. Robert Jenson develops his doctrine of the Trinity by means of a sophisticated interpretation of the divine names. His proposal falls short in part because he fails to take full account of the first category of the divine names and its metaphysical implications by focusing almost exclusively on God's historical identity descriptions. See Scott R. Swain, *The God of the Gospel: Robert Jenson's Trinitarian Theology* (Downers Grove, IL: IVP Academic, 2013).

24. The nature of Jewish and early Christian monotheism is a highly debated topic. For a good introduction to the issues, see Carey C. Newman, James R. Davila, and Gladys S. Lewis, eds., *The Jewish Roots of Christological Monotheism* (Leiden: Brill, 1999). The following two works are particularly helpful in thinking about this topic: Paul Rainbow, "Monotheism and Christology in 1 Corinthians 8:4–6" (DPhil diss., Oxford University, 1987); and Richard Bauckham, "Biblical Theology and the Problems of Monotheism," in *Out of Egypt: Biblical Theology and Biblical Interpretation*, ed. Craig Bartholomew, Mary Healy, Karl Möller, and Robin Parry (Grand Rapids: Zondervan, 2004), 5:187–229.

25. Bauckham, "Biblical Theology and the Problems of Monotheism," 218–29; and Larry Hurtado, *One God, One Lord: Early Christian Devotion and Ancient Jewish Monotheism* (Philadelphia: Fortress, 1988).

New Testament appropriates the Septuagint's standard "surrogate"[26] for God's proper name, "the Lord," and affirms that "the Lord is one" (Mark 12:29) and that "there is no other besides him" (Mark 12:32). "Although there may be so-called gods in heaven or on earth," Paul confesses that "for us there is one God . . . and one Lord" (1 Cor. 8:5–6). The New Testament not only confirms the Lord's identity as the only true God; it also expands the Old Testament's witness to his unique and indivisible nature. Following patterns of discourse present in Second Temple Jewish literature, the New Testament employs the language of Greek "natural theology" to distinguish the nature of the one true God—immortal, invisible, immutable, "having neither beginning of days nor end of life" (Heb. 7:3; Rom. 1:20, 23; 1 Tim. 1:17; Heb. 11:27; James 1:17; Rev. 1:4)—from so-called gods "that by nature are not gods" (1 Cor. 8:5; Gal. 4:8).[27] The biblical identification of the Lord God as one, and as this sort of one, is the root of "metaphysical monotheism," that is, the belief that, properly speaking, there is only one true and living God and that which distinguishes the true God from false gods (and also from all other creatures) is God's unique and incommunicable nature.[28] The Lord "alone has immortality" and "dwells in unapproachable light" (1 Tim. 6:16). Belief in this kind of monotheism is the aura within which trinitarian theology emerges.[29]

We do not exhaust the significance of the name into which we are baptized by noting its singularity. Returning to the peculiar grammar of God's triune name, we observe not only that this name is *one* but also that it belongs to *three*. It is the name "of the Father and of the Son and of the Holy Spirit" (Matt. 28:19). The Father, the Son, and the Spirit bear the unique name and nature of the Lord God, and they do so in an irreducibly threefold way.

"Jesus is Lord" constitutes the primal Christian confession (Rom. 10:9; 1 Cor. 12:3; Phil. 2:11). To call on Jesus's name is to call on "the name of the Lord" (Rom. 10:9–13)—yet another implicit reference to the Tetragrammaton.[30]

26. Soulen, *Divine Name(s)*, 12.

27. I discuss this phenomenon more fully, with accompanying documentation, in Swain, *God of the Gospel*, 173–79.

28. Katherine Sonderegger rightly identifies the importance of metaphysical monotheism for the doctrine of God: "God's uniqueness cannot simply be exhausted by an unsubstitutable identity: this, after all, is the identity condition of any finite being. . . . No, God's unique identity must be conceptualized in such a way that we could mark off his Being substantially from all other being. His Reality must be unique to him, his life" ("The Absolute Infinity of God," in *The Reality of Faith in Theology: Studies on Karl Barth Princeton-Kampen Consultation, 2005*, ed. Bruce McCormack and Gerrit Neven [Bern: Peter Lang, 2007], 48).

29. Bruce D. Marshall, "The Unity of the Triune God: Reviving an Ancient Question," *The Thomist* 74 (2010): 1–32.

30. C. Kavin Rowe, "Romans 10:13: What Is the Name of the Lord?," *Horizons in Biblical Theology* 22 (2000): 135–73.

Along with the name of the Lord, the New Testament identifies Jesus by means of other identity descriptions characteristic of the one true God. Jesus is identified as the sole creator and ruler of all things (John 1:3; Col. 1:16–17; Heb. 1:2–3) and as the covenant God of Israel (John 20:28; 1 Cor. 8:6).[31] In addition to this, the distinguishing marks of God's unique nature are applied to Jesus. Jesus is self-existent: he has "life in himself" (John 5:26). Jesus is immutable: he is "the same yesterday and today and forever" (Heb. 13:8; with 1:12). Jesus is eternal: he declares, "Before Abraham was, I am" (John 8:58), an unmistakable instance of the Tetragrammaton in its sovereign self-announcement and self-exposition (Exod 3:14; see also John 4:26; 6:20; 8:24, 28; 13:19; 18:5–6, 8).[32] As in the case of the Lord Jesus, the New Testament identifies the Father and the Spirit with the name, nature, and activity of the one true God as well. "The name . . . of the Son" is also "the name of the Father . . . and of the Holy Spirit" (Matt. 28:19).[33]

God's Personal Names

While the New Testament *identifies* the Father, the Son, and the Spirit *with* the one true God, it preserves real *distinctions* between the three as well. Unlike the distinction between Creator and creature, the distinctions between the three do not indicate division between any one of the three and the divine nature. Nor do these distinctions indicate any diminished level of participation within God by any one of the three—an impossibility at any rate, given God's simple, indivisible nature. As noted above, the distinctions concern realities that are *internal* to God's singular name and nature and that express themselves in God's singular actions toward creatures. We may appreciate the character of these distinctions by contemplating the various "personal names"—"Father," "Son," and "Spirit"—that the New Testament applies to the three. Unlike the Tetragrammaton, which signifies that which they hold in common, the personal names signify that which distinguishes the three from one another within the singular being of God.

31. Bauckham, *God Crucified*.
32. Ibid., 55–56.
33. Space forbids exploring at greater length the identification of the Father and the Spirit as the true and living God. For further discussion, see Gordon D. Fee, "Paul and the Trinity," in *The Trinity: An Interdisciplinary Symposium on the Trinity*, ed. Stephen T. Davis, Daniel Kendall, and Gerald O'Collins (Oxford: Oxford University Press, 1999), 49–72; Ben Witherington III and Laura M. Ice, *The Shadow of the Almighty: Father, Son, and Spirit in Biblical Perspective* (Grand Rapids: Eerdmans 2002); Andreas J. Köstenberger and Scott R. Swain, *Father, Son and Spirit: The Trinity and John's Gospel* (Downers Grove, IL: IVP Academic, 2008); and Wesley Hill, *Paul and the Trinity: Persons, Relations, and the Pauline Letters* (Grand Rapids: Eerdmans, 2015).

What do these personal names signify? The classical reply continues to be the most exegetically illuminating and the most theologically satisfying among available options: personal names "signify procession."[34] In other words, the personal names of "Father," "Son," and "Spirit" indicate the mutual relations in which the three stand toward one another,[35] specifically, the personal names indicate *relations of origin*. The Father is father *to* the Son, who is his "only begotten." The Spirit is spirit *of* the Father and *of* the Son, who is breathed forth in their mutual delight and who displays the glory of their mutual love. Though it enjoys a rich pedigree among the church's closest and most careful readers of Holy Scripture, this interpretation of the personal names has not gone unchallenged in Reformed and evangelical dogmatics. Some reject this interpretation of the personal names because they believe it unwittingly suggests subordination within the divine being,[36] others because it fails to take seriously enough the kind of subordination that characterizes the mutual relations of the three.[37] We will address both viewpoints below when we consider the linguistic and metaphysical implications that follow from contemplating the grammar of God's triune name. For now it will suffice to note some of the biblical patterns of identifying the three from which this interpretation of the personal names derives.

First, consider several patterns of identification that characterize the Father-Son relationship. (1) The New Testament employs a number of illustrations, what Athanasius called "*paradeigmata*,"[38] that further amplify the relation that obtains between the Father and the Son. These illustrations are not merely ornamental. They function as indispensable conceptual tools that help faith contemplate more fully the (ultimately incomprehensible) nature of the Father-Son relation.[39] Drawing on Old Testament and other Jewish wisdom literature (e.g., Prov. 8; Wis. 7:26), the New Testament portrays the Son as the "radiance" of the Father's glory (Heb. 1:3), as the "image"

34. Thomas Aquinas, *Summa theologiae*, trans. Fathers of the English Dominican Province (New York: Benzinger Bros., 1948), Ia.27.1, resp.

35. Basil of Caesarea, *Against Eunomius* 1.5, 25; 2.22; Gregory of Nazianzus, *Or.* 29.16, in *Christology of the Later Fathers*, ed. Edward R. Hardy (Louisville: Westminster John Knox, 1954), 171; Augustine, *The Trinity*, trans. Edmund Hill (Hyde Park, NY: New City, 1991), 5.1.6.

36. For example, B. B. Warfield, "Trinity," in *The International Bible Encyclopedia*, ed. James Orr (Chicago: Howard-Severance, 1915), 5:3012–22.

37. For example, Bruce Ware, *Father, Son, and Holy Spirit: Relationships, Roles, and Relevance* (Wheaton: Crossway, 2005), chap. 4.

38. On which see Khaled Anatolios, *Athanasius* (London: Routledge, 2004), 62–67; and idem, *Retrieving Nicaea*, 110–14.

39. Athanasius, *Letters to Serapion on the Holy Spirit* 1.19–20, in *Works on the Spirit: Athanasius and Didymus*, trans. Mark DelCogliano, Andrew Radde-Gallwitz, and Lewis Ayres (Crestwood, NY: St. Vladimir's Seminary Press, 2011), 82–85.

of the invisible God (Col. 1:15), and as the "Word" of God (John 1:1; Rev. 19:13). In each instance, these illustrations indicate complete ontological correspondence between the Father and the Son: the Word of God is God (John 1:1); the image of the invisible God is the one by whom, in whom, and for whom creation exists (Col. 1:16–17); the radiance of God is the exact imprint of the Father's substance (Heb. 1:3). These illustrations also indicate that ontological correspondence between the Father and the Son obtains within the context of a relationship wherein the Father is the principle or source of the Son, who is his perfect Word, image, and radiance. (2) The New Testament also indicates that the Father and the Son share the unique divine name and nature within the context of a relation characterized by giving on the part of the Father and receiving on the part of the Son. The Father has given his name to the Son (John 17:11; Phil. 2:9–11).[40] And the Father has granted the Son to have "life in himself" just as the Father has "life in himself" (John 5:26). (3) The New Testament in various ways displays God's external actions toward his creatures as expressing the ordered relation of the Father and the Son. In God's creative and providential activity, the Father acts *through* the Son (John 1:3; 1 Cor. 8:6; Col. 1:16), and the Son acts *from* the Father (John 5:19). In similar fashion, the Son's mission to become incarnate and make atonement is a mission he fulfills at the behest of the Father who sent him (Mark 12:1–12; John 6:38; Gal. 4:4–5), and the Son's enthronement as king is an authority he receives from his Father (Matt. 11:27; 28:18; Eph. 1:20–23; Heb. 1:3–4; with Ps. 110). In each of these instances, we are not dealing with a distinction between God's action and the action of a creature. We are dealing with God's unique divine acts as creator, providential ruler, redeemer, and lord, and with a distinction that obtains *within* these unique divine acts: a distinction that expresses the ordered relation of the Father and the Son.

Second, and following from the previous examples, consider several patterns of identification that characterize the Spirit's relation to the Father and the Son. (1) The New Testament employs several paradigms or illustrations that amplify the unique nature of the Spirit's relationship to the Father and the Son. As in the case of the Father-Son relation, a number of these illustrations are drawn from the Old Testament (e.g., Isa. 44:3; Ezek. 47:1–12; Joel 2:28). Particularly instructive are illustrations that associate the Holy Spirit with water. The Spirit is identified as one who is "poured out" by the Father (Rom. 5:5) and by the Son (Acts 2:33), as the element with which Jesus baptizes his disciples (Mark 1:8; 1 Cor. 12:13), and as the living water that flows from the

---

40. Bauckham, *God Crucified*, 34; Soulen, *Divine Name(s)*, 201–6, 208–10.

throne of God and of the lamb (Rev. 22:1).[41] This rich network of imagery at once identifies the Spirit as divine source of life and as one who in his life-giving identity and mission proceeds from the Father and the Son. (2) The New Testament also indicates the nature of the Spirit's relation to the Father and the Son by virtue of the Spirit's relation to God's unique name and nature. As the Father gives the divine name to the Son, so the Spirit (who also shares the divine name: 2 Cor. 3:17) causes the Son to be acknowledged as "Lord" (1 Cor. 12:3), to the glory of God the Father (Phil. 2:11). Similarly, while the Spirit *is* "the truth" (1 John 5:6), he is also the Spirit "*of* truth" (1 John 4:6). Consequently, he is able to guide Jesus's disciplines "into all the truth" (John 16:13) because of the unique relation in which he stands to the Father and the Son: he does not speak "from himself" but only what "he hears" (John 16:13), taking what he holds in common with the Son and with the Father and declaring it to the apostles (John 16:14–15).[42] When it comes to divine truth, therefore, the distinction between the Spirit and the Father and the Son "is not in what is had, but in the order of having."[43] (3) As in the case of the Father and the Son, the Spirit's ordered relation to the Father and the Son is expressed in God's external actions toward his creatures. The Father and the Son work *through* the Spirit: the Father gives the Holy Spirit to those who ask him (Luke 11:13), and Jesus performs miracles "by the Spirit of God" (Matt. 12:28). Moreover, as the Father sends the Son to accomplish his incarnate mission, in similar fashion the Father and the Son send the Spirit to indwell God's children (John 14:26; 15:26; 16:7; Gal. 4:6) in order that, through the Son, Jew and gentile might have access "in one Spirit to the Father" (Eph. 2:18; with 1:23 and 5:18). Once again, an observable pattern emerges. The distinction between the activity of the Spirit toward creatures and the activity of the Father and the Son toward creatures is not a distinction between a creaturely act and a divine act. The distinction among the three is a distinction that is internal to the singular divine act whereby Triune God fulfills his ancient covenant promise to dwell among his people forever (John 14:16–17, 23; with Lev. 26:12), and that manifests the Spirit's ordered relation to the Father and the Son. In the coming of the Triune God to dwell among us, the Spirit comes from the Father through the Son and leads us through the Son to the Father.

41. Similarly, Athanasius links 1 Cor. 12:13 with 1 Cor. 10:4: "For it is written: *we were all made to drink of the one Spirit* [1 Cor. 12:13]. But when we drink of the Spirit, we drink of Christ. For *they drank from the spiritual Rock that followed them, and the Rock was Christ* [1 Cor. 10:4]" (Athanasius, *Letters to Serapion* 1.19.4, emphasis original).

42. For further commentary on these verses, see Didymus the Blind, *On the Holy Spirit* 170–74 (in *Works on the Holy Spirit*, 195–96).

43. Thomas Aquinas, *Commentary on the Gospel of John, Chapters 13–21*, trans. Fabian Larcher (Washington, DC: Catholic University of America Press, 2010), 145.

The Trinity and the Old Testament

The "personal names" of the Father, the Son, and the Holy Spirit identify the distinct manner in which the three relate to one another within the being and activity of the one true God. Because the incarnation of the Son and the outpouring of the Spirit provide the occasion for manifesting the mutual relations of the three "east of Eden," the grammar of God's triune name is supremely a matter of New Testament revelation. The New Testament provides both the "raw material" of the church's trinitarian doctrine and, in certain cases, "highly developed patterns of reflection on this material."[44] That said, it is important to emphasize that characterization of the Lord as triune is not merely a New Testament phenomenon.[45] As noted above, the New Testament repeatedly draws on the Old Testament in its attempts to characterize the mutual relations of the three, and the Old Testament identification of YHWH's unique name and nature is indispensable to understanding New Testament claims about YHWH's triune identity. What more can be said about the relationship between the Old Testament and the revelation of God's triune name?

Herman Bavinck speaks of an "inexplicit indication" of YHWH's triune identity in the Old Testament, and this is perhaps the best way to characterize how the Old Testament bears witness to God's triune name.[46] Though the revelation of God's tripersonal nature is primarily a New Testament phenomenon, the roots of that revelation may be found in the Old Testament by those "already acquainted with the doctrine of the Trinity."[47] In God's creative and re-creative work through his Word and Spirit, we see a triune principle of activity (Gen. 1; Pss. 33:6, 9; 104:30; Isa. 44:3; 55:10–11). Under the tutelage of the New Testament's "prosopological exegesis"[48] of Old Testament texts, we overhear in certain places a dialogue between the Father and the Son (Gen.

44. Cornelius Plantinga, "The Fourth Gospel as Trinitarian Source Then and Now," in *Biblical Hermeneutics in Historical Perspective*, ed. M. S. Burrows and P. Rorem (Grand Rapids: Eerdmans, 1991), 305.

45. Central to the Socinian strategy of undermining the status of the Trinity as a fundamental doctrine was the denial of its presence in the Old Testament. See Turretin's discussion in *Institutes of Elenctic Theology* 3.24, 26.

46. Herman Bavinck, *Reformed Dogmatics*, vol. 2, *God and Creation*, ed. John Bolt, trans. John Vriend (Grand Rapids: Baker Academic, 2004), 261. For two slightly different approaches to the issue, see Bruce D. Marshall, "Israel: Do Christians Worship the God of Israel?," in *Knowing the Triune God: The Work of the Spirit in the Practices of the Church*, ed. James J. Buckley and David S. Yeago (Grand Rapids: Eerdmans, 2001), chap. 9; and Holmes, *Quest for the Trinity*, 34–51.

47. Warfield, "Trinity," 3014.

48. Matthew W. Bates defines "prosopological exegesis" as "a reading technique whereby an interpreter seeks to overcome a real or perceived ambiguity regarding the identity of the speakers or addressees (or both) in the divinely inspired source text by assigning non-trivial prosopa (i.e., non-trivial vis-a-vis the 'plain sense' of the text) to the speakers or addressees (or both) in

1:26; Pss. 2; 110; Isa. 49:3; with Mark 12:35–37; Heb. 1:5–14; etc.). In other passages, we witness a triune naming of YHWH (Num. 6:23–27; 2 Sam. 23:2–3) and also an association of the name and glory of YHWH with a promised Davidic king (Isa. 52:13; Jer. 23:5–6), "whose coming forth is from of old, from ancient days" (Mic. 5:2, 4; Ps. 109:3 LXX). Though the interpretation of this or that text may be disputable, this should not surprise us, given the Old Testament's "inexplicit indication" of YHWH's triune name and nature. Nor should it dissuade us from reading the Old Testament in a trinitarian way, given the Old Testament's role in the unfolding economy of YHWH's self-revelation. B. B. Warfield well summarizes the matter:

> The Old Testament may be likened to a chamber richly furnished but dimly lighted; the introduction of light brings into it nothing which was not in it before; but it brings out into clearer view much of what was in it but was only dimly or even not at all perceived before. The mystery of the Trinity is not revealed in the Old Testament; but the mystery of the Trinity underlies the Old Testament revelation, and here and there almost comes into view. Thus the Old Testament revelation of God is not corrected by the fuller revelation that follows it, but only perfected, extended and enlarged.[49]

God in Three "Persons": Trinitarian Language and Metaphysics

Up to this point, we have traced the peculiar grammar that characterizes the revelation of God's triune name. As we have seen, the Bible identifies YHWH, the one true God, with the Father, the Son, and the Holy Spirit even as it distinguishes the three through relations of origin. In its attempt to render the significance of God's revealed name, and also to refute heretical misunderstandings of that name, the church has found it necessary and helpful to employ extrabiblical language.[50] This is one reason we have spoken of the doctrine of the Trinity as the church's "interpretation" of God's revealed name. For one thing, interpretation involves "saying *the same thing* in other words" in order to explicate, as far as possible, the sense of those words.[51] During the christological and trinitarian controversies of the fourth century,

---

order to make sense of the text" (*The Hermeneutics of the Apostolic Proclamation: The Center of Paul's Method of Scriptural Interpretation* [Waco: Baylor University Press, 2012], 221).

49. Warfield, "Trinity," 3014.

50. On the importance of extrabiblical language in trinitarian theology, see Calvin, *Institutes* 1.13.2–6; Zacharias Ursinus, *Commentary on the Heidelberg Catechism*, trans. G. W. Williard (Phillipsburg, NJ: P&R, 1992), 132–33; and Johann Gerhard, *On the Nature of God and On the Most Holy Mystery of the Trinity*, trans. Richard J. Dinda (St. Louis: Concordia, 2007), 2.39–40.

51. Barth, *Church Dogmatics* I.1, 345 (emphasis original).

for example, the church employed extrabiblical terms in order to specify its understanding of the Bible's normative presentation of God's triune identity and to expose the folly of those who used biblical words to convey unbiblical theologies. The resulting creedal statements of Nicaea (AD 325) and Constantinople (AD 381), and their accompanying terminology of one divine "being" (*ousia*) in three "persons" (*hypostases*), "merely formalized the rules for Christian speech already implicit in the logic of the biblical witness."[52] Along with the need to employ extrabiblical terminology, there is another, more fundamental, reason for speaking of the doctrine of the Trinity as the church's "interpretation" of God's triune name. Interpreting God's triune name also involves metaphysical reflection—or, perhaps better, metaphysical ascetics—insofar as the *sense* of biblical language about God cannot be derived from the *uses* to which that language is put in ordinary human discourse. This is not because the Bible uses an esoteric angelic language. Rather, it is because the Bible employs ordinary human language to speak of an extraordinary subject: the triune YHWH. As Augustine states, "The divine Scriptures are in the habit of making something like children's toys out of things that occur in creation, by which to entice our sickly gaze and get us step by step to seek as best we can the things that are above and to forsake the things that are below."[53] And so interpreting the biblical revelation of the Trinity requires unlearning the uses to which creaturely language ordinarily applies and learning new uses for creaturely language that correspond to the grammar of biblical discourse, which reliably reveals the incomprehensible reality of God.[54] Along with the public and private reading of Holy Scripture, the church's liturgy and Christian practices of prayer are the school within which this process of unlearning/learning to name God as Trinity occurs.[55] As an interpretation of biblical revelation, therefore, the doctrine of the Trinity is the church's attempt, under Jesus's promise of illumination, to refine its speech and thought about God in

52. J. Warren Smith, "The Trinity in the Fourth-Century Fathers," in *The Oxford Handbook of the Trinity*, ed. Gilles Emery and Matthew Levering (New York: Oxford University Press, 2011), 109–10. Similarly Ayres, *Nicaea and Its Legacy*, 88–98; Anatolios, *Retrieving Nicaea*, 127–28.

53. Augustine, *The Trinity* 1.1.2; see Anatolios's discussion of Augustine's "trinitarian epistemology" in *Retrieving Nicaea*, 242–49. See also Augustine, *The Trinity* 5.1–2.

54. As Anatolios points out, Athanasius (and, we might add, all pro-Nicene theologians) assumes "that the intertextual patterns of the scriptural naming of God must mirror, in a way accommodated to human understanding, the being of God. The patterns of scriptural divine naming must correspond to the pattern of divine being" (*Retrieving Nicaea*, 111).

55. Sarah Coakley, *God, Sexuality, and the Self: An Essay "On the Trinity"* (Cambridge: Cambridge University Press, 2013).

light of God's revealed name in order that it may bear truthful witness to the one true God.[56]

The Concept of Divine "Person"

The concept of divine "person" is one of the most compelling insights to arise from the church's interpretation of God's triune name. Originally, the Greek term *hypostasis* referred to "that which stands under," or what more recent philosophy might call a "basic particular," while the Latin term *persona* referred to an actor's mask. Eventually, both terms would be used to refer to that which distinguishes the three from one another, that is, that which makes the Father *this* one over against the Son and the Spirit, and so forth. Though indispensable contributions may be found in the theologies of several Eastern fathers, pride of place in articulating a trinitarian concept of person belongs to the tradition of reflection that stems from Augustine through Boethius and reaches its apogee in Thomas Aquinas. According to Thomas Aquinas, a divine person is to be understood as a "subsisting relation."

What might *this* mean? Augustine begins book 5 of *The Trinity* reflecting on the poverty of human speech when it comes to praising the blessed Trinity. He is aware of his own weakness in relation to this task and begins asking God to help him "understand and explain what I have in mind and to pardon any blunders I may make."[57] He is also aware of the weakness of human philosophical categories when it comes to praising the blessed Trinity. In this case, Augustine singles out Aristotle's ten categories of predication (i.e., substance, quality, quantity, relation, position, habit, place, time, action, and passion), immediately disqualifying eight of the ten categories from proper speech about God: "Thus we should understand God, if we can and as far as we can, to be good without quality, great without quantity, creative without need or necessity, presiding without position, holding all things together without possession, wholly everywhere without place, everlasting without time, without any change in himself making changeable things, and

---

56. For an alternative account of the metaphysics of the Trinity, see William Hasker, *Metaphysics and the Tri-Personal God* (Oxford: Oxford University Press, 2013), along with Matthew Levering's incisive critique in his review of Hasker's book in *The Journal of Analytic Theology* 2 (2014): 294–98. For a broader introduction to discussions of the Trinity within contemporary analytic philosophy, see Michael Rea, ed., *Oxford Readings in Philosophical Theology*, vol. 1, *Trinity, Incarnation, and Atonement* (Oxford: Oxford University Press, 2009); and Thomas H. McCall, *Which Trinity? Whose Monotheism? Philosophical and Systematic Theologians on the Metaphysics of Trinitarian Theology* (Grand Rapids: Eerdmans, 2010).

57. Augustine, *The Trinity* 5.1.

undergoing nothing."[58] According to Augustine, only two of these categories apply when it comes to the praise of the Trinity, *substance* and *relation*, and these only after purging them of their ordinary creaturely senses, which entail limitation, change, and temporality.[59]

God's self-revelation to Moses in Exodus 3 provides Augustine with sufficient warrant for predicating things of God "substance-wise": "There is at least no doubt that God is substance, or perhaps a better word would be being; at any rate what the Greeks call *ousia*. . . . And who can more be than he that said to his servant, *I am who I am*, and, *Tell the sons of Israel, He who is sent me to you* (Exod. 3:14)?"[60] According to Augustine, substantial predication includes not only predications that affirm *that* God exists; substantial predication also includes predications that affirm *what sort of one* he is (e.g., great, good, etc.). Furthermore, these predications apply to the Father, the Son, and the Spirit in the singular. Just as we confess the Father is God, the Son is God, and the Spirit is God, and yet we do not confess the existence of three gods, "likewise the Father is great, the Son is great, the Holy Spirit too is great; yet there are not three great ones but one great one."[61] Along with substantial predication, Scripture mandates that we speak of God "relationship-wise." For Augustine, this mandate arises from "personal names" such as "Father," "Son," and "Holy Spirit." Relational predication does not refer (at least directly) to the singular divine substance but to that by which the three are distinguished from one another, that is, their *relations*: "not everything that is said of him is said substance-wise. Some things are said with reference to something else, like Father with reference to Son and Son with reference to Father."[62] Significantly for Augustine and his later interpreters, because relational predication identifies someone *with reference to someone else* while substantial predication identifies someone *with reference to himself*, these two categories of predication allow us to observe real distinctions between the three while maintaining their unity as one God: considered in relation to the Son and the Spirit, the Father is really and truly distinct; considered in himself, the Father is simply the one true God; and so

58. Augustine, *The Trinity* 5.2. See also Boethius, *De trinitate* 4.1–9; and Peter Lombard, *The Sentences*, book 1: *The Mystery of the Trinity*, trans. Giulio Silano, Medieval Sources in Translation 42 (Toronto: Pontifical Institute of Medieval Studies, 2007), 1.8.6–8. Augustine goes on to acknowledge that these predications may be applied to God "by way of metaphor and simile," as Scripture repeatedly does (*The Trinity* 5.2.9).

59. Augustine, *The Trinity* 5.1.3–8.

60. Augustine, *The Trinity* 5.1.3 (emphasis original).

61. Augustine, *The Trinity* 5.2.9.

62. Augustine, *The Trinity* 5.1.6. See also Thomas Aquinas, *Summa theologiae* Ia.29.4, resp., and commentary below.

forth.[63] Boethius, a later student of Augustine, summarizes the significance of this twofold pattern of predication: "the substance preserves the unity, the relation makes up the Trinity."[64]

It should be noted here that, in Augustine's judgment, one of the chief failures of "Arian" biblical interpretation is its inability to distinguish "substantial" from "relational" predication. This failure is responsible for the erroneous Arian judgment that the Son's distinct identity as the Father's "only begotten" signifies a *distinct* and therefore *different substance* from the Father rather than the *distinct relationship* in which he stands to the Father *within one divine substance*.[65] Conversely, one of the chief problems with "Sabellian" biblical interpretation is its failure to acknowledge any real distinction between the three: "In very truth, because the Father is not the Son and the Son is not the Father, and the Holy Spirit who is also called *the gift of God* (Acts 8:20; John 4:10) is neither the Father nor the Son, they are certainly three. That is why it is said in the plural *I and the Father are one* (John 10:30). He did not say 'is one,' which the Sabellians say, but 'are one.'"[66] Augustine's purgation and subsequent application of Aristotle's categories to the Trinity thus function both to clarify, as far as possible, biblical language about the Trinity and to refute inadequate interpretations of that language.[67]

Along with Augustine's distinction between relational and substantial predication, Boethius's definition of person as "the individual substance of a rational nature"[68] provides an essential backdrop to understanding Thomas's

63. Augustine, *The Trinity* 5.1.6; see also Boethius, *De trinitate* 5.

64. Boethius, *De trinitate* 6.7–9; Bonaventure, *Breviloquium* 1.4.2; Thomas Aquinas, *Summa theologiae* Ia.28.3, *sed contra*. Boethius regards his work on the Trinity as "fruit" of "the seeds of argument" sown in his mind by Augustine's work on the Trinity (*De trinitate* prologue 31–33).

65. Augustine, *The Trinity* 5.1.4, 7.

66. Augustine, *The Trinity* 5.2.10 (emphasis original).

67. In similar fashion, John of Damascus links the tritheistic error of certain monophysite theologians to their undue allegiance to "St. Aristotle's" categories (*Contra jacobitas* 10; with Andrew Louth, "Late Patristic Developments in the East," in Emery and Levering, *Oxford Handbook of the Trinity*, 143).

68. Boethius, *Contra Eutychen et Nestorium* 3.4–5. Though not a direct commentary on Boethius's definition, Zacharias Ursinus's discussion of "person" provides a fairly representative Reformed account of the various features of personhood signaled by Boethius's definition:

Person is that which subsists, is individual, living, intelligent, incommunicable, not sustained in another, nor part of another. *Subsisting*, by which we mean that it is not an accident, or a thought, or a decree, or a vanishing sound, or a created quality or motion. *Individual*, that is, not man generically, but individually, as this man. *Living*, something different from that which is inanimate, as a stone. *Intelligent*, not irrational, as the animal, which although it may have life and feeling, is nevertheless devoid of personality. *Incommunicable*, it cannot be communicated, as the divine essence, which may be in more than one, and be common to more than one—personality, however, is incommunicable. *Not sustained by another*, because it subsists by itself; for the human

conception of divine persons as "subsisting relations." When Thomas addresses the questions of *whether* the term "person" applies to God and *how* the term "person" applies to God, and thereby unpacks his conception of divine persons as "subsisting relations," it is Boethius's definition of person that he has in mind.

The question of *whether* the term "person" applies to God is not a trivial one.[69] Taken in its ordinary application to humans, Boethius's definition of person might lead us to think of the three persons of the Trinity in a tritheistic manner—as three divine individuals with three distinct centers of consciousness whose relationship to one another is merely a matter of the common nature they share (e.g., as Peter and Paul share a common human nature) and the common agenda they engage (e.g., as Peter and Paul engage in a common apostolic mission). Despite its potential for misunderstanding, Thomas insists that the term "person" should be applied to God. Not only does the term have ecclesiastical warrant (Thomas here appeals to the so called Athanasian Creed)[70] but it is also useful in conveying the sense of Scripture and confuting heretics.[71] Furthermore, the term "person" signifies something *true* about God's most excellent being: because the term "person" signifies a perfection, and because God contains every perfection in a preeminent way, the term "person" "is fittingly applied to God."[72] The point is worth emphasizing: though we may derive the *term* "person" from ordinary human discourse, the *supreme meaning* of that term derives from God, the most perfect being.[73] Therefore, it is appropriate to apply the term "person" to God, provided that we apply it to him in a divine and not a creaturely way.[74]

Granted *that* the term "person" should be applied to God, the question remains concerning *how* it applies to God. Again, the question is not a trivial

---

nature of Christ is subsisting, individual, incommunicable, intelligent, and yet it is no person, because it is sustained by the Word. So the soul of man subsists by itself, is intelligent, and not sustained by another, and yet it is no person, for the reason that it is a part of another subsisting individual. It is, therefore, added in the definition, *nor part of another.* (*Commentary*, 130)

69. On the medieval debate regarding whether "person" primarily indicates substance or relation, see Gilles Emery, *The Trinitarian Theology of St. Thomas Aquinas*, trans. Francesca Aran Murphy (New York: Oxford University Press, 2007), 114–17.

70. Thomas Aquinas, *Summa theologiae* Ia.29.3, *sed contra*.

71. Thomas Aquinas, *Summa theologiae* Ia.29.3, ad 1.

72. Thomas Aquinas, *Summa theologiae* Ia.29.3, resp.; and *De potentia* 9.3; with Gilles Emery, "The Dignity of Being a Substance: Being, Subsistence, and Nature," *Nova et Vetera* 9 (2011): 991–1001.

73. Thomas Aquinas, *Summa theologiae* Ia.29.3, resp., ad 2–3. In making this point, Thomas assumes his earlier discussion of the nature of divine naming in Ia.13, on which see Rudi te Velde, *Aquinas on God: The "Divine Science" of the* Summa theologiae (Farnham, UK: Ashgate, 2006), chap. 4.

74. Contra Barth, *Church Dogmatics* I/1, 353–68.

one. We often speak of God as a "personal" God, implying that he knows us and loves us, that he speaks to us through his Word, and so forth. This is not (primarily at least) what it means to speak of the Father, the Son, and the Spirit as divine "persons," however.[75] Drawing on Boethius's venerable definition, Thomas argues that because "person" refers to a particular *individual*, that is, to that which *distinguishes* "this one" from "that one" within a common classification of nature, "person" must apply in God's case "relationship-wise" because it is the *relations of origin* that distinguish the three from one another.[76] In medieval terminology, it is the "personal properties" of the three that constitute them as divine persons.[77] *Paternity* is the Father's personal property because he and he alone is father *to* the Son. *Filiation* or *generation* is the Son's personal property because he and he alone is son *of* the Father. *Procession* is the Spirit's personal property because he and he alone proceeds *from* the Father and the Son.[78] Because personal properties are what distinguish the Father, the Son, and the Spirit from one another, Thomas defines divine persons as "subsisting *relations*."

This is not the whole story, however, and here we may appreciate more fully what it means to apply the term "person" to God in a distinctively divine way. Because we are speaking of a *divine* person, that is, of a person who is the simple and self-existent God, Thomas defines a divine person as a "*subsisting* relation."[79] To grasp the point, we may contrast human paternity with divine paternity. When it comes to human persons, "paternity" is only an accidental property. One is a human person before and after one becomes a human father, and one can be a human person without ever becoming a human father. Paternity is, metaphysically speaking, an "add on" (to be sure, an important one!) to human persons. When it comes to God, however, God's *being God* and God's *being Father* "completely coincide."[80] The relation of

75. Rudi A. te Velde, "The Divine Person(s): Trinity, Person, and Analogous Naming," in Emery and Levering, *Oxford Handbook of the Trinity*, 359–61.

76. Thomas Aquinas, *Summa theologiae* Ia.29.4, *sed contra*.

77. Thomas Aquinas, *Summa theologiae* Ia.28.1, *sed contra*; Bonaventure, *Breviloquium* 1.3.6. The language of "personal properties" found its way into the Reformed confessions as well. See Westminster Larger Catechism, Q. 9–10.

78. These three "personal properties" are a subset of five "characteristics" or "notions" that exist in God: unbegottenness, paternity, filiation, spiration, and procession (see, e.g., Bonaventure, *Breviloquium* 1.3.1). Only paternity, filiation, and spiration count as personal properties because only these constitute *distinct relational features* of the persons. The Father's status as "unbegotten" is not a relational feature; it is the denial of one (i.e., he is *not* the Son). "Spiration," though indicating a relational feature, is not unique to any single person but is common to the Father and the Son who eternally breathe forth the Spirit as from one principle.

79. Thomas Aquinas, *Summa theologiae* Ia.29.4, resp.

80. Bavinck, *Reformed Dogmatics*, 2:305.

"paternity" *subsists* in God. God exists essentially and actually as God *the Father* of the Son, as God *the Son* of the Father, and as God *the Holy Spirit* who proceeds from them both; God has no concrete existence apart from his threefold subsistence as the Father, the Son, and the Holy Spirit. While each divine person is *really distinct from* the others on the basis of his personal property—the personal properties are "incommunicable"[81]—each divine person is *identical with* the self-existent being and essence of the one true God. God *is* three persons all the way down.[82]

With this conception of divine person in place, we may conclude this section with a summary of the personal properties and characteristics by which the three persons are identified and that manifest their distinct personal perfections.[83]

God the Father

The personal property of the Father is paternity: from eternity, the First Person of the Trinity is Father to his only begotten Son, who is the radiance of his glory and the exact imprint of his being (Heb. 1:3). With the Son, the Father shares the characteristic of spiration: from eternity, the Father and the Son breathe forth the Spirit, who shines forth in the glory of their mutual love. Paternity and spiration identify the Father as the *principle* or fontal source of the Son and (with the Son) of the Spirit. The Father is also characterized by the fact that he is unbegotten or without principle, but this is more a statement of what he is not (i.e., the Son) than it is a statement about his personal perfection.

When it comes to the Father's status as principle of the Son and the Spirit, we must speak of the Father as a "principle without priority." The Father is the fontal source of the Son and the Spirit, and these relations manifest his distinct personal perfection. However, the Father's identity as fontal source of the Son and the Spirit is not (even logically) *prior* to the existence of the Son and the Spirit but is rather constituted *by* his eternal relations to the Son and the Spirit.[84] "The original plenitude of the Father is not a potentiality of the divine essence that would find some kind of partial actuation through the generation of the Son and in the procession of the Spirit. The plenitude and

81. The "incommunicable" nature of the divine personal properties reflects Richard of St. Victor's modification of Boethius's definition of person (*On the Trinity* 4.6, 18), a modification adopted by Thomas Aquinas (*Summa theologiae* Ia.29.4, ad 4).

82. Canon 2 of the Fourth Lateran Council (1215) condemned any attempt to construe the common substance of the persons as a fourth entity within the Trinity.

83. For the distinction between personal properties and characteristics, see note 78 above.

84. For an introduction to medieval debate over this point, see Russell L. Friedman, *Medieval Trinitarian Thought from Aquinas to Ockham* (Cambridge: Cambridge University Press, 2010).

fruitfulness of the Father are perfectly actualized and are entirely manifested in these two eternal acts of the Father."[85] For this reason, we cannot ascribe any priority to the Father in relation to the Son and the Spirit in terms of either being or hierarchy.

God the Son

The personal property of the Son is filiation or generation: from eternity, the Second Person of the Trinity subsists as the Son, Word, and radiance of the Father: light of light, true God of true God, consubstantial with the Father.

> He is the true, proper, and natural Son of God, begotten from the essence of the Father. And if he is begotten from the essence of God, the same is, therefore, communicated to him whole and entire, since the divine essence is infinite, indivisible, and not communicated in part. Therefore, inasmuch as the Son has the whole essence communicated to him, he is, for this reason, equal with the Father, and, consequently, true God.[86]

With the Father, the Son shares the characteristic of spiration: he too breathes forth the Spirit. Filiation and spiration identify the Son as perfect filial product of the Father and common principle of the Spirit.

Speaking appropriately of the Son as the perfect filial "product" of the Father demands great care. The Nicene Creed confesses in this regard that the Son is "begotten not made," signaling the vital distinction that exists between the eternal generation of the Son and the temporal production of creatures and requiring that the latter not be treated as the measure of the former. Whereas the Son is generated *within* the divine being, creatures are produced *outside* the divine being. Furthermore, unlike the process of human begetting, the eternal generation of the Son is "without passion, partition, division, and temporality."[87] Though the Scriptures compel us in various ways

---

85. Emmanuel Durand, "A Theology of God the Father," in Emery and Levering, *Oxford Handbook of the Trinity*, 382. For further discussion of the fatherhood of God from a Thomistic perspective, see the excellent study of John Baptist Ku, *God the Father in the Theology of St. Thomas Aquinas* (New York: Peter Lang, 2013).

86. Ursinus, *Commentary*, 193. There is a long history of debate in Reformed dogmatics about (1) whether eternal generation is what constitutes the Son's personhood and, if so, (2) what eternal generation entails. The latter debate concerns whether eternal generation involves a communication of the divine essence from the Father to the Son. The majority argues that it does, and a notable minority argues that it does not. For the history of this debate, along with a sophisticated but ultimately unconvincing case for the minority position, see Brannon Ellis, *Calvin, Classical Trinitarianism, and the Aseity of the Son* (Oxford: Oxford University Press, 2012).

87. Basil of Caesarea, *Against Eunomius* 2.16.

to affirm the eternal generation of the Son, and though the Scriptures furnish us with various paradigms or illustrations of this glorious reality,

> they cannot set forth a full and accurate determination of the mode of this generation. Hence here (if anywhere) we must be wise with sobriety so that content with the fact (*tō hoti*) (which is clear in the Scriptures), we should not anxiously busy our thoughts with defining or even searching into the mode (which is altogether incomprehensible), but leave it to God who alone most perfectly knows himself.[88]

God the Holy Spirit

The personal property of the Spirit is procession: from eternity, the Third Person of the Trinity subsists as the Spirit of the Father (Matt. 10:20) and of his Son (Gal. 4:6). Like the Son, the procession of the Spirit is an eternal communication of the divine essence that is internal to the being of God (1 Cor. 2:11); unlike the Son, the procession of the Spirit flows from two persons rather than from one, albeit as from one spirating principle.[89] As the Spirit of the Father and the Son, the Spirit is the perfect product of their mutual love,[90] being in his person the glory of the love they shared before the foundation of the world (John 17:5, 24; with Matt. 3:16–17). He is therefore in his person the bond that completes the "perfect fecundity" that is God's tripersonal nature.[91]

The dual procession of the Spirit continues to be a source of significant controversy between Eastern and Western churches.[92] With the rest of the Western church, Reformed churches historically have confessed that the Spirit proceeds from the Father and from the Son.[93] In appropriating this confession, Reformed dogmatics must differentiate between ecclesiastical and theological

---

88. Turretin, *Institutes of Elenctic Theology* 3.29.31.

89. Augustine, *The Trinity* 5.3.15; 15.5.29; 6.47–48; Turretin, *Institutes of Elenctic Theology* 3.31.1–3.

90. Thomas Aquinas, *Summa theologiae* Ia.37.2.

91. Thomas Aquinas, *Summa theologiae* Ia.27.5, ad 3.

92. For a recent account of the history, see A. Edward Siecienski, *The Filioque: History of a Doctrinal Controversy* (Oxford: Oxford University Press, 2010).

93. For example, Westminster Confession of Faith, 2.3. Reformed theologians have engaged in significant attempts at rapprochement with the East. See, e.g., Jürgen Moltmann, "Theological Proposals Toward the Resolution of the *Filioque* Controversy," in *Spirit of God, Spirit of Christ*, ed. Lukas Vischer (London: SPCK, 1981), 164–73; and Thomas F. Torrance, *Trinitarian Perspectives: Toward Doctrinal Agreement* (Edinburgh: T&T Clark, 1994); idem, ed., *Theological Dialogue between Orthodox and Reformed Churches*, vol. 1 (Edinburgh: Scottish Academic Press, 1985); idem, ed., *Theological Dialogue between Orthodox and Reformed Churches*, vol. 2 (Edinburgh: Scottish Academic Press, 1993).

issues. The former issue concerns whether the dual procession of the Spirit warrants ecclesiastical division. The latter issue concerns whether the dual procession of the Spirit constitutes a valid interpretation of Scripture. Turretin well distinguishes and summarizes what is at stake:

> Although the Greeks ought not to have been charged with heresy on account of their opinion, nor ought it to have been the occasion of a schism arising or continuing, still the opinion of the Latins may be properly retained as more agreeable to the words of Scripture and the truer. (1) The Holy Spirit is sent from the Son as well as from the Father (John 16:7). He therefore ought to proceed from him because he cannot be sent by the Son unless he proceeds from him. (2) He is called the Spirit of the Son as well as the Father (Gal. 4:6). (3) Whatever the Spirit has, he has from the Son no less than from the Father (John 16:13–15), and as the Son is said to be from the Father because he does not speak of himself, but of the Father (from whom he receives all things), so the Spirit ought to be said to be and to proceed from the Son because he hears and speaks from him. (4) He breathed the Holy Spirit on his disciples in time (John 20:22). Therefore he breathed him from eternity; for temporal procession presupposes an eternal.[94]

Three Applications of Trinitarian Doctrine

It would be perverse to construct a doctrine of the Trinity on the basis of its perceived relevance to the needs of creatures rather than from the resources of divine self-revelation. Nonetheless, because the doctrine of the Trinity is the supreme mystery of revelation, it has much light to shed on a host of doctrinal and practical matters. In drawing the present chapter toward its conclusion, we may mention three.

The Trinity and Divine Perfection

As noted in the introduction, the revisionist program of modern trinitarian theology sought to detach reflection on the three persons from classical understandings of God's simple perfection in its quest for "a new formulation of the concept of God." In doing so, it committed a twofold error. Not only did it fail to grasp how integral God's simple perfection is to the church's confession of God as Trinity;[95] it also failed to appreciate the way in which the

94. Turretin, *Institutes of Elenctic Theology* 3.31.5. See also Dolf te Velde, ed., *Synopsis Purioris Theologiae/Synopsis of a Purer Theology: Latin Text and English Translation* (Leiden: Brill, 2014), 9.19–20.

95. To put the matter baldly: there was and is no need for the doctrine of the Trinity if God is not simple, for there were and are plenty of sophisticated and unsophisticated ways

doctrine of the Trinity enriches our understanding of God's simple perfection. The Trinity reveals to us that God's perfect nature is at once *indivisible* (i.e., simple) *and* supremely *communicable*. Thus Bonaventure: "The first and supreme Principle, by the very fact of its being first, is utterly simple; by the very fact that it is supreme, utterly perfect. Being utterly perfect, it communicates itself with total perfection; being utterly simple, it remains completely undivided."[96] He also states:

> Now our thought would not be the most elevated if we did not believe that God could communicate himself in the most complete way, and it would not be the most loving if, believing him to be able, we thought him unwilling to do so. Hence, if we are to think of God most loftily and most lovingly, faith tells us that God totally communicates himself by eternally having a beloved and another who is loved by both. In this way God is both one and three.[97]

Given the bliss that characterizes God's tripersonal life of communication and communion, we may better appreciate why God's external works in creation and redemption cannot possibly add anything to God's perfection. Moreover, we may better appreciate how these works extend God's blessedness to others, manifesting the glory of God's triune grace.[98] This leads to our second application.

The Trinity and Divine Action

As Gilles Emery suggests, a better understanding of the Trinity leads to a deeper understanding of divine action because "God acts according to what he is in himself."[99] God's triune identity informs our understanding of God's triune action in two areas, both of which specify in different ways how the three persons relate to one another within the context of their indivisible activity toward creatures. (1) *The doctrine of appropriations* helps us to appreciate why the Scriptures characteristically appropriate (for example) the act of predestination to the Father (Eph. 1:4–6; 1 Pet. 1:1–2; etc.) even though each divine person is an agent of this act (John 6:70; 13:18; 1 Cor. 2:7–11; etc.). The reason distinct divine acts are appropriated to distinct divine persons is not

of conceiving how three persons may comprise one complex divine being or community. For a recent dogmatic argument regarding the importance of divine simplicity for understanding the divine persons, see James E. Dolezal, "Trinity, Simplicity, and the Status of God's Personal Relations," *International Journal of Systematic Theology* 16 (2014): 79–98.
96. Bonaventure, *Breviloquium* 1.3.2 (translation altered).
97. Bonaventure, *Breviloquium* 1.2.3.
98. Thomas Aquinas, *Summa theologiae* Ia.32.2, ad 3.
99. Gilles Emery, *The Trinity: An Introduction to Catholic Doctrine on the Triune God*, trans. Matthew Levering (Washington, DC: Catholic University of America Press, 2011), 161.

because God's actions toward his creatures are divided between the persons: *opera Trinitatis ad extra indivisa sunt*. The reason is due to the ways in which the personal properties and characteristics of the three manifest themselves within their common, indivisible action. Thus as the Father is the principle of the Son and the Spirit, his personal character shines forth in a special way in predestination, the principle act of the Trinity in salvation. Similarly, because the Son is eternally generated by the Father and because he eternally breathes forth the Spirit, the Son's personal character shines forth in a special way in the work of redemption, since the work of redemption flows from divine predestination and issues in the work of sanctification (Eph. 1:3–14). Finally, because the Spirit eternally proceeds from the Father and the Son as the personal bond of God's tripersonal perfection, his personal character shines forth in a special way in the work of sanctification, since the work of sanctification brings the works of predestination and adoption to their divinely appointed goal (Eph. 1:4; 5:27), making us a habitation for the Triune God (John 14:16–17, 23).

More clearly than in the doctrine of appropriations, (2) *the doctrine of divine missions* reveals how the mystery of God's tripersonal being shines forth in God's tripersonal actions toward his creatures. As noted earlier in the discussion of the "personal names" of the Trinity, the sending of the Son to redeem us and the outpouring of the Spirit to sanctify us follow a very specific pattern: the Father sends the Son to accomplish his redemptive mission, and the Father, with the Son, sends the Spirit to accomplish his sanctifying mission. This missional pattern in turn corresponds to the relations of origin that constitute the divine persons: the Father eternally generates the Son and the Father, with the Son, eternally breathes the Spirit. As insightful as this correspondence is, it does not fully capture the wonderful reality expressed in the doctrine of the divine missions. The relations of origin constitute the "whence" of the divine missions, the latter being the temporal embassy and extension of the former. The relations of origin also constitute the "whither" of the divine missions insofar as they provide the divine exemplars and goals of those missions: the goal of the Son's redemptive mission is to make *us* sons and daughters in order that *he* might be the firstborn among many brothers and sisters (Rom. 8:29; Gal. 4:5); the goal of the Spirit's sanctifying mission is to embrace *us* within the fellowship of the Father and the Son, pouring out the Father's love into our hearts (Rom. 5:5), and awakening within us the Son's filial cry of "Abba! Father!" (Gal. 4:6). Formally stated, we may summarize the law of God's triune action as follows: the internal relations of the Trinity are inflected in their undivided external operations, even as the external operations of the Trinity extend their internal relations to elect creatures.[100]

---

100. *Knowledge* of this law follows from contemplation of God's triune name as revealed in Holy Scripture, not from transcendental arguments derived from the economic surface of

The Trinity and Communion with God

As God's triune identity informs our understanding of God's triune action, so must it inform our understanding of that action's blessed consequence: our communion with God. No Reformed theologian has reflected more fully on the trinitarian shape of communion with God than John Owen in his work *Of Communion with God the Father, Son, and Holy Ghost*, an extensive theological-spiritual commentary on the trinitarian benediction found in 2 Corinthians 13:14. According to Owen, communion with God consists in "his *communication of himself unto us, with our returnal unto him* of that which he requireth and accepteth, flowing from that *union* which in Jesus Christ we have with him."[101] Although the three persons act inseparably in the gracious work of restoring us to communion with God, we nevertheless enjoy communion with each person distinctly in accordance with the ways in which each person distinctly shines forth in this gracious work. We have communion with the Father in love, communion with the Son in grace, and communion with the Holy Spirit in consolation.[102]

Conclusion

This chapter does not pretend to explain the mystery of the blessed Trinity, which must forever remain "exalted above all blessing and praise" (Neh. 9:5).

> For the divinity is not handed down through logical demonstration and arguments, as has been said, but by faith and by pious reasoning with reverence. If Paul preached the saving cross *not in the wisdom of words, but in the demonstration of spirit and power* [1 Cor. 2:4], and *he heard secret words* in paradise *which it is not possible to speak* [2 Cor. 12:4], then who can make declarations about the Holy Trinity?[103]

Acknowledging the limitations of human speech and reason need not quench our ambition to know God's triune name, however, since God has bid us to

---

divine action. See Nicholas Healy, "Karl Barth, German-Language Theology, and the Catholic Tradition," in *Trinity and Election in Contemporary Theology*, ed. Michael Dempsey (Grand Rapids: Eerdmans, 2011), 237–43.

101. John Owen, *Of Communion with God the Father, Son, and Holy Ghost*, in *The Works of John Owen*, vol. 2, ed. William H. Goold (Edinburgh: Banner of Truth, 1965), 8–9 (emphasis original).

102. Ibid., 9–17. Space precludes further comment upon Owen's great work, for which a commendation to read is at any rate more important.

103. Athanasius, *Letters to Serapion* 1.20.3 (emphasis original).

seek his face (Ps. 27:8), and since it is through the revelation of this name that the blessed Trinity graciously extends the bliss of his perfect life to us, perfecting our creaturely lives through fellowship with his: the life of the Father, and of the Son, and of the Holy Spirit.[104]

104. I am grateful to Fred Sanders for offering helpful comments on an earlier draft of this chapter.

5

Covenant of Redemption

SCOTT R. SWAIN

Introduction

In turning to the doctrine of God's eternal decree, and specifically to its christo-logical concentration in the covenant of redemption, we direct our attention to the infinite (and hence unsearchable) depths of God's wisdom and judgments, from which all of God's works flow, by which they move, and to which they run (Rom. 11:33–36). Under the guidance of Holy Scripture, this tract of Christian teaching instructs us to trace all things back to the one "who works all things according to the counsel of his will" (Eph. 1:11) and who directs all things toward their consummation in Jesus Christ to the praise of his glory (Eph. 1:10–12). The doctrine of the decree does not concern the beginning of God, because God has no beginning.[1] The doctrine of the decree concerns the beginning of all things that exist outside of God. In more technical idiom: the divine decree is the internal work of the Triune God (*opera Dei interna*) that moves and directs the external works of the Triune God (*operationes Dei externae*). Thus understood, the divine decree functions as a hinge between theology's two great themes: God and all things in relation to God. The decree is both the free expression of God's

I am grateful to Howard Griffith and Laurence O'Donnell for offering helpful comments on an earlier draft of the present chapter.

1. Karl Barth, *Church Dogmatics* II/2, ed. T. F. Torrance and G. W. Bromiley (Edinburgh: T&T Clark, 1965), 102.

triune perfection, which is its principle and source, and the eternal foundation of the economy of nature, grace, and glory, which is its effect.

Though integrally related due to the simplicity of the divine decree, the covenant of redemption (also called the "counsel of peace" and the "*pactum salutis*") may be distinguished conceptually from God's decree regarding the creation and providential government of creatures, and also from God's decree regarding the election and reprobation of fallen human beings. As we will see more fully below, its specific focus is the eternal self-determination of the Triune God to manifest his glory in making sons and daughters of elect sinners through the mediation of Jesus Christ.

The doctrine of the covenant of redemption emerged as a distinct locus within Reformed systematic theology in the seventeenth century (ca. 1638–45) as the consequence of a complex array of exegetical and doctrinal influences and within the context of debates with Arminians and Socinians regarding the nature of saving grace.[2] Whether identified as a third covenant distinct from the covenant of works and the covenant of grace or as a subset of the latter, the covenant of redemption represents the pinnacle of Reformed thinking in the era of orthodoxy regarding the eternal foundation of our salvation in Jesus Christ.[3] More recently, the doctrine has been subjected to severe criticism, often by voices from within Reformed theology.[4] Some conclude that the doctrine is the fruit of vain speculation, lacking in biblical warrant: "To speak concretely of an intertrinitarian 'covenant' with terms and conditions between Father and Son mutually endorsed before the foundation of the world is to extend the bounds of scriptural evidence beyond propriety."[5] Others argue that the doctrine is implicitly tritheistic and that it rests on a metaphysical conception of God insufficiently informed by the gospel.[6] Karl

2. Carl R. Trueman, *The Claims of Truth: John Owen's Trinitarian Theology* (Carlisle, UK: Paternoster, 1998), 133–39, 206–26; idem, "From Calvin to Gillespie on Covenant: Mythological Excess or an Exercise in Doctrinal Development?," *International Journal of Systematic Theology* 11 (2009): 378–97; Willem J. van Asselt, *The Federal Theology of Johannes Cocceius* (Leiden: Brill, 2001), chap. 10 and appendix 1; Richard A. Muller, "Toward the *Pactum Salutis*: Locating the Origins of a Concept," *Mid-America Journal of Theology* 18 (2007): 11–65.

3. See, e.g., Herman Witsius, *The Economy of the Covenants between God and Man: Comprehending a Complete Body of Divinity* (Kingsburg, CA: den Dulk Christian Foundation, 1990); and Francis Turretin, *Institutes of Elenctic Theology*, ed. James T. Dennison Jr., trans. George Musgrave Giger (Phillipsburg, NJ: P&R, 1992), 12.2.11.

4. A helpful survey of and response to such criticisms may be found in J. Mark Beach, "The Doctrine of the *Pactum Salutis* in the Covenant Theology of Herman Witsius," *Mid-America Journal of Theology* 13 (2002): 101–42.

5. O. Palmer Robertson, *The Christ of the Covenants* (Phillipsburg, NJ: P&R, 1980), 54.

6. Barth, *Church Dogmatics* IV/1, 65; Robert Letham, *The Westminster Assembly: Reading Its Theology in Historical Context* (Phillipsburg, NJ: P&R, 2009), 235–36.

Barth's reformulated doctrine of election provides the most notable and influential consequence of this line of criticism.[7] Although these objections to the covenant of redemption are serious, they are not insurmountable, not least because many contemporary objections rest on misunderstanding and caricature,[8] but, more important, also because the doctrine exhibits a faithful biblical judgment regarding the merciful purpose of the Triune God—from whom, through whom, and to whom all things proceed.

The goal of this chapter is to expound the doctrine of the *pactum salutis*, the most glorious branch in the tree of life that springs from God's free and sovereign decree.[9] The following dogmatic thesis will guide our discussion: *The covenant of redemption is the eternal self-determination of the blessed Trinity, who wills to communicate the bliss of his triune life to elect sinners through the mediation of Jesus Christ for the glory of Jesus Christ. The doctrine is a faithful conceptual gloss of biblical teaching regarding the eternal appointment of the Son of God, by way of covenant, to become the incarnate redeemer and head of his adopted siblings. Because it faithfully renders the eternal mystery of our salvation, once hidden but now revealed through the gospel, the doctrine not only orients our understanding of the broader economy of God's works to its divine source, but it also enables us to perceive that economy in relation to its trinitarian and christological ends.*

First, we will address the identity of the decreeing God in general, considering the one who is the author and end of the covenant of redemption. Next, we will consider the doctrine of the *pactum salutis* in particular, providing an overview of its basic features and addressing two major contemporary objections to the doctrine that have arisen from within Reformed dogmatics. Finally, we will round out our discussion by considering how this doctrine contributes to a fuller appreciation of the christological ends of God's decree.

7. Barth, *Church Dogmatics* II/2, and IV/1, 63–66. More recently, see Myk Habets, "There Is No God behind the Back of Jesus Christ," in *Evangelical Calvinism: Essays Resourcing the Continuing Reformation of the Church*, ed. Myk Habets and Bobby Grow (Eugene, OR: Wipf & Stock, 2012), 173–97. For the reception and debate surrounding Barth's reformulation of the doctrine of election, particularly as his reformulation impinges on the doctrine of God, see Michael T. Dempsey, ed., *Trinity and Election in Contemporary Theology* (Grand Rapids: Eerdmans, 2011); and Scott R. Swain, *The God of the Gospel: Robert Jenson's Trinitarian Theology* (Downers Grove, IL: IVP Academic, 2013), chap. 2.

8. Beach, "Doctrine of the *Pactum Salutis*," 137. See also Richard A. Muller, "God as Absolute and Relative, Necessary, Free, and Contingent: The *Ad Intra–Ad Extra* Movement of Seventeenth-Century Reformed Language about God," in *Always Reformed: Essays in Honor of W. Robert Godfrey*, ed. R. Scott Clark and Joel E. Kim (Escondido, CA: Westminster Seminary California), 56–73.

9. The imagery, if not the precise point, is that of Jerome Zanchius, *Absolute Predestination* (Grand Rapids: Sovereign Grace, 1971), 24.

The Decreeing God

The blessed Trinity is the decreeing God. The covenant of redemption is the consequence of *his* good pleasure: the one who *is* Father, Son, and Spirit eternally wills to become *our* Father, through the Son, in the Spirit, to the praise of his glorious grace. To appreciate the nature of the *pactum salutis*, we must consider more closely the identity of the decreeing God and, specifically, the nature of his decretive will.

God's sovereign will is the first and supreme cause of all things that come to pass outside of God in nature, grace, and glory. The apostle Paul blesses the God and Father of our Lord Jesus Christ "who works all things according to the counsel of his will" (Eph. 1:11). In similar fashion, the saints on high praise the Lord God Almighty who brought all things into being by his will (Rev. 4:11), and they bless the Lamb who has proven himself worthy "to take the scroll and to open its seals"—to effect God's sovereign decree for history—through his sacrificial death (Rev. 5:9). The psalmist declares, "The counsel of the Lord stands forever, the plans of his heart to all generations" (Ps. 33:11). Following on biblical teaching such as this, Christian theology came to regard the causal relationship between the divine will and the divine economy as a defining feature of orthodox Christianity over against both heathen and heretical viewpoints. Basil of Caesarea blames the failures of Greek philosophers "to explain nature" on their refusal to rise to the acknowledgment "that an intelligent cause presided at the birth of the universe."[10] Conversely, Augustine rebukes the Manichees for attempting to ascend beyond "the causes of God's will" in explaining the cosmos "when God's will is itself the cause of everything."[11] Jerome Zanchius well summarizes the broad consensus of Christian teaching on this point: "The will of God is so the cause of all things, as to be itself without cause, for nothing can be the cause of that which is the cause of everything. So that the Divine will is the *ne plus ultra* of all our inquiries: when we ascend to that, we can go no farther."[12]

Some worry that using the language of "causality" to describe God's relation to the world threatens to distort gospel teaching about God by means of an alien natural theology and to import an unhealthy determinism into the God-world relation.[13] This worry need not distract us for two reasons. First,

10. Basil of Caesarea, *The Hexaemeron*, in vol. 8 of *Nicene and Post-Nicene Fathers*, series 2, ed. Philip Schaff and Henry Wace (Grand Rapids: Eerdmans, 1980), 1.2.

11. Augustine, *The Literal Meaning of Genesis*, in *On Genesis*, trans. Edmund Hill (Hyde Park, NY: New City, 2002), 1.2.4.

12. Zanchius, *Absolute Predestination*, 16–17.

13. Colin E. Gunton, *The Triune Creator: A Historical and Systematic Study* (Grand Rapids: Eerdmans, 1998), 146–56. More recently, Habets, "There Is No God behind the Back of Jesus Christ," 177.

Christian theology's use of causal language in the doctrine of God's decree follows from New Testament usage of that language.[14] Second, causal language is theologically underdetermined. That is to say, causal language, in and of itself, does not entail specific theological judgments about the God-world relation. Evidence of this may be seen in that Thomas Aquinas, John Duns Scotus, Francisco Suárez, Simon Episcopius, Francis Turretin, René Descartes, Benedict Spinoza, and Jonathan Edwards all used causal language and causal analysis in articulating quite different understandings of the God-world relation with quite different senses of what it might or might not mean to say that God's sovereign will is responsible for everything that comes to pass.[15] It is one thing to assert that the divine will is the first and supreme cause of God's external works and quite another thing to characterize that will appropriately.

What then may be said about the nature of the divine will that lies at the foundation of all things? Space permits only the briefest sketch of an answer.[16] (1) *Given divine simplicity, God's free and sovereign good pleasure concerning all things outside of himself is inseparable from the eternal pleasure he takes in himself as Father, Son, and Holy Spirit.* Because the blessed Trinity is the decreeing God, we must identify the love that produces and guides all creatures to their appointed ends with the love that resides in the Father, the Son, and the Holy Spirit. "God wills himself and his creatures with one and the same simple act."[17] (2) *Although God's will is simple, we may distinguish nevertheless between the various objects of his will: God himself on the one hand, and his creatures on the other hand.* Turretin explains, "Because good is either uncreated and infinite or finite and created, a twofold object can be assigned to the will: a primary (viz., God) as the infinite good; but the secondary (all created things out of God, holding the relation of finite good which also out of himself God wills, but not in the same manner)."[18] God

---

14. On which see Robert M. Grant, "Causation and 'The Ancient World View,'" *Journal of Biblical Literature* 83 (1964): 34–40; George E. Sterling, "Prepositional Metaphysics in Jewish Wisdom Speculation and Early Christological Hymns," *Studia Philonica Annual* 9 (1997): 219–38; Sean M. McDonough, *Christ as Creator: Origins of a New Testament Doctrine* (Oxford: Oxford University Press, 2009).

15. Kenneth C. Clatterbaugh, *The Causation Debate in Modern Philosophy, 1637–1739* (New York: Routledge, 1999); J. Martin Bac, *Perfect Will Theology: Divine Agency in Reformed Scholasticism as against Suárez, Episcopius, Descartes, and Spinoza* (Leiden: Brill, 2010).

16. For fuller discussion, see Thomas Aquinas, *Summa theologiae* Ia.19; Amandus Polanus, *Syntagma Theologiae Christianae* (Hanoviae, 1610), 1.4.6; and Turretin, *Institutes of Elenctic Theology* 3.14–18; 4.1–18. See also Herman Bavinck's fine overview of biblical teaching on this topic in *Reformed Dogmatics*, ed. John Bolt, trans. John Vriend, 4 vols. (Grand Rapids: Baker Academic, 2003–8), 2:343–47.

17. Bavinck, *Reformed Dogmatics*, 2:233.

18. Turretin, *Institutes of Elenctic Theology* 3.14.1.

wills himself and his creatures in one and the same simple act, but he does so in two different ways.

(3) *God eternally wills himself—that is, his most excellent being and his tripersonal subsistence as Father, Son, and Spirit—by his necessary or natural will, not by his decretive will.* By nature the Triune God eternally and necessarily delights in himself: God cannot fail to affirm his own perfect existence, nor can he will his nonexistence.[19] Although the necessity of God's self-affirmation is therefore absolute, this necessity does not arise from external compulsion or from internal poverty but is concomitant with the spontaneity in which God eternally reposes in himself as Father, Son, and Holy Spirit.[20] (4) *God wills all things outside of himself by virtue of his free and sovereign decree.* Here a couple of qualifications are in order. (a) As in God's natural and necessary will in relation to himself, God's decretive will in relation to his external works is characterized by spontaneity: God is not moved by external compulsion or internal indigence to decree what he decrees. (b) However, because the object of God's decretive will is the creature and not the blessed Trinity, God's decretive will is not merely *spontaneous*, but it is also *undetermined* ("indifferent"): God is free to decree or to refrain from decreeing the world ("liberty of contradiction"), and God is free to decree this or that world ("liberty of contrariety").[21] The undetermined nature of God's decretive will follows both from his infinite power, which presents to the divine will an infinite range of possibilities that it may freely enact or refrain from enacting,[22] and from his infinite self-sufficiency, as Turretin states: "This indifference of the divine will, so far from lowering the majesty of God, is the greatest proof of his perfection who, as an independent being, needs nothing out of himself."[23] Thus while spontaneity is consistent with necessity of nature, the kind of freedom that characterizes God's decretive will is not: "For only one thing results from a natural active thing, while a voluntary active thing can produce different things."[24]

God's decretive will may be further specified in terms of its relationship to the works that follow therefrom and in terms of its relationship to its

19. Amandus Polanus, *Syntagma*, 1.4.6.12; Turretin, *Institutes of Elenctic Theology* 3.14.
20. Bonaventure, *Disputed Questions on the Mystery of the Trinity* 7.a.1–2.
21. Turretin, *Institutes of Elenctic Theology* 3.14.3, 5–6; 4.1.13, 2.13. See also Muller, "God as Absolute," 64.
22. Thomas Aquinas, *Compendium of Theology*, trans. Richard J. Regan (Oxford: Oxford University Press, 2009), 1.96. See also Zanchius, *Absolute Predestination*, 12, 28–29.
23. Turretin, *Institutes of Elenctic Theology* 3.14.7.
24. Thomas Aquinas, *Compendium of Theology* 1.96. Similarly John Owen, *Christologia*, in *Works of John Owen*, ed. William H. Goold (Edinburgh: Banner of Truth, 1966), 1:59.

principle or source, that is, God's triune perfection. (5) *God's external works necessarily follow from God's eternal decree due to his unchangeable purpose and infinite power.*[25] Following "Augustine and the schoolmen," Zanchius describes God's will as the "most omnipotent will" (*voluntus omnipotentissima*) "because whatever God wills cannot fail of being effected."[26] Again several qualifications are in order. (a) The necessity attached to the things decreed is not "absolute" but "hypothetical." On the supposition that God wills this or that, it must necessarily come to pass, given God's unchangeable purpose and unbounded power. But this or that does not come to pass because it necessarily emanates from God (God could have decreed otherwise), nor does this or that come to pass because all secondary causes operate via natural necessity (i.e., as causes that are predetermined in themselves to singular effects); though some secondary causes operate by natural necessity, many operate as free and contingent causes.[27] (b) Furthermore, while God's decree is unconditional in relation to the things he decrees, and while God does not decree one thing on the basis of his foreknowledge of another thing, nevertheless, in their temporal unfolding, the things God has decreed hold numerous causal relations relative to one another, and also serve as means and ends in relation to one another.[28] To say that God's decree is the first and unconditioned cause of all things outside himself is not to say that it is the only cause of all things outside of himself. Through his decree, God establishes secondary causes and commits himself to empowering and directing them to their appointed ends by cooperating with them through his providence.[29] (c) Finally, while all things outside of God necessarily follow from God's decree, some follow as things that he has decreed to do, others as things he has permitted to be done by secondary causes.[30] "So although sin necessarily follows the decree, it cannot be said to flow from the decree. The decree does not flow into the thing, nor is it effective of evil, but only permissive and directive."[31] In other words, God is not the author of sin.

(6) *The decree arises from the love of the Father for the Son in the Spirit, which is its sole principle, and directs all things to the love of the Father for*

25. Zanchius, *Absolute Predestination*, 25–28.

26. Ibid., 15.

27. Augustine, *The Literal Meaning of Genesis* 8.23.44; 8.24.45; 9.14.24–25; 9.17.32; Zanchius, *Absolute Predestination*, 22; William Perkins, *A Golden Chaine* (Edinburgh: Robert Walde-Grave, 1592), 6; Turretin, *Institutes of Elenctic Theology* 3.14.2; 4.2.13; 4.4.4.

28. Johannes Wollebius, *Compendium of Christian Theology*, 3.3.11, in *Reformed Dogmatics*, ed. John Beardslee (Eugene, OR: Wipf & Stock, 2009).

29. See John Webster's chapter on providence, chap. 7 in this book.

30. Amandus Polanus, *The Substance of Christian Religion* (London, 1595), 1.6.

31. Turretin, *Institutes of Elenctic Theology* 4.4.10.

the Son in the Spirit, which is their supreme end. The present statement can be divided into two points. (a) The divine decree concerning all things outside of God flows *from* the eternal love of the Triune God. As we noted above, the decree does not flow from God by natural necessity but requires the exercise of God's free choice. However, as we also noted above, while we may distinguish the *objects* of God's will (i.e., God himself and God's creatures), God's will in itself is indivisible. Again to quote Herman Bavinck, "God wills himself and his creatures with one and the same simple act."[32] The divine love that decrees the production and perfection of creatures is thus to be understood as the free and faithful expression *of* the divine love that *is* God's eternal and triune bliss.[33]

The older dogmatics described the Trinity as the "principle" of the divine decree to make this precise point.[34] On the one hand, they spoke of the divine decree as the "cause" of all things outside of God and thereby introduced a *real distinction* between God and the things he brings into existence. On the other hand, they spoke of the Triune God as the "principle" of God's decree to indicate that *no real distinction* exists between God and his decree: the decree just *is* God in his free self-determination to create, guide, and perfect creatures. And here we may address Barth's great concern that describing God's decree as "absolute" (*decretum absolutum*) means that the decree is determined by an undefined, "naked," and therefore dark and menacing divine will.[35] Nothing could be farther from the truth. The language of the *decretum absolutum* does not apply to the relation between God and his decree but to the relation between God's decree and the things he decrees: as stated above, God's decree is "absolute" in the sense that it is unconditioned by his creatures. That said, it would be incorrect to say that God's decree is unconditioned by God.[36] Quite to the contrary: God's decree *is* God—the Triune God, resplendent in eternal goodness and glory—in his free self-determination to act outside of himself as the one he is. There is no other God "behind" God's decree than the blessed Trinity.

(b) By virtue of God's free and sovereign decree, all things outside of God flow *to* the eternal love of the Triune God.[37] Because God's decree is the free

32. Bavinck, *Reformed Dogmatics*, 2:233.
33. According to Owen, the intratrinitarian love and delight of the three persons is "the womb of all the eternal counsels of God" (Owen, *Christologia*, in *Works*, 1:60).
34. Turretin, *Institutes of Elenctic Theology* 4.1.12–16; Owen, *Christologia*, in *Works*, 1:59.
35. Barth asks, "How can the doctrine of predestination be anything but 'dark' and obscure if in its very first tenet, the tenet which determines all the rest, it can speak only of a *decretum absolutum*?" (*Church Dogmatics* II/2, 104).
36. Note Barth's worry in ibid., 134.
37. Along with Bavinck, I take exception to the tradition of describing the ultimate end of all things as the glorification of God's mercy in election and the glorification of God's justice

expression of his sovereign will, it is a purposive act: "everything acting by its intellect and will acts for the sake of an end."[38] Moreover, because God's inherent goodness is the supreme object of his will, God's goodness is also the supreme end toward which he directs all that he decrees: "God doth all things for himself. He can have no ultimate end in anything but himself alone, unless there should be any thing better than himself or above himself."[39] That said, it is important to emphasize that God does not decree all things in order to *increase* his goodness (which would be impossible) but in order to *communicate* to creatures a share in his goodness.[40] Thus Wilhelmus à Brakel: "God is all-sufficient in himself, having had no need to create any of his creatures. The creature can neither add glory nor felicity to him; however, it pleased the Lord to create creatures in order to communicate his goodness to them and consequently to render them happy."[41] We should add here that God takes particular delight in his eternal decree to bless creatures in this way.[42] The end of God's decree is to manifest his glory by communicating to us a share in his goodness, and God *delights in* his decree to manifest his glory by communicating to us a share in his goodness.

The present point has special application to God's decree regarding humans. According to John Owen, God's distinctly *trinitarian* goodness and glory is the ultimate end of his decree to create and redeem humans. Owen states, "Man was peculiarly created unto the glory of the Trinity,

in reprobation (Bavinck, *Reformed Dogmatics*, 2:389). The glorification of God's saving love toward sinners is *a* great end indeed, but it is not *the* greatest end toward which God directs all things: that honor belongs to the glory of the Father's love for the Son in the Spirit. To put matters this way, I should add, is not to fall prey to the sentimental modern trap of elevating divine love over the other divine perfections for the simple reason that what the Father loves in the Son, and what the Father desires to put on display in and before all creatures, is the full array of divine perfections as they shine forth in the one who is the radiance of his glory and the exact imprint of his being (Heb. 1:3). The question naturally arises, though, how it can be said that *all things* flow to the love of the Triune God when God decrees that some creatures will inherit eternal condemnation for their sins. Following Tony Lane, we may suggest that even God's wrath is an aspect of God's love: while God's wrath on impenitent sinners may not be an exhibition of love *toward those sinners*, it is nevertheless an exhibition of the Father's love *for the Son* (Ps. 2) and *for those who are elect in the Son* (Ps. 36:10–12) (Lane, "The Wrath of God as an Aspect of the Love of God," in *Nothing Greater, Nothing Better: Theological Essays on the Love of God*, ed. Kevin J. Vanhoozer [Grand Rapids: Eerdmans, 2001], 138–67).

38. Thomas Aquinas, *Compendium* 1.100.

39. John Owen, *Exercitation* 28.16 in *An Exposition of the Epistle to the Hebrews*, vol. 2, ed. W. H. Goold (Grand Rapids: Baker, 1980). See also Thomas Aquinas, *Compendium* 1.101.

40. Thomas Aquinas, *Compendium* 1.103; Turretin, *Institutes of Elenctic Theology* 3.14.8; Owen, *Exercitation* 28.16.

41. Wilhelmus à Brakel, *The Christian's Reasonable Service*, 4 vols., trans. Bartel Elshout (Grand Rapids: Reformation Heritage Books, 1992–95), 1:193–94.

42. See Owen's discussion in *Works*, 1:56–60.

or God as three in one. Hence in all things concerning him there is not only an intimation of those distinct subsistences, but also of their distinct actings with respect unto him."[43] In other words, the supreme end of God's decree regarding the creation and redemption of humans is to manifest the glorious bliss of his triune life by causing humans to share in the glorious bliss of his triune life. To put the matter in its native biblical idiom: the supreme end of all God's ways toward his creatures is that the Father's eternally begotten, eternally beloved Son might be preeminent as the firstborn among many redeemed siblings (Rom. 8:29; Col. 1:15–16; Heb. 1:2), "to the praise of his glorious grace, with which he has blessed us in the Beloved" (Eph. 1:6).[44]

God's eternal decree arises from the love of the Father for the Son in the Spirit, which is its principle and source, and directs all things to the love of the Father for the Son in the Spirit, which is their supreme end. The love of the Triune God is thus the alpha and the omega of all things outside of God. With our discussion of the decreeing God in place, we turn now to the *pactum salutis*, the divinely appointed means whereby God brings elect sinners out of the misery of Adam into the bliss of his beloved Son.

The Covenant of Redemption

We may locate the covenant of redemption within God's eternal decree via conceptual gloss on Ephesians 1:5–6: "He predestined us for adoption as sons through Jesus Christ unto himself, according to the purpose of his will, to the praise of his glorious grace with which he has blessed us in the beloved" (ESV, trans. altered). According to this text, the *efficient or impulsive cause* of predestination is "the purpose of his will," the *formal cause* of predestination is our "adoption as sons" in union with "the beloved" Son, and the *final cause* of predestination is "the praise of his glorious grace." Within this divine scheme, the covenant of redemption concerns the *means* or *instrumental cause* whereby the decree of predestination is to be executed: God ordains to accomplish his son-making purpose "through Jesus Christ." The covenant of redemption thus concerns the

43. Owen, *Exercitation* 28.8. Elsewhere Owen states, "When God designed the glorious work of recovering fallen man, he appointed two great means thereof: The one was, 'the giving his Son for them'; and the other was, 'the giving his Spirit to them.' And hereby a way was opened for the manifestation of the glory of the whole blessed Trinity; which is the utmost end of all the works of God" (*Pneumatologia or, A Discourse Concerning the Holy Spirit* [Philadelphia: Tower and Hogan, 1827], 12).
44. Swain, *God of the Gospel*, 157–61.

divinely ordained, messianic means whereby the Father, "for whom and by whom all things exist," seeks to manifest his glory by "bringing many sons to glory" (Heb. 2:10).[45]

What is the substance of this covenant? Turretin provides a representative statement:

> The pact between the Father and the Son contains the will of the Father giving his Son as *lytrōtēn* (Redeemer and head of his mystical body) and the will of the Son offering himself as sponsor for his members to work out redemption (*apolytrōsin*). For thus the Scriptures represent to us the Father in the economy of salvation as stipulating the obedience of the Son even unto death, and for it promising in return a name above every name that he might be the head of the elect in glory; the Son as offering himself to do the Father's will, promising a faithful and constant performance of the duty required of him and restipulating the kingdom and glory promised to him.[46]

According to this description, the covenant of redemption is characterized by four main features: (1) the will of the Father and of the Son, expressed by way of a covenant, regarding (2) the incarnate Son's obedience unto death (3) on behalf of his elect siblings, for whom he serves as redeemer and head, and (4) the eternal glory promised by the Father to the Son as a reward for his incarnate obedience.[47]

Points (2) and (4) are the least disputed among catholic Christians, given the broad scriptural attestation to the Son's redemptive work as a work of obedience to his Father and to the Son's ensuing glory as his Father's reward for that obedience (e.g., Isa. 52:13–53:12; John 17:4–5; Phil. 2:6–11; Heb. 2:9; 5:7–8; etc.). Point (3), which concerns the representative nature of the Son's redeeming work, is more widely debated, with the Reformed limiting Christ's representation to his elect siblings and other systems of doctrine positing various models of universal representation. Because the debate over point (3) may be more profitably addressed in discussions of the accomplishment and application of redemption, we leave it to other chapters in the present

---

45. Owen, *Exercitation* 28.15.

46. Turretin, *Institutes of Elenctic Theology* 12.2.13. Witsius offers a description of the *pactum salutis* nearly identical to that of Turretin, whom he appears to follow (*Economy*, 1:165–66). See also Owen, *Exercitation* 28.8.

47. The role (or lack thereof) of the Holy Spirit in the *pactum salutis* has become a significant topic of discussion in more recent studies of the doctrine. For a helpful overview of the issues, as well as a presentation of the way Owen incorporates the Spirit within the *pactum*, see Laurence R. O'Donnell III, "The Holy Spirit's Role in John Owen's 'Covenant of the Mediator' Formulation: A Case Study in Reformed Orthodox Formulations of the *Pactum Salutis*," *Presbyterian and Reformed Journal* 4 (2012): 91–115.

volume to address those topics.[48] As noted in the introduction to the present chapter, point (1) has become a source of contention in more recent Reformed dogmatics. The question concerns whether or not it is dogmatically appropriate to root the Son's redeeming work on behalf of his people, as well as its accompanying reward, within an eternal pact between the Father and the Son. This question has a hermeneutical dimension: Does the doctrine have biblical warrant, and what does it mean to say that the doctrine has biblical warrant? This question also has a theological dimension insofar as some worry that the *pactum salutis* implies tritheism. In the two sections that follow, we will address both dimensions of the question.

The Covenant of Redemption as Biblical Reasoning

Before addressing the biblical bases of the covenant of redemption, we must consider two potential pitfalls that are to be avoided. On the one hand, there is the pitfall of *overinterpretation*. According to Owen, we must "carefully avoid all curiosity, or vain attempts to be wise above what is written." On the other hand, there is the pitfall of *underinterpretation*. Again, according to Owen, we must "study with sober diligence to declare and give light unto what is revealed" in the Scriptures concerning this doctrine, "to the end that we should so increase in knowledge as to be established in faith and obedience."[49] We noted earlier that contemporary critics of the doctrine, such as O. Palmer Robertson, believe that the doctrine extends "the bounds of scriptural evidence beyond propriety."[50] Seventeenth-century proponents of the doctrine would likely charge its modern critics with failing to avoid the pitfall of underinterpretation, convinced as they were that the doctrine is "expressly declared . . . in the Scripture."[51] Given the controversy that exists among Reformed interpreters regarding the doctrine's biblical bases, the task of dogmatics in

48. See also David Gibson and Jonathan Gibson, ed., *From Heaven He Came and Sought Her: Definite Atonement in Historical, Biblical, Theological, and Pastoral Perspective* (Wheaton: Crossway, 2013); and Richard Muller, *Calvin and the Reformed Tradition: On the Work of Christ and the Order of Salvation* (Grand Rapids: Baker Academic, 2012).
49. Owen, *Exercitation* 27.1. Likewise, James Durham cautions against applying the language of human covenant making univocally when considering the covenant of redemption ("Sermon 23," in Durham, *Christ Crucified: or, the Marrow of the Gospel Evidently Holden Forth in Seventy Two Sermons on the Whole Fifty Third Chapter of Isaiah*, 6th ed. [Glasgow: Archibald McLean and Joseph Galbraith, 1761], 149), and Bavinck warns against the propensity for "scholastic subtlety" in propounding this doctrine (*Reformed Dogmatics*, 3:213).
50. Robertson, *Christ of the Covenants*, 54.
51. Owen, *Exercitation* 27.1. Similarly, Turretin argues that the doctrine of the covenant of redemption may be "plainly gathered from the Scriptures," and goes on to elaborate on the following texts as exegetical bases for the doctrine: Pss. 2:8; 110:4; Isa. 42:1, 6; 49:1–6, 8; 53:10; 61:2; Luke 22:29; John 17:4–5, 11, 17; Gal. 4:4; Heb. 10:5, 7 (*Institutes of Elenctic Theology*

relation to the covenant of redemption is not simply to indicate the biblical texts from which this doctrine arises but also to explicate, as far as possible, the pattern of biblical reasoning by which it emerges.

The doctrine of the *pactum salutis* follows from biblical teaching regarding the Father's eternal appointment of the Son, by way of covenant, to serve as mediator. The New Testament portrays the work of the Son incarnate as a mission he received from the Father (e.g., Mark 12:1–12; John 4:34; 5:30; 6:38; Gal. 4:4; Heb. 10:5–10) and as an appointment to an office, variously described under the title and functions of "servant of the Lord" (e.g., Matt. 12:18) and under the priestly, kingly, and prophetic functions of the Lord's "anointed" (e.g., Acts 2:34–36; 3:22–26; Heb. 5:5–6). The Son of God "gave himself for our sins," Paul declares, "according to the will of our God and Father" (Gal. 1:4). Furthermore, unlike prophets and apostles, who are consecrated to their offices from their mothers' wombs (Jer. 1:5; Gal. 1:15), the Son of God is consecrated to his office from eternity: he is one "whom the Father consecrated and sent into the world" (John 10:36) and the lamb "foreknown before the foundation of the world" (1 Pet. 1:20).[52] God *chose* us in Christ Jesus (Eph. 1:4) in accordance with "his own purpose and grace, which he *gave* us in Christ Jesus before the ages began" (2 Tim. 1:9; emphasis mine). Bavinck summarizes New Testament teaching in this regard: "To conceive of the work of Christ as the exercise of an office is to relate that work to the eternal counsel. He bears the name Messiah, Christ, the Anointed, because he has been ordained of the Father from eternity and has in time been anointed by him with the Holy Spirit."[53]

This is well and good. But by what warrants may we say that the Son's eternal messianic appointment occurs *per modum foederis*, "by way of covenant"? Certainly texts that describe the Son's eternal appointment to his incarnate mission (e.g., John 10:36; Eph. 1:4–5; 2 Tim. 1:9; 1 Pet. 1:20) do not contain the kind of covenantal language that would compel us to draw this conclusion. Whence, then, is biblical warrant for the *pactum salutis* derived? Wilhelmus à Brakel's response is instructive: "It will be easier to comprehend this matter if we primarily consider *the execution* of this covenant rather than *the decree from which it proceeds*. . . . The manner in which the Lord executes it *in this*

12.2.14). For an informative survey of the broader exegetical discussion surrounding the doctrine among Reformed orthodox interpreters, see Muller, "Toward the *Pactum Salutis*."

52. Following Simon Gathercole's study of Jesus's preexistence according to the Synoptic Gospels, we may suggest also that Jesus's "I have come" sayings (e.g., Mark 10:45) imply a preexistent appointment to his earthly mission (Gathercole, *The Preexistent Son: Recovering the Christologies of Matthew, Mark, and Luke* [Grand Rapids: Eerdmans, 2006]).

53. Herman Bavinck, *Our Reasonable Faith: A Survey of Christian Doctrine*, trans. Henry Zylstra (Grand Rapids: Baker, 1977), 333–34.

time state is consistent with the manner in which he *eternally decreed* it."[54] In other words, though the Scriptures are relatively reticent to speak of the Son's *eternal appointment* by the Father in covenantal terms, the Scriptures speak quite liberally about the Son's *historical execution* of that appointment in covenantal terms. And this language, when coupled with other biblical teaching about the eternal nature of the Son's messianic appointment, constitutes sufficient biblical warrant for the doctrine of the covenant of redemption.[55]

Two patterns of New Testament christological discourse confirm Brakel's observation. First, the New Testament speaks on a number of occasions of Jesus as one who is both *recipient* and *mediator* of the Father's covenant promises. In Luke 22:29, Jesus says, "I assign to you, as my Father assigned to me, a kingdom."[56] Similarly, in Acts 2:33, the ascended Jesus is described as one who has "received from the Father the promise of the Holy Spirit" in order to pour out the promised Spirit to his people. Furthermore, in Galatians 3:16–29, Jesus is described as the heir of the promises God made to Abraham and as the one in and through whom believers become heirs of the same covenant promises. Jesus is the one in whom all of God's promises are "yes" because he is at once the heir and the mediator of the Father's promised covenant blessings (2 Cor. 1:20–22).

Second, by means of "prosopological exegesis,"[57] the New Testament repeatedly employs Old Testament covenant language to portray the mutual dialogue between the Father and the Son regarding the latter's messianic mission and reward. Hebrews 1 uses the covenantal language of 2 Samuel 7; Psalm 1; and Psalm 110 to describe the covenantal honor bestowed by the Father on the Son. Thus the Father declares, "You are my Son, today I have begotten you" (Heb. 1:5, citing Ps. 2:7); "I will be to him a father, and he shall be to me a son" (Heb. 1:5, citing 2 Sam. 7:14); and, "Sit at my right hand until I make your enemies a footstool for your feet" (Heb. 1:13, citing Ps. 110:1). Moreover, as Hebrews goes on to argue, Old Testament texts such as these, read in the light of Christ's appearing, demonstrate that Christ's appointment as high priest did not occur through self-exaltation (Heb. 5:5–6) but through an oath: "The Lord has sworn and will not change his mind, 'You are a priest forever'" (Heb. 7:21). The Son's eternal and irrevocable appointment to be our

54. Brakel, *Christian's Reasonable Service*, 1:252 (emphasis mine).

55. Note that this methodological observation comports well with the historical development of the doctrine in Reformed exegesis. According to Muller, "The notion of an eternal covenant of redemption between the Father and the Son is established primarily by way of conclusions drawn from a collation of various texts that present the nature of the work of redemption" (Muller, "Toward the *Pactum Salutis*," 19, see also 28).

56. The word used by Jesus in this text, διατίθεμαι, carries covenantal/testamentary overtones.

57. See chap. 4, note 48.

great high priest, and his ensuing enthronement at the Father's right hand, is rooted in an eternal and irrevocable covenant oath.[58] When we further consider that Psalm 110 is the most commonly cited Old Testament text in the New Testament, the covenantal nature of the Son's messianic mission and reward becomes unavoidable.

The Covenant of Redemption as Trinitarian Reasoning[59]

As noted in the introduction, some recent Reformed theologians worry that the covenant of redemption potentially undermines orthodox trinitarianism. Thus Barth asks, "Can we really think of the first and second persons of the Triune Godhead as two distinct subjects and therefore as two legal subjects who can have dealings and enter into obligations one with another?"[60] Robert Letham offers what he deems the inevitable answer to this question:

> To describe the relations of the three persons in the Trinity as a covenant, or to affirm that there is a need for them to enter into covenantal—even contractual—arrangements is to open the door to heresy. The will of the Trinity is one; the works of the Trinity are indivisible. For all the good intentions of those who proposed it, the construal of the relations of the three persons of the Trinity in covenantal terms is a departure from classic trinitarian orthodoxy.[61]

This is quite a charge! How should we respond?

It is important to observe that proponents of the doctrine of the *pactum salutis* long ago acknowledged and answered the tritheistic objection. So, for example, to the question of how it can be said "that the will of the Father and the will of the Son did concur distinctly in the making of this covenant," given the unity of God's will, Owen responds,

> Such is the distinction of the persons in the unity of the divine essence, as that they act in natural and essential acts *reciprocally* one towards another—namely, in understanding, love, and the like; they know and mutually love each other.

58. Consider also Heb. 1:2, where the Son's *eternal* appointment as "heir of all things" likely reflects an allusion to the covenantal bequest of Ps. 2:8.
59. It should be noted that "trinitarian reasoning" is a subset of "biblical reasoning" insofar as creedal trinitarian theology is derived from biblical exegesis. Thus, to ask whether the doctrine of the *pactum salutis* is consistent with orthodox trinitarianism is to ask whether the biblical exegesis discussed in the previous section is consistent with the biblical exegesis from which the church's doctrine of the Trinity is derived (on which, see chap. 4, "Because That Is How God Is Revealed in God's Own Word"). In other words, to discern whether the *pactum salutis* is consistent with orthodox trinitarianism is to engage the analogy of Scripture.
60. Barth, *Church Dogmatics* IV/1, 65.
61. Letham, *Westminster Assembly*, 236.

And as they subsist distinctly, so they also act distinctly in those works which are of external operation. . . . The will of God as to the peculiar actings of the Father in this matter is the will of the Father, and the will of God with regard unto the peculiar actings of the Son is the will of the Son; not by a distinction of sundry wills, but by the distinct application of the same will unto its *distinct acts* in the persons of the Father and the Son.[62]

Brakel addresses the issue in similar fashion.

Since the Father and the Son are one in essence and thus have one will and one objective, how can there possibly be a covenant transaction between the two, as such a transaction requires the mutual involvement of two wills? Are we then not separating the persons of the Godhead too much? To this I reply that as far as personhood is concerned the Father is not the Son and the Son is not the Father. From this consideration the one divine will can be viewed from a twofold perspective. It is the Father's will to redeem by the agency of the second person as surety, and it is the will of the Son to redeem by his own agency as surety.[63]

In other words, when it comes to the relationship between the *pactum salutis* and the divine will, we must consider not only that will's unity, but we must also consider that will's tripersonal manner of subsistence if we are to appreciate the doctrine's status as an instance of orthodox trinitarian reasoning.[64]

Far from undermining orthodox trinitarian theology, therefore, the doctrine of the covenant of redemption should be seen as an application of orthodox trinitarian principles to the locus of God's eternal decree. Because the Son is consubstantial with the Father, God's redemptive will cannot be limited to the Father; the Son too must be the agent of God's redemptive will.[65] Moreover, because the Son eternally proceeds from the Father in his personal manner of subsisting, so too does his personal manner of willing proceed from the Father.[66] The Son's willing submission to the Father in the *pactum salutis* is thus a faithful expression of his divine filial identity.[67]

62. Owen, *Exercitation* 27.13 (emphasis original).

63. Brakel, *Christian's Reasonable Service*, 1:252.

64. Recall the discussion of appropriations in chap. 4, under "The Trinity and Divine Action."

65. Polanus, *Syntagma* 6.13; Owen, *Exercitation* 28.12; with Muller, "Toward the *Pactum Salutis*," 55–56.

66. Perkins, *Golden Chaine* 18; with Muller, "Toward the *Pactum Salutis*," 54. Note also the discussion of Thomas Aquinas in his *Commentary on the Gospel of John, Chapters 1–5*, trans. Fabian Larcher (Washington, DC: Catholic University of America Press, 2010), 294–95.

67. The trinitarian metaphysics underlying the present point are developed at length in Scott Swain and Michael Allen, "The Obedience of the Eternal Son," *International Journal of Systematic Theology* 15 (2013): 114–34.

"That in Everything He Might Be Preeminent": The Covenant of Redemption and the Ends of God's Decree

The doctrine of the covenant of redemption is one of the most profound expressions of the mutual love and commitment of the Father to the Son in the Spirit in planning and executing God's redemptive decree. As we draw this chapter toward its conclusion, it is worth reflecting on the relationship between the first part of this chapter (where we argued that the divine decree that flows from the love of the Father for the Son in the Spirit directs all things to the love of the Father for the Son in the Spirit) and the second part of this chapter (where we argued that the *pactum salutis* is a species of faithful biblical and trinitarian reasoning). Here I want to suggest that, along with its contribution to a proper understanding of several key doctrines (including the covenant of grace, the person and work of Christ, and the application of salvation), the doctrine of the covenant of redemption also helps us to appreciate the ultimate christological end that God has decreed for his creatures. The doctrine of the covenant of redemption helps us to better appreciate what it means to say that God's sovereign decree directs all things toward their fulfillment in Jesus Christ in order that he might be preeminent in all things (Eph. 1:10–12; Col. 1:18).[68]

Holy Scripture indicates that the Father appointed the Son as redeemer and head of the elect not merely out of his desire to redeem sinners but also ultimately out of his desire to manifest the glory of his beloved Son in and among his creatures. "I will tell of the decree: The LORD said to me, 'You are my Son; today I have begotten you. Ask of me, and I will make the nations your heritage, and the ends of the earth your possession'" (Ps. 2:7–8). The Father has appointed the Son as messianic "heir of all things" (Heb. 1:2) in order that "in everything he might be preeminent" (Col. 1:18). This is the Father's "plan for the fullness of times" (Eph. 1:10); this is "the mystery of his will . . . which he set forth in Christ" (Eph. 1:9). Thomas Goodwin summarizes the significance of this line of biblical teaching: "God's chief end was not to bring Christ into the world for us, but us for Christ. He is worth all creatures. And God contrived all things that do fall out, and even redemption itself, for the setting forth of Christ's glory, more than our salvation."[69]

---

68. In more esoteric terms, the *pactum salutis* promotes a "supralapsarian Christology." In making this argument, I am indebted to Edwin Chr. van Driel, *Incarnation Anyway: Arguments for Supralapsarian Christology* (Oxford: Oxford University Press, 2008); and especially Mark Jones, "Thomas Goodwin's Christological Supralapsarianism," in Joel R. Beeke and Mark Jones, *A Puritan Theology: Doctrine for Life* (Grand Rapids: Reformation Heritage Books, 2012), chap. 9.

69. Thomas Goodwin, *An Exposition of the First Chapter of the Epistle to the Ephesians* in *The Works of Thomas Goodwin* (Edinburgh: James Nichol, 1861), 1:100.

It is important to clarify this claim. To ascribe an ultimate christological end to the *pactum salutis* is not to speak of what God decrees "apart from and prior to the 'Fall' or even the creation itself."[70] God's decree concerning all things outside of himself is one. Therefore, to speak of Christ's preeminence with respect to God's decree is not to speak of Christ *apart from* or *prior to* other elements of that decree; it is rather to speak *inter praedestinandum* regarding Christ's relationships to the various other elements *within* God's decree.[71] Nor does positing an ultimate christological motive to the *pactum salutis* require us to say that creation and the fall are *means* to an ultimate christological *end*, as those who hold supralapsarian views of election are wont to speak.[72] To speak of an ultimate christological end in the covenant of redemption is simply to suggest that the Father's love for the Son in the Spirit provides his ultimate reason for freely appointing the Son to be our messianic redeemer and head.

Such an assertion holds compelling implications not only for theological understanding of the unfolding economy of creation, redemption, and consummation but also for the Christian life: "For the love of Christ controls us, because we have concluded this: that one has died for all, therefore all have died; and he died for all, that those who live might no longer live for themselves but for him who for their sake died and was raised" (2 Cor. 5:14–15). The doctrine of the *pactum salutis* instructs us that we and all things exist for the greater glory of Jesus Christ.

Conclusion

These are the deep things of God. We conclude our discussion with Brakel's wise counsel regarding how we should think about such matters: "One should not be of the opinion that all this is mere intellectual speculation, and that, having perceived all this, one can let the matter rest, for it is the foundation for all sure comfort, joy, holy amazement, and the magnification of God."[73] The deepest caverns of contemplation often yield the richest theological treasures, which in turn are occasions for wonder and worship:

70. Contra Myk Habets and Bobby Grow, "Theses on a Theme," in *Evangelical Calvinism*, 437.

71. Goodwin, *Ephesians*, 102.

72. Thus, e.g., Perkins, *Golden Chaine*, 6. For compelling criticisms of such language, see Turretin, *Institutes of Elenctic Theology* 4.9. For further discussion of the issue in relation to supralapsarian Christology, see Jones, "Thomas Goodwin's Christological Supralapsarianism," 155–56.

73. Brakel, *Christian's Reasonable Service*, 1:261.

Oh, the depth of the riches and wisdom and knowledge of God! How unsearchable are his judgments and how inscrutable his ways!

> "For who has known the mind of the Lord,
>   or who has been his counselor?
> Or who has given a gift to him
>   that he might be repaid?"

For from him and through him and to him are all things. To him be glory forever. Amen. (Rom. 11:33–36)

6

Creation out of Nothing

JOHN WEBSTER

The doctrine of creation out of nothing takes its rise in rational contemplation of the unfathomable mystery of God's free work in which, on the basis of his love and goodness alone, he brought into being reality other than himself. Theological contemplation of this mystery is directed by Holy Scripture, in which we may find prophetic instruction, an embassy from the Holy Spirit that reveals what no eye has seen or ear heard. The primary end of such contemplation is the edification of the saints, that they may better praise the one who is their hope and help, the Lord God who made heaven and earth (Ps. 146:5–6).

What follows is an exercise in positive or descriptive dogmatics. Recent reflection on the theology of creation has been much occupied with countering metaphysical error by genealogy and by the elaboration of a better philosophy of being and causation. It may readily be granted that some "modern"[1] deformities of Christian teaching about creation derive in part from metaphysical disorder, which is made more acute when theology shies away from handling speculative topics. But overinvestment in combating malign philosophy is not wise. If Christian teaching about creation is to be set on a firmer footing and

1. Whether "modern" means post-Scotus or post-Kant is a matter of debate.

to be given an intellectually and spiritually cogent exposition, we do well to direct our expectations rather to biblical exegesis and dogmatics, the double preoccupation of well-ordered theology.

We begin by (1) locating the doctrine of creation in general and, more specifically, creation out of nothing, within the corpus of Christian teaching. We then move (2) to consider three necessary preliminaries: the ineffability of the act of creation out of nothing, its relation to Holy Scripture, and the necessity of addressing some topics in speculative divinity. From here we turn to dogmatic exposition, considering (3) the triune agent and his act of creation, and, thereafter, (4) the particular qualities of the act of creation out of nothing. The argument closes with some reflection on the practical-spiritual extensions of the doctrine.

Creation in Christian Teaching

Systematic theology communicates a sense of the whole. Like all articles of Christian teaching, the doctrine of creation out of nothing is best approached by first looking at it from some distance in order to see it in its proper setting within the wider domain of Christian dogmatics. This involves envisaging this particular act of God in relation to its agent and to the economy of acts that this agent undertakes, of which the work of creation forms a part. The deep purpose of this systematic impulse is spiritual, so that theological reason may come to be captivated by the harmony, beauty, and order of the acts of God: "Great are the works of the Lord, studied by all who have pleasure in them" (Ps. 111:2 RSV). But a more immediate reason for seeing doctrines in their dogmatic milieu is to hinder misplacement or disproportion. Time spent on the placement and proportion of individual doctrines is never wasted. Far from being dispensable formalities, such matters help to conduct us to the material concerns of dogmatics and protect doctrines from strain or distortion when they are pressed into service for the wrong task or made to do too little (or too much) work. Teaching about creation has been markedly vulnerable, misshaped by being annexed to deistic apologetics or stripped of its cosmological content and turned into a mythological preface to soteriology. One remedy is sensitivity to the dramatic and conceptual structure of Christian teaching as a whole, which a system of Christian doctrine seeks to furnish.

The doctrine of creation out of nothing finds its place in consideration of the works of the Triune God. These works can be divided as God's inner works (*operationes Dei internae*)—that is, the divine processions that are God's inner life in his perfect bliss—and his outer works (*operationes Dei externae*)—that is, God's "transitive" acts whose term lies outside the divine being. These external works can then be further divided as the work of nature (*opus naturae*), oriented to all creatures and their natural ends, and the work of grace (*opus gratiae*), oriented to the children of Adam and their supernatural end of fellowship with their creator and redeemer. Along with providence or conservation, creation is part of the divine work of nature. In the course of generating a conceptual schema for contemplating and elaborating the scriptural testimonies, the doctrine of creation treats three matters in a definite sequence: God the Holy Trinity, who is the maker of heaven and earth; the act of creation; and the natures and ends of created being. (The sequence reflects the facts that the double subject matter of Christian dogmatics is the Triune God and his works, and that the doctrine of the Trinity is to be treated first, as that on which all else depends.) In speaking to the second element in the sequence—the act of creation—dogmatics considers both the *production* of all things and their *ordering*, that is, the coming-to-be of created reality and its appointment to an office or end in the creator's purpose. Creation out of nothing is, finally, a topic within the treatment of the production of all things and offers a specification of the act of God by which, as Lombard put it, "new things have stood forth."[2]

A number of aspects of the Christian doctrine of creation acquire special visibility when treating creation out of nothing, and not without reason; it has from the second century often served as an index of the Christian authenticity of teaching about creation. At the formal level, the doctrine of creation out of nothing is a gauge of the scriptural character of the dogmatics of creation. Materially too it reflects some primary features of this dogmatic topic. It draws attention to the fundamental role played by prior teaching about the simplicity and perfection of God's triune life in himself; it sets before the mind the absolute distinction between uncreated and created being on which much else in Christian doctrine turns; it displays how the doctrine of creation reaches back into the being of God but also reaches forward into the works of conservation and redemption; it demonstrates the necessary speculative impulse in Christian dogmatics. All this means that reflection on creation out of nothing unfolds a topic that may legitimately be regarded as, if not "the decisive point of the Christian doctrine of creation,"[3] at least a point where its chief concerns coalesce.

2. Peter Lombard, *The Sentences*, book 2: *On Creation*, trans. Giulio Silano, Medieval Sources in Translation 43 (Toronto: Pontifical Institute of Medieval Studies, 2008), 1.1.3.

3. Reinhard Hütter, "'*Creatio ex nihilo*': Promise of the Gift: Remembering the Doctrine of Creation in Troubled Times," *Currents in Theology and Mission* 19 (1992): 90. On the dogmatic importance of *creatio ex nihilo*, see Janet Martin Soskice, "Athens and Jerusalem, Alexandria

Over the course of its history, it has also proved to be a point at which theology has been required (and on occasions failed) to resist philosophical superintendence in order to maintain Christian integrity. Put a bit more sharply: when given a trinitarian exposition, creation out of nothing is very far from being what Charles Hodge, in a weak moment, called "this great doctrine of natural" (as well as, he conceded, revealed) "religion," a "self-evident truth," or "universally admitted axiom."[4] On the contrary, to reflect on creation out of nothing is to be reminded of the special sense that terms such as "creator," "creation," and "creature" bear in Christian belief, of that fact that "it is not the case that . . . creation and monotheism constitute a common ground, a common genus for Christianity and many other religions and philosophies."[5] This does not proscribe the exercise of speculative divinity—indeed, the display of Christian particularity is one of the chief tasks of speculation—but it does require that speculative inquiry be governed by Scripture and dogma.

Three Necessary Preliminaries

Before turning to dogmatic exposition of this distinguishing feature of the Christian confession, three preliminaries need to be dispatched.

(1) Creation out of nothing is inconceivable and ineffable to finite minds; in this matter, even the best instructed and most prayerfully exercised theological reason is compelled to acknowledge its indigence.

Ex nihilo creation is a postbiblical conception, refined from the second-century apologists onward and prompted by controversies in which Christian theology found itself pressed to explicate its understanding of the divine creator against notions of eternal matter.[6] The controversies were both cosmological and theological in that they made explicit a radical conception of the difference between God and the world deeply embedded in the Judeo-Christian tradition, most of all in its teaching about election, covenant, and incarnation. The notion of creation out of nothing served to spell out the ontological entailments of the distinction between the eternal creator and

---

and Edessa: Is there a Metaphysics of Scripture?," *International Journal of Systematic Theology* 8 (2005): 149–62.

4. Charles Hodge, *Systematic Theology* (New York: Scribner, Armstrong, 1877), 1:550.

5. Robert Sokolowski, "Creation and Christian Understanding," in *God and Creation: An Ecumenical Symposium*, ed. David B. Burrell and Bernard McGinn (Notre Dame, IN: University of Notre Dame Press, 1990), 180.

6. The most compact account of the early history remains Gerhard May, *Creatio Ex Nihilo: The Doctrine of "Creation Out of Nothing" in Early Christian Thought* (Edinburgh: T&T Clark, 1994).

the temporal, contingent creatures who are the objects of his saving regard, resisting ideas of the creator as one who merely gave form to coeval matter, and so accentuating the limitless capacity and freedom of God.

Yet creation out of nothing is much more than a polemical gambit; as often in the history of Christian theology (most notably in teaching about the Trinity and the person of Christ), controversy proved the occasion for discovery and display of the deep logic of the Christian confession. Refuting Platonic and gnostic cosmogonies prompted more precise identification of the mystery of creation that underlies God's saving presence. Note that this is an "identification," not "explanation." *Creatio ex nihilo* does not clarify the course of the world's coming-to-be, lifting the lid on a hitherto arcane event and showing how it works. Even with the concept of creation out of nothing in place, finite intelligence remains stunned; that to which the concept directs us turns out to defy our understanding. Reading the mature patristic treatments of the theme, one is struck by the sheer bafflement that is expressed, the sense that reason runs up against a limit it cannot pass. Creation out of nothing is inconceivable, and the inconceivability is *material* rather than *contextual*. It is not just a matter of the unavailability of ideas about divine creation in a reduced set of cultural circumstances—in which, for example, talk of a creator-agent is "no longer intelligible."[7] Much more is it that comprehensive understanding of the divine act of creation eludes the creature's capacity *tout court*. When he reads the words "In the beginning," Basil tells us, "I stop struck with admiration at this thought."[8] Why so?

Partly it is because the act of creation is not an object of experience or understanding but the precondition for all experience and understanding, functioning more like a category than a concept—something that we cannot get behind or look at from an independent vantage point. But there is something more: creation out of nothing drives theological reason to attend to a coming-to-be that wholly exceeds any pattern of causality we are able to conceive. As we shall see, *creatio ex nihilo* is not a change brought about in one entity by another, since in creation there is only the creator and his act, and no material cause. To create in the Christian sense is to cross an absolute gulf, to bring about being, not merely to modify it. And this, Anselm notes, is "quite unintelligible," because by long metaphysical habit we assume that "what comes to be, comes to be out of something,"[9] and that, conversely, *ex*

7. Gordon Kaufman, *In the Beginning . . . Creativity* (Minneapolis: Fortress, 2004), 55.

8. Basil of Caesarea, *The Hexameron*, in vol. 8 of *Nicene and Post-Nicene Fathers*, series 2, ed. Philip Schaff and Henry Wace (Peabody, MA: Hendrickson, 2004), 1.2.

9. Anselm, *Monologion* in *Anselm of Canterbury: The Major Works*, ed. B. Davies and G. R. Evans (Oxford: Oxford University Press, 1998), 8.

nihilo nihil fit. If, then, creation out of nothing is to become at least provision-
ally intelligible, we need somehow to come to terms not simply with the utter
nonexistence of all things apart from the will, love, and goodness of God but
also with the fact that in his simplicity and entire sufficiency God would be
wholly himself were there no world.

Making this adjustment requires us to dismantle a good deal of metaphysical apparatus—a demand the church fathers considered as much a matter of
the affections as the intellect. We have to climb out of the "naïve assumption
that the world is simply there,"[10] out of the view of things in which the world
is a given, a quasi-eternal correlate of the being of God, constituting the *sup-
positum* of all thought and action. Because we are fallen, absorbed by the
temporal, we *love* this view of things. Augustine says, "It is a great and very
rare thing for a man, after he has contemplated the whole creation, corporeal
and incorporeal, and has discerned its mutability, to pass beyond it, and, by
the continued soaring of his mind, to attain to the unchangeable substance
of God, and, in the height of contemplation, to learn from God himself that
none but he has made all that is not of the divine essence."[11] This "pressing
beyond" is a struggle not simply against intellectual error (failure to grasp
that everything but God has come to be) but also against disorders of the
soul: excessive, instinctual attachment to the weightiness of the world, what
Robert Grosseteste in his *Hexameron* thinks of as a kind of fantasy that created reality possesses infinite extension and so can provide infinite satisfaction.
The ancients, he writes, were led astray "into claiming that the world had
no beginning" by "a false use of the imagination. This made them imagine
before any given time, another time." And "to cleanse oneself of this error,
one can only cleanse the affection of one's mind [*affectus mentis*] of its love of
temporal things, so that the glance of the mind [*aspectus mentis*], untouched
by images, can go beyond time and grasp the simplicity of eternity."[12] If we
are to feel the force of creation out of nothing, what must be broken is our
powerful attraction to the idea that created being is *necessary*, indeed more
certain than the being of God.[13]

Yet even when such spiritual virtues are exercised, creation out of nothing
remains out of our reach. "To unfold the history of the creation of the world

10. David B. Burrell, "Creation or Emanation: Two Paradigms of Reason," in Burrell and
McGinn, eds., *God and Creation*, 28.

11. Augustine, *City of God*, in vol. 2 of *Nicene and Post-Nicene Fathers*, series 1, ed. Philip
Schaff (repr. Peabody, MA: Hendrickson, 2004), 2.11.2.

12. Robert Grosseteste, *On the Six Days of Creation* (Oxford: Oxford University Press,
1996), 59.

13. See here Karl Barth, *Church Dogmatics* III/1, trans. T. F. Torrance and Geoffrey Bromiley
(Edinburgh: T&T Clark, 1958), 6.

in terms equal to its dignity," Calvin reminds his readers at the beginning of his Genesis commentary, is "absolutely impossible."[14] In slightly different terms, theological inquiry into the act of creation remains in the ectypal realm, and so comprehension eludes us. We have to be in deadly earnest here! Theology *in via* cannot hope to generate an adequate intellectual schema of the way in which things came to be. No doctrine of creation out of nothing may claim any worth unless it is first silenced by the creator's question: "Where were you when I laid the foundations of the earth? Tell me, if you have understanding" (Job 38:4). The unanswerability of the question must pervade the rhetoric and modes of argument of theology at this point; brisk confidence must give way to "a sober, docile, mild and humble spirit."[15]

(2) Knowledge of creation out of nothing is derived from God's self-witness through the prophets and apostles. Creation is mystery, apprehended only as the mind's affections are cut free from the assumption that the world is basic, that *from* which we begin. Liberation depends on a prior divine movement in which the one who creates all things also creates knowledge of his creative work. Knowledge that the world was created out of nothing is "revealed" knowledge, gained from God's uncaused communicative presence and the faith it evokes. "By faith we understand that the world was created by the word of God, so that what is seen was made out of things which do not appear" (Heb. 11:3). Revelation alone, with faith as its correlate, can span the cognitive gap between *invisibilia* and *visibilia*. The principle here is that *knowledge* of the creation's having-come-to-be shares the character of the *being* of creation; it is knowledge *ex nihilo*, not a hypothesis or postulate or deduction from experience but the reduplication of the order of being in the order of intelligence. Knowledge that all things are created is an element of prophetic faith, not natural religion. And so the doctrine of creation out of nothing of necessity takes the form of reflection on Holy Scripture.

But how is this reflection to proceed? How does the dogmatic concept of creation out of nothing emerge from consideration of the biblical texts? By way of answer, a distinction may be drawn between two ways of reading the biblical materials on creation.

We could make an approach through the history of religion, envisaging the biblical texts as generated by and a means of access to the religious practices and ideation underlying them. The interpreter's task here is to disclose the history of religious culture the texts signify (in however occluded a way) using comparative historical methods and literary skills of tradition analysis. The

---

14. John Calvin, *Genesis* (Edinburgh: Banner of Truth, 1965), 1:57.
15. Calvin, *Genesis*, 1:57.

approach may yield different accounts of whether, for example, the so-called priestly narrative of creation entertains a notion of creation out of nothing and of the kinds of negotiations with ambient religious cultures that can be glimpsed in the text's creation myth.

We might, however, follow the guidance of the patristic *hexamera* and of later works shaped by them and read the biblical creation stories not primarily as an item in the history of religion (though that they undoubtedly are) but as prophetic address. This approach differs from the first in a couple of ways.

First, it does not treat the human process of authorship as a closed natural occurrence, with the author as no more than product of and agent within the history of ancient religious culture. Authorship is "open" not only laterally to cultural formation but also vertically to the self-communication of God. Indeed, authorship is generated by that self-communication, of which it is a created auxiliary. It is not immediately generated, that is, not in a way that suspends the cultural-ideational processes of production. But those processes are a function of and assistant to a divine act of communication. The author is "patient," one to whom has been granted both divine revelation and the grace to "contemplate," that is, to be selflessly attentive to the instruction of divine wisdom, and this grace continues in the commissioning of the "prophetic" author to testify to and extend divine revelation. The prophets were certainly nothing more than creatures: they "were not when the world came into existence,"[16] and the creation of the world remains inapprehensible to them too. Yet this void in their creaturely knowledge is not filled by myth making but by the operation of creative, divine wisdom through whom the prophets know and speak.

> That God made the world we can believe from no-one more safely than from God himself. But where have we heard him? Nowhere more distinctly than in the Holy Scriptures, where his prophet said: "In the beginning God created the heavens and the earth." Was the prophet present when God made the heavens and the earth? No: but the wisdom of God, by whom all things were made, was there, and wisdom insinuates itself into holy souls, and makes them into friends of God and his prophets, and noiselessly informs them of all his works.[17]

"Prophet" is a more basic category than "author" to describe the human agents of the biblical creation texts, for "prophet" catches the divinely ordered movement of elevation, instruction, and commissioned speech out of which

16. Theophilus of Antioch, *Ad Autolycum*, in vol. 2 of *Fathers of the Second Century*, ed. A. Cleveland Coxe (Peabody, MA: Hendrickson, 2004), 2.10.
17. Augustine, *City of God* 11.4.

the texts emerge. The category of prophet does not eliminate the category of author: prophetic Scripture remains a natural text, but a natural text in an economy of signs, in which created speakers stand in the service of the divine Word. Ambrose tells us how God tore Moses away from worldly pleasure to "divine contemplation," in which "there was bestowed on him the gift of the divine presence," as a consequence of which Moses "opened his mouth and uttered what the Lord spoke."[18]

Second, this entails a different account of the reader of the biblical text, who is, like the prophetic author, "patient," receptive toward the text's signifying and ambassadorial functions. Such patience is not inactive; the reader's activity is caught up in God's instruction and inspiration of the prophets and God's sanctification of the prophets' audiences. The commanding reader, busy about the tasks of literary and cultural explanation of the text in its natural domain, can make little headway here, for what is required is a set of Spirit-produced virtues: friendship with God and his prophets, readiness to "follow" the prophet "who knew both the Author and the Ruler,"[19] but more than anything the docility whose source is *holiness*. As he embarks on the first homily in the hexameron, Basil asks, "What ear is worthy to hear such a tale? How earnestly the soul should prepare itself to receive such high lessons! How pure it should be from carnal affections, how unclouded by worldly disquietudes."[20]

How do these two features (the text as prophetic testimony to divine wisdom, the reader as sanctified recipient of its instruction) affect the reading of the biblical creation texts? There are two primary ways in which reason, made pliable to the divine Word by the Spirit, "follows" the text's instruction and reads it as a sign from God. We may call them exegetical and dogmatic reasoning. Exegetical reasoning is the attempt to construe the plain sense of the text, to follow the *connexio verborum*. *Verba* refers to all the natural properties of the text: linguistic, grammatical, and literary. But, unlike the post-Spinoza tradition of biblical study, exegetical reasoning does not treat these properties as exclusively natural, as clues for the reconstruction of natural religious history. The *verba* of the text are commissioned by the divine Word or wisdom, and in tracing the movement of their literary form, we receive divine communication.

Dogmatic reasoning is a further act of following in which, directed by the prophetic testimony and with the aid of the Spirit's sanctifying grace,

18. Ambrose, *Hexameron* in *Hexameron, Paradise, Cain and Abel*, ed. J. J. Savage, Fathers of the Church 42 (Washington: Catholic University of America Press, 1961), 1.1.2.
19. Ambrose, *Hexameron* 1.1.2.
20. Basil, *Hexameron* 1.1.

theological reason endeavors to build a conceptual account of the matter that the scriptural words present, to elaborate or enlarge on the scriptural *res*. Because it attempts to reconceive what it hears in Holy Scripture, dogmatics does not necessarily retain the rhetorical sequence of particular biblical texts, or the narrative-dramatic order of the canon as a whole, or the soteriological idiom of a good deal of the biblical creation material. Rather, as reconception and enlargement, it seeks to display the anatomy of the prophetic word by transposing it into a conceptual idiom, ordering it systematically so that its unity and interconnections become more immediately visible. Dogmatic reconception gives formal clarity to what is usually informally or occasionally expressed in Scripture by elaborating, for example, the identities of the agents of the canonical drama or by tracing its metaphysical implications. Yet in doing this, dogmatics is not improving on Scripture, which retains its primacy as prophetic instruction; nor is dogmatics modifying the material substance of what the prophets say. And, even at points of maximal indirectness or abstraction from the biblical texts, dogmatics must always lead back to the *verba* of Scripture. The rule that ensures the subservience of dogmatics to the prophetic word is, "If the weakness of our intelligence does not allow us to penetrate the depth of the thoughts of the [prophet], yet we shall be involuntarily drawn to give faith to his words by the force of his authority."[21]

Once again, theology must be in deadly earnest here. No doctrine of creation out of nothing can retain its Christian character unless it cleaves to the words of the prophets and expects those words to decide matters. Nor will any doctrine of creation be of much worth unless it is prepared for the ignominy that routinely comes its way when it attends to the prophetic embassy: how, our cultured despisers ask us, can an ancient Semitic story offer metaphysical instruction concerning the origin of all things? But that is precisely what the prophetic word tenders and why it commands reason's consideration.

(3) Theological contemplation of the scriptural mystery of creation necessarily requires speculative attention to the being and acts of the Triune God. As it developed in the Christian tradition, the doctrine of creation out of nothing brought together exegesis and speculative dogmatics with some (modest) metaphysical interests. Much modern biblical, historical, and systematic theology has been decidedly reluctant to address the speculative question of God's life in himself on the grounds that the center of gravity of the biblical texts lies in the economy of salvation.[22] A radical (and not entirely temperate)

21. Basil, *Hexameron* 1.1.
22. Leo Scheffczyk, *Creation and Providence* (New York: Herder and Herder, 1970) is a thorough survey of the biblical and historical materials from this point of view.

account was presented in the mid-1990s by Jon Levenson in *Creation and the Persistence of Evil*.[23] Levenson urged that talk of God's antecedent perfection seriously distorts the Old Testament creation materials, which concern Yahweh's mastery of the forces of disorder and his dramatic establishment of Israel's persistence at Israel's behest.

But is theological attention to God *in se* always an intrusion? There is, doubtless, a certain advantage to subsuming creation under redemption: it indicates, if somewhat clumsily, the unitary character of God's action in relation to what is not himself, and that the work of creation has a teleological dimension. God's work of creation is not only the production of matter but also the establishment of temporally unfolding fellowship between the creator and Adam's race—a point sometimes lost in deistic metaphysics of creation. Nevertheless, the dualist assumption that the salvation-historical or economic is necessarily opposed to the speculative ought not to pass unchallenged. Modern theologies of salvation history commonly assume that the temporal economy of God's outer works can be grasped without reference to its ground in the perfect life of God in himself. In this, they are instinctively, though not often consciously, Kantian, countering the apparent abstraction of theological metaphysics by appeal to the activity of God in the phenomenal realm. It ought not to be forgotten that part of the cogency of this salvation-historical emphasis is its echoes of the antispeculative strain in Luther and Calvin. "We know God, who is himself invisible, only through his works," Calvin announces at the beginning of his Genesis commentary; "as for those who proudly soar above the world to seek God in his unveiled essence, it is impossible but that at length they should entangle themselves in a multitude of absurd figments."[24] Calvin wants to inculcate humble acceptance of the condition of creatures, to resist attempts at accessing the inmost divine essence apart from the way in which God is "visible to us in his works."[25] Yet he is inhibited by associating speculation with prideful attempts to circumvent God's appointed means of self-communication. Properly conducted, speculative divinity simply draws attention to God *in se* as the founding condition of God *pro nobis*. Further, there is a loss sustained when eliminating the speculative, one that seriously undermines our capacity to contemplate God's saving acts: the loss of a sense that God's external works reach out to us from his entire simplicity and his

23. Jon D. Levenson, *Creation and the Persistence of Evil: The Jewish Drama of Divine Omnipotence* (Princeton, NJ: Princeton University Press, 1994); see also Richard J. Clifford's earlier article "The Hebrew Scriptures and the Theology of Creation," *Theological Studies* 46 (1985): 507–23.

24. Calvin, *Genesis*, 1:59.

25. Calvin, *Genesis*, 1:58.

unfathomable blessedness and satisfaction. Dietrich Bonhoeffer comments that we cannot ask whether the "beginning" of Genesis 1:1 is "God's own beginning or God's beginning with the world," dismissing the question immediately: "We can know nothing at all of *this* God except as the creator of our world. . . . There is no possible question that could go back behind this God who created in the beginning."[26] But no: there *is* such a question, the question of speculative theology, and if it is not kept alive, the relation of creator and creatures may be distorted. The speculative is not an alternative to the drama of covenantal history; it is an indication of what takes place in the covenant, and of how the covenant reaches back into the infinite glory of the one who needs no creature and who creates out of inherent goodness.

The Trinity and Creation

"In the beginning God created the heavens and the earth." A dogmatic gloss on this unutterable mystery must follow a sequence of thoughts beginning with the agent of creation, moving to the properties of the creator's act of creation, and then turning to speak of creation out of nothing. Laid out in that order, the material proffers itself to our understanding; if we try to leap over one element in the sequence, the thoughts turn to dust in our hands.

(1) Teaching about creation out of nothing is a function of the Christian confession of the identity of the creator. It is cosmological teaching, but only as a corollary of teaching about God's triune perfection—this is an application of the rule (nowadays widely ignored) that first the agent, then the act, is specified.

Though only a full presentation of the doctrine of the Trinity would suffice at this point, two fundamentals need to be identified. First, God the creator wholly exceeds the act of creation, which in no way constitutes, perfects, or extends the perfection of his life as Father, Son, and Spirit. God's inner works (the relations of origin: paternity, filiation, and spiration) are wholly sufficient; God is entirely realized without potentiality. This severely beautiful thought is embedded very deeply in the structure of how Christian dogmatics thinks of the relation between creator and creatures. God is entirely himself behind and before the work of creation. The coming-to-be of all that is not God—that there is now not one order of (divine) being but two orders of being (uncreated and created)—can be thrown into relief only against the background of the repleteness and simplicity of God. Further, the act of creation does

---

26. Dietrich Bonhoeffer, *Creation and Fall: A Theological Exposition of Genesis 1–3*, ed. John W. de Gruchy, trans. Douglas Steven Bax, vol. 3 of *Dietrich Bonhoeffer Works*, ed. Wayne Whitson Floyd Jr. (Minneapolis: Fortress, 1997), 31.

not bring about a state of affairs in which God's fullness now includes his relation to creatures. As creator God does not cease to be perfectly alive and active without the creature; he remains supereminently himself apart from what he has made. The "beginning" of heaven and earth is no beginning for God. "The doctrine of creation flows from the infinite perfection of God."[27]

Second, creation is a work of God's free love and boundless goodness. Supremely, of course, God loves himself in the mutual delight and regard of the three persons in which is his entire satisfaction. But his love is also known in generosity, in the external work of love whose "tendency" is to impart "substantive existence,"[28] to bestow being. God does not do this to make good some deficiency in his bliss, for creation does not enhance or satisfy him. God creates not to make himself entire but because he is already entire, and so entirely free to create without loss. As Father, Son, and Spirit he is infinite, unconstrained by any need to retain his identity by, as it were, drawing a boundary around himself and denying being to what lies beyond the boundary. God is not to be reduced to the status of a stupendously large being over against other, smaller beings. Precisely as the one who is uncreated, God is creative. Possessing unlimited blessedness, God does not have his being in competition, reserving being and life to himself. Beyond threat, God is also beyond envy, no other possible reality having the capacity to enhance or diminish his perfection. As the one who has life in himself he can give life to the world, he can be infinitely generous without self-depletion. "God is good—or rather the source of goodness—and the good has no envy for anything. Thus, because he envies nothing its existence, he made everything from nothing through his own Word, our Lord Jesus Christ."[29]

(2) What may be said more specifically about the act of creation? Once again, a complete presentation would require discussion of some trinitarian technicalities concerning essential and relative predication in the outer works of God.[30] Here we must content ourselves with identifying properties of the work of creation that draw attention to the fact that all that is required for creation to come to be is God himself.

(a) The act of creation is "personal" action, the action of the Triune God as inalienable personal subject in the unity and differentiation of his outer work. The act of creation is a "work," not the mere operation of a force abstract from

27. C. Hodge, *Systematic Theology* (Grand Rapids: Eerdmans, 1940), 1:561.

28. Isaak A. Dorner, *A System of Christian Doctrine* (Edinburgh: T&T Clark, 1881), 2:39.

29. Athanasius, *On the Incarnation* in *Contra Gentes and De Incarnatione*, ed. R. W. Thomson (Oxford: Oxford University Press, 1971), 3.

30. On which see John Webster, "Trinity and Creation," *International Journal of Systematic Theology* 12 (2010): 4–19.

a subject. "God" and "creativity" are not (as Kaufman proposes) convertible terms; we may not just say "creation happens."[31] The principle here is that to contemplate the work is to contemplate the worker in his work; accordingly, the doctrine of creation is first a doctrine of the creator, and everything else that we say to characterize his work is derivative from what is said of his being. Basil catches the point: "It is he, beneficent nature, goodness without measure, a worthy object of love for all beings endowed with reason, the beauty most to be desired, the origin of all that exists, the source of life, intellectual light, impenetrable wisdom—he it is who 'in the beginning created heaven and earth.'"[32]

Always bearing in mind the impenetrability of this act, what may be said of it by way of dogmatic paraphrase? The act begs description, for it is a *sui generis* act of making, a bringing-about that, like the being of its agent, is not commensurate with the ways in which creatures make, most of all because there is here no "motion," no element of laborious coming-to-realization, and no "acting-upon" but simply the untrammeled exercise and limitless effectiveness of divine goodness.

(b) The act of creation is an act of God's freedom. Negatively, this reinforces the nonnecessity of creation for God, who does not create in response to inner need or outer constraint and who could, without loss of perfection, refrain from creating. The negative is, however, the antechamber to a richly positive conception of divine freedom. We do not exhaust the character of God's freedom merely by speaking of his indeterminacy. Indeed, talk of indeterminacy may prove hazardous, for pressed in certain directions it can engender a notion of the divine will as merely arbitrary, merely devoid of restriction—a pattern of thought that, paradoxically, threatens to make God finite by detaching his freedom from his nature. Say rather that God's freedom, including his freedom exercised in the making of all things, is his freedom to enact his counsel or loving purpose. In creating, God acts according to his nature and will. The necessity for God to create is not external but "consequent" on his being the one he is. Put somewhat differently, antecedent to creation, there is simply God and God's "ideas" or "counsel." God's ideas or counsel are not "objective"—that is, external notions by which God takes his bearings and shapes his actions. They are simply his "deliberate" nature. Creation, we might say, results from something like a decision, in that as creator God is wholly self-determining. But again, this self-determination is not arbitrary self-causation but simply God being the one he is, the one characterized by unrestricted goodness. "Will" and "goodness," like "freedom" and "necessity" or "nature," are identical in God.

31. Kaufman, *In the Beginning*, 56, 72–74.
32. Basil, *Hexameron* 1.2.

(c) The act of creation enacts the divine counsel instantaneously and without effort. Ambrose says, "He who in a momentary exercise of his will completed such a majestic work employed no art or skill so that those things which were not were so quickly brought into existence; the will did not outrun the creation nor the creation, the will."[33] Why stress the "incomprehensible swiftness of God's action as creator, that there is 'no succession in the action'"?[34] Partly because the creative act of the eternal God is the condition for there being temporal sequence; God's act is not an element within that sequence or its first event. Partly in order to signify that the act of creation is not discursive—deliberation followed by labor. There is no interstice between willing and bringing about that will, a point reinforced by the idiom of creation through a word of command: "He spoke, and it came to be; he commanded, and it stood firm" (Ps. 33:9). When talking of the act of creation as God's "work," we have to clear the concept of "work" of associations of a plotted succession of activity. Creation is not protracted toil but an act whereby "at the will of God the world arose in less than an instant."[35]

This is why the act of creation is effortless. "The LORD is the everlasting God, the Creator of the ends of the earth. He does not faint or grow weary" (Isa. 40:28). This is worth pausing over, since it relates closely to creation out of nothing. Creation is effortless because God is at rest not only *after* but also *in* this work. "Rest" signifies completeness, God's being beyond augmentation. His rest is what Augustine calls "eternal tranquility,"[36] which is God's being fully himself anterior to all outward acts; this is rooted in that "he himself is his own beatitude" for "he is not made happy by making things, but through being all-sufficient to himself and needing not the things he made."[37] To work and to be at rest are the same in God.

A corollary here is the need for caution when speaking of the act of creation as the strenuous exercise of divine power. God's omnipotence as creator is not just immense force, creaturely power infinitely magnified. The disproportion between uncreated and created power is one of quality, not quantity,[38] the difference being that God's creative work is without strain and requires

33. Ambrose, *Hexameron* 1.1.3.
34. Grosseteste, *On the Six Days of Creation*, 66.
35. Basil, *Hexameron* 1.6.
36. Augustine, *The Literal Meaning of Genesis 4.24* in *On Genesis*, ed. J. E. Rotelle (Hyde Park, NY: New City, 2002), 255.
37. Thomas Aquinas, *Quaestiones disputatae de potentia Dei* in *On Creation*, trans. S. C. Selner-Wright (Washington, DC: Catholic University of America Press, 2011), 4.2, ad 5; see also *Summa theologiae* Ia.73.2.
38. Ludwig Feuerbach's critique of creation out of nothing trades on precisely this assumption of proportionality (*The Essence of Christianity* [New York: Harper, 1957], 101).

no application of resistance to a countervailing force. To talk of creation as an act of power, then, may neglect that as creator God does not act "on anything."[39] This already hints at one strand of the particular character of the notion of creation that is introduced by the "out of nothing" qualifier, namely, that God acts "against nothing": God is infinitely and antecedently capable and so beyond contest or exertion.

(d) There is an absence of motion or agitation in the divine act of creation. Notice how Lombard in the *Sentences* teases apart the peculiar logic of talk of God creating. "According to what reckoning are words of this kind, 'to do,' 'to make,' said of God?" he asks. His answer runs, "These words, namely 'to create,' 'to make,' and 'to do,' and others of this kind cannot be said of God according to that reckoning by which they are said of creatures." The difference can be identified in these terms: "When we say that [God] makes something, we do not understand that there is any movement in him in operating, nor any passion in working, just as there is accustomed to befall us, but we signify that there is some new effect of his sempiternal will, that is, something new exists by his eternal will." In God the work of creation involves *nihil novi*, no "motion or mutation." "God is said 'to act' or 'to make' something, because he is the cause of things newly existing, so long as the new things, which before were not, start to be according to his will, apart from his own agitation; so that it is not able to be properly said to be an 'act,' since . . . the act of everything consists in movement, but in God it is no movement."[40] This, to forestall an objection, is not an assertion of divine immobility but rather of its opposite: "pure" (wholly realized) motion, *life*.

In short: God's act of creation is *sui generis*, and as we make our approach to it we have to check the impulse to think of it as one act of immeasurably great effectiveness in a field of other agents, acts, and objects. The act of creation is the beginning of all other being and action, not an act alongside or on them.

(e) We may draw together much of what has been said so far with Anselm's (deceptively abstract) formulation: in the work of creation the "supreme essence" acts "alone and through itself."[41] More concretely, "I am the LORD, who made all things, who alone stretched out the heavens, who spread out the earth by myself" (Isa. 44:24; cf. 40:12). Creation is an absolute beginning, and so there cannot be multiple *initia*—no material cause, no agent but the

---

39. Rowan Williams, "On Being Creatures," in *On Christian Theology* (Oxford: Blackwell, 2000), 68.

40. Lombard, *Sentences* 2.1.1.3; see Turretin's parallel account of creation by "volition alone": *Institutes of Elenctic Theology*, ed. James T. Dennison Jr., trans. George M. Giger (Phillipsburg, NJ: P&R, 1992), 5.3.13.

41. Anselm, *Monologion* 7.

creator alone. If there were any such, then "creation" would be "formation," not God acting out of utter simplicity and singularity. "Almighty God did not need the help of any kind of thing at all which he himself had not made, in order to carry out what he wishes. If . . . for making the things he wished, he was being assisted by some actual thing which he had not made himself, then he was not almighty; and to think that is sacrilege."[42] The act of creation distinguishes the one God from the many gods (Ps. 96:5; Jer. 10:11–12).

God's power to create is thus incommunicable and exercised immediately. Creation is not a communicable act but proper to God alone. In part this is because the work of creation requires infinite capacity since it crosses the absolute gulf between nonbeing and being; God creates, and creatures simply make. More basically, the power to create cannot be communicated to some instrument because any instrument is itself created. It is different in order of being from the creator, and so capable only of making out of other created elements it finds alongside itself, of bestowing form but not substance. "Creation . . . is the production of anything in the totality of its substance, presupposing nothing that is either uncreated or created by another. Whence it follows that no-one is capable of creating except God alone, who is the first cause."[43]

God therefore creates without intermediaries; in the beginning, God. In the work of creation there is no instrumental cause. When we say that the Father creates through the Son and the Spirit, we do not speak of them as intermediaries but as the personal modes of the external work of the undivided divine essence common to the three. To say that through the Son and the Spirit God the Father makes heaven and earth is to repeat that God acts alone in creating.

All of the above is simply an extended gloss on Thomas Aquinas's exquisite summary of the doctrine of creation (itself, of course, a gloss on Genesis 1): God alone is "the all-embracing cause of existence entire."[44]

Particular Qualities of the Act of Creation

(1) By now it should be clear that, once the act of creation is understood as absolute initiation, "out of nothing" follows quite naturally. If creation is, as Thomas Aquinas has it, "the introduction of being entirely,"[45] then we talk of it by talking of God and nothing besides.

42. Augustine, *On Genesis: A Refutation of the Manichees* 1.10, in *On Genesis*, 45.
43. Thomas Aquinas, *Summa theologiae* Ia.65.3, resp.
44. Thomas Aquinas, *Summa theologiae* Ia.45.2, resp.
45. Thomas Aquinas, *Summa theologiae* Ia.45.1.

The qualifier *ex nihilo* distinguishes the act of creation from other divine acts. Creation out of nothing differs from the *immanent processions* of the Godhead, which are internal, not transitive, works, the way in which God eternally is, the actuality of his perfect aliveness in which the persons do not bestow being on one another but are simply God in communion with himself. As an *ad extra* operation, creation is not "constitutional";[46] it does not "perfect the operator."[47] It is a secondary, gracious, and free act, a further work beyond the eternal inner activities of giving and receiving.

Creation out of nothing thus differs from *emanation*. Creation is the "introduction" of being, not simply an overflow of the divine being. Creation out of nothing is not creation out of God, creation by extension or diffusion. Indeed, "introduction" pulls us in quite a different direction from "extension" or "diffusion" in highlighting the gulf between nonbeing and being. The language of emanation inevitably struggles to speak of the voluntary character of the act by which all things came to be and can lead to the thought that creation is a necessary element of the divine being, a kind of potentiality in God.

Lastly, creation out of nothing differs from the work of *conservation* by which God maintains what he has made and brings it to perfection. The two works of nature, creation and conservation, are certainly related: creation is not only initiatory but also teleological, for the creator purposes the ordered temporal unfolding of created reality under his care. But the two works are not to be confused. Creation is a completed act—what Barth called an "incomparable perfect"[48]—whereas conservation is a continuing activity of sustaining. Moreover, because creation is out of nothing, it is directed to no "patient entity,"[49] there being no existing subject or recipient of the divine work of creation. Creation introduces, and conservation governs and upholds.

(2) Because creation "introduces" being in its entirety, created reality is not eternal, even in some inchoate state. It has temporal origination. Teaching about *creatio ex nihilo* is "a claim about cosmogony and not only about cosmology,"[50] not just a way of advertising the world's present state of ontological dependence on God but a pointer to the ineffable act by which it came about that there is a world to be dependent on him. To counter Greek notions of eternal matter, classical Christian divinity made much of what was taken to

---

46. W. G. T. Shedd, *Dogmatic Theology* (Phillipsburg, NJ: P&R, 2003), 370.

47. Turretin, *Institutes of Elenctic Theology* 5.3.13.

48. Barth, *Church Dogmatics* III/1, 13.

49. Paul Copan and William L. Craig, *Creation Out of Nothing: A Biblical, Philosophical, and Scientific Inquiry* (Grand Rapids: Baker Academic, 2004), 147–65.

50. David Kelsey, "The Doctrine of Creation from Nothing," in *Evolution and Creation*, ed. Ernan McMullin (Notre Dame, IN: University of Notre Dame Press, 1985), 181.

be the absolute sentence at the beginning of the Genesis account. In Genesis 1:1, Basil tells us, Moses the prophet "first establishes a beginning, so that it might not be supposed that the world never had a beginning."[51] This is why *creatio ex nihilo* has as its corollary *creatio de novo*, the "newness" of the world signifying its noneternity.[52] Both notions serve to underline the sheer divide between uncreated/creative being and created being. Part of what distanced early Christian theologians from philosophical teaching about preexistent matter was a sense that a god with whom matter is coeval would lack simplicity and radical categorical difference from the world, and so would be reduced to being a craftsman rather than a creator. There cannot be two infinites.

(3) The denial of the eternity of matter takes us a little closer to what is meant by speaking of creation out of *nothing*. In glossing the opening words of Genesis, we may say something like the following: When we speak of creation out of nothing, we say that "while something has indeed been made, there is not some thing from which it was made."[53] "Nothing" is not an odd sort of something, characterless *prima materia* later formed by God. It signifies an entire absence. Talk of the "nothing" out of which God creates simply confirms and reiterates the force of the word "create"; it does not indicate some substance, potentiality, or any other kind of material cause. There is no "preexisting subject" to the act of creation because "creation makes and posits its subject, but does not suppose it."[54] The *nihil* is thus *nihil negativum, materiam excludens*, negative nothingness, excluding matter.

All that is required for creation to take place is God, who is the all-sufficient "hypostasis of all being."[55] A notion of eternal matter, on the contrary, cannot avoid imputing "weakness" to God.[56] Something of the same point is reinforced in the familiar contrast between the creator who brings into being and the craftsman (*factor, artifex*) who forms what already is.[57] "That God made matter out of nothing, and did not make the world out of unmade matter . . . we can know from this: that the creator would not be almighty if he

---

51. Basil, *Hexameron* 1.2.

52. On the relation of *creatio ex nihilo* and *creatio de novo*, see William Dunphy, "Maimonides and Aquinas on Creation: A Critique of Their Historians," in *Graceful Reason: Essays in Ancient and Mediaeval Philosophy Presented to Joseph Owens, CSSR*, ed. Lloyd P. Gerson (Toronto: Pontifical Institute of Mediaeval Studies, 1983), 361–79; David Burrell, *Faith and Freedom: An Interfaith Perspective* (Oxford: Blackwell, 2004), 156, 232.

53. Anselm, *Monologion* 8.

54. Turretin, *Institutes of Elenctic Theology* 5.3.13; see there also his interpretation of the *invisibilia* of Heb. 11:3.

55. Tatian, *Address to the Greeks* in *Fathers of the Second Century*, 5.

56. Athanasius, *On the Incarnation* 2.

57. See, representatively, Basil, *Hexameron* 2.2.3; Athanasius, *On the Incarnation* 2; Lombard, *Sentences* 2.1.1.2.

needed previously available matter, as a craftsman does, to work on: he would be truly in need and imperfect."[58] The negative point here is the obverse of a theological perception of singular force and beauty, namely, that created reality *is* on the basis of nothing other than the power, wisdom, understanding, and voice of the Lord of hosts: "It is he who made the earth by his power, who established the world by his wisdom, and by his understanding stretched out the heavens. When he utters his voice there is a tumult of waters in the heavens" (Jer. 10:12–13).

(4) Creation out of nothing is not a causal relation or an act that brings about a change, for creation effects the coming-to-be of created reality rather than a passage from one state of being to another. Divine creating out of nothing is not a *causal* relation in anything other than a very informal sense, because part of the force of "out of nothing" is to state that in the act of creation there is only one subject and no entity on which he is at work. The idiom of worldly causation soon reaches a limit here; at the very least, it has to be stretched virtually beyond recognition, evacuated of the associations of anterior and posterior that subsume cause and effect within a single order of being. Infinitely different from the creature, the creator does not occupy a place—even primary place—in a causal chain. As "first" cause, God is not first in a sequence but the one because of whom there is a sequence at all.[59]

Similarly, the act of creation out of nothing is not a *change*, because "change" suggests some sort of constant persisting through the process of coming-to-be. Thomas Aquinas notes, "In creation, non-being is not converted into being"; the reason for this is that "one of the extremes [i.e., nonbeing] does not pass into the other." In describing creation out of nothing, we have to say "there is no underlying subject of change," whereas in instances of natural change we can say "there you have a subject."[60] Nothingness, nonbeing, is not a state of a subject but the absence of any subject, "the non-being which is nothing at all."[61]

58. Grosseteste, *On the Six Days of Creation*, 70.

59. See the penetrating comments in David Braine, *The Reality of Time and the Existence of God: The Project of Proving God's Existence* (Oxford: Clarendon, 1988), 16.

60. Thomas Aquinas, *Summa theologiae* IIIa.75.8, resp. The context is a discussion of eucharistic transubstantiation, which draws on what Thomas Aquinas has already said in the treatment of creation in Ia.45.2, ad 2.

61. Thomas Aquinas, *Summa theologiae* Ia.45.1, resp.; further on this aspect of creation, see Thomas Weinandy, *Does God Change? The Word's Becoming in the Incarnation* (Still River, MA: St. Bede's, 1985), 88–96; idem, *Does God Suffer?* (Edinburgh: T&T Clark, 2000), 113–46; idem, "God and Human Suffering: His Act of Creation and His Acts in History," in *Divine Impassibility and the Mystery of Human Suffering*, ed. James F. Keating and Thomas J. White (Grand Rapids: Eerdmans, 2009), 99–116.

Moreover, talk of change may lead us to suppose that the act of creation is some sort of process. But, as we have already noted in speaking of creation as instantaneous, there is no "event" of creation, no staggeringly large happening with an agent of immense powers and a number of patients. Creation out of nothing means that there is God alone, and then by his will and goodness there is also created reality. If we draw back from the language of causality, it is because creation out of nothing suspends what Grosseteste calls "the rule of the co-existence of cause and caused."[62] God needs "absolutely nothing to start with."[63]

(5) This "absolutely nothing" also means that there is no adversary. Creation out of nothing is not an agonistic process, because before the act of creation there is no reality outside God with which God must do battle. Creation is effortless and unopposed, achieved not by titanic effort but by the most casual word of command. As Barth puts it, creation out of nothing is "a pure act of creativity, unhindered by any opposition, unlimited by any presupposition, not requiring the cooperation of any other agent and excluding any idea either of the cooperation of any existent reality or of conflict against it."[64]

This offers further purchase against Levenson's proposal that divine creation is to be thought of as "mastery"[65] of chaotic forces, a mastery that is not unthreatened, still less complete, but rather a dramatic event in need of ceaseless renewal: Levenson's creator has his being in the struggle between chaos and salvific order. Much might be said by way of response about the assimilation of creation to saving preservation, the absorption of the divine into the sociopragmatics of religion, or the unsupportable price of dismissing substance metaphysics. One question, however, must be pressed: how can Yahweh save if he is not beyond rivalry? Is a "comparative" deity really divine? The assumption is that for God to act in time is for God to be constituted by time and its conflicts; yet this simply makes God into one of the gods who did not make the heavens and the earth (Jer. 10:11): but "not like these is he who is the portion of Jacob, for he is the one who formed all things" (Jer. 10:16). It is the "not like these"—the incomparability of God to a finite agent locked in combat—that is part of the import of creation out of nothing.

(6) The threads may be drawn together with four summary points. First, the preposition *ex* in *creatio ex nihilo* does not designate but excludes any material, *non designat sed excludit materiam*. *Ex* does not refer to a process involving an agent and a material cause but to a logical (but not temporal)

---

62. Grosseteste, *On the Six Days of Creation*, 60.
63. Thomas Aquinas, *Summa theologiae* IIIa.75.8, resp.
64. Barth, *Church Dogmatics* III/1, 100.
65. J. Levenson, *Creation and the Persistence of Evil*, 3.

sequence, in which what once was not now is.[66] *Ex nihilo* means *post nihilum*. Second, therefore, glossing Holy Scripture aright requires us to think something that largely eludes us, namely, the thought of absolute initiation that creation out of nothing indicates and that blocks attempts to bring uncreated/ creative being into the same ontological order as created being. Third, the act of absolute initiation shows that the relation of creator and creature is a nonreciprocal or "mixed" relation, real on the side of the creature but not on the side of the creator, who remains unaffected by the creature's existence or nonexistence alike. In view of much anguished but muddled protest, it ought to be added that the creator's immutability is not the absence of love for creatures but the ground of that love's absolute durability. Only a creator free *from* time and matter is free *for* them, capable of creative love because inexhaustible and without agitation. Fourth, as subsistent being the creator's life is utterly sufficient and so creates "indifferently," out of excess rather than need for a complement to itself. "It is meaningful to say that the one pure act of *esse subsistens* could 'be' all alone. . . . The contrast to *esse subsistens* is not differentiation, but nothing other at all. That there is, in fact, anything other than the one pure act of *esse subsistens* is due not to the necessity of being coupled and paired . . . but to the unnecessitated choice exercised by the creator."[67] The difference between God and the world is not a difference *within* the world; the creation of the world out of nothing is not something that happens *to* the world but the effortless act of the one who alone can bestow being. "From him . . . are all things. To him be glory for ever" (Rom. 11:36).

66. See Thomas Aquinas, *Summa theologiae* Ia.45.1, ad 3.
67. R. Sokolowski, *Presence and Absence: A Philosophical Investigation of Language and Being* (Bloomington: Indiana University Press, 1978), 179.

7

Providence

JOHN WEBSTER

Providence is that work of divine love for temporal creatures whereby God ordains and executes their fulfillment in fellowship with himself. God loves creatures and so he orders their course to perfection: *mundum per se ipsum regit, quem per se ipsum condidit.*[1] A doctrine of providence is, accordingly, a conceptual meditation on the consolation and hope that this work of love generates. But it has commonly proved a point at which the gospel's consolation is difficult to commend or receive, and the scandal is such that doing justice to the doctrine demands a greater than usual measure of resolution and clarity of mind in understanding the constraints and opportunities that attend its exposition. Providence is a permanently contrary doctrine. It is too simple to proceed on the assumption that the contrariety issues from an acute sense of unprecedented crisis—loss of confidence in epic readings of human history, a sense that we have witnessed a scale of horror unfelt by our forebears. If theology takes such outrage and unbelief seriously, it cannot placate them by modifying its concepts or eliminating embarrassing accretions; the contrariety is *material*, of the nature of the case, and it must be seen through to the end or there can be no advance.

1. Gregory the Great, *Moralia in Iob* 24.20 (Turnhout: Brepols, 1985), 1222.

Theodicy is a case in point. A theology of providence need not and cannot wait on demonstration of the divine righteousness, because providence is not asserted on the basis of the insignificance of evil but on the basis of the belief that God outbids any and all evil. What makes evil problematic for providence is not its existence but the fact that we resist applying belief in providence to cases of it, especially those in which we are concerned. Theological answers to this will therefore be as much ascetic as argumentative: we need to learn what it is to apply belief in providence, and how to apply it, in order to be persuaded of the viability and fruitfulness of making the application. Reconciling providence and horrors is a task within fellowship with God; inability to commend and receive the proffered reconciliation indicates estrangement. "When my soul was embittered, when I was pricked in heart, I was stupid and ignorant, I was like a beast toward thee. Nevertheless I am continually with thee; thou dost hold my right hand" (Ps. 73:21–23 RSV).

This is not a matter of theology evading responsibility to its setting but exercising it in the only way it knows. The task of a Christian theology of providence can be undertaken only by drawing on the resources given to it by the gospel; it can only hear the prophets and apostles, and only speak after such hearing—otherwise it has nothing to say. What it is not permitted to do is to respond to its contrary situation by suspending its talk of providence until better instructed, until better warrants are provided to ensure a more fluent, less crisis-laden exposition. Release from the misery and dishonor of making this particular confession can come only at the price of abandoning the entire undertaking. The law of theology is the law of the matter, not that of its occasion. To follow the law of the matter and bear its contrariety is not self-protection but evangelical charity. "Since we have such a hope, we are very bold" (2 Cor. 3:12).

Three Formal Features of Providence

First, three formal matters: the location of the doctrine of providence, the relation of *expositio* to *disputatio*, and the Christian specificity required in its exposition.

(1) Christian dogmatics has a double theme: God and the work of God, theology proper and economy. Though in the order of exposition the economy may be treated first and with great elaboration, in the material order theology proper is primary, and all other Christian teaching is suspended from it. This means that all Christian doctrines are functions of the doctrine of the Trinity (though it should quickly be added that this is to appeal not to some abstract

principle of relationality but to the pure originality of God's perfect life). God's immanent triune perfection is the first and last object of Christian theological reflection and governs all else. And that perfection is abundant, giving life to and sustaining that which is not God and which is the object of economic reflection.

Providence is a distributed doctrine, straddling both theology and economy, because its theme is God's government of created reality in execution of his will for creatures—what Thomas Aquinas calls *ratio ordinis* and *dispositio et executio ordinis*.[2] It pervades dogmatics, because dogmatics treats the history of fellowship between the creator and his creatures in which God perfects that to which he has given life. Like the history of redemption that it accompanies and supports, providence is ubiquitous. Because of this, a materially separate treatment can be only for the purposes of exposition and must not be allowed to obscure the linkages across the system of Christian teaching. This distributed character is something that providence shares with most other Christian doctrines; conceptual-topical treatment must be undertaken in such a way that the primary historical order of the canon in which all doctrines are being treated all the time is not set aside.

Moreover, distributed in this way, providence is informed by other tracts of Christian teaching—most of all the doctrine of God but also, for example, creation, soteriology, and anthropology. Attending to these connections helps to preserve Christian specificity; their neglect can issue in one of the most common disorders in an account of providence, namely, dominance by questions or modes of argument not derived from the Christian confession. Particularly since the eclipse of classical Christian cosmology, providence has attracted to itself a set of problems for which the solution has been considered essential to a plausible account of the doctrine. Such problems include theodicy, the nature of divine action, or the freedom of creatures in relation to divine determination. Of such problems, the Christian doctrine of providence is considered an instance. Proposed solutions are often descriptively slender, making little appeal to the resources of Christian teaching, and instead looking for help—for example—to better theories of causality. The result is a stripped-down account of providence in which the identities of the agents—God and creatures—and the historical unfolding of their relations carry insufficient weight. The most effective counter to this is to resist the isolation and problematization of the doctrine: providence cannot be extracted from the corpus, cleaned up, and then reinserted, for dogmatics is a whole, not an assemblage of discrete parts.

---

2. Thomas Aquinas, *Summa theologiae*, trans. Thomas Gilby, Blackfriars 5 (Oxford: Blackfriars, 1967), Ia.22.1, ad 1.

Where, then, should providence be located? It can be divided between the doctrine of God and the doctrine of creation, as it is by Thomas Aquinas, who treats providence proper in the context of discussing the divine will,[3] government in relation to creation,[4] and fate in connection with the order of the world.[5] Or it can be reserved for unified treatment as part of the doctrine of God's relation to creation, usually after predestination. The former placement has the considerable contemporary advantage of underscoring the relation of providence to the eternal divine counsel.[6] The latter is probably most convenient, however, to display the coherence of the doctrine provided that the all-important backward connection to the doctrine of God is retained. Retaining this backward connection is crucial to prevent the soteriological subjectivization of providence that we find in, for example, Friedrich Schleiermacher. Like John Calvin, Schleiermacher is entirely correct to emphasize that the saving preservation of the community of redemption is the creaturely core of the doctrine of providence.[7] But he lacks Calvin's reference to the eternal divine will; though he speaks of "the Divine All-Sovereignty,"[8] providence falls under the rule that "for a Christian consciousness, all the things have existence only as they are related to the efficacy of redemption."[9] The lack of a theology of divine perfection eventually leads to the absorption of the doctrine into morals or history or attitude to life. Moreover, placing providence after the doctrine of creation has the further advantage of ensuring that the doctrine of creation is not simply an account of origins but inseparable from God's establishment of creatures with movement toward finality, superintended by his care.

(2) As with all dogmatics, *disputatio* is subordinate to *expositio*. Dogmatics has a twofold task: an analytic-expository task, in which it attempts orderly

---

3. Thomas Aquinas, *Summa theologiae* Ia.22.

4. Thomas Aquinas, *Summa theologiae* Ia.103–9.

5. Thomas Aquinas, *Summa theologiae* Ia.116.

6. Karl Barth mounts a curious objection to Lombard and Bonaventure for placing the doctrine of providence in the doctrine of God, arguing that this imports God's relation to the creation "in the being of God as though the creature too were eternally in God": *Church Dogmatics* III/3, trans. Geoffrey Bromiley and T. F. Torrance (Edinburgh: T&T Clark, 1961), 5. He is certainly correct to argue that God "would be no less God if the whole of creation had never been done, if there were no creatures, and if the whole doctrine of providence were therefore irrelevant" (ibid.). But to go on from there to say that "there can be no place for this doctrine in that of the being of God" (ibid.) is an overstatement—as he implies when he argues that as an *opus ad extra* providence rests on the *opus Dei internum*, the election of grace in Jesus Christ (ibid., 6).

7. Friedrich Schleiermacher, *The Christian Faith* (Edinburgh: T&T Clark, 1928), 723.

8. Ibid., 144.

9. Ibid., 723.

conceptual representation of the content of the Christian gospel as it is laid out in the scriptural witnesses, and a polemical-apologetic task, in which it explores the justification and value of Christian truth claims. The latter, external orientation is necessary but derivative of the first; it may not without serious damage become the ground of exposition. This is, once again, to prevent the problematization of Christian doctrine in which material dogmatic content is suspended rather than applied to make headway with disputed questions. This we shall try to indicate in the relation of providence to creaturely freedom. Further, dogmatics will have a free relation to the necessary conceptualities and languages of which it makes use in explicating its material and will not expect them to bear all the weight in *disputatio*. Both dogmatic and apologetic problems can rarely be eased conceptually or by the improvement of terms: most often what is required is the clearing away of some dominant theory or conceptuality by dogmatic description. In the doctrine of providence, the language of causality and agency is a matter in point, because refinement of such language is sometimes thought to be essential to successful exposition. The doctrine cannot, of course, manage without such language—all theology has is borrowings from elsewhere. But good dogmatics will be keen to retain a sense that the borrowing is ad hoc, not principled, and to let the real work be done by the matter itself. A doctrine of providence will best be conducted as an exercise in biblical reasoning, a conceptual, schematic representation of what theology is told by the prophets and apostles.

(3) These first two points serve to indicate the Christian specificity required of a Christian doctrine of providence: at each point, the cogency of the presentation depends on deployment of and governance by the Christian doctrine of God and its economic entailments. A Christian doctrine of providence is only derivatively a theory of history, a cosmology, or an account of divine action in the world; most properly it is a representation of how the Father's plan for the fullness of time is set forth in Christ and made actual by the Holy Spirit among the children of Adam. In other words, the identities of the agents in the history of providence—this God and his creatures—are fundamental to determining its course and character. (Karl Barth's insistence on providence as God's "fatherly lordship" is surely the most extended modern attempt to account for this.)[10] Again, Christian specificity about the ends of providence is crucial to grasping its nature, for providence is not mere static world maintenance but teleological, the fulfillment of the ordered fellowship with God, which is the creature's perfected happiness. The key questions are

10. See Barth, *Church Dogmatics* III/3, 3–288; a classic statement is, of course, that in the Heidelberg Catechism, Lord's Day 10, Q. 27.

not cosmological but theological, and their answers derive from specifications of the enacted name of God.

A natural extension of this is the need for caution regarding the derivation of teaching about providence from the general concept of deity, which forms part of a natural philosophy. Huldrych Zwingli's *De providentia* is commonly held up as an example of this, because—despite its trinitarian content and its practical conclusion—it insists on the *necessity* of providence if there is a supreme good:

> For since it is of the nature of supreme truth to see through all things clearly, inasmuch as that which is divinity must see all things, and since it is of the nature of supreme might to be able to do what it sees, nay, to do all things, and, finally, since it is of the nature of the supreme good to will by its goodness to do what it clearly sees and can do, it follows that he who can do all things must provide for all things.[11]

The worry is reinforced by Zwingli's appeal to Giovanni Pico della Mirandola's oration with its talk of God as "the great master workman."[12] Others stumble here: Francis Turretin's penetrating analysis is superb but shadowed by a posteriori demonstration of providence from a doctrine of God as supreme ruler, and by a concept of motion lacking in the required equivocation.[13] If a theology of providence is to identify and steer away from the problem, it requires that analytic powers be set in the service of dramatic-historical description: only in this way can the identities and agents of the history of providence, their modes of actions and ends, be protected from formalization. The rule is: *he* upholds the universe by his word of power.[14]

The Knowledge of Providence

"We struggle and waiver in the matter of providence," Zwingli tells us. "When it presents itself before our eyes so plainly that we are forced even against our

11. Huldrych Zwingli, *The Production from Memory of a Sermon on the Providence of God*, in *On Providence and Other Essays*, ed. W. J. Hinke (Durham, NC: Labyrinth, 1983), 132.
12. See Zwingli, *On the Providence of God*, 160.
13. Francis Turretin, *Institutes of Elenctic Theology*, vol. 1, *First through Tenth Topics* (Phillipsburg, NJ: P&R, 1992), 6.1.7.
14. The examples from Zwingli and Turretin suggest that the roots of what Charles Taylor calls "providential deism" reach back into the theology of the sixteenth and seventeenth centuries, and so we require a rather more probing analysis of the theological disorder that cleared a space for deistic doctrines of the world order; see Taylor, *A Secular Age* (Cambridge, MA: Harvard University Press, 2007), 221–69.

will to see it, regard it, and execute its commands, we yet bid ourselves to hope for results according to our own desires."[15] Knowledge of providence, that is, is always a matter of mortification and vivification, the chastening and reordering of desire; the application of the intellect in the matter involves its renovation and illumination by the Spirit's grace. Only in that movement of disappointment and trust is providence known. This is simply to say that the knowledge of providence is knowledge of faith: "It is not after the manner of men, or by the natural sense, that in our miseries we acknowledge God to have regard of us, but we take hold of his invisible providence by faith."[16]

Faith is creaturely knowledge, assent, and trust, which correspond to the free communicative presence and action of God. Such knowledge accords with the essential character of creaturely being, which is not *a se* and *in se* but *ab extra*, enjoyed and exercised not in the mode of possession but in an act of the referring of creaturely intellect to God. Providence is knowledge of God, and known as God is known, in the act of faith. The creaturely act of faith is the work of the Holy Spirit, a point at which reason is caught up in an antecedent, gracious causality that enables the intellect to see God and all things in God by locating its operations *coram Deo*. This is why faith in providence is only derivatively "subjective," an interpretation of and attitude toward the world. Primarily and strictly it is *objective*, generated and sustained by a movement from outside reason. Its objectivity is of a special kind, in that it is derived from "revelation," that is, from those acts in which God makes himself present to disordered creatures in such a way that they are caused to know that against which they have blinded themselves. To acquire "objectivity" in knowledge—truthful attention to reality—we are required to submit to chastening and correction. Objectivity is not self-generated knowledge, though we wish it were and are restless when we discover that it is not; the restlessness is a further sign of the intellect's disorder. To know providence, we need to be taught by the Spirit for, again, we know providence as we know God.

One of the conditions under which faith exists is that of created temporality (this is why hope is faith's extension of itself into the future). The knowledge of faith is not available apart from its acquisition and deployment over time, yet because faith is faith in the omnipresence of God to whom all occasions are seasons of mercy, faith in providence is knowledge of what will be true in all occasions, namely, "*necesse est ponere providentiam in Deo*."[17] Without knowing our future course, faith in providence confesses that God orders our time.

15. Zwingli, *On the Providence of God*, 231.
16. John Calvin, *A Commentary on the Psalms* (London: Clark, 1965), 1:141 (on Ps. 13:1).
17. Thomas Aquinas, *Summa theologiae* Ia.22.1.

A cogent theology of providence will respect this particular kind of temporal objectivity. Bad doctrines of providence extricate knowledge of providence from the corruptions of temporality—by giving easy access to synchronic accounts of history, by neglecting the believer's stance *in medias res*, by supplying history with a frame.[18] Bad doctrines of providence abound, as do bad responses to them that try to reintroduce an element of indeterminacy by subtracting from divine determination or omnicausality. But faith's knowledge of providence will neither underdetermine nor overdetermine. It will not allow that provisionality goes all the way down (this simply makes a doctrine of providence redundant), nor will it import the notion of the tragic to disrupt complacent teleologies of history (because God is, there is lament but no tragedy). And, equally, faith in providence will be unwilling to associate certain knowledge of providence with knowledge secured by proofs (certainty contingent on proof is not possible for proofs are not of infinite range or applicability). Instead, if it follows the movement of faith in God's providence, dogmatics will pay attention to the particular kind of certainty of divine providence that is given to faith. That certainty originates wholly outside the believing subject; it is given to the believer as he or she attends to the works of God.

> We know that in everything God works for good with those who love him, who are called according to his purpose. For those whom he foreknew, he also predestined to be conformed to the image of his Son in order that he might be the firstborn among many brethren. And those whom he predestined he also called; and those whom he called he also justified; and those whom he justified he also glorified. (Rom. 8:28–30 RSV)

"We know" is a function of God, who is *for us* and shows himself such by not sparing his Son. To know providence is to know that event in its infinite range—God "gave him up for us all," and so "will he not also give us all things with him?" (Rom. 8:32 RSV). It is possible to say no to Paul's question, or to say that we do not know, but those are not possibilities for faith in providence, which can say only that "If God is for us, who is against us?" (Rom. 8:31 RSV). Providence is known as God is known—in liberation from mistrust and anxious uncertainty, from paralysis and hubris, a liberation effected by the glory of Jesus Christ by which all created being and time is illuminated.

18. For an articulate reflection on these temptations, see Ben Quash, *Theology and the Drama of History* (Cambridge: Cambridge University Press, 2005). Further, see Rowan Williams, *Wrestling with Angels: Conversations in Modern Theology* (London: SCM, 2007), 35–76.

Faith, then, confesses what Calvin calls God's "invisible providence":[19] "by faith we take hold of God's grace, which is hidden from the understanding of the flesh."[20] Providence is mystery, and it is known as such. Its invisibility does not entail lack of intelligibility; rather, it is a summons to a particular act of intelligence, one conformed to the manner in which God cares for creatures—not all at once, in the midst of their conflicts, miseries, and distractions, drawing them to direct themselves to God in "sighs and prayers."[21] Through faith in providence we may come to attain the conviction of things not seen (Heb. 11:1).

Knowledge of providence is practical knowledge, a work of reason whose end is attitudes and activities in which our creaturely vocation is enacted. It is a practical perception of the origin and order of temporal episodes, not simply an observation of the nature of things or a "world picture."[22] This is not to say that knowledge of providence is not *scientia* but to specify the kind of *scientia* that it is. Ernst Troeltsch suggests that because belief in providence is religious belief, it "can by no means serve to explain the world" and "does not infringe on the scientific explanation of the world."[23] But faith is knowledge, and by it we may venture judgments. These judgments are not "pure": they are aspects of disposing of ourselves in time. By them we attempt to read human time as the history of fellowship between the creator and his creatures, seeing particular episodes as instances of judgment and blessing, seeing the whole as directed to our good, deriving consolation from the order that is discerned but not imposed. Belief in providence is not simply a gloss on the course of nature, which could quite adequately be interpreted without reference to the divine plan and its execution. Rather, it is a belief that time *is* (and is not merely taken to be) "under [God's] hand," that it cannot be enclosed "within the stream of nature,"[24] and so to learn how to live in time.[25]

This being so, it is scarcely possible to suggest that the doctrine of providence is a "mixed article," discernible partly by natural reason, partly by

19. Calvin, *Commentary on the Psalms*, 1:141.
20. Calvin, *Commentary on the Psalms*, 1:144.
21. Calvin, *Commentary on the Psalms*, 1:141.
22. See Barth, *Church Dogmatics* III/3, 18.
23. Ernst Troeltsch, *The Christian Faith* (Minneapolis: Augsburg, 1991), 205.
24. John Calvin, *Institutes of the Christian Religion*, ed. John T. McNeill, trans. Ford Lewis Battles (London: SCM, 1960), 1.11.3.
25. On this aspect of Calvin, see Randall Zachmann, *Image and Word in the Theology of John Calvin* (Notre Dame, IN: University of Notre Dame Press, 2007), 73–104; and more generally, Cornelis van der Kooi, *As in a Mirror: John Calvin and Karl Barth on Knowing God* (Leiden: Brill, 2005).

faith; it is faithful reason's receiving of the consolation that, from before the foundation of the world and through all its course, God is for us.

The Material Content of Providence

God ordains that there should be an order to creaturely being and creaturely history, and administers or regulates creaturely being and history so that they attain their perfection. "It is not only in the substance of created things that goodness lies," Thomas Aquinas tells us, "but also in their being ordained to an end, above all to their final end which is the divine goodness. This good order existing in created things is itself part of God's creation."[26] Providence is the divine work that enacts this order, both the immanent divine action of establishing the distinction of all things and the transitive divine action of temporal government.[27]

The doctrine of providence begins from the doctrine of God, of which it is a function. It is important to begin far back in the doctrine of God—not simply with, for example, divine power or intelligence but with God's perfect life, which he is from and in himself as Father, Son, and Spirit, that is, with the eternal plenitude of the divine processions in which consists the divine blessedness. Providence is an aspect of the uncaused wonder of the overflow of God's abundant life. God's perfection includes his infinite love; he is in himself an inexhaustible fountain of life; he bestows life in limitless generosity. That is, God is the maker of heaven and earth, and of all things visible and invisible.

The free, loving work of creation is *ex nihilo*: it is a work of absolute initiation and entails no compromise of the unqualified aseity of God's life. God does not create out of something, nor does he create out of need, nor does his bestowal of life entail any impoverishment or loss, for it is ingredient within his perfection. "Since he is in need of nothing, is rich in all things, and is good and kind, nay is the Father of all the things he has made, it follows that he cannot be wearied or exhausted through giving, that he rejoices in giving, that he cannot help giving."[28] In this act of generosity, God wills, establishes, and perfects a reality beyond himself as a further object of his love.

God's acts of creating and governing are inseparable. Indeed, providence is in a certain way the special dimension of Christian belief in God the creator, because it specifies the act of creation as the beginning not simply of contingency but also of faithful care. Calvin notes that "unless we pass on to his providence . . . we do not yet properly grasp what it means to say 'God is creator.' Carnal

26. Thomas Aquinas, *Summa theologiae* Ia.22.
27. Turretin, *Institutes of Elenctic Theology* 6.1.2.
28. Zwingli, *On the Providence of God*, 136.

sense, once confronted with the power of God in the very creation, stops here, and at most weighs and contemplates only the wisdom, power and goodness of the author in accomplishing such handiwork."[29] Creation, we might say, is not simply *making*. This can be seen in relation both to the creator and to the creation.

In relation to the creator, the doctrine of providence indicates that God is no "momentary creator";[30] his relation to creatures is not simply initial but temporally extended. He gives not only *substantia* but also *finis*; that is, creatures have a historical nature, being that is ordained to acquire a particular perfection over its course. This perfection is fellowship with God. Creation is the love of God that bestows life in order that this fellowship may be (love as *creativity*); providence is the love of God that, corresponding to creativity, superintends the historical order of created being so that its relation to the creator may flourish (love as *fidelity*). As ordination, divine fidelity purposes the history of fellowship; as government, providence is that history's execution.

If we stand back a bit, two things are to be understood about these affirmations. First, like the doctrine of creation, the doctrine of providence is not only an aspect of cosmology. Although both treat the metaphysics of the world order, neither can be restricted to that field. This is because, for the Christian confession, created being is not indeterminate but has a nature ordered toward relation to God. Creation is not simply making; providence is not simply maintaining. Both have to be viewed in relation to the specific Christian confession that the history of the creation serves the history of grace, because that is the kind of creation to which God gives being, a creation that may enjoy relation to him. Second, therefore, once again a great deal hangs on the identity of the maker and governor of all things—on seeing creation as love issuing in fidelity rather than as manufacture. God does not simply provide the initial motion of nature, setting its inclination then allowing it to take its course; he is not a mere observer of creaturely time but an agent, one whose providence, as Calvin puts it, "pertains no less to his hands than to his eyes."[31] Providence cannot be restricted to foreknowledge, for God is "the ruler and governor of all things, who in accordance with his wisdom has from the farthest limits of eternity decreed what he was going to do, and now by his singular might carries out what he has decreed."[32] And this is so

29. Calvin, *Institutes* 1.16.1.
30. Calvin, *Institutes* 1.16.1; see also Turretin, *Institutes of Elenctic Theology* 6.1.5.
31. Calvin, *Institutes* 1.16.4.
32. Calvin, *Institutes* 1.16.8. Herman Bavinck is thus correct to note that providence is to be attributed not only to the divine intellect but also to the divine will: *Reformed Dogmatics*, vol. 2, *God and Creation*, ed. John Bolt, trans. John Vriend (Grand Rapids: Baker Academic, 2004), 596.

because God is triune; his works *ad extra*, though indivisible, manifest the properties of the persons to whom they may especially be appropriated. The Father determines the course of created time; the Spirit causes creaturely causes; the Son intervenes to draw creation back from ruin so that it may attain its end. Only because God is *thus* does creation issue in providence.

That creation is not simply making can be seen, second, in relation to the creature. God creates what is not himself, life that is not *in se*, having no principle of life other than that of the continuing fidelity of the creator. Creaturely being needs conservation. "The *esse* of all creaturely beings so depends upon God that they could not continue to exist even for a moment, but would fall away into nothingness unless they were sustained in existence by his power."[33] To be a creature is to depend on the creator not merely for coming-to-be but also for historical persistence. This is not to espouse a theology of continuous creation in the strong sense that the world is remade moment by moment (a weaker sense of ontological dependence sometimes goes under the same term). Creation bestows being and does not merely tantalize with the possibility of being. Once bestowed, the being of creation has its own relative independence; it needs no further creating (for to create is to call into existence) but does need to be sustained by providential care. Providence thus confirms created being but does not secure it, as if it were ontologically precarious. Further, as a reality with its own being, creation cooperates with God under God in its own persistence in a way in which it could not cooperate in its own coming-to-be. And so again, the creator is not otiose once the act of creation is complete but continues his love as the governor of what he has made.

So much, then, by way of the relation between creation and providence. "Since it belongs to the same cause to give a thing its being and to bring it to completeness, i.e., to govern it, the way God is the governor of things matches the way he is their cause."[34] The Triune God is both creation's efficient and also its final cause.[35]

How is God's loving work of administration of the history of creation to be conceived? Once again, everything depends on the identity of the agent and his ends in determining the nature of his acts. That a theological metaphysics of divine action is required is unquestionable (without it, belief in providence shrinks to a subjective disposition), but the metaphysics must follow the confession it explicates and so take some care to register the fact that words such

---

33. Thomas Aquinas, *Summa theologiae* Ia.104.
34. Thomas Aquinas, *Summa theologiae* Ia.103.5, resp.
35. This is how Isaak Dorner relates the creative and providential works of God: *System of Christian Doctrine* (Edinburgh: T&T Clark, 1880–82), 2:44.

as "motion" or "cause" are simply ministerial and not principial. With this in mind, something like the following might be said.

(1) God's administration of creation is the execution of his "plan for the fullness of time" (Eph. 1:10). "The divine mind must preconceive the whole pattern of things moving to their end."[36] This seemingly dark and forboding truth is of the essence of the gospel. How is it so?

It is so because the pattern of things preexists, as Thomas Aquinas puts it, in *mente divina*, in the divine mind. This mind is the mind of "the God and Father of our Lord Jesus Christ" (Eph. 1:3), the one who wills our good, who "destines us in love" (Eph. 1:5), and whose works issue in "the praise of his glorious grace" (Eph. 1:6). God's external acts are in accordance with his inner nature; his providence expresses his omnipotent holiness and goodness and wisdom, his infinite resourcefulness in being for us. And so to speak of God's plan is to indicate God's determination to bless creatures. For Calvin, to live by virtue of "a certain and deliberate will," that is, "God's ordinance and command," is not a matter of fear or resentment but of comfort, for it means to be "under [God's] hand."[37] This is why the Christian tradition spent much effort on distinguishing faith in providence from fatalism. Fate is untrustworthy and capricious and has no goodness. But by divine determination, creatures are "destined and appointed to live" (Eph. 1:12 RSV), to fulfillment of being in praising the creator's glory. That providence, in the strict sense of the divine plan, is not bleak; destiny is above all decided in the fact that it is in *him*, in Christ—the one who is both the origin (Eph. 1:4) and the goal (Eph. 1:10) of what God's love establishes for creatures. Providence is not a world system but the assurance that creaturely time has depth and direction, that it does indeed work for good.

(2) God exercises his plan (*providentia*) in his work of caring for creatures (*procuratio*). This work is ceaseless and universal in scope. God's love for creatures is infinite; it is not possible for there to be a creaturely occasion in which it is not at work, for providence is operative *non in universali tantum sed etiam in singulari*.[38] "All things work together for good." But because the end of creation that providence protects is the fellowship of God's rational creatures with himself, general and special providence (that is, God's care for the world in general, and for all humankind) are subordinate to singular providence (God's care for the elect or the church). Calvin judged that providence is particularly God's "vigilance in ruling the church,"[39] and his judgment was a hallmark of

36. Thomas Aquinas, *Summa theologiae* Ia.22.1.
37. Calvin, *Institutes* 1.16.3.
38. Thomas Aquinas, *Summa theologiae* Ia.22.2.
39. Calvin, *Institutes* 1.17.1.

Reformed theologies of providence.[40] This is emphatically not to undermine the universality of providence but to say that the church is the special object of God's care because it is the interim realization of the goal of rational creatures, namely, fellowship with the creator. In the church, the end of creation is being reached; that is why the history of the church is the meaning of the world's history, which is the unification of all things in Christ (Eph. 1:10).

(3) Providence is thus directed to the creature's good. With this we return to the rock of offense. How can this be when we suffer or watch inexplicable horrors? Here the gospel counsels us to endurance, in which we may attain knowledge. Again: how can the governance of our ways be good if its cost is the creature's freedom? How may believers with a good conscience take and offer gospel comfort? Here the gospel returns a longer answer.

Creation (and therefore providence) is a work of love, that is, of divine power ordered to the bestowal of life on another and to the perfection of that life, for God's "power is the minister of God's love and wisdom. It works with a teleological reference."[41] This already sets a theology of providence in the proper direction. If God is *thus*—if he is the Father who wills our good, the Spirit who gives integrity to created being, the Son who rescues it from self-chosen ruin—then how can the divine regulation of all things not be for our good? We do not need to win freedom back from God, because God is its ground, not its denial.

> Because it belongs to the best sort of being to achieve the best sort of effects, failure to direct the beings created to their perfection is not consonant with God's absolute goodness. Now the highest perfection of any being consists in the attaining of its end. Hence it is appropriate to God's goodness that, as he has brought things into being, he also guides them towards their end. That is what governing them means.[42]

To see this, however, requires that we strip the notion of "moving" of any abstract ideas of sheer causal force, maximize its equivocal character, and fill out its form with reference to the canonical portrait of the Lord of the covenant. Moreover, we need to deploy conceptual resources to try to show how the freedom and dignity of creatures are caught up in, not suppressed or eliminated by, the rule of God. God's governance secures the creature's freedom. If this fails to commend itself, it is because it contravenes a destructive convention according to which true freedom is indeterminacy and absolute spontaneity or nothing at all. To say that is to deny creatureliness. Freedom is existence in

---

40. See, e.g., Schleiermacher, *The Christian Faith*, 723; Barth, *Church Dogmatics* III/3, 38.
41. Dorner, *System of Christian Doctrine*, 2.53.
42. Thomas Aquinas, *Summa theologiae* Ia.103.1.

accordance with created nature and toward created ends, not self-authorship or aseity. This means that freedom is reception but not passivity—that it is permission and summons, spoken not *by* me, but *to* me by God. "God is the abiding cause of man's being a cause able to determine the character of his existence."[43] The free person fulfills him- or herself by perfecting a given nature. That perfecting is the work of providence that does not constrain but fulfills the creature's self-determination, because God's providence moves the creature's will by what Thomas Aquinas calls an "interior movement."[44] Can a moved will be free? Yes, because "to be moved voluntarily is to be moved of one's own accord, i.e., from a resource within. That inner resource, however, may derive from some other, outward source. In this sense, there is no contradiction between being moved of one's own accord and being moved by another."[45] If we are to see that Thomas Aquinas's argument is evangelically well judged, we need to grasp that divine providential acts are not simple compulsion (the archer sending the arrow) but rather intrinsic to the creature whom God moves, what Thomas Aquinas calls "a necessity of nature"[46] in which the creature is activated and not diminished.[47] And to see this we also need to see that—as that astute reader of Thomas Aquinas, Turretin, puts it at the beginning of the modern period—"the fount of error is the measuring of the nature of liberty from equilibrium and making indifference essential to it. Liberty must be defined by willingness and spontaneity."[48]

This points us to how, in the light of the gospel, providence dignifies creatures. As with creaturely freedom, so with creaturely dignity: it does not consist only in being *agens seipsum*, one's own director.[49] To be moved by divine government is not to be beaten but to be moved to act.

Here the conceptuality of secondary causality proves immensely resourceful. God's providential activity is omnicausal but not *solely* causal. His ordering of the history of creation includes the employment of creaturely ministers. Their ministerial operations do not threaten but draw life from divine sovereignty; divine sovereignty does not eliminate but generates creaturely operation. That creatures are so drawn into the ordering and moving of their own histories is a gift of love; it is of "the abundance of his goodness"

43. Dorner, *System of Christian Doctrine*, 2.51.
44. Thomas Aquinas, *Summa theologiae* Ia.104.4.
45. Thomas Aquinas, *Summa theologiae* Ia.104.4.
46. Thomas Aquinas, *Summa theologiae* Ia.103.1, ad 1.
47. Bavinck (*Reformed Dogmatics*, 2:608) comments, "The world and every creature in it have received their own existence, but increase in reality, freedom, and authenticity to the extent that they are more dependent on God and exist from moment to moment from, through, and to God."
48. Turretin, *Institutes of Elenctic Theology* 6.5.11.
49. Thomas Aquinas, *Summa theologiae* Ia.103.1, ad 1.

that God "imparts to creatures also the dignity of causing."[50] For not only is "operation . . . the goal of created being," but "to deprive creation of its pattern of cause and effect . . . would imply lack of power in the creator, since an agent power is the source of its giving an effect a causative capability."[51] The creature's "intrinsic power to act" does not exclude "the extrinsic pre-motion of God."[52]

Part, then, of seeing that providence is God's goodness is grasping that God's love of creatures includes his creation of them with a particular nature. They are creatures who are not *a se*. They possess causality, and this causality is secondary or medial. As medial causes they are themselves caused, but—because God is who God is, the life-giver—caused causes are not noncauses but causes that exercise a specific mode of causality. "Secondariness" is not a deficiency, a violation of creaturely agency, but a specification of the agency lovingly bestowed on us by God who summons us into his service. And further, self-subsistent agency, curved in on itself, is not our dignity but our resistance to nature.

(4) From all this, we may sketch in the most minimal way the modes of divine providential activity. God is faithful to the creature, calling it into his service and guarding it against disorder so that it may obtain its promised glory. That is, through the Son and the Spirit, God preserves, acts with, and governs the creature in its passage into the eternal kingdom of God.

God loves creatures faithfully in his work of preservation. He freely associates his being with that of the creature, continuing to bear up creaturely reality because he does not will that the creature should fail to attain its perfection. Creaturely history is thus stretched between its source and its end in God, yet its passage, though hidden, is not insecure because it exists under the divine promise. The inner court in which that promise is fulfilled is, of course, the mission of the Son, but its outer court is God's providential service, which makes possible the creature's continuance in its goal of fellowship.

God loves the creature in his work of concurrence. His agency does not cease with the last day of creation, nor does he preserve created reality merely as its passive ontological *principium*. He acts in partnership with the acts of creatures, serving them by determining them for his service. "As the creature has itself in being with respect to God, so also it ought to have itself in working, for the mode of working follows the mode of being . . . now every creature depends upon God in being, therefore also in working."[53]

---

50. Thomas Aquinas, *Summa theologiae* Ia.22.3.

51. Thomas Aquinas, *Summa theologiae* Ia.105.5.

52. Turretin, *Institutes of Elenctic Theology* 6.5.13; see further Dorner, *System of Christian Doctrine*, 2.45–49.

53. Turretin, *Institutes of Elenctic Theology* 6.4.9.

God loves the creature in his work of governance. Creaturely self-government is destructive and enslaving because it exchanges the necessity for some other self-imposed necessity, which is often less wise and loving than that appointed by God, and leading not to our happiness but to decay. In his providence God overrules this; he so orders creaturely history that—without our knowledge or consent—we are set free for our inheritance. This inheritance is not received apart from the saving missions of the Son and the Spirit. But these works, by which God's kingdom is established, are anticipated by his providential government, which also accompanies and furthers the benefits that flow from them until in the fullness of time all things are united in God.

Proper Uses

Providence is gospel consolation, ignorance of which is, Calvin tells us, "the ultimate of all miseries."[54] Trust in providence signals the end of the evil self-responsibility that so afflicts much of our civil life (this we might expect) and ecclesial life (of this we should be ashamed). To embrace and trust ourselves to divine government is not resignation but hopeful action toward the end secured for us by a loving creator. Calvin brooded on the fragility and transience of human life. "A man cannot go about unburdened by many forms of his own destruction, and without drawing out a life enveloped, as it were, with death. . . . Yet, when the light of divine providence has once shone upon a godly man, he is then relieved and set free not only from the extreme anxiety and fear that were pressing him before, but from every care."[55]

We must reach that comfort at the right pace—not too fast, lest we treat it lightly; not too slowly, lest we be overtaken by melancholy. We are instructed by the doctrine of providence to look to God for comfort; to cast ourselves in a tragic role, to allow ourselves to think that there is no comfort, is to fall prey to unbelief. But belief is learned, not given all at once. No small part of the office of dogma is to assist in that learning of the promises of God, describing them well and letting their goodness fill our sails.

> O God, whose never-failing providence ordereth all things both in heaven and earth; we humbly beseech thee to put away from us all hurtful things, and to give us those things which be profitable for us; through Jesus Christ our Lord.

54. Calvin, *Institutes* 1.17.11.
55. Calvin, *Institutes* 1.17.11.

8

Anthropology

KELLY M. KAPIC

For the fullness of our happiness, beyond which there is none else, is this: to enjoy God the Three in whose image we were made.

Augustine[1]

God created man good and in his image, that is, in true righteousness and holiness, so that he might rightly know God his Creator, love him with his whole heart, and live with him in eternal blessedness, praising and glorifying him.

Heidelberg Catechism, Q. 6[2]

Introduction

"Anthropology," as commonly understood in a contemporary academic setting, represents the study of humans, giving special attention to the biological

1. Augustine, *The Trinity*, trans. Edmund Hill (Hyde Park, NY: New City, 1991), 1.3.18.
2. Heidelberg Catechism, Q. 6, in Jaroslav Pelikan, *Creeds and Confessions of Faith in the Christian Tradition*, 4 vols. (New Haven: Yale University Press, 2003), 2:430. Hereafter CCFCT.

and social sciences: it is fundamentally an empirical study. *Theological* anthropology, however, works from a different set of questions and presuppositions, which, while overlapping at points with general anthropology, nevertheless shapes its discourse in a particular way. Paul Jewett observes why the
theological is needed: "The problem . . . is not that we seek to understand
ourselves, but that we seek such understanding in terms of ourselves alone.
Such a procedure is doomed to failure because only God, who made us, truly
knows who we are and can disclose to us the mystery of our existence."[3] This
chapter will explore that mystery.

Christian anthropology draws its guidance from revelation: here we discover
the Triune Creator, the human creature, and the particular call and response
that hold together this Lord and his image bearers, by looking to the incarnate Christ. A *theological* anthropology, therefore, faithfully reflects God's
purposes as well as the reality of current human existence—including dignity
and struggle, universality and particularity, relationality and personal identity,
all understood within the framework of love and communion.

Rather than delivering a historical survey or exhaustive review of various
interpretations of anthropology, this chapter makes a constructive proposal
rooted in classic orthodoxy. The opening proposition establishes some larger
theological connections. Subsequently, I then unpack five particular thesis
statements that are facets of a properly constructed Christian anthropology.
The chapter cites a wide variety of creedal and confessional statements to
show connections within Christian orthodoxy.

An Opening Proposition

*Christian anthropology recognizes that we never embody God's image more
clearly than when we love, delight in, and commune with his incarnate Son,
who has reconciled all things in himself. Simply put, we are never more like
God than when we love his Son through his Spirit.*

In a short homily offered before serving the Lord's supper, John Owen
(1616–83) makes a brief comment about humans imaging God: *to be like
God is to love Jesus Christ.* We focus on four points.

First, Owen reflects classic orthodox conceptions of the immanent (*ad
intra*) Trinity, arguing that from all eternity there was "an essential blessedness of the holy Trinity" that "consists in the mutual love of the Father and

3. Paul K. Jewett, *Who We Are: Our Dignity as Human* (Grand Rapids: Eerdmans, 1996),
17. Cf. John Calvin, *Institutes of the Christian Religion*, ed. John T. McNeill, trans. Ford Lewis
Battles (Philadelphia: Westminster, 1960), 2.1.1.

the Son, by the Holy Ghost; which is the love of them both." Even before the incarnation, the Son is "the only full, resting, complete object of the love of God the Father."[4]

Second, "it is in the nature of rational creatures" to experience love in such a way that "it might shadow and represent the ineffable, eternal love that the Father had unto the Son, and the Son unto the Father, by the Spirit." All love experienced and known outside this intratrinitarian love is a "free emanation from this eternal love between the Father and the Son."[5]

Third, Owen believes that the "first act of the love of God the Father wherein there is any thing *ad extra*, or *without the divine essence*, is the person of Christ considered as invested with our nature."[6] Strange as it may appear given temporal considerations, Owen argues that the Father's distinctive first love of his creation is the human nature that is assumed by the Son. Since God is eternal, when we speak of God's acts in relation to time, the language of first, second, and the like has more to do with preeminence than with temporal succession. Because of Christ's preeminence in God's creative acts, the meaning of all creation centers on Christ. Here Owen connects what he calls the first and second creation, understood in terms of humanity and anchored in the love of God: "From the first eternal love of God [*ad intra*] proceeds all love that was in the first creation; and from this second love of God [*ad extra*], to the person of Christ as incarnate, proceeds all the love in the second creation."[7] Owen here attempts to bring heaven and earth together in the incarnate Christ, all understood within terms of divine love. Listening carefully to the designation "Beloved Son" (e.g., Matt. 3:17; 17:5; Mark 1:11; 9:7; 12:6; Col. 1:13; 2 Pet. 1:17) given to Jesus, Owen hears in these words God's invitation: "Let the sons of men . . . take notice of this, that the infinite love of my whole soul is fixed on the person of Jesus Christ *as incarnate*."[8] Now having taken on a human body and soul, the Son becomes the great delight of the Father who fills his incarnate Son with his Spirit. Here in Jesus is God's great *yes* to creation in general, and humanity in particular. And in Jesus, God actualizes his call to us to enter communion with him through the Son and by the Spirit.

4. See John Owen, "Discourse 22," in *The Works of John Owen*, vol. 9, ed. William H. Goold (London: Banner of Truth, 1965), 612–15; here 613.

5. Ibid., 613.

6. Ibid., 614 (emphasis original).

7. Ibid., 614. Cf. Karl Barth's view of how the election of Jesus Christ can be seen as God's first movement *ad extra*, yet some potential ambiguity and challenges that arise, e.g., Edwin Chr. Van Driel, "Karl Barth on the Eternal Existence of Jesus Christ," *Scottish Journal of Theology* 60, no. 1 (2007): 45–61.

8. Owen, "Discourse 22," 614–15.

Owen's fourth and final point employs the ideas of love and communion in such a way that he beautifully weaves together Christology, anthropology, and sanctification.

> Proportional to the renovation of the image and likeness of God upon any of our souls, is *our love to Jesus Christ*. He that knows Jesus Christ most, is most like unto God: for there the soul of God rests . . . and *if we would be like to God . . . it must be in the gracious exercise of our love to the person of Jesus Christ.* . . . If we return to God by the renovation of his image, we do not exercise our love to God immediately as God, but our love to God by and in Christ. Here is a trail . . . of our return to God, and of the renovation of his image in us—namely, in our love to Jesus Christ.[9]

Owen concludes that we are never more like God than when we love the Son incarnate. Because Jesus is the fullness of God's self-revelation, we reflect God to the degree that we love the incarnate Son who is the great object of the Father's love, for Christ is the one "adequate, complete object of the love of God, and of the whole creation that bears the image of God."[10] In this love for Jesus the Messiah, "there God and man do meet."[11]

Following these ideas expressed by Owen, the "opening proposition" above, used as a starting point for theological anthropology, sets the discipline in clear relation to other doctrines (Trinity, Christology, sanctification, etc.) and places love and communion with God in Christ at the center for further construction.

Constructing a Christian Anthropology

There is a long Christian tradition that frames discussions about anthropology around the language of the *imago Dei*. While the use of the Latin (rather than Hebrew or Greek) may have resulted from the dominance of the Vulgate, especially in the West, one might take this persistent Latin use as a reminder that we are dealing with a theologically constructed concept. Indeed, at its best, the church never intended to reduce anthropology to a mere study of how this particular phrase ("image [and likeness] of God") is used in Scripture

9. Ibid., 615 (emphasis mine).
10. Ibid., 612–13. See Kelly M. Kapic, *Communion with God: The Divine and the Human in the Theology of John Owen* (Grand Rapids: Baker Academic, 2007), 233. That book as a whole deals with Owen's anthropology; pp. 228–33 examine this particular Lord's supper discourse and how these ideas are developed in Owen's work.
11. Owen, "Discourse 22," 615.

(e.g., Gen. 1:26–27; 9:6; cf. 1 Cor. 11:7; James 3:9).[12] The phrase "imago Dei" often served as shorthand for the whole doctrine of humanity, a doctrine that required a much larger perspective than studying the particular context in which one finds these key words in the Bible. Until this basic observation is fully appreciated, biblical scholars will continue to misunderstand theologians, believing they are reading far too much into this rarely used though significantly placed biblical expression.

An oft-repeated account of historical approaches to the *imago Dei* goes something like this. From the early church and even up into the premodern period, God's image was normally linked to a particular human faculty. For many, if not most, *reason* was that faculty. Having rational capacities appeared to set humans apart from other creatures. Sure, monkeys and dolphins are clever, but humans are "not brutelike" and thus can know God in a distinctive way.[13] Other options occasionally surfaced, such as *volition*: having a will might be the thing that distinguished humans in a way that mirrored God.

The basic impulse for any of these approaches, we are told, was to locate the image in a human capacity, or some mix of capabilities. Occasionally other theologians took a different route by emphasizing the call for Adam and Eve to exercise dominion over the earth (Gen. 1:28–30). Making this move identified the *imago* with humanity's role to *steward* the earth, thus representing the Lord to the rest of the creaturely realm. Finally, as the story is commonly stated, modern theology brilliantly moved past earlier, naive

---

12. Cf. G. L. Bray, "The Significance of God's Image in Man," *Tyndale Bulletin* 42, no. 2 (1991): 195–225; D. J. A. Clines, "The Image of God in Man," *Tyndale Bulletin* 19 (1968): 53–103. For a sampling of general studies on theological anthropology, see Karl Barth, *Church Dogmatics* III/2, ed. G. W. Bromiley and T. F. Torrance (Edinburgh: T&T Clark, 1960); Herman Bavinck, *Reformed Dogmatics*, vol. 2, *God and Creation*, ed. John Bolt, trans. John Vriend (Grand Rapids: Baker Academic, 2004), 511–88; G. C. Berkouwer, *Man: The Image of God* (Grand Rapids: Eerdmans, 1962); Marc Cortez, *Theological Anthropology: A Guide for the Perplexed* (London: T&T Clark, 2010); Anthony A. Hoekema, *Created in God's Image* (Grand Rapids: Eerdmans, 1986); David H. Kelsey, *Eccentric Existence: A Theological Anthropology*, 2 vols. (Louisville: Westminster John Knox, 2009); Reinhold Niebuhr, *The Nature and Destiny of Man: A Christian Interpretation* (New York: C. Scribner's Sons, 1949); Wolfhart Pannenberg, *Anthropology in Theological Perspective* (Philadelphia: Westminster, 1985); Christoph Schwöbel and Colin E. Gunton, *Persons, Divine, and Human* (Edinburgh: T&T Clark, 1991); Charles Sherlock, *The Doctrine of Humanity* (Downers Grove, IL: InterVarsity, 1996); John D. Zizioulas, *Being as Communion: Studies in Personhood and the Church* (Crestwood, NY: St. Vladimir's Seminary Press, 1985).

13. "A Brief Statement," Evangelical Lutheran Synod of Missouri, Ohio (1932), 6, in *CCFCT*, 3:489. The fuller statement expands and clarifies a bit: while humans are "not brutelike nor merely capable of intellectual development," as image bearers they can know God in righteousness and holiness in a way that sets them apart.

essentialist accounts that tried to locate the image in a human faculty.[14] God's image is not about the faculties, or about exercising dominion (which could mask abuses of power), but relationality. Much of modern theological anthropology argues that we *relate* to God and others, and that is the heart of being in God's image.

While I am extremely sympathetic with the concerns of contemporary theology, I fear that the focus on relationality may be an example of where we are living on borrowed capital. Current conceptions of relationality, it appears to me, actually require some of the insights found in earlier theological expressions. Relationality will be key to any Christian anthropology, but one must still ask what relationality assumes, how it takes place, and so on. I believe there is something important in each of these emphases (faculties, dominion, relationality), but without one another they suffer from incompleteness, and overemphasis of any one can undermine a full theological anthropology. By including human faculties, representation, and relationality in our discussion, we can have a robust anthropology that is recognizable to Christians across the centuries as well as faithful to the key biblical and contemporary concerns.

Thesis One

Christian anthropology is shaped by protological concerns that call us to seek a holistic account of the human creature.

The whole person matters. For many, the most important anthropological questions are historical. These focus on the "beginnings" of the human species, concentrate on when and how they lived, and give special attention to physiological development. While these questions are interesting and indeed important, theological anthropology begins with a different set of concerns that take priority over cultural, archaeological, and genetic studies, though a complete anthropology must, of course, take into account these studies in due time.

History *does* matter to theological anthropology. More precisely, a Christian anthropology repeatedly moves between the protological and the eschatological. *Protology* is primarily concerned with the creation of humans, whereas *eschatology* is concerned with their end or goal (*telos*). One focuses on the beginning as propelling us toward the present, while the other examines the

14. While this way of describing the past comes in various forms, one sample is in Stanley Grenz, *The Social God and the Relational Self: A Trinitarian Theology of the Imago Dei* (Louisville: Westminster John Knox, 2001), esp. 141–82. Grenz's volume is stimulating and rich in many ways, but it can further an overly stereotyped view of the past and overlooks insightful theological instincts found in these earlier reflections.

future pulling at the present. These are not properly pitted against each other; rather, they are complementary. Biblically, both are concerned with and governed by God's purpose for human creatures. This first thesis will focus on protological concerns.

A long tradition in the church's confession argued that humanity is a kind of bridge between the heavenly and the earthly. Angels serve as the great representatives of the former, and the crawling beasts characterize the latter. After creating angels and beasts to populate heaven and earth, argues the twelfth-century Lateran Creed (*De fide catholica* of 1215), God "created human beings composed as it were of both spirit and body in common."[15] Petrus Van Mastricht, in the early seventeenth century, argued similarly that the human creature had a special place in the entire universe. Certainly God delighted in all of his creation, from the beavers to the archangels, yet something distinctive was true about humanity in its particular ability "to experience the goodness of all creatures in himself and to render thanks to God accordingly."[16] Consequently, even from the beginning the created order described in Genesis shows God's ability "to recapitulate all created things . . . in one man and to present the sum of this vast universe in a stupendous work of art in such a tiny compass and as a sort of μικρόκοσμος."[17] Because of the distinctly human position as *microcosmos*, the Son's assumption of a human nature will have cosmic significance on account of that humanity, but we must wait to discuss this in more detail.

John of Damascus (676–749) represents an example of classic orthodoxy in how he articulates the dignity and uniqueness of the human creature made in God's image and likeness. Often thought of as the last of the Greek fathers, he consolidates and summarizes the main Eastern (and often Western) consensus on most matters. Here he briefly connects the Creator with our human distinctness and our creaturely *telos*. "From the earth He formed his body and His own inbreathing gave him a rational and understanding soul, which last we say is the divine image—for the 'according to His image' means the intellect and free will, while the 'according to His likeness' means such likeness in virtue as is possible."[18] While contemporary scholarship is quick to point out that making a hard distinction between "image" and "likeness"

15. The Doctrinal Decree of the Fourth Lateran Council (*De fide catholica*) 1, in CCFCT, 1:741.

16. Mastricht, quoted by Heinrich Heppe, *Reformed Dogmatics: Set Out and Illustrated from the Sources*, ed. Ernst Bizer, trans. G. T. Thomson (Grand Rapids: Baker, 1978), 221.

17. Heppe, *Reformed Dogmatics*, 220. Cf. John of Damascus, *Writings: The Orthodox Faith*, trans. Chase F. Hathaway (Washington, DC: Catholic University of America Press, 1958), 2.12. He also claims "man is a microcosm."

18. John of Damascus, *Orthodox Faith* 2.12.

requires exegetical gymnastics that we should properly avoid, we should also not hastily dismiss this older way of thinking through the concept of the image.[19] Notice the twofold assumption behind this statement and assertions like it. It would be a mistake to treat these faculties (mind, will, body) as entities unto themselves, because they function according to their specific purpose of responding to the Creator in a way that faithfully represents God to the rest of his creation. Central to that vision was a life of communion, which we develop in the next thesis. For now, note that such communion (or relationality) is distinctly human, engaging the mind, moving the will, stirring the affections, and affirming the body. John here emphasizes the mind and will, as most of his contemporaries did. Yet elsewhere he highlights physicality, such as when he focuses on how a full incarnation includes Jesus's body: he had a real face that could be touched and eyes that could be gazed upon. Rather than a passing observation, this recognition of the physical has a significant role in John's argument for the legitimate place of icons imaging Christ.[20] In sum, a generous reading exposes the underlying concerns John and his contemporaries often had for a holistic response to God, one embodied and enjoyed by Jesus.

This comprehensive vision of human nature can be found a millennium later in the Canons of the Synod of Dort (1618–19), which state that being made in God's image originally meant that this creature was "furnished in his mind with a true and salutary knowledge of his Creator and things spiritual, in his will and heart with righteousness, and in all his emotions with purity; indeed, the whole man was holy."[21] Such a statement demonstrates not only a full protological appreciation of human faculties but also brings into view the eschatological concern for their proper functioning (more on that in the next thesis). To appreciate more fully how this language of the faculties connects well with a holistic approach to being human, we need to turn to early Christian debates about the Son's assumption of a full human nature, thus connecting anthropology with Christology.

The classic orthodox creeds were the result of a sense that understanding the person of Jesus was vital to faithful Christian teaching. For example, it was important to state that, when the Son humbled himself and "became

19. While John of Damascus represents a patristic example of making this distinction, it carries on, as represented by Thomas Aquinas, *Summa theologiae* (Cambridge: Blackfriars, 1963–80), Ia.93.2.

20. Verna E. F. Harrison, *God's Many-Splendored Image: Theological Anthropology for Christian Formation* (Grand Rapids: Baker Academic, 2010), 161.

21. Canons of the Synod of Dort, 3/4.1, in *CCFCT*, 2:583. Only after he turns from God and rejects the goodness of his creaturely designs has he "deprived himself of these outstanding gifts."

man," he did so in a way that embraced the fullness of *being* human. Put differently, the Son does not assume *some* human characteristics while avoiding other ones. Whatever was essential to being human must also be true of the nature assumed by the eternal Son.[22] Accordingly, in the incarnation the eternal Son not only continues to be *homoousios* with the Father in his deity, but the Son also became *homoousios* with us in our humanity as a result of his assumption of a true human nature.

The concern behind this recurrent debate is the danger of latent Apollinarianism.[23] Part of the Apollinarian argument was that if the Son of God truly assumed a full human nature with all of its faculties, then the Son would necessarily be sinful. Humans, he believed, were composed of body (the material structure), lower soul (meant to convey nonmaterial personality), and mind (*nous*, which later is often referred to by tradition as the "reasonable soul").[24] It was sometimes assumed that sin resided in the mind or spirit; consequently, to have a human "mind" would compromise the sinless integrity of the incarnate Savior. Therefore, the Apollinarian position argued that the eternal Son assumed a human body and lower soul, but the divine Logos took the place of the *nous*. The hope was that this would protect an uncompromising affirmation of the full divinity of the Son and his perfect holiness. However, it became widely believed that formulating a position in this way compromised the church's soteriological hopes. As Gregory of Nazianzus memorably quipped, "The unassumed is the unhealed. . . . Had half of Adam fallen, what was assumed and is being saved would have been half too; but if the whole fell he is united to the whole of what was born and is being saved wholly."[25] This is what is behind Nicaea's earlier statement on

---

22. It should be noted that "sinning" would not have been considered essential to human nature, although the possibility of sinning would be: Adam was fully human without sinning, and in glory persons will not cease to be human even though they cease to sin. Debates about the Son's assumption of a "fallen" human nature often get confused on this point, and theologians on both sides of this debate often talk past one another. See Kelly M. Kapic, "The Son's Assumption of a Human Nature: A Call for Clarity," *International Journal of Systematic Theology* 3, no. 2 (2001): 154–66; Oliver Crisp, *Divinity and Humanity: The Incarnation Reconsidered* (Cambridge: Cambridge University Press, 2007), 90–117; Ian A. McFarland, "Fallen or Unfallen? Christ's Human Nature and the Ontology of Human Sinfulness," *International Journal of Systematic Theology* 10, no. 4 (2008): 399–415.

23. See Aloys Grillmeier, *Christ in Christian Tradition: From the Apostolic Age to Chalcedon (451)*, trans. J. S. Bowden, 2 vols. (London: Mowbray, 1965), 1:329–60; Charles E. Raven, *Apollinarianism: An Essay on the Christology of the Early Church* (Cambridge: Cambridge University Press, 1923).

24. Raven, *Apollinarianism*, 198–99.

25. Gregory of Nazianzus, *On God and Christ: The Five Theological Orations and Two Letters to Cledonius*, trans. Frederick Williams and Lionel R. Wickham (Crestwood, NY: St. Vladimir's Seminary Press, 2002), 101.5.

the salvific importance of the incarnation: "Who for us men, and for our salvation, came down and was incarnate and was made man."[26]

Fundamental to humans was not merely a physical body but also a "reasonable soul." Metrophanes Kritopoulos, a Greek theologian who traveled in western Europe in the early 1600s, argues (1625) that Apollinarian approaches lead people astray: that the heretic "stupidly asserted, that our Lord took to himself a mindless and unreasonable and mortal soul, such as inanimate animals possess."[27] Instead, both Eastern and Western expressions of orthodoxy argued that the Son assumed "a true body and a reasonable soul."[28] Thus for a true incarnation the Son must assume a real physical body and all else—whatever language one uses—that captures the fullness of being human. References to heart, soul,[29] spirit, mind, and will were meant to comprehend the whole of human nature (e.g., Lev. 17:11; Deut. 6:5; 1 Sam. 25:37–38; 2 Chron. 15:12; Pss. 51:10; 84:2; Ezek. 37:5–6; Matt. 22:37; Luke 10:27; 1 Cor. 7:34; 1 Thess. 5:23; Heb. 4:12; etc.), a nature assumed by the eternal Son and created for a distinct communion with God.

A similar concern, although less universally accepted in the ancient church, sought to discern how many "wills" the Son has: one or two? Arguing for a single will might avoid a sense of conflict within Jesus's person. Concluding that the incarnate Son simply had a divine will might protect against a strange case of multiple personality disorder, but theologians such as Maximus the Confessor (580–662) worried that this view risked docetism by undermining a genuine and complete incarnation. The abiding concern was if Jesus does not have a human will, injustice is done to the portrait of him presented in the Gospels, most memorably as he struggles in the garden of Gethsemane.[30] A delicately constructed view was developed that concluded that the Son assumed a human will and that he freely submitted to the divine will of the

---

26. For Gregory of Nyssa, "Christology really is a soteriology." Brian E. Daley, "'Heavenly Man' and 'Eternal Christ': Apollinarius and Gregory of Nyssa on the Personal Identity of the Savior," *Journal of Early Christian Studies* 10, no. 4 (2002): 469–88, quote from 484. Similar claims could be made of other orthodox fathers.

27. Matrophanes Kritopoulos, 2.6, in *CCFCT*, 1:500.

28. Westminster Shorter Catechism (1657), Q. 22.

29. Biblically, the "soul" is often highlighting not immateriality but rather a full human person in his or her entirety (e.g., Matt. 16:25–26; John 15:13; Acts 2:41), though at other times the "spirituality" of a person is the focus (e.g., Matt. 10:28; 26:38; John 12:27). See *Catechism of the Catholic Church* (Vatican City: Libreria Editrice Vaticana, 1994), 93.

30. For further theological and historical reflections on this, with background on St. Maximus, see Demetrios Bathrellos, "The Sinlessness of Jesus: A Theological Exploration in the Light of Trinitarian Theology," in *Trinitarian Soundings in Systematic Theology*, ed. Paul Louis Metzger (London: T&T Clark, 2005), 113–26; idem, *The Byzantine Christ: Person, Nature, and Will in the Christology of Saint Maximus the Confessor* (New York: Oxford University Press, 2004).

One Triune God. Behind this view are similar concerns as noted in the Apollinarian debate: our salvation required that the Son be fully human, and since
a biblical anthropology places emphasis on the call to respond to God, "fully
human" includes having a creaturely will.

Since it is more often taken for granted than emphasized, we do not always
appreciate how important physicality is to being human. Thankfully a renewal
of focus has been occurring in contemporary theology. For the ancient church,
however, this point was again normally highlighted when christological questions arose, and we are here reminded that anthropology and Christology
go together. Irenaeus and Tertullian are two early church examples. Without
apology, they argued that being human meant having real flesh, and thus when
the Son became man he necessarily experienced all the realities of human
bodily existence.[31] The Son becomes incarnate to save, and those he saves are
"fleshly" creatures, unquestionably physical beings. James B. Nelson more
recently concludes, "The body is instrument of communion. The body is
language. As such, the body is not merely the necessary physical substructure
through which the spoken and written word must come . . . the body can be
word itself—as Christians recognize in Jesus Christ, the word made flesh."[32]

Hans Walter Wolff's study *Anthropology of the Old Testament* reminds
us that while there are a variety of Hebrew terms employed, the common assumption is that humans are earthly creatures.[33] Despite certain later tendencies in the church, the Scriptures do not belittle human physicality but instead
assume the body is a gift from God. And for our purposes, our bodies were
meant to foster communion and love rather than undermine them.

Accordingly, sexuality is part of any Christian anthropology: "When God
created man, he made him in the likeness of God. Male and female he created them, and he blessed them and named them Man [*Adam*] when they
were created" (Gen. 5:1b–2; cf. 1:27). It should not escape our notice that
no sexual differentiation is reported in the creation of animals, indicating
that "human sexuality is of a wholly different order from that of the beast."[34]
There is something about male and female that gives us the full picture of

---

31. See Robert M. Grant, *Irenaeus of Lyons* (London: Routledge, 1997), e.g., 168–70 (from
Against Heresies 5.14.1–4); Gustaf Wingren, *Man and the Incarnation: A Study of the Biblical
Theology of Irenaeus*, trans. Ross Mackenzie (London: Oliver and Boyd, 1959), esp. 79–112;
Tertullian, *Tertullian's Treatise on the Incarnation* [De Carne Christi] (London: SPCK, 1956).

32. James B. Nelson, *Embodiment: An Approach to Sexuality and Christian Theology* (Minneapolis: Augsburg, 1978), 35.

33. Hans Walter Wolff, *Anthropology of the Old Testament* (Philadelphia: Fortress, 1974),
esp. 7–79. Cf. Aubrey R. Johnson, *The Vitality of the Individual in the Thought of Ancient
Israel* (Cardiff: University of Wales Press, 1949).

34. Nahum M. Sarna, *Genesis* (Philadelphia: Jewish Publication Society, 1989), 13.

humanity as image bearers in the Genesis narrative.[35] Coming in the context of a strongly patriarchal culture, this idea of women as bearing God's image was originally scandalous yet beautifully revolutionary. Sadly, in many ways the persistence of dehumanizing views of the body in general, and women in particular, continue to haunt us, even within the church.[36] While we do not have space here to properly explore human sexuality and embodiment, we can at least recognize that communion and love again provide the framework for understanding them. Our physicality, including our sexuality, is not to be demeaned or neglected, for we are psycho*somatic* beings whose experience of this world is as embodied creatures called to one another, to the earth, but ultimately to the Creator Lord.

Whether talking about a "reasonable soul," a human will, or a physical body, the principle, here given in Gregory of Nazianzus's voice, remains the same: "For all our sakes [the Son] became *all that we are*, sin apart—body, soul, mind, and all that death pervades."[37] The Spirit, from Jesus's conception, filled Jesus the Messiah beyond measure (Luke 1:15; 4:1, 14, 18; John 1:33) and enabled Jesus to remain always holy and faithful in communion with his Father, even unto death.[38] And this same Spirit, the Spirit of Christ, now fills God's people and renews them in the image of the incarnate Son.[39]

Even if some classical discussions of the image of God in us did identify one isolated element of our nature (e.g., our reason) as the place or content of that image, the foregoing paragraphs show that the classical disputes about the human nature as assumed by Christ, even emphasizing as it did particular human faculties (mind, will, affections, body), did not—at least at best—isolate any one faculty from the others or from its proper function in our communion with God. To be fair, in some ways patristic Christology was sometimes more consistent in regard to holistic concerns than was its anthropology (which could move in a partitive direction), and so our anthropology benefits from these christological observations. While we may now use

35. For a recent though somewhat controversial attempt to highlight this dynamic, see Karl Barth, *Church Dogmatics* III/1, ed. G. W. Bromiley and T. F. Torrance (Edinburgh: T&T Clark, 1960), 195, and *Church Dogmatics* III/4, 116–240, esp. 169–70. Cf. Katherine Sonderegger, "Barth and Feminism," in *The Cambridge Companion to Karl Barth*, ed. John Webster (Cambridge: Cambridge University Press, 2000), 258–73.

36. Elizabeth Lewis Hall, "What Are Bodies For? An Integrative Examination of Embodiment," *Christian Scholars Review* 39, no. 2 (2010): 159–76, esp. 164–65.

37. Gregory of Nazianzus, *On God and Christ* 111 [Or. 30:21] (emphasis mine).

38. See Gerald F. Hawthorne, *The Presence and the Power* (Dallas: Word, 1991); Sinclair B. Ferguson, *The Holy Spirit* (Downers Grove, IL: InterVarsity, 1996), 35–56.

39. Yves Congar, *I Believe in the Holy Spirit*, 3 vols. (New York: Crossroad, 1997), 2:67–141.

different terms or frame matters in somewhat different ways, our predecessors shared with us an underlying concern to be holistic.

Thesis Two

Christian anthropology includes an eschatological orientation that is governed by love and communion.

Agency and purpose matter. Theological anthropology must examine the original creation (Genesis = Greek γένεσις = origin), in which God marked humans out for great dignity and distinctive relations with their Lord and the rest of creation (Gen. 1–2). Yet those beginnings were always meant to be just that—*beginnings*, not endings. Thus from the start—even before sin's entrance into the human experience (Gen. 3)—there was an eschatological pull on humankind. As the early twentieth century Princeton theologian Geerhardus Vos argued, "Eschatology aims at consummation rather than restoration."[40] Purpose, development, and growth were always part of God's design. Sin does not determine the end, *telos*, for which humanity was created, but it does introduce the need for a redemptive aspect to it. Yet it remains that the theological discussion of eschatology "must be restorative and consummative" because "it does not aim at the original state, but at the transcendental state of man."[41] Humans cannot be understood apart from appreciating their beginnings with the very Word and Spirit of God (Gen. 1:2–3). These beginnings, however, always indicated a crescendo that anticipates a great and final cadence. The sweep of Scripture gives us both a portrait of the formation of human creatures and a vision of their final, perfected purpose. There is a *telos* not merely for humanity in general (historically) but a *telos* for each human life—we each are designed for communion with God, neighbor, and the earth. The universal and particular must always be kept in mind when considering humanity in general.

Yahweh's intentions and purposes for human creatures are consistent, from Adam to Abraham to Israel. Throughout the Scriptures Israel consistently hears this defining claim: "You shall love the LORD your God with all your heart and with all your soul and with all your might" (Deut. 6:5; cf. 11:1, 13; 13:3; 30:6; Josh. 22:5; Ps. 31:23). They were beckoned to a love and communion with God for which they were originally created, a call that was not meant to take them beyond being fully human but rather to the heart of it. It is wrong to understand this call as something extra or "spiritual" added to a

---

40. Geerhardus Vos, *The Eschatology of the Old Testament*, ed. James T. Dennison Jr. (Phillipsburg, NJ: P&R, 2001), 73–76.
41. Ibid., 74.

preexistent way of life. This call to "love God" was a call to be truly and freely a human creature, created "very good" so as to enjoy harmonious relations with the Creator and the rest of his creation.

Being human in God's image is fundamentally about communion, loving God and neighbor. That is always an embodied love, a love that fully engages the whole human being. Traditionally, as we have seen, attempts to capture a holistic approach were commonly articulated in terms of our psychological faculties. If we approach the language and imagery of the faculties from the eschatological perspective of love and communion, the conversation quickly changes in important ways. We do not merely *have* bodies or faculties, but rather, as embodied psychosomatic creatures, we are called into the relationships that define us through our bodies and faculties. To put it differently, if merely the *capacity* to reason is the key attribute that makes one human, then one would be reduced to one's IQ. However, if we treat the faculties not in terms of "norms" or forms of intelligence but in terms of love and communion, then the criteria are all changed.

What makes us human is our distinctive ability to love and commune with God, other humans, and the earth. Such love and communion normally takes place in a body and through the "faculties," no matter what level they "function" at. Someone with an IQ that barely registers may nevertheless profoundly know and love God, sensing his presence and responding to his kindness. Those who cannot verbally communicate, or who have other "disabilities," may nonetheless have profound communion with other human creatures.[42] While speaking in particular of those with serious intellectual frailties, Jean Vanier addresses the common human condition: "Communion is mutual trust, mutual belonging; it is the to-and-fro movement of love between two people where each gives and each one receives. . . . Communion is at the heart of the mystery of our humanity."[43] And, as Vanier states, this mystery of communion can be enjoyed and participated in by all humans, no matter the level of their cognitive or emotional functionality. We encounter a great mystery at this point, but for our purposes we just need to recognize that love and communion theologically reorient how we understand and evaluate our bodies and their faculties: we see them relationally rather than reductively. An eschatological perspective, highlighting the *telos* of humanity, considers the breadth of human experience, abilities, and limits without losing sight of their united purpose.

42. Cf. Henri J. M. Nouwen, *Adam, God's Beloved* (Maryknoll, NY: Orbis, 1997); Thomas E. Reynolds, *Vulnerable Communion: A Theology of Disability and Hospitality* (Grand Rapids: Brazos, 2008).

43. Jean Vanier, *Becoming Human* (Mahwah, NJ: Paulist Press, 2008), 28.

A person's mind, will, affections, and body represent the whole person, the way in which one relates to God and the rest of creation as a creature. These faculties are judged not by mechanistic efficiency but by how they are used—to foster or hinder loving communion. This can help to explain the horror of murder (Gen. 9:6; Exod. 20:13; Deut. 5:17). Intentionally killing a fellow creature made in God's image is an attack against the very possibility of love between a person and others (including God and fellow humans). For example, when people describe someone like Hitler, they often resort to language like "beast" or "animal." Does this mean that Hitler started to function intellectually more like an animal than a human? Not at all. We interpret such comments to refer to Hitler's complete lack of concern for love and communion.

Even if one rejects classical "faculty psychology," one should still find in those traditions the insight that what made us distinctively human was not simply that God gave us these faculties but our loving response to God with whatever ability we do have. The usefulness of looking at these faculties lies not in one's emotional or mental brilliance, or unbendable willpower, but instead in God's purposes of genuine loving communion between the Creator and his creation in particular, human terms. The teleological or eschatological perspective of human creatures shows this. Specific instances of communion may look very different because humans are each in their own way particular and unique creatures, and yet these differences are all united as they find their source and ultimate response to the Triune God. Again we must highlight the importance of christological concerns for theological anthropology.

Biblically, while it is true that humanity is uniquely made *in* God's image, Jesus the Son of God *is* God's image. Christ alone "is the image of God" (2 Cor. 4:4; cf. Heb. 1:3), the "image of the invisible God, the firstborn of all creation" (Col. 1:15). Believers are given the great promise that they are being renewed and conformed into the "image of God's [incarnate] Son . . . the firstborn among many brothers and sisters" (Rom. 8:29 NIV; cf. Eph. 4:22–24). The promise is not merely that we will once again become like the original Adam, but rather we shall "also bear the image of the man of heaven" (1 Cor. 15:49; cf. 2 Cor. 3:18; Phil. 3:21; 1 John 3:2). This is not a promise of escaping physicality but rather of becoming like the ascended Christ, who not only receives our praises but also leads our worship (cf. Heb. 2:11–18). The Spirit unites us to the incarnate Son, who becomes both our elder brother and high priest, allowing us to again bask in the love of the Father. Because we shall be eschatologically renewed by the Word and Spirit, we shall then love God with all our heart, soul, mind, and strength (Mark 12:30).

Scripture speaks of two Adams: the first Adam (1 Cor. 15:45a) of the early chapters of Genesis, and the "last" (*eschatos*) or eschatological Adam (1 Cor. 15:45b), who has come to carry out the work of a new creation. Whereas in Genesis the narrative moves from the cosmos to the microcosm of humanity, now in the incarnation the movement is reversed. Humanity takes center stage again, only now instead of serving as the culmination of the original creation, "man" is the beginning of its restoration. The early church father Tertullian connected this creation to divine love and the incarnation:

> Imagine God wholly absorbed in the creation of human beings—in his hand, his eye, his labor, his purpose, his wisdom, his providence, and most of all, his love. All these things were shaping the outlines of humankind, for whatever form and expression he gave to the clay of the earth, it was always in his mind that one day Christ would become a man. . . . For the Father had already said to the Son, "Let us make humankind in our image, after our likeness."[44] And God made humankind after his image, which is the image of Christ. . . . Therefore that clay that was even then putting on the image of Christ, who was to come in the flesh, was not only the work but also the pledge and surety of God.[45]

This last Adam is not a picture of some primitive human creature but rather the one who alone is able to serve as the representative of humanity who consummates its purpose. Coming as it were from the future, the last Adam breaks into the present to give humanity a taste of the expected shalom and to hold it secure in that reality even before it has yet been fully realized. Jesus the Messiah is the new Adam: his life, death, and, most crucial, his resurrection begin the movement in reverse of recapitulating creation in its re-creation, so that now it moves from him (the microcosm) to the entire cosmos (cf. Eph. 1:9–10; Col. 1:15–20). Just as what happened with the first Adam somehow was understood to affect the entire world (Rom. 5:12–14), so Jesus's life-giving reality, which has overcome death itself, now promises to affect the entire cosmos (Rom. 5:15–21). Thesis four will describe how sin affects human creatures. For now we state that in Jesus the Messiah we meet the true and full human creature, the one who loves God and neighbor with his whole being, so that when he acts, it affects the entire cosmos.

44. As is well known, the "our image" of Gen. 1:26 has been often read as a trinitarian reference. While even in the patristic period other readings of this text were known (e.g., the "our" refers to angels), most still saw this as pointing to intratrinitarian relations.

45. Tertullian, *On the Resurrection of the Flesh* 6, in Gerald Bray, *We Believe in One God*, 5 vols. (Downers Grove, IL: IVP Academic, 2009), 1:121.

Thesis Three

Christian anthropology affirms that humanity was created good and for good.

Relational growth matters. A potential concern with a protological and eschatological perspective relates to questions of goodness. Fundamental to the biblical account—and it could be argued this is one of the most important contributions Scripture made to ancient conceptions of humanity—is that the entire material world, everything God created, is good. From the stars to the snails, from the clouds to the sea creatures of the deep, everything that God made was unequivocally declared "good" (Gen. 1:4, 9, 12, 18, 21, 25). It is important to note that the word "good" here, as Gerhard von Rad explains, "contains less an aesthetic judgment than the designation of purpose and correspondence."[46] All was fitting, right, and with an appropriate *telos*. Again and again we hear this positive affirmation, with Adam (*adam* = "man") as the high point: "very good" (Gen. 1:31). Yet if all was good, "perfectly" good, how could there then be the possibility of change or development?

To speak of growth or the eschatological even before one speaks of sin's presence might to some hearers seem to deny that Yahweh's creation was completely good.[47] Such a view tends to assume a static rather than dynamic or relational view of the human person. This conflicts with the biblical testimony, according to which there is an expectation of human development. God made humans "good" and "in his image," but not immutable. Just as God planted the garden to grow, so he planted Adam in the midst of that garden—*to grow*. Humankind could and would change, either growing in beautiful communion with God and the rest of creation, being fruitful and multiplying, or turning from Yahweh and thus compromising their intended human *telos*.[48] We were created good with the expectation of growing in that goodness.

Created good and upright (Eccles. 7:29; cf. Gen. 1:26 and Eph. 4:24), the human creature was nevertheless mutable and thus capable of sinning.[49] All of this is part of the biblical narrative that tells of God walking with Adam

46. Gerhard von Rad, *Genesis: A Commentary* (Philadelphia: Westminster, 1961), 50.

47. This involves the (false) assumption that to formulate a Christian anthropology we must simply learn about how or when our first parents were created. Two deeper incorrect assumptions are also involved here: (1) that an extrabiblical conception of "good" controls the theological use of the word, and (2) that "good" must be a static condition.

48. Cf. Theophilus of Antioch's comment: "Humanity was therefore neither mortal nor immortal but capable of becoming either," which was all dependent on whether they continued to turn toward the life of God or turned toward "the things of death, disobeying God" (*To Autolycus* 2.27, quoted in Bray, *We Believe*, 1:120).

49. John of Damascus, *Orthodox Faith* 2.12. Cf. "Westminster Confession of Faith," 4.2, in *CCFCT*, 2:611; "Savory Declaration," 4.2, in *CCFCT*, 3:110.

and Eve, speaking with them, inviting them to enjoy and care for the rest of his handiwork. Rather than apathetic or even neutral, humanity was made "free therefore and not indifferent," for true freedom is expressed and enjoyed as one lives in communion with God and in harmony with the rest of the motions of the world.[50] This entails that "it was necessary for man's will to be created such that it might love God in freedom and so be able to be happy by continuing in that love."[51]

"Original righteousness" is language that often shows up in creeds and confessions as shorthand for the key principle that humans in their entirety (soul, mind, will, affections, and even their body) were made for communion with God. God did not create humans evil, or even simply impartial. Rather, from the beginning God made them positively "good" in that they were rightly ordered and properly placed within the structure of God's overall creation. Such goodness consisted in their loving communion with the Creator, a relationship that would foster human flourishing and joy. Communion has the dynamic of giving, receiving, and returning in love, and this is at the core of original goodness.

The classical language of original goodness should be taken as referring to the human person as a holistic relational being. Our understanding and use of the biblical language of heart, soul, mind, and strength should not be limited to a discussion of a hierarchy of faculties, but it should include the *telos* of our loving communion with God and his creation. Humans are distinctly made to respond to God with a level of intimacy that distinguishes them from the rest of the creaturely realm. We are created for a "noble end, that is, to know God, to love him, and to glorify him (Rom. 1:19–21), which is the essence of all true godliness (Jon. 17:3; Jer. 9:23, 24)."[52] This does not undermine the goodness of the rest of the creation, but it does highlight the particular goodness of humanity. We were protologicaly designed for communion and are eschatologically drawn toward an ever-greater enjoyment of it.

Attempts at connecting capacity and action were almost always behind creedal references to the faculties. For example, the Mennonite Articles of Faith discern the "holy and good condition" of "our first parents," so that they were clearly "glorious and happy creatures, endowed and adorned with exalted wisdom, pure affections and impulses, and with a free will whereby they could (under God's permission) accept without compulsion . . . what

---

50. J. Heinrich Heidegger, *Corpus Theologiae*, 6.100, quoted by Heppe, *Reformed Dogmatics*, 242–43.

51. Ibid.

52. Mennonite Articles of Faith (1766/1895/1902), 5.2, in *CCFCT*, 3:159.

was presented to them."[53] This was the human condition, in which "they doubtless enjoyed a perfect and intimate converse with God (Gen. 3:8) in childlike love and reverence, which, had they continued therein, could have issued only in a pure blessedness for soul and body in all eternity."[54] Or, as the nineteenth-century "Commission" Creed summarized, we were made to "know, love, and obey God, and enjoy him forever."[55]

Saint Catherine of Siena once prayerfully asked why God made humanity with such great dignity and goodness. Her prayer continues, "Certainly the incalculable love by which you have looked on your creature in yourself! You are taken with love for her; for by love indeed you created her, by love you have given her a being capable of tasting your eternal Good."[56] Humans were created for communion with God, a communion that was meant to be mutual and vibrant rather than unidirectional and simply passive. As the "Statement of Faith" from the Philippines affirms, "We believe that persons are created in the image of God and destined to live in community with God, and with other persons and with all creation."[57] Our problem now is that sin has disrupted the *telos* and experience of humanity that was created as good and for good.

To recognize the goodness of humans one looks not only backward, or simply to the present, but also forward. Nevertheless, that eschatological dimension is always harmonious with the original trajectory of creation. Without looking to the beginning and ending, our anthropological vision might suffer all manner of problems. For example, detached from the earthly account of Genesis, where Adam is formed from the very dust of the ground (Gen. 2:7), it has been tempting (e.g., gnostic impulses) to "spiritualize" humans in a way that belittles their creaturely reality or distorts their eschatological expectations. We are made good and for good. (This will be unpacked more fully below when we turn our attention to the idea of representation.) Different problems surface if we look only at the current empirical evidence of wars, jealousy, self-deception, and grief: it might be tempting to become overly cynical, imagining that common distortions represent humankind in its fullness and concluding that to be human *is* to live a flawed existence in a tragic world. What then becomes of God's original benediction of good over humanity? What becomes of the "Beloved Son," who is himself both fully human and yet

53. Mennonite Articles of Faith, 7.1, in *CCFCT*, 3:159.

54. Mennonite Articles of Faith, 7.2, in *CCFCT*, 3:159–60.

55. Congregational Church in America, The "Commission" Creed (1883/1913), 3, in *CCFCT*, 3:373.

56. Quoted in *Catechism of the Catholic Church*, 6.1.356. Here again we are reminded of Owen's observation that when we love the incarnate Christ, our love and God's love meet.

57. "Statement of Faith," the United Church of Christ in the Philippines (1986/92), 2, in *CCFCT*, 3:847.

free from personal sin (Heb. 4:15; 1 Pet. 2:22; 1 John 3:5)? To employ classical language, sin and its consequences are accidental rather than essential to being human, a point that Scripture reinforces both in terms of the goodness of the original creation and the promise of glorification. Finally, without the biblical testimony one might reduce *homo sapiens* to merely another member of the kingdom *animalia*, with no justifiable distinction or particular calling from the Creator Lord. A strong biblical protology and eschatology reminds us of the inherent goodness of being human: we are creatures particularly called by God into communion with him and specifically made by him to bear his image before the entire cosmos (Gen. 1:26–27).

Thesis Four

Christian anthropology confesses that human goodness has been compromised and distorted, and this tragedy must be understood in a holistic way.

Sin matters. God did give his human creatures restrictions, having made them able to understand and flourish, but also able to rebel by turning from his original goodness and perverting it. Such a distortion was possible even in God's good creation because the Triune Lord made humanity for the purpose of free, joyful, and meaningful communion. Any Christian discussions about human "free will" and possible distortions or even "bondage" of our will must always be read against this background. Original communion was meant to be mutual, open, and unhindered, but sin now affects all such possibilities. As Wolfhart Pannenberg argues, "Misery . . . is the lot of those who are deprived of the fellowship with God that is the destiny of human life."[58] Sin warps the human relational creature.

Like all other questions in theological anthropology, the analysis of sin has love and communion as its frame. Sin so disrupted humanity's created dynamic of fellowship with God that their lives became disordered, affecting them inside and out, body and soul. Saint Paul wrote that as a result of our condition, "There is none who does good" (Rom. 3:10b–18; drawing from Pss. 5:9; 10:7 [LXX]; 14:1–3; 36:1; 53:1–3; 140:3; Prov. 1:6; Isa. 59:7–8). If we define "good" simply in terms of an act itself (e.g., making an anonymous donation to a charity), then the statement would be rendered false. But since our being is grounded in a loving communion with God, it follows that all actions taken apart from that basic communion in an attempted godless

58. He continues, "Alienation from this destiny does not abolish it. Its continued presence is the basis of our misery, for in alienation from God we are robbed of our true identity." Wolfhart Pannenberg, *Systematic Theology*, trans. Geoffrey W. Bromiley (Grand Rapids: Eerdmans, 1991), 2:178–79.

autonomy must be seen as worthless for the purpose of that mutual loving communion.[59] Yes, it is far preferable that people live orderly, generous lives. But even the moral lives that hold God at a distance are still self-destructive, although perhaps at a slower rate. For this reason the church has declared that "good works" are impossible apart from God's grace of new creation.[60] Since the "goodness" of creation was not merely about a static thing but its *telos* and relations, this influences how truly "good works" for human creatures are understood. "Wise and virtuous men through the ages have sought the highest good in devotion to freedom, justice, peace, truth, and beauty. Yet all human virtue, when seen in the light of God's love in Jesus Christ, is found to be infected by self-interest and hostility."[61] We were created to act always in response to the loving presence of God so that the love moved from the Father through his creatures (by the Word) and then back to him (in the Spirit).[62] Sin has now distorted us at the core—it has disordered our loves so that doing the "good"—understood in terms of communion with the Triune God—becomes impossible for those still alienated from him.[63] When people no longer freely receive divine love, then divine love extended through them involves some distortion.[64] Many creedal statements have treated the character of this distortion.

The Synod of Orange (529), as an early example, asserted that true freedom of the will ceases with sin's entrance, so that the "free will of all men has been weakened through sin of the first man."[65] Peter Mogila's [Eastern]

---

59. Cf. Augustine: "The true honor of man is the image and likeness of God, which is not preserved except in relation to him by whom it is impressed." *The Trinity* 12.11.16. Thanks to Scott Swain for this reference.

60. Cf. First Helvetic Confession, 9, in *CCFCT*, 2.284.

61. *Confession* (1967) of The United Presbyterian Church in the United States, 9.13, in *CCFCT*, 3:717. The *Confession* continues, "All men, good and bad alike, are in the wrong before God and helpless without his forgiveness. Thus all fall under God's judgment. No one is more subject to that judgment than the man who assumes that he is guiltless before God or morally superior to others."

62. Cf. Rom. 11:6.

63. In sin humans "lose their humanity in futile striving and are left in rebellion, despair, and isolation." *Confession* (1967), United Presbyterian Church in the United States, 9.12.

64. This, as Martin Luther argues, can be understood in terms of the "flesh" and the "spirit": the point is not material vs. nonmaterial but the life under the *Creator Spiritus* or the non-Spirit-led life. The Father sent his Son "in the likeness of sinful flesh and for sin" in order that the rightness of communion with God could be restored: sins would be forgiven, freedom from condemnation enjoyed, and new life by the Spirit experienced (Rom. 8:1–11). New life would be found only by a new Adam, one who was fully human (body, soul, mind, will, affections) but who also never broke the loving communion with his Father in the Spirit. See *Augsburg Confession*, 18–20, in *CCFCT*, 2.68–75; Luther, "Instructions for the Visitors of Parish Pastors," in *Church and Ministry 2*, ed. Conrad Dergendoff, vol. 40 of *Luther's Works* (St. Louis: Concordia, 1958), 301–5.

65. Synod of Orange, "Canon 8," in *CCFCT*, 1:694.

Orthodox Confession (1639/1642), drawing on Romans 6:23 ("the wages of sin is death"), concludes that when our first parents sinned and were removed from the garden, this sin affected the whole person. He refers to the whole person in speaking of the mind and will: "Presently losing the perfection of his reason and understanding" with the fall, now the human creature's "will became prone to evil rather than good. Thus the state of innocence and integrity, by man tasting of evil, became a state of sin."[66]

Early Protestant confessions contain similar statements. Discussing "Human Powers," the Swiss Second Helvetic Confession (1566) states that the human condition changed at the fall. Originally the human creature was "upright and free, so that he could either continue in goodness or decline toward evil,"[67] asserting that God made humanity "good," not neutral, and called us to continue in that goodness, growing in grace and truth. Our fall into sin, however, involved not only Adam, but through him as representative, the "whole human race [fell] in sin and death," thus shaping the current human experience. This change compromised and profoundly endangered humanity. Neither his reason nor will is taken from Adam, clarifies the Second Helvetic Confession, and "he was not entirely changed into a stone or a tree." He did not cease to be human, but his condition was disordered and weakened now so that people are unable to "do what they could before the fall," namely, freely enjoy God's holy presence and uninterrupted communion with him.[68]

The French Confession (1559/1571) warns that because of original sin, humanity ("man") has become "blinded in mind, and depraved in heart" so that now "he has lost all integrity, and there is no good in him."[69] Although those who grow anxious with the language of depravity might be quick to cringe here, worrying that such a view might see humanity only in purely negative terms, the real concern was about what might be called the wholeness or integrity of the human person relating to the Lord of humanity.[70] The French Confession elsewhere observes that people "can still discern good

66. Peter Mogila, "Orthodox Confession of the Catholic and Apostolic Eastern Church," 1.23, in *CCFCT*, 1:573.
67. Second Helvetic Confession, 9.1–2, in *CCFCT*, 2:471.
68. Second Helvetic Confession, 9.3, in *CCFCT*, 2:471. Mogila argues that God created humanity with "honors and favors," but with humanity's rebellion against God, its distinction from the animal realm fades. Quoting from Ps. 49:20, he concludes, "Man that is in honor, and understandeth not, is like the beasts that perish." Mogila, "Orthodox Confession," 1.22, in *CCFCT*, 1:572.
69. French Confession (1559), 9, in *CCFCT*, 2:377.
70. The language of "integrity" is often used to present a holistic portrait of humanity as originally created, but the Belgic Confession reflects another common way of speaking when it employs the phrase "entire nature." Belgic Confession, 14, in *CCFCT*, 2:412.

and evil," so it doesn't—despite stereotypes—claim that they have lost all moral sensitivity or conscience; however, their "light" acts as a sort of darkness that no longer naturally leads them to God by their "intelligence and reason."[71] Neither does their will—which they retain—freely respond to and enjoy God's holy presence, for genuine human liberty, rooted in its communion with God, has been lost.[72] And the body now groans and suffers from sin's presence in this world.

These creedal statements repeatedly affirm both the original goodness of humanity and the radical effects of sin on it. "Our [fallen] nature is [now] enfeebled and became so inclined to sin that, unless it is restored by the Spirit of God, man neither does nor wants to do anything good of himself."[73] Just as the goodness of human creatures needs to be examined and stated in a holistic way, so our understanding of sin must understand all the dimensions of its effects on the whole person, including body, mind, will, affections, and the like. To connect the dots with earlier discussions relating anthropology to Christology, let us conclude that just as no part of the human creature escapes the distortions of sin, so no part of human nature (body, mind, will, affections, etc.) is unassumed by the Son. Since sin has affected us "universally"—that is, not just each and every person, but each person in his or her whole self—redemption of the whole person is required: this means the Son's full and true incarnation as well as the Spirit's holistic work of sanctification are both necessary.[74]

Thesis Five

Christian anthropology affirms humanity's distinctive role as God's image, which entails great dignity and profound responsibility.

Representation and solidarity matter. While I have argued that theological anthropology must draw on far more than the biblical texts that explicitly mention the *imago Dei*, recent biblical scholarship on Genesis 1 has helped to provide us with a much richer conception of what it might mean to represent God in the ancient world. J. Richard Middleton offers an extended treatment of this material in his excellent volume, *The Liberating Image*. Bringing together recent findings in ancient Near Eastern background, biblical

71. French Confession, 9, in *CCFCT*, 2:377.

72. French Confession, 9, in *CCFCT*, 2:378. See also Scots Confession (1560), 2.

73. First Confession of Basel (1534), 2, in *CCFCT*, 2:274. Biblical texts commonly given in support of these positions include Gen. 1:17–18; 3:6; 5:3; 6:5; 8:21; Ps. 143:1; John 3:5–6; Rom. 3:10–12; 5:12, 15, 19; 1 Cor. 15:21–22; Eph. 2:1–5; 4:24.

74. John Owen, "The Greater Catechism," 20.5, in *Works*, 1:488. He gives his own proof texts.

commentary, and ethical reflection, he helps us to more fully understand the powerful, even revolutionary scriptural portrait. Humanity is presented not merely like God but as his chosen stewards who are to carry out "the royal-priestly vocation of representing God's rule on earth by their exercise of cultural power."[75] They function like "idols" of God himself, that is, to cause those who see and dwell with humans to have a vision of the Creator King. Middleton stresses what is sometimes called a "functional" or "missional" reading of humanity as image bearers. While we cannot here unpack how he sees Genesis 1 working against certain ancient Near Eastern views of violence and evil, it is worth noting that in Scripture we are presented with a radical portrait of divine generosity, with humanity given special place of privilege to embody and extend divine goodness and grace. This portrayal also has a radical democratizing effect,[76] which cuts against ethnic, social, economic, and other differences that so separate humanity from one another and also pit persons against the earth. Human creatures were made as interconnected beings, linked to the earth and one another, even as they represented Yahweh to the rest of creation.

Accordingly, humans were created to live not as isolated, autonomous individuals but in community with one another and in life-giving connection with the material world as the environment for communion with God. This provides the necessary space in theological anthropology for both human unity and particularity. Our common origin, as attested in the biblical narrative, affirms a unity in the story of our existence (Acts 17:26; Rom. 5:12, 19; 1 Cor. 15:21, 22).[77] Thus, deduces the Catholic Catechism, "'This law of human solidarity and charity,' without excluding the rich variety of persons, cultures, and peoples, assures us that all [people] are truly brethren." While all living beings relate in some way to everything else, humans have distinctive relationships that include certain responsibilities, and this "differentiates mankind from the other creatures."[78] A few samples from other recent ecclesial confessions and statements follow.

The *Credo* (1980), which is part of The Mass of the Marginalized People, originating in Honduras, identifies the Son's incarnation with the "least of these." Speaking in the first person voice, it affirms that the worshiper is to

75. J. Richard Middleton, *The Liberating Image: The* Imago Dei *in Genesis 1* (Grand Rapids: Brazos, 2005), 235.
76. See J. Maxwell Miller, "In the Image and Likeness of God," *Journal of Biblical Literature* 91 (1972): 289–304; H. L. Creager, "The Divine Image," in *A Light unto My Path: Old Testament Studies in Honor of Jacob M. Myers*, ed. H. N. Bream et al. (Philadelphia: Temple University Press, 1974), 103–18.
77. See L. Berkhof, *Systematic Theology*, 4th ed. (Grand Rapids: Eerdmans, 1994), 188.
78. *Catechism of the Catholic Church*, 92.

praise God's great condescension that leads to restoration for human dignity and purpose.

> I believe that you became human
> in the womb of Mary,
> a village woman, a poor woman,
> a virgin dedicated to God.
> You give people
> new dignity and value,
> restoring in us the image in which we were made by God.[79]

To understand what God really thinks about humanity, we must not overlook the Virgin's womb. There God shows his concern for the peril of our human situation by caring for the most vulnerable among us. God repeatedly tells his people, who are his image and his representatives to the watching world, that they must care for the orphan, widow, and the poor and weak. And this care must be holistic, not simply for "spiritual" needs but for their physical, emotional, and mental health as well. To belittle their earthly needs is to belittle the Creator's love for his human creatures as he made them.

The recent Confession of the Church of Toraja, Indonesia, similarly attempts to reflect the biblical emphasis on human interdependence and obligation. "The image of God is the relationship of responsibility with God, with his fellow men and with the whole of the natural world, in true knowledge and in holiness, truth, and love." This confession, by implication, puts all people on the same level and calls them "to a life of mutual love."[80] So what is God to do in light of human rebellion and sin, in which humanity tried to "become like God"? The answer is as simple as it is powerful: "The faithful love of God was so great that he restored the true relationship with his mankind again in Jesus Christ, the true and genuine man."[81] Again, humanity's *telos* and singular solution is found only in the Incarnate One. He not only dwelled in perfect loving communion with his Father in the Spirit, but he also embodied the deepest love for fellow humanity, most clearly expressed on the cross and through his bodily resurrection. Those who are renewed in the image of Christ are to take up concern for the rest of humanity, seeking to point them—by word and deed—to the true Man who alone can offer hope to fallen humanity.

---

79. "The Credo," from The Mass of the Marginalized People, Honduras (1980), 1, in *CCFCT*, 3:796.

80. "The Confession," Church of Toraja, Indonesia (1981), 3.1–9, esp. 1–3, in *CCFCT*, 3:800–801.

81. "The Confession," Church of Toraja, Indonesia (1981), 3.9, in *CCFCT*, 3:801.

The Lausanne Covenant of 1974, which came out of the International Congress on World Evangelization, reminded the church that each human is part of the whole of humanity, for all derive their being from God himself. Issues of social responsibility and justice, therefore, grow naturally out of an applied theological anthropology. "Because mankind is made in the image of God, every person, regardless of race, religion, color, culture, class, sex, or age, has an intrinsic dignity because of which he should be respected and served, not exploited."[82] This then informs how "salvation" is described, for the new birth means entering God's kingdom and includes loving his world rightly, thus "transforming us in the totality of our personal and social responsibilities."[83] Accordingly, the reminder that "faith without works is dead" is best understood as an admonition to foster an Eden-like environment of communion with God, anticipating now the fullness of shalom that is to come. We anticipate in part, here and now, the future banquet in honor of the King and our joy in it. This is the hope of a fully restored humanity that is centered on God's incarnate Son.

Humanity was always meant to lead the worship of God, with its praises echoed and enhanced by the rest of creation. Further, as they lived in harmony with the earth and the creatures it teemed with, humans were to foster the distinctive way in which the rest of the creation could reflect and praise God. John Owen observed, for example, that humanity was given a peculiar role in equipping the rest of creation in their ability to glorify God. Creation was "as an harmonious, well-tuned instrument, which gives no sound unless there be a skillful hand to move and act it."[84] Music, for example, normally requires the cooperation of persons and the earth, most clearly exemplified through the formation of instruments. Agriculture, construction, sport, and countless other human endeavors were meant to occur within and congruent with the rest of creation. But if humanity will not practice the art of loving representation in which the rest of creation is helped to praise God, then, even amid its current groans (Rom. 8:22; cf. Jer. 12:4, 11), it will find ways on its own: the rocks and the trees will cry out (Ps. 98:7–9; Isa. 55:12; Hab. 2:11; Matt. 3:9; 27:51–54; Luke 19:40). Such concerns are partly behind why St. Francis (1181–1226), when he read Jesus's command to "go into all the world and proclaim the gospel *to the whole creation*" (Mark 16:15; emphasis mine), thought it was appropriate to declare the good news to the birds and trees that lived under the weight of the accusations (cf. Micah

82. Lausanne Covenant (1974), 5, in *CCFCT*, 3:756.
83. Lausanne Covenant (1974), 5, in *CCFCT*, 3:756.
84. Owen, *Works*, 1:183.

6:1–2).[85] Originally all creation, led by humanity, was intended to join together in robust and harmonious praise echoing throughout God's good creation.[86] Again, only through the incarnation, when the Son of God assumes the creaturely to himself, can this rightful function be restored for humanity and even the earth. In this way, it is worth keeping in mind that the Son incarnate is understood not simply as worthy of our worship, but also as uniquely the lead worshiper.[87]

In the incarnate Christ, we are also reconnected to one another. Emphasizing the human significance of social relations, the Presbyterian-Reformed Church in Cuba's confession argues that those who are born again do not cease to be human, but in this new birth the believer is finally able to "realize his full humanity, liberated from the chains that bound him irremissibly to the anti-human, sinful past."[88] Building on its argument that we are necessarily sociopolitical creatures, each connected to others in and through community, this creed states that sin caused "disintegrating distortion" in our interpersonal relations. Now that sin has polluted humanity, the person-in-community steps into the "battleground where hatred and jealousy, envy and selfishness produce fratricidal struggle, crime, and the 'exploitation of man by man.'"[89] Thus, in some fundamental ways, a Christian vision of salvation for the human person must include "the reconstruction of his being in community."[90] While this particular creedal statement treats this idea in a way that strongly reflects the 1970s context of liberation theology growing out of Latin America, the fundamental instinct is right: being human does not properly result in autonomous, self-constructed realities but rather in right relations that foster community and mutual dependence, especially in the church.

Finally, to love Christ is to love his kingdom. Scholars commonly agree that the message of the kingdom of God was central to Jesus's entire life and

---

85. Friar Leo, *The Mirror of Perfection* (London: Dent, 1963), e.g., 289–95; Timothy J. Johnson, "Francis and Creation," in *The Cambridge Companion to Francis of Assisi*, ed. Michael J. P. Robson (New York: Cambridge University Press, 2012), 143–58.

86. Charles Sherlock observes that while Christianity affirms a unique place for humanity "in relation to otherkind, and so, it must be admitted, is anthropocentric in some sense," contemporary Christians must "adopt a 'chastened, sober anthropocentrism' which recognizes the unique place of human beings *among* the creatures." Sherlock, *The Doctrine of Humanity*, Contours of Christian Theology (Downers Grove, IL: InterVarsity, 1996), 125 (emphasis original).

87. James B. Torrance, "The Vicarious Humanity of Christ," in *The Incarnation*, ed. T. F. Torrance (Edinburgh: Handsel, 1981); idem, *Worship, Community and the Triune God of Grace* (Downers Grove, IL: InterVarsity, 1996).

88. Presbyterian-Reformed Church in Cuba, "Confession of Faith" (1977), 3.B, in *CCFCT*, 3:771–72.

89. Presbyterian-Reformed Church in Cuba, "Confession of Faith," 2.B, in *CCFCT*, 3:767–68.

90. Presbyterian-Reformed Church in Cuba, "Confession of Faith," 3.C, in *CCFCT*, 3:773.

ministry.[91] And this kingdom, for Jesus, was necessarily eschatological—a taste of the future breaking into the present. As he spoke and acted, as he preached and healed, Jesus was giving a taste not simply of what was before the fall but of what will be after restoration. The profound temptations that the Messiah faced in the wilderness (cf., Mark 1:12–13 // Matt. 4:1–11 // Luke 4:1–13) pointed back and also forward, since by his faithfulness as the second Adam he was beginning to reverse the cosmic tragedy of humanity's fall (Gen. 3). Similarly, as he gathered his disciples and initiated what we now call the Lord's supper (Matt. 26:17–30 // Mark 14:12–26 // Luke 22:14–20; 1 Cor. 11:17–34), he was not only anticipating his coming death and resurrection but ultimately painting an eschatological vision of a heavenly feast (cf. Isa. 25:6–8; Zech. 14:16–19; Rev. 19:9–10) in which humanity and the Triune God would enjoy unhindered mutual love and delight. In other words, his words and deeds pointed back toward the goodness of the original garden,[92] even as he also pointed ahead to the future feast of shared shalom. Jesus calls us to enter his kingdom; not only does his teaching include a call to live in our true humanity but his action as savior also re-creates that humanity and connects us with it in him (John 15:1–6; Gal. 2:20; 2 Cor. 5:17).

Conclusion

In the fact of the incarnation we come to see our humanity in new ways. With the Son's assumption of a human nature, the significance and value of our physicality is profoundly affirmed, and in his life we encounter the embodiment of the call to "love the Lord your God" with our full creaturely selves, including our hearts, souls, minds, and strength (Matt. 22:37; cf. Mark 12:30; Luke 10:27). In the final Adam, we see how protology and eschatology are brought together: we are created as holistic, psychosomatic creatures who are distinctly called, in great dignity, to communion with God. We were created good and for good, a good that is compromised by the persistent presence of sin that undermines our freedom to enjoy the fullness of fellowship with God. No longer do our hearts, minds, wills, or even bodies, naturally move toward the Creator Lord.

91. E.g., N. T. Wright, *Jesus and the Victory of God* (Minneapolis: Fortress, 1996), esp. 145–474; for a more accessible treatment, see his *How God Became King: The Forgotten Story of the Gospels* (New York: HarperOne, 2012).
92. Geerhardus Vos observes that even with all the calls of conversion and emphasis on the Spirit, "the preeminence of the natural (physical) element in biblical eschatology" is vital, because such calls always maintain their protological grounding. Vos, *Eschatology of the Old Testament*, 74.

But this God has come; the Father sends the Son by the Spirit, and he assumed a true and genuine human nature, becoming like us in all ways yet without sin. Jesus, the Son of God, thus becomes not merely the object of worship but also the lead worshiper. Now those who are united to the risen Lord are "new creatures" (2 Cor. 5:17; cf. Gal. 6:15), set free to be fully human again in their love and communion with God, one another and the earth. In this way, we now go out as those who bear his image, declaring the good news that our true humanity is restored in Christ, a proclamation that is carried out holistically in word and deed, for we have discovered how humanity is most like God: it is in our love for the incarnate Son. In Jesus, God and humanity meet. In Jesus, humanity is realized and restored. And so in our love for Christ, we find ourselves swept into the Father's love for his incarnate Son even as we are filled with his Spirit. Here is real love, real communion realized and enjoyed. And for us, here is our real humanity.[93]

93. I would like to thank Cameron Moran, John Yates, and David Strobolakos Jr. for their helpful feedback on earlier versions of this chapter.

9

Sin

OLIVER D. CRISP

According to the Westminster Shorter Catechism, sin is "any want of conformity unto, or transgression of, the law of God" (Answer to Question 14). That seems like a useful working definition with which to begin. We might distinguish further between sin in general, or sin *simpliciter*, and original sin, that morally vitiated state into which all humans barring Christ are born as a consequence of the actions of our first parents. Clearly, one need not hold to the doctrine of original sin in order to have an account of sin *simpliciter*, and there have been thinkers who embraced the latter while rejecting the former. Immanuel Kant may be the best-known philosophical exemplar of this sort of view; Pelagius is surely the most notorious theological representative. While it is tempting to restrict the scope of this chapter to sin *simpliciter*, that is not really feasible in a theological account of the notion. For, as I understand it, the traditional theological position is that human sin obtains because of the presence of original sin in creation, and without original sin there would not be individual acts of human sin because there would be no human sin per se. Original sin obtains because of the sin of an individual—at least, on traditional versions of the doctrine, as we shall see presently. But this primal or first act of sin gives rise to the condition of original sin with which we are all generated. Thus sin exists in the world because of the fault of an individual—an act of sin—but it is this fault that is transmitted in the condition of original sin from which all human beings now suffer, and that gives rise to all subsequent individual acts of sin.[1] Hence, a theological account of human sin must place it in the wider context of a doctrine of original sin in which it is properly situated, dogmatically speaking.

In what follows we shall address what I take to be the central dogmatic constituents of the doctrine of original sin with primary reference to theology in the Reformed tradition. In the course of this discussion I shall offer a defense of one neglected strand of this tradition that is quite distinct from the majority report—the doctrine offered by the Swiss magisterial reformer Huldrych Zwingli (1484–1531). Or, more precisely, I shall outline a constructive account of original sin in the course of presenting the dogmatic lay of the land from a Reformed perspective that draws on a broadly Zwinglian version of the doctrine as one viable way forward for contemporary Reformed theology.[2] A defense is not an endorsement, of course (ask any attorney). But a Zwinglian account of original sin certainly merits more attention than it typically receives in textbooks of dogmatics like this one.

Methodological Preamble

There are broadly two sorts of theological approaches to original sin. The first attempts to shore up the traditional doctrine. The second revises it. There are different versions of the doctrine in the Christian tradition, and today there are significant doctrinal differences between, say, Protestant theologians, Orthodox theologians, and Roman Catholic theologians on this topic—not to mention differences between theologians in a given branch of the tradition, especially among Protestants.[3] Consequently, it might be thought that

1. Possibly there would still be sin in the creation if there is an angelic fall prior to the human one. But that is a matter we shall not delve into here.

2. I say "Zwinglian" because this is not an exposition of Zwingli's account but the use of some ideas that are central to it. For instance, no account will be given here of the relationship between sacramental theology and original sin, or predestination and the ordering of the divine decrees and original sin, though these are both matters that would be important if we were giving an exposition of Zwingli's doctrine.

3. On the debate about the development of the Augustinian view, see N. P. Williams, *The Ideas of the Fall and of Original Sin* (London: Longmans, Green, and Co., 1927); and Pier Franco Beatrice, *The Transmission of Sin: Augustine and the Pre-Augustinian Sources* (New York: Oxford University Press, 2013). For a recent sophisticated restatement of the Augustinian position, see Jesse Couenhoven, *Stricken by Sin, Cured by Christ: Agency, Necessity, and Culpability in Augustinian Theology* (New York: Oxford University Press, 2013). A classic attempt to restate a broadly modern Augustinian account of original sin can be found in Reinhold Neibuhr, *The Nature and Destiny of Man*, vol. 1, *Human Nature* (New York: Charles Scribner and Sons,

to refer to *the* traditional doctrine is question-begging: Which doctrine is the traditional one? Aren't there many traditional versions of the doctrine? Part of the reason for this is that there is no canonical definition of the doctrine as there is for some other Christian tenets such as the two-natures doctrine of the incarnation. (Some Roman Catholics might dispute this, given that the Council of Trent pronounced on the doctrine. However, with deepest respect to those who might take such a view, the deliverances of one branch of the Christian church cannot constitute an ecumenical consensus on the matter, and therefore cannot be binding on all Christians in the way that members of the different communions of the church are bound to accept some other dogma on which there is such universal agreement, such as the Nicene view of the Trinity.[4])

Nevertheless, although there are not insignificant differences of opinion on the matter of the nature of original sin and its transmission (and what it is that is transmitted from some putative first humans to their progeny), there is broadly historic ecumenical agreement on the following matters: *first*, that there was an original pair from whom we are all descended; *second*, that this pair introduced the morally vitiated condition from which all subsequent humans suffer; and *third*, that all humans after the fall of the original pair possess the condition of original sin and are in need of salvation, without which they will perish. Some theologians (particularly in the Augustinian tradition) want to add to this the claim that all humans after the fall (barring Christ) bear the guilt of Adam's sin, so that in addition to possessing the

---

1945). For a digest of scholastic Lutheran views, see Heinrich Schmid, *The Doctrinal Theology of the Evangelical Lutheran Church* (Philadelphia: Lutheran Publication Society, 1876); for a digest of Reformed views, see Heinrich Heppe, *Reformed Dogmatics* (London: Collins, 1950). For a readable modern Orthodox view, see John S. Romanides, *The Ancestral Sin* (Ridgewood, NJ: Zephyr, 1998). In addition to the *Catechism of the Catholic Church* (New York: Doubleday, 1995), Ludwig Ott's *Fundamentals of Catholic Dogma* (Rockford, IL: Tan Books, 1955) is a useful field guide to Roman Catholic teaching on the subject. An example of a moderate contemporary Reformed restatement of the doctrine can be found in Marguerite Shuster, *The Fall and Sin: What We Have Become as Sinners* (Grand Rapids: Eerdmans, 2004). A much more revisionist recent Protestant account is given in Patricia A. Williams, *Doing without Adam and Eve: Sociobiology and Original Sin* (Minneapolis: Augsburg Fortress, 2001).

4. Here I presume a distinction between a doctrine or teaching of Christian theology, such as the atonement, and a dogma, which is a doctrine that has some canonical definition, as the doctrine of the Trinity does in the ecumenical creeds shared between all Christian communions. I take it that the conciliar decisions of Roman Catholic councils and synods have a dogmatic status in some ways analogous to that of the confessions and synodical decisions of Protestant churches. They are analogous but not the same, for Protestants still hold that confessions, though good and useful summaries of the faith, are subject to Scripture and may err, whereas Roman Catholics ought to believe what the church promulgates in its canonical decisions, including decisions by councils like Lateran IV or Trent.

condition of original depravity they also bear original guilt. However, this is not a doctrine universally affirmed and has generated a number of significant problems, as we shall see.[5]

For present purposes, when I refer to "the traditional doctrine of original sin" in what follows, I mean by this the concatenation of these three doctrinal tenets without any commitment to the doctrine of original guilt. These three tenets are fairly broad and dogmatically unspecific enough to encompass most of the different communions of historic Christianity. Although my usage is a term of art that will not satisfy everyone, it will be easier to use this shorthand rather than give a potted version of the long and convoluted historical narrative that gave rise to these three tenets of the traditional doctrine.[6]

The Nature of Original Sin

Having dealt with these methodological concerns, we may turn to exposition. The doctrine of original sin has several parts. Some theologians argue that original sin is a moral corruption that affects humans in such a way that they are prone to sin. However, the sort of doctrine I am interested in stipulates that the moral corruption affecting humans means they will *inevitably* fall into actual sin on at least one occasion. This needs to be parsed a little more finely, however. What is this corruption, and what does it mean to "fall into sin" if one already possesses such a moral corruption?

As to the first matter, I take it that original sin is a condition that affects all humans (barring Christ).[7] Zwingli characterized original sin as analogous

5. In his recent study, Ian McFarland carves up the doctrine in a similar fashion. He divides it according to (1) the degree to which the story of the fall in Genesis 1–3 should be interpreted literally; (2) whether the story told there implicates the rest of the human race; and (3) whether or to what extent the sin of our first parents affects the freedom of subsequent humans (McFarland, *In Adam's Fall: A Meditation on the Christian Doctrine of Original Sin* [Oxford: Wiley-Blackwell, 2010], 32). By contrast, Richard Swinburne writes of the proneness to sin in all humans; the question of its cause (and whether that has to be an original human pair); and whether guilt for this original sin distributes to all other humans. Swinburne, *Responsibility and Atonement* (Oxford: Oxford University Press, 1989), chap. 9.

6. For the historical development of the doctrine, N. P. Williams, *The Ideas of the Fall*, is still the benchmark. A more recent account can be found in Tatha Wiley, *Original Sin: Origins, Development, Contemporary Meanings* (Mahwah, NJ: Paulist Press, 2002). Alan Jacobs's *Original Sin: A Cultural History* (San Francisco: HarperOne, 2008) also bears scrutiny. An interesting constructive account of the doctrine that takes account of evolutionary biology is Robin Collins, "Evolution and Original Sin," in *Perspectives on an Evolving Creation*, ed. Keith B. Miller (Grand Rapids: Eerdmans, 2003), 469–501.

7. Roman Catholics will want to include Mary *Theotokos* as another sinless post-fall human and perhaps her mother, Anne. Such Christians are invited to make the relevant adjustment in what follows.

to an inherited disease or defect that inevitably gives rise to actual sin, for which humans are culpable. Possession of original sin was not itself culpable, Zwingli said, any more than being born a slave is a circumstance for which one is culpable. Yet it implies a separation from God that leads to damnation and (inevitably) to actual sin for which the individual is culpable in the sight of God. What is more, those born with original sin will perish and be separated from God without the interposition of divine grace in Christ.[8] He sums up his view: "Original sin, as it is in the children of Adam, is not properly sin . . . for it is not a misdeed contrary to law. It is, therefore, properly a disease and condition—a disease, because just as he fell through self-love, so do we also; a condition, because just as he became a slave and liable to death, so also are we both slaves and children of wrath . . . and liable to death."[9]

Later Reformed theology spoke of original sin in rather different terms as a deformity of the soul, or *macula*,[10] possession of which is itself grounds for culpability (see, e.g., Westminster Confession of Faith, 6.5). It is tempting to try to locate this condition, much as one might want to locate specific recessive genes that may affect a person adversely. However, although original sin does have perceptible consequences—for instance, in the manifestation of moral corruption evident in the lives of sinners—it has no location because it is not a physical thing. Rather, it is a property that, when instantiated, gives rise to a particular moral condition in a person. Much as a human may be born with the property of being capable of conscious thought, so, on this way of thinking, fallen humans are bearers of a property that means they are morally disordered in some fundamental respect, such that they will inevitably sin on at least one occasion. The condition of sin with which we are generated gives rise to acts of sin. Usually such acts of sin are distinguished from the moral condition of original sin as actual sins that are performed because a person is in a state of sin, that is, that proceed from the moral condition of original sin.

Does this mean that fallen humans are guilty only for the actual sins they (inevitably) commit because they are born with the moral condition of original sin? There is not one answer to this question. Much of the Western (Catholic)

---

8. Zwingli touches on original sin in several places in his works. The most developed account is in his *Declaration of Huldreich Zwingli Regarding Original Sin, Addressed to Urbanus Rhegius, August 15, 1526*. He summarizes this view in *An Account of The Faith of Huldreich Zwingli, Submitted to The German Emperor Charles V, at The Diet of Augsburg. July 3, 1530*. Both works are translated in *On Providence and Other Essays*, ed. Samuel Macauley Jackson (Durham, NC: Labyrinth, 1983). A useful digest of Zwingli's views can be found in W. P. Stephens, *Zwingli: An Introduction to His Thought* (Oxford: Oxford University Press, 1992), chap. 7.

9. Zwingli, *Account of the Faith to Charles V*, in *On Providence and Other Essays*, 40.

10. See Heppe, *Reformed Dogmatics*, 325.

tradition replies in the affirmative, for instance, St. Anselm of Canterbury in his work *On the Virginal Conception and Original Sin*. And, as we have already noted, there are Protestant defenders of much the same view—Zwingli being the best known among the orthodox. However, at least since St. Augustine, there has been a presumption in much theology that has followed his lead that possession of the condition of original sin is itself sufficient for culpability independent of any actual sin committed. The performance of actual sins is a reason for additional culpability.

We shall consider the objections to this sort of view in a moment when considering the transmission of original sin. For now it is important to note that there is a significant difference of opinion on the nature of original sin that turns on whether fallen humans are culpable for being in a state of original sin. This question of innate culpability implies that fallen humans bear Adam's sin *and guilt*. Often, textbook accounts from a more Augustinian or Reformed perspective suggest that original guilt is a constituent of the doctrine (or ought to be) and that alternative accounts that have no doctrine of original guilt are defective. However, Zwingli and St. Anselm (to name but two theologians that defend a doctrine without original guilt) are hardly liminal or unorthodox figures in Western theology. Nor are they non-Augustinian in the general thrust of their thinking. Yet both presume that fallen humans do not possess original guilt, though (in the case of Zwingli at least) they are in a serious condition that will yield spiritual death without saving grace in Christ.[11] Although the Reformed confessions by and large do not support Zwingli's position and, as they developed, moved away from Zwingli's view to include original guilt, this is not true of *all* Reformed symbols. For instance, Article 9 of the Thirty-Nine Articles of Religion states,

> Original sin . . . is the fault and corruption of the Nature of every man, that naturally is engendered of the offspring of Adam; whereby man is very far gone from original righteousness, and is of his own nature inclined to evil, so that the flesh lusteth always contrary to the Spirit; and therefore in every person born into this world, it deserveth God's wrath and damnation. And this infection of nature doth remain, yea in them that are regenerated; whereby the lust of the flesh, called in Greek, *phronema sarkos* . . . is not subject to the Law of God. And although there is no condemnation for them that believe and are

11. To be fair, the language of infection that Zwingli utilizes can also be found in Augustine. See, e.g., "Made an exile from thence after his sin, he [Adam] bound also his offspring, whom by sinning he had marred in himself as root in the penalty and death of damnation: with the result that all the children born of him . . . were infected with original sin." Augustine, *Enchiridion*, trans. Ernest Evans (London: SPCK, 1953), 26.24.

baptized; yet the Apostle doth confess, that concupiscence and lust hath of itself the nature of sin.[12]

This is very like Zwingli's view in what it affirms about the nature of original sin as corruption as well as what it omits, for instance, original guilt. It is my view that such a Zwinglian account is underappreciated in Reformed thought. What is more, given the problems associated with defending a doctrine according to which I am guilty for the sin of an ancestor many generations removed from me whose action I did not concur with or approve, there does appear to be a significant moral objection to those Augustinian and Reformed views that include original guilt. If a strong doctrine of original sin can be had that does not include this element, it might be preferable to the stronger alternative including original guilt, at least in part because it does not have to circumvent this significant moral objection. (It may incur other objections, of course, but these are, I think, less serious in part because the doctrine is weaker in what it asserts about the moral consequences of original sin for fallen humans.) There are a number of places where the traditional doctrine of original sin *plus* original guilt is defended.[13] In the next section, dealing with the transmission of original sin, I shall outline the major views from a broadly Reformed perspective and end up offering a defense of the Zwinglian view as a viable alternative that the Reformed (and other interested theologians) might want to reconsider.

The Transmission of Original Sin

There are two related but distinct dogmatic questions pertaining to the transmission of original sin. The first of these has to do with the nature of the union between Adam and his progeny on the basis of which original sin is transmitted. The second has to do with the imputation of original guilt. Some theologians argue that original guilt is applied *immediately* so that the condition of original sin is (somehow) communicated to all of Adam's progeny

12. Compare Article 15 of the Belgic Confession, which, like the Thirty-Nine Articles, has no clear doctrine of original guilt. It states original sin "is a corruption of the whole human nature—an inherited depravity which even infects small infants in their mother's womb, and the root which produces in humanity every sort of sin. It is therefore so vile and enormous in God's sight that it is enough to condemn the human race, and it is not abolished or wholly uprooted even by baptism, seeing that sin constantly boils forth as though from a contaminated spring." It goes on, "Nevertheless, it is not imputed to God's children for their condemnation but is forgiven by his grace and mercy."

13. John Murray's little study, *The Imputation of Adam's Sin* (Grand Rapids: Eerdmans, 1959), is perhaps the best place to begin.

on commission of the primal sin. Others claim that it obtains *mediately*, as we shall see.

Concerning the Union between Adam and His Progeny

We turn to the matter of the union between Adam and his progeny first. In Reformed theology there have been two important strands of thought on the question of the mode of transmission of original sin. The first of these is often called "federalism," since it depends on a story about different covenants between God and humans (the Latin term for such a covenant being *foedus*), beginning with a "covenant of works." This had as its condition that Adam and Eve refrain from eating of the tree of the knowledge of good and evil that stood in the midst of the garden of Eden (Gen. 2:17).[14] This view is also sometimes called "representationalism," for the central theological claim here is that Adam represents the rest of the human race in committing the primal sin; he acts on our behalf, and God imputes his sin to us as a consequence. The other main view in Reformed theology is Augustinian realism, so-called because it was thought to originate with St. Augustine of Hippo.[15] On this way of thinking, Adam's progeny are somehow really present with Adam when he commits his first sin so that the culpability for that sin is transmitted from Adam to his progeny who are united with him at that moment, either seminally (in his loins, so to speak) or in some other mysterious manner, often thought to be beyond our ken.

We have already mentioned in passing the two main concerns that the transmission of sin raises, namely, the apparent immorality and injustice involved in ascribing the sin and guilt of one person to another. How can I be guilty of Adam's sin if he lived many hundreds of years ago and I had no say in his wickedness? How is it moral for me to suffer for the sin of a long-dead ancestor?[16] The thought here is this: guilt cannot be ascribed to a person who

14. Federalism is "first" in that it is the more widespread view in Reformed thought even though, as a matter of fact, it postdates realism in theological discussions of the matter.

15. For instance,

> In fact, because of the magnitude of that offence, the condemnation changed human nature for the worse; so that what first happened as a matter of punishment in the case of the first human beings, continued in their posterity as something natural and congenital. . . . Therefore the whole human race was in the first man, and it was to pass from him through the woman into his progeny, when the married pair had received the divine sentence of condemnation. And it was not man as first made, but what man became after his sin and punishment, that was thus begotten, as far as concerns the origin of sin and death. (Augustine, *City of God*, trans. Henry Bettenson [Harmondsworth, UK: Penguin, 1984], 13.3)

16. The nineteenth-century Southern Presbyterian Robert Dabney puts it like this: "The grand objection of all Pelagians and skeptics . . . is still repeated: How can it be justice, for me, who gave no consent to the federal arrangement, for me, who was not present when Adam

has not authorized or otherwise participated in the sin of another individual. Yet this is just what is said to obtain in the case of the imputation of Adam's guilt to his offspring in the doctrine of original guilt.

Federalists developed two related lines of argument that attempt to rebut these worries. The first of these depends on the claim that Adam acts as the head of the human race in sinning as he does. There is a natural union between him and us because he is the first human, and we are his offspring. So, the tragic events in Eden that led to the primal sin have consequences for all subsequent humans because he was the natural head of the race. Had he been born several centuries after the first humans, then he would not have been the natural head of the race, and his primal sin would not have been distributed to all humanity. Some humans would have lived and died before him, and not all humanity would have proceeded from him. The second line of reasoning depends on the claim that there is a legal bond between Adam and his progeny. God justly imputes Adam's sin to us because Adam is our legal representative, acting on our behalf. When he sins, this act has the legal ramifications of committing those with whom he has this legal bond to the consequences attending his primal sin, namely, condemnation and the inheritance of the condition of original sin. In a similar manner, if Jones engages Smith to act as his legal representative in certain matters, then Smith's actions in that capacity are binding on Jones. He is legally warranted to act on behalf of Jones in these matters. Something similar obtains with Adam and his progeny on this view. His action in primal sin is binding on his progeny because he is warranted by divine fiat to be our legal representative.

So, according to the federalist, it is just that Adam acts on our behalf in his primal sin because God has authorized him to act in this manner, both as the natural head of the race so that the moral effects of his action may distribute to all subsequent humans, and as our public representative, whose fall has legally binding consequences for the rest of the human race that proceeds from him. Clearly these two lines of argument are related though distinct.

However, there are several significant drawbacks to the federalist view. Perhaps the most serious problem is that the appointment of Adam as our legal representative is dependent on the divine will alone. This means that the grounds for Adam being our natural and legal head is divine convention, nothing more. God makes truth in this matter, not merely in the sense that he creates a world in which a certain person, Adam, is the first human

---

sinned, and took no share in it, save in a sense purely fictitious and imaginary, to be so terribly punished for another man's deeds?" Dabney, *Lectures in Theology* (aka *Systematic Theology*) (Edinburgh: Banner of Truth, 1985), 338.

(according to traditional theology, at least). He additionally makes it the case that Adam acts as a legal representative of the human race when he commits the primal sin. In other words, it is God alone who is responsible for the state of affairs in which Adam commits the primal sin, which is communicated to his offspring. And God alone is responsible for ordaining that original sin is communicated from Adam to his progeny as well as the mechanism by means of which original sin is transmitted from Adam to his progeny. So God alone is responsible for bringing about what appears to be a deeply immoral and unjust arrangement whereby all those who come after Adam are culpable and punishable for his primal sin—a sin they did not commit and did not authorize a representative to commit either. But God cannot bring about a state of affairs for which he is solely responsible that is both unjust and immoral (Deut. 32:4; Hab. 1:13; 1 John 1:15). Hence, there must be something amiss with the federalist account of the transmission of sin. Call this *the arbitrary divine will objection.*

A second problem is closely related to the first, though it may be distinguished from it. Call it *the authorization objection.* It goes like this: I have not authorized Adam to act on my behalf as Jones authorizes Smith. Whether I would have done the same had I been in Adam's place is irrelevant for the purposes of establishing a proper legal warrant. Normally we would expect that someone who acts on behalf of another individual or on behalf of another group does so because he is authorized to do so by some appropriate authority. Although it might be claimed that God is the relevant authority here, it is not clear that anyone has the authority to make Adam the legal representative of a whole race that has no say in the matter—which yields the divine arbitrary will objection once more. It is not clear that God has the authority to impute the consequences of Adam's primal sin to the rest of humanity, given that they have not authorized him to act on their behalf, have not colluded with him, or otherwise been a party to his sinful action. The fact that Adam is said to be the natural head of the race does not work in resolving this legal problem, of course, since this aspect of the federalist argument does not depend on any established legal arrangement independent of the divine will. What is more, the imputation of the moral consequences of the primal sin of the first human to the rest of humanity is itself a seemingly arbitrary arrangement. (Why the first sin only? Why the first sin of the first human only? And so on. The first virtuous act of Adam isn't imputed to all his offspring in a similar manner. So this seems arbitrary.) On the face of it, defenders of the federalist argument appear to be saddled with a rather difficult version of the injustice problem for the transmission of original sin.

Might the federalist notion that original sin is imputed from Adam to his progeny help alleviate the moral problem of the transmission of original sin? Not obviously. For clearly we would normally think it is immoral to impute sin and guilt from one party who is culpable to another who is innocent. Adam is the agent that commits the primal sin; the rest of humanity does not. They are innocent of committing the primal sin for which they are said to be culpable and punishable. Consequently, it appears that the federalist is in a bind regarding both the legal and moral objections to the transmission of original sin because Adam's progeny have not authorized or otherwise approved his action on their behalf.

Finally, it seems that the federalist scheme rests on what we might call a legal and moral fiction, generating *the fiction objection*: God imputes Adam's sin to his progeny; he holds them responsible for Adam's sin—or at least, he holds them jointly culpable with Adam because they are punishable for his sin by virtue of possessing original sin quite apart from any actual sin they may perform. But clearly Adam's progeny are not the ones guilty of performing the act of primal sin; Adam is. So imputing it to them involves a fiction, one that has both a legal and a moral dimension given the federalist argument. However, that God is said to impute original sin to Adam's progeny on the basis of a natural and legal union with Adam does not make this act any more appropriate. Often defenders of the federalist view argue that because God is an absolute sovereign he may distribute matters as he sees fit, and we are not to question him in this regard (relying in part on St. Paul's comments in Rom. 9). Furthermore, that an entity is an absolute sovereign in and of itself conveys no moral *imprimatur* to that entity's actions.[17] Such an entity could be a tyrant, after all, with his acts evidence of megrim. The fact is, the federalist account hangs upon the divine will, and what God decides to bring about according to his good will and pleasure. Yet this alone is an insufficient ground for an argument for the conclusion that the transmission of original sin is just and moral unless one is willing to embrace the view that God *makes* certain things just and moral. Even if one factors in the divine character so that the argument is not purely voluntarist (i.e., stemming from the divine will alone) but intellectualist (i.e., involving God acting as he does because of

---

17. Suppose Adam didn't sin. Would it have been unjust for God to have granted eternal life to all of Adam's progeny on the basis of his obedience? Maybe not. However, I am attracted to the view that without union with Christ eternal life is impossible even for those who are sinless. If that is right, then the incarnation would have happened irrespective of Adam's primal sin. For recent discussion of this matter, see Edwin Christian van Driel, *Incarnation Anyway: Arguments for Supralapsarian Christology* (New York: Oxford University Press, 2008); and Marilyn McCord Adams, *Christ and Horrors: The Coherence of Christology* (Cambridge: Cambridge University Press, 2006), chap. 7.

the character he has), it is still not clear how this provides any moral or legal justification for the act of transmitting original sin. Something more needs to be said. If, in the final analysis, the federalist appeals beyond the divine will to mystery or antinomy, it is not clear how this will help. For in the case of the imputation of a thing from one party to another, we have deep-seated moral intuitions about what is morally and legally appropriate, such that it would be clear in a more mundane context that such an arrangement as that given by the federalist for the transmission of original sin would be unjust and immoral.[18]

For these reasons, I judge that the federalist argument, taken on its own merits and without augmentation by appeal to other accounts of the transmission of sin, fails to overcome the moral and legal problems with which we began our assessment.[19]

18. The federalist may reply that this objection proves too much. In undercutting reasons for the imputation of Adam's sin, we also undercut reasons for thinking that Christ's righteousness may be imputed also. But we don't want to set aside the imputation of Christ's righteousness in redemption, so we have a christological reason for thinking that imputation obtains in the case of Christ's work and that a similar sort of reasoning obtains, *mutatis mutandis*, with respect to the imputation of Adam's sin. Here the federalist can appeal to Rom. 5:12–19, which turns on the parallel between the work of both Adam and Christ.

One line of response here is to point out that there are significant dissimilarities between the work of Adam and Christ that bear on the question of imputation. Adam's headship is natural and legal (according to federalism); Christ's is neither. Perhaps the imputation of sin on the basis of a natural and legal headship is problematic (for the reasons given above), whereas the supernatural basis for the imputation of Christ's righteousness is not. This is the realist way of distinguishing between the two "Adams." (See, e.g., William Shedd's *A Critical and Doctrinal Commentary on the Epistle of St. Paul to the Romans* [Eugene, OR: Wipf & Stock, 2001].) Another answer involves acceding to the federalist objection and appealing to a doctrine of atonement that does not include the notion that Christ's righteousness is imputed to the saints. One historic example of this is Anselm's doctrine of atonement in *Cur Deus homo*. Given his influence in historic Reformed theology, this seems to be an alternative to penal substitution worth exploring. I have attempted a different (more modern) version of a consistent realist response in "Original Sin and Atonement" in *The Oxford Handbook of Philosophical Theology*, ed. Thomas P. Flint and Michael C. Rea (Oxford: Oxford University Press, 2009), chap. 19.

19. One could augment the federalist account with a realist account, as some Reformed theologians seem to have done, e.g., Jonathan Edwards. In such cases the federalist account is no longer doing all the metaphysical heavy lifting. It may be that such hybrid doctrines are able to avoid the problems set forth here. For further discussion, see Oliver D. Crisp, "Jonathan Edwards on the Imputation of Sin," in *Retrieving Doctrine: Essays in Reformed Theology* (Downers Grove, IL: IVP Academic, 2011), chap. 3. Some early Reformed accounts of the imputation of sin are not clearly federalist or realist having aspects of both later accounts, e.g., John Calvin, *Institutes of the Christian Religion*, ed. John T. McNeill, trans. Ford Lewis Battles (Philadelphia: Westminster, 1960), 1.2.7. Some federalists maintain that their position doesn't fall foul of the arbitrariness objection because imputation is grounded in an existing natural union between Adam and his offspring. Suppose that is right. The fiction objection still obtains because God has to ascribe to Adam's offspring a property they do not naturally possess. If the federalist

What of the realist alternative? According to at least one recent treatment of the Reformed doctrine of original sin, this is very much a minority report in the tradition, associated with one nineteenth-century American Presbyterian theologian in particular, namely, William Shedd.[20] But as Shedd argues in his *Dogmatic Theology*, the realist position is found in much earlier Reformed theology, at least implicitly, and is present in the work of several other eighteenth- and nineteenth-century theologians, including Samuel Baird, James Thornwell, and the Reformed Baptist Augustus Strong. There are strong overtones of this view in the work of others too, for instance, Robert Dabney and Robert Landis, as well as Jonathan Edwards.[21]

According to the realist view, the way to avoid the moral and legal problems that beset the transmission of original sin is to opt for a real union between Adam and his progeny rather than a union that is a moral and legal construct. Making good on this claim is a tall order, however. There are several historic realist arguments for this conclusion. The first of these we may call *the seminal argument*, since the idea is that somehow all of Adam's descendants were seminally present with him in his act of primal sin. Appeal is often made to Hebrews 7:9–10, where Levi is said to have been in the loins of Abraham when he was blessed by Melchizedek, so that he may be said to have paid out a tithe with Abraham, figuratively speaking. Just as Levi was in the loins of Abraham, so we were in the loins of Adam. And just as Levi paid out a tithe via his ancestor to Melchizedek, so we sinned in Adam.

The problems with such a view are obvious. First of all, the passage in Hebrews does not require that Levi was actually seminally present in Abraham's loins, so it is a frail reed upon which to rest an argument for the conclusion that all humanity was really present in Adam's loins. Moreover, given what we now know of human biology and procreation, the seminal argument is a nonstarter. Furthermore, even if some sense could be made of it, it doesn't solve the moral problem for the transmission of original sin because a seminally present entity is not an entity that can authorize the sin of Adam or participate in his sin.

---

wants to argue that God does transmit Adam's sin to his offspring as parts of a natural or organic whole, then this begins to look much more like a realist view.

20. See Donald Macleod, "Original Sin in Reformed Theology," in *Adam, the Fall, and Original Sin: Theological, Biblical, and Scientific Perspectives*, ed. Hans Madueme and Michael Reeves (Grand Rapids: Baker Academic, 2014), 129–46.

21. For discussion of this, see George P. Hutchinson, *The Problem of Original Sin in American Presbyterian Theology* (Phillipsburg, NJ: P&R, 1972). Augustus Strong's views are set forth in his *Systematic Theology* (Valley Forge, PA: Judson, 1907). Jonathan Edwards's views are not straightforwardly realist but could be characterized as a sort of rogue realism. See his *Original Sin*, in *The Works of Jonathan Edwards, Vol. 3*, ed. Clyde A. Holbrook (New Haven: Yale University Press, 1970), 4.3.

Another realist argument is that Adam's human nature is a sort of mass from which all subsequent human natures are drawn. His nature is either fissiparous or parturient so that subsequent human natures are individualized from his greater nature as a piece of clay is taken from a lump and fashioned into a particular artifact. On this view, then, we are literally chips off the old Adamic block! Parts of Adam's human nature are passed on from him to his children; they in turn pass on a part of their human nature to their children, and so on down through the generations. Each subsequent instance of human nature is individualized as it is generated from the substance of the parent human nature, just as one might take a piece of clay from the lump, and then another piece from the smaller lump, and another piece, and so on, fashioning each individual lump into a particular artifact. Let us call this *the unindividualized nature argument*. This version of realism appears to require the doctrine of traducianism, according to which human souls are passed down the generations in a manner analogous to the passing on of genetic material from parents to children. On this realist account, human nature (whatever that is, exactly) is passed down through natural generation.

The benefit of this unindividualized nature realist argument is that it can provide an argument that ameliorates the moral problem of the transmission of original sin. We really were "in" Adam because we were literally parts of his human nature, which is the Ur-nature for all humanity that is passed down the generations and individualized in each of us in part. However, for most contemporary theologians, the cost of this solution will be too high. Few modern theologians want to embrace traducianism in any form, and the notion that Adam has some sort of Ur-nature or Ur-soul from which all subsequent humans are derived is, to say the least, fanciful—provided some sense can be made of the notion of a fissiparous Ur-nature.

A recent peroration on this Ur-nature realist argument that draws on the work of Jonathan Edwards claims that we literally sin "in" Adam because we all share a temporal part or stage with Adam—the part or stage that commits primal sin. The idea is something like this. Suppose that we are all four-dimensional beings that persist through time in virtue of having temporal parts or, perhaps, stages that are segued together, on analogy with the physical parts that make a human person.[22] Just as I have a hand and foot as distinct physical parts, so perhaps I have distinct temporal parts: the part of me that

---

22. I am skating over an important difference between stage theory and temporal parts theory, two ways to carve up distinct, four-dimensional wholes. I have had to do this in the interest of space. The distinction is clearly set forth in Sally Haslanger, "Persistence through Time," in *The Oxford Handbook of Metaphysics*, ed. Michael J. Loux and Dean W. Zimmerman (Oxford: Oxford University Press, 2003), chap. 11.

existed yesterday, the part that existed thirty years ago today, and so forth. Now, assume that this is true of all humans, Adam included. Then he has a temporal part or stage that committed primal sin. Imagine that at the moment of primal sin that stage fissures into innumerable stages that are qualitatively identical to one another though numerically distinct. These innumerable stages or parts become the first part or stage of the lives of subsequent humans so that each and every human (barring Christ, perhaps) shares a fissured stage with Adam. Then, the first moment of our lives, so to speak, is a stage that obtains thousands of years ago when Adam sinned. Like other realist arguments, this one involves the claim that somehow I have a preexistence before my conception in the womb. Unlike the Ur-soul argument, however, on this view that which preexists my first moment in the womb is a fissured stage or temporal part that is shared with Adam.

This updating of a sort of realist view uses contemporary metaphysical discussion of persistence through time to make a case for a real union between Adam and his progeny. But it has a considerable cost, and many will think the notion that I have a fissured part that I derive from Adam, though possible, is not terribly plausible and begs other important questions about my preexistence "in" Adam and about so-called gappy existence (for then I would have a temporal part or stage shared with Adam, and a huge temporal gap between it and my next temporal part or stage that obtains when I begin to exist in my mother's womb). If one has independent reasons for thinking an entity cannot have two beginnings of existence or cannot have a gappy existence like this, then one will find little attractive about this modern relative of a realist solution—what we might call *the fission argument*.[23]

Yet another peroration on a realist theme (and one that also draws on the work of Edwards) is what we might call *the participation argument*.[24] On this view, sin is "transmitted" from some first human community to all subsequent humans (barring Christ) because God constitutes the part of this human community that sins and all subsequent human beings (barring Christ) as one metaphysical whole, with myriad different parts scattered across space-time. You and I are both "parts" of this one whole entity, so that we share together certain properties in common, much as a composite whole has parts that

23. The argument is found in Michael C. Rea's essay, "The Metaphysics of Original Sin," in *Persons: Human and Divine*, ed. Peter van Inwagen and Dean Zimmerman (Oxford: Oxford University Press, 2007), chap. 14. It is discussed by Hud Hudson in *The Fall and Hypertime* (Oxford: Oxford University Press, 2014), who finds problems with it, though he thinks it a remarkable piece of metaphysics. As will be clear from a perusal of Rea's paper, his argument is inspired by Edwards's discussion in *Original Sin* 4.3.
24. For elaboration of this argument see Crisp, "Original Sin and Atonement."

share properties in common, though not all properties and not all parts. For instance, consider my cat, Tigger. He is a ginger cat. He is a composite whole made up of many parts. Some of those parts share in common the property "being ginger," which is why we think of him as a ginger cat. However, not all his parts have the property "being ginger," for not all his parts are ginger. His whiskers are not ginger, nor are his claws, his bones, his intestines, and so on. Yet he is a ginger cat. In a similar way, perhaps humanity is a whole entity that is scattered across space and time. Some of its constituent members share the property of original sin just as some of Tigger's parts share the property of "being ginger." Not all the parts of this four-dimensional whole that we might call composite humanity are fallen (e.g., Adam and Eve prior to their primal sin, or Christ). Yet many members have this property. Together they comprise a scattered entity, which shares certain parts and properties in common.

Like other versions of realism, the participation argument presumes that there must be some real unity between Adam and his progeny on the basis of which God is able to "transmit" original sin from one part of the composite whole of humanity to the others. This real unity is ordained by God, of course. But he has set up the world so that, in addition to conventional artifacts like tables and chairs, there are unconventional or exotic entities like composite humanity. Like the federalist arguments, there is a reason why this involves the "transmission" of the moral condition generated by the primal sin of the first human, Adam, rather than some later sin of a later human. Only the primal sin can infect all the later stages of composite humanity, just as only an infected acorn can be the cause of the chronic disease afflicting the oak tree at each and every stage of its later development. To change the metaphor, if one introduces a flaw into the blueprints for a new vehicle, then that flaw will be present in every production-line model of the motorcar. The same would not be true if the flaw occurred on the production line of one of the factories manufacturing the vehicle as a consequence of equipment failure. In that case there are other factories making the same model that remain unaffected by the mechanical failure at the first factory, and examples of the model being driven around that would not have the flaw. *Mutatis mutandis*, Adam's primal sin must be the sin that is communicated to the other parts of composite humanity if it is to be "transmitted" via natural generation.

But we must ask: Does the participation argument offer a moral or a just arrangement (more moral and more just than the realist alternatives)? And does it overcome the problems of the transmission of original sin? Edwards thinks it is just for God to do as he pleases, because God "makes truth in affairs of this nature." This seems too strong, and it has the unintended outcome of collapsing Edwards's four-dimensionalist argument for the transmission of original sin into a matter of divine fiat. Nevertheless, God may arrange matters so that Adam and his progeny constitute one scattered composite whole much as, in a soteriological context, Christ and his elect constitute another scattered whole comprising the Savior and those united to him by the secret working of the Holy Spirit. The union is different, of course. In the case of Adam and his progeny, it is a natural union between the first human and his sin and later humans. In the case of Christ and the elect, the union is not a natural one but a supernatural one that has a proleptic component: Christ is the firstborn from the dead, the firstfruits of resurrection, the new Adam, and the head of a new race of those who, through union with him, are redeemed (as the Pauline language of the New Testament makes clear), including those saints who lived prior to Christ.

Recall that a worry raised with seminal and unindividualized nature versions of realism were that they did not address the matter of the culpability of Adam's progeny in his sin, since seminal or unindividualized presence with Adam is hardly the same as being complicit in the sin of Adam and cannot include the notion of agreeing with Adam in his sin (for seminal and unindividualized presence does not include agency on the part of those seminally present or present in an unindividualized state). Does the participation argument fare any better on this score? It certainly involves Adam's progeny as agents capable of acceding to Adam's sin. But they do not actually accede to his sin on this version of realism. So it might appear that the argument fails to overcome the moral problem for transmission of original sin. But such a judgment would be overhasty. The participation argument presumes that Adam and his progeny form one organic whole, composite humanity.[25] What the first part does in the act of primal sin has implications for later parts of the same entity scattered across space and time because composite humanity is an aggregated object. God treats as one what is one aggregated object for the purposes of the transmission of original sin. There are parallels to such arrangements in corporate law where the different assets of a particular company can be treated as parts of one legal entity for certain legal purposes. The difference in the case of the participation argument is

25. Aren't Adam and his progeny one composite whole according to federalism as well? He is the natural and legal head of the race, and his sin is imputed to them. But this is a different arrangement than the realist one. Adam and his offspring are not one organism or one organic whole; the union envisaged in federalism is more like that of an artifact than an organism, that is, more like a collection of distinct parts organized into a whole than it is a whole that has certain parts. This would be similar to the difference between, say, a chair made of wooden parts fashioned into a serviceable object, and a tree, which is an organism made of wood.

that Adam and his progeny are not merely a legal entity (as with federalism) but a real, four-dimensional, metaphysical whole. Nevertheless, like the legal corporate entity, the metaphysical four-dimensional entity that is composite humanity can have ascribed to some of its parts the moral properties of other parts because they are parts of one entity.

We have been using the language of the traditional account of original sin here deliberately and in the interests of economy of style. However, if one thought of "Adam" as a placeholder for some early human community, the argument could still be run with only minor changes being made. Nor does it matter that "Adam" is not the first hominid. What matters for the purposes of the participation argument is that "Adam" is the first member or the first community of the whole that comprises composite humanity. God certainly "makes truth" in that respect: he decides which hominid community will be the community on which he bestows his image, and with which he enters into covenant relationship.[26]

Concerning the Guilt Transmitted

A final matter remains to be explored. This is the question of the manner of the transmission of original sin. Does God transmit it immediately on the commission of the primal sin so that once Adam sins, God transmits original sin to all subsequent humans, as it were, automatically and prior to the existence of subsequent human natures? This is a common view in Reformed theology.[27] But it has some significant drawbacks. On this view, the immediate imputation of original guilt logically precedes and is the cause of inherent corruption. But this means that I am born in a state of sin, possessing original sin, because God imputes the guilt of another individual to me logically prior to me becoming a moral agent. For reasons already touched on, this seems intolerable, the sort of arrangement that would never be thought just or moral in more mundane circumstances.

The alternative view developed by the theologians of the post-Reformation French Saumur Academy, and Josue Placeus in particular, is mediate imputation. In this view the inheritance of a corrupt nature gives rise to the guilt

---

26. Does this not fall foul of the arbitrary divine will objection? Perhaps it does. But perhaps not in quite the same ways as federalism. The worry with federalism is that it attributes an arbitrariness to God that raises moral objections. The same objections cannot be raised here because (we presume) no hominid group deserves special treatment by God, and God may elect according to his good pleasure and will (Eph. 1:9; Rom. 8:28–30; 9:6–18).

27. See Westminster Confession of Faith, 6.3; The Formula Consensus Helvetica of 1675 also takes a firm stand against the mediate view of the Saumur theologians in favor of immediate imputation.

of Adam's sin. That is, guilt for Adam's sin is consequent on possessing the corrupt nature inherited from Adam. Placeus's view was censured at the Synod of Charenton, though in clarifying his view after the censure, Placeus made it clear that his position was not identical to the one the Synod had condemned. Nevertheless, though it is intriguing, mediate imputation has remained relatively undeveloped in subsequent Reformed theology.[28]

The Zwinglian Alternative

Zwingli's view, to which we have already made reference, is that humans inherit a disease or defect, a moral condition from fallen Adam that includes no guilt at all. We are not culpable for the corruption that we are generated with and bring with us into the world. On the Zwinglian view, neither immediate nor mediate imputation applies, for two reasons. First, Adam's guilt is not transmitted to his progeny; second, the condition of original sin is inherited, passed down the generations like genes. It is not imputed; it is a disease consequent on Adam's primal sin, akin to contracting a chronic and debilitating malady that is then passed on to one's offspring through natural generation. Being born in sin, on this Zwinglian view, involves having moral corruption—that much is held in common with other Reformed thinkers. But without a doctrine of imputed original guilt, there is no need for elaborate metaphysical distinctions between immediate or mediate imputation, or between the punishable aspect of original guilt and the inherent aspect, or even explicit commitment to four-dimensional parts and wholes. So his view, or a variant of it, has a certain theological parsimony in making sense of the transmission of original sin that is attractive and perhaps preferable to the alternatives.

Does it overcome the moral problem and the injustice problem for the transmission of original sin? Does it fare any better than federalism or realism in this regard? In answer to the immorality objection to the transmission of original sin, the Zwinglian can say that it is not immoral for God to allow Adam to freely choose to commit the primal sin. Nor is it immoral that the consequences of this act are transferred to all his progeny as a spiritual disease, moral defect, and inherited condition on analogy with the inheritance of serious medical conditions that are recessive in nature. This is just the natural outworking of Adam's primal sin, just as, in a different context, the selling of oneself into slavery is the reason why one's offspring and their offspring, and so on, are

---

28. See Philip Schaff, *Creeds of Christendom*, vol. 1, *The History of the Creeds* (New York: Harper and Brothers, 1877), 484–85; Anthony A. Hoekema, *Created in God's Image* (Grand Rapids: Eerdmans, 1986), 156–57; G. C. Berkouwer, *Sin* (Grand Rapids: Eerdmans, 1971), 454–58.

all born into slavery. In a sense, and metaphorically speaking, that is just what Adam has done: he has sold his offspring into a condition of bondage to sin. This means that each of his offspring (barring Christ) is generated with original sin, a condition that will lead to spiritual death if left unaddressed.[29]

What about the injustice objection to the transmission of original sin? Here too Zwingli's position has distinct advantages. Zwingli can say something different from federalism and realism. God justly transmits Adam's sinful condition to me through natural inheritance. (Perhaps, we might think, God does this via some sort of spiritually recessive "gene" that both parents of any fallen person possess—though this goes beyond what Zwingli actually says.) He does not transmit Adam's guilt to me, so the condition in which I find myself (i.e., being born with the condition of original sin) is not one for which I am culpable, though it will lead to my death without the interposition of divine grace, just as some inherited conditions lead to death without medical intervention.

Note that Zwingli clearly does endorse original sin. He is not a Pelagian (*pace* Luther), for Pelagians deny the doctrine of inherited sin, opting instead for the view that sin obtains by imitation, not imputation (or inheritance).[30] Clearly, Zwingli does think sin obtains through inheritance, the inheritance of a vitiated moral condition that leads inevitably to acts of sin. Is he semi-Pelagian? Semi-Pelagians hold to a doctrine of synergism in the matter of salvation. That is, they teach that humans are able to exercise their free will independent of divine grace in order to cooperate with divine grace in bringing about their own salvation. But Zwingli emphatically denies this, and the Zwinglian can do the same: salvation is entirely a matter of divine grace for which fallen humans can do nothing to prepare themselves. This Zwinglian view is clearly monergistic and therefore not semi-Pelagian.[31]

29. Granted, the federalist and realist can use similar language about Adam selling his descendants into slavery, but the theological account of the transmission of sin underpinning this trope is quite different.

30. For Pelagius's writings, see B. R. Rees, trans., *The Letters of Pelagius and His Followers* (Woodbridge: Boydell, 1991); and idem, *Pelagius's Commentary on St. Paul's Epistle to the Romans*, trans. Theodore de Bruyn (Oxford: Oxford University Press, 1993). For a brief introduction to Pelagius, see John Ferguson, *Pelagius: A Historical and Theological Study* (Cambridge: W. Heffer and Sons, 1956).

31. There are aspects of Zwingli's position that are less attractive. In *On the Providence of God* he argues that hard determinism obtains; that human free will and agency is an illusion; and that God is the only real cause of all that takes place in the world. He also advocates a strong version of supralapsarianism that will not appeal to everyone. However, one can extract his doctrine of original sin from these wider, though related, theological commitments in which it is embedded without damaging the substantive claims he makes about original sin and its transmission. That is what I am proposing here.

Other things about the Zwinglian view seem appealing as well. Although Zwingli thought of original sin as originating with a historic human pair, it might be that a broadly Zwinglian account of original sin could be had that makes room for a more expansive understanding of the acquisition of original sin. Perhaps the disease is introduced by the actions of more than one pair or by the action of a community (i.e., by "Adam"). It comes to afflict all the members of the community and, as a consequence, is passed on to all their offspring through the generations.

Such a peroration on the Zwinglian position would not require that the humans from which all have descended were specially created or were the only hominids at the time the primal sin was committed. And it could provide a plausible account of the transmission of original sin down through the years via (or accompanying) natural generation.[32] It would offer a strong doctrine of human moral disorder, but one that does not have the problems that the more metaphysically elaborate notions of federalism or realism require. Without imputation and original guilt, such a Zwinglian doctrine is also freed from the need to defend implausible or objectionable notions such as moral and legal fictionalism, or the culpability of the innocent. It is not without cost, of course. But it may be that a Zwinglian doctrine taken along these lines has more to be said for it in a post-Darwinian world than does the sort of doctrine beloved of many Reformed divines after Zwingli. Their views are encumbered by various elements that make them much less attractive or straightforward, much of which stems from their inclusion of a doctrine of original guilt.

Conclusions

Can a traditional account of original sin be defended? Recall that we character-ized the three constituents of the traditional view as follows: first, that there was an original pair from whom we are all descended; second, that this pair introduced the morally vitiated condition from which all subsequent humans suffer; and third, that all humans after the fall of the original pair possess the condition of original sin and are in need of salvation, without which they will perish. Clearly some Reformed account can be given of the doctrine that does satisfy these three criteria, though I have indicated that a more expansive understanding of the first constituent is required given what we now know about human evolution. I have also commended the Zwinglian view as one that has certain obvious advantages over extant alternatives in the Reformed

32. Here I have in mind the notion of a hominid community chosen by God from which all subsequent humans are descended.

tradition, chief among which is that it does not require a doctrine of original guilt. Not only is original guilt not a constituent of the traditional view as set forth here, but it also generates significant dogmatic problems for the federalist and realist doctrines that presume it. Does something like the Zwinglian alternative seem plausible—perhaps *more plausible* than the alternatives that presume original guilt? I have answered in the affirmative. What is more, a version of this Zwinglian story of original sin can be had that is consistent with much of the story of human development told by contemporary biology and allied sciences. If that is right, then this neglected strand of Reformed anthropology may well be both dogmatically and scientifically plausible—or at least, dogmatically plausible and not scientifically *im*plausible, and at least as plausible as the alternatives and perhaps more plausible on balance. That may be the best one can ask for when considering such a difficult and perplexing theological topic.

10

Incarnation

DANIEL J. TREIER

Modern Christology often begins with Jesus's question, "Who do you say I am?" (Matt. 16:15). Yet the context of Peter's response involves not just human opinions or personal seeking but divine revelation. Already evoking the Old Testament, Jesus dubbed himself Son of Man in his initial question (Matt. 16:13). The prominent answers of the time (Matt. 16:14) already evoked the Old Testament salvation history as well. When Peter—already having followed Jesus for some time—responded, "You are the Messiah, the Son of the living God" (Matt. 16:16 NIV), Israel's long-awaited hope was reaching fulfillment. The church truly understands God's self-disclosure in Christ only in the context of Israel's story (Matt. 16:17–20).

After Jesus's passion and the Spirit's outpouring, the church could begin to more fully interpret this divine self-disclosure. Even then, the Son of God becoming one of us fulfilled Israel's hopes beyond all human understanding. Centuries of reflection on the apostolic witness became necessary to honor this mystery. Hence Christology's reflection on Scripture, its final authority, depends on Christian tradition—no mere test of time but ultimately the Spirit's provision. The church needed to discern the basic grammar of the mystery underlying its worship, exploring its meaning without expecting to exhaust its fullness.

Dogmatic Christology's proper context—divine self-revelation and its heritage of churchly responses—prioritizes "who" Jesus Christ is, avoiding undue preoccupation with "what" kind of being he is or "how" he could be divine and human.[1] Only followers—hearing the Incarnate One call—can identify him truly. Yet this call, precisely because it is authentically personal, elicits respect for the church's heritage and suspicion of endless speculation: "Jesus Christ is the same yesterday, today, and forever" (Heb. 13:8 NIV). Hebrews assures the church of an enduring answer to our "Who?" question, a constant companion on our pilgrimage. After all, the Gospels query how responsive disciples are as much as how they identify their Lord. Appropriately wondering about the mystery of the incarnation does not mean seeking explanations as if left to ourselves, apart from Christ's revelatory presence.

Therefore Christian dogmatics in the Reformed tradition is particularly attentive to how divine self-revelation unfolds in the Bible's redemptive history.[2] First, this scriptural unfolding places the *meaning* of incarnation within the real movement of earthly history. Next, its fullness of meaning involves *presuppositions*, *entailments*, and *implications*, discerned in submission to Scripture and early catholic dogma, then expressed in distinctive confessional terms.[3] Finally, *further possibilities* arise for deeper understanding or even necessary reform as revelation elicits faithful creativity. The eight theses of this chapter embody such churchly faith seeking fuller understanding. In humble dependence on divine revelation, we begin with the meaning of "incarnation" itself.

1. *"Incarnation" means* becoming embodied, referring theologically to the Son of God becoming fully human in Jesus Christ. *The root metaphor of being in flesh generates the regular christological concept of assuming full humanity: if God takes upon himself even our embodiment, then this ultimate divine self-revelation surely embraces all aspects of human life. The beginning—the initial becoming—of this incarnate state was the event of the Holy Spirit accomplishing Christ's virginal conception in Mary.*

John 1:14 provides the root metaphor: "The Word became flesh and made his dwelling among us" (NIV). The incarnation is an event with a beginning:

1. Dietrich Bonhoeffer, "Lectures on Christology (Student Notes)," in *Berlin: 1932–1933*, ed. Larry L. Rasmussen, trans. Isabel Best and David Higgins (Minneapolis: Fortress, 2009), 299–360.
2. This chapter interacts with, though it cannot represent, the breadth of those who might self-identify as Reformed without assuming that self-identification or churchly association either sets or erases simple boundaries.
3. J. L. Austin (*How to Do Things with Words* [Oxford: Oxford University Press, 1962], 47–48) speaks of successful speech acts involving other claims; given background conditions, meaning incorporates what verbal expression presupposes, what is entailed by it, and then what it implies. The Reformed heritage does not indulge "proof-texting" without context, but beyond explicit teaching Scripture invites doctrinal discernment from sanctified reason.

"became." The incarnation is an event with a human body: "flesh." The incarnation is an event with a subsequent history, an enduring life: "made his dwelling among us." The incarnation is an event with revelatory significance: "the Word," whose glory the first disciples saw, overflowing with the "grace and truth" glimpsed by Moses. The incarnation is therefore a singular event, having no earthly analogies that could sustain full explanation. The incarnation is a reality with its own mysterious rationality, having its cogency in the Logos through whom all creation came to exist and comes to light.

All language originates in metaphor, thinking of something in terms that suggest something else.[4] Concepts are dead metaphors: somewhat language-independent habits associating particular ideas or objects with words.[5] Various concepts can express similar or shared theological judgments; the same concept could inform various judgments.[6] The root metaphor of Word becoming flesh primarily appears in John's Gospel, yet related judgments in other biblical texts evoke conceptual similarity. Incarnation understandably became the most central, regular way for Christian dogmatics to name the advent of Jesus Christ.

The canonical biographies—the fourfold Gospel—of the Incarnate One begin variously. Yet whether their narratives begin before creation itself, or with a genealogy drawn from Israel's covenant history, or with John the Baptizer preparing the way, or with extraordinary births, they draw prominently on Isaiah (notably chaps. 49, 52–53, and 61): Jesus is the anticipated, Spirit-anointed Servant who is ultimately God's Son coming personally to heal God's servant Israel. In that context Jesus's virginal conception in Mary is especially fitting.

It is easy to reach the facile conclusion that any difference from other human births precludes Jesus's full humanity. Such suspicion of the "virgin birth" rests on two major claims.[7] First, the New Testament contains multiple, contradictory depictions of Jesus's origins, with the virginal conception in Luke and probably Matthew a "minority report."[8] These depictions bear marks of literary creativity that mitigate straightforward historical claims. Second, whereas ancient anthropologies had Mary providing the fullness of Jesus's

---

4. Janet Martin Soskice, *Metaphor and Religious Language* (Oxford: Clarendon, 1985).

5. See Kathleen Callow, *Man and Message: A Guide to Meaning-Based Text Analysis* (Lanham, MD: University Press of America, 1998); this is treated further in Daniel J. Treier, *Virtue and the Voice of God: Toward Theology as Wisdom* (Grand Rapids: Eerdmans, 2006).

6. David S. Yeago, "The New Testament and the Nicene Dogma: A Contribution to the Recovery of Theological Exegesis," in *The Theological Interpretation of Scripture: Classic and Contemporary Readings*, ed. Stephen E. Fowl (Oxford: Blackwell, 1997), 87–100.

7. See Andrew T. Lincoln, *Born of a Virgin? Reconceiving Jesus in the Bible, Tradition, and Theology* (Grand Rapids: Eerdmans, 2013); see fuller counterarguments in Daniel J. Treier, "Virgin Territory?," *Pro Ecclesia* 23, no. 4 (Fall 2014): 373–79.

8. Lincoln, *Born of a Virgin?*, 39.

humanity—virginal conception actually resisting "docetic" tendencies—modern genetics requires a male Y chromosome for Jesus to be fully human. So, some say, those who would remain orthodox today should jettison the virginal conception—as biblical variety authorizes doing.

It is important to identify assumptions in play. The first claim, about biblical diversity, rests on a tradition-historical approach that is inconsistent with classical Christian teaching about Scripture. The second claim, about theological difficulty, rests on assumptions about full humanity. To focus on this theological challenge, precisely because of differences between ancient anthropologies and modern genetics, no one should assume that a divinely provided Y chromosome precludes the Son *becoming* fully human. After all, "Adam" was fully human without exactly the same origins as his progeny; even nonliteralistic interpretations of Genesis posit a distinctive beginning for the image of God. Moreover, the "anhypostatic" character of the Son's humanity—that it is fully personal only in the Logos who assumed it and not independently—resists tying its fullness to its origination.[9] The Son's personal assumption of humanity is what gives life to *this* individual. For the theological objection to stick, any alternative would need to show how, with a complete human person from the very genetic beginning, one could avoid a sophisticated form of "adoptionism." At minimum there is good reason not to accept the incomplete-humanity objection *prima facie*.

The Son assumes full humanity to identify sinlessly with our helpless condition,[10] but the Word becomes flesh in a creative act. As a sign, the virginal

9. Complexities regarding "anhypostatic" and "enhypostatic" terminology are highlighted in Oliver D. Crisp, *Divinity and Humanity* (Cambridge: Cambridge University Press, 2007), chap. 3. The ambiguity of the latter term leads to its avoidance here.

10. Did the Son assume "fallen" human nature? Surveying that debate are Kelly Kapic, "The Son's Assumption of a Human Nature: A Call for Clarity," *International Journal of Systematic Theology* 3 (2001): 154–66; and discussions by Crisp, whose *God Incarnate: Explorations in Christology* (New York: T&T Clark, 2009), chap. 6, defends the Son's impeccability. Michael Allen proposes that the Son's assumed humanity is "from" (*a quo*; via Mary), but not "of" or "to" (*ad quem*), a fallen nature—being immediately sanctified by the Holy Spirit. See Allen, *The Christ's Faith: A Dogmatic Account* (London: T&T Clark, 2011), and "Christ," in *The T&T Clark Companion to Sin*, ed. Keith Johnson and David Lauber (forthcoming).

Moreover, without nuanced meanings of "fallen" and "human nature" the apparent dilemma may be false. Metaphysically, human nature did not clearly change after our fall into sin. Salvation-historically, human capacities for responding to God did change, leaving no direct ontological access to our pre-curse state. If "fallen" focuses corporately on embracing this human situation—Christ assuming physical weakness and cultural contingency alongside our guilt—the adjective is cause for rejoicing. But if "fallen" focuses singly on negating created nature in his case—implicating him in wayward desire itself—the adjective is unhelpfully confusing at best. The Son identifies with our creation and history, but not so entirely with our plight that he cannot make all things new. He is fully human as we were made to be.

conception bears eloquent witness to this divine act, with the *origin* of Jesus's humanity inevitably remaining distinct from ours; many modern Christologies assume what "full humanity" must mean without providing adequate argument. They leave behind companion truths—the Son's full divinity and personal unity—without which "incarnation" is meaningless. True, virginal conception is not required for the Son's sinlessness; no account of sin's transmission attained creedal consensus. Instead, the virginal conception announces God's fresh visitation of his people, via the Father's initiative and the Spirit's overshadowing (Isa. 59:21; 61:1–3).

With God nothing is impossible (Luke 1:37)—not even a virginal conception that joins together divine initiative, faithful human response, and full identification with broken humanity. As such a sign, the virginal conception indicates the Son's "impeccability," overshadowed by the Holy Spirit. From conception to the completion of his mission, there is *communicatio gratiarum*: divine communication of gracious empowerment by the Spirit to the Son's humanity. Inability to sin did not make the Son less authentically human, for someday our humanity will become sinless like his (1 John 3:1–3). Meanwhile, he suffered our panoply of temptation (Heb. 4:14–16), and his obedience, though inevitable, was genuinely voluntary in the Spirit.[11]

As a sign, the virginal conception indicates still another reality, pervasively neglected in modern scholarship. Whatever the Incarnate One heard directly from Joseph or Mary or John the Baptizer, or discerned indirectly from scandalous rumors, his extraordinary birth profoundly influenced his self-understanding. The nearly pervasive Isaianic background for New Testament Christology makes sense not merely as a late ecclesial invention but as the early heart of Jesus's identity. Hence it is hardly astonishing, mystery notwithstanding, for the God-man to recognize himself as the embodied Servant of YHWH, to expect rejection and atoning death, and to hope for resurrection by which he would renew Israel and reach the gentiles. Once he read his strange beginning in light of Isaiah 7:14, Isaiah 40–66 understandably followed.

"Incarnation" is an event in time, whatever the nature of divine eternity. The Logos cannot simply be *ensarkos*, in flesh, eternally; there must be a "prior" *Logos asarkos*, without flesh, to fit the incarnation's narrative shape—as a temporal happening lovingly willed in the divine decree, not to mention having its earthly climax in the ascension. Humans are creatures with beginnings,

---

11. Perennial theological debates aside, for philosophically keeping mistaken concepts of "libertarian" freedom at bay, see Harry G. Frankfurt, "Freedom of the Will and the Concept of a Person," *Journal of Philosophy* 68 (1971): 5–20. Moral responsibility can pertain even when a person cannot do otherwise.

with bodies that are born. Old Testament theophanies in general, perhaps the angel of the Lord in particular, may involve the person of the Son; they may anticipate the incarnation with human forms. But they are not incarnation. Nor is the Son of God already human in heaven sans Jesus's body or by rebirth as Jesus. The "preexistent" Logos is not *incarnatus* but *incarnandus*—the One who elects, sent by the Father and enabled by the Spirit, to become incarnate in time, whose eternity makes room for sequence in fellowship with us.

This "incarnation" involves extraordinary reality. The incarnation has no exact parallel with any precursor, analogue, or successor. The incarnation is not just a myth, even if understanding its mystery involves metaphor.[12] By its very nature, although mysterious enough to transcend human logic—even to render any full explanation heretical—still the incarnation relates God and earthly history.

2. *The incarnation presupposes* Scripture's widespread identification of Jesus Christ with YHWH, Israel's God. *Eternally alive with the Father "before" his Spirit-empowered ministry in earthly time, as God-man the Son will share the unceasing glory of God being all in all.*

Each Gospel narrates Jesus being uniquely from God yet fully human. Whether the virginal conception begins a particular biography, Jesus follows a path from God prepared by John the Baptizer. The rest of the New Testament likewise frequently names Jesus in light of the divine identity implied by Isaiah's fulfillment. Philippians 2:5–11 provides a crucial example, cohering with the judgments in John 1:1–18.

John 1 has the language of incarnation, whereas Philippians 2 does not. Yet Paul appeals to Isaiah 45:21–24, one of the Old Testament's strongest monotheistic texts, to proclaim Jesus's identity with YHWH/*Kyrios*, Israel's God. Given this appeal, Philippians 2 undergirds patristic orthodoxy, fitting within incarnation's conceptual range even without the root metaphor. Interminably debating whether Paul's words are directly ontological should give way to recognizing common patterns between creedal and canonical judgments. Varying language aside, the creeds provoke questions that scriptural concepts clearly answer.[13]

---

12. See Sarah Coakley's overview of approaches to the creeds' truth, along with her suggestion that they make claims like "riddles," in "What Does Chalcedon Solve and What Does It Not? Some Reflections on the Status and Meaning of the Chalcedonian 'Definition,'" in *The Incarnation: An Interdisciplinary Symposium on the Incarnation of the Son of God*, ed. Stephen T. Davis et al. (Oxford: Oxford University Press, 2002), 143–63.

13. On this passage, see further Daniel J. Treier, "Christology and Commentaries: Examining and Enhancing Theological Exegesis," in *On the Writing of New Testament Commentaries: Festschrift for Grant R. Osborne on the Occasion of his 70th Birthday*, ed. Stanley E. Porter and Eckhard J. Schnabel (Leiden: Brill, 2013), 299–316. Contributing most crucially to upholding

The text does not say that Christ refused to grab hold of divinity, but rather he refused to take advantage or hold on to the glory that was already eternally his. The resulting earthly descent is narrated as revelatory unveiling-and-veiling of his real identity: the Son unveils YHWH more fully by taking human form; paradoxically, though, earthly accessibility veils the fullness of divine glory. Again in the background stands Isaiah, including chapters 52–53, with the Son's obedience upon the cross serving the expectation that the Servant's intervention would reveal Israel's God. The category of divine identity proves helpful. Neither Paul nor later creeds are forced by preset Greek concepts to move from Jesus's messianic functions toward mistakenly granting him ontological "divinity" of some kind. In a context involving worship—for instance, the Philippians "hymn"—identity relates self-understanding and social interaction, naming and narrative, with nature. Sharing the divine name, Jesus properly receives worship; hence he *is* apparently identified with the Creator who one day will reestablish comprehensive sovereignty. Since Christ's work brings to its climax the history of Israel's salvation, this narrative identification with YHWH has ontological implications.

What about the other drama in Philippians 2, the self-emptying (*kenōsis*)? To begin with, Western exegetes consistently project masculinist assumptions about power onto the term: self-emptying reflects condescension necessary for—because opposite of—a God viewed as a lordly male.[14] Given the paraenetic thrust and poetic context, plus ambiguities of the verb and its object "himself," it is ironically easy for some to make too little of ontology elsewhere in the passage and too much here. But the Son cannot divest himself of divine attributes he supposedly never had. If, however, he is divine, then self-divestiture neither reassures us about salvation nor establishes a pattern to follow. Paul does not call Christians to empty their true identity but rather to realize it by giving up self-preference.[15] In due course important questions follow about the Son's divinity vis-à-vis his incarnate state, yet Philippians 2 presents neither a theory nor even a convenient label concerning them. Appeals to *kenōsis* should not be glib, stemming largely from cultural assumptions about full humanity related to patriarchal assumptions about divine perfection.

"early high Christology" elsewhere are Richard Bauckham, Simon Gathercole, Sigurd Grindheim, and Larry Hurtado.

14. Sarah Coakley, "*Kenōsis* and Subversion: On the Repression of 'Vulnerability' in Christian Feminist Writing," in *Powers and Submissions: Spirituality, Philosophy and Gender* (Oxford: Blackwell, 2002), 3–39.

15. On healthy self-sacrifice, see Ruth Groenhout, "Kenosis and Feminist Theory," in *Exploring Kenotic Christology: The Self-Emptying of God*, ed. C. Stephen Evans (Oxford: Oxford University Press, 2006), 291–312.

Meanwhile, today "incarnational" paradigms for literature, church ministry, and the like laud the redemptive virtue of self-giving (often, "kenotic") embodiment. Philippians 2 indeed calls for imitation of Christ; however, incarnational paradigms pay inadequate attention to cultural dynamics of appealing to "self-giving" or "embodiment" as general principles or using "redemptive" language for human activity. It is dangerously easy to downplay the incarnation's uniqueness. Neglecting power dynamics while putting ourselves in Christ's place, we as Christians lapse into unhealthy condescension.

Philippians 2 presents paradigmatically early high Christology in which Jesus is identified with Israel's God. His exaltation indicates "preexistence" as the divine Son. Strictly speaking, that term is inadequate for an eternal identity transcending time and never ending. Still, in human perspective, to speak of his divine life "before" the incarnation gestures at the crucial claim. His exaltation has a new element too, for the Son returns to glory as the God-man, having completed his self-giving mission while remaining human. Now Christian God-language operates in two registers, depending on the relational context: "God" is the proper name for the Father of whom Jesus is the Son in his humanity, and "God" also properly names Father and Son with the Holy Spirit who binds them together in the love they lavish on us.

If such Pauline texts complement Johannine incarnational theology, what about the rest of the New Testament? Although some epistles do not make clear ontological identifications, both the divine revelation and human solidarity of the Son appear when they oppose false teachers. Plus older dogmatic appeals to names or "titles" of Christ are not without merit, since patterns emerge in light of the Old Testament background.[16] "Son of Man" indicates an apocalyptic dimension more than mere humanity while identifying Jesus with his people. "Messiah" indicates transcendent fulfillment of any previous figure(s) in this Anointed One while identifying Jesus with particular offices through which God led his people. Moving beyond mere respect, "Lord" indicates supplanting Caesar's pretense of ultimate authority while identifying Jesus with the authority of Israel's God, YHWH/*Kyrios*. Not straightforwardly connoting full divinity, "Son of God" indicates trajectories, such as sharing the work of one's father, that prepare for identifying the Son more directly with "God." (Romans 9:5 is a notoriously disputed but credible example.)

Two final claims conclude this gesture at the high biblical Christology. First, even in the Synoptic Gospels Jesus frequently does what YHWH uniquely identifies himself having done or promised. These "passion narratives with

---

16. For contemporary surveys of such biblical-theological subjects, see Joel B. Green, ed., *Dictionary of Jesus and the Gospels*, 2nd ed. (Downers Grove, IL: IVP Academic, 2013).

extended introductions" not only announce God's kingdom coming into our midst in Jesus; their endings also depict what he does and undergoes so uniquely as to identify God profoundly with him and him with God.[17] Second, Hebrews paradoxically contains some of the most seemingly adoptionist, along with the most straightforwardly preexistent, christological moments: the High Priest, who fully identifies with fellow humans as their once-for-all sacrifice, must be the eternal divine Son to offer himself in the heavenly temple. The climactic identifier, holding together these names Son and High Priest, is "mediator of a new covenant" (12:24)—a vocation holding together divine and human, eternity and time, Israel and church, in ways that entail what became the traditional dogma of the incarnation.[18]

3. *The incarnation entails the truth of catholic, creedal dogma. Jesus Christ is the self-existent, fully divine Son who has taken full human life into personal union with the Triune God.*

Ecumenical dogma gradually discerned and reaffirmed this biblical teaching. Within God's providence, heresies arose even among those who appealed to the full scope of Scripture. These heresies became provocations for the church to specify christological boundaries guiding worship and gospel proclamation.

Heresies and Creedal Definition

The Ebionites, apparently a sect with Judaizing tendencies, provoked early recognition that "Messiah" does not exhaust Jesus's identity: he is more than merely a special human. Various gnostic heretics, with their special knowledge claims docetically treating Jesus as apparently but not actually human, provoked exclusion of the other extreme: Jesus is not just a divine "Christ" either; he became an embodied human. Otherwise the cross was strangely patripassian, too bluntly inserted into the divine life—if even redeeming at all—seemingly crucifying God himself without remainder. Such a God is too monarchian—only one kingly Father—and/or modalistic, with Son and Spirit merely being ways of appearing to us.

The next phase of heretical provocation centered on the Arian controversy leading to and from Nicaea in AD 325, with the church learning to insist on the full divinity of the incarnate Son. The church could not settle for special

17. Hans W. Frei, *The Identity of Jesus Christ: The Hermeneutical Bases of Dogmatic Theology* (Eugene, OR: Wipf & Stock, 2000).

18. Knowing *God*—personally—is integral to the superiority of the New Covenant, which has dogmatic implications for Christ's identity as mediator, not just an intermediary.

humanity, or even partial divinity or divine likeness—for merely *homoiousios*, strong similarity to the Father. That Arian settlement seems sensible, hence its periodic revivals ever since. Protecting divine transcendence that way, the church could easily treat the Son as "firstborn over all creation" (Col. 1:15 NIV), that is, his creation inaugurating time as we know it. Two theological concerns, however, eventually enabled the church to resist that temptation, affirming instead that the Son is *homoousios* ("of one being") with the Father (and likewise with the Spirit, as clarified later).

The first concern is worship: *lex orandi lex credendi* ("the law of prayer is the law of faith"). Honoring Jesus Christ as Son of God without acknowledging him to be fully divine would commit idolatry; a third kind of being, quasi-divine, would intrude on the distinction between Creator and creature.[19] What needed protection was not divine transcendence in a Greek sense; according to that Arian tendency, the Creator must keep his hands from getting dirty with the world through a mediating, less divine, Son. To the contrary, what needs protecting is the divine transcendence associated with biblical worship; only the Creator God may be honored as such. Worship demonstrated the church's belief that the Son is not merely a quasi-divine intermediary but the mediator who embodies fully divine initiative.

The second concern is salvation. If the Son were only a quasi-divine intermediary, then how could humans confidently face the God "to whom we must give account" (Heb. 4:13)? Various paradigms notwithstanding, salvation means encountering God personally in reconciling love. If in Jesus Christ humans do not encounter God directly, then they cannot confidently embrace this love. Furthermore, worrying that God hides behind an emissary, humans treat salvation as reaching toward God via this quasi-divine intermediary instead of receiving divine grace.

Soon the Apollinarian heresy reached the flip side of Arianism while sharing some anthropological assumptions. Nicaea recognized, and in AD 381 Constantinople reaffirmed, that we must not merely associate Jesus Christ with divinity but acknowledge him to be fully divine. Rejecting Apollinarianism, Constantinople further recognized that we must not merely associate Jesus Christ with human embodiment but acknowledge him to be fully human. Apollinarianism expressed latent implications from the widespread Alexandrian anthropology: if the Logos filled the usual place of the *psychē* as active life-principle, then it was natural to deny the full humanity of the Incarnate

19. Interpretations of biblical "monotheism" remain contested. Nonetheless, Christian dogmatics can appeal to evidence from Richard Bauckham and others for outlining a Creator-creature distinction.

One's mind or spirit.[20] After all, the Logos took flesh precisely because of human fallenness, so why not conclude that psychic substitution was for the best, preventing corruption of the Incarnate One? Eventually, however, the church recognized this subtler provocation for what it was: another threat to the integrity of salvation. If some aspect of human life is irredeemable in principle, then we remain dead in sin. The relevant rallying cry had been uttered earlier, but now its full implications became recognizable: "What is not assumed is not healed."

By this point heretical pendulum swings were no longer as wide. From denying either meaningful divinity or humanity of the Son at all, to denying either his full divinity or humanity, the church came to affirm both "natures." Yet struggle ensued, and has ever since, over how they relate. One more round of heretical provocation and creedal definition became ecumenically basic. Nestorius denied the term *Theotokos*, "God-bearer," to Mary, preferring *Christotokos*. Nestorianism became the latest, but not necessarily subtlest, form of "adoptionism" wherein a special human is taken up into God's redemptive history. For Nestorianism the union between the two natures was moral or relational but not essential. Yet, without speaking of Mary as *Theotokos*, the church speaks too separately of the Son's humanity and divinity—threatening the integrity of the person they characterize. As Cyril of Alexandria recognized, in that case Christ's divinity becomes logically subsequent to his humanity.

Provoked by Nestorianism, Eutyches overreacted by saying that the Son's nature was both divine and human—a *tertium quid*, a hybrid mixing the two. Eutychianism was another, again not necessarily the subtlest, form of monophysitism according to which every person, including the Son, must have only one nature. Monophysitism so carefully protects the union of the person, and the divine identity and initiative of the Son, as to lose the integrity of his humanity.

Influenced by Cyril and the christological *Tome* of Pope Leo I, the Chalcedonian Definition of 451 rejected both Nestorian and Eutychian accounts. They threaten not just the personal unity and distinct natures but even Christ's divinity (in an adoptionist direction) or humanity (in a monophysite direction). The church insists therefore on the "hypostatic union" of fully divine and fully human natures in one person (*hypostasis*). This insistence is largely stated negatively:

20. On this history see Aloys Grillmeier, SJ, *Christ in Christian Tradition*, vol. 1, *From the Apostolic Age to Chalcedon (451)*, trans. John Bowden, 2nd rev. ed. (Atlanta: John Knox, 1975); and the sketch of "pro-Nicene" Christology (despite overzealous strictures on systematic theology) in Lewis Ayres, *Nicaea and Its Legacy: An Approach to Fourth-Century Trinitarian Theology* (Oxford: Oxford University Press, 2004).

one and only Christ—Son, Lord, only-begotten—in two natures [*duo physesin*]; [and we do this] without confusing the two natures [*asunkutōs*], without transmuting one nature into the other [*atreptōs*], without dividing them into two separate categories [*adiairetōs*], without contrasting them according to area or function [*achōristos*]. The distinctiveness of each nature is not nullified by the union.[21]

Such boundary statements actually free the church to worship and to explore faithful possibilities for further witness. Their minimalism offers no comprehensive theory since mystery is fitting, given the nature of their claim: *God with us.*

Complexities and Confessions

Still, complexities ensued from this ecumenically orthodox settlement. Nestorian and monophysite groups broke away, their tendencies periodically reappearing within orthodox circles. The church struggled over Chalcedon's implications for Christ's agency, concluding at the Third Council of Constantinople in AD 681 that monothelitism was heretical: Christ must possess two wills, his choices counting as both divine and human. The church further struggled over Chalcedon's implications for icons, concluding at the Second Council of Nicaea in AD 787 that iconoclasm was heretical. On this mainstream account, the incarnation authorizes representing the divine Son via human forms; accordingly, "veneration" of icons directs "worship" to God.

However, early Protestant Christianity and much subsequent Reformed theology have been uncomfortable with that conclusion. The Decalogue's prohibition remains: "You shall not make for yourself an image. . . . You shall not bow down to them or worship them" (Exod. 20:4–5 NIV). Without ongoing access to the visible form of the Incarnate One, icons risk supplanting worship of the Creator with unauthorized—culturally self-aggrandizing—creaturely representation. Although Protestants must respectfully discern the import of the Second Council of Nicaea vis-à-vis Chalcedon, church councils remain subordinate to the Scriptures they sought to understand. Admittedly, if the Reformed tradition has a besetting sin, it lies on the Nestorian side: aggressively celebrating the fullness of the Son's humanity, insisting that the finite is incapable of containing the infinite (*finitum non capax infiniti*). Even so, these cautions do not negate the Reformed witness concerning the distinctiveness of the incarnation: might the Second Council of Nicaea have been

21. John H. Leith, ed., *Creeds of the Churches*, 3rd ed. (Louisville: John Knox, 1982), 36.

overzealous in rejecting iconoclasm out of hand? Whatever the contingencies of the original controversy, might ecumenical space now be appropriate for those who bear witness to an alternative understanding of the incarnation's revelatory implications?

After all, Reformed confessions firmly uphold the verities of Chalcedonian Christology, with particular emphasis on the Son being our mediator. Reformed theology expounds these verities with scriptural freedom. In particular, John Calvin's trinitarian theology—distinct from both classical precursors and scholastic successors—maintains that the Son is *autotheos*, God in and of himself. Classical trinitarians predicated such aseity of the Son insofar as self-existence pertains to the shared divine essence.[22] Classical trinitarians also insisted that communication of the shared essence from Father to Son in "eternal generation" undergirds their essential unity and relational distinction. Unlike some later Calvinist and evangelical rejections of eternal generation as unbiblical and dangerously subordinationist, Calvin retained the doctrine. However, Calvin jettisoned essential communication—developing, neither simply repristinating nor rejecting, the tradition.

It is fundamentally misguided to move from isolated exegetical discoveries, such as *monogenēs* in texts like John 1:18 not necessarily denoting "begotten," toward denying eternal generation. Various biblical texts still lend themselves to this doctrine, which the denials misunderstand.[23] Of course eternal generation is metaphorical; it does not literally refer to human, physical begetting. Without this ubiquitous metaphor, though, God's proper naming gives way to radical alteration, since "Father" and "Son" become arbitrary conventions. Instead, most minimally, eternal generation specifies processions or relations of origin that define the distinct personhood of Father and Son. The persons are the same in essence but not absolutely the same, having distinct relations appropriate to the economy of divine acts.[24] The proper names do not make God sexual, or even masculine in terms of socially constructed gender. Nor do they preclude feminine imagery for divine activity, which the Old Testament associates with God (e.g., Isa. 42:14; 49:15; 66:13) and the New Testament associates with the Son in his male flesh (Matt. 23:37). What these proper names, and the metaphorical reality to which they point, reveal is a personal

22. This is true at least adjectivally, though maybe not adverbially, according to Brannon Ellis, *Calvin, Classical Trinitarianism, and the Aseity of the Son* (Oxford: Oxford University Press, 2012), 34, which informs the surrounding discussion.

23. On Prov. 8:22–36, a key text influencing early Christians, see Daniel J. Treier, *Proverbs and Ecclesiastes* (Grand Rapids: Brazos, 2011), 44–57.

24. In *Calvin, Classical Trinitarianism*, Ellis calls for "*abiding and intrinsic* relative predication" (56, emphasis original).

God, with one person particularly prepared to embrace human embodiment in all its messy history.

Essential communication may go too far in explaining ineffable trinitarian relations, so mainstream Reformed assimilation of Calvin's *autotheos* to this classical doctrine may be unnecessary. Yet the venerable tradition merits respect, not least for respecting God's proper naming. For the ecumenical moment, the Son's being *autotheos* may be "understood quite strictly in terms of *external essential independence*":[25] the Son is Creator, not just creature, with the Father's blessing sharing the divine liveliness before coming to share our humanity.

4. *The incarnation implies* that earthly history has a redemptive consummation with Jesus Christ at its center. *In humbling himself to assume full humanity, the Son of God fulfills three primary offices while remaining the ever-present Lord of the cosmos.*

The Reformed confessions and their ecclesial tradition go beyond providing for Chalcedonian catechesis and discipline. They uniquely emphasize biblical revelation's unfolding redemptive drama. At best, their emphasis on the incarnate Lord's full humanity resists both earlier and later dualisms,[26] partly due to a distinctive account of the *communicatio idiomatum*, the communication of the properties of the Son's divine and human natures. As article 8 of the Westminster Confession states, "Christ, in the work of mediation, acts according to both natures, by each nature doing that which is proper to itself; yet, by reason of the unity of the person, that which is proper to one nature is sometimes in Scripture attributed to the person denominated by the other nature."[27] Contra the Lutheran account, the Reformed version of the *communicatio* transpires only in and at the level of the one person, not between the natures directly, preserving the ontological integrity of Creator and creature. While divinity and humanity must not be construed simply in

25. Ellis, *Calvin, Classical Trinitarianism*, 159, describing mainstream Reformed allowance for essential communication (which he rejects).

26. Debatable specifics aside, resisting dualism is an insightful theme of Colin E. Gunton, *Yesterday and Today: A Study of Continuities in Christology* (London: Darton, Longman, & Todd, 1983). Gunton recognizes that "whereas the ancient world was tempted to *eternalize* the human Jesus" (perhaps due to overly metaphysical accounts of divinity), "we are tempted to eternalize the *human* Jesus" (ibid., 206) (having overly psychological preoccupations). Scott R. Swain, *The God of the Gospel: Robert Jenson's Trinitarian Theology* (Downers Grove, IL: IVP Academic, 2013), 185, cautions against treating divinity and humanity as metaphysically polar. Minimally the *imago Dei* resists such polarity, although modern versions of the natures' intrinsic mutuality need resistance too.

27. Quoted in Joel R. Beeke and Sinclair R. Ferguson, *Reformed Confessions Harmonized* (Grand Rapids: Baker, 1999), 66–67, with the confessions' Chalcedonian consistency appearing throughout the documents on 62–85.

terms of contrast, the incarnation does not confirm a general truth about the finite being either capable or incapable of the infinite. Instead, its indication is simply that the infinite is capable of the finite.[28]

The Reformed *communicatio*, perhaps counterintuitively, fosters chaste engagement with metaphysical language. Respecting divine providence, Reformed orthodoxy uses classical terminology, refusing to assume that Greek philosophy is inherently corrupt. If the incarnation occurred at the fullness of time (Gal. 4:4), then such language has its uses. Respecting revelation's cultural limits and any language's need for redemptive transformation, though, Reformed theology refuses a priori notions of divinity and humanity apart from Scripture. By focusing the *communicatio* on the person, the Reformed version could avoid metaphysical dichotomies about the natures' properties. Thus being attentive to the person's history and identity in light of Scripture brings into relief three distinctive concepts concerning the Incarnate One's earthly ministry prior to its atoning climax and heavenly aftermath.

Three Offices

First, Christ's *munus triplex*, or "threefold office," became particularly, though not exclusively, important to the Reformed tradition. Its grounds lie in the "anointing" associated with each office, which Jesus the Messiah fulfills in addressing sinners' needs.

As prophet, Christ is the revelatory mediator representing God to humanity and addressing our ignorance. The church receives a prophetic ministry by extension (Joel 2:28; Acts 2:17–21), so overemphasizing this office leads toward moralism and/or rationalism.[29] As priest, Jesus is the redemptive mediator representing humanity before God by offering himself as a once-for-all sacrifice and addressing our enmity. Baptism anoints believers into royal priesthood, and the church mysteriously participates (nonredemptively) in Christ's suffering (Col. 1:24), so overemphasizing this office leads toward pietism and/or mysticism. As king, Christ mediates divine rule as both God and man, addressing our bondage.[30] The mediator brings divine rule to bear

28. So Christoph Schwöbel, "Christ for Us—Yesterday and Today: A Response to 'The Person of Christ,'" in *The Person of Christ*, ed. Stephen R. Holmes and Murray A. Rae (New York: T&T Clark, 2005), 182–201, at 194, 197.

29. So Geoffrey Wainwright, *For Our Salvation: Two Approaches to the Work of Christ* (Grand Rapids: Eerdmans, 1997), 174–75, suggests from W. A. Visser't Hooft, *The Kingship of Christ* (New York: Harper, 1948), 17.

30. Royal priesthood tempts us to marginalize the prophetic office. Yet, although prophets confronted the other two from outside, as it were, overlap also appears—e.g., in David, who is juxtaposed with Saul's arrogation of priesthood, or Moses, who anticipates kingly rule as

on the entire cosmos, his humanity initiating our priestly participation (e.g., Ps. 89:35–37; Eph. 1:22–23; Phil. 2:9–11). Overemphasizing this office leads the church toward utopianism and/or apocalypticism. Indeed, far from being triumphalist, the Son's subsequent revelation of his glory in exercising these offices involved prior earthly suffering: no crown without the cross.

Two States

A second Reformed characterization of the Incarnate One's earthly ministry involves two states: humiliation and exaltation. On the one hand, Christ exercises all his offices in both; he is not simply prophet and priest prior to the resurrection and king afterward. God's kingdom is in our midst from the incarnation onward, and Jesus's prophetic preparation of his disciples intensifies between his resurrection and ascension. His priestly self-offering incorporates his exalted return to the Father and ongoing intercession for us. On the other hand, while the states may not merely be sequential, this doctrine includes narrative movement. A descent-ascent pattern commences in the very incarnation itself, culminating in the resurrection and its aftermath (besides Phil. 2:5–11; see Eph. 4:8–10). Humility pervades the Son's earthly life—having no place to lay his head—in solidarity with cursed humanity and culminates in sacrificial obedience on the cross. Exaltation vindicates this humble completion of the earthly mission as his unique glory. The Son remains incarnate now in his heavenly session, yet his glory is no longer hidden while now being humanly shared.

The two states' narrative sequence requires dialectical juxtaposition along with their paradoxical, nonsequential overlap. Speaking of the humiliation of the Son of God emphasizes that "the Son of God is Jesus of Nazareth"; speaking of the exaltation of the Son of Man emphasizes that "Jesus of Nazareth is the Son of God."[31] Whether in specific cases of Johannine irony or in broader connections between Synoptic and Johannine patterns, the Bible does contain examples of nonsequential, unexpected humiliation and exaltation.[32] Yet, ironically enough, these patterns still tell a story—not of

---

the paradigmatic prophet while remaining distinct from Aaron's priesthood. Near Eastern associations of priesthood and kingship are secondary in importance to biblical reticence about unifying any of these offices—only to unify them all definitively in Jesus Christ, partially or proleptically in figures that typify him.

31. George Hunsinger, "Karl Barth's Christology: Its Basic Chalcedonian Character," in *Disruptive Grace: Studies in the Theology of Karl Barth* (Grand Rapids: Eerdmans, 2000), 131–47, at 143.

32. Karl Barth, in his daring *Church Dogmatics* IV, advocates a nonsequential account of the *status duplex*. Barth also famously champions the history of Jesus Christ. Yet such "actualism"

metaphysical subtraction but of the divine Son assuming human sonship and recapitulating its covenant history.

The Extra Calvinisticum

Similarly, a third paradigm explicates what was implicitly widespread within classical orthodoxy. This third paradigm, the so-called *extra Calvinisticum*, concerns the manner in which Jesus Christ conducts his earthly ministry without giving up divine lordship "outside" the limitations of his flesh:

> For even if the Word in his immeasurable essence united with the nature of man into one person, we do not imagine that he was confined therein. Here is something marvelous: the Son of God descended from heaven in such a way that, without leaving heaven, he willed to be borne in the virgin's womb, to go about the earth, and to hang upon the cross; yet he continuously filled the world even as he had done from the beginning![33]

The *extra* has fallen on hard modern times, supposedly threatening the integrity of Jesus's humanity in favor of abstract notions regarding divinity. Orthodox commitment to the *extra*, however, properly stems not from metaphysics but from creedal resistance to jeopardizing the Son's mediation.[34] As in earlier resistance to Arianism and Nestorianism, so here the church must insist that in the Incarnate One humanity encounters God himself—not least on earth—or else a hidden God looms. The *extra* seems counterintuitive, since opponents fear a hidden God; fearing a metaphysical *Logos asarkos*, they reject the Incarnate One's cosmic lordship. Ironically, though, overindulging these fears separates the cosmic creator and ruler from the enfleshed one, threatening to deny that he is God incarnate. Far from hiding God or risking Nestorianism, the *extra* undergirds the incarnational dialectic of unveiling and veiling. When the Son remains present throughout the universe beyond the human body of Jesus on earth, he is not sneaking around on another

---

actually requires maintaining sequential aspects of the two states; otherwise the "movement" Barth prefers (to the "calm" of the classic doctrine; see Barth, *Church Dogmatics* IV/2, trans. G. W. Bromiley [Edinburgh: T&T Clark, 1958], 105–10) gets lost. Without sequence dialectically included, Barth's treatment of the entire history of Jesus Christ as one "act" can supplant the internal dynamism of the narrative with paradoxical abstraction about obedient divinity and exalted humanity.

33. John Calvin, *Institutes of the Christian Religion*, ed. John T. McNeill, trans. Ford Lewis Battles (Philadelphia: Westminster, 1960), 2.13.4.

34. Bruce McCormack routinely cautions against "metaphysical" speculation in abstraction from the history of Jesus Christ; however, ontological language of divine perfections, revealed within that history's surrounding biblical framework, does not violate legitimate cautions.

project; in the unity of his Spirit with the Father, he continues to participate in divine sustenance of creation and restoration of its proper rule. The Son's bringing this rule into our earthly midst reveals the divine benevolence of the redemption at hand.

5. *The incarnation initiates* the ultimate redemption of God's covenant people. *Though not atoning in itself, the incarnation inaugurates, embodies, enables, and thereby participates in God's reconciling action.*

Since atonement is a distinct dogmatic locus, this chapter must be restricted to four brief comments specifically about its complexities vis-à-vis the incarnation. The first complexity concerns the Son's "person" and "work." Does this traditional distinction too easily separate what God joined together? After all, the church discerned the identity of Jesus Christ partly from his saving mission—both its truly divine initiative and its full identification with humanity. Epistemologically speaking, it is impossible to understand the incarnation apart from atonement.

The second complexity concerns necessity. Would the incarnation have occurred without the fall, or is it inherently redemptive? Reformed theologians have often been leery of the tradition's minority report that insists on incarnation regardless of the fall, making it ontologically possible to understand apart from atonement. The question is speculative, risking movement behind God's revelatory history of redemption. Still, the question of how the incarnation relates to divine self-revelation remains. If revelation is meaningfully personal, then (how) would humans have come to know the Triune God otherwise? (How) does divine fellowship with humans from the very beginning anticipate the ultimate happening of "God with us"? At minimum, dogmatics must reflect on the significance of divine self-disclosure unfolding through a redemptive-historical incarnation; at maximum we may wonder if incarnation is simply ingredient to *this* God's self-revelation.

The third complexity concerns meaning. Does "atonement" refer to ransom or victory, payment of a debt, provision of an example or transforming influence, satisfaction of a penalty, restoration of proper moral order, and/or something else? Reformed orthodoxy associates atonement with expiation or propitiation; according to such narrower treatment of biblical concepts focused on the cross, the incarnation itself is not atoning. If, however, atonement more broadly involves all God does in restoring sinful humans to covenant fellowship, then alongside the Son's active and passive obedience, the incarnation may join his kingdom proclamation, resurrection, ascension, and outpouring of the Holy Spirit in a more comprehensive picture of reconciliation.

A fourth complexity concerns the subject(s). Who is being reconciled to whom? If atonement concerns only reconciling us, overcoming enmity toward

God, then the incarnation may share the label "atoning." If atonement also (hence ultimately) concerns reconciling God to us—at God's loving initiative overcoming our expectation of divine judgment—then the incarnation cannot be crucially atoning; what "must needs be" (e.g., Acts 2:23) will be the crux, even if the cross integrally relates to the rest of Jesus's earthly history. Thus Reformed dogmatics traditionally distinguishes incarnation from atonement, restricting the latter to accomplishing and perhaps applying salvation.

By contrast, some contemporary Reformed circles, with ecumenical respect for patristic emphases, treat the incarnation as atoning to acknowledge ontological dimensions of salvation.[35] Salvation becomes participation in the divine nature via union with Christ. If reconciliation deals with not just the sins and status of individual persons but the state of humanity as a whole, then the divine Son's solidarity with us in the incarnation initiates reconciliation. There is healthy provocation here to integrate all aspects of Christ's identity and story, avoiding overly "contractual" connotations into which popular atonement theology often falls. In such flawed connotations, the Son's suffering for our sake creates a breach within the Triune God: the Father's loving initiative and the Son's divine embrace of this mission drop out, overshadowed by divine wrath poured on the human Jesus.

Nevertheless, a properly trinitarian account of propitiation—satisfaction of divine wrath expressing God's holy love—avoids contractualism while honoring biblical truth about covenant relationship. The Bible hardly treats the incarnation itself as atoning. When God the Son comes to be with us (Matt. 1:23), his name, Jesus, indicates that he *will* save his people from their sins (Matt. 1:21). This salvation focally required the cross, even if its benefits appeared earlier—even in the Old Testament—by anticipation. The cross enacts the eternally loving will of the Triune God. The Father and Son, together in the Spirit, lovingly choose for the Son to face the estrangement from God that humans deserved. Accordingly, the Son became human

35. See, e.g., the "evangelical Calvinism" associated with T. F. Torrance (see Myk Habets and Bobby Grow, eds., *Evangelical Calvinism: Essays Resourcing the Continuing Reformation of the Church* [Eugene, OR: Pickwick, 2012]); the "sacramental" emphasis of Hans Boersma, *Heavenly Participation: The Weaving of a Sacramental Tapestry* (Grand Rapids: Eerdmans, 2011); or Kathryn Tanner, *Christ the Key* (Cambridge: Cambridge University Press, 2010). Indeed, union with Christ is vital to Calvin, as evident in J. Todd Billings, *Calvin, Participation, and the Gift: The Activity of Believers in Union with Christ* (New York: Oxford University Press, 2007); and Julie Canlis, *Calvin's Ladder: A Spiritual Theology of Ascent and Ascension* (Grand Rapids: Eerdmans, 2010)—although their perspectives differ from the other thinkers noted here. For still another Reformed christological framework attentive to such interests but covenantally rather than ontologically oriented, see Michael S. Horton, *Lord and Servant: A Covenant Christology* (Louisville: Westminster John Knox, 2005).

while undergoing this estrangement as the mediator for many with justice
and benevolence that could only be divine. Ultimately, then, the incarnation
participates in God's reconciling action, yet it is unnecessarily misleading to
call the incarnation itself atoning.

6. *The incarnation endures* forever as the Son retains full (now glorified)
humanity. *When he returned to divine glory after descending into hell, he ascended as the God-man in whom the church begins to enjoy divine fellowship
on earth—in prayerful dependence on his intercession, obedient listening to
his speech, and eucharistic celebration of his presence—anticipating complete
restoration of divine rule over creation.*

At the climax of its earthly phase, the incarnation leads to the cross. Resurrection and ascension follow, indicating the incarnation's continuation.
Meanwhile, the Apostles' Creed narrates an additional phase of the Son's
earthly career: descent into hell. Some Calvinist and evangelical thinkers reject the phrase, pointing to exegetical complexities, not least over when the
referent is "Hades" as the realm of the dead versus "hell" anticipating final
judgment. Actually a crucial passage, 1 Peter 3:18–22, instead concerns Christ's
proclamation of victory over all hostile spirits—proclamation made in the
spiritual realm as Jesus ascended after his resurrection.[36] A proper response to
such exegetical complexities, however, affirms the creedal phrase while notic-
ing its location: at the extreme point emphasizing Christ's humiliation unto
death, leading into resurrection and exaltation. The descent, per the Protestant
Reformers, underscores the Son's full identification with sinful humanity's
plight—even mysteriously undergoing our alienation from God.[37] Descent
into hell completes the descent begun in the manger. Its dogmatic function
is captured by Romans 8:38–39: "Neither death nor life, neither angels nor
demons, neither the present nor the future, nor any powers, neither height
nor depth, nor anything else in all creation, will be able to separate us from
the love of God that is in Christ Jesus our Lord" (NIV).

In the ascension Jesus visibly—even liturgically—marks the end of this
earthly descent and announces his future return. On his resurrection—a theological chapter all its own, were not our focus necessarily limited—he completes the ascending trajectory of his divinely vindicated mission. The Triune
God is so committed to the incarnation that by the Spirit the Father restores

36. The classic study remains W. J. Dalton, *Christ's Proclamation to the Spirits: A Study of
1 Peter 3:18–4:6*, 2nd rev. ed. (Roma: Editrice Pontifico Istituto Biblico, 1989).

37. As Jacques Ellul suggests provocatively, "It is unthinkable. . . . How can Jesus, the Son of
the Father, be abandoned and no longer call him 'Father' and instead address him as 'God,' like
any man abandoned by God?" (*If You Are the Son of God: The Sufferings and Temptations of
Jesus*, trans. Anne-Marie Andreasson-Hogg [Eugene, OR: Cascade, 2014], 50).

the Son to embodied human life, albeit with transformation as the firstfruits of the new creation. Since this Son returns to prior glory, the new element of exaltation is his identity as the God-man. For *Jesus* to share in the name above every name exalts a human life to inaugurate our promised participation in God's reign. Now the Son of Man anticipated in Daniel 7 receives authority in God the Father's presence, inaugurating everlasting dominion in which the church will participate.[38]

The ascension initiates Christ's heavenly session. He rules over his regathered form of Israel called "church," thereby advancing his earthly rule. This royal priesthood experiences his presence and absence dialectically. Because the Son remains incarnate, he is physically absent from earth; indeed, the church does not know where "heaven" is. When the church fails to acknowledge Jesus's absence adequately, it becomes unduly triumphant about the earthly mediation of Christ's presence. Yet it enjoys a new form of divine presence poured out in the Holy Spirit. This new form is less tangible—apart from the sacraments—but more universally immediate and intimate. The Spirit can make the risen Christ present to anyone whereas if the Son remained on earth, that form of presence would be locally limited.

The ascension indicates—even enacts—divine vindication of the Son's reconciling mission. A new phase unfolds. He makes a heavenly presentation of his once-for-all sacrifice, entering into a ministry of intercession on behalf of his people. They draw near with boldness, confident of God's welcome in Jesus's name. When the church fails to acknowledge adequately Jesus's presence with God the Father, it fears the Son as too divine to be of earthly saving good. Accordingly it threatens to displace the one mediator between God and humanity (1 Tim. 2:5) with additional intermediaries—Mary, the saints, and the like. But if in Christ faithful covenant partnership is always already present before God, Christians can participate in that heavenly worship in anticipation of the fullness of future glory. On his second advent, when all things will finally be under his feet (Heb. 2:8) so that God will be all in all (1 Cor. 15:26–28), then the church shall enjoy divine communion face-to-face (1 Cor. 13:12)—for God will show his face as well as the marks of his wounds for us in Jesus.

7. *The incarnation elicits* churchly faith seeking understanding. *In testimony, catechesis, nurture, discipline, debate, apologetics, and contemplation, with creative fidelity the Reformed tradition exhibits perennial tendencies and correspondingly faces particular theological challenges.*

38. Influential here is Douglas Farrow, *Ascension and Ecclesia: On the Significance of the Doctrine of the Ascension for Ecclesiology and Christian Cosmology* (Grand Rapids: Eerdmans, 1999).

Until Christ returns, Reformed faith seeks catholic understanding of the incarnation's singular reality and rationality. Certain preoccupations result: particularly, to repeat, the redemptive history presented in biblical revelation; accordingly, the full, ongoing humanity of Christ; simultaneously, the full equality of the Incarnate Son with the Father and the Spirit. These preoccupations evoke periodic tension; their compatibility is not naturally obvious. Further tension arises between allergies to "speculation" beyond clear biblical revelation and "scholastic" reflection on its traditional entailments.[39] Reformed catholicity seeks the right blend of covenantal apophaticism: apophatic respect for the limits of biblical revelation and human finitude before an infinitely perfect God, yet with covenantal knowledge of God evoking such respect and its acknowledgment of the ecumenical creeds.

Covenantal apophaticism can actually be a source of theological creativity. The church is "always reforming," yet always "according to the Word of God," which is the same yesterday, today, and forever. While humans cannot know God's essence, the church can really know God in his self-revelation. The incarnation is therefore not just something known but the basis for knowing. Mere humans cannot share in God's "archetypal" self-knowledge, but Christ does as the God-man. The mediator reveals an "ectypal" form of theological knowledge in the divine economy and its scriptural witness.

Today's myriad Reformed christological debates arise from these distinctive concerns and resulting tensions. To illustrate this claim, one final debate merits further attention: whether to underscore the Incarnate Son's full humanity by means of a "kenotic" theory—whether suitably modified from Lutheran origins or philosophical—such as "two-minds" theory or simply rest in apparent "paradox." The *extra Calvinisticum* clearly precludes any ontological kenotic theory, and Philippians 2 does not teach one. Even strongly Spirit-oriented Christologies—when orthodox—happily affirm that the Son performed works of extraordinary power distinguishing him from other humans.[40] So debates over omnipresence and omnipotence move largely to the side. The remaining crux concerns omniscience—the Son's knowledge, particularly his self-consciousness as the God-man, both initially during his earthly sojourn and climactically in his passion. Modernity, congratulating

39. Swain, *God of the Gospel*, 168, differentiates between empty speculation and ontological submission to Scripture regarding the Son.

40. Some Spirit Christologies are pitted against Logos Christologies, seemingly emphasizing the Spirit's empowerment of the human Jesus to an extent that creates tension with Chalcedon. However, such emphasis can be helpfully biblical and orthodox, not to mention authentically Reformed—as in John Owen, profiled by Tyler Wittman, "The End of the Incarnation: John Owen, Trinitarian Agency and Christology," *International Journal of Systematic Theology* 15 (2013): 284–300.

itself for newfound preoccupation with the historical human subject, poses this challenge stridently.

In response, the philosophical two-minds theory solves little while risking much. Its apparent virtue lies in consistency with two wills.[41] However, despite the tradition's eventual embrace of dyothelitism, it remains possible to appreciate the subsequent lack of further metaphysical specification. Does the Son's incarnate thinking, like his choosing, count as both divine and human? Surely yes. Is there sufficient definition of "mind" or anthropological faculties in general to authorize the next step of specifying two minds? Likely not. Indeed, once two-minds theory purports to explain aspects of the Incarnate Son's self-consciousness, it quickly associates him with apparently unhealthy ("bipolar") ways of life.

But is the alternative classical preference for paradox adequate when it suggests that the Son can be both omniscient by virtue of divinity and ignorant by virtue of humanity—with Scripture passages interpreted in terms of one or the other nature's activity being predicated of the one personal Subject? When the Heidelberg Catechism addresses the parallel question of omnipresence— "But if His human nature is not present, wherever His Godhead is, are not then these two natures in Christ separated from one another?"—its framing already seems unfortunate. The answer—"Not at all, for since the Godhead is illimitable and omnipresent, it must necessarily follow that the same is beyond the limits of the human nature He assumed, and yet is nevertheless in this human nature, and remains personally united to it"—may be true as far as it goes, but it threatens to turn the human nature into something like a *hypostasis*, a primary substance if not a person, and to preclude the Son's presence as God-man alongside localizing his human body.[42] It seems

---

41. Affirming "two willings, two knowings, two workings, and so on," Stephen R. Holmes notices that our culture "conflates the personal and the psychological," whereas "in conciliar Christology the union is hypostatic, not psychological, however, and what establishes the person as one is not psychology but ontology": the omniscient Word knows the thoughts of Jesus Christ *as his own* ("Reformed Varieties of the *Communicatio Idiomatum*," in *Person of Christ*, ed. Holmes and Rae, 86). Ironically, dyothelitism has been unpopular among modern thinkers even as they prioritize the Son's human self-consciousness. A dyothelite account such as Thomas Joseph White, OP, "Dyothelitism and the Instrumental Human Consciousness of Jesus," *Pro Ecclesia* 17, no. 4 (Fall 2008): 396–422, seems necessary, yet its need to distinguish having two grammatical (orthodox) from different ontological (Nestorian) subjects of operation—plus handling "instrumental" language carefully—demonstrates the rhetorical complexities.

42. See Question 48, quoted in Beeke and Ferguson, *Reformed Confessions Harmonized*, 80. In an Aristotelian framework, a primary substance is a single instantiation (a dog), and a secondary substance an abstract universal (dogness). However often the earlier tradition may have spoken of Christ's human nature concretely, and therefore in the former sense, modern association of human nature with personality or personhood is so strong that treating Jesus's human nature as a primary substance can connote Nestorianism.

better to focus on the truth that by virtue of divinity the God-man is present everywhere (as human, not just divine, even if not locally). But by virtue of humanity he is also particularly, bodily present (as divine, not just human, and therefore wholly but not exhaustively) at the Father's right hand. The eucharist involves the Spirit making the Son's presence real by taking us up proleptically, as it were, to wherever heaven may be. Yet this is not to say that the *extra Calvinisticum* stopped being true at the ascension or that his humanity is only a function of his body—which, for all its locatedness, may have been transformed in its newfound glory.

Notions of God as "pure act," on the one hand, and of divine "attributes," on the other hand, may create some of the relevant difficulties, since both— fairly or unfairly—can convey static polarities inconsistent with personal acts in history. There should be room to find better conceptualities for Reformed confessional commitments, and *perfections* and *powers* may be pertinent. The Son gave up neither omnipresence nor omnipotence in the incarnation; however, these "perfections" do not entail either the same form of presence or maximally supernatural exercise of power at every point. Instead, these perfections involve "powers" to act in whatever way is necessary and to be present in whatever form is appropriate. Thus, regarding omnipresence, action can occur in and through the natural, and God does not use power in percentages. So too with omnipresence: God is spiritually everywhere and able to be variously anywhere. Ultimately these are perfections of One who is Spirit; accordingly, the powers transcend human conceptions of presence and agency.

Likewise, then, omniscience. The Son remains perfectly wise, with all powers of knowing at his disposal. The underlying spiritual reality is that the Son's knowledge, whether of self or other, is not exhausted by the operation of his physical brain. By virtue of his humanity Jesus could develop in self-understanding, lack focal attention to items of knowledge, and so forth. By virtue of divinity, however, "beyond" his brain the Son still knew himself vis-à-vis the Father and the Spirit,[43] possessing access to any and all knowledge content necessary for wisdom. Mark 13 even signals this extra knowledge. Just before

---

A concrete-nature view is by no means automatically Nestorian, as Crisp (*Divinity and Humanity*, chap. 2) demonstrates. Nonetheless, its frequent connotation is a real problem for those who find theology to have significant rhetorical dimensions. Alternatively, Alvin Plantinga's account of an abstract-nature view is not simplistically monothelite, despite Crisp's treatment (ibid., 58–60). For all its emphasis on full humanity and distinct natures, Reformed dogmatics finally should prioritize Cyril's single-subject Christology, from which hesitation about certain metaphysical initiatives may follow.

43. Schwöbel insists that treating christological concepts in a vacuum separate from trinitarian theology leads inevitably to problems ("Christ for Us," 186), and here may be an illustration:

the infamous demurral of verse 32 regarding eschatological knowledge, verses 28–31 contain powerful claims about the Son's privileged divine knowledge, not least regarding who has what knowledge and when the desired events will occur. Moreover, subsequent verses identify Jesus with the owner of the house who will suddenly return.

Hence the Son does not empty himself of divine perfections. He does not even categorically empty himself of the use of certain powers, as in weaker, functional, kenotic theories. There may be *krypsis*, hiddenness concerning the Son's divine nature and how its powers might operate.[44] Yet revelatory veiling and unveiling may be enough to account for this aspect of the incarnation without additional terminology. It would better unleash Reformed insights to speak of what the Son does "by virtue of" divinity or humanity rather than "in" his divine or human natures—or, put differently, to follow the tradition of using "natures" language adverbially rather than nominally. The latter language more readily sounds Nestorian by treating the natures as primary substances or allowing them to sound like subjects of action. The former, adverbial language, being less metaphysically loaded, rightly focuses on the person of the Son and his active history—not hypostatizing the human nature while honoring his exercise of the powers attending his perfections. Without speaking of perfections, there is hardly a subject to whom the narrative can attribute—even within its frame of reference—a history. Yet the providentially provided ontological language of these perfections needs thoroughly Christian transformation to honor how God actually exercises their powers.

To recall, contra almost the entire drift of modern Christology, the virginal conception indicates that the Son—even as human—knew himself to be the divine visitation of the covenant people that Isaiah anticipated. It is impossible to explain how he understood his divine identity humanly or exercised divine powers with respect for human limitations. We should be suspicious of purported explanations for such mysteries. We should also

---

problems for kenotic theories of the Son's self-knowledge—whether ontological or functional—are considerable given the reciprocal self-consciousness of the perichoretic triune persons.

44. So Crisp, in his helpful critique of kenotic theories in *Divinity and Humanity* (esp. 121, 150–53). However, some conceptual features (e.g., Oliver D. Crisp, *Revisioning Christology* [Surrey, UK: Ashgate, 2011], 108) remain unclear, or unhelpful if focus rests not on hiddenness or revelation of the Son's divine nature vis-à-vis humans but instead turns to communication (or not) between Christ's two natures. Is specifying that the human nature is initially restricted from sharing in divine properties—then undergoes limited "nature-perichoresis," gaining some access to them (*Divinity and Humanity*, 33)—an instance of metaphysical parsing that eventually creates Nestorian-like problems (or seemingly Lutheran ones, in the subsequent nature-perichoresis)?

be as suspicious of our own cultural predilections as those of prior generations. Perhaps they were tempted by static, abstract, metaphysical notions of divine transcendence; we are tempted by dynamic, concrete, perhaps no less "metaphysical" notions of personhood. Our dogmatic task is neither rejecting nor reaffirming the modern self but rather bearing witness to the Son's embrace of our true humanity.

8. *The incarnation invites* followers of Jesus to share in costly love as forgiven sinners. *As Christ's identification with all humans reminds us, God loves without any partiality based on sex or gender, race or ethnicity, wealth or status, abilities or challenges. Imitating this self-involving love we encounter in Christ, the church bears witness to the singularly redemptive divine self-revelation.*

Thus we conclude where we began: hearing a call to find new life in following the Incarnate One. The New Testament refuses to reduce "incarnation" to a principle of philosophy or piety or even, more fashionably these days, church practice.[45] The incarnation is a singular and enduring, revelatory and redemptive, event: God coming to dwell with us. Strictly speaking, there can be no parallel, least of all in the failed humanity from which the Incarnate One came to rescue us. Far too often in Christendom "Christ" became identified with a prized principle of a dominant culture, while more recently "incarnation" generates a broad principle of inclusion. Instead, recognizing the unique nature of the incarnation begins with Jesus's Jewishness, locating him within God's covenant history with Israel. Therefore, sexism, racism, classism, and the like indeed have no place—to the church's frequent shame.[46] God lovingly addresses everyone in their particularity while addressing redemption as a universal need. The incarnation offers no general hope rooted in the histories or loves of earthly cultures, revealing instead that they need divine reconciliation.

Extraordinarily, though, the humiliation-exaltation pattern of the incarnation both welcomes and obligates those who would be rescued: "Have the same mindset as Christ Jesus" (Phil. 2:5 NIV), namely, "in humility value others above yourselves, not looking to your own interests but each of you to the

---

45. On this concern, see J. Todd Billings, *Union with Christ: Reframing Theology and Ministry for the Church* (Grand Rapids: Baker Academic, 2011).

46. J. Kameron Carter, *Race: A Theological Account* (New York: Oxford University Press, 2008) demonstrates the correlation between European development of "race" as a concept and anti-Semitic de-Judaizing of Jesus in favor of a more gnostic "Christ." While this chapter focuses on traditional dogmatics, we must become more attentive to the incarnation's social implications; for one illustration of the challenges involved, see Richard J. Mouw and Douglas A. Sweeney, *The Suffering and Victorious Christ: Toward a More Compassionate Christology* (Grand Rapids: Baker Academic, 2013).

interests of the others" (Phil. 2:3–4 NIV). In light of God highly exalting this Incarnate One, "continue to work out your salvation with fear and trembling, for it is God who works in you" (Phil. 2:12–13 NIV), and he "will carry it on to completion until the day of Christ Jesus" (Phil. 1:6 NIV). "Jesus Christ is the same yesterday and today and forever" (Heb. 13:8 NIV).[47]

47. Thanks to my colleague Marc Cortez and PhD student James Gordon for constructive criticisms of this chapter. James's dissertation defending the *extra Calvinisticum* makes a promising contribution.

11

The Work of Christ Accomplished

DONALD MACLEOD

Approaching the Atonement

The most fundamental of all questions with regard to the atonement is the question of direction. To whom is the great atoning act, the cross, directed? God or humanity? The question is seen at its most acute in relation to the Pauline concept of reconciliation. The current consensus is that the estrangement lies entirely on our human side and that there is no barrier to peace and fellowship on God's side. We are at enmity with him; he is not at enmity with us. Reconciliation, therefore, means our being reconciled to God, not his being reconciled to us. The plausibility of this construction rests on three factors.

The first factor is the reality of our enmity against God. Scripture bears abundant testimony to it. Paul, who alone among New Testament writers uses the vocabulary of reconciliation (*katallagē* and its cognates), takes the reality of our enmity against God for granted. Not only, he says, is the mind of the flesh at enmity with God, it *is* enmity (*echthra*) toward God (Rom. 8:7). Earlier in the same epistle (Rom. 5:10) he writes that the great demonstration of God's love was that he had given his Son to die for us while we were still his enemies, and in Colossians 1:21 he describes us as enemies to God because of our evil behavior.

But the evidence for our hostility to God is not limited to such explicit passages. It also includes those that speak of humans as haters of God, others that describe us as wishing there were no God (Ps. 14:1), others that charge us with habitual disobedience to his commands, and the many that accuse us of ignoring and defying his Word. Among these we must reckon Romans 1:18–32, which portrays us as suppressing and perverting the knowledge God gives through general revelation. On a broader canvas still, human history in its entirety is a sustained testimony to human resistance to divine truth, our refusal to give God the place that is his due, and our hatred of his representatives on earth. Clearly, then, reconciliation must include a revolution in the human heart, changing hatred to love and repugnance to longing.

The second factor that suggests there is no obstacle on God's side is the repeated emphasis of the New Testament that the atonement is an expression of the divine love, not its cause. Never is there even a hint that the cross secured God's love or persuaded him to change from hating us to loving us. All the key passages (John 3:16; Rom. 5:8; 2 Cor. 5:18; 1 John 4:10) speak instead of the divine love as taking the initiative. This love has no cause external to God himself and never appears as a response to any human initiative. Since God is love, his love could have no beginning: he never was, without loving the world.

Yet, while never capricious, God's love for us was an expression of the divine freedom. It was eternal yet contingent: not, like the love of the Father for the Son, an essential feature of the very being of the Triune God but sovereign and gracious, so that we share in it only as those who have to say, "It pleased God" (Gal. 1:15).

Does this not make God's love arbitrary and evacuate it of all moral significance? This is often suggested. Bruce McCormack, for example, argues that if God's decision to turn toward the human race was contingent, then it does not reflect what God is essentially.[1] But can we really accept that only an action performed by necessity of nature provides a true reflection of the divine character? This is certainly not how we judge human actions. On the contrary, only actions performed in freedom are deemed to have moral significance, and far from viewing our free actions as arbitrary, we see them as the true reflections of moral character. There is no reason to think that the opposite applies in the case of God and that his free actions tell us nothing about his true character. True, it may be beyond us to understand how there

---

1. See Bruce McCormack, "Grace and Being: The Role of God's Gracious Election in Karl Barth's Theological Ontology," in *The Cambridge Companion to Karl Barth*, ed. John Webster (Cambridge: Cambridge University Press, 2000), 97.

can be a love that is both contingent and eternal, but contingent God's love certainly was, just as his decision to create the world was contingent.

But what matters for this chapter is that precisely because it was the divine love that provided the atonement, it can be no part of the function of the cross to turn God into a God of love. The love is already there before the cross, before the incarnation, and before the creation of the world.

The third factor lending support to the view that the problems are all on humanity's side is that the New Testament never speaks of God being reconciled to humanity but only of humanity being reconciled to God. In 2 Corinthians 5:20, for example, it is to us that the appeal is directed, "Be reconciled to God." Similarly, in Romans 5:10 we are said to have been reconciled to God through the death of his Son, while in Colossians 1:22 God is said to have reconciled *us* (to himself) by Christ's physical body. These are powerful arguments, especially when taken together. Yet there are clear indications that the primary impact of the cross was directed toward God, not toward humanity.

First, while Paul in 2 Corinthians 5:18–21 certainly makes it plain that it was God, the offended party, and not humanity, the offender, who took the peace-making initiative, he defines reconciliation in a way that rules out the idea that it amounted to no more than a change in the sinner's attitude toward God. "God," he writes, "was reconciling the world to himself in Christ, *not counting men's sins against them*" (2 Cor. 5:19 NIV; emphasis mine). This is no merely subjective change. Instead it parallels what Paul has already said in Romans 8:1: "Therefore, there is *now* no condemnation for those who are in Christ Jesus" (NIV; emphasis mine). The point is not that the reconciled no longer hold anything against God but that God no longer holds anything against them. This is why in Romans 5:11 Paul can speak of reconciliation as something that we "receive"—not a change of heart but a divine pardon. This is also why the idea of reconciliation shades easily into the idea of justification, as appears in, for example, Romans 5:9–10, where being "justified by his [Christ's] blood" is parallel to "being reconciled to him through the death of his Son." "The righteousness of faith," Calvin writes, "is reconciliation with God, which consists solely in the forgiveness of sins."[2]

Second, this "not counting men's sins against them" rests on a remarkable foundation. God did not cancel sin on the ground of some subjective change in the sinner. Nor did he dismiss it as a mere trifle. Nor, yet again, did his love proceed directly to reconciliation. Instead he took what seems to us an extraordinarily circuitous route. He proceeded *via* the cross of Calvary and

---

2. John Calvin, *Institutes,* ed. John T. McNeill, trans. Ford Lewis Battles (Philadelphia: Westminster, 1960), 3.11.21.

there laid an astonishing basis for reconciliation. He made Christ, the one who alone was utterly innocent of sin, to be "sin" for us—identifying with it, answering for it, suffering in our place all that our godlessness, self-centeredness, and violence deserved. And conversely, we who are utterly devoid of righteousness become God's righteousness in Christ: as righteous as God himself (2 Cor. 5:21).

It is not, then, to sinners simply as such that God is reconciled, any more than it is the "wicked" simply as such who are justified (Rom. 4:5). It is with sinners "in Christ" that he is reconciled. The reconciliation consists in God no longer condemning us, and the reason he no longer condemns us is that our sin received its doom in the flesh of his own Son (Rom. 8:3).

It is becoming increasingly common to describe this death as a purely intratrinitarian transaction between the Father and the Son, as if God himself bore the whole cost of atonement without any human involvement. This has an important element of truth. But Jesus was not only the Son of God; he was also the last Adam, and it was in this capacity as "the man, Christ Jesus" (1 Tim. 2:5) that he offered to God the obedience through which "the many" are made righteous (Rom. 5:19). Our "no condemnation," therefore, does not rest on an indulgent divine love but on the fact that Christ, who shared our flesh and blood, offered himself in place of his "children" (Heb. 2:13).

Third, the appeal "be reconciled to God" is no decisive proof that all the barriers to reconciliation are on our side and that there are none on God's. The same form of words occurs in the principle laid down by Jesus in Matthew 5:24: "First be reconciled to your brother, and then come and offer your gift." What is interesting here is the context. Jesus is addressing the case of someone who knows that another person has something against him. His appeal is not made, however, to the person who holds the grievance, telling him to change his attitude. It is made to the person who is the victim of the attitude: "Go and be reconciled to the brother who has something against you." This means, at the very least, that when Paul says, "Be reconciled to God," it is far from self-evident that he means, "Lay aside your animosity to God." On the contrary, the use of the same expression by Jesus strongly suggests that what the apostle means is, "Be reconciled to God, who has something against you."

It was exactly this perception of the relationship between God and humanity that lay behind the prayer of the publican: "God, have mercy on me, a sinner" (Luke 18:13 NIV). He is not showing mercy toward God; he is asking God to have mercy on him, a sinner who has nothing to say in his own defense and can appeal only to the divine clemency. The same situation is assumed in 1 John 2:1–2, which portrays Christ as an attorney representing sinners before

God the Father and resting his whole case on the fact that he, personally, has atoned for their sins. Why do we need an advocate with God if the barriers to peace and reconciliation are entirely on our side? If they were, then it would be God who needed an attorney to plead his case before us. And as if all this were not enough, there is the solemn principle laid down in Hebrews 9:22: "without the shedding of blood there is no forgiveness." Without forgiveness there is no reconciliation, and without the shedding of blood there can be no forgiveness. It is precisely this fact, that God cannot condone sin, that creates the necessity for an objective atonement directed toward the forgiver, not the forgiven—one that will satisfy the judge of all the earth that it is right to give remission to sinners.

Finally, the Scriptures clearly portray the death of Christ as a sacrifice, and it was implicit in the very notion of sacrifice that it was offered to God, not to humanity. Even the pagans spoke of "sacrificing to the gods," and the generic term "offering" (Greek *prosphora*) assumes that the sacrifice is placed before the deity and yielded up to him. This is why the Old Testament frequently appends to the prescriptions for sacrifice the promise "and he shall be forgiven" (e.g., Lev. 4:26, 31, 35). Who can forgive sins save God only (Mark 4:6)?

But the idea of sacrifice directed toward God is not only implicit; it is also explicit. This appears, for example, in such a passage as Ephesians 5:2, which speaks of Christ as giving himself up for us "as a fragrant offering and sacrifice *to God*" (NIV; emphasis mine). Clearly, the fragrance of the offering is a fragrance in the nostrils of the deity, not in the nostrils of the offerer or of the onlookers. This same Godward emphasis is equally explicit in Hebrews 9:14, which declares that Christ through the eternal Spirit offered himself unblemished *to God*. But this is no isolated verse. Throughout Hebrews, and particularly in chapters 4–10, the idea of the Godward action of Christ is emphasized in the writer's typological interpretation of the tabernacle.[3] Jesus, our High Priest, went into the holy of holies carrying his own blood in order to present it before the divine presence. It is impossible to interpret this as being directed toward humanity. Apart from the high priest himself, there was no human observer in the holy of holies. The atoning moment was a transaction between the mediator and God, and its effect was "to do away with sin by the sacrifice of himself" (Heb. 9:26 NIV).

Such an understanding of the cross as a sacrifice offered to God in order to reconcile him to the sinner clearly raises serious questions about traditional

---

3. While Hebrews warrants such an interpretation of the Levitical order, we should heed Calvin's warning about "looking for some sublime mystery in every nail" (John Calvin, *The Epistle of Paul the Apostle to the Hebrews and The First and Second Epistles of St Peter*, trans. William B. Johnston [Grand Rapids: Eerdmans, 1963], 107).

ideas of divine immutability and divine impassibility. But is there not a danger that these are human constructs, or at least that we construct them in a human way? It is tempting to dismiss the idea of divine passibility as a transient theological fad, but the language of revelation (and theologians must take their cue from this) leaves us in no doubt that God is affected by events outside himself.[4] He is not only proactive (e.g., as the one who sovereignly creates) but *reactive*. Nor is this a marginal biblical theme to be grudgingly conceded. It runs throughout Scripture. At the most basic level it is reflected in the fact that God responds to prayer, but it also becomes clear at key moments in biblical history. God expelled Adam and Eve from paradise in response to their disobedience; he responded to the godless violence of the antediluvians by sending the flood; he responded to the cries of his people in Egypt by sending them a deliverer; he responded to the apostasy of Judah by sending them into exile. Even more significantly, the idea of divine responsiveness underlies the whole Old Testament *cultus*. The sacrifices were not merely reflexive in their impact, having no effect beyond making the offerer feel better (as is sometimes said to be the value of prayer). On the contrary, as we have already noted, they had a clear objective impact, spelled out time and again in Leviticus; they secured forgiveness. This can hardly be a case of sinners forgiving themselves. It can mean only, "And God will forgive him." He responds to the sacrifice by remitting the sin, or, as it is expressed in relation to the Passover, "When I see the blood, I will pass over you" (Exod. 12:13).

The cross is the supreme example of God being affected by events outside himself, and no understanding of the atonement is possible on any other principle. The historic (and historical) obedience of the last Adam reconciles him to those with whom he could not otherwise be at peace.

The Covenant

It was clearly in such objective terms that Jesus understood his own death. "This," he says, "is my blood of the [new] covenant, which is poured out for many for the forgiveness of sins" (Matt. 26:28). Here, once again, the Godward effect is clearly uppermost: in response to the shedding of Jesus's blood, God will forgive sin. But now a new element is introduced, the

4. Calvin wrestled with this but adhered to the traditional view, arguing that both the idea that God was angry with those he loved and that his attitude was modified by the sacrifice of Christ were but "accommodations" to our human capacity. See Paul Helm, *John Calvin's Ideas* (Oxford: Oxford University Press, 2004), 389–416.

covenant, and it is no isolated reference.[5] Jesus clearly hints at a pretemporal covenant when he speaks of a commandment given to him by God the Father (John 10:18) and again when he refers to a work given him to do (John 17:4). Peter also hints at it in 1 Peter 1:2, where he speaks of the elect being sprinkled with the blood of Christ (an allusion to the confirmation of the covenant in Exod. 24:8, when Moses "threw" the blood of the sacrifice on the people). But it becomes explicit again in the Epistle to the Hebrews, especially in chapters 8–10, where Christ is both the mediator (Heb. 9:15) and the surety (Heb. 7:22) of the covenant, serves as high priest under a superior covenant (Heb. 8:6), and inherits the "better promises" of a better covenant (Heb. 8:6).

The whole life and ministry of Jesus must be seen within this covenant framework. He comes as a "sent" one with a definite mission, definite rules of engagement, and definite promises. This does not mean, of course, that the Father, the Son, and the Holy Spirit sat around a table and engaged in long, protracted negotiations. They lived in perfect, wordless communion, one in love as they were one in being, and united in commitment to the salvation of the world. The covenant reflects this profound oneness of mind. Yet while all three are involved in the work of redemption, each is involved in his own way, and each makes his own distinctive contribution. The Son, and he alone, will become flesh and live in the world as the Lord in servant form, but he comes in covenant with the Father and the Spirit. His death is the climax of his covenant obedience, fulfilling the purpose for which he came, namely, to lay down his life for his sheep. His relationship with his people is a covenant relationship, constituting him not only their brother through a common humanity but their surety, representative, and substitute. And the promise made to him is a covenant promise. His obedience and sacrifice will be accepted as an expiation for sin, satisfying God that it is right to justify the ungodly (Rom. 1:5 KJV).

It was within the terms of this covenant that Christ offered himself to God, confident that his death would be rewarded with the blessings that had been agreed, and rewarded not only because such was the agreement but also because in the eternal covenant itself the intrinsic worth of his self-sacrifice had been fully recognized. To every charge against his people, it would be said *autos hilasmos*: "He himself is the expiation for their sins" (1 John 2:2, my translation).

---

5. For an excellent modern statement of the covenant background to the work of Christ, see J. I. Packer's introduction to Herman Witsius, *The Economy of the Covenants between God and Man* (Phillipsburg, NJ: P&R, 1990).

Propitiation

But what, precisely, was the Godward impact of the cross? The key biblical answer is *propitiation*. It is important, however, not to drive a wedge between this concept and the idea of *expiation*. Evangelicals, jealous for the doctrine of divine anger, have sometimes fallen into this trap laid for them by C. H. Dodd's contention that the *hilaskomai* word group must always be rendered "propitiate" and never "expiate." Going to the other extreme and arguing that it must always be translated "propitiate" and never "expiate" is not the answer. The two concepts imply each other, and it is on the basis that sin has been expiated that God is propitiated. True though it is that in pagan usage *hilaskomai* and its cognates always denote appeasement (usually of the gods), and true though it also is that in Romans 3:25 (where Paul refers to Christ as a *hilasterion*) "the wrath of God revealed from heaven" (Rom. 1:18) is very much on the apostle's mind, nevertheless in all the New Testament occurrences of the *hilaskomai* word group the more direct reference is not to divine anger but to human sin.

The clearest instance of this is Hebrews 2:17, which speaks of the need for Christ to be a merciful and faithful high priest "to make atonement for the sins of the people." Here, "sins" is in the accusative, and while it can be argued that it is an "accusative of respect" yielding the sense "with respect to the sins of the people," it is hardly necessary. The natural translation is "to expiate the sins of the people," and this gathers support from the fact that the root meaning of the underlying Hebrew term, *kipper*, is "to cover." The obedience of Christ (culminating in his self-sacrifice on the cross of Calvary) covers our disobedience (Rom. 5:19).

In 1 John 2:2, similarly, the direct link is between the *hilasmos* and our sins. John's purpose in writing the epistle is "so that you will not sin" (1 John 2:1). But if anybody does sin, what then? It is to that problem, the sin problem, that the *hilasmos* provides the answer. Our attorney, representing us before the Father, is able to argue that our sins, real though they are, have been expiated by no less a person than the advocate himself, Jesus Christ, the Righteous One. Not only has he actively expiated them, but he is himself the expiation, the covering for our sins.

The same close link between the *hilaskomai* word group and sin appears in Romans 3:25. Here, the precise form is *hilasterion*, and its precise meaning in this context has been much disputed. The NIV follows the majority view in rendering it "a sacrifice of atonement" (ESV has "propitiation"), but in the Septuagint *hilasterion* is the uniform translation for the "mercy-seat" (Hebrew *kapporeth*), and that should not be lightly set aside. This is clearly its meaning in the only other New Testament occurrence of the word, Hebrews 9:5, where the KJV has "the mercy-seat" and the NIV has "the atonement cover." At first sight, the image of Christ as the mercy seat is incongruous, particularly in view of the reference to his blood. In the Old Testament the blood was sprinkled on the mercy seat. If Christ is the *hilastērion*, is the blood sprinkled, then, on him? But the mercy seat should not be seen independently of the blood. Separately, neither the blood nor the mercy seat had any efficacy. It was "the blood-sprinkled mercy-seat" that had the atoning value, and since the function of the mercy seat (the lid of the ark) was to cover the tablets of the broken law, it served as a powerful symbol of expiation. When the glory enthroned between the cherubim (1 Sam. 4:4) looked down, he saw not the broken law but the blood. In Romans 3:25, this link between the *hilastērion* and sin is further reinforced by the following sentence, where Paul argues that the whole point of God's action in putting Christ forward as a *hilastērion* was that this justified him in leaving unpunished the sins of those believers who had died before the coming of Christ.

The link with sin is never far away, then, in New Testament occurrences of the *hilaskomai* word group, and at the level of mere translation it would be perfectly defensible to use "expiate" and "expiation" as the English equivalent. It remains, however, that expiation is incomplete as a theological concept. Far from being an end in itself, its whole purpose was to restore the fractured relationship between God and humanity. God is angry with sin, Christ expiates it, and by expiating it he propitiates God—or, in modern English usage, he placates or appeases him. Whichever term we use, however, the presupposition is clear: the anger of God against sin and sinners is a solemn reality. There is no need at this juncture to prove that this is the biblical position. Over against the influential denials of C. H. Dodd,[6] such scholars as Leon Morris and Roger Nicole have demonstrated beyond the shadow of a doubt that the divine anger is not only a well-attested biblical concept but also a pervasive and prominent one, and that to suppress it would throw Christian theology into hopeless confusion.[7]

Yet it is important to note the truth that Dodd has highlighted: the anger of the God and Father of our Lord Jesus Christ is a very different anger from that of the gods of Olympus. The pagan deities were irascible, and their anger irrational, unpredictable, and vindictive—a reflection of human anger at its

---

6. See C. H. Dodd, *The Bible and the Greeks* (London: Hodder and Stoughton, 1954), 82–95; idem, *The Epistle of Paul to the Romans*, 46–55, 78–80.

7. Leon Morris, *The Apostolic Preaching of the Cross*, 2nd ed. (London: Tyndale, 1960), 125–85; Roger Nicole, *Standing Forth: Collected Writings of Roger Nicole* (Fearn, UK: Christian Focus, 2002), 343–85.

worst. The God of Scripture, by contrast, is slow to anger and reluctant to punish, as Hosea makes brilliantly clear (Hosea 11:8, 9); his wrath, far from being unpredictable, is covenantal, leaving us in no doubt as to what will provoke it. It is the measured response of his broken heart to the evil he sees in the world and the contempt and defiance he experiences at its hands.

But is this anger a matter of the divine will or of the divine nature? Could he have chosen not to be angry with sin and simply overlook it without atonement?

This recalls the mind-set of Anselm's dialogue partner, Boso, to whose suggestion that he might cancel sin by a single moment of repentance Anselm famously replied, "You have not yet considered how heavy the weight of sin is."[8] We quickly reduce sin to mere peccadillos and, having no concept of the majesty of God, cannot understand why he should take blasphemy and idolatry so seriously; nor can we grasp the destructive nature of our own covetousness, envy, and lust.

God did not sit down, deliberate carefully, and then decide that on balance he should hate evil. Nor is his freedom circumscribed by some law of retribution external to himself, like some human judge bound, even when he disapproves of them, by the laws passed by his national legislature. "Just" is what God *is*. "Angry with sin" is what he *is*. It is his whole nature, his very being, to recoil from it and condemn it. It is unimaginable that he should place idolatry, blasphemy, murder, rape, child abuse, greed, deceit, and exploitation outside the law, ignoring the pain they cause and the havoc they wreak. No human society places evil outside the law, and it is one of the paradoxes of this whole discourse that those who cry out most loudly for justice (against, e.g., child abusers and rapists) are often the very ones who deny the Almighty any judicial function. Yet our human systems of justice can have no legitimacy except as ordained by God, and while postmodernism may calmly discuss "Whose justice?," our sanctions against crime clearly presuppose the validity of law and of appropriate retribution. We cannot deny to the Judge of all the earth the prerogatives we concede to our own petty judicatories. It is precisely because we are made in his image that we ourselves feel revulsion in the presence of evil.

It is only from this perspective of a Creator who hates sin that we can hope to justify the ways of God with Jesus Christ. Why does the sword fall here? What gives the question special poignancy is the prominence given to the role of God the Father in the story of the crucifixion. It was he who *gave* his one and only Son (John 3:16); he who did not spare him but *delivered him up*

8. Anselm, *Cur Deus homo* 1.21, in *Anselm of Canterbury: The Major Works*, ed. Brian Davies and G. R. Evans (Oxford: Oxford University Press, 1998), 395.

(Rom. 8:32); he who *made him sin* (2 Cor. 5:21); he who showed his love for us by sending his Son as an expiation for our sins (1 John 4:10).

What these passages bring out, and bring out so strongly, is that we must see the cross not only in terms of the action of Jesus but also in terms of the action of God the Father; every doctrine of the atonement has to take this into account. This in no way detracts from the loving action of the Son. *He* gave his life as a ransom; *he* laid down his life for his sheep; *he* loved Saul of Tarsus and gave himself for him (Gal. 2:2). Here is the priesthood of God the Son, who not only "gives" himself but gives himself as a "bloody sacrifice" (*thusia*; Eph. 5:2). By this blood, by this act of priestly obedience, he expiates the world's sin, and on this basis he serves as our advocate (1 John 2:1). On Good Friday, just outside Jerusalem, he descended into hell in our place.

But then, such verses as John 3:16; Romans 8:32; and 1 John 4:10 speak of another priesthood: the priesthood of God the Father. Here is the heavenly archetype of the story of Abraham and Isaac, where the Father delivers up his *jachid*, his beloved Son, and where Father and Son together proclaim that there is no length to which they will not go to save the world. This is what "theories" of the atonement have to wrestle with: the cross not only as a demonstration of the love of Jesus but also as a demonstration of the love of God the Father. *His*, ultimately, was the cost, and *his* the loss. It is *his* Son who bleeds and dies. It is from his own Son that he must hide his face, to his cry he must turn a deaf ear, to him whom he can extend no comfort and offer no hint of recognition.

Why can the Father not spare him? Because he *bears* the sin of the world, and because he *is* the sin of the world. He carries it in his body to the tree (1 Pet. 2:24), and God executes his judgment (Rom. 8:3). It is not a pain he personally deserves. But he is "for us." That is why the sword falls here. It falls here because it is right, and before the cross can be anything, it has to be right. It cannot be an act of caprice or malice. It cannot be a mere demonstration. In the hand of God the sword can fall only where it is deserved, and it is deserved here at Calvary because it is what those whom Christ represents deserve: the wages of sin, which he receives not merely "with us" but in our place. He is condemned so that there is no condemnation for those who are in Christ Jesus (Rom. 8:1). "It is finished!," Christ cries in triumph. The debt is fully paid, and the children are free! The cost of redemption is indeed borne by humanity, but it is the humanity of God, and it highlights not only the love of the Given One but the love of the Giver. "*God* so loved the world."

The whole case for this understanding of the atonement rests on Scripture. Here the wisdom that crucified Christ is disqualified from speaking. Here there can be only one word, the apostolic word (*logos*) of the cross (1 Cor.

1:18), which proudly put the crucifixion at the very forefront of its message and proclaimed the Crucified the Savior of the world, bearing in himself the pain that evil deserved.

An Unbiblical Notion of Justice?

It is suggested, however, that this whole construction rests on a totally un-biblical notion of justice. Joel Green and Mark Baker even go so far as to suggest that Charles Hodge's doctrine of penal substitution simply reflects nineteenth-century American notions of criminal justice, and they contrast these with a biblical understanding that sees justice as covenantal, relational, and virtually synonymous with faithfulness.[9]

This echoes the argument that there is a fundamental difference between the classical (Greek and Roman) concept of justice and the biblical one. The classical notion was summarized in the Ciceronian principle *suum cuique* ("to each his own"), which meant giving everyone his or her due, including retribution if that was what the person deserved. The Hebrew or biblical no-tion, we are told, is fundamentally different.[10] But is it? True, it is covenantal, which means that God will be faithful to his promises. This is why, in the Old Testament, righteousness is frequently paired with love (e.g., Ps. 103:17) and salvation (e.g., Isa. 51:6), and this is why the "righteousness of God" held none of the dread for the author of Psalm 4:1 that it held for Martin Luther. But covenant faithfulness also means that God will fulfill his threats, includ-ing the threat, "Cursed is everyone who does not continue to do everything written in the Book of the Law" (Gal. 3:10 NIV; Deut. 27:26). That curse hangs over the whole human race because, individually and collectively, we are all covenant breakers and, therefore, liable to the curse. It was that curse, demanded by God's covenant faithfulness, that Christ bore at Calvary, and from that curse that he redeemed us (Gal. 3:13).

It is true too that God's faithfulness means that he rights wrongs.[11] But does this rule out his also punishing wrongs? It is precisely God's justice (*sedaqah*) that leads him to perform those acts of judgment (*mishpatim*) in which he

9. Joel B. Green and Mark D. Baker, *Recovering the Scandal of the Cross: Atonement in New Testament and Contemporary Contexts* (Milton Keynes, UK: Paternoster, 2000), 147.

10. See the discussion in Alister E. McGrath, *Iustitia Dei: A History of the Christian Doctrine of Justification*, 2nd ed. (Cambridge: Cambridge University Press, 1998), 4–16.

11. In their widely cited article, "For God So Loved the World," Joanne Carlson Brown and Rebecca Parker criticize Anselm because "his view of justice is not that wrong should be righted but that wrongs should be punished." See Joanne Carlson Brown and Carole R. Bohn, eds., *Christianity, Patriarchy and Abuse: A Feminist Critique* (New York: Pilgrim, 1989), 7.

rights wrongs. According to Psalm 72:4, for example, God's rescuing of the needy inevitably involves the destruction of their oppressors, and this is the consistent message of Scripture. If God is going to right wrongs, he must act against the forces of evil, destroy them (Heb. 2:14), disarm them (Col. 2:15), bind them (Rev. 20:2), and finally banish them to the outer darkness (Matt. 8:12) where evil can work its malice against only itself. That is a destiny in which all covenant breakers will share unless we find an advocate to plead for us (1 John 2:1).

Substitution

Retributive justice, then, far from being incompatible with covenant faithfulness, lies at its very heart. And far from being an invention of nineteenth-century America, it was already very much in evidence when Yahweh drowned the forces of the pharaoh in the Red Sea. But what of the idea of *vicarious* retribution? Is it morally tolerable that the innocent should take the place of the guilty and suffer as his substitute?

The first point to be borne in mind here is that there are no appropriate human analogies to the self-sacrifice of Christ. It is, of course, true that a man may lay down his life for his friends. It is even true that Jesus expects our love for one another to rise to this level of self-sacrifice: we are to love one another as he loved us (John 3:34). Yet the self-sacrifice of Jesus differs radically from all human self-sacrifice. Calvary is not a case of one human laying down his or her life for another. It is a case of the one and only Son of God deliberately assuming human nature in order to put himself in a position where he can lay down *his* life. Nor is it a case of a man laying down his life for his friends: Jesus lays down his life for his enemies. Nor yet again is it a case of him sacrificing himself to rescue someone in merely temporal peril. Jesus lays down his life for those in eternal spiritual peril, and the death he tastes is not merely death in the physical sense but death unmitigated. He must endure the curse pronounced by heaven against human evil (Gal. 3:13).

Above all, Jesus's death was a death of universal significance. He was not a mother laying down her life for her child, or a soldier sacrificing himself for his comrades, or a patriot dying to save his or her city. He died to expiate sin, and the benefits of that expiation were to extend to the whole world (1 John 2:2).

Second, it is ironic that humanity has no sooner objected to God being restricted by an "external law" of retribution than it proceeds to hedge him in with a host of other external laws. One external law says that God must *not* visit guilt with retribution. Another lays down that guilt is nontransferable, and yet another pronounces that the innocent may not suffer in the place of the guilty. Still another decrees that God may not inflict on his own Son the curse due to sinners. In other words (to adapt the language of Karl Barth), the judge has no right to let himself be judged in our place, the attorney has no right to take his client's place in the dock, and God has no right to make our mortal peril his mortal peril.[12] Even less does he have a right to purchase his church with blood: a horrid idea (Acts 20:28)!

It is far wiser, surely, to stand back, listen to the narrative of how God did save his people, and accept his own explanation (*logos*) of the necessity for the death of the Lord of Glory. Here more than anywhere theology has to be content with exegesis. The atonement can be neither deduced from nor limited by human first principles.

Third, the capacity in which Christ died has no bearing whatsoever on the depth and intensity of his agony. Whether he suffered as example, martyr, suicide, or substitute, the floggings, the crown of thorns, the nails, and the descent into hell were the same. The question is, "Why?" And to suggest that he suffered either as a mere example to us or simply in solidarity with us gets us nowhere. Why has God placed his Son there on the garbage heap between two thieves?[13] Why is the suffering of the Son a "must," and why, for all the earnestness of his prayer, can the cup not pass (Mark 14:35)? It can only be because there was no other way to restore order to God's sin-violated universe.

Fourth, Christ was not an innocent third party dragged against his will into a quarrel that was none of his concern. If the words of the Baptist (John 1:29) were true, far from being "innocent," he was bearing the sin of the world, and far from being a third party, he was closely connected with both parties. We might even say that he *was* both parties: both God and Adam. He was himself the God who had been defied and hated by man, and at the same time he was in the fullest and most complete sense a member of the human race, sharing in the flesh and blood of his "children" (Heb. 2:14). And he was no reluctant sufferer. "No one," he said, "takes my life from me, but I lay it down of my own accord." True, he was laying it down in obedience to his Father's command, but it was a most willing obedience: he delighted to do his Father's will (Ps. 40:8; Heb. 10:7). But it was also (at the risk of repetition) a covenanted obedience. In his eternal form he was no servant, but he had covenanted to take a servant's form (*morphē*, Phil. 2:7), and in that form to

12. This phraseology is borrowed from Karl Barth's discussion of "The Judge Judged in Our Place," in *Church Dogmatics* IV/1, ed. G. W. Bromiley and T. F. Torrance (Edinburgh: T&T Clark, 1956), 211–83.

13. The language of George F. Macleod, founder of the Iona Community, in *Only One Way Left* (Glasgow: Iona Community, 2000).

act with the Father and the Spirit for the salvation of his people. The ultimate impulse of his mission was his love for the world. The Son loved and gave himself (Gal. 2:20); the Father loved and gave his Son; and the Son's sacrifice of himself was as voluntary as the Father's sacrifice of his Son.

Finally, far from representing God as an unyielding Shylock demanding his pound of flesh, the substitutionary sacrifice of Christ underlines the eternal goodwill of God toward the human race. In terms of strict law, each individual sinner should die for his own sin; it was grace to concede that one should die for all (2 Cor. 5:14), and it was grace that the temporary sufferings of the One should be accepted in place of the endless sufferings of the many. Yet it was a grace that involved no compromise because the sacrifice offered was one in which God could take infinite satisfaction—not because it was a quid pro quo, or because the weight of Jesus's suffering perfectly balanced the weight of human sin, but because it was the obedience of a "one and only Son" (John 1:14). Here, for each person of the Trinity, there was satisfaction. The Son was satisfied and cried, "*Tetelestai!*" The Spirit was satisfied, having upheld the Son through all the challenges of his self-offering.

And the Father was satisfied. Yes, there was pain in it: the pain of not sparing him, and the pain of not being able to respond to his anguished "Why?" But the Son's act was in itself so glorious that the angels peered down to look (1 Pet. 1:12), and the Father was so thrilled with it that he commands every knee to bow and every tongue to confess the Crucified as the King of Glory (Phil. 2:10, 11)! His Son's obedience and blood hide all our transgressions from view.

Redemptive Violence

But it is not only the concepts of retribution and substitution that have drawn the fire of critics. Others have been appalled by the idea of "redemptive violence," which, they say, lies at the heart of the Christian doctrine of atonement. Joanne Carlson Brown and Rebecca Parker have even spoken of Christianity as "an abusive theology that glorifies suffering": "Is it any wonder that there is so much abuse in modern society when the predominant image or theology of the culture is of 'divine child abuse'—the Father demanding and carrying out the suffering and death of his own son?"[14] Christianity needs to be liberated from this theology, they argue. Otherwise, far from bringing liberty to the oppressed, it represents the very acme of oppression and of the abuse of power.

14. Brown and Parker, "For God So Loved," 26.

When St. Paul spoke, then, of glorying in the cross (Gal. 6:14), was he
glorying in violence, saying, in effect, how proud he was that God's Son, his
"holy child," had been abused? There can certainly be no denying the violence. Nor can there be any denying the abuse of power. But the question for
the theologian is not whether the cross is an instance of gratuitous violence
from the perspective of radical Christian feminists for whom the fundamental
human problem is not their own sin but patriarchal oppression, and who see
Jesus as no more than a prophet who fell victim to his own faithfulness. The
question is whether the cross is an instance of violent patriarchal abuse when
taken on its own terms, including the doctrines of the incarnation and the
Trinity, and including too the guilt of our revolt against God and our myriad
personal contributions to the violence that has filled the earth.

We note, first of all, that Jesus was not a child. He was a full-grown man
who made his own choices and who, as such, had clearly chosen the way of
the cross. More fundamentally still, that he was in the world at all was his
own personal choice. Originally "rich beyond all splendor" (2 Cor. 8:9), he
had chosen not to cling to his prerogatives and immunities but to come instead
into this dark world of sin not in divine but servant form, his glory veiled
by the meanness of his humanity. In that humanity he had made the further
choice to descend even lower, all the way to Calvary.

This was no helpless victim, then, and certainly no abused child. Nor was
he simply facing the inevitable and meekly accepting his fate. He need not
have been in the world at all, and being in the world, he need never have made
that last somber journey to Jerusalem or let himself be betrayed and arrested.
Paradoxical though it sounds, Pilate held the power to condemn him only
from the prisoner himself (John 19:11).

Besides, Jesus had a very clear understanding of the necessity and nature
of his own death. "The Son of Man," he declared, "*must* suffer and be killed"
(Mark 8:31), and in Gethsemane, he had looked into the cup, shuddered, and
recoiled. Yet he took it. Not only did Jesus choose the way of the cross and
reaffirm that choice time and again; he also had a very clear idea where that
cross fit into the eternal purpose of God. He was laying down his life for
his sheep (John 10:15), giving his soul as a ransom for many (Mark 10:45),
and shedding his blood for the remission of sins (Matt. 26:28). His apostles
would eventually develop the *logos* of the cross in even greater detail, but all
its essentials, including the particular and the substitutionary, were already
present in the teaching of Jesus himself. The real problem is that the authors
of the New Testament and the editors of *Christianity, Patriarchy, and Abuse*
have radically different worldviews. On the Bible's terms, the violence Jesus
suffered vicariously makes perfect, if dreadful, sense.

Even as the clouds gather, there is not a hint in the Gospels that Jesus ever doubted his Father's love, and certainly none to suggest that he felt himself hated or abused by a patriarchal deity. It is on his last journey (from Caesarea Philippi to Jerusalem) that he receives "honor and glory" on the Mount of Transfiguration: a key psychological moment when the Father reaffirms the assurance given at his baptism: "This is my Son, whom I love" (Mark 9:7 NIV) And in that sublime moment in the upper room when he washes the feet of the disciples, he does so knowing not only that Judas was set to betray him but also that he had come from God and would soon be returning to God (John 13:1). Indeed, he repeatedly represents his death as a homecoming (John 14:2, 12). Even in Gethsemane, he still has the assurance that God is "*Abba*," and while that may have been momentarily eclipsed when he cried, "*Eloi, Eloi, lema sabachthani?*," the last cry on his dying lips is one of serenity and triumph: "*Abba*, into your hands I commit my spirit" (Luke 23:46).

Of course, all this assumes that the Gospels, including the Gospel of John, give us an authentic account of the inner as well as the outer life of Christ. If he was the victim of "divine child abuse," he was clearly unaware of it. On the contrary, he knew that beyond the cross lay glory: the days of humiliation would be followed by hyperexaltation (Phil. 2). He died satisfied: satisfied with the quality of his obedience; satisfied with the glory of the church he had purchased with his blood; and satisfied, above all, with the loving approbation of his Father giving up his Son.

But then, can we really equate God's "giving up" his Son (the terminology of the New Testament) with God "abusing" his Son? Our surest guide is the language used by Peter on the day of Pentecost: "This man was handed over to you by God's set purpose and foreknowledge; and you, with the help of wicked men, put him to death by nailing him to the cross" (Acts 2:23 NIV). The preceding verse makes plain that God had borne clear and loving witness to his Son, attesting him as the Messiah by "miracles, wonders, and signs." But it is also clear that the Father had foreknowledge of Jesus's death and had even indeed foreordained it. The crucifixion had happened by "God's set purpose and foreknowledge" (*hōrismenē boulē*). Similar language is used in Acts 4:28: those who conspired against Jesus had done what God's power and will had decided beforehand.

We must, however, draw a clear line between what God foreordains and what God personally does, otherwise the Almighty will have to bear sole responsibility for every crime in history.[15] There is a clear difference between,

15. This echoes the distinction (used, for example, by John Calvin) between remote and proximate causality. See Carl Trueman and R. S. Clark, eds., *Protestant Scholasticism: Essays in Reassessment* (Carlisle, UK: Paternoster, 1999), 55.

for example, the agency of God in the crucifixion of Jesus and his agency in the resurrection. The resurrection was an immediate, supernatural divine act. God raised him from the dead without any created means or agency. It was an act of pure divine power using no secondary causes. But in the crucifixion, as Peter makes clear, human agency stood in the foreground. It was not God who betrayed Jesus or flogged him or spat on him or nailed him to the cross. On the contrary, "his own people" (John 1:10) had handed him over to "men without law" (*anomōn*; Acts 2:23), and it was they who violently abused him and nailed him to the cross. That their action was foreordained by God did not absolve them of moral responsibility. It was a sin, a malicious and barbaric abuse of power, which is why Jesus prays, "Father, forgive them" (Luke 23:34).

Not only is there human agency here; there is also satanic agency. The cross was the hour when darkness reigned (Luke 22:53): hell at its most foul and most violent, but also at its most maddened and insane, blind to the fact that the cross would be its destruction.

We find, then, God fulfilling his purposes through three agencies: the willing self-surrender of his Son, the malice of men, and the fury of hell. What Paul calls the "curse of the law" (Gal. 3:13) and Calvin described as "the terrible torments of a condemned and forsaken man"[16] were administered through a corrupt human judiciary and a malignant devil. The "wrath" was not a factor additional to his circumstances. It was *in* his circumstances, not only in their horrific cruelty but also in the fact that he had been abandoned to them and that when he cried to his Father, there was no response. No relief came, nor any answering voice. He was forsaken in his circumstances, as foreshadowed in Psalm 22:2, with no sense of the Father's love, presence, or approbation—and perhaps (if only momentarily) no understanding of the "Why?"

God, then, did not merely foreordain the sufferings of his Son; he delivered him up to them, and he forsook him in them. Yet the Father did not hand him over unreservedly. "Crucifixion," Martin Hengel remarks, "was a punishment in which the caprice and sadism of the executioners was given full rein."[17] In the case of Jesus, however, and without in any way diminishing his sufferings, it is clear that the executioners were not permitted to do their worst. He died relatively quickly, and in the moment of his dying, his great atoning act was completed, as is indicated in the cry, "*Tetelestai!*"

---

16. Calvin, *Institutes* 2.16.10.

17. Martin Hengel, *Crucifixion in the Ancient World and the Folly of the Message of the Cross* (Philadelphia: Fortress, 1977), 25.

Here, therefore, the humiliation of Christ ends, and with his last breath his exaltation begins. The Father says, "Enough!," and so not a bone is broken (John 19:36), his body is lovingly anointed and reverently entombed, and death is told that though it may briefly hold him, it can work no corruption. Above all, death was not allowed to detain him. The loving, adoring Father, struck with the glory of his Son's obedience, brings him back to life, raises him up, and seats him in the heavenlies (Eph. 2:5–6). He places that humanity, so abused by men, in the glory the Son had with the Father before the world was (John 17:5).

At the heart of the cross lies the death of the immortal. Here the blood of God is shed, and here the Son of God tastes death (Heb. 2:9). But as in every outgoing act of the Trinity, all three persons are involved. The pain of the Son cannot, therefore, be external to God the Father. They are one and the same in being (*homoousioi*), and in each the other dwells (John 14:10).[18] The affliction of the Son is the affliction of the Three, though of each in his own way. The Father was not crucified, nor was he made a curse, yet it is to him that the New Testament characteristically traces back the cost of Calvary, as if it were of *his* love that the cross speaks above all. But how, if he felt it not at all? If he has compassion for us, his children (Ps. 103), had he no pity for his Son? Did he not long to intervene as he did in the case of Abraham, and cry, "Don't lay a hand on the boy!"?

The greatest indictment of sin is that even the divine love and wisdom could save the world only at the cost of God sacrificing his own Son. It was, indeed, a free and loving initiative, yet once it was embarked on, the sacrifice became a necessity. There was no other way. The cup could not pass (Mark 14:35), and it was a sacrifice for both the Father and the Son. They went up, "both of them together" (Gen. 22:6, 8), not as helpless victims of an unavoidable destiny but as divine persons who had covenanted together to share the cost of saving the world and were now walking together toward the pain. For the Son, there was the pain of laying down his life; for the Father, the pain was of not sparing him and having to turn a deaf ear to his anguished cry. Yet it was through such shared pain that God disarmed and disgraced the powers of darkness. At the very point where he provides an atonement for sin, he exposes it at its most barbaric and ridiculous. "Oh, the depth of the riches of the wisdom and knowledge of God!" (Rom. 11:33).[19]

18. This fact is reflected in the classic patristic doctrine of *enperichōrēsis*, from the Greek *chōreō* ("I dwell").

19. I have addressed this question in a little more detail in the chapter, "Can God Suffer?," in Donald Macleod, *Behold Your God*, rev. and exp. ed. (Fearn, UK: Christian Focus, 1995), 31–38.

Models and Metaphors

Is it not the case, however, that what we have in the New Testament is not one coherent doctrine of the atonement but a variety of models and metaphors that is impossible to reduce to any sort of unity?

Part of the response to this must be that the concept of "model" is ill-adapted to theological use. It suits the naval architect who wants to see a three-dimensional scale model of what he has designed, and it suits the geneticist who wants to see a visible representation of the DNA molecule (the famous double helix). But the very point of such models is visibility, and theology does not deal with visibles. The closest we have to a model of the atonement is the Lord's supper, but this is far removed from what the concept means to an engineer.

However, it is true that some of the key concepts used in the doctrine of the atonement involve significant elements of metaphor. For example, the idea of expiation is linked to the idea of covering (from the Hebrew *kipper*, "to cover"). Such ideas as reconciliation and propitiation (placating) are familiar to us from interpersonal relationships; the idea of redemption had close links to the manumission of slaves and the ransoming of prisoners of war; and the portrayal of the cross as a victory clearly deploys a military metaphor.

It is sometimes suggested that the "penal substitution theory" draws on only one metaphor, expiation, and ignores the others.[20] But whether we think of Anselm, Luther, Calvin, or their successors, all proposed a doctrine of the atonement that incorporates all the "metaphors." If the idea of expiation seems unduly prominent, this is because it is the idea that has attracted most attack. We must also note, however, that expiation is the foundation on which all the other metaphors stand. It is by expiating sin that the cross propitiates God and reconciles him to sinners; it is by the expiation of sin that we are redeemed from the curse of the law; and it is by the expiation of sin that Christ secures his victory over the devil.

Victory

The clearest statement of this link between expiation and victory is given in Hebrews 2:14–15, where the writer speaks of Christ as destroying, through death, the one who had the power of death. Gustav Aulèn, in his influential

---

20. We should note in passing that a "model" that draws on only one metaphor cannot be a "model" at all. The whole point of a model is that it gives multidimensional expression to a design or idea.

book *Christus Victor*,[21] argued that the Western church, apart from Luther, abandoned the "classic" view of the atonement as a conquering of sin, death, and the devil, and replaced it with the very different concept of the atonement as a juridical satisfaction to divine justice. Yet in post-Reformation thought the one concept was never adopted to the exclusion of the other. The idea of the cross as a victory is clearly present in, for example, Calvin's commentary on Hebrews 2:14–15, where he states that "not only has the tyranny of Satan been broken by the death of Christ, but that the devil himself has been laid so low as to be of no more account."[22] It is interesting too that while in later (post-1539) editions of the *Institutes* Calvin writes of a threefold office of Christ as prophet, priest, and king, in the first edition (1536) he refers only to a twofold office of priest and king.[23]

It is precisely this twofold office that is implied in Hebrews 2:14–18, and both are closely linked to his assumption of human nature. In verse 17 Christ is said to have been "made like" his brothers and sisters in all things "in order that he might become a merciful and faithful high priest" (NIV); according to verse 14, he took flesh and blood "so that by death he might destroy him who holds the power of death" (my translation). Here the two offices are inextricably linked. It is by means of his priestly act of atonement that the king destroys the devil. The expiation of sin delivers the fatal blow to the devil's kingdom, depriving him of the power to take "the children" (v. 13) down to hell with him. Far from being antitheses, the expiation "metaphor" and the victory "metaphor" are interlocked as complementary elements in one great act of reconciliation and atonement. This is why the great nineteenth-century Scottish theologian Hugh Martin could describe the cross as simultaneously "an altar of priestly agency" and "a chariot of victory and triumph."[24]

Is it possible to put any detail on this concept of the cross as victory?

First, Satan is no longer the prince of this world. He has been driven out (John 12:31), and in Revelation 20:1 (assuming a nonmillennial interpretation) he is already bound with a great chain. This may sound like an extremely rash claim in view of the evil that still stalks the world. But the immediate import of the chain is made clear in verse 3: he deceives the nations no more. It would be foolish to pretend that the passage presents no exegetical difficulties, but

21. Gustav Aulén, *Christus Victor: An Historical Study of the Three Main Types of the Idea of the Atonement*, trans. A. G. Herbert (London: SPCK, 1965), chaps. 5, 7.

22. Calvin, *The Epistle of Paul the Apostle*, 31.

23. John Calvin, *Institutes of the Christian Religion, 1536 Edition*, ed. and trans. Ford Lewis Battles, rev. ed. (Grand Rapids: Eerdmans, 1986), 2.14.

24. Hugh Martin, *The Atonement: In Its Relations to the Covenant, the Priesthood, the Intercession of Our Lord* (Edinburgh: Banner of Truth, 2013), 55.

there is good reason to believe that "the nations" are the gentiles and that the passage is pointing to a new, post–Old Testament age in which God fulfills his promise to Abraham that in him all the nations of the earth would be blessed (Gen. 22:18). It was to these same gentiles that Paul alluded when he spoke of being sent "to open their eyes and turn them . . . from the power of Satan to God" (Acts 26:18 NIV). Above all, it was to them that the Lord sent the apostles when he commissioned them to make disciples of "all nations" (again, *ta ethnē*; Matt. 28:19). From this perspective, the great presupposition of all Christian mission is that Satan is bound and can no longer claim the entire non-Jewish world as his own. Millions of gentiles have already turned from darkness to light (Acts 26:18), and there are millions more still to come.

Second, following the triumph of Christ, the world is now under new governance. The Son of God, crucified in weakness, has been installed as Son of God with power (Rom. 1:4), occupies the center of the throne (Rev. 5:6), and exercises universal dominion (Matt. 28:18). This is why, in the words of Abraham Kuyper, "There is not a square inch in the whole domain of human existence over which Christ, who is Sovereign Lord of *all*, does not cry, 'Mine!'"[25]

Granted, the end is not yet: we are still waiting for the new heaven and the new earth (Rev. 21:1). But we may well avail ourselves of Oscar Cullmann's famous analogy between the climax of salvation history and the climax of World War II.[26] VE-Day (Victory in Europe Day) came on May 8, 1945, but the decisive moment had come almost a year earlier, on D-Day (June 6, 1944), when the Allied Forces established themselves on the mainland of Europe. There was much fighting to follow, and still much opposition to overcome, and there would be moments when stout hearts almost failed. But the decisive victory had been won.

It is so with the all-conquering Redeemer. His archenemy may still rage, and pandemonium still seems unsubdued. But he is a bound devil, already chained to Christ's triumphal car (Col. 2:15). His empire is doomed (Jude 6).

A Merely External Righteousness?

Does the doctrine of penal substitution, with its concomitant doctrine of an imputed righteousness, not lead to an understanding of salvation as something

25. Quoted in John Bolt, *A Free Church, A Holy Nation: Abraham Kuyper's American Public Theology* (Grand Rapids: Eerdmans, 2001), 21.

26. Oscar Cullmann: "The decisive battle in a war may already have occurred at a relatively early stage of the war, and yet the war still continues" (*Christ and Time*, rev. ed. [London: SCM, 1962], 84).

that leaves the sinner unchanged—forgiven (in the legal sense) but in no way transformed?

The criticism is made explicitly by Joel Green and Mark Baker, who claim that in terms of the penal substitution "model," all that changes is a legal ruling: "an individual could be saved through penal substitution without experiencing a fundamental reorientation of his or her life."[27] A similar point is made, though from a different perspective, by T. F. Torrance: "In Western Christianity the atonement tends to be interpreted almost exclusively in terms of external forensic relations as a judicial transaction in the transference of the penalty for sin from the sinner to the sin-bearer."[28]

The first response to this must be that the idea of a forensic righteousness is not to be dismissed lightly. It is, after all, what Paul meant by "justification," and it was to it that Luther referred when he declared that "if the article of justification is lost, the whole of Christian doctrine is lost."[29] Nor is the idea of "external" righteousness to be readily abandoned. It is neither more nor less than the *iustitia aliena* (the righteousness of another) that lay at the very heart of Reformation theology. Tried on our own record, we have no hope of acquittal but face certain condemnation. Only "in Christ" are we righteous (2 Cor. 5:21), and his righteousness is always an alternative to our own (Phil. 3:9).

We would do well, then, to heed Emil Brunner's warning that "it is no sign of great fidelity to the Scriptures nor of a deep understanding of Christian truth to think that we can attack any dogmatic formulae simply by using the word 'forensic' as a term of reproach."[30] Our relation to the law, and to God as Judge, matters, and there are only two possible ways by which we can be right with God. Either we can put God in *our* debt (by our own personal righteousness), or we can put ourselves in *his* debt (by accepting his free gift of justification; Rom. 3:24).

Yet the forensic can never be disjoined from the transformational and ontological, which then leaves us with the questions: What is the relation between them? How does the work of Christ bear on sanctification?

One possibility is the doctrine of incarnational redemption proposed by Thomas Torrance: Christ by his assumption of human nature and by his obedient life sanctified humanity, transforming it internally and ontologically.

27. Green and Baker, *Recovering the Scandal of the Cross*, 149.
28. Thomas F. Torrance, *The Mediation of Christ* (Grand Rapids: Eerdmans, 1983), 50.
29. Martin Luther, *Lectures on Galatians, 1535, Chapters 1–4*, ed. Walter A. Hansen, vol. 26 of *Luther's Works* (St. Louis: Concordia, 1963), 9.
30. Emil Brunner, *The Mediator: A Study of the Central Doctrine of the Christian Faith*, trans. Olive Wyon (London: Lutterworth, 1934), 466.

"From his birth to his death and resurrection on our behalf," Torrance writes, "he sanctified what he assumed through his own self-consecration as the incarnate Son to the Father."[31]

The immediate problem with this is that "our fallen and estranged humanity" (to use another of Torrance's phrases) is an abstraction: the essence of humanity, not actual humans. If Christ by his incarnation (including his incarnate life) sanctified humanity, does this mean that he completely undid the results of the fall and that everyone is born sanctified? Does it mean, as Torrance suggests, that all humans were born again at the cross of Calvary, and that all share in the baptism with the Holy Spirit experienced by Christ at his baptism in the Jordan?

The facts do not bear it out. Christ's own individual humanity was created holy, but there is not the least evidence that post-nativity humanity in general differs radically from pre-nativity humanity in general; nor is there any evidence that every human was sanctified by the incarnation. Judas Iscariot was certainly not "healed" when Jesus assumed human nature in the womb of the Virgin. Besides, there is the wider issue that the sanctification of human nature as such would logically imply the universal salvation of humanity as such. This is not a step Scripture allows us to take, nor was it a step Torrance himself was prepared to take (any more than was his mentor, Barth).

Let us return, then, to penal substitution. Is its impact limited to merely changing our external, forensic relations with God? Most emphatically not! The New Testament repeatedly emphasizes the link between the cross and sanctification. As we have already seen, the crucifixion is set within "God's set purpose" (Acts 2:23), and the heart of that purpose is exposed to us in Romans 8:29 (NIV): "those God foreknew he also predestined to be conformed to the likeness of his Son." The cross has to be seen within this purpose, focused not only on expiating sin but also on transforming sinners. It was in pursuit of this purpose that God, "his Son not sparing," delivered him up "for" us all. In accordance with this, Paul later points to a direct link between the self-sacrifice of Christ and the sanctification of the church. He died not only to redeem it by his blood (Eph. 1:6) but also to make it holy, to cleanse it, and to present it to himself as a radiant church without stain or blemish (Eph. 5:26–27).

And as a further link in the chain we have the direct connection between the substitutionary suffering of Christ and the ministry of the Holy Spirit. Christ became a curse "for" us (Gal. 3:13). But why? Not merely to redeem us from the curse of the law, immensely important though that was, but to

31. Torrance, *Mediation of Christ*, 50.

secure for gentiles "the blessing given to Abraham." And what was that blessing? The promise of the Spirit (Gal. 3:14)! The cross, as forensic, reconciles us to God, and the immediate consequence of that restored relationship is the ministry of the Holy Spirit, a ministry received by the very same faith that justifies (Gal. 3:2). It is this ministry that bears in the lives of Christians the fruit described by Paul in Galatians 5:22–23 (NASB): "love, joy, peace, patience, kindness, goodness, faithfulness, gentleness, and self-control." The communion with God that was lost in the fall is restored in the reconciliation secured by the substitutionary suffering of Christ, and the Holy Spirit returns to his long-desolate temple.

Underlying all this is the doctrine of union with Christ: not merely an external, federal union but an intimate, spiritual one. Only "in Christ," only as members of his body, are we justified. But equally, we cannot be "in Christ" without also being transformed: vivified, empowered, and ennobled by his Holy Spirit.

Union with Christ—crucified, risen, and indwelling—always means, as John Calvin insisted, a *duplex gratia*: the inseparable graces of justification and sanctification.[32] Indeed, there is a *triplex gratia*, because we must also add adoption, again directly traceable to the cross (Gal. 4:5).

Here, in union with Christ, there is no possibility of a salvation that does not transform. And there is no possibility of cheap grace received by a faith divorced from repentance. Here, the man who was dead in sin dies. Here the new man rises to a vibrant life.

---

32. Calvin, *Institutes* 3.11.1: "By partaking of him, we principally receive a double grace: namely, that being reconciled to God through Christ's blamelessness, we may have in heaven instead of a Judge a gracious Father; and secondly, that sanctified by Christ's Spirit we may cultivate blamelessness and purity of life."

12

The Work of Christ Applied

RICHARD GAFFIN

First, we must understand that as long as Christ remains outside of us, and we are separated from him, all that he has suffered and done for the salvation of the human race remains useless and of no value to us.

John Calvin[1]

Without application, redemption is not redemption.

Herman Bavinck[2]

In his state of exaltation there still remains much for Christ to do.

Herman Bavinck[3]

1. John Calvin, *Institutes of the Christian Religion*, ed. John T. McNeill, trans. Ford Lewis Battles (Philadelphia: Westminster, 1960), 3.1.1.

2. Herman Bavinck, "*Dempta applicatione, redemptio non est redemptio*"; quoted without attribution in Bavinck, *Gereformeerde Dogmatiek* (Kampen: Kok, 1976), 3:520; the English translation (see note 3), 523–24, varies slightly.

3. Herman Bavinck, *Reformed Dogmatics*, ed. J. Bolt, trans. J. Vriend, 4 vols. (Grand Rapids: Baker Academic, 2003–8), 3:568.

The Work of Christ Applied as the Work of Christ

Reformed theology, this volume included, characteristically considers the work of Christ applied together with the work of Christ accomplished. Further, Christ's work applied is addressed as Christ is the eternal Son of God become man—true God and true man, "in two distinct natures, and one person, forever"[4]—and the only mediator between God and sinners, the savior-redeemer of his people, the elect given him from eternity (1 Tim. 2:5–6; Eph. 1:4).

Treatments of this mediatorial activity are sometimes structured in terms of Christ's threefold office of prophet, priest, and king, exercised in his states of humiliation and exaltation. The former state begins at the incarnation and continues through his death and remaining dead for a time. The latter begins with his resurrection and ensuing ascension to his present heavenly session, continuing until his future return for final judgment, and will last forever (Phil. 2:6–11; Heb. 9:26–28).

Within this overall framework,[5] the work of Christ applied may be profitably considered as *the work of Christ in his state of exaltation*. This will be the vantage point explored in this chapter. The work of Christ applied involves his own distinctive activity. In his glorified state Christ's work consists primarily in his ongoing application to his people, individually and corporately, of the salvation accomplished for them, once for all, both in his state of humiliation and, as we will see, in his state of exaltation.

Redemption applied is often seen as the work of the Holy Spirit in distinction from redemption accomplished as the work of Christ. This viewpoint has some validity, for in applying Christ's finished work, the Spirit is active in a preeminent and unprecedented way. A liability, however, attaches to this way of distinguishing. On the one hand, it can lead to minimizing the important work of the Spirit during Christ's earthly ministry and his work accomplished then. On the other hand, it can obscure that, as expressed by Bavinck above, "in the state of exaltation there still remains much for Christ to do."

The "it is finished" of the cross (John 19:30) is true—decisively, preciously true. Atonement for sin has been made and does not need to be repeated. The work of propitiating sin is complete. It is surely difficult, then, to overstate the truth of this dying declaration. Still, in all its momentous significance, its truth is not absolute but relative—relative in particular to the considerable work that remains for the exalted Christ.

---

4. Westminster Shorter Catechism, A. 21.
5. Captured with admirable succinctness and clarity in Westminster Shorter Catechism, 21–29. These distinctions (in terms of offices and states) are valid and helpful as they can be shown to arise from the text of Scripture and are not made to function as a grid imposed on the text.

270 Richard Gaffin

Of course, God the Father is also integrally involved in salvation applied (e.g., Acts 2:32–36; Gal. 1:1). God is one, and the activities distinctive to each of the three persons related to creation and redemption are undivided. Still, only the Son—neither the Father nor the Spirit—is the mediator, and that mediatorial role involves his singular and indispensable centrality for salvation—not only in its accomplishment but also its application.

Historia Salutis and Ordo Salutis

Consideration of the application of salvation is largely concerned with the *ordo salutis* (order of salvation), so much so that the *ordo salutis* and *historia salutis* are often viewed as virtually coterminous. The order of salvation has in view (1) that the application of the salvation accomplished by Christ has a fullness marked by multiple elements or aspects, and (2) that these are not received as an arbitrary or chaotic mix but in a set pattern with fixed connections among them. The failure to recognize the existence of such a pattern with its interrelationships runs the risk of misrepresenting individual aspects or acts and so distorting the work of Christ applied as a whole.[6]

In his important work on the theology of Paul, Herman Ridderbos has coined the Latin *historia salutis* (history of salvation) to contrast with *ordo salutis* to show that Paul's controlling interest is the former, not the latter.[7] In other words, for Ridderbos, Paul's central concern is the once-for-all accomplishment of salvation, not its ongoing application.

The expression *historia salutis* is useful particularly because it serves to highlight not only that salvation is historical, not to be sought above or beyond time, but also that Christ's work in history is not to be considered by itself, more or less in isolation. Rather, his work is the culmination of the history that began already at the fall (Gen. 3:15) and continues, incorporating in its unfolding the history of Israel, God's covenant people, until Christ's coming in "the fullness of time" (Gal. 4:4). The salvation revealed in Christ is nothing less than the "last days" climax of that long redemptive or covenant history (Heb. 1:1–2a). As we will see, it is paramount to keep in view

6. Assuming the secondary sources are correct, the first occurrence of the technical term *ordo salutis* in this sense is in the eighteenth century within emerging pietism, from where it is taken over and becomes widely current in both Lutheran and Reformed orthodoxy.
7. The distinction first appears in Herman Ridderbos, "The Redemptive-Historical Character of Paul's Preaching," in *When the Time Had Fully Come: Studies in New Testament Theology* (Grand Rapids: Eerdmans, 1957), 48–49; it occurs repeatedly in idem, *Paul: An Outline of His Theology*, trans. J. de Witt (Grand Rapids: Eerdmans, 1975), e.g., 14, 45, 63, 91.

the redemptive-historical, eschatological nature of Christ's work and what it entails for a sound understanding of its ongoing application.

An Essential Distinction

The distinction between salvation accomplished and applied may appear to be self-evident. That is certainly the case for the theology that flows from the Reformation, including Lutheran and Reformed orthodoxy. More recently, however, it has been challenged, a challenge that needs to be addressed, because—this does not put it too strongly—the integrity of the gospel itself stands or falls with maintaining this distinction, as the first of the Herman Bavinck quotes above indicates.

What is at stake here can be seen by considering briefly Karl Barth's rejection of both this very distinction and of the *ordo salutis* itself as found in Protestant orthodoxy.[8] His dismissal, probably the most influential to date, turns on his idea of *Geschichte* ("historicity" or "historicness"), involving the undivided contemporaneity of salvation as a single event, the radical simultaneity of all its aspects (in this sense often termed "the Christ-event").

This notion excludes the distinction between accomplishment and application. It has no place for a finished salvation accomplished in history two thousand years ago and as such having its own integrity yet distinct from its ongoing appropriation. Accordingly, Barth rejects the idea of an *ordo salutis*, maintaining that it leads inevitably to psychologizing and individualizing distortions of Christian existence.

Furthermore, as Barth's idea of *Geschichte* leaves no room for the accomplishment/application distinction, it involves a radical recasting of the work of Christ. Significantly, it excludes that a temporal sequence between the two states of Christ is determinative for salvation. Barth denies that their saving efficacy resides in the fact of their historical before and after, and that in history Christ's exaltation followed his humiliation.[9] He sees, quite rightly, that the distinction between accomplishment and application is given with the historical sequence of humiliation followed by exaltation. To affirm or deny the latter is to affirm or deny the former; they stand or fall together.

8. Karl Barth, *Church Dogmatics* IV/2, ed. G. W. Bromiley and T. F. Torrance (Edinburgh: T&T Clark, 1958), 502–3; and IV/3, 505–6.

9. Barth, *Church Dogmatics* IV/2, 502. Correlatively, Barth denies as well the historicity of the fall in the sense of the historical sequence of creation (a time of original beatitude at the beginning of human history where sin was not yet present) and fall; e.g., "There never was a golden age. There is no point in looking back to one. The first man was immediately the first sinner" (*Church Dogmatics* IV/1, 508).

This view, it should be clear, involves a radical departure from biblical revelation, one that strikes at the very heart of the gospel. Christ's state of exaltation is separate from and subsequent to his state of humiliation; his being "highly exalted" and "given the name above every name" follows, temporally, his "obedience unto death" (Phil. 2:8–9). Christ, having become incarnate in history, for a definite time in the past endured and satisfied God's just wrath on the sins of his people, but now, subsequently and permanently, for all eternity future, is no longer under God's wrath but restored to his favor under conditions of eschatological life. If that is not the case, then, as Cornelius Van Til, for one, has pointed out in critiquing Barth's theology, "there is no transition from wrath to grace in history."[10]

But if in Christ that transition has not taken place, then his people are still in their sins (1 Cor. 15:17). The gospel, the salvation of sinners, stands or falls with the historical before and after of Christ's humiliation and exaltation. This *is* the gospel at its core (what is "of first importance"), as 1 Corinthians 15:3–4, for one, makes clear.

Accordingly, with that before and after, with the historical sequence from the one state to the other, is given the irreducible distinction between redemption accomplished and applied, between *historia salutis* and *ordo salutis*, where neither one may be allowed to diminish or eclipse the other. The question of application, of the *ordo salutis* and what constitutes it, may not be dismissed: How does the then-and-there of Christ's transition from wrath to favor relate to the here-and-now of the sinner's transition from wrath to grace? How do Christ's death and subsequent resurrection, then and there, benefit sinners here and now? What are those benefits, and what is the pattern (*ordo*) in which they are communicated to sinners? This is the controlling question in considering the work of Christ applied, the work of Christ in his state of exaltation.

Salvation Applied (the Ordo Salutis) and Sin

Salvation evidently has no meaning apart from sin. The gospel is not good news apart from the bad news of human sin. Salvation applied is more than negative in this sense, but it is at least and essentially that. We will be clear about salvation and its application only as we are clear about sin and its consequences. To the extent we are unclear about sin and its gravity, we will be unclear about salvation and its glory.

10. Cornelius Van Til, *Christianity and Barthianism* (Philadelphia: P&R, 1962), vii; the same observation is made by G. C. Berkouwer, *The Triumph of Grace in the Theology of Karl Barth* (Grand Rapids: Eerdmans, 1956), 257, 380; cf. also 234–36, 370.

Summarized briefly for our purposes, sin is *theocentric* and *relational*; it is primarily against God and then, derivatively, against humans, including the self. Sin is essentially hostility toward God, the image-bearing creature's rebellious renunciation of fellowship with God as creator. Inevitably, then, sin is idolatrous, the exchange of "the truth of God for a lie," consisting in worshiping and serving "the creature rather than the Creator" (Rom. 1:25). Sin is the rejection of God's will and the failure to delight in what pleases him. In this sense, sin is *illegal*, "any want of conformity unto, or transgression of, the law of God."[11]

Sin, further, is *universal*; Jew as well as non-Jew, "all have sinned" (Rom. 3:23; 5:12). That is so not only because inevitably all humans actually sin but also because, in union with Adam and by natural descent from him as their representative, all enter the world accountable for his first transgression and with an inborn disposition to sin, which is itself sinful and therefore culpable (Rom. 5:12–19). Scripture knows of no sin, whether as imputed, innate disposition, or actual commission, that does not entail guilt as well as liability for its consequences.[12]

The destructive results of sin are virtually incalculable. Still, as we consider the full misery of human sin, it is important to recognize that all of its consequences are basically twofold. First, sin affects the sinner's *status* before God; it renders sinners *guilty*, liable to his just judgment and condemnation. Second, it affects the *condition* of the sinner; it leaves sinners thoroughly *corrupt and enslaved* to Satan and sin as the power that dominates their lives. The depth of their sinful state is such that all sinners, left to themselves apart from God's saving grace, are nothing less than "dead in . . . transgressions and sins" (Eph. 2:1, 5). In sum, sin renders the sinner inexcusably guilty and helplessly enslaved.

"But where sin abounded, grace abounded much more" (Rom. 5:20 NKJV). The extensive effects of sin are surpassed by the even more abundant benefits of salvation applied. At the same time, in all their fullness, these benefits have a corresponding twofold profile as they redress the fundamentally twofold effect of sin. Expressed in terms of the elements usually considered in the *ordo salutis*, there are those benefits that concern the sinner's *status* before God—*judicial* (or legal or forensic) benefits. These are *justification* and *adoption*. In distinction from these benefits are those that concern the sinner's personal *condition—re-creative* (or renovative,

---

11. The language of Westminster Shorter Catechism, A. 14.

12. See the summary of the aspects constituting human sinfulness in Westminster Shorter Catechism, A. 18.

transforming) benefits. These, prominently, are *effectual calling, regenera-tion*, and *sanctification*.[13]

All these benefits—judicial and re-creative—take effect instantaneously at the initial moment of application, when the sinner passes from being under God's just wrath to being a recipient of his saving grace; now God is no longer the sinner's condemning judge but merciful Father. The ongoing state that stems from this first moment further includes *perseverance* toward *glorifica-tion*. All these benefits are ultimately, from beginning to end, the sovereign, self-sufficient work of God.

Insofar as that working also engages the sinner's response and activity it involves *repentance* and *faith*—turning from sin to Christ (*conversion*), and since repentant faith stems from the new disposition, a heart for God at the core of the sinner's being given by regeneration, it results in a life necessarily marked, however imperfectly, by *obedience* ("faith working through love"; Gal. 5:6; cf. Eph. 2:10).

Surveying or even summarizing the extensive discussion that each of these elements of salvation in the *ordo salutis* has received is beyond the scope of this chapter.[14] Here the reader's basic familiarity with the elements just enumerated will be assumed for the most part as in light of the preceding observations. We turn first to consider the application of salvation as the work of Christ in his state of exaltation and then to give some attention to several matters of overall importance for the *ordo salutis* and how various elements within it are related to one another.

The Exaltation of Christ and the Work of Christ Applied

Essential for the work of Christ in his state of exaltation in applying what he accomplished in his state of humiliation is the significance of the exalta-tion for Christ personally. What was done for and in him in being exalted qualifies him for his ongoing activity as exalted (Heb. 7:16). In that regard, what especially needs to be considered is the relationship between Christ and the Holy Spirit that results from his resurrection. This new relationship has two basic aspects. These are inseparable yet distinguishable in terms of the twofold profile—judicial and renovative—on the benefits of salvation applied.

---

13. Adoption is overarching, both a forensic and a transformative reality. For the latter aspect, see the discussion of Rom. 8:29 toward the close of this chapter.

14. Numerous valuable resources are available. Among these in Reformed theology I es-pecially commend, in the following reading order: John Murray, *Redemption: Accomplished and Applied* (Grand Rapids: Eerdmans, 1955), 93–224; and Bavinck, *Reformed Dogmatics*, 3:483–595 and 4:27–270.

Justified in the Spirit

Christ's resurrection has forensic significance for him personally.[15] The contrasting parallelism between Adam and Christ in Romans 5:12–19 makes clear that on the one side, human death is not a normal natural phenomenon but has judicial significance; sin incurs God's just condemnation resulting in death. Accordingly, on the other side of the contrast, life, antithetical to death, likewise has judicial significance. Specifically, Christ brings "justification of life" (v. 18 NKJV). "Eternal life" in verse 21 as well as parallel statements in 1 Corinthians 15:21–22 show that this life derives from his resurrection. Whether "justification of life" means that justification consists in resurrection life as de facto justification, or, alternatively, that it is the consequence of justification, the life in view is inalienably forensic.

The judicial import of Christ's resurrection enters the argument of Romans earlier in the summary statement of 4:25, "who was delivered up for our trespasses and was raised for our justification." Here a direct connection is drawn from Christ's resurrection to justification. How is that so? As the representative sin bearer and righteous substitute (Rom. 3:25; 8:3; 2 Cor. 5:21), in his full life of obedience culminating in his death (Phil. 2:8), Christ's resurrection is his own justification in the sense that the resurrection is God's de facto declarative recognition, on the ground of that obedience, of his righteousness (cf. 1 Cor. 1:30). As an event, his resurrection "speaks," and it does so judicially, in a legal manner.

Confirming this is 1 Timothy 3:16, where Christ is described as "manifested in the flesh, justified in the Spirit." This almost certainly has in view the Holy Spirit's activity in raising Jesus from the dead (cf. Rom. 8:11), as the response warranted by the righteousness manifested in his obedience "in the flesh" during his earthly life prior to the resurrection.[16]

Christ's own resurrection-justification is not merely or even primarily for his own sake but "for our justification." Just how his justification becomes ours we will consider below, except to note here that Christ's justification, unlike that of Christians, does not involve the imputation to him of the righteousness of another. The ground of his being declared righteous, unlike theirs, is his own righteousness.

---

15. The following comments adapt material from Richard Gaffin, *By Faith, Not by Sight: Paul and the Order of Salvation*, 2nd ed. (Phillipsburg, NJ: P&R, 2013), esp. 97–98.

16. Many translations have "vindicated" instead of "justified." But there is no need or compelling reason to abandon "justified," the sense the verb almost always has elsewhere. The same is true for the King James Version (KJV), American Standard Version (ASV), and NKJV. "Shown to be righteous" (New Living Translation [NLT]) also gets at the sense.

Life-Giving Spirit

"The last Adam became life-giving Spirit" (1 Cor. 15:45). Though the meaning of this statement is disputed, in particular whether the reference of the
Greek noun *pneuma* is to the Spirit or to "spirit" in some other sense, detailed
exegesis leaves little doubt, if any, that (1) it refers to the person of the Holy
Spirit, and (2) Christ's resurrection is the time of "becoming" in view.[17] Further, within the immediate context (vv. 42–49), the last Adam, as resurrected,
is also in view as ascended. He is "the second man . . . from heaven" (v. 47)[18]
and in that sense, "the man of heaven" (v. 48).

Expressed here, then, is the momentous, epochal significance of his exaltation for Christ personally. His own climactic transformation by the Spirit in
his resurrection results is a new and permanent relationship between them,
a functional unity in their activity of such closeness, that it is captured most
adequately by saying he has become "the life-giving Spirit."

This is not to deny that prior to the resurrection the Spirit was present and
at work with Christ. Now, however, dating from his resurrection and as he
is ascended, their joint life-giving action is given its stable and consummate
basis in the history of redemption (*historia salutis*). Now, at last, such action
is a crowning consequence of the work of the incarnate Christ actually and
definitively accomplished in history.

While the immediate context has in view primarily Christ's future life-giving
action by the Spirit in the bodily resurrection of believers (cf. 1 Cor. 15:22,
49; Rom. 8:11), his present activity is surely intimated as well. His resurrection is not an isolated event in the past but the inaugurating "firstfruits" of
the eschatological resurrection harvest (1 Cor. 15:20, 23), so that for believers
their place in that harvest is present as well as future. Christ, as resurrected,
is already active in the church in the resurrection power of the Spirit. The

17. For an extensive treatment of this statement, see Richard Gaffin, "The Last Adam,
the Life-Giving Spirit," in *The Forgotten Christ: Exploring the Majesty and Mystery of God
Incarnate*, ed. Stephen Clark (Nottingham, UK: Apollos, 2007), 191–231.

Apparently, most English translations have "spirit" (lowercase) because to capitalize it, as the
reference to the Holy Spirit requires, seems to lend credence to an antitrinitarian reading. But
it is entirely unwarranted to find here a denial of the personal distinction between Christ and
the Spirit irreconcilable with later church formulation of trinitarian doctrine. The scope, the
salvation-historical focus, of the argument in this context needs to be kept in view. The point is
not who Christ is essentially—eternally and unchangeably—but what he "became" historically
as "the last Adam" and "the second man" (1 Cor. 15:47); in view is what has happened to him
in history as incarnate, in terms of his true humanity. Cf. in the same sense, "the Lord is the
Spirit" (2 Cor. 3:17), where in context "the Lord" is almost certainly the exalted Christ. The
"is" in this statement is based on and is the result of "became" in 1 Cor. 15:45.

18. Given the immediate context, "from heaven" is almost certainly an exaltation predicate,
not a reference to Christ's origin, say, out of preexistence at the incarnation.

resurrection life of the believer, in union with Christ, is not only future but present (e.g., Gal. 2:20; Col. 2:12–13; 3:1–4). Inwardly, at the core of their being, believers are already resurrected, while outwardly, bodily, they are not yet resurrected (cf. 2 Cor. 4:16).

Pentecost

The latter part of 1 Corinthians 15:45 is, in effect, a one-sentence commentary on Pentecost and its significance. Toward the conclusion of Peter's Pentecost sermon, its focus on the earthly activity, death, and especially the resurrection of Jesus (Acts 2:22–31) leads to the following culminating sequence (Acts 2:32–33): resurrection, ascension, reception of the Spirit, outpouring of the Spirit. The last of these events, Pentecost, is linked with the others; it is in view as it belongs together with them. Pentecost is climactic and final on the order that they are and as such is no more in need of being repeated than they are. Resurrection, ascension, and Pentecost, though temporally distinct, constitute a unified complex of events, a once-for-all, unified series in redemptive history, such that they are indivisible; the one is given with the others. In 1 Corinthians 15:45 this unified event complex is compressed and given its central focus.

The sequence in Acts speaks of Jesus having received the Spirit following his ascension (2:33). How is this reception to be understood since Luke has previously reported that Jesus already received the Spirit at the Jordan when he was baptized by John (Luke 3:22) and that he was conceived by the Spirit (Luke 1:35), so that throughout his ministry prior to his resurrection he was filled and empowered by the Spirit (Luke 4:1, 14, 18; 10:21)?

The answer lies in the analogy between the Jordan and Pentecost, an analogy particularly significant for the application of salvation. At the Jordan Jesus as the Messiah receives the Spirit as endowment and equipping essential for the impending kingdom task that will take him through the path of mediatorial obedience and suffering that ends on the cross in dying for the sins of his people. In his ascension, in contrast, as resurrected by the Spirit he receives the Spirit as the reward deserved for that kingdom task now completed. This climactic reward he does not keep for himself but, in turn, is the great gift that he shares with his people at Pentecost. Pentecost reveals Christ as the exalted receiver-giver of the Spirit, the life-giving Spirit.

These observations are reinforced by the ascension-based sending of the Spirit promised by Jesus in John's Gospel (14:12–26; 15:26–27; 16:13–19; cf. 20:17, 22). The Spirit's coming will be the presence of Jesus himself ("I will not leave you as orphans; I will come to you"; 14:18). The Spirit is the "vicar" of Christ. He has no agenda of his own; his role in the church is basically self-effacing and Christ-enhancing (16:13–14 especially points to that), so much so that his presence and activity within the church is, vicariously, the presence of the ascended Jesus.

Earlier the Evangelist comments, "For the Spirit was not yet given, because Jesus was not yet glorified" (John 7:39). It is important not to soften the absoluteness of "not yet" in this categorical assertion, notwithstanding clear indications of the Spirit's presence and activity in various ways prior to Jesus's glorification during his earthly ministry and throughout the Old Testament. Expressed is what is true for the once-for-all accomplishment of salvation (*historia salutis*), not its ongoing application (*ordo salutis*). The Spirit's presence in view here pivots on Jesus's glorification; the former is a function and fruit of the latter. Here Pentecost has the same epochal, once-for-all significance as his death, resurrection, and ascension seen in Luke-Acts and Paul.

In a virtually identical vein, Jesus, who in his resurrection has been "given"[19] universal authority, declares, "I am with you always, to the end of the age" (Matt. 28:20). This claim is best taken not primarily as an affirmation of divine omnipresence, though that is implicit, but as a promise of Pentecost soon to come, with its enduring consequences. Here again the presence of the Spirit is the presence of Christ; Jesus will be with the church to the very end in the power of the Spirit. If it means anything, Pentecost means the exalted Jesus is here to stay, permanently, with his church.

In conclusion, essential for Christ's role in applying salvation in his state of exaltation is his own climactic transformation by and possession of the Holy Spirit resulting from his resurrection. What Christ now does rests in part on what was done to him and what he has become in being exalted. Pointedly, by his resurrection he was "justified in the Spirit" and "became the life-giving Spirit."

The single action of the Spirit in raising Christ from the dead (cf. Rom. 8:11) constitutes him as the source of both the forensic and renovative aspects of salvation: notably justification that removes condemnation and entitles to life in the Spirit, and regenerating and sanctifying life in the Spirit that eradicates the power and corruption of sin and death.

While these two aspects are inseparable, the judicial aspect has an essential and decisive priority. Because his obedience unto death is the requisite judicial ground for his resurrection, his becoming the life-giving Spirit presupposes his being justified in the Spirit, not the reverse. Further, it may be noted at this

---

19. That is, universal authority that he did not have previously prior to the resurrection but now does as resurrected.

point, Christ's obedience and atoning death also provide the requisite prior forensic basis for regeneration (the resurrection-enlivening of sinners that creates faith) to precede justification (by faith) in the Reformed *ordo salutis*.

Seen in terms of this relationship between the exalted Christ and the Spirit, Pentecost is an integral event in the *historia salutis*, not an aspect of the *ordo salutis*. Pentecost has its primary place in the once-for-all, completed accomplishment of redemption, not as a model for individual Christian experience. It does not go too far to say that *without Pentecost there is no salvation, for without Pentecost the definitive, unrepeatable work of Christ is incomplete*.

The mediatorial task set before Christ as the last Adam was not only to secure the remission of sin, as important and absolutely necessary as that is, but also, more ultimately and as the grand outcome of his lifetime of obedience and atoning death, to obtain life—eternal, eschatological, resurrection life (e.g., John 10:10; 11:25; 2 Tim. 1:10), life in the Spirit.[20] Without that life "salvation" is obviously not only truncated but also meaningless. And it is just that life, that completed salvation, and Christ as now qualified to be its giver that is openly revealed at Pentecost.[21]

Heavenly Intercession

Nothing is more essential and central in the activity of the exalted Christ in applying salvation than his ongoing intercession. This ministry deserves much greater attention than we can give it here. It is an integral part of his priestly office. In Hebrews this heavenly (high) priestly activity is as much as any the letter's "main point" (8:1 NASB). The priesthood of Christ is in view not so much for what he did in the past on earth in making a once-for-all sacrifice for sin (7:27; 9:26) as in what he is doing now in heaven. There, in

---

20. The use of metaphors for the Spirit as "deposit" (2 Cor. 1:22; 5:5; Eph. 1:14) and "firstfruits" (Rom. 8:23) highlights the inherently eschatological nature of his presence and work in the church. The Spirit, as the singular gift that came at Pentecost, is the source and substance of eschatological blessing. "On the one hand the Spirit is the resurrection-source, on the other He appears as the substratum of the resurrection-life, the element, as it were, in which, as in its circumambient atmosphere the life of the coming aeon shall be lived. He produces the event and in continuance underlies the state which is the result of it" (G. Vos, *The Pauline Eschatology* [Grand Rapids: Baker, 1979], 163; cf. 59, 165, 169).

21. Soteriologically, the "newness" of Pentecost is not individual-experiential but christological and ecclesiological-missiological. (1) The Spirit is now present and active, at last, on the basis of the finished work of Christ; he is the *eschatological* Spirit. (2) The Spirit is now "poured out on all flesh" (Acts 2:17), gentiles as well as Jews; he is the *universal* Spirit. For a fuller discussion of the redemptive-historical significance of Pentecost, see Richard Gaffin, *Perspectives on Pentecost* (Phillipsburg, NJ: P&R, 1979), 13–41.

the heavenly sanctuary, the place of ultimate justice and efficacy, he appears as the living exhibition of the righteousness that avails for his people, and where, consequently, he "always lives to make intercession for them," an intercession by which "he is able to save to the uttermost those who draw near to God through him" (7:25).[22]

A particularly striking and compelling instance of this unfailing intercession concerns justification. In Romans 8:34, not only is it relevant for justification that Christ is the one "who died" but it is also relevant ("more than that") that Christ, as resurrected, is "indeed interceding for us" "at the right hand of God." That intercession, abiding and unwavering, explains, in part, why those justified "can never fall from the state of justification."[23] Christ's exalted intercession is indispensable for the application of salvation, and, just so, our justification is inviolable and unshakable. In terms of the *ordo salutis*, this intercession is the key and the ultimately decisive consideration for the *perseverance* of believers.[24]

Union with Christ[25]

Essential to the significance of Christ as the last Adam is the union or solidarity that exists between him and believers. Apart from those "in him," he would not be the last Adam. He is "the man of heaven" only together with "those who are of heaven," believers, and as in their own bodily resurrection they will bear (fully) "the image of the man of heaven" (1 Cor. 15:48–49). Union with Christ is at the heart of the work of Christ applied.

Though the expression "union with Christ" does not occur in the Bible, it describes the central and overarching reality of salvation. For those "in

22. Is this intercession the reality of his being at God's right hand as priest, his presence there as inherently intercessory, or does it also involve a specific and ongoing praying activity? A plausible case can be made for both; e.g., the answer to question 55 of the Westminster Larger Catechism ("How doth Christ make intercession?") appears to include both aspects.

23. Westminster Confession of Faith, 11.5.

24. On Christ's exaltation priesthood, see Richard Gaffin, "The Priesthood of Christ, a Servant in the Sanctuary," in *The Perfect Saviour: Key Themes in Hebrews*, ed. Jonathan Griffiths (Nottingham, UK: IVP, 2012), 49–68; and idem, "'More Than That'—Christ's Exaltation and Justification," in *The People's Theologian: Writings in Honour of Donald Macleod*, ed. Iain Campbell and Malcolm Maclean (Ross-shire, UK: Christian Focus, 2011), 135–51.

25. For a particularly helpful overview of biblical teaching on union with Christ, see Murray, *Redemption: Accomplished and Applied*, 201–13; see also, reflecting on Murray's discussion, Richard Gaffin, "Union with Christ: Some Biblical and Theological Reflections," in *Always Reforming: Explorations in Systematic Theology*, ed. A. McGowan (Downers Grove, IL: IVP Academic, 2006), 271–88. My discussion here, building on Murray, utilizes material found on 272–75.

Christ," this union or solidarity is all-encompassing; it extends from eternity to eternity. They are united to Christ not only in their present possession of salvation but also in its past, once-for-all accomplishment (e.g., Rom. 6:3–7; Gal. 2:20; Eph. 2:5–6; Col. 3:1–4), in their election "before the creation of the world" (Eph. 1:4, 9), and in their still future glorification (Rom. 8:17; 1 Cor. 15:22). Accordingly, we may fairly categorize being "in Christ" as either *predestinarian* (Eph. 1:4), *past* or *redemptive-historical*—the union involved in the once-for-all accomplishment of salvation—or *present*, looking toward Christ's return: union in the actual possession or application of salvation, in that sense *existential* union.[26]

In making these distinctions it is important to keep in mind that they refer to different aspects or phases of the same union, not different or separable unions.[27] At the same time, it is no less important to maintain each of them and to do so without equivocating on them, either by denying any one aspect or blurring the distinction between them.

Focusing now on present union, union in the actual appropriation of salvation presupposes the continuation of the representative or substitutionary nature of union in both its predestinarian and past redemptive-historical aspects[28] and is now further marked by four interrelated aspects: mystical, spiritual, vital, and indissoluble.

Both *mystical*, a standard, classical designation, and *spiritual* are subject to misunderstanding. In view is not a mysticism of ecstatic experience at odds with or indifferent to reasoned understanding. Rather, union with Christ is a mystery in the New Testament sense of what has been hidden with God in his eternal purposes but now, finally, has been revealed in Christ, particularly in his death and resurrection, and is appropriated by faith (Rom. 16:25–26; Col. 1:26–27; 2:2).[29]

Ephesians 5:32 highlights the intimacy of this union ("a profound mystery"; NIV) by comparing it to the relationship between husband and wife.

---

26. Sinclair Ferguson distinguishes these three "moments" of union as "the eternal, the incarnational and the existential" (*The Holy Spirit* [Leicester: Inter-Varsity Press, 1996], 109).

27. One ought not to think in terms of two unions in the application of salvation, one legal and representative, the other mystical and spiritual, in the sense of being renovative. To do so loses the integral unity of the Bible's outlook. There is only a single union in application with distinguishable but inseparable legal and renovative aspects.

28. To see Christ as a representative, especially as no more than an example, but not also as a substitute seriously distorts biblical teaching.

29. Certainly, the full dimensions of this mystery are beyond the believer's comprehension. Involved here as much as anywhere is the hallmark of all true theological understanding that knowledge of Christ's love "that surpasses knowledge," the knowledge of what in its depths is beyond all human knowing (Eph. 3:18–19; cf. 1 Cor. 2:9).

Elsewhere in the New Testament other relational analogies picture this union: the foundation's cornerstone together with the other stones of a building (Eph. 2:19–22; 1 Pet. 2:5), a vine and its branches (John 15:1–7), the head and the other members of the human body (1 Cor. 12:12–27), the genetic tie between Adam and his posterity (Rom. 5:12–19). But the climactic comparison is to the ontological union, the unique eternal oneness in being, between Father, Son, and Spirit (John 17:20–23).

Similarity is not identity, but especially this inner-trinitarian analogy shows that the highest kind of union that exists for an image-bearing creature is the union of believers with the exalted Christ. "But the greatest mystery of creaturely relations is the union of the people of God with Christ. And the mystery of it is attested by nothing more than this that it is compared to the union between the Father and the Son in the unity of the Godhead."[30]

Mystical union is spiritual. This is so not in an immaterial, idealistic sense but because of the activity and indwelling of the Holy Spirit. This circumscribes the mystery and protects against confusing it with other kinds of union. As spiritual (i.e., effected by the Holy Spirit), it is neither ontological, like that between the persons of the Trinity; nor hypostatic or unipersonal, like that between Christ's two natures; nor psychosomatic, like that between body and soul in human personality; nor somatic ("one flesh"; Gen. 2:24), like that between husband and wife; nor merely intellectual and moral, a unity in understanding, affections, and purpose.

Spiritual union stems from the climactic and intimate relationship, the consummate oneness between Christ and the Holy Spirit in their working given with his exaltation, already discussed. As "spiritual,"[31] mystical union has a reciprocal character. Not only are believers "in Christ," he is "in them" (John 14:20; 17:23, 26); "Christ in you" is "the hope of glory" (Col. 1:27). Correlatively, to be in Christ is to be in the Spirit and the indwelling of the Spirit is the indwelling of Christ (Rom. 8:9–10; Eph. 3:16–17).

Union, accordingly, is also inherently *vital*, a life-union ("the law of the Spirit of life in Christ Jesus"; Rom. 8:2 NASB). Christ indwelling by the Spirit is the very life of the believer: "I no longer live, but Christ lives in me" (Gal. 2:20); "your life is hid with Christ in God" (Col. 3:4). Finally, it is *indissoluble*, rooted as it is in the unconditional and immutable decree of divine election "in [Christ] before the creation of the world" (Eph. 1:4). The salvation eternally purposed for believers "in Christ" is infallibly certain of reaching its

---

30. Murray, *Redemption: Accomplished and Applied*, 209.
31. There is some value in capitalizing the adjective, at least mentally, to keep clear that the work of the Holy Spirit, not some immaterial and merely internalized state of affairs, is in view.

eschatological consummation in their future resurrection-glorification "in Christ."

Union with Christ and the *Ordo Salutis*

Union with Christ and Twofold Grace (Judicial and Re-creative)

The importance of Calvin's statement highlighted at the beginning of this chapter can hardly be overstated for a sound understanding of the work of Christ applied, both as a whole and for how its specific elements are inter-related: "First, we must understand that as long as Christ remains outside of us, and we are separated from him, all that he has suffered and done for the salvation of the human race remains useless and of no value to us."[32] We can do no better here than attend to Calvin's further comments in its immediate context.

These words, coming at the outset of book 3 of the *Institutes*,[33] which deals at length with salvation applied, assert what is "first" in the sense of what is most fundamental, that consideration antecedent to all others. Put negatively, what is crucial is that Christ not remain "outside us," that we not be "separated from him," or, expressed positively a little later, that "we grow into one body with him." In view, then, is the union that exists between Christ and believers.

This union is so central, so pivotal, that without it the saving work of Christ, the once-for-all redemption he has accomplished, "remains useless and of no value." Union is the all-or-nothing reality on which everything depends in the application of salvation. I must have Christ or I have nothing—that underlies and gives rise to everything else. Without union, the benefits that flow from it are otherwise nonexistent or irrelevant.

This union, further, is not a partial union, as if one can share in some benefits without others. Unless I share in all of his benefits, I share in none of them. If I do not have the whole Christ, I have no Christ. Or, as Calvin puts it memorably elsewhere, Christ "cannot be divided into pieces."[34] We must not "shamefully rend Christ asunder," referring to those "who imagine that gratuitous righteousness is given us by him, apart from newness of life."[35]

---

32. Calvin, *Institutes* 3.1.1.

33. Titled "The Way in Which We Receive the Grace of Christ: What Benefits Come to Us from It, and What Effects Follow."

34. Calvin, *Institutes* 3.16.1.

35. John Calvin, *Commentary on the Epistle to the Romans*, ed. and trans. John Owen (Grand Rapids: Eerdmans, 1948), 217.

Judicial and re-creative benefits, justification and sanctification, cannot possibly be separated because, while distinct, they are coincidentally inseparable
aspects of union with Christ.

This union, Calvin immediately goes on to make clear, is "obtained by
faith." In other words, in terms of the threefold distinction made earlier, in
view is present or existential union, union as it does not exist apart from or
prior to faith but is given with and is inseparable from faith.

This key role accorded to faith prompts Calvin, still within this opening section, to touch on what has become a central question in subsequent
discussions about the *ordo salutis*, namely, the origin of faith, giving rise
eventually in Reformed theology, especially in response to the emergence of
Arminianism, to its doctrine of regeneration. We observe, he says, "that not
all indiscriminately embrace that communion with Christ which is offered
through the gospel."[36] Why? Not because of some differentiating factor or
capability on the side of the sinner; not because of themselves some ultimately
will to accept Christ while others do not. Rather, consistent with the pervasive teaching of Scripture about the total inability of the will due to sin, we
must "climb higher" and consider "the secret energy of the Spirit."[37] Faith is
Spirit-worked, sovereignly and efficaciously.

Union with Christ, then, is forged by the Spirit's working faith in the sinner, a faith that "puts on" Christ (Gal. 3:27), that embraces Christ as he is
offered to faith in the gospel. Faith is the bond of spiritual union seen from
the side of the believer. "To sum up, the Holy Spirit is the bond by which
Christ effectually unites us to himself."[38] This, then, is the core of salvation
applied, the heart of the *ordo salutis*: union with Christ by Spirit-worked faith.

At the same time, as Calvin makes clear elsewhere,[39] the basic profile of
application is marked by "twofold grace,"[40] the grace that flows from this
union and consists of justification, definitive and settled, and sanctification,
definitive and ongoing—the forensic and the renovative aspects—each as distinct as it is inseparable from the other.

Calvin uses a metaphor that seems hard to improve on to capture this tri-
angular relationship between union, justification, and sanctification—both
their simultaneity as well as union as the source of the latter two, without
either separation or confusion: Christ, our righteousness, is like the sun;

36. Calvin, *Institutes* 3.1.1.
37. Calvin, *Institutes* 3.1.1.
38. Calvin, *Institutes* 3.1.1.
39. In numerous places, for instance, and notably at the beginning of his treatment of justification in *Institutes* 3.11.1.
40. Note the singular, highlighting the integral inseparability of the two aspects involved.

justification, its light; sanctification, its heat. The sun is at once the source of both, so that light and heat are inseparable. But only light illumines, and only heat warms, not the reverse. Both are always present without the one becoming the other.[41]

This analogy is hardly arbitrary or random. Whatever may have prompted its use by Calvin, it is appropriate to the biblical truth that the Son as God's "last days" speech and "the exact imprint of his nature" is also "the radiance of his glory" (Heb. 1:1–3). The "sun" of salvation is the Son. This analogy disposes the church to see how the Son, "the Lord of glory" (1 Cor. 2:8), is central in the ongoing application of salvation as well as in its once-for-all, finished accomplishment.[42]

With an eye to current ongoing discussions, where charges of antinomianism and legalism are often exchanged—sometimes warranted, sometimes not—it will help to keep clear that in its application salvation is neither justification-centered nor sanctification-centered but is and has to be *both* because it is *Christ-centered*. Both justification and sanctification are central to the gospel, because union with Christ in all his benefits is its center.

That Spirit-worked union by faith is the source or matrix of all other benefits in redemption applied is not merely the view of individual theologians like Calvin but also has an integral place in the Reformed confessions. This can be seen, for instance, in the Westminster standards. To the question, "How does the Spirit apply to us the redemption purchased by Christ?," Shorter Catechism 30 answers, "The Spirit applies to us the redemption purchased by Christ, by working faith in us, and thereby uniting us to Christ in our effectual calling." Then the immediately following questions and answers, beginning with 32, specify the particular benefits of this union brought about by effectual calling: justification, adoption, and sanctification, with attendant benefits. The answer to Larger Catechism 69 is even more explicit: "The communion in grace which the members of the invisible church have with Christ, is their partaking of the virtue of his mediation, in their justification, adoption, sanctification, and whatever else, in this life, *manifests their union with him*" (emphasis mine).

41. Calvin, *Institutes* 3.11.6; one need not get distracted by the physics involved in this metaphor to appreciate its validity!

42. Within the considerable literature on union with Christ in Calvin, see esp. Mark Garcia, *Life in Christ: Union with Christ and Twofold Grace in Calvin's Theology* (Milton Keynes, UK: Paternoster, 2008); and Cornelius Venema, *Accepted and Renewed in Christ: The "Twofold Grace of God" and the Interpretation of Calvin's Theology* (Göttingen: Vandenhoeck & Ruprectht, 2007). An informative treatment of recent assessments of Calvin on union outside the context of confessional Reformed orthodoxy is provided by J. Todd Billings, *Calvin, Participation, and the Gift: The Activity of Believers in Union with Christ* (Oxford: Oxford University Press, 2007).

An *ordo salutis* that seeks to account for and highlight the central and controlling place of union with Christ in the application of salvation may be formulated along the following lines. Calling is effectual, first and foremost, in drawing sinners into the fellowship bond of union with Christ (1 Cor. 1:9). In that moment of uniting to Christ a new state is effected that is nothing less than one of being resurrected (re-created, regenerated) in Christ, and the core reflexive expression of that state and the bond of union seen from the side of the regenerated sinner is faith. By repentant faith sinners lay hold of Christ in response to his sovereign initiative in laying hold of them.[43] Coincident with that initial moment of calling-effected union by faith, the further benefits of salvation resident in his person, forensic and transforming—justification, adoption, and sanctification in its definitive aspect[44]—are applied to believers as manifestations of their union with him. And as that unbreakable Christ-initiated mutual embrace continues, sanctification and perseverance continue infallibly toward glorification.[45]

Union and Imputation[46]

It might appear that union as justifying excludes imputation as unnecessary. Union, however, does not destroy the personal distinction between Christ and the believer. The "in him" does not eliminate the "for us/me" that Christ remains just for those in union with him. There is a very real sense in which in union with Christ, Christ remains "outside" the believer.

At issue here is the ground of the believer's justification in union with Christ, the basis of being reckoned righteous in him. There are three conceivable options: (1) Christ's own righteousness, complete and finished in his obedience culminating on the cross, the righteousness that he now is and embodies in his exaltation (1 Cor. 1:30); (2) the union itself, the uniting bond as such; or (3) the righteousness and obedience being produced by the transforming work of the Spirit in those united with Christ. In short, in union with Christ

43. Utilizing the language, if not the exact thought, of Phil. 3:12, "that I may lay hold of that for which also I was laid hold of by Christ Jesus" (NASB; cf. as well in this context vv. 8–14, esp. 8–9).

44. At the moment of being united to Christ—important well beyond its brief mention here—believers experience decisive, once-for-all deliverance not only from the guilt of sin but also from its enslaving power. Previously they were dead *in* sin (Eph. 2:1, 5); now, as their lord and master, they are dead *to* sin (Rom. 6:2) and alive to God and righteousness (vv. 16–22). For them sin remains indwelling, but it is no longer overpowering. Sanctification as an ongoing, lifelong process is rooted in this definitive transition in lordship; on sanctification as definitive, see esp. John Murray, *Collected Writings* (Edinburgh: Banner of Truth, 1977), 2:277–93.

45. For a full and helpful discussion along the lines sketched in this paragraph, see Ferguson, *Holy Spirit*, 93–113 ("The Spirit of Order").

46. This subsection utilizes material from Gaffin, *By Faith, Not by Sight*, 57–59.

the ground of justification is resident either (1) in Christ as distinct from the believer; (2) in the uniting bond itself between Christ and the believer as distinct from either; or (3) in the believer as distinct from Christ.

Neither (2) nor (3) is sustainable biblically. The relationship as such, no matter how real and intimate, distinct from the persons in that relationship cannot be the basis of justification. Not the relational bond in itself but a person justifies, specifically the person of "the Son of God, who loved me and gave himself for me" (Gal. 2:20).

Nor does Scripture teach that justification is based on the ongoing renovating work of the Spirit in the believer. Certainly the Spirit's re-creative work is involved in justification, specifically in producing faith as its sole instrument, but that work is not its ground (cf. Westminster Confession of Faith 11.1; Westminster Larger Catechism 73; Heidelberg Catechism 61). Justification includes the free remission of all sin—past, present, and future. But present, ongoing renewal can hardly secure remission for bygone sins and also leaves future remission uncertain at best. Christ's sacrifice for me, not the Spirit's work in me, is the basis of my being forgiven, fully and perfectly.

The only viable option is the first one above. In union with Christ, his righteousness is the ground of my being justified. That is, in my justification his righteousness becomes my righteousness. But this is virtually and necessarily to arrive at the notion of imputation. His righteousness is reckoned as mine. An imputative aspect is integral and indispensable to the justification given in union with Christ.

Calvin is worth quoting here. "This is a wonderful plan of justification that . . . they [believers] should be accounted righteous outside themselves."[47] A little earlier, before coming to this summary conclusion, he expresses how he understands, and does not understand, Christ being "outside" believers:

> Therefore, that joining together of Head and members, that indwelling of Christ in our hearts—in short, that mystical union—are accorded by us the highest degree of importance, so that Christ, having been made ours, makes us sharers with him in the gifts with which he has been endowed. *We do not, therefore, contemplate him outside ourselves from afar in order that his righteousness may be imputed to us but because we put on Christ and are engrafted into his body—in short, because he deigns to make us one with him.* For this reason, we glory that we have *fellowship of righteousness* with him.[48]

It is difficult to see how the matter could be stated any better than that.

47. Calvin, *Institutes* 3.11.11.
48. Calvin, *Institutes* 3.11.10 (emphasis mine).

Union with Christ and the Unity of the Covenant

Union with the exalted Christ as the source of the benefits of his work applied raises the issue of salvation under the old covenant. How were sinners saved before Christ's death and resurrection, when union with him *as exalted* was not yet a reality? The answer lies in recognizing that union with the exalted Christ is fellowship in covenant with God in its ultimate, eschatological form. This bond of covenantal fellowship between God and his people has existed previously, in its provisional and less than climactic form, beginning already at the fall with his commitment to be their God and Savior (e.g., Gen. 3:15; Isa. 49:26).

Under the old covenant salvation was by way of trusting the promise to be fulfilled in the future coming of the Messiah, Jesus, who "will save his people from their sins" (Matt. 1:21). So certain was the future fulfillment of that divine promise in Christ's once-for-all work (*historia salutis*) that basic benefits of that work—both judicial and renovative—were applied to old covenant believers ahead of time, prospectively, in anticipation of its accomplishment (*ordo salutis*).

So in the New Testament primary examples of justification by faith are Abraham (Rom. 4; Gal. 3) and David (Rom. 4). Further, their justifying faith is hardly something they had of themselves or in their own strength but only because they had been regenerated by the Spirit. Both old and new covenant believers are "children of promise," as both have been "born according to the Spirit" (Gal. 4:28–29).

There is fundamental continuity in application and the *ordo salutis* between the old and new covenants. Under both, the benefits of Christ's work are received within the bond of covenanted fellowship with the Triune God (cf. Westminster Confession of Faith 7.5–6; 11.6). The great difference, without precedent, is that new covenant believers are privileged to enjoy that fellowship bond in its consummate and most intimate form as union with Christ as he has been exalted.

The Ordo Salutis *in Ultimate Perspective*

The classic proof text for the *ordo salutis* is Romans 8:30. Here the so-called golden chain of salvation extends from eternity to eternity, beginning with predestination and culminating in glorification. For salvation applied, verse 30 affirms the priority of calling to justification and, in turn, of justification to glorification.

Not to be missed, however, is what happens in verse 29. Prior to the forging of individual links in the chain in verse 30, that linkage is compressed, as it were, in a way that focuses the design and purpose of the chain as a whole.

First, being foreknown and predestined is to the end, all told, that believers might be "conformed to the image of his [God's] Son" (Rom. 8:29). Note that here the goal of election for believers is not salvation generally. Nor, more specifically, is it justification and the forgiveness of sins. Rather, that overall goal is image-bearing conformity to the Son, for which, as verse 30 shows, having been justified is absolutely essential. Believers have been chosen *in Christ* "before the foundation of the world" (Eph. 1:4) to the ultimate end that they be *like Christ*. In view, in other words, is their sanctification, which will culminate in their glorification, the final link of the chain in verse 30.

Second, this ultimate goal of being conformed to the image of Christ is to the further end "that he might be firstborn among many brothers" (Rom. 8:29). Image-conformity to Christ is essentially familial; adoption is in view. To be sure, adoption is forensic, a matter of legal identity and entitlement as heirs, nothing less than coheirs with Christ as God's children (Gal. 4:5–6; Eph. 1:5; Rom. 8:14–17). Here, however, a further and more ultimate dimension comes into view: full Spirit-worked family resemblance to Christ. This is an adoption unlike any other; at the core of their being those adopted have been given the same Spirit-generated DNA, as it were, as their firstborn brother according to his exalted human nature.

Third, here this adoptive conformity to Christ's image is in view in its consummate realization in the still future glorification of believers (Rom. 8:30), to be realized in their bodily resurrection at Christ's return (cf. esp. 1 Cor. 15:49; Phil. 3:21); their bodily resurrection will be their "adoption" (Rom. 8:23), its open manifestation. But this adoption-tethered and sanctification-qualified image-bearing glorification is not only future. Already "we all, with unveiled face, beholding the glory of the Lord, are being transformed [by his Spirit] into the same image from one degree of glory to another" (2 Cor. 3:18). Even now believers are being made over into this image as their "inner man is being renewed day by day" (2 Cor. 4:16 NASB). "Until Christ is formed in you" (Gal. 4:19) is a paramount concern for the present life of the church.

Here it is apparent that salvation applied entails far more than reversal of the effects of the fall. Application involves the realization, according to the present-future structure just noted, of nothing less than the eschatological destiny of those elect in Christ—that destiny of image bearers forfeited in Adam and attained by the last Adam. Further, that destiny, as the immediate context makes clear—though here we hardly give it the attention it deserves—has cosmic dimensions as the impersonal nonimage-bearing creation "eagerly awaits," with believers, its deliverance from "being subjected to futility" and "bondage to decay"—the environmental consequences of the curse on human sin (cf. Gen. 3)—to its own sharing in "the freedom of the glory of the children of God" (Rom. 8:19–21). In the sense of this passage, then, consonant with what Scripture teaches elsewhere, redemption restores and also perfects creation.

Finally, it would be remiss not to highlight that in the summary encapsulation of God's predestinating purpose in Rom. 8:29, the ultimate goal for believers is really no more than penultimate. Their conformity to the image of the Son with all we have seen that involves, serves an even more ultimate end: that "among many brothers he might be firstborn." This, we may fairly say, purposed from all eternity, is what is at stake for the Son personally, what he has invested for himself in his work accomplished and applied. This as much as anything is why Christ became incarnate, suffered, and died: that as resurrected "firstborn from the dead" (Col. 1:18), he might be "firstborn among many brothers," that their glorification, due entirely to him, might serve to magnify his own preeminent exaltation glory.

There can be no more ultimate perspective on the work of Christ applied and the *ordo salutis* than this.

13

The Law of God
and Christian Ethics

PAUL T. NIMMO

Introduction

The gospel of Jesus Christ declares that those who believe in him are justified by grace through faith, and not by any merit or work of their own. Yet against the backdrop of this confession, within which the *sola gratia* of salvation is emphatically affirmed, it is far from the case that the activity of Christians is considered irrelevant. The faithful may now be declared free from the law of sin and death, but instead they are called to existence under the law of the Spirit of life in Christ Jesus (Rom. 8:2). Thus it is precisely within this context of restored covenant relationship with God that the church and its members are repeatedly and unavoidably confronted by the core question of Christian ethics: "What shall we do?"

Christian ethics ought to be a central consideration within the field of Christian dogmatic enquiry. Karl Barth correspondingly observes, "The theme of dogmatics is always the Word of God and nothing else. But the theme of the Word is human existence, human life and volition and action. . . . Neither theology nor dogmatics can be true to itself if it is not genuinely ready at the same time to be ethics."[1] In truth, this insight that accounts of Christian faith and accounts of Christian life belong together attests a central and long-standing conviction in the Reformed tradition, as a conviction attested by, among many others, John Calvin, Friedrich Schleiermacher, and many confessions and catechisms.[2] The corollary of this conviction is that one can also unproblematically make the claim that Christian dogmatics ought to be a central consideration within the field of Christian ethical enquiry. In practice, however, and particularly through the Enlightenment and post-Enlightenment periods, there has been a widespread temptation to seek to ground Christian ethics on broader or even universal foundations that have no necessary connection to the content of Christian dogmatics. Such tendencies are to the detriment of both disciplines.

To explore this vast doctrinal terrain in somewhat orderly fashion, this chapter attends first to the character and source of the law of God, then relates these to the Gospel, Scripture, and Jesus Christ, and concludes with some outline reflections on the shape of Christian ethics.

The Law of God

The law of God in its most basic form refers to the divine rule in the government of all things external to God.[3] More narrowly, and as it more commonly finds use in the field of systematic theology (and in this chapter), it refers to a divine address to humanity, declaring the divine will—in the forms of both command and prohibition—in respect of human activity. As it effects this particular task, it correspondingly provides humans with a moral discrimen between right and wrong. The Second Helvetic Confession summarizes both these points succinctly: "We teach that the will of God is explained for us in the law of God, what he wills or does not will us to do, what is good and just, or what is evil and unjust."[4] Moreover, as the confession continues later, "the whole will of God and all necessary precepts for every sphere of life are

1. Karl Barth, *Church Dogmatics* I/1, ed. G. W. Bromiley and T. F. Torrance (Edinburgh: T&T Clark, 1956), 793.

2. John Calvin, *Institutes of the Christian Religion*, ed. John T. McNeill, trans. Ford Lewis Battles (Philadelphia: Westminster, 1960), 3.6–8; Friedrich Schleiermacher, *The Christian Faith*, ed. H. R. Mackintosh and J. S. Stewart (Edinburgh: T&T Clark, 1999), 26.2; and (as examples) the "Second Helvetic Confession" (1566), 16, in *Reformed Confessions of the 16th Century*, ed. Arthur C. Cochrane (Philadelphia: Westminster, 1966), 257–61; and the "Heidelberg Catechism" (1563), 90–115, in *Reformed Confessions*, 322–28.

3. Cf. Thomas Aquinas, *Summa theologiae*, translated by Fathers of the English Dominican Province (Notre Dame, IN: Christian Classics, 1981), IaIIae.91.1, resp., and 93.3, resp.

4. Second Helvetic Confession (1566), 12, in *Reformed Confessions*, 247.

taught in this law."[5] There is thus no sphere of life that is not addressed by the law of God, and no other source than the law of God from which the will of God can be deduced. The law of God can then be said to be sufficient: there is no need for the Christian to fabricate or speculate in this connection, or to seek elsewhere than here for ethical instruction.

The law of God is not given after the manner of caprice. The divine will in respect of human activity is but one aspect of the divine will in general, which is perfectly aligned with the essence of God and is indeed not distinct from that essence. Thomas Aquinas posits in this connection that the eternal law (in the broader sense) is "the type of Divine Wisdom, as directing all actions and movements."[6] As a corollary of this, the law is by nature good, holy, and spiritual—something in which to delight (cf. Rom. 7). And it is hence no surprise to find Jesus Christ declaring that he has not come to abolish but to fulfill the law, and that "until heaven and earth pass away, not one letter, not one stroke of a letter, will pass from the law until all is accomplished" (Matt. 5:17–18).[7]

The law of God is also not to be received after the manner of caprice. The divine will is the will of the One who creates and preserves all things—and specifically human beings. In this sense, the law of God is not an alien or distant imposition on human action: just as the law of God in its reference to humanity reflects the true nature of God, so too it reflects the true nature of humanity as the rule and order of their true being as creatures who are brought into existence by God their Creator and called into covenant by their Lord (cf. Ps. 119:73). Far from seeking to repress or to oppress humanity, then, the law seeks to defend and preserve their freedom, dignity, and interest. It is a sign of the faithfulness of God and of God's provision for and accommodation to God's creatures.

The law of God is not to be sought in the creation or in the conscience. On a common account of the matter, there is implanted in humanity in the divine act of creation a moral law—a so-called law of nature—that provides humans with knowledge of the will of God and with awareness of the obedience or disobedience with which that will has been followed. Heinrich Bullinger offers an exemplary statement of this position. Drawing on Romans 2:14–16, he writes, "God has imprinted or engraven in our minds some knowledge, and certain general principles of religion, justice, and goodness, which, because they be grafted in us and born together with us, do therefore seem to

---

5. Ibid.
6. Thomas Aquinas, *Summa theologiae* IaIIae.93.1, resp.
7. This and all further citations from Scripture in this chapter are from the NRSV.

be naturally in us." This law of nature has, for Bullinger, "the same office that the written law has . . . [i.e.,] to direct men, and to teach them, and also to discern between good and evil, and to be able to judge of sin."[8] According to this line of thinking, this knowledge of the moral law is not entirely obliterated even after the fall of humanity. By contrast, this implanted law continues to stir the consciences of all people so that no one is left without excuse for sin before God.

Bullinger continues that this law of nature functions to instruct the conscience, such that the latter "accuses and condemns the evil committed."[9] This function of the law (commonly referred to as the "second" use of the law by Lutherans[10] and as the "first" use of the law by Reformed[11]) is known as the *usus theologicus* or *elenchticus* or *paedagogicus*. Its effect is said to be to lead the individual to despair and terror in respect of their inability to fulfill the law of God and thus to lead them to a recognition of their sinfulness. This is true for both the unregenerate and the regenerate: for the latter only, however, does this use of the law direct the individual to the embrace of Jesus Christ.

In passing, it is well to mention the "second" use of the law in Reformed reckoning—the "first" use of the law according to Lutherans—which is the *usus civilis* or *politicus*. The function of the law under this rubric is, according to Francis Turretin, that of "restraint, restraining and checking men by its commands and threatenings, so that they who feel no regard for justice and rectitude unless compelled . . . may be restrained at least by the fear of punishment."[12] This use of the law does not depend on the same created imparting of the law as the previous use, and its further treatment thus belongs elsewhere: perhaps to the divine providence or to political theology, where it may more properly belong.

Yet this understanding of the once implanted and still effective moral law is to be at least marginalized and at best resisted. It undercuts the best Protestant instincts concerning the radical dependence of the human being on the grace of God, and it risks the worst Protestant excesses concerning an inflated understanding of the innate abilities of the human being. In opposition to this view, then, as Barth argues, "There is no law and commandment of God inherent in the creatureliness of humanity as such, or written and revealed

8. Heinrich Bullinger, *Decades*, ed. Thomas Harding (Cambridge: Cambridge University Press, 1849–1852), 2.1 (translation revised).

9. Bullinger, *Decades* 2.1.

10. Formula of Concord, 6, in *The Book of Concord: The Confessions of the Evangelical Lutheran Church*, ed. Robert Kolb and Timothy J. Wengert (Minneapolis: Fortress, 2000), 502.

11. Calvin, *Institutes* 2.7.6.

12. Francis Turretin, *Institutes of Elenctic Theology*, ed. James T. Dennison Jr., trans. George Musgrave Giger (Phillipsburg, NJ: P&R, 1992), 11.22.9.

in the stars as a law of the cosmos, so that the transgression of it makes a human being a sinner."[13]

The wider theological issue at stake in this resistance is the question of general revelation. It is true that many of the first theologians in the Reformed tradition—and much of the subsequent tradition—advocated a general revelation of God to humanity. The French Confession, for example, speaks of God's self-revelation "firstly, in [God's] works, in their creation, as well as in their preservation and control. . . . Secondly, and more clearly, in his Word."[14] This view is reiterated in the Belgic Confession of 1561[15] and is endorsed by Calvin and Turretin and many others in the tradition who clearly affirm the same.[16]

However, some of the confessions point in a rather different direction. The Ten Theses of Bern are both definite and instructive here: "Thesis I. The holy, Christian church, whose only Head is Christ, is born of the Word of God, abides in the same, and does not listen to the voice of a stranger. Thesis II. The Church of Christ makes no laws or commandments without God's Word."[17] The First Confession of Basel insists, "We confess that just as no one may require things which Christ has not commanded, so in the same way no one may forbid what He has not forbidden."[18] And the First Helvetic Confession affirms that "the holy, divine, Biblical Scripture . . . is the most ancient, most perfect and loftiest teaching and alone deals with everything that serves the true knowledge, love and honour of God, as well as true piety and the making of a godly, honest and blessed life."[19] These confessions do not seem to accord any place of note or of esteem to general revelation. The issue of the place of general revelation in the Reformed tradition arose with particular ferocity in the period immediately preceding World War II, in heated exchanges between the Swiss theologians Emil Brunner and Karl Barth.[20] At the heart of exploring this debate further would be a patient and informed exposition of Scripture, particularly the pertinent material in the opening chapter of Paul's Epistle to the Romans. A careful defense of the position affirmed here is provided by Barth, who explores these and other significant texts cited by proponents of general revelation as part of his work.[21]

13. Barth, *Church Dogmatics* IV/1, 140.
14. French Confession (1559), 2, in *Reformed Confessions*, 144.
15. Belgic Confession (1561), 2, in *Reformed Confessions*, 189–90.
16. Calvin, *Institutes* 1.3; Turretin, *Institutes of Elenctic Theology*, 1.1–3.
17. Ten Theses of Bern (1528), 1–2, in *Reformed Confessions*, 49.
18. First Confession of Basel (1534), 11, in *Reformed Confessions*, 95.
19. First Helvetic Confession (1536), 1, in *Reformed Confessions*, 100.
20. See Emil Brunner and Karl Barth, *Natural Theology* (Eugene, OR: Wipf & Stock, 2002).
21. Barth, *Church Dogmatics* II/1, 85–128.

Law and Gospel

The law of God is instead to be sought in the Word of God, addressed to those called to be the covenant people of God and attested in the texts of Holy Scripture. The Word of God is not a simple word, but a double one, communicating not only law but also gospel. As the gospel declares the good news of reconciliation to all people (cf. John 12:32), so the law of God claims, determines, and judges the response of those who are reconciled to God in faith.

This instinct is behind Barth's famous formulation: "The one Word of God is both Gospel *and* Law. . . . In its content, it is Gospel; in its form and fashion, it is Law."[22] But the instinct that the law is not alien to the gospel is deep-seated in the Reformed tradition, and finds particular expression in the so-called third use of the Law—the *usus didacticus* or *normativus*. Calvin writes that this is the "third and principal use," which, "pertain[ing] more closely to the proper purpose of the law, finds its place among believers in whose hearts the Spirit of God already lives and reigns."[23] Thus even if one insists that the previous "uses" also belong to the purpose of the law, it is here—for Reformed theology at least—that the true and central function of the law resides. In this vein, the Second Helvetic Confession posits "that the written law when explained by the Gospel is useful to the Church, and that therefore its reading is not to be banished from the Church."[24]

At different points, this has led to conflict with Lutheran theologians, some of whom have feared that the third use of the law implies a reprise of a theology of justification by works. And indeed some Reformed preaching may on occasion so emphatically emphasize the role of sanctification in the Christian life that such an impression might erroneously be given. But in truth nothing could be further from the Reformed position, which always, emphatically, and unequivocally insists on justification by faith alone. The Westminster Confession explicitly clarifies that "true believers [are] not under the law, as a covenant of works, to be thereby justified, or condemned."[25] And indeed both Luther and the tradition after him spoke positively of the use of the law in the Christian life: the Formula of Concord explicitly affirms the third use of the law for the purpose that the reborn "may have a sure guide, according to which they can orient and conduct their entire life."[26]

22. Barth, *Church Dogmatics* II/2, 511 (emphasis original).
23. Calvin, *Institutes* 2.7.12.
24. Second Helvetic Confession, 12, in *Reformed Confessions*, 249.
25. Westminster Confession (1647), 19.6, in *The Confession of Faith and the Larger and Shorter Catechisms* (Glasgow: Free Presbyterian Publications, 1973), 82.
26. Formula of Concord, 6.1, in *Book of Concord*, 502.

One corollary of this is that there is no easy distinction between the Old Testament and the law on the one hand and the New Testament and the gospel on the other hand. By contrast, the Old Testament is far from devoid of the gospel: as the Second Helvetic Confession states, "It is most certain that those who were before the law and under the law were not altogether destitute of the Gospel [for] they had extraordinary evangelical promises."[27]

This recognition explains why when Thomas Aquinas distinguishes between "Old Law" and "New Law," he does not relate this distinction to the division of the Old and New Testaments. For Thomas Aquinas, the new law as "perfect" surpasses the old law as "imperfect" because it is directed toward "heavenly and intelligible good" rather than "sensible and earthly good," because "it directs our internal acts," and because it induces obedience "by love" rather than by "the fear of punishment."[28] However, he observes, some under the old law belong to the New Testament, and some under the new law to the Old Testament.[29] Yet this distinction is not one that is regularly made in the Reformed tradition, which—as will be seen—has generally thought in terms of a specific material continuity in the law.

Texts such as the "proto-evangelium" (Gen. 3:15) and diverse messianic prophecies (Isa. 9:6; Mic. 5:2) offer substantive objections to any Marcionism at this point. And, as the abundant paraenetic material found in all parts of the New Testament attests, the law of God in its communication of the will of God is full of relevance for the lives of Christians, even after the incarnation and work of Jesus Christ. The Heidelberg Catechism is particularly instructive on this matter as it details the ways in which the law remains useful to Christians.

> Question 115: Why, then, does God have the ten commandments preached so strictly since no one can keep them in this life?

> Answer: First, that all our life long we may become increasingly aware of our sinfulness, and therefore more eagerly seek forgiveness of sins and righteousness in Christ. Second, that we may constantly and diligently pray to God for the grace of the Holy Spirit, so that more and more we may be renewed in the image of God, until we attain the goal of full perfection after this life.[30]

Furthermore, the Westminster Confession indicates clearly that there is no competition or dissonance between the law and the gospel: "Neither are the

---

27. Second Helvetic Confession (1566), 13, in *Reformed Confessions*, 249.
28. Thomas Aquinas, *Summa theologiae* IaIIae.91.5, resp.
29. Thomas Aquinas, *Summa theologiae* IaIIae.107.1, resp., ad 2.
30. Heidelberg Catechism (1563), Q. 115, in *Reformed Confessions*, 328.

forementioned uses of the law contrary to the grace of the Gospel, but do sweetly comply with it."[31]

Thus there is no place in the Christian theology for antinomianism—the understanding that as Christians are justified by faith, so there is no need for them to attend to the obligations of the law of God, as these have been either discontinued entirely or simply abrogated in their particular case. In this connection, the French Confession strikes an appropriate and cautionary note of wisdom: "The ordinances of the law came to an end at the advent of Jesus Christ; but . . . we must seek aid from the law and the prophets for the ruling of our lives, as well as for our confirmation in the promises of the gospel."[32]

At the same time, a clear distinction must be registered between the law and the gospel. As already mentioned, the law has no power to save or to justify; the message of salvation by grace through the justification by faith pertains to the gospel and not to the law.

It is abundantly clear from the testimony of Scripture that prior to Jesus Christ no one—whether inside or outside a covenant relationship with God— was able to fulfill all the commandments of the law or (the same thing) to obey all the precepts of God's will. As Paul writes, "All have sinned and fall short of the glory of God" (Rom. 3:23). For this reason, the possibility of a "justification by works" was only ever a hypothetical possibility. Calvin reflects that "righteousness is taught in vain by the commandments until Christ confers it by free imputation and by the Spirit of regeneration."[33]

There is also to be registered a clear ordering of law and gospel—functionally, logically, and teleologically. In respect of the first, the law serves the gospel; in respect of the second, the law follows the gospel; and in respect of the third, the gospel is the final Word of God. For these reasons, gospel and law cannot simply be identified, though to speak of an opposition of law and gospel may be too bold, or to require at the least careful further specification.

The Second Helvetic Confession writes that "the Gospel is . . . opposed to the law. For the law works wrath and announces a curse, whereas the Gospel preaches grace and blessing."[34] Yet if the setting for the law of God is firmly within the covenant, this view falters somewhat: while the law may still represent the inability of humans to obey the will of God, any divine wrath against such sinful failure is in one measure already expiated by the work of Jesus

31. Westminster Confession (1647), 29.7, in *The Confession of Faith*, 84.
32. French Confession (1559), 23, in *Reformed Confessions*, 152.
33. Calvin, *Institutes* 2.7.2.
34. Second Helvetic Confession (1566), 13, in *Reformed Confessions*, 249.

Christ and its curse correspondingly lifted and abrogated. And hence within the context of the covenant, the Second Helvetic Confession continues, "the law of God, which is his will, prescribes for us the pattern of good works."[35]

A further corollary of the connection of law and gospel is that there is no recognition of sin without the message of the gospel: sin can be recognized only after grace has been received. Again, there is an esteemed tradition of theological inquiry within the Reformed tradition that would disagree on this point. Indeed, as explored above, the first (in the Reformed reckoning) use of the law depends on a person's ability to be convicted of sin by means of a conscience informed by the law of nature implanted by God at creation. Herman Bavinck thus comprehensively notes that "what sin is is finally determined not by the church (Rome), nor by the state (Hobbes), nor by an autonomous moral law (Grotius), nor by the autonomous Self (Kant), nor by humanity as a whole (Comte), nor by social instincts (Darwin), but solely and exclusively by the law of God."[36] Yet this law has, for Bavinck, no necessary reference to the Word of God or to the gospel.

Barth contends that this first use of the law seems to advocate "the knowledge of God in His basic relationship with humanity—as distinct from His presence, action and revelation in Jesus Christ."[37] But for Barth, precisely this venerable position is "alien to the biblical knowledge of God and cannot, therefore, be put to any Christian use."[38] Indeed, the idea that the human knows such a law of nature and can measure human conduct by it is conceived by Dietrich Bonhoeffer as in itself a sinful consequence of the fall: "human beings who know about good and evil have permanently cut themselves off from life, that is, from the real life that flows out of God's choice."[39]

More specifically, sin can be recognized only in light of its defeat in the work of Jesus Christ—the One who is made sin on behalf of sinful humanity (2 Cor. 5:21) so that sin might be condemned in the flesh (Rom. 8:3). The christological import of these beliefs will be explored in detail below. For the present, there are evident here grounds for skepticism in respect to the validity of the responses of the unregenerate conscience, and grounds for hesitation in respect to Christian apologetic attempts to secure shared foundations for ethical thinking.

35. Second Helvetic Confession (1566), 16, in *Reformed Confessions*, 258.
36. Herman Bavinck, *Reformed Dogmatics*, vol. 3, *Sin and Salvation in Christ*, ed. John Bolt, trans. John Vriend (Grand Rapids: Baker Academic, 2006), 140–41.
37. Barth, *Church Dogmatics* IV/1, 362.
38. Ibid., 363. For his underlying exegesis, see ibid., 392–96.
39. Dietrich Bonhoeffer, *Ethics*, ed. Clifford J. Green, trans. Reinhard Krauss, Charles C. West, and Douglas W. Stott, vol. 6 of *Dietrich Bonhoeffer Works*, ed. Wayne Whitson Floyd Jr. (Minneapolis: Fortress, 2005), 302.

In light of the inseparability of law and gospel, the content of the law of God—that is, what God wills of humanity—thus takes on a very particular shape within a very particular framework, and both are rooted in Christology rather than in creation. Such a Christocentric understanding of the law of God has clear implications for how the ostensibly ethical texts of Scripture are to be read and conceived, with a series of issues emerging in respect of the relevant texts from both Old and New Testaments.

In the first place, it is clear that a significant amount of Old Testament material—foremost among which are, of course, the Ten Commandments (Exod. 20:1–17)—relates God setting out a series of commands and prohibitions for the people of Israel to obey. According to Calvin, the reason why the prophets and apostles employ "so many admonitions, commandments, [and] exhortations" is that these are all "nothing but mere expositions of the law, which conduct us into obedience to the law, rather than lead us from it."[40] In the history of the Reformed tradition, all this ethical instruction was directly related to and materially identified with the innate natural law. The Second Helvetic Confession, for example, states that the law of God, which had been "written in the hearts of men by the finger of God," was also "inscribed by his finger on the two Tables of Moses, and eloquently expounded in the books of Moses."[41]

The existence of this innate natural law has already been questioned above. But it is worth noting additionally here that the material identification of the innate natural law with the biblical Mosaic law that is suggested by this trajectory of the tradition seems to be rather lacking in foundation in Scripture itself. Indeed, the text "I am the LORD your God" (Exod. 20:2), which introduces the Ten Commandments, serves not so much as a rhetorical preamble but as the fundamental presupposition of all the ethical material that follows. As Otto Weber notes, then, the law "is not something like the application of general norms to this special people, but is the expression of the fact that this 'nation' which has its national substance solely in relation to God is Yahweh's people."[42] Against this backdrop, the material from Romans 1:18–3:20 is to be understood only against the backdrop of the revelation of Jesus Christ. Barth poses the crucial question starkly: "Does [Paul's] knowledge of the judgment under which the Jews stand alongside the heathen, the heathen alongside the Jews, come from the fact that he sees it in the light

40. John Calvin, "Catechism of the Church of Geneva" (1545), in *John Calvin: Theological Treatises*, trans. J. K. S. Reid (London: SCM, 1954), 119.

41. Second Helvetic Confession (1566), 12, in *Reformed Confessions*, 247.

42. Otto Weber, *Foundations of Dogmatics*, trans. Darrell Guder, 2 vols. (Grand Rapids: Eerdmans, 1981–83), 1:294.

of the cross and resurrection of Jesus Christ? Or does he arrive at it on the basis of religio-ethical observations and principles acquired independently of what happened in Christ?"[43]

In terms of the scriptural material itself, the Mosaic law (with the Ten Commandments) contains a variety of types of law—moral, ceremonial, and judicial.[44] The judicial precepts of the Mosaic law in their particularity were abrogated with the demise of the (biblical) state of Israel,[45] although the broader issue of the relationship between civil law and Christian dogmatics remains of profound import (and beyond the purview of this chapter).

The abrogation of the judicial law at this point—and thus of any easy identity between the law of God and the law of a nation—secures a legitimate pathway to the theories of civil resistance that led ultimately to the confessions of Barmen (1934) and Belhar (1986). Moreover, with the coming of Jesus Christ, the ceremonial aspects of the Mosaic law have also been abrogated.[46] However, though the form of the ceremonial laws has been discontinued in the church, their chief concern and primary interest have not been lost—such a loss might have implied that they had been deleterious to the covenant people of God prior to Jesus Christ. Instead, as the French Confession states, "the ceremonies are no more in use, yet their substance and truth remain in the person of him in whom they are fulfilled."[47]

Calvin writes that "Christ by his coming has terminated [the ceremonies], but has not deprived them of anything of their sanctity; rather, he has approved and honoured it."[48] This understanding is clearly visible in the traditional view of the sacraments in the Reformed tradition, whereby baptism is related to circumcision and the eucharist is related to the Passover. The Scots Confession does not distinguish between the two dispensations of old and new covenant in respect of the purpose of the sacraments:

> These sacraments, both of the Old Testament and of the New, were instituted by God not only to make a visible distinction between His people and those who were without the Covenant, but also to exercise the faith of His children and, by participation of these sacraments, to seal in their hearts the assurance of His promise, and of that most blessed conjunction, unity, and society, which the chosen have with their Head, Christ Jesus.[49]

43. Barth, *Church Dogmatics* II/1, 119.
44. Cf. Second Helvetic Confession (1566), 12, in *Reformed Confessions*, 247.
45. Cf. Westminster Confession (1647), 19.4, in *Confession of Faith*, 81.
46. Cf. Westminster Confession (1647), 19.3, in *Confession of Faith*, 81.
47. French Confession (1559), 23, in *Reformed Confessions*, 152.
48. Calvin, *Institutes* 2.7.16.
49. Scots Confession (1560), 21, in *Reformed Confessions*, 179.

The meaning of the ceremonial aspects of the Mosaic law thus now resides in the person of Jesus Christ. As for the moral law present in the Mosaic law, there has generally been assumed in the Reformed tradition to be something of a continuity between the requirements of a life in covenant with God before and after the incarnation.

In the second place, then, and following on directly, there is a variety of New Testament material that sets out at diverse points teaching in respect of how Christians are called to respond to the gospel of Jesus Christ. Indeed the Heidelberg Catechism articulates the contours of the content of the law of God with direct reference to the words of Jesus Christ.

Question 4: What does the Law of God require of us?

Answer: Jesus Christ teaches this in a summary in Matthew 22:37–40: "You shall love the Lord your God with all your heart, and with all your soul, and with all your mind [Deut. 6:5]. This is the great and first commandment. And a second is like it, you shall love your neighbour as yourself [Lev. 19:18]. On these two commandments depend all the law and the prophets (cf. Luke 10:27)."[50]

This answer of Jesus Christ to the question of which commandment is the greatest, citing the Old Testament Scriptures, is significant in affirming the diachronic continuity of the covenant relationship between God and the people of God in respect of the law. And indeed Jesus Christ further states, "If you wish to enter into life, keep the commandments" (Matt. 19:17).

Christ as the End of the Law

There is no small measure of complexity to the relationship between Jesus Christ and the law. On the one hand, there is exhibited in his teaching and practice a certain religious conservatism—he is keen to uphold the law (cf. Matt. 5:17; 23:1–3) and to recognize it even as he intensifies its demands (cf. Matt. 5:21, 27, 33, 38, 43). On the other hand, there is also exhibited a certain religious freedom, for example in respect of fasting (Mark 2:18–19), purification ritual (Mark 7:1–4), and the Sabbath (Mark 2:23–28). In an effort to assert the consistency of Jesus's practice with the moral law, it might be observed that the latter examples concern only aspects of the abrogated ceremonial law—even though some might posit Sabbath observance as a moral rather than a ceremonial affair. Yet this assertion of consistency may fail to be fully

50. Heidelberg Catechism (1563), Q. 4, in *Reformed Confessions*, 305.

satisfactory insofar as it may underplay the radicality of the invasion of the kingdom of God, which takes place in Jesus Christ, and of its consequences for Christian understanding of the will and law of God.

These dominical references to the commandments, together with the extensive paraenetic material in the New Testament beyond the four Gospels, evidence clearly the compatibility of gospel and law outlined previously in respect of the explicit presence and ongoing validity of the "third use" of the law and do so with specific reference to the teaching of Jesus Christ.

Yet a christological understanding of the law of God has clear implications beyond the interpretation of the ostensibly ethical texts of Scripture, even those of the New Testament. To rest here would be to court the danger of eliding the compatibility of law and gospel into a confused identity, as if the gospel consisted in nothing more than the New Testament reiterating a series of ethical demands from the Old Testament without further specification.

The New Testament message does not reach its center either with the abrogation of the ceremonial (and judicial) law or with the reconfirmation of the moral law. Instead, what the New Testament announces is first and foremost the gospel: the inbreaking in Jesus Christ of the long-promised and now-arrived kingdom of God (Luke 8:1). As indicated above, this message is far from absent in the Old Testament, but in the New Testament one has to do with the reality over the sign, the realization over the promise. In this way, the New Testament declares both that this Jesus Christ has come to "fulfill" the law (Matt. 5:17), and that he is "the end of the law" (Rom. 10:4). Both statements require further elucidation.

First, to argue that Jesus Christ fulfills the law is to recognize that he and he alone has obediently followed the law of God at all times, surrendering himself for the sake of humanity "to the point of death, even death on a cross" (Phil. 2:8). And thus Paul writes that "Christ redeemed us from the curse of the law by becoming a curse for us—for it is written, 'Cursed is everyone who hangs on a tree'" (Gal. 3:13). The vicarious and obedient fulfillment of the law by Jesus Christ is centered on his "passive" fulfillment of the will of God evident in voluntarily taking on the sin of humanity, becoming sin, and undergoing crucifixion (2 Cor. 5:21). However, the scope of his obedient fulfillment of the law is not limited to the hour of his passion and death. Rather, it also embraces the "active" obedience to the law that is evident at every point throughout his life. Jesus Christ thus not only teaches and hence reveals the law; he also enacts and embodies it in his life and work as a whole. As Calvin correspondingly notes, "Paul extends the basis of the pardon that frees us from the curse of the law to the whole life of Christ."[51] Only Jesus Christ, the One who is alone without sin, could fulfill the law perfectly by obeying the will of God at every turn and in the face of every temptation (Matt. 4:1–11).

Second, because the law of God has been fulfilled in Jesus Christ, this means that he is, in one sense, "the end of the law." This statement indicates that the condemnation that would be due to those who fail to obey the law of God is now abrogated. Paul writes, "There is therefore now no condemnation for those who are in Christ Jesus. For the law of the Spirit of life in Christ Jesus has set you free from the law of sin and of death" (Rom. 8:1–2). These verses make it clear that the accusatory and punitive functions of the law have no place in the covenant relationship with God established in Jesus Christ. The guilty sentence to which all humanity (except Jesus Christ) would be liable on account of failing to obey the will of God no longer pertains to those who believe in him. The Scots Confession is particularly insightful here in relating how this sentence is expiated by the work of Jesus Christ.

> It is therefore essential for us to lay hold on Christ Jesus, in His righteousness and His atonement, since He is the end and consummation of the Law and since it is by Him that we are set at liberty so that the curse of God may not fall upon us, even though we do not fulfill the Law in all points. For as God the Father beholds us in the body of His Son Christ Jesus, He accepts our imperfect obedience as if it were perfect, and covers our works, which are defiled with many stains, with the righteousness of His Son.[52]

Third, however, and immediately following this, it must be insisted that the claim that Jesus Christ is "the end of the law" cannot be taken to mean that there is no longer a place for the law of God, insofar as God still commands and prohibits in respect of Christian action. There thus remains a place for "law" in the new order—the law referred to by Paul as the "law of the Spirit of life in Christ Jesus" (Rom. 8:2). This insistence not only reaffirms the close interconnectedness of law and gospel outlined above and expressed in the affirmation of the "third use" of the law but also confirms that the covenant relationship between God and humanity brings with it a clear call to an obedient response to the gospel. At the same time, clearly, justification and salvation do not directly depend on such obedience, and there is a recognition that even within the covenant, true obedience will remain beyond the faithful.

Fourth, Jesus Christ is "the end of the law" in a further sense because he is the original and ultimate expression of the purpose of the law of God as

51. Calvin, *Institutes* 2.16.5.
52. Scots Confession (1560), 15, in *Reformed Confessions*, 174.

the will of God. The fulfillment of the law he effected is rooted and purposed in God's eternal election to be for humanity in Jesus Christ: "[God] chose us in Christ before the foundation of the world to be holy and blameless before him in love" (Eph. 1:4). What this means further is that to identify the will of God with the sending of Jesus Christ is in one sense to posit Jesus Christ as the law of God. Bonhoeffer draws some of these strands of reflection together helpfully when he observes that "since God . . . as ultimate reality is no other than the self-announcing, self-witnessing, self-revealing God in Jesus Christ, the question of good can only find its answer in Jesus Christ."[53] In light of this, the earlier identification that the law of God reflects the divine nature can be enhanced materially with the observation that the "divine nature" in view is that of the God who decides in all eternity to become incarnate in Jesus Christ for the sake of humanity.

Fifth, and both drawing on the last point and returning to the first point above, to argue that Jesus Christ fulfills the law and corresponds to the divine nature in so doing indicates something very particular about the way in which God chooses to work in the economy. The direction that the perfect obedience of Jesus Christ—the very image of God (Col. 1:15)—takes in fulfilling the law of God is a very particular one. The writer of Philippians states, "Being found in human form, [Christ Jesus] humbled himself and became obedient to the point of death" (Phil. 2:7–8). The connection between this profound abnegation and the *fact* of the fulfillment of the law has been noted above; here, it is the connection between this profound abnegation and the *manner* of the fulfillment of the law that is of interest. To effect salvation, the will of God is to choose humiliation in the person of his Son.

Barth writes in this connection that "Jesus Christ was not led to [the cross], nor did he go to this place, in contradiction of the fact that he was the royal man. On the contrary, it was in a sense His coronation as this man."[54] Relating this to the law directly, Otto Weber posits that "in the law, . . . God accepts his partner in just the same way he gives himself. The direction of the law is self-sacrifice, not personal security. This is how Jesus functioned under the law. . . . In obeying absolutely, Jesus asserts the validity of the law."[55] This conception of the work of Jesus Christ will inform the account of Christian ethics to follow. This trajectory is not simply a reflection of an economic subordination of the Son; it is also a material indication of the particular path chosen for and by Jesus Christ en route to the cross.

53. Bonhoeffer, *Ethics*, 49.
54. Barth, *Church Dogmatics* IV/2, 252.
55. Weber, *Foundations of Dogmatics*, 1:298.

These reflections on what it means for Jesus Christ to fulfill the law of God and be the end of the law of God lead naturally to the question of what it means for a Christian to fulfill the law of God and thus to issues surrounding the discipline of Christian ethics. Given the constraints of space, only certain initial reflections can be propounded here.

First, the fact that the law has already been fulfilled in Jesus Christ, and that justification is by grace through faith, means that Christian ethics is not about striving for salvation. In this sense, good works are not necessary for salvation. It is Jesus Christ who fulfills the law of God perfectly, imaging and effecting the will of God in his person and work. At the same time, however, it should be noted that there remains a real sense in the Reformed tradition in which good works are necessary as *evidence* of salvation. And this is rooted in the view that the grace received by the believer from Jesus Christ is two-fold—justification and sanctification.

The Westminster Confession is further typical in this regard in its affirmation that "good works, done in obedience to God's commandments, are the fruits and evidences of a true and lively faith."[56] It is along these lines that there was usually explained the potentially awkward material emphasizing the significance of works in James 2:14–26. Lest there be any confusion, the Confession continues:

> We cannot by our best works merit pardon of sin, or eternal life at the hand of God, by reason of the great disproportion that is between them and the glory to come; and the infinite distance that is between us and God . . . and because, as they are good, they proceed from his Spirit; and as they are wrought by us, they are defiled, and mixed with so much weakness and imperfection.[57]

A danger still exists in the Reformed tradition that the desire for evidence of good works in an individual life may be unhealthily related to a desire to prove (or disprove) the divine election of that person unto salvation. Traces of the roots of this problem lie in texts such as the Heidelberg Catechism, which, in answer to the question "Why must we do good works?," states:

> Because just as Christ has redeemed us with his blood he also renews us through his Holy Spirit according to his own image, so that with our whole life we may show ourselves grateful to God for his goodness and that he may be glorified through us; and further, so that we ourselves may be assured of our faith by its fruits and by our reverent behaviour may win our neighbours to Christ.[58]

56. Westminster Confession (1647), 16.2, in *Confession of Faith*, 68.
57. Westminster Confession (1647), 16.5, in *Confession of Faith*, 70–71.
58. Heidelberg Catechism (1563), Q. 86, in *Reformed Confessions*, 322.

There is much here to approve without hesitation, but the idea that good works allow a person to be assured of their faith (and thus his or her election)—the so-called *syllogismus practicus*—is not without potential issues theologically, let alone pastorally. It may be more beneficial to rely on Jesus Christ as a mirror in which to contemplate election.[59] The Belgic Confession certainly offers a stark warning here: "We should always be in doubt, tossed to and fro without any certainty, and our poor consciences would be continually vexed, if they relied not on the merits of the suffering and death of our Saviour."[60]

It is a central instinct of the Reformed tradition that the good works of the Christian are not self-generated and thus are not meritorious. Rather, as the Scots Confession states, "The cause of good works . . . is not our free will, but the Spirit of the Lord Jesus, who dwells in our hearts by true faith, [and] brings forth such works as God has prepared for us to walk in."[61] The ongoing triumph of the Spirit over the flesh, even in the regenerate, is necessary for this achievement of good works. The Westminster Confession correspondingly writes of "the Spirit of Christ subduing and enabling the will of [the individual] to do that freely, and cheerfully, which the will of God, revealed in the law, requires to be done."[62] Moreover, it is a core tenet that the good works of the Christian are accepted not because of their abundant felicity. By contrast, as the Westminster Confession states, they are accepted because God, "looking upon them in his Son, is pleased to accept and reward that which is sincere, although accompanied with many weaknesses and imperfections."[63]

Second, it is clear that the basic contours of Christian ethics in a material sense are available in the text of Scripture. The Ten Commandments of the Mosaic law, aptly summarized in the two dominical commandments of Jesus Christ,[64] and together with the other ethical material in the Old and New Testaments, reveal to the covenant people of God the commands and prohibitions by means of which God has sought to govern the ethical shape of the covenant and thus the delineated paths along which their ethical thinking should develop in the present. It is clear that certain texts in the New Testament present the reader with ethical encouragement, clear commands, and firm prohibitions, sometimes related explicitly to the concrete context of those addressed (e.g.,

---

59. Cf. Calvin, *Institutes* (1559), 3.24.5.
60. Belgic Confession (1561), 24, in *Reformed Confessions*, 206.
61. Scots Confession (1560), 13, in *Reformed Confessions*, 172.
62. Westminster Confession, 29.7, in *Confession of Faith*, 84.
63. Westminster Confession, 16.6, in *Confession of Faith*, 71.
64. Cf. Calvin, "Catechism of the Church of Geneva" (1545), in *Theological Treatises*, 117.

2 Cor. 5; Eph. 4–5; and Phil. 2:12–15). These indicate the historical paths along which the command of God has traveled, and consequently a trajectory of reference for considering the command of God today.

Yet it should also be noted that it is the unanimous witness of Scripture that, in Barth's words, people "always learn by the direct instruction of God or His messengers and servants, of Jesus Himself or the Holy Spirit, either to do this or not to do that in a definite historical situation."[65] What this means is that the witness of Scripture emphatically identifies, first, the one who commands as the God of Israel and the Father of Jesus Christ; second, the one who is commanded as the person or community called to covenant partnership with this commander; and third, the contours of the ethical relationship that has subsisted between them.

To suggest this is neither to devalue the relevance or trustworthiness of Scripture in terms of ethical matters, nor to suggest any kind of ethical relativism or occasionalism. It is simply to recognize that the narrative of Scripture indicates at every juncture that the God of Israel and the church is a living God, a God who speaks. At different times, in different places, God offers specific commands and prohibitions to God's covenant people. And if God is a living God, then it cannot be the case in covenant history only that *Deus dixit*; it must also be the case that even today *Deus dicit*. Hence in the practice of Christian ethics, the ongoing discipline of prayerful discernment remains of paramount importance.

Correspondingly, the texts of Scripture that contain ethical instruction cannot simply be used for the abstraction of universal laws of Christian conduct that fall thenceforth under the jurisdiction of the Christian or the church. To do so would be to abstract from the God who commanded then—the same God who commands now. Foremost among Christian engagement with such material should therefore not simply be to consider the texts insofar as they might erect a new law or reissue an existing law. Instead, a more holistic understanding of these texts might be gained by contemplating the way in which they contribute to the wider description of the divine action toward humanity in the history of the covenant, and by attending to the way in which the practical activities called forth by specific commands exemplify a particular covenantal disposition toward God.

The contours of this response to the covenant relationship might be variously articulated. One might, for example, explore the implications of the dominical command through the ways in which love of God can be expressed in adoration and gratitude, and love of neighbor can be expressed in a concern

---

65. Barth, *Church Dogmatics* III/4, 12.

for justice and mercy.[66] One might, alternatively, describe the complementary moral ramifications of the three distinct spheres of the covenant relationship between God and humanity—creation, reconciliation, and redemption.[67] A further option might be to develop an account of the life of Christian discipleship under the rubric of the three theological "virtues" of faith, love, and hope.[68]

Whichever particular organizing rubric is chosen for the presentation of Christian ethics, the center of the covenant relationship between God and humanity is Jesus Christ, the one mediator between God and humanity (1 Tim. 2:5). And so Barth correspondingly contends that "what right conduct is for humanity is determined absolutely in the right conduct of God. It is determined in Jesus Christ."[69] This is nothing other than to reiterate the paraenesis of the writer of Philippians, "Let the same mind be in you that was in Christ Jesus" (Phil. 2:5), or of the writer of Ephesians, "Therefore be imitators of God, as beloved children" (Eph. 5:1). Such verses explicitly encourage a certain kind of imitation—of the way of Jesus Christ, of the way of God, a covenantal response that goes beyond simply obeying ethical prescriptions.

At this point, then, the manner of the way in which Jesus Christ achieved salvation returns to the center of attention. It was noted above that on the road toward passion and crucifixion on behalf of the faithful, Jesus Christ journeyed on a path of self-abasement and self-sacrifice. And it was also noted that on this journey he embodied and enacted the divine law, obediently accepting and treading his elected path of humiliation. So too, then, the Christian is called to a journey of discipleship that evidences that same downward trajectory—of humility rather than pride, of service rather than arrogation, and of sacrifice rather than exploitation. To seek to imitate Jesus Christ against the backdrop of this understanding is indeed to ask what Jesus would do, but to do so within the framework of his lowliness and self-offering.

The contours of this disposition are discernible also in the words of the prophet Micah, "What does the Lord require of you but to do justice, and to love kindness, and to walk humbly with your God?" (Mic. 6:8), or in Paul's description of the fruit of the Spirit, "Love, joy, peace, patience, kindness, generosity, faithfulness, gentleness, and self-control. There is no law against such things" (Gal. 5:22–23). Also in the background here is the teaching of Jesus Christ that "the least among all of you is the greatest" (Luke 9:48).

---

66. This possibility is implicit in the work of Eberhard Busch, *Reformiert* (Zürich: TVZ, 2007), 111.

67. This trajectory is followed by Barth in *Church Dogmatics* III/4 and IV/4.

68. This trajectory is followed by Oliver O'Donovan in *Finding and Seeking*, vol. 2 of *Ethics as Theology* (Grand Rapids: Eerdmans, 2014).

69. Barth, *Church Dogmatics* IV/2, 538.

In short, the Christian seeking ethical instruction is primarily confronted by the words of Jesus Christ: "If any want to become my followers, let them deny themselves and take up their cross and follow me" (Matt. 16:24). But this is not merely an ethical option or a moral recommendation; by contrast, that Christians "stand under the sign and direction of [the] cross," Barth observes, "is not so much a matter of morals as ontology."[70] To be united with Jesus Christ is to be united in solidarity with him, standing under the shadow of his crucifixion, setting forth in witness a faint yet meaningful reflection of his life and work.

But just as the cross did not have the final word in the history of Jesus Christ, so too the shadow of the cross does not have the final word in the history of the Christian. As Paul writes, "If we have been united with him in a death like his, we will certainly be united with him in a resurrection like his" (Rom. 6:5). This resurrection is the source of the hope that underlies the disciples of Jesus Christ as they strive to uphold and obey the law of God even in the most adverse or adversarial of circumstances. And as in obedience to the law of God they pursue "righteousness, godliness, faith, love, endurance, [and] gentleness," so they "fight the good fight of the faith" and "take hold of the eternal life" to which they were called (1 Tim. 6:11–12). The words of the Scots Confession offer a fitting conclusion: "As we willingly disclaim any honour and glory from our own creation and redemption, so do we willingly also for our regeneration and sanctification; for by ourselves we are not capable of thinking one good thought, but he who has begun the work in us alone continues us in it, to the praise and glory of his undeserved grace."[71]

70. Ibid., 264.
71. Scots Confession (1560), 12, in *Reformed Confessions*, 172.

14

The Church

MICHAEL HORTON

Anglican Paul Avis observes, "Reformation theology is largely dominated by two questions: 'How can I obtain a gracious God?' and 'Where can I find the true Church?' The two questions are inseparably related."[1] Martin Luther was not the first person in church history to have asked these questions, but the Reformation was a vote of no confidence in Rome as providing the right answers to either. The Roman Catholic Church preserves and proclaims the true gospel, according to the pope. No, Reformers like Luther and Calvin replied: find the true gospel and you will find the true church. The ministry determines the right ministers, not vice versa.

With the ecumenical consensus, churches of the Reformation embraced the *attributes* of the church as "one, holy, catholic, and apostolic." However, they also added *marks* of the true church: "the Word rightly preached and the sacraments rightly administered according to Christ's institution." Reformed and Presbyterian confessions add discipline as a third mark.[2] According to the Roman Catholic Church, the attributes *are* the marks. After all, the true

---

1. Paul D. L. Avis, *The Church in the Theology of the Reformers* (Atlanta: John Knox, 1981), 1.
2. Interestingly, Martin Luther included church discipline as a mark in *On Councils and the Church* (1539), but it is not included in the Book of Concord; John Calvin did not regard it as a mark of the being but only of the well-being of the church, but it is the third mark in

church does not have to be identified by certain conditions; it is simply identical with the Roman Catholic Church.

As Joseph Cardinal Ratzinger (later, Pope Benedict XVI) observes, "If Orthodoxy starts from the bishop and from the Eucharistic community over which he presides, the point on which the Reformed position is built is the Word: the Word of God gathers men and creates 'community.' The proclamation of the Gospel produces—so they say—congregation, and this congregation is the 'Church.'" However, Rome teaches that unity with the pope is constitutive. "*Communio* is catholic, or it simply does not exist at all."[3] One may go so far as to say that discipline is *the* mark, since identifying the true church depends on whether it is the one that is in submission to the pope as its visible head. The Roman Catholic Church simply *is* the one, holy, catholic, and apostolic church, and therefore its ministry is valid for all time.

Radical Protestants have contributed their own distinctive emphases to the definition of the church. Though consisting of diverse groups, Anabaptists, pietists, and independents reflect a shared view of the visible church as a pure church of the truly converted.[4] Often, the search for the fellowship of true believers takes precedence over the ministry of Word and sacrament as definitive.[5] The emphasis on church discipline as a means of separating wheat and tares is one of the reasons that John Calvin demurred from Martin Bucer's conviction (later endorsed by the Reformed confessions) that it was a mark of the church. From a Lutheran and Reformed perspective, this shifts the locus of the church's being from the objectivity of God's saving action through the means of grace to the subjective faith and piety of its members. Where

---

Reformed confessions (Belgic and Westminster). In this decision, the Reformed churches follow the view of Martin Bucer.

3. Joseph Cardinal Ratzinger, *Called to Communion: Understanding the Church Today*, trans. Adrian Walker (San Francisco: Ignatius, 1996), 80–82.

4. Representing the Swiss and southern German Anabaptists, the Schleitheim Confession (1527) is brief and focuses chiefly on the separation of the righteous from the unrighteous. In the first article, infant baptism is regarded as "the highest and chief abomination of the pope" and the other articles concern the discipline required to maintain a fellowship of pure saints. According to the Dordrecht Confession (1632) adopted by the Mennonites, the true church consists of "those who, as has been said before, truly repent and believe, and are rightly baptized." The true church is therefore known by the marks of "Scriptural faith, doctrine, love, and godly conversation as also by the fruitful observance, practice and maintenance of the true ordinances of Christ" (8). Hence, once again, discipline is central ("On the Ban," 16, and "On Shunning," 17). With the Savoy Declaration (1658), the English Independents (Congregationalists) revised the Westminster Confession, omitting the inclusion of the children of believers in the visible church and defining the visible church as a regenerate body. Yet the baptism of covenant children was still practiced. See the helpful comparison between these two confessions at http://reformed .org/master/index.html?mainframe=/documents/Savoy_Declaration/index.html.

5. This is in evidence especially among the more radical independents, e.g., John Robinson.

Christ is at work by his Spirit through the gospel, there will be repentance, faith, love, mission, and good works. Nevertheless, the *source* of the church's continual existence is the ministry of Christ himself, by his Spirit, through his word and sacraments.

I interact elsewhere with other traditions, including orthodoxy, on this topic.[6] For this chapter, however, I restrict my focus to summarizing chief elements of Reformed ecclesiology especially as found in our confessions. I begin with the marks because they identify the source of the church's existence.

"*Creatura Verbi*": Where Reformed Ecclesiology Begins

The church is the *creatura verbi* or "creature of the Word."[7] Scripture refers to the "Word of God" in three senses: Jesus Christ, who is the Word of the Father in his essence; the Word written (Scripture); and the preached Word. It is the third sense that is in view here.

God's speech is "living and active" (Heb. 4:12–13). The Triune God called creation into being and sustains it by his Word that "goes forth" (Gen. 1:3, 6; Pss. 33:6; 104:30; 148:5; Heb. 11:3). While the eternal Son is God in essence (John 1:1–5, 14; Col. 1:15–20), God's speech—from the Father, in the Son, by the Spirit—is God's energies or activity: creating, providing, judging and justifying, convicting and faith-producing. There is not first of all a church and then certain activities in which it engages, such as preaching and baptizing and communing. Through the Word the Spirit brings the church into existence—and keeps it in existence. It is specifically through the gospel that we are born again into the new creation (Rom. 1:16; 10:17; 1 Pet. 1:23–25; James 1:18). Since "faith comes from hearing and hearing through the word of Christ" (Rom. 10:17), the church is always on the receiving end of its existence. As in the first creation, so in the new: the Father speaks, the Son is the saving content, and the Spirit creates faith in the hearts of his elect through this gospel and confirms his promise by his sacraments (Heidelberg Catechism, Q. 65). For this reason, God's Word always achieves its purpose (Isa. 55:1).

The proclaimed Word is not simply the sermon, but the faith that is announced, confessed, sung, and witnessed to by the church—by those called to special office but also by all the whole body in its general office as prophets,

6. Especially in Michael Horton, *People and Place: A Covenant Ecclesiology* (Louisville: Westminster John Knox, 2008).

7. See, e.g., "Reformed–R. C. Dialogue" in *Growth in Agreement II: Reports and Agreed Statements of Ecumenical Conversations on a World Level, 1982–1998*, ed. Jeffrey Gros, Harding Meyer, and William G. Rusch (Grand Rapids: Eerdmans, 2000), 802.

priests, and kings in Christ. Even singing in church is a form of proclamation: "Let the word of Christ dwell in you richly, teaching and admonishing one another in all wisdom, singing psalms and hymns and spiritual songs, with thankfulness in your hearts to God" (Col. 3:16; cf. Eph. 5:19). Nevertheless, it is especially in its official preaching that this Word is a *verbum sacramentale* (sacramental Word).[8]

Although everything that the church says and does is to be determined by the Scriptures, it is especially the preached Word that we have in mind. It is called the *verbum sacramentale*—sacramental Word—because it is chiefly in this public form of proclamation that the Word is considered a means of grace.[9] Even the sacraments of baptism and the Lord's supper are made effective by the Spirit *through the Word*. They confirm and ratify God's promise of salvation in Christ. Just as hearing is a receptive act, so we receive baptism and the Lord's supper. It is God who is at work, serving us: the Father, in the Son, by the Spirit, bringing a church into being, sustaining its existence and growth.

At the outset, certain ecclesiological options are foreclosed, expressed here as extremes. Each of these extremes that I have identified as overcome by a view of the church as "creature of the Word" cuts across diverse traditions and denominations. Nevertheless, they reflect general tendencies of Roman Catholic and radical Protestant ecclesiologies, respectively.

First, there can be no *confusion* of the Word of God with the church's speech, much less a priority of the church over the Word. It is common in Roman Catholic theology—and in some Protestant circles—to hear references to the Bible as "the Church's Book." Of course, Reformed churches have never denied that the church came before the written Scriptures. Long before the first letters were inscribed, the church already had its existence as the covenant people who began to "call on the name of the LORD" (Gen. 4:26). However, it was the Word proclaimed to Adam and Eve after the fall—the promise of salvation (Gen. 3:15)—that gave birth to the church. Wherever it exists, in any time and place, the church exists as a communion of *hearers* of God's promise. The church does not speak itself into being. It does not grow and fulfill its mission by its own pronouncements and pious actions. Jesus Christ himself is the only King and Head of his church, judging, saving, and guiding his church by his royal Word. The church has ministerial authority to declare and to apply God's Word but not magisterial authority to speak and act in Christ's name apart from Scripture.

8. John Calvin, *Institutes of the Christian Religion*, ed. J. T. McNeill, trans. F. L. Battles (Philadelphia: Westminster, 1960), 4.14.4. See also the Westminster Larger Catechism, Q. 155.

9. For a broader summary of this view (with citations from the Reformers and the confessions), see Horton, *People and Place*, 37–98.

Second, there can be no *separation* of the Word of God from the church's speech. God could speak to us today apart from human mediation, but he has chosen instead to address us through other sinners whose mouth he consecrates: first the prophets, then the apostles, and now "by ministers lawfully called" so that we should not doubt that what they preach "is to be received as the word of God." Indeed, "the preached Word is the Word of God."[10] As Calvin puts the matter, "The means that God uses do not take anything away from his primary operation."[11] Although Christ the King alone possesses magisterial authority, he gives church officers—in local and broader assemblies—genuine ministerial authority through the exercise of the keys of the kingdom through preaching, sacraments, and discipline (Matt. 16:17–19; 18:18). After his resurrection, Jesus told his disciples, "'Peace be with you. As the Father has sent me, even so I am sending you.' And when he had said this, he breathed on them and said to them, 'Receive the Holy Spirit. If you forgive the sins of any, they are forgiven them; if you withhold forgiveness of any, it is withheld'" (John 20:21–23).

Third, because the church has its origin in the decision of the Triune God and is created by God's Word, the church is not the mere product of history. It is born "from above" as the creature of his redemptive speech. It is not a co-redeemer alongside Christ, but is redeemed by Christ. Thus the church may never take its existence for granted. Not only an apostle or angel from heaven but certainly also any living pastor, magisterium, or movement today can be anathema—and a church "unchurched"—by preaching another gospel (Gal. 1:6–10). Only by constant invocation of the Spirit to bless his means of grace can a church exist; otherwise, any particular church can have its "candlestick" removed (Rev. 2:5). A historical pedigree or succession of ministers is never by itself a mark of the church. Nor is the presence of an alleged prophet or apostle. Not even the presence of the Spirit is a mark of the church, since the Spirit is pleased to identify his presence with his Word.

Fourth, because God speaks his Word through the ministry of creatures, even using the media of creaturely language, water, bread, and wine, the church is not only spiritual and invisible but also physical and visible. Though it is not the product of history, it lives and grows within history. Indeed, it is a historical institution. In many ways, the church shares striking similarities with other human institutions. There is a divinely ordained structure to its ministry, its worship, and its government. The church has officers and meetings. As a human institution, it transcends the particular egos of individuals

10. Second Helvetic Confession, in *The Book of Confessions* (Louisville: PCUSA General Assembly, 1991), chap. 1.

11. Calvin, *Institutes* 4.14.17.

and continues "from generation to generation." Only because it is called into being by the Spirit through the Word that it hears and by which its doctrines and life are normed can this continuation be something more than a social club or voluntary association.

Fifth, because the church is a creation of the Word, it cannot be reduced to a numerical unity. The precious union of Christ and his members is constituted not by their being fused into one personal entity represented visibly by one pastor. Each of us hears, receives, and obeys the Word that is spoken and ratified to each one individually in baptism and eucharist.

Yet, sixth, because this speech is a public event in which Christ draws us into his holy communion through a proclamation that makes us co-hearers and co-heirs, the believer's relation to Christ is personal but never private. As Dietrich Bonhoeffer observed, the proclamation of the Word is "the sociological principle of the church."[12] "One Lord, one faith, one baptism": the unifying factor is not a pyramid of ecclesial grace cascading from the magisterium to the bottom (Eph. 4:4–6). Paul does not mention "one pastor." Rather, it is the unifying action of the Father in the Son through the Spirit that builds us up into Christ the head through the ministry of the Word (Eph. 4:11–16).

Like the preaching of the Word, the sacraments derive their efficacy neither from the ministers themselves by virtue of their personal charisma, holiness, knowledge, or a habit infused into them at their ordination, nor from the response of the recipients. Rather, they derive their efficacy from the Spirit and the Word. The proclamation remains the Word of God, and the baptism and the Lord's supper remain God's ratification of his covenantal promise regardless of what we think, feel, or do. They do not operate automatically in and of themselves, but are means of the Spirit's work of uniting us to Christ and of confirming us in that union. They are public acts of God, but they are also personal, as we see in our Lord's words of institution: "given for you" (1 Cor. 11:24). The sort of creature that these actions create is therefore public and corporate as well as personal but never private.

By including believers' children in the covenant of grace, God underscores once more that the church is always on the receiving end of his grace. The inclusion of children in baptism is an essential aspect and guarantee of the church as the creation of the Word: "born from above," yet a promise that creates a historical succession "to you and your children" as well as a mission "to those who are far off" (Acts 2:39). The church is born—and lives—not from the

---

12. Dietrich Bonhoeffer, *Sanctorum Communio: A Theological Study of the Sociology of the Church*, ed. Clifford J. Green, trans. Reinhard Krauss and Nancy Lukens, vol. 1 of *Dietrich Bonhoeffer Works*, ed. Wayne Whitson Floyd Jr. (Minneapolis: Fortress, 1998), 158, 230, 247.

decision of the one church or from the decision of the many believers but from the electing, redeeming, promising, and preserving initiative of the Triune God.

The Covenantal Identity of Reformed Ecclesiology

Everything that I have said so far shares a great deal with the Lutheran Reformation. However, a distinctively Reformed contribution is the deep grounding in the biblical notion of "covenant." This not only casts a particular mold on what "church" means but also contributes important insights on such matters as the outward form of worship and government of the church, which many Lutheran and even Reformed churches before Calvin regarded as "indifferent."

A biblical-theological analysis of the church involves a stimulating trek through a forest of analogies. The church is a city, a building—in fact, a temple. It is also a body, growing up into Christ as its head, or living branches united to the vine. Especially in the New Testament, architectural and organic analogies are often jumbled together. This should not be surprising, since the church is both a place and a people. The covenantal relationship between YHWH and his church is also likened to a marriage, especially in Ezekiel 16; the book of Hosea; Ephesians 5:25–32; and Revelation 21:2 and 22:17.

There are other analogies: that of a shepherd and his sheep, for example. "You are my sheep, the sheep of my pasture, and I am your God, says the LORD God" (Ezek. 34:11–16, 23–26, 28–31). The shepherd-king's "rod and staff" that comfort the psalmist (Ps. 23) are like the scepter and mace ceremonially held in coronations of European royalty. In this covenantal context, our Lord's announcement that he is "the Good Shepherd" (John 10:7–16) would have been heard as equivalent to the claim that he is YHWH—the Great King.

Many of these analogies were already in wide use in ancient Near Eastern and Greco-Roman politics. When a city or smaller kingdom was threatened, a greater ruler would often intervene. Rescued from the jaws of disaster, the beneficiary was hardly in a negotiating position; the treaty was simply imposed by the suzerain who now annexed the vassal kingdom to his empire. At least in the Hittite and Assyrian treaties, the suzerain did not make promises. It was understood that he would provide security for every part of his empire, but it was the vassal who accepted the terms of the treaty or covenant (its stipulations) and its sanctions (death or life for fealty). And yet, it was understood that the suzerain would rise to the defense of a loyal vassal that invoked his name alone. Analogous to the more modern mace and scepter, the suzerain's "rod and staff" comforted the lesser kingdom that depended on his "strong arm" to save in times of trouble.

Indeed, the covenant is not merely an analogy; it is the concrete basis for YHWH's relationship to his people. In other nations, the gods were called on as *witnesses* to the treaty or covenant between the great king (suzerain) and his new client-state (vassal). Only in Israel was the deity also the suzerain himself. The covenant (treaty) is the root metaphor for the church from which most if not all other analogies are derived. It is not surprising that God freely draws on familiar analogies of everyday life that his own providence placed in history for his use. What is striking is the dominance of a political concept—"covenant"—as the basis of the relationship between God and his people.

Even "the body of Christ" is to be understood in covenantal terms. Neither metaphysics nor religion yields a biblical account of such a metaphor, since it is drawn from the realm of politics. Paul's description of the integral and organic relationship of each member to the others, with Christ as the head (esp. 1 Cor. 12:12–31), closely resembles Stoic political philosophy. However, as I have argued above, the long-standing covenant concept is already sufficient to account for Paul's appeal to this image. Avery Cardinal Dulles observes that, like other analogies (such as "people of God"), "The root of the [Body of Christ] metaphor is the kind of treaty relationship into which a suzerain state entered with a vassal state in the ancient Near East. That kind of military and political treaty afforded the raw material out of which the concept of 'People of God' was fashioned."[13] If we fail to see this broader covenantal background, Dulles observes, the analogy of the body of Christ can lead "to an unhealthy divinization of the Church," as if the union "is therefore a biological and hypostatic one" and all actions of the church are *ipso facto* actions of Christ and the Spirit.[14]

In the words of the Westminster Confession, "The distance between God and the creature is so great, that although reasonable creatures do owe obedience unto Him as their Creator, yet they could never have any fruition of Him as their blessedness and reward, but by some voluntary condescension on God's part, which he has been pleased to express by way of covenant."[15] There are different covenants in Scripture and each provides the concrete framework for God's relationship with creatures. Reflecting the mature Reformed consensus, the Westminster Confession continues,

II. The first covenant made with man was a covenant of works, wherein life was promised to Adam; and in him to his posterity, upon condition of perfect

13. Avery Dulles, *Models of the Church* (New York: Doubleday, 1974), 50.
14. Ibid., 51.
15. Westminster Confession of Faith, 7.1, in *Trinity Hymnal*, rev. ed. (Atlanta: Great Commission Publications, 1990).

and personal obedience. III. Man, by his fall, having made himself incapable of life by that covenant, the Lord was pleased to make a second, commonly called the covenant of grace; wherein He freely offers unto sinners life and salvation by Jesus Christ; requiring of them faith in Him, that they may be saved, and promising to give unto all those that are ordained unto eternal life His Holy Spirit, to make them willing and able to believe. IV. This covenant of grace is frequently set forth in scripture by the name of a testament, in reference to the death of Jesus Christ the Testator, and to the everlasting inheritance, with all things belonging to it, therein bequeathed.[16]

The covenant of works provides the framework within which the New Testament contrast between Adam and Christ, law and promise, personal performance and representative substitution operates. "Law" has its determinative effect over human destinies only as the stipulations of a covenant. Because Christ fulfilled all righteousness according to the covenant of works, he can now dispense it to his co-heirs in a covenant of grace.

Because the shadows of the old covenant directed faith to Christ, the covenant of grace is the unifying factor of both testaments. The Westminster Confession draws a clear distinction between the old and new covenants: "in the time of the law and in the time of the Gospel." The former proclaimed God's covenant of grace "by promises, prophecies, sacrifices, circumcision, the paschal lamb, and other types and ordinances to the people of the Jews, all fore-signifying Christ to come." These "were, for that time, sufficient and efficacious, through the operation of the Spirit, to instruct and build up the elect in faith in the promised Messiah, by whom they had full remission of sins, and eternal salvation."[17] But now the covenant of grace "is dispensed" by "the preaching of the Word and the administration of the sacraments of Baptism and the Lord's Supper." Though less glorious outwardly, these New Testament means of grace hold forth the gospel "in more fullness, evidence, and spiritual efficacy to all nations, both Jews and Gentiles." There is, therefore, no Marcionite opposition between Old and New Testaments. From the promise of redemption in Genesis 3:15 to the consummation in Revelation 22, the church finds its only existence in a covenant of grace. "There are not therefore two covenants of grace, differing in substance, but one and the same, under various dispensations."[18]

Christian theology has traditionally regarded the church as one people of God from Old Testament promise to New Testament fulfillment. Nevertheless,

16. Westminster Confession of Faith, 7.2–4.
17. Westminster Confession of Faith, 7.5.
18. Westminster Confession of Faith, 7.6.

the Sinai covenant established a typological interlude—a parable—of God's
overarching purposes. The church became also a nation, a geopolitical entity
with YHWH as King. With the coming of Christ, the shadows gave way to
the reality. The church continues, as it had since God announced his promise
to Adam and Eve (Gen. 3:15). Even in its theocratic era, the church fed on the
promise of a worldwide family in Christ, Abraham's offspring.

> It does not say, "And to offsprings," referring to many, but referring to one,
> "And to your offspring," who is Christ. This is what I mean: the law [Sinai cov-
> enant], which came 430 years afterward, does not annul a covenant previously
> ratified by God so as to make the promise void. For if the inheritance comes
> by the law, it no longer comes by promise, but God gave it to Abraham by a
> promise. (Gal. 3:16–18)

The law is not opposed to the promise, but serves it by having "impris-
oned everything under sin, so that the promise by faith in Jesus Christ might
be given to those who believe" (Gal. 3:21–22). These are "two covenants,"
represented by two mothers (Hagar and Sarah) and two Jerusalems (earthly
and heavenly). "One is from Mount Sinai, bearing children for slavery; she is
Hagar," corresponding "to the present Jerusalem, for she is in slavery with her
children. But the Jerusalem above is free, and she is our mother" (Gal. 4:24–26).
The same distinctions are drawn in Hebrews, where the imperfection or
incompleteness of the Sinai covenant in comparison with the Abrahamic
promise is set out in bold relief. Joshua did not give that perfect rest that
remains open for us through faith in Christ today (Heb. 4:1–13). The law
did not appoint a high priest who could himself be the sacrifice as well as
mediator to take away sins forever. Yet this is precisely what Jesus has done
(Heb. 5:1–10). "For when God made a promise to Abraham, since he had
no one greater by whom to swear, he swore by himself, saying, 'Surely I will
bless you and multiply you'" (Heb. 6:13–14). Since this covenant is based on
God's oath, "the unchangeable character of his purpose," we have "a sure
and steadfast anchor" (vv. 17–19). Whether Jews or gentiles, new covenant
believers have not come to Mount Sinai. "But you have come to Mount Zion
and to the city of the living God, the heavenly Jerusalem" (Heb. 12:22). The
whole fabric of the old covenant cult was temporary and typological: like an
architectural drawing rather than the building itself (Heb. 8:5). "But as it is,
Christ has obtained a ministry that is as much more excellent than the old
as the covenant he mediates is better, since it is enacted on better promises"
(v. 6). Appealing to Jeremiah 31, the writer concludes, "In speaking of a new
covenant, he makes the first one obsolete" (v. 13a).

Whenever God calls the prophets to execute his covenant lawsuit against Israel, it is on the basis of the Sinai covenant. "Like Adam, they broke my covenant" (Hosea 6:7). Yet even in exile, they hear an evangelical word that transcends the vicissitudes of their conduct in the land. God tells the same prophets to announce comfort in a greater promise of worldwide blessing through the Messiah. It is only in this way that Israel is restored not to the position of the old covenant theocracy but to something much greater. Instead of being limited to a sliver of real estate, his people "shall inherit the earth" (Matt. 5:5). Beyond temporal health, wealth, and happiness, they will live forever with joy in the presence of the Triune God. Far more than a geopolitical nation, the church will flourish as a spiritual kingdom whose subjects from all nations will be co-heirs with the King himself. Their sins will be forgiven, they will be justified, and the Spirit will be poured out on all flesh to indwell and renew his elect.

Throughout the prophets we find this paradox: on the one hand, the true Israel is a remnant of the nation, and yet, on the other hand, it is also far larger than Israel had ever been. Its tents have been enlarged. The gospel now goes out to the ends of the earth. All of this, which is clearly found in the prophets, is announced by the apostles as fulfilled in Christ. Thus it becomes clearer that we are not dealing with two peoples but one (cf. Eph. 2:11–22) and not with a displacement of Israel but its enlargement. While the national covenant (i.e., the theocracy) has come to an end, the Abrahamic covenant, according to which all nations will be blessed in Abraham and his seed, has reached its appointed goal. Jew and gentile in Christ form one flock with one shepherd (Gal. 3:13–18, 27–29), not a replacement for the ancient people of God but "the Israel of God" indeed (Gal. 6:16).

The inclusion of believing gentiles is simply the realization of the promise made to the patriarchs and prophets: a promise to the Jews that is realized as blessing for the whole world (Gen. 12:3a). In establishing his "everlasting covenant" with David, YHWH promises:

> I will be a father to him, and he shall be a son to me. When he commits iniquity, I will punish him with a rod such as mortals use, with blows inflicted by human beings. But I will not take my steadfast love from him, as I took it from Saul, whom I put away from before you. Your house and your kingdom shall be made sure forever before me; your throne shall be established forever. (2 Sam. 7:14–16)

In this light, Paul refers to the church as "the household of God" (1 Tim. 3:15), as Peter does as well (1 Pet. 4:17). There is one Father over the house, and a Son who is represented as our elder brother, legal heir of the whole estate that he nevertheless enjoys as a public (representative) person only to dispense to his co-heirs (Rom. 8:17). Once again, the traditional political and legal practices undergo modification as analogies in this new covenant relationship, since it is after all Christ who in this case is the "firstborn son" and "heir of all things" (Heb. 1:2). As he has made us his joint heirs, he has made Jews and gentiles "fellow heirs" of the promises made to Abraham (Gal. 3:29; 1 Pet. 3:7). All of those united to Christ, who is the very "image of the invisible God" (Col. 1:15), are adopted as God's children (Rom. 8:23; Gal. 4:5) and therefore are being transformed into the likeness of Christ's image: "For those whom he foreknew he also predestined to be conformed to the image of his Son, in order that he might be the firstborn within a large family" (Rom. 8:29 NRSV). The body of Christ is a commonwealth, Paul tells gentiles. Though formerly "without Christ, being aliens from the commonwealth of Israel, and strangers to the covenants of promise, having no hope and without God in the world" (Eph. 2:12 NKJV) they are now "brought near by the blood of Christ" (Eph. 2:13). Only with the passing of the old covenant is the new covenant promise able to be fulfilled, making one new body out of two (Eph. 2:12–16, 19–21).

Just as the New Testament church is complete only as it grows out of the Old Testament church, the Israel of God only attains its eschatological form with the inclusion of the nations: "Yet all these [OT saints], though they were commended for their faith, did not receive what was promised, since God had provided something better so that they would not, apart from us, be made perfect" (Heb. 11:39–40 NRSV). Paul states, "For I tell you that Christ has become a servant of the circumcised on behalf of the truth of God in order that he might confirm the promises given to the patriarchs, and in order that the Gentiles might glorify God for his mercy" (Rom. 15:8–9 NRSV). "And if you belong to Christ, then you are Abraham's offspring, heirs according to the promise" (Gal. 3:29 NRSV). The whole *ekklēsia*, then, is "the Israel of God" (Gal. 6:16; cf. Rom. 11).

Attributes of the Church

Only after having considered the marks from which the church takes its life and the covenantal context of the church's existence through redemptive history can we now define the nature of the church.

Unity and Catholicity

Catholic means "universal," but in its actual use it has a richer meaning, especially as a summary term for the communion of the redeemed as one body.

The principalities and powers of this present evil age seek to control our desires, longings, and hopes by dividing us according to its false catholicities. Yet in Christ every racial barrier (beginning with the Jew/gentile distinction), every socioeconomic wall, every demographic profile and generational niche, and every political-ideological partition that defines this present age disintegrates as the rays of the age to come penetrate. Wherever the Word and Spirit—"one Lord, one faith, one baptism" (Eph. 4:5)—break up the givens of this age and reconstitute a new people, there is a piece of the catholic church.

Behind, above, and underneath all evidences of visible unity in the body of Christ lies the original, inviolable, and largely hidden unity of that body in God's eternal election. According to the Heidelberg Catechism, to affirm "one holy catholic church" means, "I believe that the Son of God, through his Spirit and Word, out of the entire human race, from the beginning of the world to its end, gathers, protects, and preserves for himself a community chosen for eternal life and united in true faith. And of this community I am and always will be a living member."[19]

Taking the catholicity of the church entirely out of our hands, election proscribes all overrealized eschatologies, whether they identify the pure church with a universal institution or with the sum total of the regenerate. Although it is truly a proleptic anticipation, only in the eschaton will the visible church, strictly speaking, be *identical* with the catholic church. The union of Christ and his body—that is, the one, holy, catholic, and apostolic church—is the eschatological communion of the elect, chosen "in Christ before the foundation of the world to be holy and blameless before him in love" (Eph. 1:4 NRSV).

God's election remains largely hidden, but it does manifest itself in the redemption, justification, and sanctification of actual people in time and space. We do not make the church; the church makes us—rather, God makes us through the church's ministry. This means that its visibility in the world occurs through God's fulfillment of his promise to work through preaching and sacrament, regardless of the imperfections and ambiguities of personal and corporate unity.

Thus, "invisible" and "visible" refer not to two different churches (much less do they correspond to true and false) but to the body of Christ as known to God in eternity and as known to us now as a mixed assembly. The Westminster Confession first defines the catholic church as *invisible*," which "consists of the whole number of the elect, that have been, are, or shall be gathered into

---

19. The Heidelberg Catechism, Lord's Day 21, Q. 54, in *The Psalter Hymnal: Doctrinal Standards and Liturgy of the Christian Reformed Church* (Grand Rapids: Board of Publications of the CRC, 1976), 27.

one, under Christ the Head thereof; and is the spouse, the body, the fullness of him that filleth all in all." Yet in the next article, "The *visible* church, which is *also catholic* or universal under the gospel (not confined to one nation, as before, under the law), consists of all those throughout the world that profess the true religion; and of their children: and is the kingdom of the Lord Jesus Christ, the house and family of God, out of which there is no ordinary possibility of salvation."[20] As such, it truly participates in the thing signified, but is not yet identical with it as one day it will be. "For the creation waits with eager longing for the revealing of the children of God" (Rom. 8:19 NRSV) and despite the confusion, error, and dissension that have always plagued the church, "God's firm foundation stands, bearing this inscription: 'The Lord knows those who are his'" (2 Tim. 2:19 NRSV).

With good reason, Edmund P. Clowney warns against appealing to "invisible" unity as a cop-out for recognizing the visible unity of the church.[21] Precisely because it is already given as a gift—because, in other words, Christ himself "is our peace" (Eph. 2:14), in whom "the covenant of peace" (Ezek. 34:25) is realized—we are called "to keep the bond of peace" (Eph. 4:3). In Scripture, announcements of what God has accomplished for us in his Son are the basis for its exhortations to grow and live in line with the truth. In its essence, then, catholic unity is not a human task but a divine gift. Nevertheless, God's electing and redeeming grace should provoke us daily to long for and work toward greater visible unity.

Also, in both Ephesians 4 and 1 Corinthians 8–14, the supper (along with baptism and preaching) plays a critical role. It is not just common doctrine ("one faith") that creates ecclesial unity but "one baptism," sharing "one loaf," and drinking one cup. However, nothing in these seminal passages suggests that this unity and catholicity is generated by a particular church order (much less a papal office) or the decision of individuals to belong to it. Neither the church nor the individual is creating this new reality in the world; it is the work of God. In Ephesians, the communion that each of the elect enjoys with Christ (chap. 1) simultaneously creates on the horizontal register (to which Christ also belongs as head) a communion of saints that defies the divisions of both Athens and Jerusalem. In the work of the Spirit through the event of Word and sacrament, the church is not simply reminded or brought to a new awareness of its unity but becomes more and more the catholic church in truth (1 Cor. 10:17).

In Roman Catholic ecclesiology, the "one" has ontological priority. In his *Confessions*, Augustine coins the phrase *totus Christus* ("whole Christ") to refer

20. The Westminster Confession, 25, in *Trinity Hymnal*, 863 (emphasis mine).
21. Edmund P. Clowney, *The Church* (Downers Grove, IL: InterVarsity, 1995), 78.

to the union of Christ with his body. Believers are not made merely one with and in Christ together, but are made one "Christ."[22] This idea was worked out in medieval theology in unwholesome ways. Kingdom and church, head and members, eschatology and history began to merge. Especially in the Counter-Reformation, the concept of the church that came to dominate the late medieval period was that of a legal, juridical institution under "the one vicar of Christ on earth, the Roman pontiff."[23] There was nothing questionable, ambiguous, or precarious about the church's location or identity in this age. It was simply the kingdom of God—the historical replacement for the natural body of Christ.

If anything, the emphasis on the church as one personal entity became even stronger as late nineteenth-century "reform Catholicism" turned from legal to more organic analogies for the "fusion" of existences (both Christ's and ours). As the continuation of the incarnation, the Roman Catholic Church is "the realisation on earth of the Kingdom of God," Karl Adam writes.[24] "Christ the Lord is the real self of the Church," and the church and Christ are "one and the same person, one Christ, the whole Christ."[25] The church—that is, the Roman Catholic Church—is "the incarnation of Christ in the faithful."[26] Yet the *totus Christus* is hierarchically constituted according to Rome, descending from the pope as its visible head. Through this hierarchy, "*the divine is objectivised, is incarnated in the community*, and precisely and only in so far as it is a community. . . . So the Church possesses the Spirit of Christ, not as a many of single individuals, nor as a sum of spiritual personalities, but as the compact unity of the faithful, as a community that transcends the individual personalities, . . . *the many as one*." Christ's mission is "to reunite to God mankind as a unity, as a whole, *and not this or that individual man*."[27] Adam asserts that "the community and not the individual is the bearer of the Spirit of Jesus," which entails a visible head, the pope: the symbol of numerical unicity.[28] In a somewhat chilling illustration of his time and place, Adam passionately asserts, "One God, one faith, one love, one single man: that is the stirring thought which inspires the Church's pageantry and gives it artistic form."[29]

22. Augustine, *Confessions* 13.28.
23. Robert Bellarmine, *De controversies* 2.3; *De ecclesia militante* 2; *De definitione Ecclesiae* (Naples: Giuliano, 1857), 2:75.
24. Karl Adam, *The Spirit of Catholicism* (New York: Crossroad, 1997), 14.
25. Ibid., 15.
26. Ibid., 20.
27. Ibid., 31–32 (emphasis mine).
28. Ibid., 38.
29. Ibid., 41. Like many Catholic and Protestant theologians of his generation, Adam at first welcomed Hitler's ascendancy. According to Robert Krieg, after declaring for Hitler, six months later Adam criticized the regime (xii).

Joseph Cardinal Ratzinger (later, Pope Benedict XVI) writes, "The temporal and ontological priority lies with the universal Church; a Church that was not catholic would not even have ecclesial reality."[30] And this unity and catholicity have their unity in the papal office. Here, the difference between the "not yet" of unity is simply collapsed into the "already." Genuine catholicity is attained only in union with the pope.[31]

However, wherever it occurs, the Pauline phrase "body of Christ" is deployed to affirm plurality as much as unity, as in 1 Corinthians 12:12: "For just as the body is one and has many members, and all the members of the body, though many, are one body, so it is with Christ" (NRSV). Not only are the many and the one treated with the same ontological weight, but also the formula itself expresses a simile: "just as . . . so it is with Christ." Christ forms his own body, it is true; but it remains no less "many members" than "one body." "For the body does not consist of one member but of many" (1 Cor. 12:14).

At the other extreme stands radical Protestantism: Anabaptist, radical pietist, and independent ecclesiologies. In this trajectory, "the many"—truly converted believers—are ontologically primary in defining the church. "Church" exists only as a local assembly and is constituted as such by the mutual covenanting of believers. Stanley Grenz observes, "The post-Reformation discussion of the *vera ecclesia* formed the historical context for the emergence of the covenant idea as the focal understanding of the nature of the church."[32] With its insistence on the marks of the church, "the Reformers shifted the focus to Word and Sacrament," but the Anabaptists and Baptists "took yet a further step," advocating a congregational ecclesiology. "This view asserts that the true church is essentially people standing in voluntary covenant with God."[33] Obviously, this means that the covenant is at least chiefly something that the individual makes with God rather than vice versa. Consequently, not only are children of believers excluded in the new covenant (unlike the old); the church consists only of genuine believers. A *voluntary* covenant not only entails the independence of local churches but also the independence of individuals within them until they mutually agree on the terms of that relationship. "No longer did the corporate whole take precedence over the individual as in the medieval model," Grenz notes. Rather, individuals formed the church. "As a result, in the order of salvation the believer—and not the

30. Ratzinger, *Called to Communion*, 44.
31. Ibid., 79–80.
32. Stanley Grenz, *Theology for the Community of God* (Nashville: Broadman & Holman, 1997), 609.
33. Ibid., 610–11.

church—stands first in priority."[34] "Because the coming together of believers in mutual covenant constitutes the church, it is the covenant community of individuals," although it has a history as well.[35]

At least in more popular forms (e.g., Anglo-American revivalism), evangelicalism has frequently adopted a contractual more than covenantal view both of union (soteriology) and communion (ecclesiology). Especially when wedded to an Arminian soteriology, a voluntaristic emphasis emerges, with human decision as the contractual basis for both conversion and ecclesial existence. Rather than means of grace, the sacraments become "means of commitment."[36] Taken to its extreme, contractual thinking easily leads to the view expressed by George Barna, an evangelical pioneer of church marketing: "Think of your church not as a religious meeting place, but as a service agency—an entity that exists to satisfy people's needs."[37] Not surprisingly, Barna has recently suggested that the institutional church is no longer relevant and should be replaced by informal gatherings for fellowship and internet communities. He has introduced a new demographic: the "Revolutionaries," the "millions of believers" who "have moved beyond the established church and chosen to be the church instead."[38] Barna explains his use of "church" (small *c*) to refer to "the congregation-based faith experience, which involves a formal structure, a hierarchy of leadership, and a specific group of believers" and "Church" (capital *c*) to denote "all believers in Jesus Christ, comprising the population of heaven-bound individuals who are connected by faith in Christ, regardless of their local church connections or involvement."[39] The Revolutionaries have found that in order to pursue an authentic faith they had to abandon the church.[40] To be sure, Barna's vision is a long way from the Pietist conventicle, and Grenz encourages a more traditional congregationalist model. Yet the emphasis on the human (and individual) side of the covenant connects both approaches.

Karl Barth would have rejected many aspects of this trajectory.[41] However, especially in his earlier work, absolute contrasts between the "Church of

34. Ibid., 611.
35. Ibid., 614.
36. For example, Grenz introduces baptism and the supper as "Community Acts of Commitment" and argues that in Baptist theology, the sacraments "are basically human, and not divine acts" (ibid., 670).
37. George Barna, *Marketing the Church* (Colorado Springs: NavPress, 1988), 37.
38. George Barna, *Revolution: Finding Vibrant Faith beyond the Walls of the Sanctuary* (Carol Stream, IL: Tyndale House, 2005), back cover copy.
39. Ibid., x.
40. Ibid., 17.
41. These differences are recounted and interpreted in fascinating detail in Eberhard Busch, *Karl Barth and the Pietists*, trans. Daniel W. Bloesch (Downers Grove, IL: InterVarsity, 2004).

Jacob" and the "Church of Esau" follow the usual course of radical Protestant-ism. Where the Augustinian and Reformed distinction between the invisible and visible church referred to the church as it is known only to God and the church as we know it now, Barth nearly identifies the former with the true church and the latter with the false (or merely apparent) church.[42] He is alert to the dangers of confusing the church with Jesus—the assimilation of "the many" to "the one." "What constitutes the being of man in this [covenantal] sphere is not a oneness of being but a genuine togetherness of being with God."[43] Nevertheless, if Rome too nearly identifies Christ's authority and work with the church's ministry, the sign with the reality, the "not-yet" with the "already," and the body with its sovereign head, Barth tends to separate them—even to set them in opposition.

This antithesis between divine and human action is seen even in Barth's latest phase of the *Church Dogmatics*. There is no such thing as "means of grace."[44] Baptism and the supper stand on the "human witnessing" side of the chasm between divine and human action.[45] Christ is the only sacrament, "standing over against all Christian action, including Christian faith and Chris-tian baptism."[46] Hence his attraction to an independent ecclesiology, criticism of the triumph of "Calvin's sacramentalism" in the Reformed confessions over against Huldrych Zwingli's better insights, and, finally, his explicit rejection of infant baptism in *Church Dogmatics* IV/4.[47] The true church appears to enter into history in merely momentary flashes of eschatological events. Consistent with his actualist ontology, the church for Barth is something that happens, rather than a divinely ordained institution that exists through history. Barth's discomfort with associating divine grace with creaturely mediation in the final fragment is marked, compared with the earlier volumes. "In Luther's insistence on the literal force of the 'is' in the words of institution," Bruce McCormack observes, "Barth saw the opening of a door to every direct identification of revelation and history."[48] It was a door that he determined to shut.

In view of these extremes, the challenge before us is to identify something between conflation and separation. Although Reformed theology also appeals

42. Karl Barth, *The Epistle to the Romans*, trans. Edwyn C. Hoskyns, 6th ed. (London: Oxford University Press, 1933), 36, 304, 396.

43. Karl Barth, *Church Dogmatics* III/2, ed. G. W. Bromiley and T. F. Torrance (Edinburgh: T&T Clark, 1960), 141.

44. Barth, *Church Dogmatics* IV/4, 106, 129–30.

45. Barth, *Church Dogmatics* IV/1, 296.

46. Barth, *Church Dogmatics* IV/4, 88.

47. Ibid., 73, 102.

48. Bruce McCormack, *Karl Barth's Critically Realistic Dialectical Theology* (Oxford: Clar-endon, 1995), 392.

to Augustine's *totus Christus* motif without scruple, it is always connected with the historical economy: sharing in Christ's death and resurrection so that what has happened to Jesus will also happen to us. Christ is the representative head in a covenant, not the "corporate personality" in whom his own identity as well as ours is surrendered to the whole. The ascension keeps this version from substituting either a pyramid-like church or a cosmic body for Christ and directs us to the work of the Spirit in uniting us to Christ so that there is real affinity despite real difference. In Calvin's words,

> This is the highest honour of the Church, that, until He is united to us, the Son of God reckons himself in some measure imperfect. What consolation is it for us to learn, that, not until we are along with him, does he possess all his parts, or wish to be regarded as complete! Hence, in the First Epistle to the Corinthians, when the apostle discusses largely the metaphor of a human body, he includes under the single name of Christ the whole Church.[49]

It is no wonder, then, that Calvin insisted on stronger language for *koinōnia* (fellowship) than Erasmus's *societas* (society); this also measures the reformer's distance from Barth on this point. Nevertheless, for Calvin and his heirs, this version of *totus Christus* is eschatologically oriented: "the Son of God reckons himself in some measure imperfect" or incomplete only because he is the firstfruits of the harvest, the head of a body. What he possesses perfectly and completely in himself is at present only imperfectly and incompletely realized in his body. Though chosen and redeemed, the whole body has not yet been gathered and justified. Even those who are justified only begin that progress in sanctification that will be fully realized eventually in their glorification.

Yet the visible church does participate proleptically in the eschatological reality, namely, the whole communion of the elect in all times and places. One cannot help but observe at this point how crucial the practice of infant baptism is to a covenantal view of the communion of saints more generally. The inclusion of believers' children underscores the priority of God's sovereign grace in ecclesiology as well as soteriology, challenging all voluntaristic and contractual interpretations that contribute to an individualistic faith and practice. When construed in the context of a covenantal theology, the baptism of believers together with their children underscores (1) the priority of divine activity in creating the church (i.e., covenant over contract); (2) the "mixed" character of the body of Christ at present, which subverts overrealized eschatologies;

---

49. John Calvin, *Commentaries on the Epistles of Paul to the Galatians and Ephesians*, trans. William Pringle (Grand Rapids: Eerdmans, 1957), 218 (on Eph. 1:23).

and (3) the importance of personal faith as well as communal mediation in the nurture of faith and repentance.

If Reformed ecclesiology is designated "church as covenant," it is not surprising that the form of its outward organization is *connective*. This is to say that "the church" refers not only to particular (local) churches, or to the clerical hierarchy, but also to local congregations, broader assemblies (regional and ecumenical), and to the whole communion of professing believers and their children in all times and places. The New Testament refers to the church as wider than a local congregation (Acts 9:31; 1 Cor. 12:28; Eph. 4:4–16), and the churches addressed in the Epistles (though in the singular) consisted of more than one local congregation (Acts 20:20; Rom. 16:5; Philem. 2). It is important to say at the outset that although I am discussing church government under the broader rubric of the essential attributes of the church, it is only because it is an implication of what I regard as a New Testament view of church unity, not because I regard a particular polity (presbyterian) as essential to the being of the church.

A covenantal ecclesiology suggests a concrete praxis, which is neither hierarchical nor democratic. "Presbyterian" comes from the word *presbyteros* ("elder"), with the New Testament term for a broader assembly of elders as a *presbyterion* ("presbytery"). We will examine specific passages, but first the main outlines of a presbyterian polity can be seen in the Council of Jerusalem in Acts 15, where a local church dispute was taken to the broader assembly of the church. It is striking that several times the report refers to "the apostles and the elders" as the decision-making body. Commissioners (including Paul and Barnabas) were sent from the local church in Antioch to the wider assembly convened at Jerusalem. It was James, rather than Peter, who said, for his part, "Therefore I have reached the decision that we should not trouble those Gentiles who are turning to God" (Acts 15:19 NRSV). Still, the final verdict awaited the assent of the full assembly. "Then the apostles and the elders, with the consent of the whole church, decided to choose men from among their members and to send them to Antioch with Paul and Barnabas," to relate the written decision to that local church (vv. 22–29 NRSV).

At the Jerusalem Council, the unity that the Spirit had established at Pentecost was preserved visibly not by the sacrifice of the one to the many or the many to the one but by the consent of the many as one. The covenant community *functioned covenantally* in its outward and interpersonal government, in mutual submission rather than hierarchical unity or independent plurality. Already in the following chapter of Acts we see the salutary practical effects of this council in the mission to the gentiles, when Timothy joined Paul and Silas. "As they went on their way through the cities, they delivered to them for observance the decisions [*dogmata*] that had been reached by the apostles and elders who were in Jerusalem. So the churches were strengthened in the faith, and they increased in numbers daily" (Acts 16:4–5). These emissaries were delivering decisions to be observed by the whole body, not merely godly advice that churches could either accept or reject. At the same time, they were not imposed hierarchically but arrived at ecumenically by representatives of the broader church. The whole visible church was present federally (covenantally) at the Jerusalem Council.

A covenantal ecclesiology challenges both realist/idealist as well as voluntarist formulations of catholicity. Insisting that the church in its local and wider assemblies consist representatively of ministers and elders (following the repeated reference to the "apostles and elders" gathered at the Jerusalem Council), with elders being ordained laypeople, presbyterian polity avoids clericalism. Placing the rule of the church in ministers and elders not only provides important checks and balances on ecclesiastical power, but it also ensures that the title of "church" refers to the whole body and not simply to a magisterium of clergy while nevertheless affirming the real authority of local and broader assemblies.

As constituted "from above" by the always surprising and disruptive announcement of the gospel, the covenant community receives its catholicity along with its entire being *extra nos*, outside itself, in spite of its own history of unfaithfulness. As constituted "from below" in history ("to a thousand generations"), catholicity is mediated through the faithful ministry of word and sacrament, yielding a succession of faith from one generation to another across all times and places.

Taking its bearings from both of these coordinates—the eschatological and the historical—a covenantal ecclesiology affirms that just as each believer must be joined to the visible body and each generation must be connected to those who precede and follow it, particular (local) churches must make "every effort to maintain the unity of the Spirit in the bond of peace" (Eph. 4:3) by ever wider and deeper solidarity that expresses itself in concrete, visible, and enduring structures. Because this catholic unity of the church is already a perfect gift of God's electing and redeeming grace, we are called to preserve its visible unity in history.

Holiness

With the Augustinian tradition, Reformation confessions maintain that until Christ returns, the visible church remains a "mixed body" of elect and nonelect and that even the regenerate are simultaneously justified and sinful.

Even when discipline is seen as a mark, there is no expectation that it can create a church that consists only of those who are truly converted. The church depends entirely for its being on the gospel proclaimed and sealed in baptism and the Lord's supper. In these means of grace, the Triune God acts, creating and confirming faith in our hearts (Heidelberg Catechism, Q. 65).

At the same time, ecclesial practice was shaped by its context. It is one thing to speak of the church as a mixed body before Christianity became the imperial religion. In Christendom, however, church membership was coterminous with being a subject or citizen of a Christian realm. Far from changing after the Reformation, this confusion of the two kingdoms was heightened as the rising nation-state now determined the confession, worship, government, and discipline of the church. The separation of the believing community from the civil community was an understandable, even if extreme, development.

Just as the church must guard against assimilating itself to a democratic and egalitarian cultural impulse today, the churches of the Reformation accommodated too much to the culture of rising nation-states. Names like the Church of England, the Church of Scotland, and the Church of Sweden reveal a constitution that is different from the addressing of churches by the apostles as "all those in Rome who are loved by God and called to be saints" (Rom. 1:7) or "the church of God that is in Corinth, to those sanctified in Christ Jesus, called to be saints together with all those who in every place call upon the name of our Lord Jesus Christ, both their Lord and ours" (1 Cor. 1:2). It is not difficult with five centuries of hindsight to see how the state church model compromised—even threatened—the holiness of the church as distinct from secular powers and affiliations.

Covenantal ecclesiology advances with an emphasis on corporate solidarity in a representative head. Just as the suzerain and vassals are united as shepherd and sheep, king and kingdom, the people are represented to the great King through the mediation of one of their own. Thus in 2 Corinthians 6:16–7:1, for example, "cleanness" is transferred from the ethnic to the ecclesial domain. Thus the church is holy not because of the inherent righteousness of each believer or of the church corporately, but because that which properly belongs exclusively to the Living Head or federal representative is *imputed* to the whole body, individually and corporately, and on this basis also becomes *imparted* from the one head to the many members (1 Cor. 1:30).

And yet, just as election of a church known to God does not cancel the imperative to preserve the visible bond of unity, so also the church's holiness in Christ cannot be a cop-out for its failure to pursue holiness. The church is called to correct errors and faults through the instruction and discipline exercised especially by its officers in local and broader assemblies. Raising church discipline to the level of a mark of the church underscores the fact that the church is truly a historical institution while distinguishing between its ministerial authority and the magisterial authority of Christ. There is a distinction between the action of Christ and that of his church, but not a separation.

Even the visible church, with all of its weeds sown among the wheat, can be regarded as a holy unity generated by the Word and Spirit, although its eschatological unity is only as yet provisional and largely hidden. The church is not only a people but also a place that the Spirit sanctifies as the sphere of his activity through his creaturely means. The Word and the sacraments do not merely pass on to us the remembrance of Jesus and what he said and did; through them, Christ is present in living speech (Rom. 10:6–17). The essence of the church's holiness is therefore to be found in the message that it hears. At the same time, the faith generated through this Word bears the fruit of love and good works. Since we are holy in Christ, we should pursue holiness. This is as true on a corporate as on an individual level. The imperfection of ecclesial sanctification is no cop-out for pursuing visible holiness.

Apostolic

With other branches of the Reformation tradition, Reformed churches lodge the apostolicity in the succession of a particular ministry rather than of particular ministers. Official Roman Catholic teaching gives the impression that a church can in all sorts of ways be corrupt in its actual ministry—its understanding of the gospel, administration of the sacraments, and discipline—and remain a church if it maintains its episcopal succession in submission to the pope.

In the New Testament, however, the apostles had no successors. To them belonged an extraordinary ministry for an extraordinary period of the church. It was the foundation-laying era (1 Cor. 3:1; Eph. 2:20) followed by the ordinary ministry of pastors and teachers (2 Tim. 2:2). The apostles speak with magisterial authority directly from Christ himself, but they instruct the ordinary pastors who follow in their wake to receive and guard the deposit of truth rather than to add to it (1 Tim. 6:20). Just as there is no mention of "one pastor" in the lists for catholic unity, there is no mention in the New Testament of a continuing apostolic office. There is certainly no list of qualifications for such an office as we find for the offices of pastor, elder, and deacon.

Although there is a distinction in office, this in no way implies a distinction in standing or quality before God. The source of ecclesiastical authority is no more the members of the local congregation than it is the bishops or the pope. Rather, it is possessed *magisterially* by Christ alone (Matt. 28:18; John 15:1–8; Eph. 1:10–23; 2:20–22; 4:15; 5:30; Col. 1:18; 2:19; 3:11; Phil. 2:10–11; Rev. 17:14; 19:16) and *ministerially* by delegated representatives (Matt. 10:1, 40; 16:18–19; 29:19–20; Mark 16:15–16; Luke 22:17–20; John 20:21–23; 1 Cor. 11:23–29; 2 Cor. 13:3; Eph. 4:11–12; 1 Tim. 3:1–15; 2:14–4:3). Although the elders function representatively in the covenant community, they represent the Lord rather than the people.

A covenantal conception of apostolicity seems at least to imply a connectional yet nonhierarchical polity: something like a presbyterian polity. Elders are to be "worthy of double honor," although for this reason, "Do not ordain anyone hastily" (1 Tim. 5:17, 22). Qualifications for ministers and elders are clearly laid out in 1 Timothy 3:1–7, distinct from the office of deacon (vv. 8–13). It is not because of his charisma, personality, communicative skills, or any other characteristics of his person but by virtue of his office that Timothy is told by Paul, "Command and teach these things" in spite of his youth. "Until I come, devote yourself to the public reading of Scripture, to exhortation, to teaching. Do not neglect the gift you have, which was given you by prophecy when the council of elders [*presbyteriou*] laid their hands on you" (1 Tim. 4:11, 13–14). So Paul can also remind Titus that he left him "behind in Crete for this reason, so that you should put in order what remained to be done, and should appoint elders in every town, as I directed you," again listing the qualifications (Titus 1:5–9 NRSV).

Even Peter can identify himself as an apostle in his salutation and yet immediately add, "To those who have obtained a faith of equal standing with ours in the righteousness of our God and Savior Jesus Christ" (2 Pet. 1:1). In his first letter, Peter says,

> Now as an elder myself and a witness of the sufferings of Christ, as well as one who shares in the glory to be revealed, I exhort the elders among you to tend the flock of God that is in your charge, exercising the oversight, not under compulsion but willingly, as God would have you do it—not for sordid gain but eagerly. Do not lord it over those in your charge, but be examples to the flock. And when the chief shepherd appears, you will win the crown of glory that never fades away. (1 Pet. 5:1–4 NRSV)

Because the majority of the elders are not ministers of Word and sacrament, the distinction between those who exercise spiritual oversight and those who are served is not the same as that between clergy and laity in the usual sense. Just as the Jerusalem Council consisted of "the apostles and the elders," broader and local assemblies are composed of ministers (teaching elders) and ruling elders together.[50]

As is evident in Peter's example, all ministers are elders but not all elders are ministers. Together they are "overseers" (*episkopoi*), which is often translated "bishops." This is evident from Acts 20, where the Ephesian elders are called *episkopous* (v. 28), as also in Philippians 1:1. In calling Titus to "appoint elders in every town," Paul uses *presbyterous* and *episkopous* interchangeably (Titus 1:5–7). Significantly, it is Peter who says that Christ is "the Shepherd and Overseer of your souls" (1 Pet. 2:25). Together with other elders, the apostles oversaw the flock under Christ as its only Chief Shepherd, but they gradually widened this pastoral ministry to the ordinary ministers who were trained and ordained for the specific office of preaching, prayer, and teaching (Eph. 4:7–16).

The Second Helvetic Confession repeats some of the patristic quotes often appealed to by the Reformers. Besides Cyprian, Jerome is cited: "Before attachment to persons in religion was begun at the instigation of the devil, the churches were governed by the common consultation of the elders," and Jerome goes so far as to suggest that the introduction of bishops as a separate order above the elders and ministers was "more from custom than from the truth of an arrangement by the Lord."[51] The significance of Peter in the apostolic college was never denied by the evangelical confessions, yet it was pointed out that Christ gave the keys of the kingdom to all of the apostles equally, and it pertained to the confession of Christ as the Son of God (Matt. 16:19; 18:18–20).

The manifold gifts that the ascended King has poured out on his church by his Spirit include not only offices pertaining to the sound instruction in the one faith and spiritual government but also the ministry to the temporal needs of the saints. To give due diligence to this important work without distracting the apostles from their work of preaching and prayer, the diaconate was created (Acts 6; cf. Phil. 1:1; 1 Tim. 3:8–12). Just as the particular offices of minister and elder equip all of the saints as witnesses in their general office as prophets, priests, and kings, "works of service" are done officially in the name of the whole church by the deacons, even though all believers are given gifts of hospitality, generosity, and mutual service in the body.

All believers are priests and, therefore, go directly to Christ without requiring pastoral mediation, edify one another, and share their faith with

---

50. Differing largely in nothing more than terminology, Presbyterian churches refer to the local session, a regional presbytery, and a national general assembly, while Dutch-influenced Reformed churches refer to these bodies as consistory, classis, and synod, respectively.

51. Second Helvetic Confession, in *The Book of Confessions* (Louisville: PCUSA General Assembly, 1991), chap. 18.

unbelievers, but not all are pastors. All believers share equally in one baptism and one Spirit, and, therefore, encourage one another in growth and service, but not all are elders or deacons. Just as no believer is an island, no local church or denomination is the one catholic church; they are only one and catholic as they exist together in Christ through faithful preaching and sacrament.

Not even the apostles acted without consulting the elders. Since elders are ordained members who are not called to the full-time ministry of prayer and preaching, the church—both in its local and broader assemblies—resists the temptation of our fallen hearts toward domination. "You know that the rulers of the Gentiles lord it over them, and their great ones exercise authority over them," Jesus told his disciples as they jockeyed for positions in his kingdom. "It shall not be so among you" (Matt. 20:25–26). Knowing our frame, Jesus instituted checks and balances. Although this outward organization cannot save a church from apostasy and tyranny, such general declensions often coincide with their gradual loss. At the same time, we are only the church with Christ as our head, from whom alone the church receives its unity and catholicity.

The Marks and the Mission

Just as the marks identify the "one holy, catholic and apostolic church," they also define the mission of the church. In his Great Commission, Jesus mandated the preaching of the gospel, baptism, and discipline in the widest sense ("teaching them to observe all that I have commanded you" [Matt. 28:20])." To fulfill this mission, then, the church is to deliver Christ's promise "for you and for your children and for all who are far off, everyone whom the Lord our God calls to himself" (Acts 2:39). The same ministry that builds up the whole body—young and old, rich and poor, Jew and gentile, male and female—goes out to those who do not yet know Christ.

The preaching of the Word and the administration of the sacraments has (or at least should have) such preeminence in the church not because of the desire for clerical dominance over the laity but rather because of the unique and essential service that this ministry provides for the health of the whole body and its mission in the world. So instead of treating the formal ministry and marks of the church as one thing and the mission of the church as another, we should regard the former not only as the source but as the same thing as the latter. Throughout the book of Acts, the growth of the church—its mission—is identified by the phrase, "And the word of God spread." The regular gathering of the saints for "the apostles' teaching and fellowship," "the breaking of bread," and "the prayers" (Acts 2:42) is not treated in Acts merely as an exercise in spiritual togetherness but as itself the sign that the kingdom had arrived in the Spirit. It is only to the extent that the whole body is shaped by this Word that all members can be witnesses.

Furthermore, the Spirit's descent issued in a community that brought wonder and awe to its neighbors. Being built up into Christ, they realized a communion with one another that crossed the lines established by this present age. Richly fed with Christ and his gifts, they shared their gifts—spiritual and temporal—with one another and with outsiders, so that the Word of Christ continued to reverberate in ever-expanding rings from pulpit, font, and table to pew and public houses. The mission of the church is to execute the marks of the church, which are the same as the keys of the kingdom. Even the attributes of the church are manifested publicly by these marks. Where the gospel is being preached, the sacraments are being administered, and the officers are caring for the flock, we may be confident that the mission is being executed, the keys are being exercised, and the attributes of "one holy, catholic, and apostolic church" are being exhibited.

If more traditional ecclesiologies can marginalize the notion of the church as people in their emphasis on the church as place, movement-driven approaches risk making the opposite mistake. A final false choice that I believe Reformed ecclesiology to mediate is of more recent vintage. Churches defined by the "marks" (preaching, sacraments, discipline) are frequently seen as purveyors of "maintenance ministry" rather than having a "missional" orientation. This forces a choice between the church as people or place: "We can't *go* to church because *we are* the church."[52] Dan Kimball writes:

> The excellent book *The Missional Church*, edited by Darrell Guder, makes the case that since the Reformation, the church unintentionally redefined itself. The Reformers, in their effort to raise the authority of the Bible and ensure sound doctrine, defined the marks of a true church: a place where the gospel is rightly preached, the sacraments are rightly administered, and church discipline is exercised. However, over time these marks narrowed the definition of the church itself as a "place where" instead of a "people who are" reality. The word church became defined as "a place where certain things happen," such as preaching and communion.[53]

While some Reformed churches have treated the church as merely a "place where" certain things happen, the missional approach represented by Kimball

---

52. Dan Kimball, *The Emerging Church: Vintage Christianity for New Generations* (Grand Rapids: Zondervan, 2003), 91.

53. Ibid., 93.

accepts the other half of this false choice. Yet we must refuse such a choice. The gospel always comes first. Christ creates his church by his Spirit through the Word and sacraments. There is no *gathering* until there is a *service*. Only because God serves us liberally with his grace is there a church at all in the first place. There is no ecclesial going and giving until there is a hearing and receiving, no sanctification without justification, and no following of Christ apart from faith in Christ. However, it is *God* who is the server, coming to us and those sitting beside us behind the mask of weak ministers. God comes to us in the Word (preached, read, sung, prayed) and in the sacraments, to convict and comfort, to kill and make alive, to judge and to justify, to bring about the effects of Christ's completed work: not only justification but sanctification; not only faith but hope and love. Because Christ fulfilled his mission, and the Spirit is fulfilling his mission today, we have a mission as well. The Word that is preached, taught, sung, and prayed along with baptism and the eucharist not only prepare us for mission but also is itself *the* missionary event as visitors are able to hear and see the gospel that it communicates and the communion that it generates. To the extent that the marks define the mission and the mission justifies the marks, the church fulfills its apostolic identity.

15

Sacraments

TODD BILLINGS

If alien space travelers could visit church communities in different eras of history—observing its vast cultural differences in diverse geographical locations—what would they discover as common among them? At the top of the list would likely be this: that Christians preach the good news of Jesus Christ from their Scripture, they baptize with water in welcoming new members into community, and they celebrate a ritual meal centered on Jesus Christ. Indeed, Andrew Walls, a historian of world Christianity, points to commonalities like these in his own thought experiment about alien visitors observing diverse Christian communities.[1] Of course, even with these three practices, there would be numerous differences. Sometimes these practices would occur among large crowds of people in the open air, accompanied by exuberant, spontaneous singing and dancing. At other times it would be a small group gathering for a liturgy behind closed doors, avoiding the attention of a persecuting state. There would be different words spoken, different uses of space and bodies, different theological convictions expressed. Nevertheless, the deep

---

1. See Andrew Walls, *The Missionary Movement in Christian History* (Maryknoll, NY: Orbis, 2000), 6–7.

significance of these three practices is signaled through a remarkable degree of commonality among diverse groups of Christians across space and time.

This chapter gives an account of Christian teaching, or dogma, concerning the Christian confession about these three fundamental characteristics of Christian identity: preaching, baptism, and the Lord's supper. These practices can be fruitfully explored from a number of different angles. We could analyze the significance of them as practices and rituals, compare the liturgical texts of various traditions, or examine the complex social history in which these practices have taken place in different contexts. In this chapter, however, we will explore these questions in relation to Christian doctrine, addressing this question specifically: *What are preaching and sacraments in relation to the God of the gospel?* The special strength of a dogmatic approach is that it avoids the temptation to reduce these acts to merely human phenomena but sees them first and foremost as participating in the work of the Triune God.

The chapter will use the following dogmatic thesis to outline and exposit a response to that question. *Rooted in the eternal love of the Triune God, the Father sends the Word to create fellowship by the Spirit with a people whom he has appointed to be a sign of his sovereign love for the whole creation. God gives the Word to his people through preaching, baptism, and the Lord's supper, which are instruments of grace received by the Spirit through faith. The sacraments are material signs and seals of God's covenant promise, through which the risen Christ communicates his person and benefits by the power of the Spirit. Baptism is the sacrament of incorporation into Christ and his body, the church; the Lord's supper is the sacrament of communion with Christ and his people, providing nourishment for grateful service to God and neighbor. Through preaching and the sacraments, the Spirit unites a community of witnesses to Jesus Christ and his kingly love for the world.*

Rooted in the eternal love of the Triune God, the Father sends the Word to create fellowship by the Spirit with a people whom he has appointed to be a sign of his sovereign love for the whole creation.

On the most basic level, the sending of the Word in its proclaimed and sacramental forms is not simply a response to sin, a way to counter the corruption of God's good creation. This sending expresses the eternal, trinitarian love of God, as God freely shows his love as "maker of heaven and earth" (Ps. 146:6; Nicene Creed). Before the first day of creation, the love of the Father, Son, and Spirit was already alive and vibrant. While preaching and the sacraments come to creatures in the midst of the drama of creation, sin, and redemption, they fundamentally express an eternal, unbreakable fellowship of the Triune God.

This extraordinary Triune God of love precedes, envelops, and is the central actor in the drama of redemption. When we pick up on the action with Jesus, the incarnation of the Word, we find that the eternal Word already "was in the beginning with God," indeed, "the Word was God," and "all things came into being through him" (John 1:1–3). The Word was in the drama long before creatures came onto the scene. What we see in the Word made flesh, the Son, is an image of this perfect, eternal love. "The Father loves the Son and has placed all things in his hands" (John 3:35 NRSV); "for God so loved the world that he gave his only Son" (John 3:16a NRSV). All of this takes place through the Spirit, for the Father has given the Son "the Spirit without measure" (3:34), and the Spirit is sent as one who will "testify" on behalf of Jesus (15:26). The Spirit incorporates sinners into this divine drama and makes believers witnesses of the Triune God's "sovereign love" in Christ. God is king, and he elects a people for the sake of blessing the whole creation, a people who are signs of the kingdom of God and representatives of Jesus Christ, for "at the name of Jesus every knee should bend, in heaven and on earth and under the earth, and every tongue should confess that Jesus Christ is Lord, to the glory of God the Father" (Phil. 2:10–11 NRSV).

Thus when congregations gather today to receive the Word in proclamation and sacraments, the central actor is not the minister or the worship leader, and the service did not start at 8:30 or 10:00 or 11:00 in the morning. The central actor in worship is the Triune God whose life and love have no beginning and no end. The central movement of worship is the movement that God himself has determined—that *the Father sends the Word to create fellowship with his people by the Holy Spirit.* The central movement of worship is not satisfying the musical preferences of the congregation or inspiring the congregation to be more healthy, happy, or successful. Rather, the central movement of worship is to participate in the ongoing action of the Father, Son, and Holy Spirit in receiving the preached Word and being incorporated into (baptism) and fed (the Lord's supper) as those who are in Christ, sent to represent God's love to the world.

This may sound all too grand for the gathering of congregations around the world today. The singing may sound more like a cacophony than a chorus of angels. We might be thinking more about how to fix the car than the psalm that we sing. And mysteries—like the eternal love of the Triune God—may seem to strike us as abstractions rather than earthy, concrete realities. But God has gone to great lengths to make his astonishing love accessible to us; preaching and the sacraments are accommodations to our bodily existence. Focusing on the sacraments, the Belgic Confession says it this way:

> We believe that our good God,
> mindful of our crudeness and weakness,
> has ordained sacraments for us
> to seal his promises in us,
> to pledge good will and grace toward us,
> and also to nourish and sustain our faith.
> God has added these to the Word of the gospel
> to represent better to our external senses
> both what God enables us to understand by the Word
> and what he does inwardly in our hearts,
> confirming in us
> the salvation he imparts to us.[2]

Thus the sacraments are gifts—gifts that communicate "the Word of the gospel" through "our external senses." God did not have to go to such lengths to communicate his promise—he does so out of love. God desires that we have his promises "sealed" to us—that we may know deeply and broadly of his desire to "pledge good will and grace toward us" and thus nourish our faith.

But does the Belgic Confession's language about our "crudeness and weakness" suggest that the sacraments were given in response to human sin? It does not. In order to understand what is meant by God accommodating to our "crudeness and weakness" in the Belgic Confession, it is helpful to look at the thought of John Calvin on this point.[3] In his commentary on Genesis 2–3, Calvin interprets the tree of life as God's loving accommodation to unite Adam to himself, a sign of God's grace. By this sign God "stretches out his hand to us, because, without assistance, we cannot ascend to him. He intended, therefore, that man, as often as he tasted the fruit of that tree, should remember whence he received his life, in order that he might acknowledge that he lives not by his own power, but by the kindness of God alone."[4]

In this commentary, Calvin is clearly using sacramental language. But significantly, it is before the fall: humans, as circumscribed, physical creatures, have an inherent need not only to hear God's Word (as Adam and Eve did in the garden) but also for physical signs of God's promise to "seal his grace to man."[5] Thus when God stoops over in love to accommodate to our

2. Belgic Confession, 33, in *Our Faith: Ecumenical Creeds, Reformed Confessions, and Other Resources* (Grand Rapids: Faith Alive, 2013), 58.
3. Calvin's theology was a central theological source for Guido De Bres in writing the Belgic Confession, and Calvin approved the confession by letter.
4. See John Calvin's commentary on Gen. 2:9 in *Commentaries on the First Book of Moses Called Genesis*, vol. 1, trans. John King (Grand Rapids: Baker, 1979), 115–18.
5. Calvin, *Commentaries on the First Book of Moses*, 182–84 (on Gen. 3:22).

weakness—using water, bread, and wine as signs and seals—this is not just an "object lesson" to illustrate a verbal point. It is profoundly appropriate for who we are as creatures. We were created to hunger and thirst for the Word of God. We *need* the physical signs of baptism and the Lord's supper to fully and wholly comprehend the loving promise of God. Ultimately, Calvin insists that the sacraments and the preached Word are complementary—they need to be held together. But the physical, sense-oriented mode of the sacraments also gives them a certain advantage for communicating the gospel promise. "But the sacraments bring the clearest promises; and they have this characteristic over and above the word [preached] because they represent them for us as painted in a picture from life."[6]

What implications does this have for the practice of worship today? It means that if the sacraments are merely a matter of mental recollection, then we are not fully entering into God's provision. We are acting as if we were disembodied, without the need of signs and seals of grace. Moreover, while the movements of sin and redemption are central to the triune drama that we enter into, if that is our *exclusive* focus in baptism and the Lord's supper, then we have missed something as well: God's eternal, astonishing love in the gift of creation and embodiment itself. Before sin, Calvin argues (along with Augustine), humans had a need not just for mental remembrance but physical signs of nourishment in God's love. For this was a "figure of Christ," a feeding on the eternal Word of God.[7] Simply as embodied creatures, we need Jesus Christ, the mediator, and physical signs of his presence. As Herman Bavinck notes, "The Son is not only the mediator of reconciliation on account of sin, but even apart from sin he is the mediator of union between God and his creation."[8] The Son is not only the rescue plan to save humans from sin. The Son is the one whom we were created to feed upon from the beginning, the mediator of union and communion with God.

God gives the Word to his people through preaching, baptism, and the Lord's supper, which are instruments of grace received by the Spirit through faith.

The Word of God generates the central action in the biblical drama and is its principal agent. It is not simply abstract information. A minister does not merely dispense information in saying "I pronounce you husband and wife" in a wedding. The words perform an action. In a similar way, God performs

---

6. John Calvin, *Institutes of the Christian Religion*, ed. John T. McNeill, trans. Ford Lewis Battles (Philadelphia: Westminster, 1960), 4.14.5.

7. Calvin, *Commentaries on the First Book of Moses* (on Gen. 2:9).

8. Herman Bavinck, *Reformed Dogmatics*, vol. 4, *Holy Spirit, Church, and New Creation*, ed. John Bolt, trans. John Vriend (Grand Rapids: Baker Academic, 2008), 685—several untranslated Latin phrases excluded.

actions through his Word—creating, covenant making, confronting, and comforting. "The word of God is living and active, sharper than any two-edged sword, piercing until it divides soul from spirit, joints from marrow; it is able to judge the thoughts and intentions of the heart" (Heb. 4:12 NRSV). God's Word is active and a site for divine action.

God's Word is the initial source for creation and covenant making, and it is still the source for life for God's people today. While good advice and devout practice may bring benefits, nothing compares with the Word of God as the source of Christian nourishment and identity. In the words of Martin Luther, "All kinds of works, even contemplation, meditation, and all that the soul can do, does not help. One thing, and only one thing, is necessary for Christian life, righteousness, and freedom. That one thing is the most holy Word of God."[9] This Word is not news that humans have generated or carefully tapped from human consciousness in general. This Word comes to us from God—an external Word, embodying a love in Christ so astonishing that we could never have imagined it. And we cannot control it. We receive the external Word as the Spirit illumines us and enables us to embrace the Word in faith, "*received by the Spirit through faith*." This Word does not need us to add to it anything that is missing. For "if it [the soul] has the Word of God it is rich and lacks nothing since it is the Word of life, truth, light, peace, righteousness, salvation, joy, liberty, wisdom, power, grace, glory, and of every incalculable blessing."[10]

How is God's Word the source of life for his people today? It does not come to us in an unmediated form but through "*instruments of grace*" given "*to his people*," the community of the church. Specifically, the Word of God comes to the body of Christ, the church, giving them fellowship with Christ their Head by the Spirit. This occurs in particular places and times as a community gathers for "*preaching, baptism, and the Lord's supper*." The Father sends the Word as an expression of the Triune God's eternal love, and the *telos* of this sending is in forming a community of witnesses to bless the whole creation in the name of Christ. But these central parts of the action take place as the people of God gather to receive the Word of God in its proclaimed and sacramental forms. To receive the Word, we need to join with others in receiving it concretely in its preached and sacramental forms. For the preached and sacramental forms of the Word share the same basic function, according to Calvin: "The sacraments have the same office as the

---

9. Martin Luther, *Luther's Works*, 55 vols., ed. Jaroslav Pelikan and Helmut T. Lehman (Philadelphia: Fortress, 1955–86), 31:345.
10. Luther, *Luther's Works*, 31:345.

Word of God [proclaimed]: to offer and set forth Christ to us, and in him the treasures of heavenly grace."[11]

Why should we speak about preaching, baptism, and the Lord's supper as instruments of grace? At the heart of it all is the promise of Jesus Christ, the eternal Word made flesh. Jesus Christ has not only *commanded* these three activities for his church, but he has *promised* to offer his presence through these acts. Jesus himself forgave sins and gave new life through his words, and he commissions his disciples to "go into all the world and proclaim the good news to the whole creation" (Mark 16:15 NRSV). And his commission is not without the promise of his presence that "I will be with you always" (Matt. 28:20). Indeed, Jesus indicates that his presence will be mediated by the Spirit as he sends his disciples as "witnesses" shortly before he ascends: "But you will receive power when the Holy Spirit has come upon you; and you will be my witnesses in Jerusalem, in all Judea and Samaria, and to the ends of the earth" (Acts 1:8 NRSV). As the book of Acts unfolds the first act of this drama in the church, preaching the good news is central to the action. Unlike the sacraments, however, preaching should be offered to believer and nonbeliever alike, even though the benefit comes "*by the Spirit through faith*," for preaching is both "an effectual means of convincing and converting sinners, and of building them up in holiness and comfort, through faith, unto salvation."[12] In the words of Paul, "But how are they to call on one in whom they have not believed? And how are they to believe in one of whom they have never heard? And how are they to hear without someone to proclaim him? . . . So faith comes from what is heard, and what is heard comes through the word of Christ" (Rom. 10:14, 17 NRSV). Thus the Reformed confessions treat preaching as a means of grace. Indeed, in the words of the Second Helvetic Confession, in preaching, "the very Word of God is preached, and received of the faithful."[13]

As with preaching, the promise of the Lord is central to why baptism and the Lord's supper are "instruments of grace." Jesus commands and also promises to make himself present through these communal, symbolic actions. In redemptive history, baptism and the Lord's supper are rooted in God's promises in the Old Testament: circumcision as a physical sign of God's covenant promise to Abraham and his descendants; Passover as a physical sign-act of God's deliverance of his covenant people from judgment in Egypt (Exod. 12).

11. Calvin, *Institutes* 4.14.17.
12. Westminster Shorter Catechism, Q. 89, in *The Creeds of Christendom*, ed. Philip Schaff and David S. Schaff, 6th ed. (Grand Rapids: Baker, 2007), 3:695–96.
13. Second Helvetic Confession, 1, in *The Creeds of Christendom*, ed. Philip Schaff, David S. Schaff, 6th ed. (Grand Rapids: Baker: 2007), 3:832.

Baptism, like circumcision, is a sign of initiation into the covenant people of God (Col. 2:11). This rite of initiation is connected to the action and promise of Jesus Christ. Jesus baptizes with the Holy Spirit (John 1:29–35) and proclaims that "no one can enter the kingdom of God without being born of water and Spirit" (John 3:5 NRSV). As a means of receiving God's promise in Christ, it is a means for union with Christ, "as many of you as were baptized into Christ have clothed yourselves with Christ" (Gal. 3:27 NRSV). Yet, as with the reception of preaching, this reception does not take place apart from faith, as the apostle indicates in the previous verse: "for in Christ Jesus you are all children of God through faith" (Gal. 3:26 NRSV).

In the Lord's supper, God's promise of forgiveness and deliverance in the Passover, and of nourishment through the "bread from heaven" (Gen. 16:4), culminates in the promise of Jesus Christ: as Jesus celebrates the Passover with his disciples (Matt. 26:17–19; Mark 14:12; Luke 22:14–15), he performs sign-actions of God's covenantal promise. "While they were eating, Jesus took a loaf of bread, and after blessing it he broke it, gave it to the disciples, and said, 'Take, eat; this is my body.' Then he took a cup, and after giving thanks he gave it to them, saying, 'Drink from it, all of you; for this is my blood of the covenant, which is poured out for many for the forgiveness of sins'" (Matt. 26:26–28 NRSV). Jesus also identifies himself as the fulfillment of God's promise for the "bread of heaven"—for "I am the bread of life" (John 6:35). "Our ancestors ate the manna in the wilderness; as it is written, 'He gave them bread from heaven to eat.' Then Jesus said to them, 'Very truly, I tell you, it was not Moses who gave you the bread from heaven, but it is my Father who gives you the true bread from heaven. For the bread of God is that which comes down from heaven and gives life to the world'" (John 6:31–33 NRSV). Jesus Christ is the embodiment of God's promises in the Passover, and with it the temple and sacrifice for sin—and he is also the embodiment of the nourishment and new life God gives to his people. We receive these promises—the Word himself, Jesus Christ—"*through instruments of grace*," namely, through preaching, baptism, and the Lord's supper received in the church community.

The language of "instruments of grace" has been troubling to some. We will consider two related concerns: the freedom of God to act anywhere he pleases, and the possibility of binding God's action to human action.

First, speaking of preaching and the sacraments as "instruments of grace" can appear to limit the freedom of God to act anywhere he pleases—as if God could *work only* through the gathered community in preaching and the sacraments. What about prayer? What about Christian fellowship? What about acts of service and witness to those in need? The Triune God does, indeed, work through all of these activities and many more. There is something right about the instinct fueling this objection, for God is indeed free. As Balaam's donkey filled with prophetic speech makes abundantly clear (Num. 22:21–39), God can encounter humans in the most unexpected places and moments.

However, if our main affirmation is that God is free, we may ask this: Should we gather together with other Christians, or just take walks in the woods as individuals if one senses that is an instrument of God? Why not just listen to music alone on the iPod? Why not just meet for coffee instead of corporate worship? These and related questions are live issues among Christians in the late modern West. But in functional terms, such questions presuppose that God has *not* promised to meet us in a special, identity-constituting way in corporate worship. Specifically, affirming preaching and the sacraments as "ordinary" instruments of grace means that we do not have the burden of trying to constantly manufacture a new "God-experience" on our own.[14]

Indeed, because of God's command and promise in Jesus Christ, Christians can gather together to receive the life-giving Word in preaching and sacraments, realizing that as instruments of grace, they do not just make us feel good; indeed, they do not just mediate a generic presence of God. Rather, through these human practices Jesus Christ promises to act, mediating nothing less than the eternal movement of divine love, for "*rooted in the eternal love of the Triune God, the Father sends the Word to create fellowship by the Spirit with a people whom he has appointed to be a sign of his sovereign love for the whole creation.*" This Word is received in trust, because faith is the proper response to God's promise in Jesus Christ. Because the good news is constituted by the person of Jesus Christ and communion with the Triune God made known in him, preaching and the sacraments have an exalted station: to mediate Jesus Christ and his benefits to humans by the Spirit, empowering his people to be representatives of his love to the world.

Thus God can and does act in many ways besides the communal actions of preaching, word, and sacrament. For example, God works through the divinely ordained covenant of marriage and in delighting in the wonders of God's creation, through which God declares his glory (Ps. 19:1). Truly, as Roman Catholic poet Gerard Manley Hopkins wrote, "The World is charged with the grandeur of God." Yes. And we need to add that this grandeur has a name: Jesus Christ, for "all things have been created through him and for him" (Col. 1:16 NIV). The restriction of the sacraments to baptism and the Lord's supper, emerging from the command and promise of Jesus Christ, is not an arbitrary restriction of God's freedom; it is a way of insisting that being

14. The term "ordinary" here simply means shared in common with the whole church.

a sacrament is constituted by the self-presentation of Christ and none other.[15] It does not demote marriage or the honoring of God's creation as genuine places where God can work in discipleship. Rather, these activities are lifted up—they come to find their true meaning in light of union with Christ, which baptism and the supper display and offer with such clarity.

If the common instruments of grace—preaching and sacraments—are not defined by their self-presentation of Christ by the Spirit, then "sacramental" can easily be degraded into a term for any vaguely "spiritual" experience. Thus prayer is central to the Christian life as a way of experiencing communion with God. Fellowship is central as well, building up one another in our identity in Christ. Service and witness are central—for they are necessary fruits of our union with Christ and with Christ's body. But the mark that distinguishes the church from all other groups is that it is constituted by God's action in sending the Word through preaching and sacraments to a gathered community. Because God's Word *precedes* all of our responses to it—in prayer, fellowship, witness, and service—the Word in its preached and sacramental forms is a "means of grace" in a distinctive way.

The sending of the Word of God is at the origin of the church—by the Spirit, the Word creates a community of fellowship, prayer, service, and witness. And this Word must be received concretely in community in its proclaimed and sacramental forms. For "even if Christ were given for us and crucified a thousand times, it would all be in vain if the Word of God were absent and were not distributed and given to me with the bidding, this is for you, take what is yours."[16] For this reason, the Lutheran and Reformed traditions have focused their definitions of the "marks" of the true church around preaching and sacraments. The community of the church can and should do other things, and God can and does work in other ways. But the "outward and ordinary means whereby Christ communicateth to us the benefits of redemption"[17] are first and foremost through the Word received in its concrete forms in preaching, baptism, and the Lord's supper.

Now, on to our second objection. Some worry that confessing that God works through material instruments of grace threatens to bind God to human action, making humans in control of the action of God. This was a common criticism from the Reformation of the Roman Catholic belief that sacraments are efficacious "from the work worked" (*ex opera operato*). The Roman

15. This corresponds with the Reformed confessional requirement for sacraments to be instituted and commanded by Jesus Christ. The Heidelberg Catechism is characteristic on this point by including its institution by Jesus Christ as part of the definition and number of the sacraments. See *Our Faith*, 92, Q. 68.
16. Luther, *Luther's Works*, 40:213.
17. Westminster Shorter Catechism, Q. 88, in *Creeds of Christendom*, 695.

Catholic teaching was meant to safeguard the objectivity of sacramental grace rather than focus on the worthiness of the priest or the recipient. But in the sixteenth-century context, it was often perceived as a way to give the clergy control over God's grace and subject to human manipulation. For example, Luther protested the practice of Roman Catholic priests who received money in performing masses for the dead (as a "work" to shorten suffering in purgatory) and the practice of private communion.[18]

In reaction to this, the Lutheran and most Reformed strands of the Reformation emphasized that the sacraments are signs of God's promise, to be received in faith. The sacraments are not works that can gain merit, but God's Word of promise to be received simply as a gift. Faith, as a mode of reception, was not a "human work" before God but a Spirit-enabled trust through which the sacramental benefit was embraced.

In addition, while the sacraments are means of grace, they need to be communally received by faith through the Spirit. Thus, particularly for the Reformed, practices such as "private communion" were condemned, for communion with Christ was inextricably connected with communion with brothers and sisters in Christ. "The cup of blessing that we bless, is it not a sharing in the blood of Christ? The bread that we break, is it not a sharing in the body of Christ? Because there is one bread, we who are many are one body, for we all partake of the one bread" (1 Cor. 10:16–17 NRSV). The sacraments were framed as inextricably ecclesial and communal.

However, Huldrych Zwingli in Zurich went further than either of these moves in response to the Roman Catholicism of the time. Zwingli denied that the sacraments were instruments of grace.

> I believe, and indeed I know, that all sacraments, so far from conferring grace, can neither impart nor bestow it. . . . For since grace is effected or given by the Spirit of God (I speak Latin, using the word "grace" in the sense of forgiveness, remission of sins, or undeserved favour), only the Spirit can bestow the gift. The Spirit needs neither guidance nor vehicle, for he is himself the power and the means by which everything is carried.[19]

Positively, Zwingli emphasized the importance of the communal dimension of celebrating the supper, an emphasis reflected by others in the Reformed

18. Gordon A. Jensen, "Luther and the Lord's Supper," in *Oxford Handbook to Martin Luther's Theology*, ed. Robert Kolb, Irene Dingel, and L'ubormir Batka (Oxford: Oxford University Press, 2014), 324.
19. Translation of Zwingli from Gottfried W. Locher, *Zwingli's Thought: New Perspectives* (Leiden: Brill, 1981), 217.

tradition. He insists that the supper is "an inward and outward union of Christian people" where we "testify to all men that we are one body and one brotherhood."[20] The supper is a communal meal, a testimony to God's work in uniting together the church as one body. But the supper is a remembrance of grace, not a present instrument of grace. As one scholar notes, for Zwingli "as opposed to Luther (and Calvin), the actor of the celebration is not Christ, but the congregation."[21] Thus the centrality of Christ and his promise to nourish his people with himself is replaced with an emphasis on the response of believers. Ultimately, while intended as a reaction to abuses in Roman Catholic practice at the time, Zwingli's approach hinged on a dualism between the material and the physical that Lutherans and Reformed (as well as Roman Catholics) sought to overcome. Although Zwingli's denial of the sacraments as instruments of grace is not taught by any major Reformed confessions, his approach has nevertheless been an influential one on the Reformed and broader evangelical traditions.

In modern theology, Karl Barth developed a neo-Zwinglian doctrine of baptism and the Lord's supper, emphatically denying the sacraments as a means of grace in his later theology.

> Baptism and the Lord's Supper are not events, institutions, mediations, or revelations of salvation. They are not representations and actualizations, emanations, repetitions, or extensions, nor indeed guarantees and seals of the work and word of God; nor are they instruments, vehicles, channels, or means of God's reconciling grace. They are not what they have been called since the second century, namely mysteries or sacraments.[22]

According to Barth, instead of "means of grace," they are human acts of gratitude; instead of instruments of divine grace, baptism and the Lord's supper are fundamentally about "ethics," "actions of obedience," and "the Christian life."[23] With Zwingli, Barth wants to guard against the arrogation of divine grace under human power. On the one hand, Barth's approach is consistent with his approach to revelation in *Church Dogmatics* I/1: "Revelation in fact does not differ from the person of Jesus Christ nor from the reconciliation accomplished in him."[24] But on the other hand, in I/1, Barth

20. W. P. Stephens, *The Theology of Huldrych Zwingli* (Oxford: Oxford University Press, 1988), 225.

21. Locher, *Zwingli's Thought*, 222.

22. Karl Barth, *Church Dogmatics* IV/4, trans. Geoffrey Bromiley (London: T&T Clark, 1981), 46.

23. Ibid., 45–46.

24. Barth, *Church Dogmatics* I/1, 119.

is more open to speaking of Scripture and proclamation as forms (and instruments) of revelation, even while holding to Jesus Christ as the one who constitutes divine revelation.[25] Barth scholars differ in their account of why his "both/and" approach in I/1 was replaced by an "either/or" approach in the later dogmatics. John Webster, a sympathetic interpreter of Barth, notes that in certain ways the concern to preserve a distinctive space for human response is a long-running concern for Barth. But in other ways, his writing in IV/4 on baptism "does not cohere with the rest of the work—neither with Barth's earlier theology of the sacraments, nor with his account of the mediation of revelation, nor, most of all, with the christologically-grounded refusal to divide divinity and humanity too sharply." In his section on baptism, he appears to affirm a dualism similar to Zwingli, making a sharp distinction between "water baptism (an exclusively human act) and baptism with the Spirit (an exclusively divine act)."[26]

What are we to make of Zwingli's and Barth's concern about the danger of making preaching and sacraments into "instruments of grace" that make God's work to be under human control? We have already noted a key affirmation that can help to avoid this danger—framing preaching and the sacraments as a Word to be received in trust, as a gift rather than a work of merit. Moreover, in the next section, exploring the sacraments as "signs and seals" of the covenant will help to ameliorate this danger as well. But there is no use in denying that the notion of preaching and sacraments as instruments of grace can be abused—that in a variety of Christian communions, they are approached as "automatic" ways to manipulate God's work. Perhaps the sermon expresses a health-and-wealth gospel and then claims to be "the Word of God," filling the coffers of the preacher. Or perhaps a parishioner acts as if participation in corporate worship is a ticket to being a "good Christian" while disregarding the ways of God in the rest of his or her life. But Zwingli and Barth do not give solutions to these abuses in a way that focuses our hearts and minds with greater clarity on the gospel. Instead, they divide the bodily and the material from the spiritual and risk displacing God's most lavish, loving accommodations of the gospel to bodily creatures like ourselves. Because of the way in which the self-presentation of Christ by the Spirit constitutes preaching, baptism, and the supper, they should be cherished and celebrated as divinely chosen instruments for conformity to the Son, means of growing into our God-given identity as the body of Christ sent forth in mission to the world.

25. Barth, *Church Dogmatics* I/1, 118.
26. John Webster, *Karl Barth* (London: Continuum, 2004), 157.

The sacraments are material signs and seals of God's covenant promise, through which the risen Christ communicates his person and benefits by the power of the Spirit.

What exactly are the sacraments, and what benefits do they bring? Baptism and the Lord's supper have both commonalities and differences. This section focuses on what they hold in common as sacraments. The Westminster Larger Catechism elegantly summarizes a characteristic Reformed position.

Question 176: Wherein do the sacraments of baptism and the Lord's supper agree?

Answer: The sacraments of baptism and the Lord's supper agree, in that the author of both is God; the spiritual part of both is Christ and his benefits; both are seals of the same covenant, are to be dispensed by ministers of the gospel, and by none other; and to be continued in the church of Christ until his second coming.[27]

Adapting the language of Westminster, we can say that the sacraments are gifts of God that signify "Christ and his benefits." The context for the sacraments is "the covenant"—thus God's covenant fellowship provides the context for understanding the sacraments as material signs and seals. Ministers, as servants of the Word and representatives of the unity of the community gathered, administer the sacraments as a sign of community unity. And the sacraments occur in this time of waiting—of union with the ascended Christ and crying out, "Come, Lord Jesus!" (Rev. 22:20) until Christ visibly returns and culminates his kingdom reign.

For a wide range of theological traditions, the most fundamental theological category for understanding what the sign-acts of baptism and the Lord's supper signify is *union with Christ*. This reflects key New Testament teachings about baptism and the Lord's supper, as well as a shared Augustinian notion of a sacrament that Roman Catholics share with magisterial Protestant traditions: that a sacrament is a sign of "invisible" grace and that Jesus Christ himself is the substance, or the signified, of the sacraments. The centrality of union with Christ is apparent in the Catholic Catechism's exposition on "the Sacraments of Salvation": "'Sacramental grace' is the grace of the Holy Spirit, given by Christ and proper to each sacrament. The Spirit heals and transforms those who receive him by conforming them to the Son of God. The fruit of the sacramental life is that the Spirit of adoption makes the faithful partakers in the divine nature (2 Pet. 1:4) by uniting them in a living union with the only Son, the Savior." Through the sacraments, the Spirit "conforms" them to the Son, "uniting them in a living union" with Jesus Christ.

27. *Book of Catechisms: Reference Edition* (Louisville: Geneva, 2001), 180.

On the other end of the sacramental spectrum, while Credo-Baptists deny that baptism and the Lord's supper signify union with Christ, they still see them as related to that reality.

> Christian baptism is the immersion of a believer in water. . . . It is an act of obedience symbolizing the believer's faith in a crucified, buried, and risen Saviour, the believer's death to sin, the burial of the old life, and the resurrection to walk in newness of life in Christ Jesus. The Lord's Supper is a symbolic act of obedience whereby members of the church, through partaking of the bread and the fruit of the vine, memorialize the death of the Redeemer and anticipate His second coming.[28]

Like Barth, the Credo-Baptist tradition sees these acts as fundamentally acts "of obedience" rather than of receiving grace, and union with Christ is not confessed as occurring through baptism and the Lord's supper as instruments. Nevertheless, union with Christ is essential to the significance of baptism and the supper. But union with Christ is the effect of "the believer's faith," which is then symbolized through these actions.

Together with Roman Catholics, the Lutheran and Reformed traditions unequivocally affirm that union with Christ (rather than the believer's faith) is the *signified* of baptism and the Lord's supper. Thus, though differing from Roman Catholic teaching in important ways, they hold in common a sense of the centrality of union with Christ. As the Genevan Catechism says, "Seeing that our Lord Jesus Christ is truth itself, there cannot be a doubt that he at the same time fulfills the promises which he there gives us, and adds the reality to the figures. Wherefore I doubt not that as he testifies by words and signs, so he also makes us partakers of his substance, that thus we may have one life with him." Jesus Christ is the "truth" or "substance" of the sacraments, and by partaking in Jesus Christ "we may have one life with him."[29] Lutheran confessions insist that the elements are effective only through the Word, and with the signified of baptism being union with the dying and rising Christ (Rom. 6:4–14): "That the old Adam in us should, by daily contrition and repentance, be drowned and die with all sins and evil lusts, and, again, a new man daily come forth and arise"; the signified of the supper is "true body and blood of our Lord Jesus Christ."[30]

---

28. "The Baptist Faith and Message," a statement of faith for the Southern Baptist Convention, www.sbc.net/bfm2000/bfm2000.asp.

29. Quoted from *Tracts Relating to the Reformation*, trans. Henry Beveridge (Edinburgh: Calvin Translation Society), 2:91.

30. Martin Luther, "The Small Catechism," in *The Book of Concord: The Confessions of the Evangelical Lutheran Church*, ed. Theodore G. Tappert (Philadelphia: Fortress, 1959), 349.

Union with Christ is also prominent as the signified of baptism and the supper in recent ecumenical statements, such as the 1982 *Baptism, Eucharist and Ministry* document, which was prepared by representatives from Reformed, Lutheran, Methodist, Anglican, and Orthodox communions. It helpfully points out how a theology of union and communion with Christ can integrate a variety of biblical portrayals: "Baptism means participating in the life, death and resurrection of Jesus Christ" (Rom. 6:3–11; Eph. 2:5–6; Col. 2:13, 3:1); this union with and participation in Christ involves "cleansing" and "justification" (Heb. 10:22; 1 Pet. 3:21; Acts 22:16; 1 Cor. 6:11), the giving of the Spirit (Acts 2), and our "incorporation into the body of Christ" involving "union with Christ, with each other, and with the Church of every time and place" (Eph. 4:4–6).[31] *Baptism, Eucharist and Ministry* has not led to full communion or agreement among the participating groups, but it does point to the ecumenical promise of recovering the centrality of a New Testament theology of union with Christ in approaching baptism and the Lord's supper.

Through the sacraments, "*the risen Christ communicates his person and benefits by the power of the Spirit.*" This affirmation is central and is to be celebrated across the wide range of Christian traditions that celebrate baptism and the Lord's supper as means of grace. Through the sacraments, the living Christ—risen from the dead—gives us himself as nourishment by the power of the Spirit. But how does this happen? Indeed, how do the words and actions with water, the bread, and the cup relate to this feeding upon Christ? This, surely, is a mystery. But since the sacraments are not mysteries in the darkness, but luminous mysteries for the sake of conforming us to Christ, we must not stop our reflection here.

There is no "ecumenical" answer about how to connect the concrete word-acts of the sacrament with union with Christ. This phrase in the dogmatic thesis displays a Reformed emphasis on setting the context for a response: the sacraments "*are material signs and seals of God's covenant promise*" and thus are sites of the action of the Triune God. What is baptism? What is the Lord's supper? For the Reformed tradition, they are not independent causes of grace but "signs" and "seals" of the covenant. As the Reformed confessions repeatedly note, Paul calls circumcision both a "sign" and "seal" of God's covenant of grace with Abraham (Rom. 4:11); similarly, baptism is "a spiritual circumcision" of union with Christ: "In him

---

31. World Council of Churches Commission on Faith and Order, *Baptism, Eucharist and Ministry* (Geneva: World Council of Churches, 1982), 2–3. These Scripture references draw on the publication's document.

also you were circumcised with a spiritual circumcision, by putting off the body of the flesh in the circumcision of Christ; when you were buried with him in baptism, you were also raised with him through faith in the power of God, who raised him from the dead" (Col. 2:11–12 NRSV).[32] Likewise, the Lord's supper is a sign-act in the tradition of Passover, the covenant meal. The covenantal connection is explicit: "This cup that is poured out for you is the new covenant in my blood" (Luke 22:20; cf. 1 Cor. 11:25). In light of this, the primary *context* for understanding the connection between the sign-acts and the signified (Jesus Christ) is not found through speculation about whether Christ gives himself through or within the elements, or whether the "substance" of the elements has changed at some point in the worship service. Rather, the primary context is covenantal—relational—how the Spirit is *"creating fellowship"* through the Word of the Father. This does not take place primarily through people coming to interact with transformed objects, but through the Triune God acting through the sign-actions of preaching, baptism, and the supper to conform his people to Christ and unite them in love to one another as Christ's body. Thus, in this covenantal context, "through Word and the sacraments, we are dislocated from this present age of sin and death 'in Adam' and are relocated 'in Christ,' as citizens of the age to come."[33]

Indeed, there is a "sacramental union" between the elements and actions as signs, and what they signify, Jesus Christ. In the words of the Belgic Confession, "They are not empty and hollow signs to fool and deceive us, for their truth is Jesus Christ, without whom they would be nothing."[34] But this union should not lead us to think that Christ has become contained in the elements. Rather, the water, bread, and cup are taken up into a larger covenantal drama *as signs and seals*. They do not control God's grace, but they are true signs and seals of God's faithful, covenantal love in Christ.

Baptism is the sacrament of incorporation into Christ and his body, the church; the Lord's supper is the sacrament of communion with Christ and his people, providing nourishment for grateful service to God and neighbor.

The French Confession of Faith (1559) beautifully summarizes what baptism signifies:

---

32. For more on the way in which the New Testament suggests that baptism replaces circumcision as a sign of covenant entry, see James V. Brownson, *The Promise of Baptism: An Introduction to Baptism in Scripture and the Reformed Tradition* (Grand Rapids: Eerdmans, 2007), 136–42.

33. Michael Horton, *The Christian Faith: A Systematic Theology for Pilgrims on the Way* (Grand Rapids: Zondervan, 2011), 783.

34. Belgic Confession, 33, in *Our Faith: Ecumenical Creeds, Reformed Confessions, and Other Resources* (Grand Rapids: Faith Alive, 2013).

Baptism is given to us as the pledge of our adoption. In Baptism we are grafted into the body of Christ, washed and cleansed by his blood, and renewed in holiness of life by his Spirit. Although we are baptized only once, the benefit it signifies lasts through life and death, so that we have an enduring testimony that Jesus Christ will be our justification and sanctification forever.[35]

As a rite of entry into the church community, sometimes baptism is associated exclusively with the forgiveness of sins. But in a fashion that reflects the theology of Calvin, it suggests that there is a "double grace" of justification and sanctification received in union with Christ—inseparable but distinct. Thus, in addition to being a pledge of "adoption" and "grafting" into the body of Christ, it is a sign of being "washed and cleansed by his blood" (justification) and "renewed in holiness of life by his Spirit" (sanctification). Therefore, "although we are baptized only once," it is a "pledge" and "enduring testimony" of our ongoing union with Jesus Christ, who "will be our justification and sanctification forever."

The Lord's supper, although different in its imagery and in its administration, also signifies the double grace of union with Christ. "We confess that the holy Supper of the Lord is a testimony of our unity with Jesus Christ. He died only once and was raised for our sake, yet we are truly fed and are nourished by his flesh and blood. Thus we are made one with him and his life is communicated to us."[36] This "testimony to our unity with Jesus Christ" involves both forensic images of salvation—that Jesus died "only once" on the cross, and "was raised for our sake." Yet, unlike baptism as a sign of incorporation and ingrafting, the mode of reception also implies ongoing nourishment and transformation: through the supper "we are truly fed and nourished by his flesh and blood." One with him, his life and benefits are "communicated to us."[37] And since the new life by the Spirit is a gift of union with Christ at the supper, the Belgic Confession can testify that "by the use of this holy sacrament we are moved to a fervent love of God and our neighbors" as an expression of this new life.[38]

Having recognized the commonalities of baptism and the Lord's supper in the previous section—and their ongoing commonalities (the double grace of union with Christ) even with different images (adoption, ingrafting, incorporation versus feeding and nourishment)—it is worthwhile considering

35. The French Confession of 1559, trans. Ellen Babinsky and Joseph D. Small for the Office of Theology and Worship, Presbyterian Church (U.S.A.), n.d. www.presbyterianmission.org /ministries/worship/frenchconfession. http://www.presbyterianmission.org/ministries/worship /frenchconfession/.
36. The French Confession of 1559.
37. The French Confession of 1559.
38. *Our Faith*, 64.

the differences in more detail. The Westminster Larger Catechism provides a helpful summary of a classical Reformed position to supplement the doctrinal thesis statement above:

Question 177: Wherein do the sacraments of baptism and the Lord's supper differ?

Answer: The sacraments of baptism and the Lord's supper differ, in that baptism is to be administered but once, with water, to be a sign and seal of our regeneration and ingrafting into Christ, and that even to infants; whereas the Lord's supper is to be administered often, in the elements of bread and wine, to represent and exhibit Christ as spiritual nourishment to the soul, and to confirm our continuance and growth in him, and that only to such as are of years and ability to examine themselves.[39]

The first contrast is between baptism as received only once, and the supper as "nourishment," thus to be received "often." The contrast is rooted in the singularity of "one baptism" in the New Testament (Eph. 4:5), where baptism is never described as being repeated but framed as a sign of entry in the community. Thus Westminster says baptism is a "sign and seal" of incorporation into Christ and his body. Even if a baptized person denies the faith and later returns to it, a repeat of the baptism is not required, for the baptism was not a "sign" of faith but a "sign" of Jesus Christ and the believer's incorporation into him. The covenant sign—like the covenant sign of circumcision—remains valid, even as it calls forth the recipient to trust in God's promise in baptism and to live into their covenant identity. Does this mean that any baptized person is automatically elect, or "saved?" No—for the Reformed that would be a category mistake. Only the Triune God saves, and baptism as an instrument of grace does not make it an *independent* instrument (under human control). Instead, it is an instrument giving a sign and seal of God's covenant promise, a promise that is to be received by faith (for all who are capable of expressing faith).

The question of who should receive these sacraments is another note of contrast between baptism and the supper. According to Westminster, baptism is to be given "even to infants" (of believers), while the supper is to be given "only to such as are of years and ability to examine themselves." Critics of the Reformed tradition have argued that this contrast is inconsistent—that infants can become members of the church through baptism, receiving the sign and seal of union with Christ, yet those same infants cannot receive the supper. What is an appropriate response to this criticism?

39. *Book of Catechisms*, 180.

First, by way of clarification, the Reformed tradition's practice of baptizing the infants of believers is not based on speculation about the ability of infants to have "faith" but rather the way in which the household was the covenantal unit in the Old Testament and the way in which there are numerous indications that this continues in the New Testament. In the prophets such as Jeremiah and Joel, the promise of God's covenant renewal is confessed to include the children of God's people (Jer. 32:38–40; Joel 2:28–32; Isa. 44:3; 59:21). Peter quotes this Joel prophecy in his Pentecost sermon in Acts 2, providing context for his statement that "this promise is for you and your children" and the household baptisms that take place in Acts. Thus, exegetically speaking, the burden of proof must be on biblical interpreters who believe that the covenantal unit has shifted from households (the "physical seed" of Abraham in the Old Testament) to the individual (as the "spiritual seed" of Abraham, as one who confesses Christ as a condition for receiving baptism) who confesses faith in Christ.[40] Yet, the Reformed position on faith should not be misconstrued: faith is still necessary for receiving the promise of salvation for all who are capable of faith. That may sound like an odd qualification, but it is a qualification that the mainstream Credo-Baptist tradition makes as well: they do not think that children are "unsaved" before they can come to explicit faith in Christ but that they are not yet accountable. Yet faith is necessary for receiving salvation once one is capable of faith. The Reformed tradition agrees with this basic point, though it does not need to postulate an "age of accountability" or require a specific "conversion experience." Rather, the Reformed tradition fits more organically with an approach where faith—as a Spirit-given mode of reception—is like a balloon that increases in accordance with the size of its capacity. But the promise of union with Christ in baptism—whether given to infants or adults—is ultimately to be received by faith unless death or a disability makes the expression of such faith as a mode of reception impossible.

However, there is some validity to the concern that critics have about the dichotomy expressed by Westminster above: children are to receive the "sign and seal" of covenant entry as members of the church. If they are members of the church, why are they not welcomed to the Lord's table? If, according to our doctrinal thesis, *baptism is the sacrament of incorporation into Christ and his body, the church*, then why should baptized children not be welcomed to the table, which is "to represent and exhibit Christ as spiritual nourishment

40. For a cogent defense of the Credo-Baptist case for discontinuity between the physical family and the individual believer as covenantal units, see Stephen J. Wellum, "Baptism and the Relationship between the Covenants," in *Believer's Baptism: Sign of the New Covenant in Christ* (Nashville: B & H Academic, 2007), 105–70; and Paul K. Jewett, *Infant Baptism and the Covenant of Grace* (Grand Rapids: Eerdmans, 1978).

to the soul, and to confirm our continuance and growth in him"? There are a variety of responses to this concern in the Reformed tradition. My own view does not advocate paedocommunion in a strict sense of the term, in which infants receive the supper by virtue of their baptism alone (as in Eastern Orthodoxy). However, I do not think that there are strong reasons for asking children to wait for the table until they are a teenager or young adult (such as a formal "profession of faith" before the congregation). Instead, I draw on the notion of age-appropriate and ability-appropriate faith to suggest that the baptized displaying this faith should be welcomed to the table.[41] Such an approach to faith and the table not only addresses the question of who should be invited to the table but also how to avoid an overly abstract, ethereal approach that can distract from the wondrous gift of Jesus Christ received by the Spirit at the supper.

The central biblical issue underlying this matter is how to interpret Paul's exhortation: "Whoever, therefore, eats the bread or drinks the cup of the Lord in an unworthy manner will be answerable for the body and blood of the Lord. Examine yourselves, and only then eat of the bread and drink of the cup. For all who eat and drink without discerning the body, eat and drink judgment against themselves" (NRSV). With Westminster, it is precisely because young children are seen as unable to "examine themselves" that they are excluded from the supper. Moreover, others would add that young children cannot "discern the body," assuming that this discerning of the body requires a cognitive understanding of the way in which the sign and signified of the supper relate to each other.

The mainstream Reformed tradition interprets this passage in Paul as setting up the conditions and qualifications for partaking of the supper along with words of judgment for those who fail to follow those conditions. But there is also a long Reformed heritage for a minority report. In the sixteenth century, Wolfgang Musculus, a reformer who was a contemporary of Calvin, outlined an argument that provided a contrasting perspective. He points out an argument that should sound familiar in light of the circumcision argument above: "the little children of Jews" took the Passover, so why should our children not partake of the "new Passover," the Lord's supper? Moreover, he questions whether Paul is listing off qualifications for receiving the supper in 1 Corinthians 11:27–29; rather than Paul seeking to exclude young children

41. I am indebted to Randy Blacketer for this section on children at the table. For an accessible account presenting a biblical and pastoral case for this approach, see the Christian Reformed Church of North America document of 2011, "Children at the Table: Toward a Guiding Principle for Biblically Faithful Celebrations of the Lord's Supper, Revised Edition." Available at www.crcna.org/sites/default/files/2011agenda_appendixC.pdf.

by speaking this way, we should note that "none of this [is] to be feared in the little children of them that do believe." Instead, the apostle is not listing a qualification to participate in the supper but a warning against abusing "the sacrament of grace." Musculus notes that young children already partake of the "signified" (union with Christ) even though the "sign" (bread and cup) are denied them. For Musculus, a case for including children can be built on the truth that "Christ is the Saviour of the whole body, that is to say of the church, and that the infants also do belong unto the integrity and wholeness of the ecclesial body."[42]

Musculus gives the basic doctrinal logic of a Reformed case for welcoming children to the table. This case is bolstered by New Testament scholarship, which has pointed to the significance of the overall context of 1 Corinthians 11, one in which failure in Corinth involved rich believers humiliating poor believers and celebrating separately (11:21–22). In the words of Richard Hays, "For Paul, 'discerning the body' means recognizing the community of believers for what it really is: the one body of Christ."[43] Thus "unworthy eating" involves the sinful exclusion of those who should be welcomed to the table, and self-examination is an imperative to examine one's hospitality. As a consequence of this, neither Paul's imperative toward "self-examination" nor "discerning the body" requires a high level of cognitive development or functioning: both warn against possible abuses of the table that would deny that communion with Christ is inherently connected to loving, unified communion in Christ's body, the church. God uses faith as an instrument for us to receive his promises. But if we overintellectualize what is involved in this faith presupposed in 1 Corinthians 11:27–29—using the standard that neither believing children nor persons with cognitive impairments can meet—then we have decentered the central reality of the sacrament itself: that the Triune God has united together unworthy sinners into one baptized body, having fellowship with Jesus Christ and one another at the supper. As Martha Moore-Keish has argued, Reformed Christians in particular can tend to reduce the table to a human act of enacting specific, intellectual beliefs.[44] Instead of this intellectualized

42. Wolfgang Musculus, *Loci communes*, trans. John Man (London, 1578).

43. Richard B. Hays, *First Corinthians* (Louisville: John Knox, 1997), 200. While I agree with Hays that "discerning the body" necessarily involves discerning the community of believers as the corporate body of Christ, this should not be seen as an exhaustive account of what "discerning the body" involves. Anthony Thiselton gives a persuasive argument that 1 Cor. 11:29 is not exclusively corporate in its focus but also involves faith in the gospel. See Thiselton, *The First Epistle to the Corinthians: A Commentary on the Greek Text* (Grand Rapids: Eerdmans, 2000), 888–94.

44. See Martha Moore-Keish, *Do This in Remembrance of Me: A Ritual Approach to Reformed Eucharistic Theology* (Grand Rapids: Eerdmans, 2008).

approach, young and old believers, "abled" and "disabled" believers alike should approach the table as a feast of delight in the gift of Jesus Christ.

Through the sacraments, the Spirit unites together a community of witnesses to Jesus Christ in the world.

Whether one invites baptized children or just professing adults to the table, the sacraments function on both vertical and horizontal planes: union with Christ by the Holy Spirit and a uniting communion with others in the body of Christ, thus being formed as a community of witnesses of God's love to the world in Christ. Tragically, at times the horizontal dimensions of the sacraments have been neglected in the Reformed tradition. In a fateful 1857 decision, the Dutch Reformed Church in South Africa moved away from their Reformed polity and allowed white members to exclude baptized black members from the Lord's supper on the basis of race. Historians have pointed to this action as a decisive move toward the eventual advocacy of racial apartheid by the Dutch Reformed Church.[45] That move was a denial of the reality of union with Christ—and of the gifts of baptism and the supper as not only instruments of communion with God in Christ but also communion with others in Christ's body. As Calvin says in speaking about the supper, "We cannot love Christ without loving him in the brethren."[46]

Indeed, actions of irreconciliation, unforgiveness, and prejudice based on race, gender, or social standing are actions of denial of the central trinitarian movement noted throughout this chapter. "God has sent the Spirit of his Son into our hearts, crying, 'Abba! Father!' So you are no longer a slave but a child, and if a child then also an heir, through God" (Gal. 4:6–7 NRSV). In this sending, the Son "came and proclaimed peace to you who were far off and peace to those who were near; for through him both of us have access in one Spirit to the Father" (Eph. 2:17–18 NRSV). Through Christ, we have corporate access to the Father as adopted children, filled with the Spirit. The unity of reconciliation and love in the church is not an optional "add-on" to the sacraments of baptism and the supper. It is part of the self-giving love that should be part of every celebration of the supper by the baptized. Indeed, for the Reformed, although the supper is not a sacrifice to atone for sin, it always involves a "sacrifice of praise" and thanksgiving: "the Lord's Supper cannot be without a sacrifice of this kind."[47]

As such, the unity of the church—in its union with Christ, the Word, in his death and resurrection—should be a key part of its witness of God's

---

45. See G. D. Cloete and D. J. Smit, *A Moment of Truth* (Grand Rapids: Eerdmans, 1984).
46. Calvin, *Institutes* 4.17.38.
47. Calvin, *Institutes* 4.18.17.

love to the world. This union with Christ, received through the instruments of preaching, baptism, and the Lord's supper, is a gift of participating in the sending of the Word from the Father through the Spirit. As a gift, however, it does not leave us passive. In the words of the Belhar Confession, written in South Africa in response to the failure of the Dutch Reformed Church to live into this reconciled union with Christ, "Unity is, therefore, both a gift and an obligation for the church of Jesus Christ; that through the working of God's Spirit it is a binding force, yet simultaneously a reality which must be earnestly pursued and sought." Indeed, for the sake of witness, "this unity must become visible so that the world may believe that separation, enmity and hatred between people and groups is sin which Christ has already conquered."[48]

The sacraments are not simply ethical actions—actions of obedience. But since the sacraments are signs and seals of union with Christ and instruments of grace, the Spirit springs us into action through the sacraments along with the preached Word. They incorporate us into the mission of the Triune God: in communal fellowship with Jesus Christ and being reconciled in Christian community; in displaying that the shape of the church's life is one of loving God and neighbor; in representing the eternal, unbroken love of the Triune God through lives of worship, service, and witness to a broken and unbelieving world. The sacraments are concrete, bodily, material actions that take place among particular people at particular moments in time. But as Christ's chosen means of exercising his kingship by the Spirit, the Word in its preached and sacramental forms staggers the imagination of pilgrims like us, seeking to discover what it means to live as adopted children of the Father.

48. *Our Faith*, 146.

16

Kingdom of God

MICHAEL HORTON

Like "church," the "kingdom of God" pulls into its orbit a variety of images or analogies. However, kingdom and covenant are not metaphors; they are the concrete basis of the Creator-creature relationship throughout history. YHWH *is* King. YHWH assumed direct suzerainty over Israel when he led his people out of Egyptian bondage and brought them to Canaan. The gods were invoked as witnesses to political treaties in the ancient Near East, but only in Israel was the deity also invoked as the suzerain lord. Therefore, the most fundamental basis of Israel's relationship to YHWH was taken from the world of politics rather than religion.

The Bible's opening scene designates Israel's ruler as the creator and lord of all things. As God's own image and viceroy, humanity was to rule, subdue, and multiply. The opening chapters of Genesis are in large part a polemic against the idols of the nations. Unlike these alleged deities, YHWH cannot be manipulated. He lives and acts in perfect freedom and transcendence. Nor is YHWH one god among many, sovereign only over his allotted department; he is the Lord of all. Also unlike the gods, YHWH freely enters into history even to the point of assuming the direct kingship over Israel. He gives the nation its laws, fusing cult and culture. In this kingdom, land and temple, geopolitics and the sacrificial system, and heaven and earth are of one piece.

Consequently, YHWH is lord of history. While pagan mythology gave birth to a cyclical view of time, YHWH's mighty acts created a sense of moving through time from promises to fulfillment. There is always the possibility of a "new thing" in history, even after disasters were brought on the people by their disobedience. In short, YHWH's kingship was anything but remote. Entering into covenant with this suzerain could bring blessings or curses, but it was never a matter merely of the inner life of the individual soul. In the Bible, the kingdom of God is a political concept that has been made the center of Israel's religious and cultic life as well.

Kingdom and Covenant

The kingdom of God is not a generic concept that can simply be applied in any epoch; its character is determined in every era of history by the covenant according to which it is administered. The Sinai covenant is preceded by a long historical prologue that begins not only with the history of Abraham, Isaac, and Jacob, but also with the creation of all things, including human beings, with Adam as the precursor of Israel as God's earthly viceroy. One way of summarizing the Bible's major theme is "the lordship of YHWH." This lordship seems to be lost after the fall, but is followed by a divine promise carried forward in the Abrahamic covenant and realized in the new covenant. Thus at least one crucial aspect of the New Testament fulfillment is the universal and cosmic lordship of YHWH, in Christ, over all things in heaven and on earth.

It has long been observed that the pattern of suzerainty treaties is evident in the Bible, particularly in the covenant that Israel swore before YHWH at Mount Sinai.[1] For example, a compact version is found in the giving of the Ten Commandments. Exodus 20 begins with a preamble: "I am YHWH your God," followed by a brief historical justification: "who brought you out of the land of Egypt, out of the house of bondage." Therefore, the stipulations follow, chief among them being the first: "You shall have no other gods besides me" (Exod. 20:1–3).

1. See, among others, G. E. Mendenhall, *Law and Covenant in Israel and the Ancient Near East* (Pittsburgh: Biblical Colloquium, 1955); Delbert Hillers, *Covenant: The History of a Biblical Idea* (Baltimore: Johns Hopkins University Press, 1969); M. G. Kline, *The Structure of Biblical Authority* (Grand Rapids: Eerdmans, 1975), esp. chap. 3; Jon Levenson, *Sinai and Zion: An Entry into the Jewish Bible* (New York: HarperOne, 1987). See also Gary N. Knoppers, "Ancient Near Eastern Land Grants and the Davidic Covenant: A Parallel?," *Journal of the American Oriental Society* 116, no. 4 (1996): 670–97. Knoppers challenges the strict typology that opposes "royal grant" and "covenant/treaty." Nevertheless, his detailed critique of this established view does not keep us from recognizing obvious differences among various biblical covenants on the basis of content.

I take the entire patriarchal history to be the prologue to the treaty that Israel swears at Mount Sinai.[2] Moses grounds the national theocracy of Israel in creation itself. The first two chapters of Genesis exhibit a treaty pattern: a prologue naming the suzerain who makes it ("In the beginning God . . ."), a historical prologue justifying his lordship (the act of creation), and the stipulations (in this case only one: refraining from eating the fruit of a particular tree) and sanctions (life for obedience, death for transgression).

As Reformed theology has maintained (with ancient precedent, especially in the second-century church father Irenaeus), God established a covenant of law with Adam as the federal (representative) head of the human race.[3] Just as the vassal-king represented his kingdom, Adam represented all of his fellow image bearers of God. It is a covenant of law (or of works). Although it was grounded in God's lavish love, it placed before Adam a task to fulfill with the help of Eve and a choice to give his ear to the word and command of YHWH or to turn inward and rely on his own inner impulses. Just as YHWH worked in creation to turn chaos into an ordered cosmos and then entered his Sabbath as the enthroned Lord of creation, Adam was to imitate this trek by his labors, endure the trial, and then enter the glorious Sabbath with all of humanity in his train. The tree of life was the sacrament of this glorification that awaited Adam and his posterity, while the tree of the knowledge of good and evil was a test of his fidelity as the vassal-king. This pattern of work (trial) and rest (enthronement) remained so central to the biblical concept of the kingdom that it structured each week of labor and Sabbath.

More than four centuries before the covenant at Sinai, God made a covenant with Abraham (Gen. 12–17).[4] It contains two promises: an earthly land and seed (as many as the stars in heaven) and a heavenly land and blessing for the nations through the single seed of Abraham and Sarah, Jesus Christ (see Gal. 3:16). Especially as we see in Genesis 15, YHWH the suzerain swears an oath and assumes the responsibility for its fulfillment. This is signified by the vision of the theophanic smoking firepot that walks between the pieces of animals cut in half. This would have been a familiar scene in ancient Near Eastern politics, where the great king would cause the lesser king to walk

2. See R. W. L. Moberly, *The Old Testament of the Old Testament* (Eugene, OR: Wipf & Stock, 2011).

3. See Ligon Duncan, "The Covenant Idea in Irenaeus of Lyons," paper delivered to the North American Patristics Society annual meeting, May 29, 1997 (Greenville, SC: Reformed Academic, 1998).

4. I omit here the covenant with Noah. Though a unilateral promise, it pertained only to common grace: God swearing never to destroy the world again by flood. The rainbow, drawn and aimed in a self-maledictory oath toward God the promise maker, would always remind God of his pledge.

between the pieces, accepting the stipulations (and sanctions). Yet what is surprising here is that it is YHWH who makes all the promises and signifies it by walking alone through the pieces. The apostle Paul interprets these "two covenants" as distinct: Sinai "law" and Abrahamic "promise." With Moses as the mediator, the former creates a nation; with Christ as the mediator, the latter creates a church. In the Old Testament, these covenants are operative simultaneously: the law determining Israel's status in the typological land, while Israelites themselves were justified through faith in the promise.[5]

This is clearly a different covenant from the oath that God made to Adam and Eve after the fall and to Abraham and Sarah. The Sinai covenant is typological and temporal, limited to the geopolitical theocracy of Israel, with Moses as its mediator. By contrast, YHWH is the promise maker with Abraham and he passes between the pieces, as if to dash the blood of judgment on himself. Rooted in God's assurance of a Savior in Genesis 3:15, it promises everlasting life through a single descendant of Abraham and Sarah, a worldwide family, and it has Jesus Christ for its mediator.

These contrasts become even more visible when Israel thoroughly violates the Sinai covenant. The prophets are God's lawyers, bringing his covenant lawsuit against the nation. There is nothing in the old covenant—that is, the Sinai covenant—that even offers a way to everlasting life. It is purely typological, as I have argued. Even the sacrificial system can do no more than to point to the remission of sins; it cannot itself bring an end to guilt and divine judgment (Heb. 10:1, 4). Whatever *everlasting* blessings believing Israelites enjoyed, it was based on the promise God made to Abraham rather than the oath that they swore at Sinai. While the nation's exile was based on its

5. While the covenant of works with Adam was a fixture of federal theology (e.g., Westminster Confession, 7), there were differences over its relation to the Sinai covenant. See, e.g., Andrew Woolsey, *Unity and Continuity in Covenant Thought* (Grand Rapids: Reformation Heritage Books, 2012). Characteristic among the Reformed orthodox on this point is the work of Herman Witsius, *Economy of the Covenants* (Charleston, SC: Nabu, 2010). Charles Hodge affirms that the Sinai covenant echoes the covenant of works in *Systematic Theology* (Grand Rapids: Eerdmans, 1946), 117–22. More recently, see Bryan Estelle, J. V. Fesko, and David VanDrunen, eds., *The Law Is Not of Faith: Essays on Works and Grace in the Mosaic Covenant* (Phillipsburg, NJ: P&R, 2009). John Murray, however, rejected an original covenant of works in "The Adamic Administration," *Collected Writings of John Murray*, vol. 2 (Edinburgh: Banner of Truth, 1977). On this debate, see Jeong Koo Jeon, *Covenant Theology: John Murray's and Meredith G. Kline's Response to the Historical Development of Federal Theology in Reformed Thought* (Lanham, MD: University Press of America, 1999). In my view, there are obvious differences between the original covenant with Adam and Sinai, although the principle inherent to both is "Do this and you shall live." Especially helpful is the recently published translation of Geerhardus Vos, *Reformed Dogmatics*, ed. R. B. Gaffin and J. R. de Witt, trans. K. Batteau, D. van der Kraan, and H. Boonstra (Bellingham, WA: Lexham, 2013), 76–80.

violation of the Sinai covenant, a wider hope for a new kingdom is held out
on the basis of the new covenant—in fulfillment of the Abrahamic promise.

"The days are coming, says YHWH, when I will make a new covenant with
the house of Israel and with the house of Judah—not according to the covenant that I made with their fathers in the day that I took them by the hand
to lead them out of the land of Egypt, my covenant which they broke, though
I was a husband to them" (Jer. 31:31–32 NKJV). How different? As different
as the Abrahamic and Sinai covenants: God will unilaterally circumcise their
hearts by grace, regenerating them. He will write his law on their hearts.
"For I will forgive their iniquity and remember their sin no more" (vv. 33–34
NRSV). Notice who is making the promises again: the covenant Lord rather
than the servant Israel. The new covenant is not, therefore, a continuation or
revival of the Sinai covenant.

Old Testament saints were justified, like Abraham, through faith alone in
the promised Messiah alone (Rom. 4:1–24; Gal. 3:5–4:31). Therefore, the law
(or Sinai covenant) was the basis for the nation's continuing existence in the
earthly land, while Israelites obtained salvation from sin and death by looking
to the promise that would be realized in Christ's life, death, and resurrection.

In his Sermon on the Mount, Jesus assumes the seat of Moses and announces a regime change. He speaks not only as the mediator who brings
God's Word, but as YHWH himself: "You have heard that it was said . . . but
I say . . ." Not because the old covenant was wrong but because it had fulfilled
its role of leading by type and shadow to Christ, the theocratic polity is no
longer in force. Instead of calling down God's judgment and driving out the
gentile nations, Jesus commands us to pray for our enemies. God no longer
sends plagues among the godless but "makes his sun rise on the evil and on
the good, and sends rain on the righteous and on the unrighteous," and expects us to imitate his kindness (Matt. 5:43–48 NIV). This is not the time to
judge our neighbors but to take the log out of our own eye (Matt. 7:1–5), to
diligently seek God's good gifts (vv. 7–11), to enter through the narrow gate
(vv. 13–14), and to bear good fruit (vv. 15–27).

When Jesus went to a Samaritan village preaching the good news and
was rejected, James and John wanted to call for fire to fall from heaven in
judgment on them. "But he turned and rebuked them. Then they went on to
another village" (Luke 9:51–56). Nicknamed "sons of thunder," James and
John, it should be remembered, were clearly looking for a kingdom of glory
all the way to the very end (Mark 10:35–45). However, Jesus was announcing
the arrival of the new covenant, which he would inaugurate in his own blood
(Matt. 26:28). The Sinai law-covenant was no longer in effect. Christ's kingdom would be, in this phase, a reign of grace. Confusing Christ's kingdom

of grace with the Sinai theocracy was precisely the error that Paul addressed especially in Galatians.

When Christ instituted the supper in the upper room, he pledged himself as their sacrifice. Instead of sprinkling the blood on them, in accordance with their oath, he swears to walk between the pieces and bear their curse: "Take, eat; this is my body. . . . Drink from [the cup] all of you. For this is my blood of the new covenant, shed for many for the remission of sins" (Matt. 26:26–28, my translation). "The law came through Moses; grace and truth came through Jesus Christ" (John 1:17, my translation).

On the one hand, we must not set the old and new covenants over against each other; the same Triune God is the author of both and they both serve the larger covenant of grace (Westminster Confession 7.5–6). On the other hand, we must not see the new covenant as a continuation of the old. These contrasts serve as the basis for the apostolic contrast between "the law" (i.e., the terms of the Sinai covenant, sworn by the people, with Moses as mediator) and "the promise" (God's unilateral oath in Christ the mediator). As the apostle says, "law" and "promise" refer to "two covenants," represented by two different mediators, two different mothers (Sarah and Hagar), and two different mountains (Sinai and Zion) (Gal. 4:23–26). This is the meaning of Paul's contrast between the letter and the Spirit in 2 Corinthians 3.

The writer to the Hebrews labors over the point that the law of Moses—and everything pertaining to it (the land, the temple, the sacrifices, and the commands governing individual and social life in the theocracy)—was a typological shadow. "But as it is, Christ has obtained a ministry that is as much more excellent than the old as the covenant he mediates is better, since it is enacted on better promises" (Heb. 8:5–6).

It is therefore because of God's pledge to Adam and Eve after the fall and to Abraham and Sarah that there was any hope of God's saving presence rather than judgment. Looking to Christ from afar, as it were, the old covenant saints could actually enjoy the heavenly blessings only together with us—that is, with the dawning of the new covenant (Heb. 11:40). Justified through faith, they were preserved and kept by the Spirit. With the advent of the reality, the shadowy administration is gone. The covenant of law (Sinai) is now designated the "old covenant." "In speaking of a new covenant, he makes the first one obsolete" (Heb. 8:13). We have not come to Mount Sinai but to Mount Zion—the heavenly Jerusalem (Heb. 12:28).

One final point may be offered concerning this eschatological transition from old to new covenant forms of the kingdom. Imagine two funnels placed end to end. The history of the kingdom begins with the widest end of the first funnel, encompassing all of humanity under Adam's representation. After the fall, there is the promise already of redemption through "the seed of the woman": one person in the future (Gen. 3:15). With Abraham too there is the promise of many heirs (as many as the stars in heaven), but also of one heir—the promised "seed"—through whom all the families of the earth will be blessed. Then at Sinai, the whole nation pledges fidelity to YHWH as sole monarch. It is family by family and the nation is a confederation of tribes under YHWH. But later in its history the people demand a human king, and God accedes. "As goes the king, so goes the kingdom." As we know, this arrangement did not go very well either. But God's promise to David—of a perpetual heir on the throne—is never forgotten. By the time John the Baptist appears, God is dividing Israel into messianic and non-messianic, but then Jesus shows up and the spotlight falls on him alone: "Behold, the Lamb of God who takes away the sin of the world" (John 1:29 NASB). Jesus is now the true Israel. Only those who are united to him by faith are the Israel of God.

But just because Israel has been narrowed in this way to one person—Jesus Christ—an expansion of his body begins that is unimaginably wider than anything that Israel had known. Now people from every nation, Jew and gentile, are Israelites, children of Abraham. The gospel now goes out from Jerusalem and Judea to Samaria and the uttermost parts of the earth. The kingdom narrows until it rests on Christ the King and then fans out again in the most universal way. While covenant history had found its center in a particular figure, his influence and significance extends to a truly universal and cosmic scope. Just as the funnel of Old Testament history narrows to Jesus Christ as the true Israel, from him it widens to engulf the families of the world.

The Kingdom and Eschatology

In Israel's history, as Gregory Beale reminds us, "The emerging domination of ungodly kingdoms over the world is sometimes described with the imagery of the outgrowth of Eden's trees as a kind of parody. . . . Such unbelieving empires plant gardens to 'enjoy the aesthetic without the ethic'; they 'collectivize themselves . . . to seek a community without a covenant.'"[6] Without the securities of suzerainty treaties (i.e., a *covenantal* relationship), life and death were managed either under *despotic* or *contractual* regimes dependent on the whim of rulers or the ruled, but not grounded in a transcendent ethical obligation. This is why the people's perennial demand for a king "like the other nations" is so tragic and untrusting of YHWH: they want "a community

6. Gregory Beale, *The Temple and the Church's Mission* (Downers Grove, IL: InterVarsity, 2004), 126, 129.

without a covenant." As the paradigmatic city of God, Eden was to expand outward from the garden itself until the glory of God filled the whole earth. This was humanity's commission in Adam.

The fall shattered this unity of cult and culture: humanity now lived east of Eden. Living under a common curse, creation also shares in God's common grace, which preserves all that God has made, even those who will not finally be preserved from God's wrath on the last day. The pseudo-temple of apostate civilization symbolized by Babel from Genesis 11 to Revelation 18 and 19 would be overthrown by the typological temple in Jerusalem but ultimately only by the true Temple that came down from heaven to create the focus city in himself, a true gathering that renders all such attempts of the earthly city as nothing more than crude parodies.

The goal of all biblical eschatology is that God's dwelling would be with humanity. After the fall, the cultural and cultic activities diverge into two distinct cities, with Cain's line and Seth's line, respectively. Cain builds a city recognized for its cultural achievements (Gen. 4:17–24), while of Seth's line we read, then "people began to invoke the name of the LORD" (v. 26 NRSV). The interaction between these two cities becomes the theater for the repeated showdowns between YHWH and his covenant people ("the seed of the woman") and Lucifer and his allies ("the seed of the serpent").

Kingdom Eschatology in the New Testament

Only with Israel's failure to preserve its typological function in the land does the occasion arise for a theology of hope after exile. This more eschatological concept of the kingdom—the expectation of a messianic ruler—emerges in the prophets (Isa. 40–55; Obad. 21; Mic. 4:3; Zeph. 3:15; Zech. 14:16–17). "The coming kingdom of God will be inaugurated by the great day of the Lord," Herman Ridderbos summarizes, "the day of judgment for the apostate part of Israel, as well as for the nations in general, and at the same time, however, by the day of deliverance and salvation for the oppressed people of the Lord."[7] We find the expectation of a last judgment, for example, in Hosea 4:3; Isaiah 2:10–22; Amos 4:12; 5:18–20; and elsewhere. The coming day of salvation, when YHWH himself acts in judgment and deliverance, is also mentioned throughout the prophetic writings (Hosea 2:17; Mic. 4:1–13; Isa. 9:1–6; 11:1–10).

The coming salvation is imperishable (Isa. 51:6); a supramundane reality will begin (Isa. 60:1); a new heaven and a new earth will come into existence

7. Herman Ridderbos, *The Coming of the Kingdom* (St. Catherines, ON: Paideia, 1979), 5.

(Isa. 60:19; 65:17; 66:22); death will be annihilated (Isa. 25:7); the dead will be raised (Isa. 26:19). In opposition to the eternal woe of the wicked there will come to be the eternal bliss of the redeemed (Isa. 66:24). Even the heathen will share the blessing with Israel (Isa. 25:6; 45:22; 51:4–6), with YHWH as the world's king in that day (Mic. 4:1).[8]

The messianic kingdom of peace is anticipated in Isaiah 9:11; 11:9–10, 32; and Micah 5:1. The redeemer king will come from David's house, enthroned in majesty (Pss. 47; 93; 96; 97; 99). Jesus himself appealed to Daniel 7 for his title as Son of Man. God *is* king in status but will one day *be* king eschatologically in all the earth.

Especially given the parody of kingship in Roman-occupied Israel, with the Second Temple period there is an intensification of messianic longing, with explicit references to the *malkuth shamaim* (Greek: *basileia tôn ouranôn*, "kingdom of heavens"). It entailed (1) God's sovereignty and (2) coming deliverance/vindication. A prayer in the Qaddish reads:

> Glorified and sanctified be his great name in the world he has created according to his own pleasure. May he establish his royal dominion and start his deliverance of his people, and may he bring his Messiah and redeem his people in the time of your life, and in your days, and in the time of the life of the whole House of Israel, with haste and in a short time; and thou shalt say Amen.[9]

At the same time, there were diverse eschatologies on offer from various groups: some emphasize restoration of Israel (e.g., Psalms of Solomon, Testaments of the Twelve Patriarchs, Assumption of Moses), while others are more apocalyptic and supernatural-transcendent irruptions (Apocalypse of Baruch, 4 Esdras). According to the latter especially, "this age" is marked by disaster and oppression, while "the age to come" by the appearance of Messiah and the resurrection of the dead. Jon Levenson has documented this connection of the age to come with the resurrection.[10]

The New Testament announces the arrival of the kingdom of God/heaven generally: "the time is fulfilled," a "great turning-point of history."[11] The two Second Temple Jewish eschatologies are clearly in view: nationalistic-messianic and prophetic-apocalyptic, yet in the New Testament this schema is too tidy. We must not begin with any eschatological a priori but allow the New Testament

---

8. Ibid., 5.

9. Quoted in ibid., 10.

10. Jon Levenson, *Resurrection and the Restoration of Israel: The Ultimate Victory of the God of Life* (New Haven: Yale University Press, 2008).

11. Ridderbos, *Coming of the Kingdom*, 13.

itself to give us the proper horizon.[12] "The coming of the kingdom is first of all the display of the divine glory, the re-assertion and maintenance of God's rights on earth in their full sense," theocentric and cosmic, not (contrary to Albrecht Ritschl and Adolf von Harnack) anthropocentric, individualistic, and limited to the moral/spiritual sphere—the "infinite value of the individual soul."[13] The kingdom cannot be reduced to the covenant or justification by faith but encompasses both as God's self-assertion over "*all* his works."[14] This should not be surprising, since all of the covenants find their fulfillment in Jesus Christ and his kingdom. The covenant of creation provides the wider cosmic horizon, while the Sinai covenant is specific to Israel. Yet both require the successful completion of the probation by the covenant servant. The postfall promise to Adam and Eve, as well as the Abrahamic, Davidic, and new covenants are fulfilled in Jesus Christ's kingdom, inasmuch as they all represent God's immutable commitment to deliver his people through the faithful seed of the woman.

Ridderbos points out that according to the New Testament, "the kingdom of God is not a state or condition, not a society created and promoted by men (the doctrine of the 'social gospel'). It will not come through an immanent earthly evolution, nor through human moral action; it is not men who prepare it for God." Rather, it is something that humans pray and wait for, "nothing less than the great divine-break-through, the 'rending of the heavens' (Isa. 64:1), the commencement of the operation of the divine *dunamis* (Mark 9:1)," the revelation of God's glory (Matt. 16:27; 24:30; Mark 8:38; 13:26).[15] It is a *dynamic* concept ("at hand," "comes," "is coming," "has come").[16] Yet it is a space of peace and a state of peace (Matt. 8:11; 22:1; 26:29; Luke 14:15), "an order of things in which there will be 'superiors and inferiors' (Matt. 5:19; 11:11; 18:1, 4)."[17]

John the Baptist's view of the kingdom transcends the political ideal. "John calls it 'the wrath to come' (Matt. 3:7), which indicates the last judgment."[18] Baptizing the outcasts, tax collectors, and prostitutes, John warned that the ax is laid at the root of the trees and that no longer can anyone claim Abraham as their father simply on the basis of ethnic descent (Luke 3:7–9). A great separation within Israel is coming. "Every tree therefore that does not

12. Ibid., 14–15.
13. Ibid., 20–21.
14. Ibid., 22–23.
15. Ibid., 24.
16. Ibid., 25.
17. Ibid., 26.
18. Ibid., 29.

bear good fruit is cut down and thrown into the fire" (v. 9). "I baptize you with water," said John, "but he who is mightier than I is coming, the strap of whose sandals I am not worthy to untie. He will baptize you with the Holy Spirit and with fire. His winnowing fork is in his hand, to clear his threshing floor and to gather the wheat into his barn, but the chaff he will burn with unquenchable fire" (vv. 16–17). Israel's remnant saved, the rest will be judged along with the world. "Salvation and perdition are the two stages into which the tremendous future will diverge according to the prophecies: first the descent of the Holy Spirit, and then the day of judgment (cf. Joel 2:28–32; Ezek. 36:26; Zech. 12:9–10)."[19]

Identifying the kingdom of God with his own role as the Son of Man, Jesus's own view, then, was in line with the prophetic-apocalyptic concept rather than the nationalistic. In the Beatitudes, Ridderbos notes, "Jesus describes the bliss of the kingdom of heaven as the inheritance of the [new] earth, as being filled with the divine righteousness, as the seeing of God, as the manifestation of the children of God, all of these expressions pointing beyond the order of this world to the state of bliss and perfection that shall be revealed in the future."[20] It exists in heaven, but we pray even now for it to come to earth (Matt. 6:10). "The coming of the kingdom is the consummation of history, not in the sense of the end of the natural development, but in that of the fulfillment of the time appointed for it by God (Mark 1:15); and of what must happen before it." Thus it is not only a vertical intrusion (*übergeschichtliche*) but an event in time (*endgeschichtliche*). "This is why the practical-existential meaning of the preaching of the coming kingdom is not only expressed by the categories of 'conversion,' 'decision,' *Entscheidung*, but no less also those of 'patience,' 'perseverance,' 'vigilance' and 'faithfulness.'"[21] In Oscar Cullmann's words (contrary to Rudolf Bultmann), "It is not *a new time* that has been created with Christ, but *a new division of time*."[22]

Geerhardus Vos observes that the new covenant is to the writer of Hebrews as limitless as the old was provisional: "It is the ocean into which all the rivers of history roll their waters from the beginning of the world."[23] It is not just forward (historical) or the reverse (futurity), but eschatological (irruption from above): "The New Covenant, then, coincides with the age to come; it brings the good things to come; it is incorporated into the eschatological scheme of

19. Ibid., 30.
20. Ibid., 44.
21. Ibid.
22. Ibid., 45.
23. Geerhardus Vos, *The Teaching of the Epistle to the Hebrews* (Eugene, OR: Wipf & Stock, 1998), 194.

thought."[24] While for Paul, "this age" and "age to come" are representative of sin and death (flesh) and righteousness and life (Spirit), for Hebrews these two ages represent two covenants: the old and the new.[25]

From thinking of the eschatological state as future, the Christian mind is led to conceive of it as actually present but situated in a higher sphere (semi-eschatological). The horizontal, dramatic way of thinking gives place in part to a process of thought moving in a perpendicular direction and distinguishing not so much between before and after but rather between higher and lower.[26] Therefore, the kingdom is "from above," created by the powers of the age to come: an eschatological inbreaking rather than an immanent historical progress.

The writer to the Hebrews explains that believers have not come to Mount Sinai but

> to Mount Zion and to the city of the living God, the heavenly Jerusalem, and to innumerable angels in festal gathering, and to the assembly of the firstborn who are enrolled in heaven, and to God the judge of all, and to the spirits of the righteous made perfect, and to Jesus, the mediator of a new covenant, and to the sprinkled blood that speaks a better word than the blood of Abel. (Heb. 12:22–24)

Unlike the earthly cities, including Jerusalem, the heavenly city cannot be shaken. It is not a kingdom that we are *building* but one that we are *receiving* (Heb. 12:26–28). "For here we have no lasting city, but we are looking for the city that is to come" (13:14 NRSV). This was true even in the case of Abraham:

> For he looked forward to the city that has foundations, whose architect and builder is God. . . . All of these [patriarchs] died in faith without having received the promises, but from a distance they saw and greeted them. They confessed that they were strangers and foreigners on the earth, for people who speak in this way make it clear that they are seeking a homeland. If they had been thinking of the land that they had left behind, they would have had opportunity to return. But as it is, they desire a better country, that is, a heavenly one. Therefore God is not ashamed to be called their God; indeed, he has prepared a city for them. (Heb. 11:10, 13–16 NRSV)

Believers are already citizens of this heavenly city, "seated with Christ in heavenly places" (Col. 3:1–4; 1:12–18; Eph. 1:3; 2:5–6; Phil. 3:19–20; Gal. 4:25–26; 1 Cor. 11:18; 14:26–28; 1 Cor. 1:2).

24. Ibid., 195.
25. Ibid., 196.
26. Ibid., 198.

Engaging Contemporary Eschatologies of the Kingdom

The challenge for us in this age is to avoid both *underrealized* and *over-realized* eschatologies of the kingdom. Although Revelation 20 is the only biblical passage that refers explicitly to a thousand-year reign, this chapter is crucial in generating different views of Christ's kingdom. There are three major positions.

According to a *premillennial* view, history will generally deteriorate until Christ returns to establish a thousand-year kingdom; thus he will return *before* the millennium. In this future era, the promises made to Israel as a nation will be fulfilled to Israel as a nation. The *postmillennial* view teaches that Christ will return *after* the millennial kingdom has gradually "Christianized" the kingdoms of this age. For those who embrace an *amillennial* interpretation, both views misunderstand the symbolic nature of numbers in apocalyptic literature generally and in the Apocalypse in particular. According to this view, the "thousand years" refers to the period between Pentecost and Christ's return. "Amillennial" is a misnomer, since those who hold this view do believe in a "millennium," symbolically understood as unfolding in the present.

However, within each of these views one discerns a spectrum of emphases. Over against *historic* premillennialism, *dispensationalists* draw a sharp distinction between Israel and the church as well as the kingdom of God and the kingdom of Christ. According to dispensationalism, covenantal history is marked by failure. Even when the Messiah came and offered the kingdom to Israel, they rejected it. Currently, the kingdom is not present; it will appear at Christ's second coming. "The kingdom, however, will also be a period of failure."[27] Thus even in this future millennial kingdom the purpose is not only to dispense Christ's gifts, which he has already won by his own trial, but "is the final form of moral testing."[28] Whenever the prophets anticipate the restoration of Israel, it is the revival as a geopolitical kingdom, with a restored temple and sacrificial system, that they have in mind. For example, Amos 9:11–12 prophesies, "'In that day I will raise up the booth of David that is fallen and repair its breaches, and raise up its ruins and rebuild it as in the days of old, that they may possess the remnant of Edom and all the nations who are called by my name,' declares the LORD who does this." They will "plant vineyards and drink their wine, and they shall make gardens and eat their fruit" (v. 14). To imagine that these promises are fulfilled in the church is to engage in a "spiritualizing" hermeneutic.

27. Lewis Sperry Chafer, *Major Bible Doctrines* (Grand Rapids: Zondervan, 1974), 136.
28. Ibid.

Amillennialists reply by referring to the way in which the apostles interpreted such passages. James cited this very prophecy (Amos 9:11–12), inserted "Gentiles" in the place of "Edom and all the nations," and announced that this was fulfilled in the calling of the gentiles after Pentecost (Acts 15:13–20). Amillennialists interpret the book of Revelation as providing snapshots of the entire history of Christ's kingdom between his two advents. From Jesus's teaching in Matthew 25–26, it is argued that this entire period is to be marked simultaneously by the victory of the gospel throughout the world and the persecution of the church until the Son of Man comes again to gather his elect and take his throne of judgment. There is simply no space in this scenario for an intervening millennial kingdom.

These historical categories are of rather recent vintage, so we should be careful of anachronism. Nevertheless, it would seem that the earliest post-apostolic eschatology followed an amillennial interpretation.[29] Having said this, there are different varieties within this view that result chiefly from different historical contexts among readers. In an era of persecution and marginalization, Jesus's teaching in Matthew 25–26 and in Revelation would have brought comfort to the oppressed, confirming the line from Tertullian that "the blood of the martyrs is the seed of the church."[30] However, this context changed radically with Constantine and Theodosius. When the church's ministers were now found dining with the emperor, the current reign of Christ could be—and was—understood as a mission to be undertaken jointly by church and empire. Reading the Old Testament conquest allegorically, the emperor could be seen as the heir of David, riding off to drive the "Canaanites" out of Christendom. Instead of being martyrs, the church's leaders collaborated in crusades against the infidel: Jews, Muslims, and dissenting sects from the church. Contrary to the judgment of many contemporary critics, this was not a failure of an amillennial position but the result of a dangerous confusion of Christ and culture, the sword of the Spirit and the sword of Caesar.

Also among postmillennialists there is a range of emphases. The gradual progress of Christ's kingdom through the advance of the gospel has been understood in terms similar to an amillennial perspective.[31] Yet it could also be interpreted as a golden age that must be brought into being by all "Christian" powers, civil and spiritual. This latter tendency can be seen in various revolutionary movements, from the early Anabaptist Thomas Müntzer to various

29. So argues Charles E. Hill, *Regnum Caelorum: Patterns of Millennial Thought in Early Christianity* (Grand Rapids: Eerdmans, 2001).
30. Tertullian, *Apologeticus* 50.
31. For example, B. B. Warfield, as noted in Fred Zaspel, *The Theology of B. B. Warfield* (Wheaton: Crossway, 2010), 533n1.

liberation theologies. In recent decades, Christian Reconstruction or Theonomy has represented what has been called "a liberation theology of the right."[32]

Any of these positions may be exploited for an overrealized eschatology. Postmillennialism seems most easily disposed to this tendency, especially when it is wedded to a secular (Western) view of progress and enlightenment. Dispensationalism tends to see contemporary events in the Middle East as a realization of imminent Armageddon and Israeli statehood in 1948 as a fulfillment of prophecy. Amillennialists can interpret the kingdom of Christ as not only present now in suffering and witness but also as triumphant in visible glory. To an even larger extent, more critical questions concern the proper relationship between spiritual and temporal power, whether redemption involves the whole creation or is reduced to individual souls, and whether the Great Commission is to be confused with the cultural mandate.

Beyond these positions, contemporary eschatologies have been influenced by broader trends. After centuries of assimilating the kingdom of Christ to the progress of secular culture, liberal Protestantism was shaken from within by the "consistent eschatology" of Albert Schweitzer (1875–1965). In sharp contrast to the idea of a gradual evolution of the kingdom of love taught by Jesus, Schweitzer argued that Jesus expected an imminent kingdom arriving from above, bringing cataclysm and judgment. However, when this kingdom did not materialize, Jesus surrendered himself to death in the hope that it would somehow provoke the Father to act on his behalf. This perspective was short-lived, however, soon to be replaced by the dialectical circle (early Rudolf Bultmann, Karl Barth, Friedrich Gogarten, and Emil Brunner) of the 1920s and '30s, with its tendency to set history and eschatology in antithesis as virtually synonymous with a time-eternity dualism.

However, by midcentury there was a flowering of renewed interest in history, even among some of Bultmann's students. Associated with a working group at Heidelberg University that included Oscar Cullmann and Gerhard von Rad (Old Testament), Gunther Bornkamm (New Testament), and Hans von Campenhausen (historical and systematic theology), renewed attention to the history of Israel and its covenant theology challenged a century of anti-Jewish (and therefore, anti–Old Testament) presuppositions of biblical scholarship, especially in Germany.

A young member of this circle, Wolfhart Pannenberg, sought to relate eschatology to history in developing his theology of the kingdom.[33] Pannenberg's eschatology is future-oriented. Only in the end is the meaning of the whole of history finally revealed. However, as the prolepsis of the end,

---

32. Richard John Neuhaus, "The Theonomist Temptation," *First Things*, May 1990, www
.firstthings.com/article/1990/05/002-why-wait-for-the-kingdom-the-theonomist-temptation.
33. Wolfhart Pannenberg, *Theology and the Kingdom of God* (Philadelphia: Westminster, 1969).

Christ's resurrection is the fully realized aspect of eschatology that warrants the Christian hope.

Jürgen Moltmann joined this broader trajectory, but with a more radical expectation of the power of Christ's future to transform the present. Indeed, eschatology is the principal theme of Moltmann's work as it is shaped by Joachim of Fiore's vision of the Age of the Spirit and influenced by German mysticism (especially Jakob Böehme) and idealism (especially Hegel and Schelling), democratic socialism, and a staunch defense of premillennialism.

Where Barth tended to see eschatology as a hope beyond history in an eternity-time dualism, Moltmann saw eschatology as the hope within history that propels us toward the future. In Barth's *Römerbrief*, the kingdom of God cannot be identified with social revolutions. God's revolution negates the state; it doesn't reform it.[34] Timothy Gorringe notes that Moltmann's *Theology of Hope* is especially directed against the "epiphany of the eternal present" that he found in Barth.[35] No more in Barth than in Augustine does the future introduce a genuine *novum* (new thing) that breaks up our own history of death, according to Moltmann. Amillennialism tends to support the status quo, he argues, while popular forms of apocalyptic premillennialism (especially dispensationalism) encourage visions of final catastrophe. He writes:

> The Thousand Years' reign of Christ, "the kingdom of peace," is hope's positive counterpart to the Antichrist's destruction of the world in a storm of fire, and is indispensable for every alternative form of life and action which will withstand the ravages of the world here and now. Without millennial hope, the Christian ethic of resistance and the consistent discipleship of Christ lose their most powerful motivation.[36]

"Christian eschatology—eschatology, that is, which is messianic, healing and saving—is millenarian eschatology."[37] Moltmann's guide is Joachim of

34. Karl Barth, *Der Römerbrief*, ed. H. Stoevesandt (Zurich: Theologische Verlag, 1985), 505–7.
35. Timothy Gorringe, "Eschatology and Political Radicalism," in *God Will Be All in All*, ed. Richard Bauckham (Edinburgh: T&T Clark, 1999), 104. Similarly, Miroslav Volf observes, "Eschatology was the heartbeat of Barth's theology. But it was an eschatology that managed to posit itself, so to speak, only by denying itself. It was an 'eternalized' eschatology, which had much to do with the present (the transcendent 'eternal Moment' in the early Barth) or with the past (the 'hour' of Christ's coming in the later Barth), but little with the future—either the future of God or the future of God's world" (Miroslav Volf, "After Moltmann," in Bauckham, *God Will Be All in All*, 233–34).
36. Jürgen Moltmann, *The Coming of God* (Minneapolis: Fortress, 2004), 201.
37. Ibid., 202. For an interesting reflection on how he developed his early foci, see Moltmann, "Can Christian Eschatology Become Post-Modern? Response to M. Volf," in Bauckham, *God Will Be All in All*:

Fiore. "Joachim's great idea was to identify the seventh day of world history with the kingdom of the Spirit. The great 'sabbath' of history, before the end of the world, and the kingdom of the Spirit mean the same thing."[38] Moltmann's exegesis—both of Scripture and historical theology—has been subjected to significant rebuttals. He sees clearly the disastrous effect of the confusion of Christ with empire, but identifies this move with amillennialism itself. As Mark C. Mattes has observed, Moltmann's widely influential views present humans almost entirely as actors rather than receivers, building the kingdom rather than receiving it. As Mattes remarks, "In Luther's view, the kingdom is promised. It is Jesus Christ in action. . . . For Luther, the kingdom is realized linguistically, not existentially, metaphysically, or politically, in the gift-word of the gospel as sheer promise."[39] By contrast, Mattes says, "Along with Engels and Bloch, who maintained that communism was indebted to Müntzer (1490–1525), Moltmann believes that the human is always an agent (*homo semper agens*), not a recipient." He continues,

> The paradoxes that help preserve faith, described by Luther (that one is simultaneously lord and servant, sinful and righteous, that God is hidden and revealed, and that Jesus Christ is human and divine), are flattened out into a "Christ transforming culture" perspective, effected, strangely enough, by means of a counterculture—"Christ against culture," to use the helpful typology of H. Richard Niebuhr (1894–1962). . . . Here, the gospel is given within the matrix of law.[40]

But this misses the important fact that "misplaced trust" is the root cause of ethical problems and can be challenged only by proclamation of the gospel.[41]

What next? is a typically modern question—generally an American one. So what comes "after" the modern? We have it: the post-modern. What comes after the post-modern? We have it: the ultra-modern. Or are these merely further instalments of modernity, which is always out to outstrip itself—a kind of post-ism? If we look at the ever-shorter "shelf-life" of what is produced, and the speeding up of time, then the post- and ultra-modern are no more than modernity in new packaging. (259)
After writing *Theology of Hope*, Moltmann says he came as a visiting professor at Duke and found that it was being used to bolster American optimism. Thereafter, "I promised friends that if I were to come back I would only talk about 'the theology of the cross.' This is what I then did in 1972 with my book, *The Crucified God*, which appeared in English in 1974" ("Can Christian Eschatology Become Post-Modern?," 260). The Reformation attack on millenarianism as a "Jewish dream" caught his attention. "The Reformation critics no doubt grasped the fact: anyone who banishes the millennium from the Christian hope has no further interest in Israel and no positive relationship to the Jews" ("Can Christian Eschatology Become Post-Modern?," 262).
38. Moltmann, *Coming of God*, 204.
39. Mark C. Mattes, *The Role of Justification in Contemporary Thought* (Grand Rapids: Eerdmans, 2004), 89–90.
40. Ibid., 91.
41. Ibid., 92.

Mattes goes so far as to call Moltmann's approach a "post-tribulation premil-
lennialist of the 'left.'"[42] Rather than unify law and gospel, Mattes argues
that we should stand with the victim because he or she is our neighbor. In
this perspective, all of our secular callings in the political kingdom are valuable (funded by God's common grace) but only the ministry of the gospel
is redemptive (proceeding by saving grace).[43] Liberated from the power and
principalities of death that turn us in on ourselves, believers are now free to
receive God's gift of salvation and, through this energy of faith, to serve their
neighbors in love.[44]

Richard Baukham raises a most trenchant concern. Moltmann assumes
that an amillennial perspective negates the renewal of the present creation in
favor of a "hope for souls in the heaven of a world beyond this one."[45] However, Bauckham finds this an odd claim, totally unsupported by the history of
amillennial interpretation. Amillennialists expect a total renewal of creation
at Christ's return and not simply in a thousand-year reign. If this is the case,
"The question we must ask is: what theological function does the millennium
fulfill which the new creation cannot?"[46] Moltmann argues, "Before the millennium there is no rule of the saints," but only the church: "the brotherly
and sisterly, charismatic, non-violent fellowship of those who wait for the
coming of the Lord."[47] However, this argument is "in danger of suggesting
that while it is premature for Christians to attempt to exercise absolutist and
violent domination over the world now, they will exercise such domination in
the coming millennium."[48] If this is so, the Anabaptist radicals were not wrong
in principle but only in their timing.[49] Furthermore, "according to Revelation,
it is not only in the millennium that the saints rule (20:4) but also in the New
Jerusalem (22:5)." Why substitute a penultimate for an ultimate realization of
the restoration of creation? "Once the new creation is understood in this way,
it is not clear why a millennium is necessary."[50] "According to Moltmann, only
the millennium supplies a 'goal of history.'"[51] However, is not this goal just

42. Ibid., 95.
43. Ibid., 105.
44. Ibid., 112.
45. Richard Bauckham, "The Millennium," in Bauckham, ed., *God Will Be All in All*, 135,
citing Moltmann, *Coming of God*, 147.
46. Bauckham, "Millennium," 135–36.
47. Moltmann, *Coming of God*, 184.
48. Ibid., 137.
49. Ibid., 138. For his statement concerning radical Anabaptists, Bauckham refers to Norman
Cohn, *The Pursuit of the Millennium*, 2nd ed. (London: Paladin, 1970), chap. 13.
50. Bauckham, "Millennium," 138.
51. Ibid.

as certainly realized—even more so—in the end of history, as amillennialism argues, as within it? "Why should it not have its goal in the new creation?"[52]

No less than millenarianism does an amillennial position anticipate the consummation of Christ's kingdom in the future. Yet it does so without an expectation of either final destruction of the cosmos (as in some popular versions of dispensationalism) or of a reduction to this wonderful condition to a millennial age. Miroslav Volf argues that "understood as transition, the millennium is not only unnecessary but *detrimental*."[53] Moltmann reduces the economy of grace to the categories of redemption and completion, with the former made subservient to the latter:

> Though on account of transgression human beings need to undergo the transforming judgment of God (eschatological judgment conceived in analogy to justification), the transgression will be taken care of above all by the overcoming of transience, because—in a reversal of the Pauline account of the matter—the cause of sin is death. Rooting sin in death is highly problematic, however. Nothing suggests that we kill, let alone commit other sins, only because we cannot endure mortality, as Moltmann argues.[54]

Redemption is more crucial, because, "With all imaginable completing done, the world will forever remain 'old.' As Paul argues in 2 Corinthians 5, the passing away of the old world and creation of a new world rests on redemption."[55]

Kingdom and Church

Roman Catholic modernist thinker Alfred Loisy writes, "Jesus expected a kingdom and in its place there appeared a church."[56] At first, the apocalyptic concept of a kingdom—especially the type of kingdom that Jesus announced—seems quite different from a historical institution extending through all times and places. Jesus promised, "I will build my church and the gates of Hades will not prevail against it" (Matt. 16:15–18 NRSV). Admittedly, however, Jesus does not often employ the noun "church" (*ekklēsia*) but refers repeatedly to the kingdom (*basileia*).

The important question, however, is whether by his words and actions he was building his church. It is clear enough from the narrative plot of the

52. Ibid., 139.
53. Ibid., 243.
54. Ibid., 249.
55. Ibid., 251.
56. Alfred Loisy, *The Gospel and the Church*, ed. Bernard B. Scott, trans. Christopher Home (Philadelphia: Fortress, 1976), 166.

Gospels that Jesus is redefining the *qahal* (assembly) of Israel. Insiders become outsiders and outsiders become insiders. Not only does Jesus describe this; by his teaching and signs he is actually bringing this reversal about in his ministry. He gathers the nucleus of the new Israel (the prophesied remnant) and promises to gather other sheep from another fold into one flock under himself as one Shepherd (John 10 as the fulfillment of Ezek. 34).

To understand the distinctiveness of the kingdom in its present phase and its relation to the church, we should first recognize the differences between the *Great Commandment* and the *Great Commission*.

All humans, even as fallen, remain God's image bearers—with the original commission to love God and neighbor. Every person, believer and unbeliever alike, receives a distinct vocation for his or her calling in the world and the Spirit equips each person for these distinct callings in common grace. We were created to subdue, rule, fill, and expand.

Only after the fall in the garden is the gospel announced, creating a new community within the human race that will be given an additional mandate: the Great Commission. They will subdue, rule, fill, and expand, but not by creating just governments and empires of cultural advancement—for this is now common rather than holy labor—but by Word and sacrament. Instead of dominating and subduing by sword, this community will fill the earth with God's glory by announcing the fulfillment of God's promise and his gathering of the remnant from all the nations to Zion.

With the Sinai covenant, however, God establishes a new theocratic kingdom, reuniting the cultural and cultic mandates. After the nation's thorough transgression of the covenant, YHWH prosecutes his case and Israel is exiled. The theocracy will be dismantled (signaled by the Spirit's evacuation from the temple, rendering it common rather than holy) and the land will be ruled by foreign oppressors, but YHWH will again hear and answer the cries of his exiled people and send his Messiah.

This Messiah has arrived. In this phase of the kingdom, with the King himself present in the flesh on the earth in humiliation and forgiveness rather than power and glory, the cult and culture once again become distinct activities. The kingdoms of this age, like Rome, pursue the cultural mandate and now believers are commanded by Jesus, "Give therefore to the emperor the things that are the emperor's, and to God the things that are God's" (Matt. 22:21 NRSV). Even oppressive rulers are "God's ministers" in the cultural sphere of our common curse and common grace alongside unbelievers; we must honor and submit to these governors (Rom. 13:1–7; 1 Pet. 2:13–17).

In the meantime, believers pursue their common vocations alongside unbelievers in the world with distinction in service and godliness, while also pursuing the aims of the Great Commission that Jesus gave to his disciples. Comparable to Joseph and Daniel, who held positions of secular leadership during periods of exile, some believers may become rulers of state. Nevertheless, like Joseph and Daniel, they are not to confuse their cultural mandate (which they share with unbelievers) and their evangelical mandate to spread God's kingdom. While refusing to accommodate their faith and practice to the idolatry of the nations they serve, such leaders also do not seek to advance and expand God's kingdom by means of the powers that they are given as secular rulers. Christ's followers will not imitate the gentile rulers "who lord it over" their people, but will instead imitate the Son of Man who "came not to be served but to serve and to give his life a ransom for many" (Matt. 20:28 NRSV). Nowhere in the New Testament is the Great Commission fused with the cultural mandate. Rather than offer a blueprint for establishing Christ's kingdom through cultural, political, or social power, Paul's instructions for daily conduct of believers in civil society seem rather modest: "to aspire to live quietly, to mind your own affairs, and to work with your hands, as we directed you, so that you may behave properly toward outsiders and be dependent on no one" (1 Thess. 4:11–12 NRSV).

Yet as citizens of the kingdom of Christ, believers are to submit to their spiritual teachers and rulers who exercise their ministry by serving rather than by dominating. Unlike the false shepherds who led Judah astray by their own alleged "words from the LORD," the true shepherds are those who have "stood in the council of the LORD" and are therefore called and sent—authorized to bring God's Word from the heavenly council chamber to the covenant people (Jer. 23:18, 22–23). The Twelve fulfill that condition, as those who have stood in this sanctuary as it is present on earth in the person and ministry of Jesus Christ. Initially sent "to the lost sheep of the house of Israel," they are commissioned to "proclaim the good news, 'The kingdom of heaven has come near,'" with attending signs of Christ's victory over the powers of darkness—the "wild animals" that terrorize the flock (Matt. 10:5–8 NRSV).

So we see already the divine authority and commission being given to Peter (representative of the disciples), the Twelve (representative of Israel), and the Seventy (representative of the whole earth, echoing the seventy included in the table of nations in Gen. 10). In Matthew 16, Jesus tells Peter upon the latter's confession, "I will give you the keys of the kingdom of heaven, and whatever you bind on earth will be bound in heaven, and whatever you loose on earth will be loosed in heaven" (vv. 17–19 NRSV). Then two chapters later we read of Jesus telling the Twelve more generally, "Truly I tell you, whatever you bind on earth will be bound in heaven, and whatever you loose on earth will be loosed in heaven. Again, truly I tell you, if two of you agree on earth bout anything you ask, it will be done for you by my Father in heaven. For where two or three are gathered in my name, I am there among them" (Matt. 18:18–20 NRSV).

Just as Ezekiel prophesied, this will involve a judgment not simply between sheep and goats (the last judgment), but sheep from sheep: the house of Israel itself will be divided and judged as the Twelve, and then also the Seventy, fulfill their commission from village to village (Luke 10:1–20). Jesus sent the Seventy (representative of the nations) in pairs (the legal rule for witnesses). Jesus tells them, "Whoever listens to you listens to me, and whoever rejects you rejects me, and whoever rejects me rejects the one who sent me" (v. 16 NRSV). They do not themselves exercise this judgment, but on the contrary "shake off the dust from [their] feet" if they are not welcomed. "Yet know this: the kingdom of God has come near. I tell you, on that day it will be more tolerable for Sodom than for that town" (vv. 11–12 NRSV). The Seventy return to announce to Jesus with jubilation, "Even the demons are subject to us in your name" (v. 17), and Jesus responds: "I watched Satan fall from heaven like a flash of lightning. See, I have given you authority to tread on snakes and scorpions, and over all the power of the enemy; and nothing will hurt you. Nevertheless, do not rejoice at this, that the spirits submit to you, but rejoice that your names are written in heaven" (Luke 10:18–20 NRSV).

In their commission, the Twelve become the under-shepherds of the Great Shepherd, bearing their Suzerain's own authority. Again, this is in contrast to the "false shepherds" of Israel: the "teachers of the law," and this contrast with respect to the authority of their respective teachings was not lost on the people (Luke 11:52; Matt. 23:1–2; John 8:33; Matt. 11:25–26). In the heavenly worship of Revelation 7, the church militant becomes the church triumphant, sheltered by the one seated on the throne in their midst. "They will hunger no more, and thirst no more; the sun will not strike them, nor any scorching heat; for the Lamb at the center of the throne will be their shepherd, and he will guide them to springs of the water of life, and God will wipe away every tear from their eyes" (Rev. 7:16–17 NRSV).

The Spirit and the Kingdom

Preparing the disciples for his departure, Jesus gave his farewell discourse: the fullest instruction on the Holy Spirit's role in the economy of grace (John 14–16). Even after this teaching, as well as his death and resurrection and the forty days of instruction that followed, the disciples were still asking even at his ascension, "Lord, will you at this time restore the kingdom to Israel?" (Acts

1:6). As faithful Jews, they would have assumed "exodus" and "conquest" as the great historical events that defined Israel's existence. After the risen Jesus appeared to them, they knew that the exodus that Jesus had accomplished in Jerusalem was far greater in scope and depth than the typological deliverance from Egypt. This side of the cross and resurrection, they now understood Christ's teaching concerning a greater exodus from death and destruction. In his conversation with the two disciples along the Emmaus road, Jesus said, "O foolish ones, and slow of heart to believe all that the prophets have spoken! Was it not necessary that the Christ should suffer these things and [then] enter into his glory?" (Luke 24:25–26). As Jesus proclaimed himself from all of the Scriptures for the next forty days, the disciples finally recognized that this was the real exodus. It was everlasting life in the resurrection, not long life in the land; liberation from death, sin, and hell, not just from Egypt; good news for the world, not just for Israel; and therefore it was about the justification of the ungodly, both Jew and gentile, in Jesus Christ. However, they were still thinking in terms of an imminent conquest with their new Joshua leading the way to a revived nation.

> Then he opened their minds to understand the Scriptures, and said to them, "Thus it is written, that the Christ should suffer and on the third day rise from the dead, *and that repentance and forgiveness of sins should be proclaimed in his name to all nations, beginning from Jerusalem. You are witnesses* of these things. And behold, I am sending the promise of my Father upon you. But *stay in the city until you are clothed with power from on high.*" (Luke 24:45–49, emphasis mine)

Jesus repeats his teaching in the farewell discourse as well as his postresurrection instruction in Luke 24 in his answer to their question in Acts 1:7–8: "'It is not for you to know times or seasons that the Father has fixed by his own authority. But you will receive power when the Holy Spirit has come upon you, and you will be my witnesses in Jerusalem and in all Judea and Samaria, and to the end of the earth.' And when he had said these things, as they were looking on, he was lifted up, and a cloud took him out of their sight" (Acts 1:7–9).

In each of these passages, Jesus's answer to "What comes next?" is the same: the outpouring of the Spirit, so that his Word will become effective in the world, uniting Jews and gentiles to himself in one body. Just as his resurrection inaugurated the new creation, Jesus's sending of the Spirit from the Father would mark the beginning of the conquest—not of Palestine, but of the nations. All of this Jesus explains in his farewell discourse. While Christ continues to exercise his threefold office from heaven, as the glorified King at the Father's right hand, the Spirit makes this office effectual on earth.

There is the *prophetic* ministry: as the Son is the sole embodiment of all truth, the Spirit will be sent "to guide you into all truth." The Spirit is the guide, while the Son is the destination. Just as the Son did not speak on his own authority, but related everything he himself heard from the Father, the Spirit "will not speak on his own, but will speak whatever he hears, and he will declare to you the things that are to come" (John 16:13 NRSV). Indeed, Jesus adds, "He will glorify me" (v. 14). The Spirit is the one who "does not in fact present himself but the absent Jesus," as Douglas Farrow notes. Through Word and sacrament, the Spirit seizes us for his future. "The Spirit's work is an infringement on our time, an eschatological reordering of our being to the fellowship of the Father and the Son, and to the new creation."[57] Christ will also exercise his *priesthood* through the Spirit's work. The Spirit will come to "prove the world wrong about sin, righteousness, and judgment," with unbelief in Christ as the focus of that conviction (John 16:8 NRSV). This is why Jesus calls the Spirit "another Advocate" (*allos paraklētos*, John 14:16–18), the same word used concerning Christ in 1 John 2:1. While Jesus intercedes for us in heaven, the Spirit intercedes within our hearts, assuring us of our adoption (Rom. 8:16). He will bring about within us a realization of our guilt before God and give us faith in Christ. They will be united to Christ as their saving mediator. Consequently, his *kingdom* will spread as he indwells his people and empowers them to be his witnesses throughout all nations. "As you have sent me into the world," Jesus prays to the Father, "so I have sent them into the world" (John 17:18 NRSV). The Father sends the Son, the Son returns to the Father to send the Spirit, and the Spirit descends to send his witnesses to the nations.

All of these promises are fulfilled at Pentecost. The signs are obvious, and they all focus on this ministry of the Spirit: flames of witness appear over each disciple; through the gift of tongues each person hears the gospel in his or her own language; and Peter proclaims Christ as the fulfillment of the prophecies of old. Not only are the witnesses clothed with power by the Spirit; those who heard Peter's sermon were "cut to the quick" as the Spirit made the convicting word effective in their hearts. Convinced of their guilt and of the gospel of Christ, they asked what to do in response. "Repent and be baptized every one of you in the name of Jesus Christ for the forgiveness of your sins, and you will receive the gift of the Holy Spirit. For the promise is for you and for your children and for all who are far off, everyone whom the Lord our God

---

57. Douglas Farrow, *Ascension and Ecclesia: On the Significance of the Doctrine of the Ascension for Ecclesiology and Christian Cosmology* (Grand Rapids: Eerdmans, 1999), 257.

calls to himself" (Acts 2:38–39). While a good many individuals ("about three thousand souls") were "cut to the heart" by this message, repented, believed, and were baptized, they were organized by the Spirit into a new human community. "And they devoted themselves to the apostles' teaching and fellowship, to the breaking of bread and the prayers" (v. 42). From this shared union with Christ, these pilgrims from faraway regions were so united with one another that the worshiping community itself was a witness to the world. "And the Lord added to their number day by day those who were being saved" (v. 47).

The prophets had identified the "last days" with the pouring out of the Spirit, particularly in the prophecy that Peter cited (Joel 2:28). At this point, it now became clear how the conquest would unfold after Jesus's ascension. Throughout the book of Acts, the growth of the kingdom is identical with the phrase, "And the word of God spread" (Acts 6:7; 12:24; 13:49; 19:20). Through the proclamation of the "living and active" Word, the Spirit convicts us of our guilt by the law and of Christ's gift of righteousness by the gospel. It is by that gospel outwardly proclaimed that the Spirit regenerates us inwardly (Acts 16:14; Rom. 10:6–17; 2 Cor. 4:6; Heb. 4:12; 1 Pet. 1:23–25).

Thus it becomes clear that, in its present phase, the kingdom of Christ is associated with the forgiveness of sins and the gift of the Spirit. As in Peter's sermon, so in many other places in the prophets and the New Testament, these twin gifts appear together. For now, the kingdom does not appear in outward glory, like the kingdoms of this age. Instead of reigning over all powers and authorities, the church suffers. Following in the train of the King who was to "suffer these things and [then] enter his glory" (Luke 24:26), Christ's kingdom is hidden under the cross until the King returns to make all things new. In the meantime, his kingdom grows through the proclamation of the gospel, the administration of the sacraments, and discipline. This is not to make a choice for Paul's "church" over Jesus's "kingdom." Rather, it is to accept our Lord's own teaching, as he associates his kingdom with the forgiveness of sins. Having accomplished his exodus, he has looted Satan's empire. He now pursues his conquest by his Spirit, giving the keys of his kingdom to his ambassadors to set the prisoners free (Matt. 16:18–19; 18:15–20). Breathing on the disciples, the risen Christ tells them, "Receive the Holy Spirit. If you forgive the sins of any, they are forgiven them; if you withhold forgiveness from any, it is withheld" (John 20:22–23). Jesus surely inaugurated his kingdom. However, if he had consummated it in his first advent, there would have been no space in history for the Spirit's ingathering of his elect Jews and gentiles. If the final resurrection and judgment of the world had taken place at Christ's resurrection, his kingdom would have had no subjects and the King would have had no co-heirs.

In this phase of the kingdom, then, we do not expect the overthrow of all oppression, injustice, war, idolatry, and immorality. Indeed, if the church itself is a "mixed body" and even the elect are simultaneously justified and sinful, then the church itself must await the consummation of the kingdom. It must patiently await Christ's return and joyfully use the productive intermission to bring good news to all people. For the time being, the church is not identical to the fully realized kingdom. At the same time, the "already" that the church has experienced is a real participation in and harbinger of the consummation. There really are signs of the age to come here and now throughout the earth. Those "dead in sin" are alive in Christ, forgiven and renewed citizens of the new creation. It is precisely because we "have the first-fruits of the Spirit" that "even we ourselves groan within ourselves, eagerly waiting for the adoption, the redemption of our body" (Rom. 8:23 NKJV; cf. Gal. 4:6). As the *arrabōn* (downpayment) of our final redemption, the Spirit gives us the "already" of our participation in Christ as the new creation, and it is the Spirit within us who gives us the aching hope for the "not yet" that awaits us in our union with Christ (Rom. 8:18–28; cf. 2 Cor. 1:22; 5:5; Eph. 1:14). The *more we receive* from the Spirit of the realities of the age to come, the *more restless we become*. Yet it is a restlessness born not of fear but of having already received a foretaste of the future. And wherever this ministry spreads, Christ's kingdom becomes truly present in the passing evil age as a city set upon a hill.

The story began with the lordship of YHWH over all creation and his commission to humanity to rule and subdue in his name. Even after the rebellion of his viceroy, God kept his kingdom alive. Cast out of paradise, Adam and Eve were given the promise of a coming kingdom. Feeding on this promise, a church emerged from Seth and his descendants who called on the name of YHWH. Then his kingdom eventually became a nation. "But like Adam, they transgressed the covenant" (Hos. 6:7). Still, after exile "east of Eden," the prophets announced a new covenant of far greater blessings based on far greater promises. From a human perspective, YHWH's lordship was by no means a forgone conclusion. On the contrary, the promise ran against the flow of history under the reign of sin and death. Yet he has demonstrated his lordship and installed his King on his holy hill and has sent his Holy Spirit to sweep the children of disobedience into his kingdom of grace. This kingdom lies hidden to the rulers of the earth. But when Christ returns, the lordship of YHWH will be unquestionably visible and realized fully in depth and scope. Only then will we hear the seventh angel announce, "The kingdom of the world has become the kingdom of our Lord and of his Christ, and he shall reign forever and ever" (Rev. 11:15).

The Kingdom's Consummation

Especially in the face of the Islamist threat, there is growing pressure for Christians to distance themselves from the Old Testament "texts of terror." Even among evangelicals, this sometimes reaches the point of a nearly Marcionite opposition of the God of Israel and the Father of Jesus Christ.[58] However, as we have seen in the Hebrew Scriptures, holy war is based on holy land. The land of Canaan belongs to YHWH, but it has been usurped by a culture of idolatry and violence. In the book of Joshua, it is stressed that YHWH is the one who cleansed the land of the "serpent" and all that defiles, giving his enemies into Israel's hand. And if the Israelites fail to keep his covenant, they will find themselves evicted as well.

The theme of holy war does not disappear in the New Testament. Rather, it reaches its fulfillment, of which the Old Testament conquests were mere previews. Echoing Moses at Mount Sinai, Jesus's Sermon on the Mount in Matthew 5 declares, "You have heard it said . . . but I say . . ." He is not condemning the law of Moses but announcing a change in administration. It is no longer a time for hating and driving out the enemies with swords but of praying for them.

However, it is hardly because Jesus is a friendlier deity than YHWH that these commands are issued. Rather, as I point out above, Jesus is announcing the polity for the interim era between his two advents. For now, "we do not wrestle against flesh and blood, but against the rulers, against the authorities, against the cosmic powers over this present darkness, against the spiritual forces of evil in the heavenly places" (Eph. 6:12–13). This battle can be waged only in the power of the Spirit through the Word, especially the gospel (vv. 14–17). The church proclaims the gospel, administers the sacraments, and cares for the flock and in this way the true and final conquest unfolds. Christ has given his church the power of the keys to bind and loose, promising that he will build the church, and the gates of hell will not be able to hold back its advance (Matt. 16:18–19).

Yet when Christ does return, it will be to raise the dead, to deliver his elect to safety, and to execute the last judgment, as Jesus prophesies in the Olivet Discourse (Matt. 25–26). The separation of sheep and goats is not merely typological this time but final, with two everlasting destinies: "eternal punishment" and "eternal life" (Matt. 25:46). Indeed, most of the explicit

58. See, e.g., C. S. Cowles, "The Case for Radical Discontinuity," in *Show Them No Mercy: Four Views on God and Canaanite Genocide*, ed. C. S. Cowles et al. (Grand Rapids: Zondervan, 2003). See more recently Peter Enns, *The Bible Tells Me So: Why Defending Scripture Has Made Us Unable to Read It* (New York: HarperOne, 2014), esp. chap. 2.

passages on eternal punishment in Scripture come from Jesus himself (Matt.
5:30; 8:10–12; 13:40–42, 49–50; 22:13; 24:51; 25:30; cf. Luke 16:19–31). The
apostles also witness to this final judgment with two everlasting destinies
(Rom. 2:5, 8–9; 1 Thess. 5:1–3; 2 Thess. 1:7–10; Jude 7, 13; 2 Pet. 3:7). It is in
the Apocalypse where we meet the war to end all wars in the person of the
Warrior-King, Jesus Christ himself (Rev. 6:15–17; 16–18; 19:1–18; 20:14–15).

In the meantime, believers long for the appearing of their Savior (2 Tim.
4:8). Though their body decays and eventually dies, their soul is being sanctified
(2 Cor. 4:16–18) and will be immediately in the presence of the Lord on death
(2 Cor. 5:8). Nevertheless, the ultimate hope is the resurrection of the body
and life everlasting in a restored cosmos—nothing short of the *palingenesis*
(re-creation) promised in Matthew 19:28: As Paul argues in 1 Corinthians 15,
the resurrection of Jesus is the beginning of this *palingenesis*-resurrection and
sweeps us into his train (cf. Rom. 8:9–30; 2 Tim. 1:10; Col. 3:1–17).

Much of patristic and medieval theology anticipated the "beatific vision."
Although Plato coined the phrase for gazing on the "One" by resolute contemplation, the church properly understood that there was indeed a final
transformation—even glorification—consequent on beholding Christ face-
to-face (2 Cor. 3:18). In Eastern Orthodoxy, *theōsis* or deification is the goal
of salvation. When we behold Christ, we will be like him in glory (1 John
3:2). Even now we are "partakers of the divine nature" (2 Pet. 1:4). According to the churches of the East, we never share in God's essence but in his
energies—that is, the activities of his grace.[59]

Early Reformed theology never shied away from these classic categories.
References to the beatific vision and even to *theōsis* abound in the Reformed
orthodox and Puritan writers. What stands out, however, is the way in which
they focused these themes on the final resurrection. In contrast with all neopla-
tonic temptations, these theologians identified the highest state of existence
not with the disembodied soul but with the clothing of our mortal bodies with
Christ's immortality. At the resurrection, we are made like God as much as
is possible for a creature. And yet, precisely as such, we are made more truly
human than ever as we share in the glorious image of God that is possessed
already by our Head. Calvin can even say, "Let us mark that the end of the
gospel is to render us eventually conformable to God, and, if we may so speak,
to deify us." He hastens to add that "the word nature is not here essence but
quality." To be "deified" is to be "partakers of divine and blessed immortality

59. Basil of Caesarea, *Doctrina partum de incarnatione verbi*, ed. Franz Diekamp, 2nd ed.
(Münster: Aschendorff, 1981), 88–89; Vladimir Lossky, *The Mystical Theology of the Eastern
Church* (Crestwood, NY: St. Vladimir's Seminary Press, 1976), 221; Timothy (Kallistos) Ware,
The Orthodox Church (New York: Penguin, 1997), 231.

and glory, so as to be as it were one with God as far as our capacities will allow . . . the image of God in holiness and righteousness."[60]

Calvin was by no means alone in such comments; it became a key theme under the topic of "glorification."[61] In our union with Christ, according to Peter van Mastricht, "there is a certain shadowing forth" of the unity of the divine persons of the Trinity.[62] "Sight, joy, and love" are the essential features of the eternal state, notes Francis Turretin, because of the "efflorescences" (energies) of God. In glorification, faith yields to sight; hope is fulfilled in joy; and love consummated "will answer to love begun" in our sanctification. "God cannot be seen without being loved; love draws joy after it because he cannot be possessed without filling with joy." Although we will not behold God in his essence, "There is nothing else than a certain effusion and emanation (*apporrōe*) of the deity upon the souls of the saints, communicating to them the image of all his perfections, *as much as they can belong unto a creature.*" In short, what is consummated is "the covenant of God."[63]

Indeed, this regeneration of all things extends to the body as well as to the soul (Westminster Shorter Catechism, Q. 38). Interpreting this question and answer of the Catechism, Thomas Watson remarks, "What a welcome will the soul give to the body! Oh, blessed body!" The soul has "*appetitus unionis*—a desire of reunion with the body and is not fully happy till it be clothed with the body." If the ultimate promise were merely for the soul, "then a believer would be only half saved." In fact, "The *dust* of a believer is part of Christ's mystic body."[64] Therefore, in Reformed theology, deification and the beatific vision converge in the glorification-resurrection that leads us into God's Sabbath rest.[65] It is a gift that is given not to some saints in this age but to all saints in the age to come.

60. *Commentaries on the Catholic Epistles*, ed. and trans. John Owen (Grand Rapids: Baker, 1996), 371 (on 2 Pet. 1:4).

61. For example, see Francis Turretin, *Institutes of Elenctic Theology*, ed. James T. Dennison Jr., trans. George Musgrave Giger (Phillipsburg, NJ: P&R, 1922), 12.9–10.

62. Peter van Mastricht, as quoted in Heinrich Heppe, *Reformed Dogmatics*, ed. Ernst Bizer, trans. G. T. Thompson (London: Allen & Unwin, 1950), 512.

63. Turretin, *Institutes of Elenctic Theology*, 20.8.6, 15 (emphasis mine).

64. Thomas Watson, *A Body of Divinity Contained in Sermons upon the Westminster Assembly's Catechism* (Edinburgh: Banner of Truth, 1986), 305–9 (emphasis mine).

65. I treat this at greater length in *The Christian Faith: A Systematic Theology for Pilgrims on the Way* (Grand Rapids: Zondervan, 2011), 692–708.

CONTRIBUTORS

Michael Allen (PhD, Wheaton College) is associate professor of systematic and historical theology at Reformed Theological Seminary in Orlando. He has written or edited several books, including *Reformed Catholicity* (with Scott Swain) and *Justification and the Gospel*.

Todd Billings (PhD, Harvard Divinity School) is the Gordon Girod Research Professor of Reformed Theology at Western Theological Seminary in Holland, Michigan. He has written several books, including *Calvin, Participation, and the Gift* and, most recently, *Rejoicing in Lament*.

Oliver Crisp (PhD, Kings College, London) is professor of systematic theology at Fuller Theological Seminary. He is a founding editor of the *Journal of Analytic Theology*. He has published widely in systematic and historical theology as well as analytic theology, including *Deviant Calvinism* and *Retrieving Doctrine*.

Richard Gaffin (ThD, Westminster Theological Seminary) is Charles Krahe Professor Emeritus of Biblical and Systematic Theology at Westminster Theological Seminary in Philadelphia. He has written widely regarding soteriology and pneumatology, including his most recent book, *By Faith, Not by Sight*.

Michael Horton (PhD, University of Coventry and Wycliffe Hall, Oxford) is the J. Gresham Machen Professor of Systematic Theology and Apologetics at Westminster Seminary California. He has published numerous books, including a systematic theology titled *The Christian Faith* and a four-volume dogmatics series.

Kelly Kapic (PhD, Kings College, London) is professor of theological studies at Covenant College. He has written and edited several books, including *Communion with God* and *A Little Book for New Theologians*.

Donald Macleod (MA, University of Glasgow) served as professor of systematic theology and principal of Free Church College in Edinburgh. He has written a number of books, most recently *Christ Crucified*.

Paul Nimmo (PhD, University of Edinburgh) is professor of systematic theology at the University of Aberdeen. He is an editor of the *International Journal of Systematic Theology*. He has written *Being in Action* and edited the *Cambridge Companion to Reformed Theology*.

Scott Swain (PhD, Trinity Evangelical Divinity School) is professor of systematic theology and academic dean at Reformed Theological Seminary in Orlando, Florida. He has written several books, including *Reformed Catholicity* (with Michael Allen) and *The God of the Gospel*.

Daniel Treier (PhD, Trinity Evangelical Divinity School) is the Blanchard Professor of Theology at Wheaton College. He has written and edited a number of books, including *Proverbs and Ecclesiastes* and *Introducing Theological Interpretation of Scripture*. He was associate editor of the award-winning *Dictionary for Theological Interpretation of the Bible*.

Kevin Vanhoozer (PhD, University of Cambridge) is research professor of systematic theology at Trinity Evangelical Divinity School, having previously taught at the University of Edinburgh and Wheaton College. He has written or edited many books, including *The Drama of Doctrine* and *Remythologizing Theology*. He was general editor of the award-winning *Dictionary for Theological Interpretation of the Bible*.

John Webster (PhD, University of Cambridge) is professor of systematic theology at the University of St Andrews, having most recently served at the University of Aberdeen and previously as Lady Margaret Professor of Divinity at the University of Oxford. He is cofounding editor of the *International Journal of Systematic Theology* and was elected a fellow of the Royal Society of Edinburgh. He has written many books on modern theology and Christian dogmatics, including *The Domain of the Word* and *God without Measure*.

SCRIPTURE INDEX

2 Samuel

7 51, 120
7:13 47
7:14 120
7:14–16 321
23:2–3 92

1 Kings

8:27 76

2 Kings

22:2–3 51

2 Chronicles

15:12 174

Ezra

9–10 51

Nehemiah

9–10 51
9:5 105

Job

28 82
38–41 11
38:1 75
40:2 75
40:6 75

Psalms

1 120
2 92, 115n37
2:7 120
2:7–8 123
2:8 118n51, 121n58
4:1 254
5:9 184
10:7 184
13:1 154n16
14:1 244
14:1–3 184
19:1 82, 347
19:14 29
22:2 260
23 317

25:14 83
27:8 106
31:23 177
33:6 84, 91, 313
33:9 84, 91, 140
33:11 110
36:1 184
36:9 14
36:10–12 115n37
40:8 256
47 371
49:20 186n68
51:10 174
53:1–3 184
72:4 255
73:21–23 149
84:2 174
89:35–37 231
93 371
96 371
96:5 142
97 371
98:7–9 190
99 371
102:25–27 85
103 261
103:7 45
103:17 254
104:30 91, 313
109:3 92
110 89, 92, 120, 121
110:1 120
110:4 118n51
113 83
119:73 293
119:105 55
119:160 52
139:7 76
140:3 184
143:1 187n73
145:1–2 28
145:3–4 28
145:4 28
145:4–6 61
145:6–7 28
145:10 61
145:10–11 28
145:12 61
145:13 61
145:16 28
145:17 61
145:21 28

146:5–6 126
146:6 340
148:5 313

Proverbs

1:6 184
8 88
8:22–36 228n23
30:4 82

Ecclesiastes

7:29 181

Isaiah

2:10–22 370
6:5 58
7:14 220
9:1 371
9:1–6 370
9:6 75, 297
11:1–10 370
11:9–10 371
11:32 371
21:6 70
25:6 371
25:6–8 192
25:7 371
26:19 371
40 74
40–48 74
40–55 370
40–66 59, 220
40:12 141
40:12–31 85
40:26 85
40:28 85, 140
42:1 118n51
42:6 118n51
42:14 228
44:3 89, 91, 358
44:24 84, 85, 141
44:24–26 84
45:14 75
45:18 85
45:21–24 75, 221
45:22 371
49 218
49:1–6 118n51
49:3 92

49:8 118n51
49:15 228
49:26 288
51:4–6 371
51:6 254, 370
52–53 218, 222
52:13 92
52:13–53:12 117
53:10 118n51
55:1 313
55:6 61
55:10–11 91
55:11 50
55:12 190
59:7–8 184
59:21 220, 358
60:1 370
60:19 371
61 218
61:1–3 220
61:2 118n51
64:1 372
65:17 371
66:13 228
66:22 371
66:24 371

Jeremiah

1:5 119
3:31–32 367
3:33–34 367
7:4 76
9:23 182
9:24 182
10:10 85
10:11 85, 146
10:11–12 142
10:12 85
10:12–13 145
10:16 146
12:4 190
12:11 190
23:5–6 92
23:18 383
23:22–23 383
23:23 76
30:18 47
30:22 44
32:38–40 358
33:2 84
37:2 48

SUBJECT INDEX

Mass of the Marginalized People, 188–89
mastery, creation and, 146
Mastricht, Petrus van, 171
matter, eternity of, 143–45
Mattes, Mark C., 379–80
McCormack, Bruce, 63–65
mediate imputation, 211–12
Mennonite Articles of Faith, 182–83
Messiah, Jesus as, 223
metaphors, theological, 262
metaphysical monotheism, 86
metaphysics, 92–102, 135–37
Middleton, J. Richard, 187–88
millennium, the, 375–81
mission, 1, 336–38
missions, doctrine of divine, 104
models, theological, 262
Moltmann, Jürgen, 378–80
Monophysitism, 226
monotheism, 83–87, 141–42
monothelitism, 227
Mosaic law, 300–302
Muller, Richard, 41
munus triplex, 230–31
Musculus, Wolfgang, 359–60
mystical, union as, 281–82

name, God's, 69–70, 73–74, 81–92
narrowing, exegetical, 20–22
National Socialism, 18–19
naturalism, hermeneutic, 32
nature, law of, 293–95, 300
Nazism. *See* National Socialism
Nestorianism, 226, 238n42
Nicene Creed, 224–26

offices, Christological, 230–31, 263, 279–80, 386
omnipotence, 68–77, 140–41, 237, 239
omnipresence, God's, 76, 237–39, 346–48
omniscience, 237–40
ontology, Scripture and, 46–47
ordo salutis, 270–74, 278–79, 283–90

origin, relations of. *See* procession
original goodness, 181–87
Orthodox Confession, 186
Owen, John, 166–68

pactum salutis, 108–25
palingenesis, 390
Pannenberg, Wolfhart, 377–78
paradox, 237–39
participationist argument, 208–11
Passover, 359–60
past union, 281
paternity, attribute of, 98–100
peace, counsel of, 108–25
Pelagianism, 213
Pentecost, 277–79, 386–87
perfection, divine, 102–3
personhood, 87–90, 92–102, 138–39
philosophy. *See* metaphysics
physicality. *See* body, physical
Placeus, Josue, 211–12
pneumatology. *See* Spirit, the
political law, 294
pope, the, 311–12
postmillennialism, 375, 376–77
praise. *See* worship
prayer, theology and, 23
preaching. *See* proclamation
predestination, 116–17, 281, 306–7, 324–25
predication, the Trinity and, 96
premillennialism, 375
presbyterian, the church as, 330–31, 334–36
presence, God's, 73–76, 237–39, 346–48
present union, 281–83
priest, Christ as, 230–31, 279–80, 386
procession, 88–90, 98–99, 101–2, 143
process theology, 63–64
proclamation, 313–17, 344–45, 351
prophecy, 43, 133–34, 230–31, 386
propitiation, 250–54
proposition, discourse and, 45–46

prosopological exegesis, 91–92, 120–21
protology. *See* creation
providence, 148–64

Rahner's Rule, 19–20
reading, Scripture and, 54, 134
realism, Augustinian, 201, 206–11
realized eschatology, 375–77
reason. *See* epistemology
reception, Scripture and, 54
reconciliation. *See* soteriology
redemption. *See* soteriology
Reformation, the, 36–38
relationality, 170
relational predication, 96
relations of origin. *See* procession
renewal, theological, 2–3
representationalism, 201–5, 210n25
rest, creation and, 140
resurrection, the, 235–36, 275–76, 289–90, 310, 389–91
retrieval, theological, 4–5
revelation
  Christ and, 17–18, 20–22
  creation and, 11–14, 132–35, 295
  God and, 75–76
  reason and, 23–26
  Scripture and, 31–34, 38–43, 54–55
  the Trinity and, 82–83, 102–3
righteousness, 181–84, 264–67
Roman Catholic Church, 311–12, 324–26, 352

Sabellianism, 96
sacraments
  the church and, 311–12, 326–30
  grace and, 343–51
  law and, 301–2
  the Trinity and, 340–43, 352–62
sacrifice, atonement and, 247–48, 255–61
salvation. *See* soteriology
sanctification, 284–86, 331–33
Satan, 263–64